# The Roots of Rural Poverty
in Central and Southern Africa

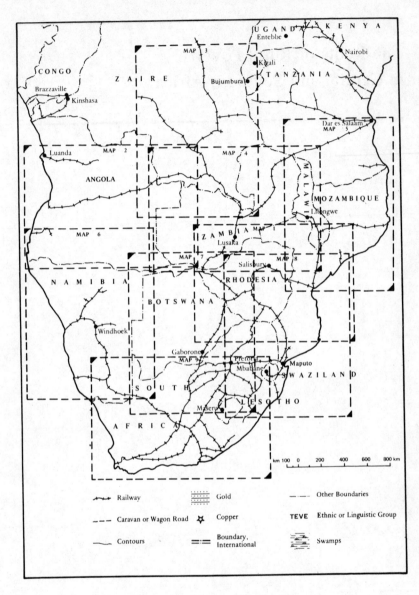

Key to Maps on pages x–xviii

# The Roots of Rural Poverty

*in Central and Southern Africa*

*Edited by*

**ROBIN PALMER**
*Senior Lecturer in History*
*University of Zambia*

**NEIL PARSONS**
*Lecturer in History, University of Zambia*
*and University of Botswana and Swaziland*

HEB


LONDON
**HEINEMANN**
IBADAN · NAIROBI · LUSAKA

Heinemann Educational Books Ltd
48 Charles Street London W1X 8AH
PMB 5205 Ibadan · PO Box 45314 Nairobi · PO Box 3966 Lusaka
EDINBURGH  MELBOURNE  TORONTO  AUCKLAND
SINGAPORE  HONG KONG  KUALA LUMPUR
NEW DELHI  KINGSTON

037 039

ISBN 0 435 94752 4 (Cased)
ISBN 0 435 94753 2 (Paper)

Phototypesetting by George Over Ltd, London and Rugby
Printed by Biddles, Guildford

# CONTENTS

# PREFACE

Governments throughout Africa talk today of the need to promote 'rural development'. The problem has proved remarkably intractable and has attracted the attention of social scientists of all disciplines, who have come to recognize that its dimensions stretch well beyond the particular expertise of the agricultural scientist. *The Roots of Rural Poverty in Central and Southern Africa* offers a historical perspective to this ongoing debate, while being in no way constrained by traditional academic boundaries.

Ideally, a work such as this should be the product of a single author, or at least a single point of view. We are conscious that published symposia of this kind are open to the criticism that they lack overall coherence, and we have endeavoured to overcome the problem by rigorous editing and by involving our contributors in a substantial exercise in mutual criticism and subsequent revision, designed to achieve maximum thematic unity. We would point out that the rural economic history of Central and Southern Africa has only just begun to be written, and that a great deal more research will be necessary before a work of synthesis comparable to A. G. Hopkins's *An Economic History of West Africa* (London, 1973) can be produced. This present book should thus be seen as a first step towards such a work for Central and Southern Africa, where studies have previously been largely industrial and national rather than peasant and regional, and as a stimulus to present and future research. *The Roots of Rural Poverty* lays its emphasis on the black rural areas previously neglected in formal history books. It moves towards a continental perspective by cutting across colonial linguistic boundaries. And it extends back into the pre-colonial era to search for the origins of underdevelopment that pre-date the formal hoisting of colonial flags.

One of our main concerns is that the contents of this book should reach, directly or indirectly, a wide audience in Africa, and that it should make a significant contribution to the growing public awareness of the problems involved in eliminating underdevelopment. We hope that in the African universities, particularly those of Central and Southern Africa, it will inform and stimulate undergraduate and postgraduate students across orthodox disciplinary lines, and in addition will also be read by those currently planning strategies of 'rural development'. We anticipate that some of the book's findings will be further refined in forthcoming academic theses by Maud Muntemba and Sherilynn Young, whose preliminary research findings are included here, and by Chipasha Luchembe, Joseph Mtisi, Mwelwa Musambachime, and Ken Vickery, who are currently working on areas within Zambia.

Finally, we wish to acknowledge the great assistance we have received from all the contributors; from the two Judys; from the postgraduate students listed above; from Ann Seidman, who encouraged us to undertake this book; and from the staff of the Geography Draughting Office of the University of Zambia, who prepared the maps. We are most grateful to the editors of *African Social Research, African Affairs,* and *Rural Africana* for permitting us to publish amended versions of articles originally published in those journals by Neil Parsons, Barry Kosmin, Ian Phimister, and Martin Chanock. On our part, we were happy to allow the chapter by Gervase Clarence-Smith and Richard Moorsom, commissioned for this book, to appear also in the *Journal of African History.*

Robin Palmer and Neil Parsons
*Lusaka and Kwaluseni*

## A Note on Currencies

Readers may find it helpful to have some comparative guide to the changing value of the various currencies mentioned by contributors to this book. This is something which is extremely difficult to assess accurately, but some rough guide must be attempted. The main unit of comparison is the International Unit (IU), based on the average purchasing power of the American dollar in the USA in the period 1925–34. It thus reflects a fully monetized consumer society rather than rural societies with a limited range of food staples. IU figures are cited here up to 1952 for the British pound, the South African pound (initially a British pound in South Africa), the Belgian franc, and the Portuguese escudo. The following table shows the comparative value (in IUs) of these four currencies at selected dates.

| Year | British pound | South African pound | Belgian franc | Portuguese escudo |
|---|---|---|---|---|
| 1895 | 11.40 | n.a. | 0.398 | n.a. |
| 1912 | 9.21 | 5.61 | n.a. | n.a. |
| 1913 | 8.94 | n.a. | 0.324 | n.a. |
| 1914 | 9.11 | n.a. | n.a. | 1.20 |
| 1920 | 3.24 | 4.30 | 0.0711 | 0.41 |
| 1927 | 5.16 | 4.46 | 0.0411 | n.a. |
| 1934 | 5.94 | 5.10 | 0.0484 | n.a. |
| 1938 | 5.40 | 4.87 | 0.0408 | 0.061 |
| 1946 | 2.968 | 3.53 | 0.01565 | n.a. |
| 1947 | 2.749 | 3.50 | 0.01538 | 0.0275 |
| 1951 | 2.195 | 2.91 | 0.01275 | 0.0280 |
| 1952 | 2.070 | 2.69 | 0.0126 | n.a. |

The British pound rose gradually from 8.76 IU in 1870 to a peak of 11.40 in 1895, then fluctuated between 11.23 and 8.94 until 1914, when it stood at 9.11. It dropped annually through the First World War to a low of 3.24 in 1920. It then climbed back steadily to reach 6.04 in 1933, from where it adjusted downwards to 5.40 in 1938. After the Second World War (for which there are no figures available) it began at 2.968 in 1946 and dropped annually to 2.070 by 1952, the last year for which IU figures are available. An alternative gauge of the purchasing power of the pound shows that goods bought for £1 in 1914 cost £2.50 in 1920, £1.56 in 1938, £2.65 in 1946, £5.47 in 1966, and £9.77 in 1974.

The fluctuations of the South African pound are illustrative first of colonial costs at metropolitan standards of living and later of South Africa's character as a 'sub-metropole' with comparative cost advantages over the rest of the world in supplying the Westernized enclave markets of Southern and Central Africa. Foreign exchange with the British pound was equal until 1967, when the British pound was devalued. Whereas the British pound was worth 3.60 IU more than the SA pound in 1912, it was worth 0.62 less by 1952, and the gap has widened in favour of the SA pound ever since. The two pounds first approached equality towards the end of the First World War, and from 1918 to 1920 the SA pound was worth a little more, but was unable to match the British pound's recovery until the Second World War. The SA pound began at 5.61 IU in 1912, dropped to a low of 3.48 in 1921 and rose gradually to 4.54 in 1925. It then hovered around 4.42 until 1930, rose gradually to 4.94 by 1933 and remained at about that level throughout the rest of the 1930s, being 4.87 in 1938. It declined annually thereafter up to 1952, being 3.53 in 1946 and 2.69 in 1952.

The Belgian franc, whose relationship to the Congolese franc is discussed in Chapter 12, climbed from 0.324 IU in 1846 to a peak of 0.398 in 1895, dropped to 0.324 in 1913, and tumbled after the First World War to 0.0711 in 1920. Unlike the two pounds it declined gradually during the 1920s, reaching 0.0367 in 1930, fluctuated between 0.048 and 0.041 in the 1930s, and stood at 0.0408 in 1938. It collapsed again during wartime, stood at 0.01565 in 1946, and had declined to 0.0126 by 1952.

The Portuguese escudo stood at 1.20 IU in 1914, but fell from 0.41 in January 1920 to 0.16 by the end of that year. By 1938 it had declined to 0.061. In the years 1947−51 it was steady at about 0.028 and closed at that figure in 1951.

Sources: C. Clark, The Conditions of Economic Progress (London, 1957), 18, 101−2, 136−41, 178, 190−2; 1976 Whitaker's Almanack (London, 1975), 1051.

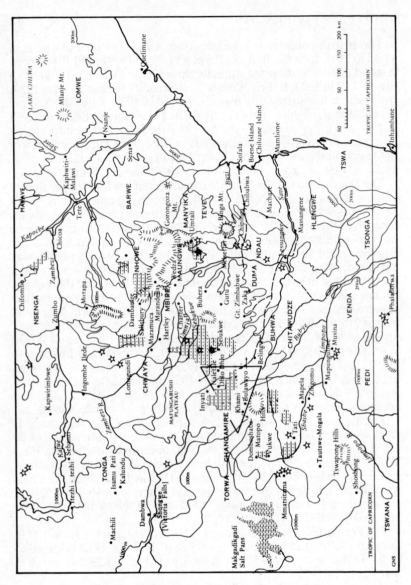

Map 1 — Zimbabwean Plateau: Pre-colonial

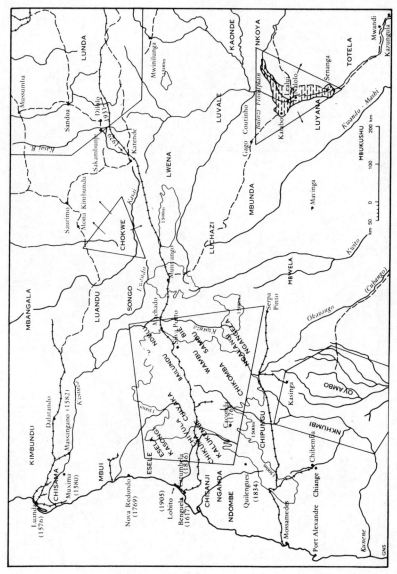

Map 2 — Angola: Ovimbundu, Chokwe, Ovambo, Nkhumbi, Luyana
(Lozi), and Lunda Kingdoms

xi

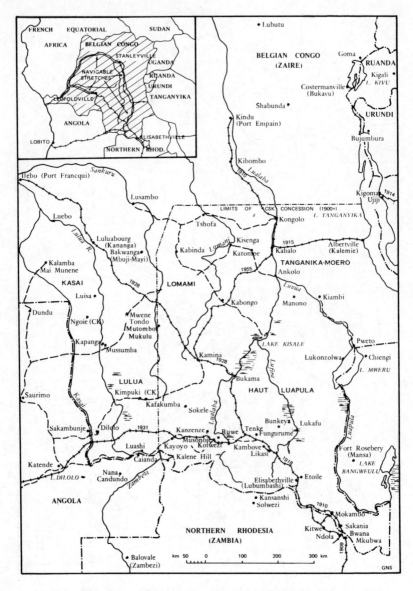

Map 3 — Zaïre (Belgian Congo): Districts as 1928

xii

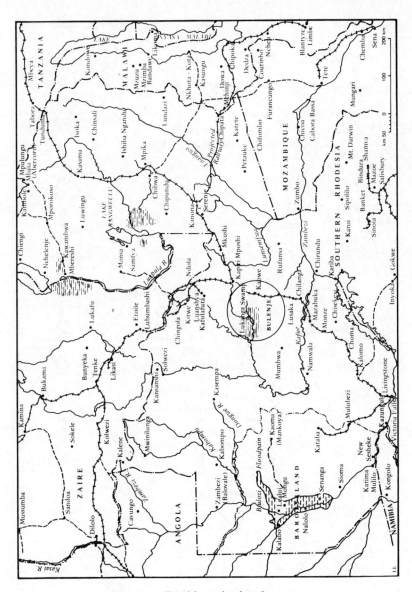

Map 4 — Zambia and related areas

xiii

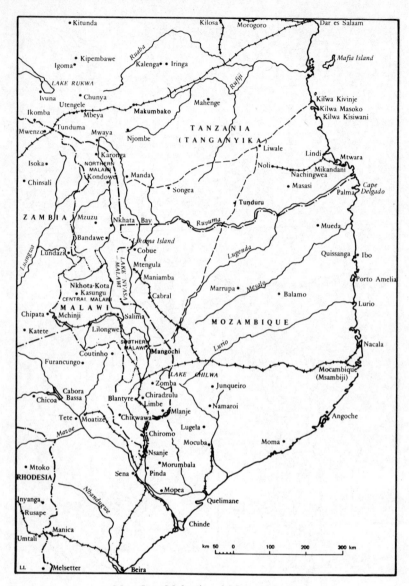

Map 5 — Malawi and Mozambique

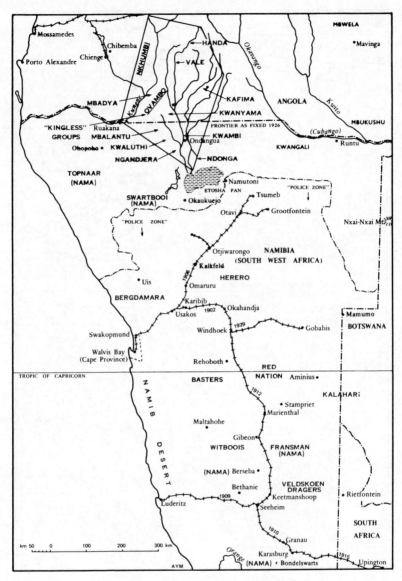

Map 6 — Namibia and Angola

XV

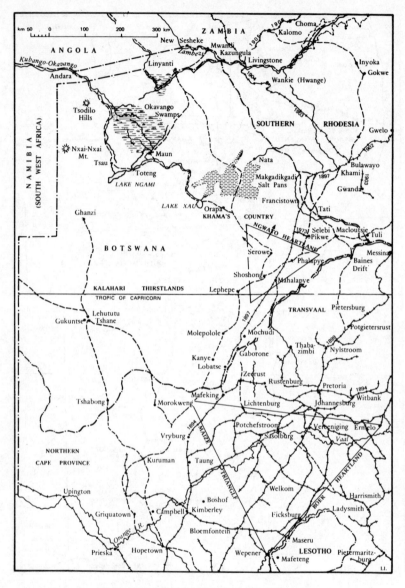

Map 7 — Botswana, South Africa and Southern Rhodesia

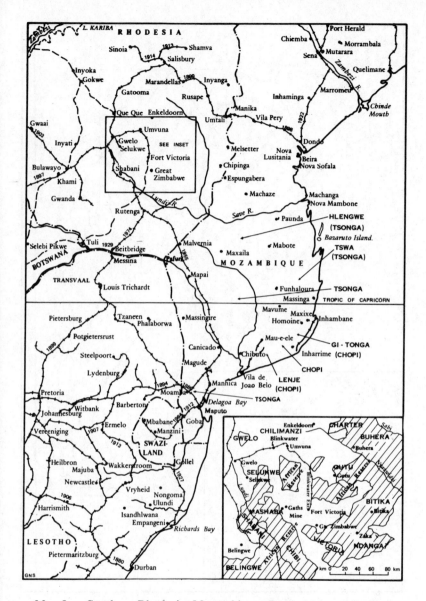

Map 8 — Southern Rhodesia, Mozambique, South Africa, Swaziland

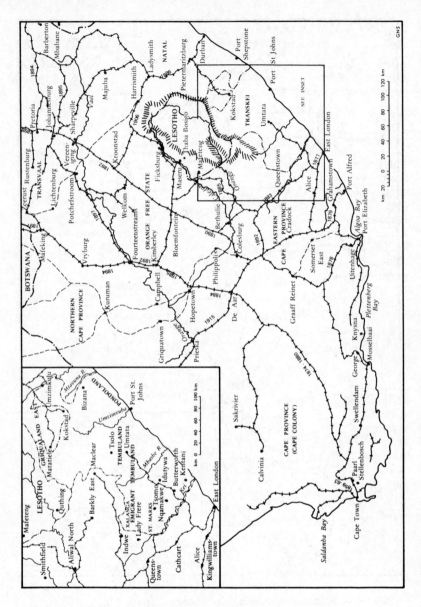

Map 9 — South Africa and Lesotho (Transkei inset)

# INTRODUCTION

## The Roots of Rural Poverty: Historical Background

## NEIL PARSONS AND ROBIN PALMER

This Introduction is divided into three sections. In the first of these, we are concerned to place this book in its historiographical context and to suggest the particular contribution which we feel it has to offer to the ongoing debate on underdevelopment. In the second section we outline key social and economic developments in Central and Southern African history essential to a proper understanding of the essays; these include discussion of the physical environment and myths pertaining to African agriculture, of the past economic history of the area, of the particular characteristics of the Southern and Central African economic regions, and of the labour supply myth on the South African mines. The third section consists of a short essay on underdevelopment in Swaziland and Lesotho, which both compensates for their lack of explicit treatment elsewhere and serves to illustrate some of the main themes which recur throughout the book. Immediately preceding the Introduction, there is a brief note on the fluctuations of the British, South African, Belgian, and Portuguese currencies.

For the purposes of this book, Central and Southern Africa is defined, very roughly, as Africa south of 8°S, a line of latitude which stretches from just north of Luanda on the Angolan coast, through southern Zaïre, crosses the southern tip of Lake Tanganyika, and leaves the east coast of Africa to the north of the Mozambique-Tanzania border. 'Central' and 'Southern' Africa will have differing connotations over time (especially pre- and post- the South African mineral revolution), but comprise essentially the savanna lands of the series of plateaux (above 1,000 m) south of the tropical forests of the Congo/Zaïre Basin.

## I

### Historiography and theory

In writing about rural poverty in the mid-1970s, our contributors have been influenced by a number of themes which have dominated recent historical writing in Africa. The oldest of these is the 'trade and politics' historiography which now dates back two decades to the publication of Dike's *Trade and Politics in the Niger Delta* in 1956, and which, for Central and Eastern Africa, reached its apogee in Gray and Birmingham's 1970 collection, *Pre-Colonial African Trade*.[1] We would like to

1

think of *The Roots of Rural Poverty* as a worthy successor to
*Pre-Colonial African Trade,* but one which also goes a long way
towards meeting Walter Rodney's critique of that work — that Gray
and Birmingham did not investigate the modes of production and social
formations beyond the 'markets' of exchange.[2] A second and related
historiography on which *Roots* clearly draws is that of 'agricultural
history', which was stimulated by the publication of 'national'
agricultural histories by the Historical Associations of Zambia,
Tanzania, and Kenya, written by Ranger, Iliffe, and van Zwanenberg.[3]
These pamphlets clearly inspired a number of the chapters in this book
and also a great deal of research which, though yet in its early stages,
should over the next few years produce a number of important doctoral
dissertations. 'Agricultural history' itself, it should be noted, drew
upon the tradition of what might be termed 'agricultural science with a
human face', best exemplified in William Allan's *The African
Husbandman* of 1965, and in the more polemical works of René
Dumont.[4]

*Roots* also owes much to the interdisciplinary concern with peasants
and peasantization, proletarians and proletarianization, stimulated by
the influential work of Giovanni Arrighi on Rhodesia, especially his
seminal 1970 article 'Labour Supplies in Historical Perspective'.[5]
Arrighi brought out the historical contradictions inherent in capitalist
development first stimulating the growth of a peasantry to supply its
foodstuffs, and then proceeding to break up that peasantry in order to
obtain its labour. A number of our contributors cite the somewhat
complex definition of African peasants adopted by Saul and Woods in
1971;[6] we feel it sufficient here to indicate to readers that 'peasants' are
small agricultural producers who intend to make a living by *selling* part
of their crops or herds, while 'proletarians' are wage earners in the hire
of an employer. Thus people as individuals or as members of a family
may be more or less one or the other: the typical colonial economy in
Central and Southern Africa put people in an intermediate position
through the phenomenon of temporary labour migration and 'the
tradition of a subsistence wage'.[7]

A further intellectual debt is owed to radical (i.e. committed to
fundamental change) social scientists writing in French on West
Africa. The widely cited Samir Amin has gone beyond both dependency theory (discussed shortly) and orthodox Marxist historical
categories into a re-analysis of the stages and varieties of capitalist
impact upon African political economies, while Meillassoux and
Terray have concentrated upon the study of pre-capitalist African
modes of production.[8] Central and Southern Africa can clearly derive
only benefit from comparison with other parts of the continent, and
indeed such comparison might well take out of its West African
vacuum the rather sterile debate about whether there was *only one*
pre-capitalist mode of production in Africa.

Most important of all however, is the debate on the 'development of
underdevelopment' which was initiated by social scientists concerned

with Latin America, then spread across the Atlantic to Africa, and which has aroused widespread interest inside and outside academic circles throughout the Third World. According to what has come to be termed 'dependency theory', Western capitalism promoted *under-development* by permeating Third World economies, reducing them to dependency, and then creaming off their surpluses. This critique, born of the Leninist theory of imperialism, contradicts the 'modernization theory' advocated by development planners in Africa in the 1950s and 1960s, who had seen capitalism as progressively spreading *development* throughout 'backward' hinterlands. Expressed thus crudely, it can be seen how 'dependency' reflects contemporary disenchantment, while 'modernization' mirrored earlier misplaced optimism.[9]

It is precisely the crude appeal of dependency theory however, which has made it controversial. Marxists and others have criticized its popularization — by André Gunder Frank, Walter Rodney, and in the rhetoric of university students — as the unscientific bowdlerization of previously precise insights and dialectical reasoning.[10] Even Radio South Africa, beaming to Black Africa, now uses a variant of dependency theory to persuade African countries to divert their trade links away from the inflation-ridden West, and towards the better terms offered by South Africa. Part of the value of this book, we feel, lies in the testing of the theory against the evidence of varied historical examples. We are convinced that dependency theory remains a useful tool, provided its crudest formulation (underdevelopment = dependence = underdevelopment) is rejected. At this point it is perhaps worth restating in a truism the real meaning of *development*: that while economic *growth* is reflected in improved production statistics, economic *development* entails improved standards of living.[11]

At various times our contributors make use of certain concepts — notably the 'core–periphery' and the 'dual economy' — without necesssarily accepting corresponding bodies of theory. The core–periphery concept has in fact been employed by both dependency and modernization theorists. Among the latter, Green and Fair's *Development in Africa,* emanating from Johannesburg in 1962, is particularly important for having popularized the idea of white settler 'islands' pumping out development into the black tributary areas of Southern and Central Africa.[12] Dependency theorists of course reverse the model from a centrifugal one to a centripetal one of the core draining the periphery. One problem with core–periphery models is how to relate the local and regional cores together in a world hierarchy, which leads to the use of terms such as 'peripheral centres' and 'semi-peripheries'. Martin Legassick, in Chapter 7, utilizes the concept of South Africa being a 'sub-metropole' of the world system, subordinate to the metropoles of Western capitalism, but possessing significant autonomy over its own periphery. A more serious danger in core–periphery explanations lies in the assumption of coherence and uniformity in the growth of the peripheries, which properly pertains only to the cores. Nevertheless, the concept has great utility in clarifying a number of questions. For example, in Chapter 12 Jean-Luc Vellut demonstrates how the very words 'rural' and 'poverty' are expressive of the deprivation of peripheries to their core areas within a single socio-economic system.

The concept of the 'dual economy' must be strongly distinguished from 'dualism theory' as an explanation of the origins and coexistence of development and underdevelopment. The term 'dual economy' is a convenient label by which to describe the system of socio-legal segregation erected on reserved land categories, which reaches its logical extreme in *apartheid,* but is still to be found in some form (based on class, rather than race) in every country in Central and Southern Africa. This system of internal colonialism — as is graphically illustrated by some of the essays in this collection — was deliberately created by the colonial authorities throughout 'Africa of the labour reserves', as Samir Amin dubs Central and Southern Africa,[13] during the period between the South African War and the Second World War, with the south setting the pace. The emerging one-sector economy previously evident in the growth of African peasant production for the industrial market — see Chapters 8–14 — was split into two on racial economic lines: a controlled market sector for Africans and a 'liberalized' sector for Europeans, with the former supplying the latter with labour and receiving goods on disadvantaged terms.[14]

However, the cumulative evidence of this book would tend to invalidate conventional 'dualism theory', with its emphasis on the clash between an imported 'modern' and an indigenous 'traditional' sector.[15] Dualism theory, essentially a variant of the modernization theory, imputes to Africa inherent economic backwardness and irrationality which is simply not supported by the evidence of this book. Dependency theory, on the other hand, has the virtue of accommodating the historical fact of the importation of capitalism to Africa as a top half (capital and skills) in search of a bottom half (resources and labour). It utilized the resources and labour of pre-colonial economic systems and itself underwent structural change, finally producing a form of capitalist economy very different from that found in the metropoles. *The Roots of Rural Poverty* goes further to demonstrate the extent to which elements of the pre-capitalist systems were deliberately permitted to survive under capitalism.

Indeed, one of the aims of this book is to put the various explanatory theories and models to the test of historical case studies which address themselves to the specifics of rural poverty. In particular, as a result of the essays collected here, we are now in a much better position to appreciate the subtleties and complexities of the process of peasantization and proletarianization. Marx's observation that in Europe 'in the sphere of agriculture, modern industry ... annihilates the peasant ... and replaces him by the wage labourer',[16] was paralleled for Africa by a contemporary, Florence Nightingale, who expressed the hope in

1880 that the Zulu people of Natal would turn into 'what they have every capacity for becoming, a first-rate working population and one of the finest peasantries . . . in the world'.[17]

*Roots* shows the diverse ways in which peasantries developed out of pre-existing agricultural systems under the impact of new markets — from the end of the sixteenth century on the Mozambique coast, but especially in the late nineteenth and early twentieth centuries, as capitalist industry began spreading into the interior. Discretionary, rather than obligatory, proletarianization in the urban areas and peasantization in the rural areas proceeded hand in hand for a while as viable alternatives, until major capitalist interests and/or settler political power intervened. This intervention did not occur solely, as the Arrighi model presupposes, through the direct use of military or legal coercion to pillage rural resources and create an unlimited labour supply for capitalist development; often it was achieved more cheaply by the use of indirect coercion to 'freeze' peasant production and proletarian incomes at the lowest levels to which they had been reduced by natural disasters — to which African rural economies were structurally more prone — and by world market trends dictated by events outside Africa. Thus between the first decade of the twentieth century in the south and the third decade in the north of our region, there were created variations of the 'dual economy' which kept African families split but constantly moving between rural and urban 'reserves' or settler estates. Peasants and proletarians were structurally dependent on each other for survival, when falling urban incomes were matched by rural impoverishment and neither sector could alone provide full subsistence and social security.

We are particularly concerned to trace connections between pre-colonial relations of production, the colonial undermining of rural self-sufficiency, and the process of peasantization. Several essays focus in particular on how during the colonial period the development of social and economic facilities for the ruling minority was intimately associated with the underdevelopment of facilities for the subordinate majority in both town and country, following an initial period of shared economic growth. Moreover, it is clearly shown that in many instances underdevelopment was not merely a matter of increasing economic distortion, dependency, and subordination for the masses of the people; it was also a matter of absolute impoverishment against previous standards of living. Wealth was being extracted, and in many cases is still being extracted, from the rural areas by force, fraud, and fiat.

In conclusion, the evidence assembled in this book argues strongly that the nature of the inherited colonial economies of Central and Southern Africa cannot be understood, and therefore be changed wittingly, without historical analysis of how and why contemporary social and economic distortions originated.

## II

## Physical environment and the European myth of African agriculture

The physical environment of Central and Southern Africa is undoubtedly a harsh one.[18] The soil is not as good as that in Europe or North America; it lacks sufficient humus and the calcium and phosphorus essential for plant growth, and it is washed away all too easily by heavy rainfall.[19] The rainfall itself, whose quantity and reliability tends to diminish as one moves from east to west, is frequently either inadequate — virtually all of South Africa, Botswana, and Namibia have less than 30 inches (762 mm) of rain per annum — or else comes with such force and over such a short period of time that its usefulness is greatly diminished. Such disabilities have led one writer to suggest that about half of Central Africa and a quarter of Southern Africa cannot be used in any form for agricultural production.[20] Consequently farming, both 'subsistence' and 'commercial', is and always has been an extremely precarious and hazardous occupation. In Chapter 1 David Beach discusses the impact of shangwa, drought or disaster, on the pre-colonial economy in Zimbabwe/Rhodesia, and his emphasis on the fragility of Shona agriculture would hold true for most of our area, with a few favoured exceptions. Colonial rule, which in the twentieth century plundered male labour, expropriated much of the best land for settlers, and usually packed Africans into 'reserves', added considerably to the people's burdens.

The inadequacy of rainfall has meant that south of the Limpopo and Kunene the land is more suited to pastoralism than to agriculture, while in much of the north the bane of the tsetse fly has precluded the keeping of cattle.[21] The fluctuations of the fly belts, together with very great local and annual variations in rainfall, have greatly influenced settlement patterns. Population movement has never been straightforward. With few exceptions, the main rivers are not navigable for any distance, and the sandy thirstlands of the Kalahari Basin have acted as a major wedge between areas of denser settlement.

The soils of Central and Southern Africa are not suited to intensive or continuous cultivation, a fact well recognized by African farmers, whose practice of 'shifting cultivation', much derided by early European observers, is now generally recognized to have been a perfectly sensible response to the environment. Indeed European administrators and settlers in their ignorance, and perhaps in their arrogance, have contrived to do much harm to the environment.[22] In particular the colonial orthodoxy of deep ploughing and emphasis on rotation rather than fallow has had disastrous ecological effects, and resulted in inferior yields until after the Second World War. Around 1900 an elderly African farmer in the Cape explained to an English agronomist why he dug a furrow only a few inches deep for his maize, while the agronomist wanted him to dig down two or three times deeper. The topsoil was only so many inches deep, most moisture came to the roots of his maize from below, and so the old man reasoned that the roots needed as much topsoil as possible beneath them. Deep furrows on the other hand opened up the topsoil to be dried by the sun, while the maize roots had to penetrate the hard infertile subsoil.[23] Few African soils have the chemical properties to sustain continuous cultivation, and continuous deep ploughing has been responsible for turning cultivable soils into sun-baked powder.[24] Hence the more fertile areas such as Lesotho and the Transkei, where peasants readily abandoned the hoe and adopted the plough and 'European' cultivation in the nineteenth century, have since been subject to massive erosion.

Similarly the introduction of American-style ranching, based on extensive fenced pastures, from which people and wildlife were expelled, led to overgrazing and unbalanced nutrition for the cattle, which in turn promoted bush encroachment. In contrast, African cattle management was more efficient, since by its intensive method of herding it was able to rotate around the local seasonal patchwork of 'sweet' and 'sour' grasses, as well as to support settlement, cultivation, or hunting on the same land.

The accumulation of cattle often provided the capital resource upon which pre-colonial political systems were built. For example, it is apparent from archaeology and linguistics that the Iron Age people of south-east Africa first based their wealth on small stock (sheep and goats), but later certain groups among them rose to power through obtaining cattle from the west in exchange for metal products. In Chapter 5 Neil Parsons shows how the Tswana chiefdoms (in modern Botswana and South Africa) derived their power from the accumulation of cattle, which were then transferred into a political resource by being loaned out to 'feudal' supporters under the *mafisa* system — variations of which were found among the Sotho, Shona, Lozi, and many other peoples.[25]

The evident political and social role of cattle led to the creation by colonial administrators of the 'cattle complex' myth, which formed part of the larger myth that Africans were 'uneconomic men', i.e. psychologically incapable of responding rationally to the market.[26] Charles van Onselen has recently demolished that part of the myth pertaining to African workers,[27] and the so-called 'cattle complex' also deserves to be put firmly in its place. According to this myth, Africans would not sell their cattle because their 'economic concern is overlaid by mystical and ritual devotion to their stock, and by the desire to accumulate merely for prestige'.[28] Studies in this book and elsewhere in fact show how cattle-keeping is an alternative system of capital investment to the cash market, and it is as wealth that cattle have cultural prestige. Robin Fielder has noted that among the Ila of Zambia, 'Cattle are regarded very much as shares and investments are in capitalist societies'. Sales to the market are regulated, quite rationally, by factors such as price levels, security of investment, and local demands for cash and consumer goods. 'Cattle are our bank' sums up the security offered by cattle-keeping: a self-regenerating investment with an annual increase of up to 15 per cent in the herd, with dividends in milk and dung, cashable in the form of meat and hides, and a currency which though cumbersome provides its own transport — and whose cash value has risen by 300 to 400 per cent since 1950. In the early and middle colonial periods, beset by disastrous droughts, stock diseases, and price slumps, the value of cattle, in terms of the capitalist market, sank very low, but in 1976 at a time of rampant inflation, and with a ton of beef fetching more on the world market than a ton of copper, cattle are 'a far more profitable investment, though more risky, than a Post Office savings account, or a building society, or most industrial shares'.[29]

A second colonial myth concerning 'traditional' agriculture was to imply that it was inefficient. This involves considerations of 'efficiency' on a number of levels — appropriate technology, scale of production, and individual and communal profit and loss.

It was not in fact until after the Second World War that Central and Southern Africa experienced a real agricultural revolution in increased production based on superior technology. Until that time peasants and settler proprietors were using essentially similar technology, though on a different scale. What had given the white farmers predominance by about 1930, as a number of the essays in this book demonstrate, was political and legal control over land, labour, and market mechanisms— a prime example of the latter being the Maize Control Acts in Rhodesia discussed by Robin Palmer in Chapter 9. In fact it is now generally conceded that in unit terms peasants were more productive farmers than settlers: large ploughed fields had a lower unit yield than careful hoe cultivation of selected soils, and even today with high cattle prices, a peasant area in Angola is more productive in terms of cattle sales than an equivalent-sized settler ranching area in Rhodesia.[30] Attempts to introduce European farming methods in Central and Southern Africa had limited success and, as we have seen, were often ecologically unsound. Up to recent times, therefore, in terms of farming methods, white farmers have been more Africanized than black farmers have been Europeanized. What distinguished the larger from the smaller scale farmer was the extent of his use of the same labour-intensive techniques. This is the essential background to the coercive recruitment of agricultural labour, the use of semi-slave or prison labour on settler estates, and the farming out of white estates to black tenant or tributary producers.

Since the Second World War the agricultural revolution of manufactured fertilizers, herbicides, and pesticides, of efficient motorized machinery, and of new crop strains, has changed the face of rural Africa decisively in favour of large-scale capital-intensive production. This is exemplified by the swing away from burley and turkish to virginia tobacco in Rhodesia, but is perhaps best illustrated by the case of maize in Zambia. The new maize hybrid SR52 introduced in the 1950s had a world record yield of over thirty bags per acre compared to the four to eight bags produced previously, and could be used 'on the vast tracts of sandveldt which had previously been considered suitable only for low-density cattle grazing and tobacco production'. But it requires dry season mechanical ploughing, much fertilizer, and the application of pesticides and herbicides with scientific exactitude. The consequent economies of scale mean that the larger the crop the greater is the unit and gross profitability. The resultant market forces have meant that maize prices, despite high cost inflation, have remained virtually the same between 1953 and 1974, while profitable production has become monopolized by large capitalist estates. Given the high capital investment required, it is only the small class of emergent commercial farmers and peri-urban plot holders among the 'peasantry' who are able to reap the advantage of SR52.[31] The resulting political dilemma of whether to adjust maize prices is discussed by Maud Muntemba in Chapter 14.

That one man's profit may be another man's loss is a maxim that underlines the hidden *social costs* to a community, which may easily be disguised beneath impressive-looking statistics. One is reminded again of the distinction between economic growth and economic development. The social costs of labour migration borne by a rural area — of providing social security and other benefits deliberately withheld from workers in the urban sector — have been explored in an extensive literature,[32] and are again touched on by a number of essays in this book. The social costs, however, of capital-intensive rural production replacing labour-intensive methods, such as ploughing with a tractor rather than an ox-team and fencing off agricultural areas from human settlement, remain to be better elucidated by rural economists.

## Central and Southern African economic history

In order to understand recent and contemporary rural history one must have some knowledge of the broad economic patterns of the past. Much of this information comes from archaeological investigation, and the intensive work carried out in Zambia, Rhodesia, and the Transvaal makes it possible to reconstruct the major economic developments in Central and Southern Africa as a whole. Local and regional 'industries' and 'cultures', named after the original sites at which they were discovered, have been classified, grouped into divisions of the Stone Age and Iron Age (i.e. technology based on stone and iron tools), and dated by the radiocarbon method. The phases of economic development evident to archaeology are the most useful starting points for historical investigation into types of socio-political formation and the dominant modes of production on which they were based.

The Iron Age spread from Central into Southern Africa over the centuries around the birth of Christ, to reach south of the Limpopo by the third or fourth century AD.[33] Closely associated with the distribution of Bantu languages, the Iron Age replaced the Late Stone Age (associated with Khoisan-speaking hunters and herders),[34] especially in those areas suited to agriculture, and spread towards the south-western corner of the continent. Iron hoes, machetes, and axes enabled Early Iron Age people to clear the land and cultivate extensively for millet and sorghum production, while people in the latest of Late Stone Age phases had been limited to the 'vegeculture' of root and leaf crops. Cereal agriculture meant the stabilization of human settlement patterns, albeit with fields shifting a little from year to year and short migrations being made when local water supplies or soils were exhausted. In time this led to the growth of larger and more dense population units under the increasing sovereignty of selected individuals or kinship groups. It is a mistake however to see the Late Stone Age/Early Iron Age changeover as necessarily marking a sharp divide in economic history. Elements of the Late Stone Age, such as the weighted digging stick and the stone mortar, have survived even to the present century, while Early Iron Age peoples adopted Late Stone Age hunting practices and the long-horned Sanga cattle of Late Stone Age herders from Namibia and the western Cape.[35]

From at least the Early Iron Age we may begin to distinguish rich and poor, in a class sense, within the same society on the basis of differential access to and control over the means of production. But though one may equate as a general rule the bringers of iron technology with its controllers, one should not assume that smiths or miners, or even Bantu-speakers, necessarily formed an aristocracy. The dark-skinned Bergdama iron-makers of Namibia were probably non-Bantu in origin and were subordinate to Khoisan cattle-herders, while mine labour — at least in the Later Iron Age — was considered to be the lowest social status apart from serfdom among the Tswana.[36]

While the Early Iron Age may be identified as a single dominant type of economy or mode of production from Kenya to the Transvaal, the Later Iron Age, evident from about the eleventh century AD, is characterized archaeologically by regional and local diversification of 'cultures', economically by variations in exchange and production, and politically by the increase in scale from chiefdoms to kingdoms.

It is into the latter part of the Later Iron Age that the agricultural economies discussed in this book fit. The Later Iron Age was a millennium in which internal exchange, productive specialization, and external trade built up to a peak in the eighteenth and nineteenth centuries, when caravan routes spanned Central and Southern Africa. For the most part human porterage was the only feasible means of transport, since the tsetse fly blocked all routes to ox-wagons except from the south. It was during the late eighteenth and the nineteenth centuries, as Jean-Luc Vellut points out in Chapter 12, that the distinctions between rich and poor, oppressors and oppressed, took on new dimensions in many areas. Societies underwent qualitative as well as quantitative change when the penetration of overseas mercantilism into the interior made slaves and ivory the most lucrative and abundant primary export commodities. The Later Iron Age witnessed an increasing degree of 'unequal exchange' in the export of primary commodities (ivory, gold, slaves, etc.) to coastal merchants in exchange for manufactured goods (cloth, ornaments, liquor, etc.) that were mainly for the prestige of the rich, and which were in fact growing ever cheaper at the source of manufacture overseas. By the eighteenth and nineteenth centuries the market values of the Indian and Atlantic Ocean trade systems had come under the control of the rapidly rising capitalism of north-western Europe which stood at the heart of an increasingly uniform world economy.[37] It became a standing joke among Europeans that Africans would accept in good faith the bead and shell currencies whose values had been maintained by genuine scarcity for centuries, but which could now be mass-produced and imported in bulk by those traders with direct access to the sources of supply.

In Chapter 1, David Beach shows how such a situation might not become structurally evident until the late nineteenth century, and the historical experience of the Shona trade complex over many centuries may be taken as a paradigm of what happened to some societies during only a matter of decades in their reduction to 'external dependency'. Chapters 4 to 12 detail how some entrepreneurial groups managed at the onset of the colonial period to use market conditions to their advantage until they were eventually deprived of independent leverage by colonial intervention.

By the nineteenth century a number of coastal-oriented trade networks converged on the area of Zambia and Zaïre; Ovimbundu and Chokwe from the west, Swahili, Yao, and Chikunda from the east, British, Griqua, and other wagoners from the south. The impact of Indian and Mediterranean mercantilism was succeeded by that of capitalism based on heavy industry in Europe, whose 'arrival' in Africa may be dated from the early 1860s when British capital accumulated in the new banks (Standard Bank, etc.) in the Cape Colony, searching for new fields of investment. This capital promoted the mining revolution, which began with diamonds at Kimberley in the 1870s, continued with gold at Johannesburg in the 1880s, and eventually totally transformed the whole of Central and Southern Africa. The extension of railway lines into the interior (see maps), every inch of which was imported until the mid-twentieth century, graphically charts the importation of the externally dependent 'Steel Age' — the secondary industrial revolution of mass production in Europe from about 1870, whose goods undercut and replaced those of the Later Iron Age throughout Central and Southern Africa.[38]

## Southern and Central Africa as economic regions

'Steel Age' penetration into Africa has been essentially a matter of enclave development — first of primary industrial enclaves linked by rail to the coast for export to Europe, secondly of enclaves of capitalist agriculture knocking out peasant competition to supply the industrial enclaves, and thirdly of secondary industrial enclaves in South Africa and partially farther north. All three required cheap and plentiful supplies of labour, which were extracted from the rural areas over the whole of Central and Southern Africa. In outlining the regional nature of colonial economic growth, it is vital to emphasize that we are distinguishing between 'Southern' and 'Central' Africa in geo-political terms based on shifting socio-economic linkages. Central Africa as a geographical term is centred on the Congo/Zaïre Basin, and in contemporary usage stretches northwards if one speaks French and southwards for English-speakers! Geo-politically one might consider Central Africa as stretching even as far as the Cape of Good Hope until the last quarter of the nineteenth century, when Southern Africa began to become a distinguishable economic region based on the Witwatersrand hub.

The development of the core of the Southern African region is discussed in detail by Martin Legassick in Chapter 7. The expansion of this region is evidenced by South Africa's capital investment in, and trade and labour links with, neighbouring countries, together with their adoption of the South African model of development/underdevelopment. Central Africa has never been a coherent region in such centralized economic terms. International rivalries have precluded the emergence of a Copperbelt/Katanga core for the region, while the 1953–63 Federation of the Rhodesias and Nyasaland was an attempt to create a second Southern Africa based on Southern Rhodesia rather than a radical Central African alternative. At this point we need to note the main characteristics of South African expansionism.

Political expansionism was implicit in the very title of the 'Union of South Africa' formed in 1910, and explicit in its constitution, which allowed for the future incorporation of Southern Rhodesia and the 'High Commission Territories'. The attendant customs union, discussed later in this Introduction in relation to Swaziland and Lesotho and by Neil Parsons in Chapter 5 in relation to Botswana, was initiated in 1889 between the Cape Colony and the Orange Free State and by 1905 stretched as far north as Barotseland, though by 1935 its northern borders were the Limpopo and the Kunene. The political history of South African attempts to incorporate the High Commission Territories is well known;[39] less well known is the fact that a 1922 referendum vote by white Southern Rhodesians not only precluded that country from joining the Union,[40] but also put an end to South African hopes of acquiring the (then copper-less) Northern Rhodesian line of rail. Smuts, who was given South West Africa (Namibia) as a League of Nations 'mandate' after the First World War, also had his eye firmly on Mozambique, Katanga, and southern Angola,[41] while economic influence, if not direct political control, was also sought in Kenya and Tanganyika, where South African Airways began operating in the 1930s.

Political ambition was mirrored in the northward expansion of mining capital, best illustrated in the 1889 creation of Cecil Rhodes's British South Africa Company, which subsequently administered both Southern and Northern Rhodesia until 1923/4.[42] One of its associate companies, Tanganyika Concessions Ltd, had a close if complex relationship with the Union Minière du Haut-Katanga, founded in 1906, while South African capital was heavily invested in the Northern Rhodesian Copperbelt, which started production in the late 1920s.

Commercial links to the north, accompanying mining capital, were reinforced in the 1940s, when South Africa experienced unprecedented growth in the manufacturing sector. In the 1940s and early 1950s numerous trade missions trekked north and diplomatic representatives were stationed in Salisbury, Nairobi, Leopoldville (Kinshasa), and Elisabethville (Lubumbashi) where the South African 'Trade Commissioner for the Central and West African Territories' resided. This last appointment unconsciously echoed a comment made in that city in 1922 by the editor of the *South African Journal of Industries,* to the effect that

> when it is remembered that the Union of South Africa is Africa's great manufacturing centre, the actual or potential producer of most of the finished goods needed by the Continent's huge population, and that the Union might well draw upon the rest of Africa for much of the raw materials which her factories need, it is evident that the development of inter-African trade relations . . . follows logically upon the Union's geographical position.[43]

Until recently, some Zambian building regulations bore the mark of former trade agreements with South Africa and Southern Rhodesia in stipulating that door and window frames had to be of imported metal rather than local ant-resistant wood.

The events of 1965 finally broke the close relationship between the Zambian and (Southern) Rhodesian economies, but this merely opened the way for South African expansion once again. Rhodesia became a client state of South Africa, South African exports to Zambia rose from £16.2 million in 1964 to a peak of £38 million in 1968, and the way was open for expansion farther north, thinly disguised as 'dialogue' or 'détente'. Central Africa on the other hand, though now possessing a mining and potential manufacturing core along the Benguela–Copperbelt–Tete axis, remains balkanized by infrastructure, industrial policies, market tariffs, and, most poignantly of all, by the Portuguese, French, and English languages.

South Africa continues to offer to the rest of Africa the model of its own 'economic miracle' as the recipe for 'co-prosperity'. What is that model? Contributors to this book would argue that it is essentially one of internal colonialism[44] which, if shorn of its racist aspects, reveals a rich minority living in enclaves of prosperity through repression of a poor majority. *Apartheid,* it may be argued, is the ultimate expression of the colonial 'dual economy', its political coercion maintaining the segregation of rich/capitalist and poor/peasant-worker sectors to maximize the use of cheap labour in the former.

## The South African mines and the labour supply myth

The South African model of rural segregation was constructed very largely as a result of political action.[45] As many of the essays in this book illustrate, the rural areas outside the industrial and settler farming enclaves were ultimately reduced to labour reserves. In the nineteenth century the diamond mines drew most of their labour from the Cape Colony and Lesotho, but only southern Mozambique — for reasons explored by Sherilynn Young in Chapter 2 — was able to satisfy the enormous and ever-increasing demand of the Witwatersrand. Indeed Lesotho and southern Mozambique have consistently contributed the largest slices of 'foreign' labour to South Africa. But in the wake of firmer colonial rule, the imposition of the 'dual economy' and of market depressions, labour began flowing in from farther afield, bearing witness to the expansion of the Southern African economic region. Migration from Botswana and Swaziland built up during the first two decades of the twentieth century, followed by direct migration from Malawi and Zambia to the Witwatersrand in the 1930s and from Angola and Tanzania in the 1940s. (Tanzania and Zambia disengaged themselves during the 1960s.) Such expansion is extraordinary, given the falling real wages paid to African miners,[46] and would appear to justify the mineowners' myth that 'The more you gave Sambo the less he worked'.[47]

This is not the place to enter into the debate concerning the causes and effects of labour migration, but some account should be given of the historically neglected period just before and after the South African War, during which the labour supply myth was assiduously developed by mining interests on the Rand. The myth was a function of the need on the part of the gold mines to lower their underground working costs after the deeper mining of low-grade ores, involving heavy investment in shafts and surface plant, became necessary from 1892. A Labour Department was set up by the Witwatersrand mines in 1893 to take 'active steps for the gradual reduction of native wages to a reasonable level'. Though the labour supply had declined when wages had been reduced in 1889–91, once the supply had climbed from 14,000 in 1891 to 51,000 in 1895, the mines decided to reduce wages once more. An average monthly wage of 63s 6d in 1895 had been reduced to a mere 20s by 1899–1902.[48]

It was the statistics for 1896–9 in particular which gave substance to the labour supply myth. These showed that while wages were cut from 63s 6d to 49s 9d, the labour supply increased from 51,000 to 97,000. Three points need to be made. First, more detailed statistics reveal that though the supply increased between 1895 and 1896 when a wage cut of under 3s was made, it remained stable at 70,000 when wages were cut again in 1897, this time by 12s, and only rose in 1898–9 when the wage was increased by about 1s. Secondly, one must remember that the years 1896–8 were years of cattle plague (rinderpest) and famine, and of land alienation and revolt, when African cultivators were forced off the land. Thirdly, the notion that African workers acquiesced meekly in these pay cuts is entirely erroneous. There was a strike of thousands ~~strikes~~ of workers across the Rand in October 1896 in sympathy with the 'hammerboys' (hand-drillers) of the Crown Reef, whose piecework rates (so much money for so many inches drilled) were being replaced by a lower flat payment for a nine-hour shift. Black labour militancy was not something new in South Africa, nor did it fade away thereafter. In 1854 there had been a strike of 'working boatmen and coolies' at Cape Town. In 1884 black diamond miners at Kimberley joined a white strike against forcible stripping and searching; in 1885 they struck against the imposition of the 'closed compound' system by the Central Company; in 1887 there were strikes at the Central Company and later at De Beers. In 1894 a workers' 'riot' was charged by the Johannesburg police; and in 1902, 1905, and again in 1913 there was African strike action on the Witwatersrand.[49]

The main refutation of the mineowners' myth lies in the years 1901–6. There was no question in South Africa of black workers sheltering in a self-sufficient subsistence economy, with their few wants satisfied, as claimed by the gold-mining interests. The South African War saw a boom in peasant production because of the high food prices stemming from military demands and the absence or destruction of competition from white farmers. The war and post-war reconstruction also created a widespread and better paid casual labour market in the building of fortifications, roads, and railways, in which an unskilled man might receive a 60s or 80s per month. The diamond mines decided to compensate their workers for temporary imprisonment with better wages and working conditions than on the gold mines, in which appalling death rates deterred workers from choosing a career in what was obviously the worst of four possible options for earning money. The mineowners' concern was illustrated by their desperate attempts to procure indentured Chinese labour. What drove workers back to the gold mines was a combination of the collapse of the post-war foodstuff and employment boom, the onset of market depression exacerbated by drought and stock disease, the resurgence of white farm production after heavy state investment in 1902–4, and the tailing off of diamond production down to a standstill by 1914.[50]

As in South Africa, so too in areas farther north, the people were reduced to a degree of rural poverty which gave them little option but to sell their labour abroad. In South Africa it was 'Gold' (the mining industry) and 'Maize' (the white farms) which were the denominators of African wage levels, and which became the pace-setters of low income and labour repression throughout the economy of Southern Africa. In Rhodesia it was predominantly 'Maize' and 'Tobacco'; in Zambia and Zaïre it was 'Copper'. But the resulting rural–industrial relations were essentially similar everywhere.

## III

By accident rather than by design there are two countries in Southern

Africa which are not touched upon by the essays in this book —
Swaziland and Lesotho. Both countries are in fact particularly
interesting to the economic historian as compact laboratories of
processes evident elsewhere. Swaziland exemplifies white settler
interpenetration and enclave development, while Lesotho is the
archetype of peasant economies reduced to peripheral labour reserves. The brief case studies which follow serve therefore as
introductions to important themes which will recur throughout *The
Roots of Rural Poverty*.

## Dualism theory and Swaziland's economic history

The spatial jigsaw of land types and of black and white landholdings
which characterizes Swaziland has encouraged the concentration of
social research there since 1937 in the academic field of economic or
human geography.[51] The sharp racial distinction of white capitalist and
black peasant sectors has also promoted the wholesale adoption of
socio-economic dualism — itself apparently integral to colonial
economic thought in Swaziland since the publication of the 1932 Pim
Report.[52] Economic geographers have thus set themselves the task of
combating Swaziland's underdevelopment in terms of conventional
dualism theory. Sufficient data on the spatial jigsaw of Swaziland has
been collected during and since a 1960 survey by the University of
Natal's Institute for Social Research to make possible multivariate
analysis by computer within the preconceptions set by dualism
theory.[53]

Consequently the almost unanimous solution to Swaziland's underdevelopment offered by contemporary social scientists has been
progressively to integrate — and thereby eliminate — the 'traditional'
sector of the 'dual economy' into the 'modern' sector, by expanding
the latter outwards from its islands of development into the sea of
backwardness.[54] In historical terms this 'modernization' thesis may
be characterized as a form of economic Darwinism — a process of
evolution in which strong modernity must swallow up weak
traditionalism. Fair, Murdoch, and Jones (1969) put their historical
assumptions thus: 'The most significant event in the economic history
of Swaziland, as in most of Africa, was the gradual introduction of the
modern money economy to a society whose economy was traditional,
subsistent, local and self-sufficient.'[55] In essence therefore the white
settlement model — if no longer white settlement itself — has been
equated with *development* in the classic usage of estate management,
to increase the immediate productive capacity and market value of land
as a capital asset and as security for further investment. The peasant
must accordingly be made more 'efficient' in estate management and
weaned away from his 'age-old farming methods'.[56]

Are such views really supported by the historical evidence? We
doubt it and present here an alternative explanation of the origins of the
'dual economy' to that offered by dualism theory — which we hope to

see tested by more detailed research.

Swaziland today is politically a resurrected pre-colonial monarchy ruling a small territory of 17,400 sq. km nestling between South Africa and the southern tip of Mozambique, with a population in 1966 of 375,000, of whom 20,000 were absent abroad. Its territorial shape and internal fragmentation dates from the period 1881–1914. Towards the end of the nineteenth century the territory was greatly coveted by Afrikaners from the Transvaal, who were seeking access to the sea between British and Portuguese coastal possessions. They succeeded in annexing to the Transvaal a great deal of Swazi territory in 1881, actually administered Swaziland itself during 1894–9, and in addition prevailed upon the Swazi king, Mbandzeni, to alienate land recklessly to individual Europeans. The British took over the administration after the South African War, and the contentious land issue was settled by the Resident Commissioner, Robert Coryndon, a man notorious for his bias in favour of settler land interests in Barotseland/North-Western Rhodesia (1897–1907), as chairman of the Southern Rhodesia Native Reserves Commission (1914–15), and as governor of Uganda (1917–22) and Kenya (1922–5).[57] Only about a third of the country (37.6 per cent) was duly confirmed as 'Native Area' under Coryndon in 1907–9. By independence in 1968, the amount of what was now 'Swazi Nation Land' had been increased to just over half the country (54.1 per cent) as a result of land purchases by the Swazi royal government and of the colonial 'Native Land Settlement Scheme'.

Swazi Nation Land is now scattered about in numerous blocks amidst individual tenure holdings — the former white reserves. The blocks are to be found in all four topographical regions of Swaziland — the mountainous *highveld* rising to 1,800 m above sea level; the transitional hills of the *middleveld*; the *lowveld* countryside rolling down below 220 m; and the Lebombo mountain chain climbing to around 600 m and separating Swaziland from the coastal flats of Mozambique.

The major thesis of conventional dualism theory is to posit a historical parallelism between two separate economies — 'modern' and 'traditional'. But the assertion that the 'traditional' economy of Swaziland is 'subsistent, local, and self-sufficient' flies fully in the face of historical evidence which shows how the Swazi have been progressively integrated into a sub-continental labour and produce market over many decades.

Leaving aside the question of whether the pre-colonial Swazi state was indeed self-sufficient, it is evident that Swazi food consumption has been dependent on imports since the 1896–7 disasters of rinderpest, drought, and famine. Before that time Swazi producers were said 'even to have furnished Europeans with grain from their own supplies'. After 1914, when many people were moved off the land alienated to Europeans and labour migration to South Africa increased, Swazi dependence on grain purchases persisted.[58] By 1918 local European farmers were visibly prospering through the sale of maize and tobacco to the Swazi, though during the 1920s settler estates began to concentrate on producing agricultural exports for South Africa, and the period witnessed a resurgence in Swazi peasant production. Thus in the years 1925–9, for example, Swazi consumption of settler-grown maize dropped by an estimated two and a half bags per family, and it is assumed that this was replaced through peasant production. Evidence of increased peasant production may be found in the great increase in the number of ploughs in Swaziland, so that by 1934 one in every two adult males possessed a plough, compared to only one in ten in 1914. But in 1930–4, in the wake of the Depression, peasant production of foodstuffs proved insufficient and was apparently able to meet only one-fifth of consumption requirements and families were forced to rely on purchases from traders for bare subsistence. The purchasing power could only be obtained through migrant labour, and by this time an average of 10,000 Swazis were working away from home each year.[59]

The collapse of agricultural producer prices associated with the Depression, coupled with the partial closure of the South African market by protectionist measures despite the common customs union, reduced African peasants and the small settler estates of Afrikaner maize farmers in the south of Swaziland to penury. By 1934 the country's tobacco production had dropped to one-sixth of its 1929 level, following market restrictions imposed by South Africa in 1930. In respect of cattle, South African protectionism against its partners in the customs union preceded the Depression. In 1924 South Africa had imposed minimum weight restrictions on cattle imports from the High Commission Territories of Basutoland, Bechuanaland, and Swaziland. Swaziland had previously suffered a partial embargo on cattle imports into South Africa between 1902 and 1916, and this had ensured that only prime African-owned cattle which were good breeding stock could be sold for export, while 'scrub cattle' of inferior quality remained at home to breed rapidly. Thus, while Swaziland's estimated cattle population doubled from 210,000 in 1921 to 420,000 in 1934, the general quality declined markedly. The weight restrictions were less rigorously applied against white ranchers — 40 per cent of them absentee landlords — who had taken over large tracts on the *lowveld* recently cleared of tsetse by the rinderpest, and supplied Johannesburg with winter-fed stock at a time of year when good slaughter stock was in short supply. The low carrying capacity of the *lowveld* pastures meant that ranching had to be on a large scale and capital–intensive in order to be profitable.[60]

Swaziland duly became an agricultural appendage of South Africa, in which only large-scale producers — often absentee owners resident in South Africa — could effectively overcome the tariff discrimination of the South African market, to which Swaziland was tied by the customs union which allocated to her only 0.149 per cent of its gross customs revenue. The most dramatic case of the use of Swaziland's natural resources in the interests of South Africa has been the treksheep farms. Transvaal sheep-owners began to trek their sheep annually to winter pasturage in Swaziland from about 1876. In 1900–20 some 300,000 to 400,000 sheep immigrated and emigrated annually in this manner, and by the 1930s no less than 360,000 hectares of mostly *highveld* farmland in Swaziland were being used exclusively for the annual sheep trek. The matter became a source of ecological and political concern which finally culminated in government restrictions after 1955. The practice of burning off old grass at the end of summer to produce young shoots for winter grazing has led to erosion of the main watershed area of Swaziland on the headwaters of the Usutu river system, which carries the greatest water capacity of any river south of the Zambezi. However, there is also evidence that the treksheep farms have provided some relief from overcrowding on Swazi Nation Land by leaving land open to squatting.[61]

The smaller settler maize and tobacco estates in Swaziland found themselves disadvantaged in supplying the South African market after the Depression, and consequently reverted to supplying the local African market. They sold maize at the same price levels as maize previously imported from the Transvaal, despite lower transport costs, and took the bulk of the social services and agricultural aid provided by the colonial administration of Swaziland up to the 1960s.[62] At the bottom of this pecking order the African population bore an annual poll tax of 35s, said to have been the highest 'south of the Nile'— a direct inheritance of the country's experience as a *de facto* colony of the South African Republic (Transvaal) in 1894–9. The need for cash income was the classic propellant of peasants from their holdings to outside labour markets, which according to Leonard Barnes in 1932 kept Swazi peasant agriculture in a 'vicious circle' of low productivity and impoverishment.[63] It remains to be established by more detailed research how general such impoverishment was among the Swazi and how it varied among different social and territorial groups.

Since 1939, and especially since the beginning of the 1960s, Swaziland has seen the setting up of large capital-intensive mining operations (asbestos and iron ore) and agro-industrial projects (sugar, forestry, and citrus) on its territory. If Lesotho, to be discussed shortly, shows that rural poverty cannot be eliminated by convention-ally understood agricultural development alone, Swaziland's experi-ence seems to show that the raising of mass living standards cannot simply be achieved by carving out enclaves of intensive capitalism and hoping for subsequent 'spread' or 'trickle off' to the benighted poor in surrounding areas. National statistics showing a healthy export surplus and a gross domestic product of R130(£73) per head inherited at independence in 1968 disguise enormous social inequalities, and rural income from peasant production is reckoned to have actually declined from over R600,000 to under R300,000 gross in the decade 1960–70.[64]

The enclaves of capitalist development carved out of Swaziland were not designed to integrate with local market conditions, but purely to produce exports for the South African and world markets, and thereby boost state and foreign private revenues rather than general income levels. Whether the capital has been British, Japanese, or South African, the effect of the development enclaves over the last three decades has merely been to divert the main geographical destination of rural labour tribute to capitalist development from South Africa to inside Swaziland. In other words, the geographical localization of 'development' from South Africa to Swaziland has not fundamentally altered the external dependency of the rural areas, but it has provided the state with revenue to alleviate rural poverty by subsidization. Swaziland, by virtue of its small scale, has been able to move nearer to the status of 'sub-metropole' of the world economic system — the conventional aim of development planning in Africa — than any other black-ruled state in Southern and Central Africa. It resembles in miniature the development pattern of South Africa, of which it has been a subsidiary growth pole. Its 'dual economy' is emphatically not one of two separate economies in parallel development. It is one of dominant and subordinate sectors within one economic system, brought into being and maintained through the legal and administrative machinery of the state.

## Peasantization and underdevelopment in Lesotho

As dramatically as any case study in this book, historical evidence suggests that peasant production in Lesotho, a 30,000 sq. km kingdom entirely surrounded by South Africa, boomed under conditions of early capitalist contact, but declined thereafter and has been in a state of chronic depression for most of the twentieth century. The Lesotho kingdom, founded as a refuge from the *Mfecane* wars of the early nineteenth 'century, owed its very origins and its expansion to Moshoeshoe's capture and concentration of the crop and cattle resources of the Caledon valley at his base of Thaba Bosiu. Royal control of surplus cattle through the *mafisa* system, mentioned earlier, and ritual and political control of agriculture was at the heart of Sotho/Tswana political expansion in general.[65] Lesotho was barren of trees except along watercourses and in mountain passes, but the Basotho recognized the fertility of different soils for cultivation. There is *selokoe,* heavy black alluvial soil up to a metre deep in the valley bottoms, very fertile in rainy years but becoming disastrously baked and crumbling in years of drought; there is *lehlohlojane,* a lighter and reddish soil, less fertile but easier to work in dry weather; and there is a grey sandy soil too light to be cultivated.[66]

Approaching Lesotho from due south in 1833, a French missionary party noted how the southern Caledon valley was bare of cultivation until they neared the military security of Thaba Bosiu, when 'The entire land lying between the river and the foot of the mountain was covered with sorghum and maize'.[67] Trade in grain with the Griqua and other *trekboers* of the Orange river around Philippolis had begun in the previous decade. In 1827, Africans from north of the Caledon came to

Philippolis 'with pack oxen to trade among the white people with corn', according to a contemporary witness, and the trade continued into the 1830s, when Basotho came to trade with the African population of Bethulie on the Orange river. By the end of the 1830s the Basotho had stored reserve supplies of millet sufficient for between four and eight years, while in the mid-1840s white farmers 'flocked' to them to buy wheat.[68]

The exact nature of the economic interactions between the Basotho and the Afrikaners who came to form the Orange Free State must be elucidated by further research. Superficially it appears that the products first exchanged were subsequently adopted into the agriculture of the other group — Basotho sorghum and maize for Afrikaner sheep and wheat. But it was land, typically, which became the crucial political issue — especially the large area west of the Caledon, a hilly patchwork of 'sweet' and 'sour' pastures with high stock-carrying capacity and soils virtually self-fertilized by the action of the rains on phosphate-bearing rocks, and able to carry ten to fifteen crops in rotation[69] — a rare occurrence indeed in Southern Africa. By the mid-1850s the Basotho were adopting intensive plough cultivation of the lowlands and the use of wagons to transport their crops to markets. In the 1860s they attempted to reoccupy the western lands with cattle, expelling Afrikaners who had turned from sheep-raising to arable farming. The climax of this struggle for land came in 1868, when Afrikaners systematically destroyed Basotho cultivation east of the Caledon.[70] By a treaty of 1869 Lesotho finally lost the 'conquered territory' west of the Caledon to the Orange Free State, a loss which has remained a touchstone of political grievance ever since.

The loss of productive land and the gain of extra population expelled east of the Caledon into a smaller Lesotho coincided with the opening up of the Kimberley diamond mines to the west in the early 1870s. The maximizing of agricultural production necessary to meet new demands of internal subsistence was combined with a vigorous response to new external market opportunities. Kimberley was quite easy to reach by wagon across 300 kilometres of mainly flat lands, provided that the Orange Free State did not interfere. As for labour migration on foot, Lesotho, like other Sotho/Tswana areas, had already become accustomed to sending migrants to farms in the Cape Colony during the annual harvest season.[71] Overpopulation on agricultural lands in terms of previously acceptable population density was an additional factor: it can be observed as early as 1861 in the number of land disputes brought to court in Lesotho.[72]

A report of 1868 put trade between Lesotho and the Cape Colony at three decades old in the importation of 'blankets, Kaffir picks, and other Kaffir truck', and added that the Basotho 'are the Jews of South Africa, and have a keen appreciation of anything that is to their advantage in a commercial point of view'.[73] By 1872 there were thirty trading stores in Lesotho, and shortly afterwards the number had increased to fifty, importing £150,000 worth of goods annually and exporting 100,000 *muids* (bags of about 84 kg each) of grain and 2,000 bales of wool in a year.[74] An indication of Lesotho's prosperity at this time is provided by the 1875 census, which revealed a population of 128,000 owning 2,700 ploughs, 300 wagons, 35,000 horses, and nearly 224,000 cattle and 300,000 sheep.[75]

Lesotho was a major supplier of labour, as well as foodstuffs, to Kimberley during the 1870s and to the Rand in the 1880s. By 1892 a total of 30,000 Basotho were working on the mines and on Cape railway construction.[76] Before the Gun War of 1879–81, a major incentive for migration had been the desire to acquire firearms; and it was these firearms, together with Sotho ponies, which ultimately enabled the Basotho to be the only formidable non-British military force to survive the South African War of 1899–1902.[77] But from the 1880s it appears that Lesotho needed to maximize the export of agricultural produce and of labour in order to finance the importation of subsistence and luxury items — such as blankets and clothing, ploughs and wagons, cooking utensils and tobacco — upon which the Lesotho economy had become dependent both for customary use and for its structural efficiency. It was therefore in this period of prosperity up to 1900 that the seeds of later underdevelopment were sown. The rising market led to overcultivation, overgrazing, and habitual labour migration, while the Afrikaners of the Orange Free State, 'responding rather belatedly to the markets for their agricultural produce', put restrictive tariffs on competitive Lesotho grain passing through to the mines. The railways made practicable the importing of cheap Australian wheat to Kimberley after 1885, and the rising market of the 1890s in turn collapsed with the coming of the rinderpest cattle disease. 'The natives are in rags, even on Sundays; they seem not only to be impoverished, but disheartened for a long time to come,' remarked an observer in 1899. The South African War revived the market once again, so that a senior colonial official giving evidence to a 1903 commission was able to describe the country as the 'great granary of South Africa', but in that same year, with the collapse of the boom and the onset of drought, Lesotho was obliged to import North American wheat in order to feed herself.[78]

The twentieth century has witnessed the progressive underdevelopment of Lesotho peasant agriculture. Ignorant of its historical background, modern commentators have been wont to dismiss Lesotho as 'a stagnant pool in the fast flowing river of South African economic progress'. The economist Leistner ironically identifies the fundamental cause of underdevelopment as 'the remarkable tenacity of traditional institutions, concepts and values'.[79] Others go further and see underdevelopment among blacks in Southern Africa as the detrimental product of communal social security arresting individual capital formation and promoting 'social and psychological inertia'.[80] Development planners have put their faith in state action which, it is hoped, will reclaim and stabilize eroded lands and improve standards of cultivation and stock-keeping. They have also debated the merits of

individual land tenure, which, they believe, will give peasant proprietors security and hence an incentive to maximize production.[81]

A rather more radical explanation of Lesotho's underdevelopment
begins its reasoning from the evident failure of rural development in
recent years. The anthropologist Wallman presents a model of the
syndrome of 'non-development', a closed circle in which rural
poverty, migration, and ideology serve to reinforce each other.
*Poverty* is evident to any Mosotho in the increasing time and energy
that has to be spent on the diminishing returns of sub-subsistence
agriculture. (There is virtually no local employment outside agriculture; a highly skilled sheep-shearer can expect to practise his trade for
only two weeks in a year.) *Migration* enables the family to survive at
subsistence level while depriving it of the productive manpower and
parental authority that could make it a viable unit of production.
Migration constantly exposes Lesotho society to the ad-mass consumer ideals of South African urban life: even imported goods like
blankets (universally worn as cloaks) and packaged goods vital for
subsistence are marketed and bought on the basis of manipulated
consumer appeal in designs and brand names. *'Ideology'* (as the
totality of ideas and attitudes) is how a Mosotho accommodates and in
fact reinforces the conditions of his economic plight. Not only
hopelessness for the future but also restlessness sets in, with constant
travel in which he looks vaguely for work and visits relatives. Social
insecurity in modern Lesotho is evidenced in widespread but
unfounded fears of night violence, and in the growing number of legal
cases in the customary courts concerning trespass.[82]

Such explanations raise questions that help the historian to put his
evidence in perspective. Can one talk of 'traditional' agriculture as one
of the continuities between pre-colonial and post-colonial society?
Should redevelopment of blighted resources by state capital be
equated with the development of peasant productivity and living
standards? What evidence is there of changes in peasant morale over
time in the intellectual history of the masses evident in popular culture?
How far can one consider the national economy of Lesotho in isolation
from that of South Africa under changing political and economic
conditions?

Fuller answers to such questions must await fuller historical
research, but available evidence does make clear certain structural
changes in the Lesotho economy during the twentieth century.
Statistics from 1909 show that the rate of imports and exports built up
from £260,000 (imports) and £353,000 (exports) in that year to a peak in
1928 of £922,000 (imports) and £1,013,000 (exports). Thereafter the
favourable relation between exports and imports was reversed, and
there was an ever-widening gap between the two until by the last year of
colonial rule, in 1965–6, only 44 per cent of local consumption was met
by local production and the trade gap stood at *minus* £8.2 million.[83]

The foregoing account of peasant growth in the later nineteenth
century suggests that the potential for underdevelopment existed

by the 1880s in the form of dependency on external markets outside Basotho control. The early twentieth-century colonial system set up to embrace Southern Africa increased these tendencies with political controls and falling market returns. But it was the 1930s which appears to have been the great era of change from viable peasant production to Wallman's syndrome of 'non-development'. The 1930s were times of disaster on two counts— the effects of the Depression on world agricultural commodity prices from 1929, and of blight culminating in the drought of 1933—4.

In 1934 the value of exports dropped to its lowest ever level of £285,000, while imports stood at £629,000 and continued thereafter to rise in cost. As elsewhere, the trade gap could only be closed through labour migration and by eating into or exporting capital assets. In 1933 the Basutoland administration issued some 52,000 passes for migrants going to the Union of South Africa. In the period 1921—36 the proportion of Basotho migrants outside the country rose from 8.7 to 15.3 per cent of the population, and the actual number involved more than doubled. Many migrants once left never returned. It has been estimated that in the years 1936—46, South Africa, then undergoing unprecedented urban and secondary industrial growth, absorbed 100,000 Basotho permanently, to which another 40,000 were added in 1946—56.[84] This represents a massive bleeding of Lesotho's capital resources not only in brawn but also in brain — the export of earlier investment in education to South Africa constituted subsidization of that country's secondary industrial growth in the form of semi-skilled and skilled mechanical and clerical labour.

The export or deterioration of capital assets, in the interests of South African economic growth, may also be seen in agriculture and on the land. Prime ponies and sheep were progressively sold off for inferior imported stock, resulting in a decline in breeding stock and in quality of wool. The 1933—4 drought was probably all the more disastrous because optimum stock- and crop-carrying capacities on the land had already been surpassed by constant use. In 1921 the number of cattle was estimated at 580,666, and of ponies and horses at 153,733; these figures had dropped dramatically by the time of the 1936 census, and have never again reached the same level. Wheat exports peaked at 256,000 bags in 1919; during the 1930s the figure ranged from 56,000 to 197,000 bags; from 1946 to 1950 it averaged 46,000 bags. Maize exports peaked at 101,000 bags in 1928; but by 1946—50 exports averaged only 18,000 bags annually. These figures cannot be explained in terms of rapid population growth consuming potential exports, for the population, albeit allowing for permanent emigration to South Africa, appears to have been remarkably static at this time.[85] It is important to realize that since the 1930s Lesotho has been an importer of the same staples as she exports. This reflects the lack of marketing and storage facilities within Lesotho — one of the consequences of open access to South Africa within a common customs union, under which Basutoland (colonial Lesotho) received 0.88575 per cent of the gross customs revenue of the union, and was made 'entirely dependent on the fiscal and economic policy' of South Africa.[86] Statistics show that what was sold off cheap was bought back dear. The state-backed South African produce-marketing boards were representative of white farming interests in the 'maize triangle' of the Transvaal and the Orange Free State. In the case of wheat, it is safe to assume that what was imported into Lesotho was inferior to the exported highland product so highly prized by millers and bakers in South Africa.

Perhaps the most important capital asset which had been 'exported', or which had at any rate deteriorated by the 1930s, was peasant self-confidence and initiative. Wallman's 'ideological' factor, though not quantifiable, should never be ignored — as the studies of Rhodesia and Katanga in Chapters 9 and 13 also illustrate.

Famine, erosion, and falling agricultural production prompted government reaction from 1935 onwards. Between 1935 and 1952, nearly 140,000 hectares of lowland were terraced and 165,000 hectares of mountain were protected from erosion with buffer grass strips, while in 1942 52,379 small dams were built and 18 million trees planted — though most of the trees failed to take root because of drought. Colonial and royal coercion combined finally to 'purify' the nation's sheep to merino standard, by eliminating inferior stock from breeding, while 12,000 vegetable plots were established with state encouragement.[87] But it is important to realize that this improvement was not achieved by state intervention alone, for the primary commodity price boom of the 1950s helped to resurrect exports. For example, 4.8m. kg of wool fetched only £329,000 in 1946, but an annual average of 3.4m. kg fetched £2.5m in the years 1951 − 5, though by 1963 the income from 4.3m. kg had declined to £2.1m.

Nevertheless, Lesotho today presents a picture of underdevelopment by any definition. The stark mountains rising to 3,600 metres, the foothills, and the lowlands are all barren of natural vegetation and rent with the scars of some of the worst erosion on the continent. At independence in 1966, Lesotho's gross domestic product stood at about £20m., while the total earnings abroad of its labour migrants stood at £21.5m., of which less than a fifth was finding its way back to Lesotho.[88] No fewer than 117,000 of its 970,000 people were absent abroad in that year. And half the resident population was crammed into a mere quarter of the territory — the lowlands — where all available land was being cultivated, and population densities ranged from the average 40 per sq. km up to 118 per sq. km in one district.[89]

In 1954 a colonial government report questioned whether there really was a land shortage in Lesotho, pointing to social inequities in the distribution of land and in control over labour and resources. Recent census analysis has shown that there is indeed a physical shortage of cultivable land in Lesotho, which is continually increasing with population growth and the lack of alternative industrial employment within the country or facilities for permanent emigration. But it has also been recognized since the agricultural census of 1960 that individual 'rural capitalists' are taking up a disproportionate share of land.[90] As elsewhere on the continent, productive farming became increasingly the prerogative of the few after the Second World War, while the many have had to compensate for impoverishment by selling the labour of their families to centres hundreds or even thousands of miles away. The nationalist movements of the 1960s in Africa tenuously combined political levelling with increasing socio-economic inequity.

The structural conditions for agricultural underdevelopment persisted in Lesotho even after the corrosion of agricultural blight had been checked by state action. A population that theoretically remained rural in Lesotho had in fact to become peri-industrial in Southern African terms. If labour migration to South Africa is accepted as an index of the structural incapacity of the rural economy, then the underdevelopment of the national economy of Lesotho has increased progressively to date. The migration of Basotho to South Africa climbed to a peak of 206,424 in 1960, representing some 23.2 per cent of the total population. Since then the imposition of South African border controls in 1963 has finally blocked the 'safety valve' of permanent emigration. An annual figure of 150,000 temporary labour migrants has been incorporated into the official planning of the independent Lesotho state, but as Williams points out, 'migration has effectively operated to delay the implementation of essential reforms not only in agricultural techniques but also in decisions affecting the entire economic environment'.[91]

The case of Lesotho thus serves to underline the intimate connections between peasant and proletarian, capital and labour, political factors and the means of production, that have built up in local areas in Central and Southern Africa, and the connections between such local areas and the world economy. Rural poverty cannot be isolated as the province of Ministries of Agriculture and 'Rural Development' alone. Its emergence and therefore its elimination must be seen as part of a larger process involving the total political economy.

## NOTES

1.  K.O. Dike, *Trade and Politics in the Niger Delta, 1830–1885* (Oxford, 1956); R. Gray and D. Birmingham (eds), *Pre-Colonial African Trade* (London, 1970).
2.  W. Rodney, review of Gray and Birmingham, *Pre-Colonial African Trade,* in *Transafrican Journal of History,* 2, 1, 1972, 124.
3.  T.O. Ranger, *The Agricultural History of Zambia,* Historical Association of Zambia Pamphlet No. 1 (Lusaka, 1971); J. Iliffe, *Agricultural Change in Modern Tanganyika,* Historical Association of Tanzania Paper No. 10 (Nairobi, 1971); R. van Zwanenberg, *The Agricultural History of Kenya to 1939,* Historical Association of Kenya Paper No. 1 (Nairobi, 1972).
4.  W. Allan, *The African Husbandman* (Edinburgh and London, 1965); R. Dumont, *Lands Alive* (London, 1965); R. Dumont, *African Agricultural Development* (New York, 1966); R. Dumont, *Types of Rural Economy* (London, 1966); R. Dumont, *False Start in Africa* (London, 1968); R. Dumont, *Socialisms and Development* (London,

1973). See also W. Allan, M. Gluckman, D. U. Peters, and C. G. Trapnell, *Land Holding and Land Usage among the Plateau Tonga of Mazabuka District* (London, 1948); W. Allan, *Studies in African Land Usage in Northern Rhodesia* (London, 1949).
5.   G. Arrighi, 'Labour Supplies in Historical Perspective: A Study of the Proletarianization of the African Peasantry in Rhodesia', *Journal of Development Studies, 6,* 1970, 197–234. This was first published in Italian in 1969. See also G. Arrighi, *The Political Economy of Rhodesia* (The Hague, 1967). These two works, together with other pieces by Arrighi and John Saul, have been gathered together in G. Arrighi and J.S. Saul, *Essays on the Political Economy of Africa* (New York and London, 1973). For Western Africa, an important article is K. Post, ' "Peasantization" and Rural Political Movements in Western Africa', *Archives Européennes de Sociologie, 13,* 1972, 223–54.
6.   J.S. Saul and R. Woods, 'African Peasantries', in T. Shanin (ed.), *Peasants and Peasant Societies* (Harmondsworth, 1971), 105. This is also to be found in Arrighi and Saul, *Essays,* 407.
7.   D. G. Bettison, 'Factors in the Determination of Wage Rates in Central Africa', *Rhodes-Livingstone Journal, 28,* 1960, 27. Cited in Arrighi, 'Labour Supplies', 200.
8.   S. Amin, 'Underdevelopment and Dependence in Black Africa — Origins and Contemporary Forms', *Journal of Modern African Studies, 10,* 1972, 503–24; S. Amin, *Accumulation on a World Scale* (New York, 1974); C. Meillassoux, 'From Reproduction to Production: A Marxist Approach to Economic Anthropology', *Economy and Society, 1,* 1972, 93–105; C. Meillassoux, 'The Social Organisation of the Peasantry: The Economic Base of Kinship', *Journal of Peasant Studies, 1,* 1973, 81–90; E. Terray, *Marxism and 'Primitive' Societies* (New York, 1972). See also P.P. Rey, *Colonialisme, neo-colonialisme et transition au capitalisme: Example de la 'Comilog' au Congo-Brazzaville* (Paris, 1971).
9.   For a lucid introduction to underdevelopment theory, see C. Leys, *Underdevelopment in Kenya* (London, 1975), 1–27. Three useful collections of essays are, H. Bernstein (ed.), *Underdevelopment and Development: The Third World Today* (Harmondsworth, 1973); C. K. Wilber (ed.), *The Political Economy of Development and Underdevelopment* (New York, 1973); I. Oxaal, T. Barnett, and D. Booth (eds), *Beyond the Sociology of Development* (London and Boston, 1975).
10.   A.G. Frank, *Capitalism and Underdevelopment in Latin America* (New York and London, 1967); A.G. Frank, *Latin America: Underdevelopment or Revolution?* (New York and London, 1969); A.G. Frank, *Lumpenbourgeoisie: Lumpendevelopment – Dependence, Class and Politics in Latin America* (New York and London, 1972); W. Rodney, *How Europe Underdeveloped Africa* (London and Dar es Salaam, 1972). For the critics see, among others, E. Laclau, 'Feudalism and Capitalism in Latin America', *New Left Review, 67,* 1971, 19–38; F.H. Cardoso, 'Dependency and Development in Latin America', *New Left Review, 74,* 1972, 83–95; F. H. Cardoso, 'Associated-Dependent Development: Theoretical and Practical Implications', in A. Stepan (ed.), *Authoritarian Brazil* (New Haven, 1973); T. Dos Santos, 'The Crisis of Development Theory and the Problem of Dependence in Latin America', in H. Bernstein (ed.), *Underdevelopment and Development,* 57–80; A. Nove, 'On Reading André Gunder Frank', *Journal of Development Studies, 10,* 1974, 445–55; D. Booth, 'André Gunder Frank: An Introduction and Appreciation', in Oxaal, Barnett, and Booth, *Beyond the Sociology,* 50–85; A.G. Hopkins, 'On Importing André Gunder Frank into Africa', *African Economic History Review, 2,* 1, 1975, 13–21.
11.   R.W. Clower, *et al., Growth without Development: An Economic Survey of Liberia* (Evanston, 1966).
12.   L.P. Green and T.J.D. Fair, *Development in Africa* (Johannesburg, 1962); T.J.D. Fair, 'The Core–Periphery Concept and Population Growth in South Africa, 1911–1960', *South African Geographical Journal, 47,* 1965, 59–71.
13.   Amin, 'Underdevelopment and Dependence', 504.
14.   We feel that the distinction between 'dual economy' as a convenient descriptive term and 'dualism theory' as an invalid historical analysis is the root of the problem

which has taxed Archie Mafeje and others. A. Mafeje, 'The Fallacy of Dual Economies', *East Africa Journal, 9,* 1972, 30–4; A. Mafeje, 'The Fallacy of "Dual Economies" Revisited', in R. Leys (ed.), *Dualism and Rural Development in East Africa* (Copenhagen, 1973).

15. The classic statements of (two world) dualism theory for our area are W.J. Barber, *The Economy of British Central Africa* (London, 1961); D.H. Houghton, *The South African Economy* (Cape Town, 1967); D.H. Houghton, 'Men of Two Worlds: Some Aspects of Migratory Labour in South Africa', *South African Journal of Economics, 28,* 1960, 177–90.

16. K. Marx, *Capital, Vol. 1* (Moscow, 1961), 505.

17. F. Nightingale, quoted in Aborigines' Protection Society to Colonial Office, 6 March 1880, in *C.2676, Further Correspondence Respecting the Affairs of South Africa* (London, 1880), 1–3.

18. We have eschewed a detailed geographical description of the whole area here, since virtually all our contributors indicate salient features at the beginning of their essays. Readers are urged to make use of the collection of maps which precedes this Introduction when reading the essays.

19. 'Tropical soils are proper and more fragile than those of temperate regions. Great care is needed in using them, if their further destruction and impoverishment are to be avoided. These conditions give tropical agriculture a precarious character which is absent from the temperate belt.' P. Gourou, *The Tropical World* (London, 1958), 13. Cited in P. Fordham, *The Geography of African Affairs* (Harmondsworth, 1968), 26.

20. R.W. Stephens, 'Population Pressures in Africa South of the Sahara', in *Population Research Project Bulletin* (Washington, 1959). Cited in M. Yudelman, *Africans on the Land* (Cambridge, Mass., 1964), 8.

21. See the excellent study, J. Ford, *The Role of the Trypanosomiases in African Ecology* (Oxford, 1971).

22. 'Many mistakes have been made because European planters and administrators were unaware that, under tropical conditions, factors require to be taken into account which are operative only to a minor degree in temperate countries, often coupled with an erroneous belief that tropical soils are of well-nigh inexhaustible fertility.' H. Tempany and D.H. Grist, *An Introduction to Tropical Agriculture* (London, 1960). Cited in R.P. Moss (ed.), *The Soil Resources of Tropical Africa* (Cambridge, 1968), 113.

23. O. Thomas, *Agricultural and Pastoral Prospects of South Africa* (London, 1904), 15–17.

24. A 1963 UNESCO report noted that 'the savannah soils present a characteristic, which, more than any other, makes them particularly vulnerable to erosion, namely the great instability of their structure as soon as they are over-cultivated. Two successive years of mechanized cultivation are enough, in a savannah zone, to degrade soil structure and to reduce permeability.' It went on to speak of 'the disastrous effect of excessively mechanized cultivation methods'. UNESCO, *A Review of the Natural Resources of the African Continent* (Paris, 1963), 234.

25. P.B. Sanders, 'Sekonyela and Moshweshwe: Failure and Success in the Aftermath of the Difaqane', *Journal of African History, 10,* 1969, 440–1, 443; S.I. Mudenge, 'The Role of Foreign Trade in the Rozvi Empire: A Reappraisal', *Journal of African History, 15,* 1974, 389–90 n. 105; E.L. Hermitte, 'An Economic History of Barotseland, 1800–1940', PhD thesis, Northwestern University, 1973, 29, 35, 124.

26. The notion of 'uneconomic man' is investigated in W.O. Jones, 'Economic Man in Africa', *Food Research Institute Studies, 1,* 1960, 107–34; S.D. Neumark, 'Economic Development and Economic Incentives', *South African Journal of Economics, 26,* 1958, 55–63; C.J. Doyle, 'Productivity, Technical Change, and the Peasant Producer: A Profile of the African Cultivator', *Food Research Institute Studies, 13,* 1974, 61–76. See also C. Hutton and R. Cohen, 'African Peasants and Resistance to Change: A Reconsideration of Sociological Approaches', in Oxaal, Barnett, and Booth, *Beyond the Sociology,* 105–30. See also Postscript, 411 below.

27.   C. van Onselen, 'Black Workers in Central African Industry: A Critical Essay on the Historiography and Sociology of Rhodesia', *Journal of Southern African Studies*, *1*, 1975, 228–46.
28.   R.J. Fielder, 'The Role of Cattle in the Ila Economy: A Conflict of Views on the Uses of Cattle by the Ila of Namwala', *African Social Research*, *15*, 1973, 327.
29.   Fielder, 'The Role of Cattle', 351–2.
30.   E.C. de Carvalho, ' "Traditional" and "Modern" Patterns of Cattle Raising in Southwestern Angola: A Critical Evaluation of Change from Pastoralism to Ranching', *Journal of Developing Areas*, *8*, 1974, 222–3.
31.   G. Scott, 'No Revolution for the Small Farmer', *African Development*, *8*, October 1974, Z.41–Z.42.
32.   See, *inter alia*, Nyasaland Protectorate, *Report of the Committee Appointed by His Excellency the Governor to Enquire into Emigrant Labour, 1935* (Zomba, 1936); A.I. Richards, *Land, Labour and Diet in Northern Rhodesia* (London, 1939); M. Read, 'Migrant Labour in Africa and its Effects on Tribal Life', *International Labour Review*, *45*, 1942, 605–31; I. Schapera, *Migrant Labour and Tribal Life* (London, 1947); J. Gugler, 'The Impact on Labour Migration on Society and Economy in Sub-Saharan Africa: Empirical Findings and Theoretical Considerations', *African Social Research*, *6*, 1968, 463–86; F. Wilson, *Migrant Labour in South Africa* (Johannesburg, 1972); R.B. Boeder, 'The Effects of Labour Emigration on Rural Life in Malawi', *Rural Africana*, *20*, 1973, 37–46; C.P. Luchembe, 'Rural Stagnation: A Case Study of the Lamba-Lima of Ndola Rural District', in R.H. Palmer (ed.), *Zambian Land and Labour Studies, Vol. 2*, National Archives of Zambia Occasional Paper 3 (Lusaka, 1974), 21–33; M.C. Musambachime, 'Labour Migration from Mweru-Luapula 1900–24: A Study of African Response to Wage Labour', in Palmer (ed.), *Zambian Land and Labour Studies, Vol. 2*, 39–65; K.N. Mponda, 'Post-Independence Labour Migration in Kaputa District and Its Effects on Tabwa Traditional Society', in Palmer (ed.), *Zambian Land and Labour Studies, Vol. 2*, 66–85; J.P. Mtisi, 'Rural Misery on the Screen: The Effects of Taxation and Colonial Labour Demands in Chipata and Petauke, 1900–1924', in R.H. Palmer (ed.), *Zambian Land and Labour Studies, Vol. 3*, National Archives of Zambia Occasional Paper 4 (Lusaka, 1977), 31–56; R.S. Kapaale, 'A Survey of Wenela in Barotseland', in Palmer (ed.), *Zambian Land and Labour Studies, Vol. 3*, 75–120; D. Parkin (ed.), *Town and Country in Central and East Africa* (London, 1976).
33.   The southward spread of the Early Iron Age may be crudely plotted by the earliest known radiocarbon dates from archaeological sites. The site at Katuruka near Lake Victoria in Tanzania has been dated to 550 BC ± 115; at Funa, near Kinshasa on the lower Zaïre river to 270 BC ± 90; at Situmpa Forest Station in Zambia immediately north of the Zambezi to AD 20 ± 100; at Calder's Cave near Gokwe in the north of Rhodesia to 20 BC ± 80; at Mabveni in south-east Rhodesia facing the Limpopo to AD 180 ± 120; at Silverleaves near Tzaneen in the north-east Transvaal to AD 270 ± 55; at Broederstroom in the western Transvaal to AD 460 ± 50; at Blackburn near Durban to AD 1050 ± 50; and at Kapako on the Okavango river on the Namibia/Angola frontier to AD 840 ± 50.
34.   'Khoisan' is a convenient linguistic envelope for the non-Bantu 'click' languages of Southern and Central Africa, including Khoikhoi, San, and possibly other linguistic groupings. E.O.J. Westphal, 'The Linguistic Prehistory of Southern Africa: Bush, Kwadi, Hottentot, and Bantu Linguistic Relationships', *Africa*, *33*, 1963, 244–5, 249–50. The habit popularized by the *Oxford History of South Africa* of translating all references to 'Hottentots' as Khoikhoi, and 'Bushmen' as San, is plainly confused: cf. S. Marks, 'Khoisan Resistance to the Dutch in the Seventeenth and Eighteenth centuries', *Journal of African History*, *13*, 1972, 55–8.
35.   I.L. Mason and J.P. Maule, *The Indigenous Livestock of Eastern and Southern Africa* (Farnham Royal, 1960).
36.   C.H.L. Hahn. H. Vedder, and L. Fourie, *The Native Tribes of South West Africa* (Cape Town, 1928), 39–78; M. Wilson, 'The Hunters and Herders' and 'The Sotho,

30                          NEIL PARSONS AND ROBIN PALMER

Venda, and Tsonga', in M. Wilson and L. Thompson (eds), *The Oxford History of South Africa, Vol. 1, South Africa to 1870* (Oxford, 1969), 40–74, 131–67.
37.    E.A. Alpers, 'Re-thinking African Economic History: A Contribution to the Discussion of the Roots of Underdevelopment', *Ufahamu, 3*, 3, 1973, 97–129; E.A. Alpers, *Ivory and Slaves in East Central Africa* (London, 1975); W. Rodney, *West Africa and the Atlantic Slave Trade*, Historical Association of Tanzania Paper No. 2 (Nairobi, 1967); E.A. Alpers, *The East African Slave Trade*, Historical Association of Tanzania Paper No. 3 (Nairobi, 1967); J.E.G. Sutton, *Early Trade in Eastern Africa*, Historical Association of Tanzania Paper No. 11 (Nairobi, 1973).
38.    On Cape Colony banking, see M.H. de Kock, *Selected Subjects in the Economic History of South Africa* (Cape Town, 1924), 367–8. We have adopted the term 'Steel Age' to emphasize the quantitative development of the Iron Age post-1870 in the secondary industrial revolution of mass production based on steel tools and machinery: see G. Barraclough, *An Introduction to Contemporary History* (Harmondsworth, 1967), 43–64. The 1880–1913 period of capital injection and export of cheap manufactures into Africa in exchange for high-cost primary products upsets the crude model of the Third World always being locked in 'unequal exchange' with Europe and America. See M.B. Brown, *The Economics of Imperialism* (Harmondsworth, 1974), 250–2, for a critique of A. Emmanuel, *Unequal Exchange* (London, 1972).
39.    R.P. Stevens, *Lesotho, Botswana and Swaziland* (London, 1967); R. Hyam, *The Failure of South African Expansionism, 1908–1948* (London, 1972); W.M. Hailey, *The Republic of South Africa and the High Commission Territories* (London, 1963); J. Halpern, *South Africa's Hostages* (Harmondsworth, 1965); S.C. Nolutshungu, *South Africa in Africa* (Manchester, 1975).
40.    M.A.G. Davies, *Incorporation in the Union of South Africa or Self-Government: Southern Rhodesia's Choice, 1922* (Pretoria, 1965); P.R. Warhurst, 'Rhodesia and her Neighbours, 1900–23', PhD thesis, Oxford University, 1970.
41.    In 1919 Smuts, 'lamenting that the British Empire was "specially poor in copper"', urged not only that most of the German colonies should be retained but also that part of Portuguese and Belgian Africa should be acquired'. W.R. Louis, *Great Britain and Germany's Lost Colonies 1914–1919* (Oxford, 1967), 159.
42.    J.S. Galbraith, *Crown and Charter* (Berkeley, Los Angeles, and London, 1974).
43.    Quoted in B. Bozzoli, 'The Origins, Development and Ideology of Local Manufacturing in South Africa', *Journal of Southern African Studies, 1*, 1975, 211.
44.    Harold Wolpe suggests that colonialism cannot be internal and is of necessity an external relationship. We would argue, however, that the 'dual economy' is an attempt to create internally conditions parallel to those of a metropole and its colony. H. Wolpe, 'The Theory of Internal Colonialism: The South African Case', in Oxaal, Barnett, and Booth, *Beyond the Sociology*, 229–52.
45.    F. Wilson, 'Farming, 1866–1966', in M. Wilson and L. Thompson (eds), *The Oxford History of South Africa, Vol. 2, South Africa 1870–1966* (Oxford, 1971), 104–71; E.B. Jones, 'South African Native Land Policy', *Bantu Studies, 14, 1939–40*, 175–97; R. Leys, 'South African Gold Mining in 1974: "The Gold of Migrant Labour"', *African Affairs, 74*, 295, 1975, 196–208.
46.    F. Wilson, *Labour in the South African Gold Mines, 1911–1969* (Cambridge, 1972), 60–7.
47.    Van Onselen, 'Black Workers', 235. See also E.J. Berg, 'Backward-Sloping Labour Supply Functions in Dual Economies — The Africa Case', *Quarterly Journal of Economics, 75*, 1961, 468–92.
48.    D. Denoon, *A Grand Illusion* (London, 1973), 156.
49.    J.M. Smallberger, 'I.D.B. and the Mining Compound System in the 1880s', *South African Journal of Economics, 42*, 1974, 398–414; *African Review, 3*, 1894, 372, *9*, 1896, 555; P. Warwick, 'Black Industrial Protest on the Witwatersrand, 1901–02', *South African Labour Bulletin, 2*, 8, 1976, 22–35; C.R. Diamond, 'The Native Grievances Enquiry, 1913–1914', *South African Journal on Economics, 36*, 1968, 211–27.
50.    Denoon, *Grand Illusion*, 127–48; Diamond, 'Native Grievances', 218–19;

Thomas, *Agricultural and Pastoral Prospects*, 165.
51.  D.M. Doveton, *The Human Geography of Swaziland* (London and Liverpool, 1937).
52.  Pim wrote that the Swazi 'are but recently emerged from a subsistence economy and have not yet adapted themselves to the new money economy, being still absolute children in money matters'. *Cmd. 4114, Financial and Economic Situation of Swaziland, Report of the Commission appointed by the Secretary of State for Dominion Affairs, January, 1932* (London, 1932), 22, 84.
53.  J.F. Holleman (ed.), *Experiment in Swaziland* (Cape Town, 1964); J.B.McI. Daniel, 'Swaziland: Some Problems of an African Rural Economy in a Developing Country', *South African Geographical Journal, 48*, 1966, 90–100; J.P. Lea, 'The Differentiation of the Rural Periphery in Swaziland: A Multivariate Analysis', *South African Geographical Journal, 54*, 1972, 105–23.
54.  See for example, T.J.D. Fair, G. Murdoch, and H.M. Jones, *Development in Swaziland* (Johannesburg, 1969). A notable exception is M. Fransman, 'Development and Underdevelopment in Swaziland: A Case Study', University of Botswana, Lesotho, and Swaziland, History Teachers' Workshop, Gaborone, 1973.
55.  Fair, Murdoch, and Jones, *Development*, 19.
56.  G.W. Whittington and J.B.McI. Daniel, 'Problems of Land Tenure and Ownership in Swaziland', in M.F. Thomas and G.W. Whittington (eds), *Environment and Land Use in Africa* (London, 1969), 454.
57.  R.H. Palmer, *Land and Racial Domination in Rhodesia* (London, 1977), 105–6.
58.  Doveton, *Human Geography*, 38.
59.  L. Barnes, *The New Boer War* (London, 1932), 93–4; H. Kuper, *The Uniform of Colour* (Johannesburg, 1947), 136–46.
60.  S. Ettinger, 'South Africa's Weight Restrictions on Cattle Exports from Bechuanaland, 1924–41', *Botswana Notes and Records, 4*, 1972, 22–3; Doveton, *Human Geography*, 39, 47–51.
61.  Doveton, *Human Geography*, 48–9; Whittington and Daniel, 'Problems of Land Tenure', 458–60.
62.  Barnes, *New Boer War*, 86–127; *Official Year Books of the Union of South Africa and of Basutoland, Bechuanaland Protectorate, and Swaziland* (Pretoria, 1918–).
63.  Barnes, *New Boer War*, 107–8.
64.  Fransman, 'Development and Underdevelopment', 17.
65.  Sanders, 'Sekonyela', 440–1, 443. See also note 25 above.
66.  E. Casalis, *The Basutos* (London, 1861), 12–13; H. Ashton, *The Basuto* (London, 1967), 121.
67.  A. Coates, *Basutoland* (London, 1966), 27, quoting in translation E. Casalis, *Mes Souvenirs* (Paris, 1930).
68.  G.M. Theal, *Basutoland Records, Vol. 2, 1853–1861* (Cape Town, 1883), 437–8; R.C. Germond, *Chronicles of Basutoland* (Morija, 1967), 438–9, 444.
69.  Thomas, *Agricultural and Pastoral Prospects*, 18–19, 227–8; Germond, *Chronicles*, 444.
70.  Theal, *Basutoland Records, Vol. 3A, 1862–1865*, 209–11, *Vol. 3B, 1865–1868*, 867, 878–82; Germond, *Chronicles*, 453–4.
71.  J.C. Williams, 'Lesotho: Economic Implications of Migrant Labour', *South African Journal of Economics, 39*, 1971, 149.
72.  C.W. de Kiewiet, 'Social and Economic Developments in Native Tribal Life', in *The Cambridge History of the British Empire, Vol. 8, South Africa, Rhodesia and the High Commission Territories* (Cambridge, 1963), 843.
73.  Theal, *Basutoland Records, Vol. 3B, 1865–1868*, 876.
74.  D.H. Houghton and J. Dagut, *Source Material on the South African Economy: 1860–1970, Vol. 1, 1860–1899* (Cape Town, 1972), 319–20; Germond, *Chronicles*, 325.
75.  E. Bradlow, 'The Cape Government's Rule of Basutoland 1871–1883', *Archives Year Book for South African History, 31, Part 2* (Johannesburg, 1968), 130.

76. Williams, 'Lesotho', 149.

77. A. Atmore and P. Sanders, 'Sotho Arms and Ammunition in the Nineteenth Century', *Journal of African History, 12,* 1971, 535−44; H.B. Jeffreys, 'The Native Races of South Africa from a Military Point of View', *Journal of the Royal United Services Institute, 51,* 1907, 1107−23.

78. F. Wilson, 'Farming, 1866−1966', 70; J.J. Guy, 'The Origins of Migrant Labour in Lesotho', *Mohlomi, 1,* 1976, in press.

79. G.M.E. Leistner, *Lesotho: Economic Structure and Growth* (Pretoria, 1966), 35−6.

80. J.L. Sadie, 'The Social Anthropology of Economic Underdevelopment', *The Economic Journal, 70,* 1960, 297−8, 301.

81. With reference to the Transkei, see G.L. Rutman, 'Asset deterioration, the Nature of Property Rights, and the "Traditional" Economic System', *South African Journal of Economics, 39,* 1971, 79−87. As Rutman points out, blight (asset or property deterioration) can scarcely be attributed to a lack of capitalist spirit in rural Africa, when it is so rampant at the heart of capitalist development in urban North America.

82. S. Wallman, 'Conditions of Non-development: The Case of Lesotho', *Journal of Development Studies, 8,* 1972, 251−61. She compares the lethargy and lifestyle of a temporarily returned labour migrant to actors in Britain 'resting' between uncertain contracts. See also S. Wallman, *Take Out Hunger: Two Case Studies of Rural Development in Basutoland* (London, 1969).

83. *Official Year Books;* T. van Waasdijk, 'The Economic Development of Lesotho', *South African Journal of Economics, 38,* 1970, 164−6.

84. Leistner, *Lesotho,* 4.

85. The figures show that population increased most rapidly during the period 1875−1904, and again after 1958. In 1921 the estimated population was 498,781, which had risen to only 563,854 by 1946. As always, one needs to take such figures with a considerable degree of caution and scepticism.

86. W.M. Hailey, *Native Administration in the British African Territories, Part V: The High Commission Territories: Basutoland, The Bechuanaland Protectorate and Swaziland* (London, 1953), 20−1.

87. *Official Year Book No. 27, 1951−2.* 1270−2. Basil Davidson quoted an American authority, Dr Lowdermilk, as describing this conservation work as 'the finest I have seen in Africa south of the Sahara', but Davidson added that 'The Basuto peasant . . . simply cannot afford soil conservation. . . . And that is where the achievements of conservation in Basutoland — admirable though they are within their limits — pall before the failure or refusal of the British to develop the land and people.' B. Davidson, *Report on Southern Africa* (London, 1952), 209, 211, 213.

88. F. Wilson, *Migrant Labour,* 110. Recent attempts by the Lesotho government to insist on partial repatriation of migrants' earnings have been bitterly resented by the migrants themselves, as a check on their purchasing power for consumer goods which are cheaper in South Africa.

89. Leistner, *Lesotho,* 3−5.

90. I. Hamnett, 'Some Problems in the Assessment of Land Shortage: A Case Study in Lesotho', *African Affairs, 72,* 286, 1973, 37−45.

91. Williams, 'Lesotho', 149−53, 167,

# PART 1

---

*Pre-Colonial Economies
and Colonial Impact*

---

The six chapters in the first part of this book are concerned with the characteristics of pre-colonial economic development, and with the subsequent impact of the imposition of colonial rule.

In Chapter 1, the scope and limitations of the typical Later Iron Age economy are illustrated in comprehensive detail by a case study of the Shona people between the Zambezi and the Limpopo. David Beach highlights the structural weakness of the agricultural base due to harsh ecology and limited technology, compounded by social and geographical maldistribution of resources. The theme of a slowly emerging peasantry is then taken up in Chapter 2 by Sherilynn Young's pioneering study of the Tsonga and Chopi peoples of the Mozambique coastal belt south of the Limpopo. She shows how female dominance in agriculture assisted the emergence of male labour migration to South Africa before full colonial rule was imposed. In Chapter 3, Fola Soremekun focuses on the role of long distance trade, servicing the world mercantile system, in developing certain aspects of a pre-colonial economy while simultaneously laying the foundations of subsequent underdevelopment. The Ovimbundu of Central Angola dominated trade over West Central Africa until they were rapidly superseded by the direct penetration of Portuguese and Belgian colonialism to seize the rubber, labour, and land of the interior.

The early colonial model of a labour-exporting peasantry is clearly shown in Chapter 4 in its emergence among the Ovambo and Nkhumbi, southern neighbours of the Ovimbundu, in Angola and Namibia. Gervase Clarence-Smith and Richard Moorsom emphasize how German, Portuguese, and South African colonialism took over and perpetuated the increasing social repression of a ruling class dependent on trade. In Chapter 5, a case study in Botswana on the main Cape to Rhodesia route demonstrates in detail how the wider market of capitalism first developed and then underdeveloped local economies. Colonialism introduced political systems that subordinated all black interests to white at a time of market depression in the early twentieth century. Neil Parsons traces the reduction of a pre-colonial state in Botswana to a colonial 'native reserve', and in Chapter 6 Laurel Van Horn rounds off this part of the book with a study of the Lozi state on the upper Zambezi in western Zambia. This state slipped from the pre-colonial Atlantic trade network into the British colonial system extending northwards from the Cape. Ecological change and political

36

manipulation are related to the questions of agricultural productivity on the Zambezi flood plain and of labour migration to the south.

## The contributors

David Beach was born in Britain and grew up in Kenya and in Rhodesia. He took his first degree at the University of Cape Town and his 1971 doctorate at the University of London. He has been a Research Fellow at the University of Rhodesia for several years, and has conducted extensive field and archival research into pre-colonial Shona history. He has published a number of articles and is currently nearing completion of a major monograph, *An Outline of Shona History*.

Sherilynn Young was born in America, and is currently a doctoral candidate at the University of California at Los Angeles. This is her first published article, and it should be noted that it was written before she commenced fieldwork in southern Mozambique towards the end of 1974.

Fola Soremekun was born in Nigeria, and lectured at the University of Zambia between 1967 and 1974, before leaving to take up a post at the University of Ife. His 1965 doctorate at Northwestern University was on American mission activity in Angola, and he has written on both Angolan history and modern Zambian politics.

Gervase Clarence-Smith took up a lectureship at the University of Zambia in 1975, having completed a University of London (SOAS) doctorate on the history of the Mossamedes hinterland in Angola. He was born in India, grew up in Eritrea, and after serving as librarian at the University of Yaoundré in Cameroon, took his first degrees at the Universities of Cambridge and Paris.

Richard Moorsom was born in Britain and grew up in South Africa, wrote a 1973 MA at the University of Sussex on the formation of the Namibian working class, and is currently working on a doctoral dissertation on proletarianization in the Eastern Cape in the nineteenth century.

Neil Parsons is co-editor of this volume. He was born in Britain and grew up there, in Egypt, and in Botswana. After taking a first degree at North-Western Polytechnic, London, he completed a doctorate on Khama III for the University of Edinburgh in 1973. From 1971 to 1975 he lectured at the University of Zambia, where he was co-editor of the journal *African Social Research*, before taking up a post at the University of Botswana and Swaziland. He has published widely on Botswana history.

Laurel Van Horn was born in America. She took her first degree at Bryn Mawr College and then studied for a year at the University of Zambia. While doing so she wrote the paper on Barotseland, which, like Sherilynn Young's, is her first publication. She is now a postgraduate student in economic history at the New School for Social Research, New York.

# CHAPTER 1

## The Shona Economy: Branches of Production

## DAVID BEACH

## Introduction

An understanding of the economic history of the Shona-speaking peoples is fundamental to any analysis of the economy of southern Zambezia. The Shona, occupying most of the area, outnumber the neighbouring Ndebele, Valley, and Lower Zambezi Tonga, Tsonga, Sotho, and Venda by a considerable margin.[1] Since 1890, the establishment of a capitalist economy based upon farming, mining, and manufacturing in the region has led to great changes in the 'traditional' economy, but it has not destroyed it. Indeed, the capitalist sector of the economy relies upon the coexistence of the 'traditional' sector to keep wages low.[2] Economic historians who are concerned with the working of the capitalist economy have drawn attention to the effect of that economy in its early stages on the African people. In particular, they have shown how a very rapid African response to the market opportunities offered by the capitalist economy led to the expansion of an African peasantry that prospered on the sale of produce until it was crushed by legislation and other measures aimed at reducing the African people to wage-labourer status.[3]

So far, historians have not paid much attention to the Shona economy as a whole in its pre-capitalist phases. Specific aspects of this economy such as mining and trade have been examined in varying detail,[4] but only recently have studies been made of entire economies from a local viewpoint.[5] The tendency of historians to concentrate on such aspects as mining and trade has been largely due to the rise of the Shona state at Zimbabwe before 1500 and the concentration of the Portuguese upon trade with its successors of Mutapa, Torwa, and Changamire. The smaller political units have largely been ignored,[6] and some analyses have come dangerously close to depicting the Shona economy as a mining, manufacturing, and trading economy.[7] This chapter will attempt to give a general account of the Shona economy over the last thousand years.

The analytical techniques of two anthropologists, Meillassoux and Terray, who studied the peoples of the Ivory Coast, provide useful concepts for the study of the Shona economy.[8] Terray points out that the identification of a 'mode of production' — an analytical tool composed of an economic base, a juridical-political structure, and an ideological superstructure — is superior to a simple description of an economy.[9] But the *mode* of production is also divisible into *branches* of production, and it is with these that we are concerned here, rather than with the *relations* of production on which Meillassoux and Terray laid such stress.[10] In other words, we are concerned with the things that people did, rather than with the size or organization of their labour forces. The analysis of branches of production is the simplest and most basic part of the total economic analysis, but unless it takes note of the most complex and refined part of the mode of production — the ideological superstructure— it can lead to a highly distorted picture. In plain English, if one lacks statistics for the Shona economy in the past, one has to rely upon oral traditions to a great extent, and these depend upon the ideological views of informants. An embittered old man, talking of the pre-colonial economy, might say: 'We grew crops in muddy areas along the river banks. We got plenty of food from there. We hunted as we liked. There was nothing which the people were not allowed to do. We did whatever we liked. . . . One could go and plough wherever one wanted. There was plenty of food in those days. Our children are now unhealthy because of shortage of food. That is what I saw in the old days. . . . '[11] A researcher into the area discussed, Chwaya on the lower Umfuli, might wonder whether riverbank fields were indeed adequate, or whether other lands had to be used, and whether good hunting was compatible with good crops. A document of 1898 would show that at least once in that old man's youth his people had been forced to abandon their land and seek refuge from drought and locusts in Shangwe.[12]

But the ideological superstructure of a people's economy can produce more serious distortions of the evidence than a simple nostalgia for a Utopian past. The Shangwe of the Mafungabusi plateau were known as tobacco-sellers,[13] the Njanja of the upper Sabi as ironworkers,[14] and so on, but it will be shown that claims such as those of the Njanja that they were *primarily* ironworkers should not be taken too seriously in an economic analysis. Indeed, Meillassoux's emphasis on the role of the elder in the 'traditional' mode of production may have owed something to the age of his informants,[15] while Terray paid a great deal of attention to a mode of production based upon communal hunting with nets which, among the Shona at least, was rather rare as a food-producing process, for reasons that probably apply to all agricultural economies, including that of the Ivory Coast Gourou.[16]

Any analysis of modes of production, therefore, must make some attempt at indicating the relative importance of each of the branches of production within each mode. This can only be done by applying historical analysis to the picture given by anthropologists and by bringing in the concept of time. This involves not only the question of the different activities in which the people spent the limited number of hours in every year, but also contrasting the activities between years, between decades, and between centuries. Except for their recognition of the importance of the crop cycle, Meillassoux and Terray make little attempt to show how change over time affected their analysis, and virtually ignore historical factors such as droughts, the economic development over the centuries of the peoples they studied, and other events that could affect the economy.[17]

## Hunting

The Early Iron Age ancestors of the (Later Iron Age) Shona accomplished the transition from a hunting and gathering economy to agriculture between c.2000 BC and c.AD 1.[18] Before this transition they had more or less perfected the techniques of hunting with spear and bow and trapping animals. These techniques accounted for a variety of animals ranging from the edible rat to the elephant, and practically nothing was forgotten.[19] But it is very difficult to calculate from oral traditions the relative importance of hunting among the Shona as a branch of production. The hunt was exciting and interesting, the traditional province of the man, and brought in meat that was highly prized for its nutritious value, as well as for by-products such as skin and horns. What we are still in ignorance of is the number of hours spent by the men of a Shona community in hunting, whether as individuals or small or large groups, and the amount of meat produced.

What we do know is that the importance given by traditions to hunting in the Shona past has been exaggerated. This is especially true of traditions about population movements in which the incoming group are depicted as hunters. This is because Shona traditions tend to concentrate on male descendants of a founding ancestor, which produces a picture of an abnormally small original group, often of only one man. Thus founding ancestors such as Mbiru of Buhera, Sabarawara of Maungwe, and Nyamubvambire of Manyika — all of whom lived at a time when Portuguese documents make it quite clear that the Shona economy was based on agriculture — in the traditions are seen as hunters.[20] The migration paths of such groups as the Duma and the Nambiya avoided dry and sandy areas unsuitable for agriculture, which suggests that they were planting crops as they went,[21] while a movement of Chimbadzwa's group from Manyika to Barwe in 1896 involved hundreds of people and was carried out between reaping and sowing seasons.[22]

Hunting by the Iron Age people, who far outnumbered their hunting and gathering predecessors of the Late Stone Age in the same area of land, had counter-productive results if pushed too far. The Shona used nets called *mambure* to catch animals of up to medium size which had been driven by a large crowd of beaters. This involved every available man in the polity, and people under several different rulers would sometimes combine together.[23] It seems to have been a hunting method of great efficiency, but the only times when it was noted were in the droughts of the early 1870s and middle 1880s, and in the dry lowlands of Buhera in 1891.[24] If a large population relied too much on hunting, it would clear out the game and thus lead to diminishing returns.

In early Shona settlements, hunting was not as prominent as cattle-keeping as a source of meat. The thirteenth- and fourteenth-century Musengezi culture relied mainly on cattle,[25] and middens at Zimbabwe and Khami show that cattle bones were more common than game bones.[26] The nineteenth century saw an increase in the hunting of small cats such as the civet and genet as tribute for the Ndebele in Belingwe, the attractive skins being used for decorative clothing and perhaps for resale to traders.[27] As firearms became more common in the Shona country, hunting grew in importance, including the hunting of elephants for ivory. In 1884 Kerr noted the effect of firearms on the game,[28] and in 1897 Chitawudze's people on the Bubye were using their firearms for mass slaughter of zebra.[29]

In short, hunting provided a valuable addition to the diet of the Shona, but it was not central to the Shona economy, and could offer only a limited amount of support to subsistence during famines.

## Gathering

The gathering of wild plants has been more important to hunting peoples than the game they killed,[30] and the Shona have continued to practise it down to the present day. Even in non-drought years, the countryside yielded a great deal of important nutrition in the form of wild fruits, vegetables, and insects that were gathered by the women and children.[31] In times of famine, the importance of gathering increased dramatically, and people sometimes relied almost exclusively on wild fruit, herbs, and insects. This was true, for example, in south Charter in 1899 and in lower Buhera in 1903.[32] Locusts, themselves the cause of crop failures, were also a source of food, but they were not equal in value to the crops they destroyed. Gathering was peripheral to the Shona economy for the same reasons as hunting: the land would not provide enough to support the larger population that had grown up as a result of agriculture, but it did provide relishes for ordinary food and a standby in emergency.

## Agriculture

The Shona communities were all basically agricultural, in that the most important activity of the greatest number of their people was the production of food by growing crops. All other activities, including mining, manufacturing, building, trade, politics, and religion, were secondary to this, and could not have been carried on without it. It is important to realize that the ancestors of the Shona had become agriculturalists over a thousand years before the Shona settled south of the Zambezi.[33]

The earliest Shona settlements were made in the south of their region round about AD 1000, the Leopards Kopje and Gumanye cultures, and in the north in about 1200, the Harare and Musengezi cultures. The Leopards Kopje, Harare, and Musengezi cultures of archaeology are almost certainly ancestral to the Kalanga, Zezuru, and Korekore dialect clusters of the modern Shona, and there are probably early Shona cultures still undiscovered in the east corresponding to the Nyanga, Manyika, Shanga, and Ndau dialect clusters.[34] Although Shona settlement was achieved over a large area within a couple of centuries, this does not imply an even spread of population over the whole southern Zambezian region at any time. Not only were there dry, sandy, saline, and frost-exposed lands that were relatively unsuitable for settlement, but over the whole period of Shona history there were major demographic movements within their region that created imbalances in population, which led in turn to further movements. Thus a build-up of population at Zimbabwe — which arose out of the Gumanye culture — led in the fifteenth and sixteenth centuries to population movements westward to Khami, where the Torwa state was founded, and northward to the edges of the main plateau and the Zambezi valley. This northward movement resulted in the sixteenth century in a reverse movement to the south-east, down to the coast. In the seventeenth century a double movement of peoples from the *moyo* nuclear area (between the Mazoe and Nyadiri rivers) to the south-west and south-east led to the foundation of the Changamire state and the *moyo* Ndau dynasties respectively. During the eighteenth century a major movement of peoples from the north and east completely resettled the south and much of the centre of the region, which had not been heavily settled since the fall of Zimbabwe over three centuries earlier.[35]

All this means that recent arguments about the soil preferences of the Shona are strictly academic, since the Shona rarely had a free choice in the matter.[36] Political units were established by many more factors than the presence of red or sandy soils. For a people whose land did not include the soil they preferred, the only choice was between making the best of what was available and emigration, which involved either conquest of the original inhabitants of their chosen area or subjection to them. Even if they had a choice, people were also constrained by the need for defensible hills in some areas, the need for water, and the need to move their fields every few years. However, given a free choice, informants have made it clear that the soil preferred depended upon the type of crop required: finger millet did better in sandy soils, and maize in red clays.[37]

The crops available to the Shona appear at first sight to have been numerous, but in fact they were rather limited. *Rukweza* or *zvivo,* finger millet; *mhunga,* bulrush millet; *mapfunde,* sorghum; *magwere* or *chibagwe,* maize; *mupunga,* rice; *nzungu,* groundnuts; *nyimo,* Bambara groundnuts; *nyemba,* cowpeas; and a very wide range of vegetables were grown. But a closer analysis shows that only the finger and bulrush millets were central to the Shona economy. The vegetables and the groundnuts and cowpeas were not staple crops in themselves. Rice was grown in well-watered areas,[38] and near Sofala in the sixteenth century it was of real importance as a crop,[39] but in most areas the riverbank fields and the marshes were too few to grow enough rice for everyone. Sorghum, on the other hand, thrived in dry areas, but in the better-watered areas it was only grown in small quantities in the women's gardens alongside the vegetables.[40] Maize appeared in the Zambezi valley in the eighteenth century and had spread throughout the region by the nineteenth century, but this American crop did not become a staple as it did in eastern Zambia. Informants have stated that it was difficult to stamp, and indeed maize when dry has a moisture content as low as 8 per cent and has to be wetted before stamping in a traditional Shona mortar. Until the Europeans began to buy it and mechanical mills became available, maize was eaten on or off the cob as a relish.[41] All these vegetables, nuts, and grains in fact were *usavi* or *muriwo*, relish, to the Shona, and were not relied upon to produce *sadza*, the stiff grain porridge that is a synonym for food itself. They were important in the diet of the people, but they were not as crucial as the two millets.

The process of cultivation itself was comparatively straightforward. The fields were prepared for planting in the dry winter months, and planted at the onset of the summer rains. The exact time of planting depended on the crop concerned. By the end of the rains the crops reached maturity and they were harvested in early winter. Mid-winter was the time for drying and threshing. Part of the crop was then put into the next cycle as seed, and the remainder was stored as food for the village. Like all agricultural cycles, this process depended upon the food supply from one crop lasting through the entire cycle until the next harvest became available. This depended upon the effectiveness of Shona methods of grain storage and the effect of the Shona environment.

The most common Shona granary was a small hut, built on a rock to keep the insects out, with a well-sealed roof and door. This could be made fairly airtight, but in the rainy season there was a general rise in humidity, and it seems that even the best built granary could not prevent a certain increase in moisture inside. This softened the grain kernals which had been dried in the winter, and made it easier for borers to eat into them. In a normal rainy season this would not be very serious, and the stored crop would dry out again in the winter. If grain was kept through two or more rainy seasons, however, it would become progressively more difficult to keep it in a good condition. In theory it was possible to make an almost totally airtight granary, and individual experiments have shown that it was possible to keep grains for a very long time, but in everyday practice it seems that few crops could be kept for more than two or three years.[42] This problem of storage was of crucial importance to the Shona economy. Sorghum could be stored for a very long time, and was very resistant to drought as a growing crop, but although it was well known to the Shona it was not grown as a staple crop in most areas; presumably there was a good reason for this.[43] Finger millet was also good for storage,[44] and it was generally the most important Shona crop. Unfortunately it suffered more than bulrush millet from drought.

*Shangwa* is the Shona word for drought, but it also means disaster or misery. Droughts are, and have been, remarkably common on the southern Zambezian plateau. It is difficult to generalize, but there is about one chance in five that a year will bring subnormal rainfall.[45] But a mere shortage of rain is not the only thing that can produce *shangwa*. Rains that come too soon or too late, too much rain, locust plagues, or even frosts and floods in some areas could destroy the crops of millet on which the people depended. *Shangwa* could not be predicted in advance: one of the major functions of Shona religions of all kinds was to bring the required rain, but no completely accurate drought-prediction method has yet been invented.[46] The effect of a *shangwa* was delayed. In a four-year sequence, if the crops sown in the early summer of Year 2 were hit by a drought, the crops sown in Year 1 and harvested in the winter of Year 2 would last until the winter of Year 3. But even if the rains of Year 3 were good, before the crop of Year 3 could be reaped in the winter of Year 4, the crop of Year 2 would have run out. The consequence of this could be terrible, and worse if there were two or more droughts in succession. It is not surprising that every year saw a certain amount of tension until it became certain that the crops were secure. Traditions stress the effect of a drought: 'At that time there was no water and so the people of Nyashanu were drinking the urine of cattle . . . ' says a tradition of the foundation of the Karivara religious cult in the eighteenth century.[47] This may be exaggerated, but traditions of movements show that at times the agricultural system simply collapsed and people had to fall back on gathering and hunting, or flee to other areas not so badly hit. Thus in the bad famines in the early nineteenth century the entire Samuriwo group abandoned their lands on the upper Umfuli and sought refuge with Nyandoro in Tsunga, to the south-west.[48] In Lomagundi in September 1895 some villages had no food left after the locusts had struck, and were living on wild fruit and roots.[49] In Charter in 1901, while some areas had done well, others had been so badly hit by locusts that gardens had been abandoned.[50] On the lower Zambezi in about 1810 it was reckoned that one-third of the year was spent in gathering wild produce when the crops were bad.[51]

These of course are extreme cases, but they show that in spite of years of experience of the southern Zambezian environment, and in spite of the wide range of crops known and the effectiveness of hoe cultivation, Shona agriculture was remarkably fragile. There were ways of countering *shangwa* within agriculture, but none of them were completely successful. One method was to plant bulrush millet, which stood up to drought far better than finger millet; unfortunately, it could not always be known if a drought was coming, and in any case bulrush millet did not store as well as finger millet.[52] Another method was to plant a second crop in the hope that it would not be hit as badly as the first. Often this worked, though presumably later crops would not be as good as the earlier ones would have been. In Charter in 1899 the first crop was destroyed by the drought, and the second one by frosts, so that by the end of the year some people were living on wild oranges.[53] There was nothing in theory to stop people from growing much larger crops: this was often done when markets became available.[54] But, unless this was done every year, the limitations of the storage system meant that a store of extra grain would eventually go bad. On the other hand, if extra crops were grown every year, what was to be done with them? Most years were not drought years, and no one needed extra grain.

Factors such as this and the difficulty of transporting grain on anything other than on the back of an extremely valuable ox or cow prevented the growth of a grain trade until mercantile and capitalist markets became available. A Shona farmer could not grow a surplus in the certainty that an area near him would be hit by a drought, and nor would he risk his valuable cattle in hawking his grain around in the hope of finding a buyer. On the other hand, those who were affected by a *shangwa* of some kind would go to those who were better off in search of grain. In 1895 around Salisbury the locusts caused a great deal of damage to the crops in some areas; and by the end of the year about half of an estimated herd of 2,000 cattle had been traded to the people in Marandellas district in return for grain, and a further 500 had been eaten.[55] It is not surprising that in 1896 the Kaguvi spirit medium, who had made his reputation as a locator of game for the *mambure* hunting nets in the droughts of the 1880s, should have been so keen on getting a new locust medicine from Mkwati in the Inyati area, a keenness that led to his involvement in the 1896 Shona Rising.[56] The shortage of grain in Manyika in 1896 is said to have been one of the reasons for the slowness of its ruler Mutasa to move against his enemy Makoni, from whom he bought his grain.[57] The people in the Zambezi valley near Sena came as far into the Shona country as Mbire when they suffered from famine, selling ivory and women.[58] The coming of the Ndebele did not create a market in grain for the Shona. In the first few years of their settlement, and in times of famine, the Ndebele raided for grain from the Shona,[59] but the Ndebele were themselves primarily agriculturalists rather than raiders and by the early 1850s they were extremely prosperous in grain.[60] Arrighi's suggestion that continual Ndebele raiding and tribute-taking stimulated Shona grain production is unsupported by the facts.[61]

Although the Shona were agriculturalists first and foremost, with many crops and centuries of experience of their environment, the problems they encountered with grain storage meant that the agricultural base of their economy was not totally secure. The contemporary record does not suggest that hunting and gathering were enough to offset totally the food shortage caused by *shangwa*. What was required was some sort of wealth that could outlast the limits of the agricultural growing and storage cycle. The rest of this chapter discusses the ways in which this wealth was sought, and their relative importance

## Herding

The keeping of domestic livestock mitigated dependence on the crop cycle for food. Sheep, goats, and cattle live much longer than grain can be stored, reproduce themselves, and can be supervised by those males who are of less use in the agricultural process, the young boys. The Early Iron Age people of southern Zambezia before AD 1000 had originally been almost entirely dependent upon sheep and goats, but later they acquired some cattle.[62] The Shona, as the Later Iron Age population of the region, were from the start the owners of herds of cattle, but goats remained important. The proportion of goats to cattle varied considerably from district to district, but generally there were at least twice as many goats as cows, and often more.[63] In such places as Bocha in the 1890s there were virtually no cows, and the people relied almost entirely on goats.[64] Sheep were much rarer, but in some areas such as Manyika they almost equalled the cattle in numbers.[65] But the cow was regarded as being the supreme domestic beast in value.

The Shona cow was generally very small, averaging round about 350 lb (160 kg), as compared with about 450 lb in the average Ndebele cow, about 600 lb in the best Ndebele cattle, and about 650 lb in Ngami cattle. Selective breeding and favourable conditions, however, could lead to a rapid increase in size,[66] and a seventeenth-century account claims that the cattle of the Torwa state (in the later Ndebele area) were so tall that one had to stand to milk them.[67] Small though the average nineteenth-century Shona cow was, it was far superior to the goat in the amount and quality of the meat it supplied. Dintweng Kousu's poetic description of cattle says disparagingly of goats and sheep, 'these are not like the real livestock [cattle]. Their meat is little and their milk is little and the work they do is little.' Kousu's account, that of a Kalanga cattle-guard, stresses the value of every part of the cow.[68] The mature cow could calve once a year, and since a heifer almost always calved by her third year and usually lived until she was sixteen or twenty, the average yield was ten to fifteen calves.[69] This represented a great increase from one cow, and careful breeding and herding could lead to a real increase in a man's wealth in a short time. Of course, factors ranging from contagious abortion to raiding could cut down this increase, but when compared with the agricultural cycle the cattle herd did much to make life more secure.

The record of cattle-herding by the Shona is a long one. The clay figurines of cattle of the Leopards Kopje and Gumanye cultures; the cattle bones in the middens of Zimbabwe and Khami; the herds of the Mutapa and the Torwa states; the cattle trade from the south-west to the Zambezi valley from the sixteenth to the nineteenth centuries; and the cattle-wealth of the Changamire all support this.[70] It is almost impossible to get a clear estimate of the total numbers of Shona cattle before the European occupation. The Ndebele, Gaza, and Ngoni raiders of the nineteenth century took many of them, and after a raid on Gutu one Ndebele man was granted 150 head for himself,[71] but Gutu was still reckoned to have 1,500 head in the colonial census of 1895.[72]

Since this census was taken by the native commissioners who were counting people and livestock in order to tax them, and who had already taken 2,611 head of cattle as tax, their count of about 16,000 head for Mashonaland was well under the real total.[73] Not only were some areas such as Melsetter and Buhera not counted at all, but in many districts the native commissioners had not visited every part. The Shona had had some decades in which to perfect their techniques of concealing themselves and their cattle from the Ndebele, so it is unlikely that the Native Department raiders had an accurate picture. On the other hand, their estimates of the proportion of people to cattle were probably accurate, and ranged from 3:1 in Victoria through 6:1 in Umtali and 8:1 in Salisbury to much higher ratios in cattle-poor districts such as Hartley and Lomagundi. Later estimates were that the basic herd in the whole country in the 1890s was 500,000 of which about 200,000 were owned by the Ndebele.[74]

'Here is one important point about cattle. When you have a kraal of cattle, you can say that you have all power; if you are given a wife, you *lovola* [give dowry] with them; if you have sons, you *lovola* for them with the same, selling some, and procuring blankets for your wife. . . . Furthermore, if you are without cattle, but have daughters, you then give them for *lovola,* cutting a cattle-kraal . . . ', wrote Kousu.[75] The social importance of cattle to the Shona is so well known that it hardly requires stating.[76] Generally, it was true that cattle were only killed on special occasions, but we have already seen how, in the Salisbury district in 1895, the people killed some and sold more for grain, in order to survive. In the last resort, the cow was insurance against the failure of the crops, and this lay at the root of its economic importance, but it acquired so much social importance that the main aim of every Shona farmer was to build up his herd.

The problem for the poorer Shona was how to acquire cattle, or at least goats, for they were not distributed equally among the people even in cattle-rich areas. As we have seen, the rate of reproduction of cattle was such that the payment of the *rovora* [*lovola* or *lobola*] bride-price need not have depleted a herd that had built up to reasonable numbers, but it could deplete smaller herds. In any Shona society, there were relatively rich and poor people. As we have seen, cattle were sold for grain by people who could get grain no other way, but it is unlikely that they would have sold their cattle for grain under normal circumstances. For the Shona farmer who lacked cattle, a number of ways of obtaining them existed. The most direct way was to steal them. The *gororo,* or professional thief, was a well-known figure in Shona lore,[77] and the Shona raiding-party was probably just as responsible for the construction of 'refuge'-type stone walls on hilltop strongholds in the centuries after 1600 as the historically much-abused Ngoni, Gaza, or Ndebele *impi.* But for many people such raiding was not practicable, and the wealth they sought had to be found in the profits of mining, manufacturing, and trade. Since in many cases the entire process and trade of the product was carried out by the same man or family group, production and trade will be considered in two classifications, that internal and that external to the region's economy.

## Internal production and trade

It has already been shown that in practice the pre-capitalist Shona economy was anything but self-sufficient in local terms. The supply of game and wild vegetables in a given area does not appear to have been enough to support an agricultural community whose crops had failed, and so grain was purchased from elsewhere. Similarly, two of the most important elements of the Shona village's economy, salt and iron, could in theory be obtained locally, but in practice they had often to be obtained through trade. Where specialist groups existed to make or sell special commodities, they sometimes added to their existing wealth by their trade, or used it to make their unfavourable environment more bearable, but in no case did these specialists rely entirely or even largely upon their specialization for their basic subsistence: they remained agriculturalists in the main, so that the term 'specialist' in the Shona economy does not imply total specialization.

Salt was an essential commodity. There were three basic ways of obtaining it. One was to burn certain plants, put their salty ashes in water, filter it, and produce salt crystals by evaporation in a specially formed pot.[78] The truly desperate could do the same with the droppings of goats.[79] But the best method used the evaporation process on the saline earths that formed around saline springs in certain areas. This produced salt of noticeably better quality, so that although salt-plants and goat's dung were available to all, a salt industry grew up at these rare saline springs that supplied people over a wide area. Some of these springs were in the Zambezi valley, and were well known to the Portuguese even in the sixteenth century.[80] In 1859 this salt industry was still operating, a large cake of salt selling for a fathom of cloth.[81] Another such salt-producing area was the Mafungabusi plateau, where the Shangwe processed and sold salt across the Umniati in Chwaya, at a rate of one chicken to a dish of salt according to one informant.[82] This industry attracted some European commercial interest at the end of the nineteenth century,[83] but it remained a fairly small-scale business. The best-known salt-producing area was the middle Sabi valley. The geological formation led to the rise of saline springs, and those people of the *moyo* and *dziva* Ndau who for various reasons were pushed out of the well-watered highlands into the dry middle Sabi lowlands found in the salt trade a compensation for their bad crops and fly-ridden herds.[84] In particular, the Chiadzwa and Chamutsa houses of the *moyo* Muwushu dynasty, who had crossed the rivers into lower Bocha and Buhera respectively, specialized in salt-manufacture. The process described above produced an *ibvi*, knee, of salt in a bark container. Some of the Bocha and Hera people descended to the lowlands to make these, but the *moyo* people produced the most, and either sold it on the spot or took it into the uplands for sale. According to Hera informants,

the Chamutsa people had to pay a tax to the Hera ruler, which reduced
the benefit of the Chamutsa salt trade, which generally brought in one
hoe for one *ibvi* of salt. This trade extended throughout Bocha and
Buhera, but north of the Sabi, west of Wedza, and in Gutu the price
asked apparently became too high, for the people there used the other
methods described to produce their own salt. The Sabi salt-traders
were specialists only in the sense that they produced more salt than
anyone else. The only evidence in 1896 that indicated any special
benefit obtained by Chiadzwa's people from the salt trade was a rather
large herd of 800 goats.[85]

The *badza* or iron hoe was the mainstay of Shona agriculture, and
regular use made it necessary to replace each hoe at intervals of two to
five years.[86] 'Iron deposits are often small, but they are widespread and
of frequent occurrence hence very many tiny iron-ore quarries are
bound to be overlooked and we can now know only the largest and most
recent.'[87] This statement by an archaeologist is supported to some
extent by traditions and documents. Traditions from Chwaya talk of
hoes 'from the mountains', though there were suggestions that they
were not of iron.[88] South of the Sabi at the Chiurwi, Shava, Bepe, and
Dorowa hills, hoes were made from the local iron ores.[89] Other
traditions refer to the iron ore of Mahugwi near Zimbabwe.[90] Other
iron mines that are known to have been worked were at Makaha in
Mtoko, Anwa in Nhowe; on the Shawasha goldfield; in Gutu; in the
Mwanesi range; at Thaba Insimbi south of the Sebakwe; on the Kwe
Kwe river; in the Mulungwane hills; near Filabusi and Gwanda; at
Buhwa mountain; and in the Matopos.[91] Still more were in Maungwe;
at fourteen places near Manyika; in Sanga; and in Teve.[92] Thus,
although not every small political unit had its own supply of iron ore,
few such units were very far from an iron mine — rarely more than fifty
miles. It is thus interesting to note the development of the Wedza iron
industry.

Wedza, a mountain at the headwaters of the upper Sabi, possessed
iron ores that were specially suited to Shona iron-smelting and
iron-working techniques.[93] Wedza ores were therefore taken to forges
as far away as Gutu, Seke, and Selukwe by the smelters of those
areas.[94] Wedza mountain originally belonged to the Hera people who
lost it to the immigrant Mbire at the end of the eighteenth century,[95] and
according to Posselt the Hera worked the iron there and made hoes
with which they paid tribute, though to whom is not stated.[96] But the
main exploiters of the iron of Wedza were to be the Njanja, a group of
people from the Zambezi valley in the north-east who settled at
Bvumbura, some way south of Wedza, in the early eighteenth century.
At the end of that century they began to expand rapidly, and in fifty
years they occupied a wide sweep of land running south-west from
Wedza.[97] The Njanja played the major part in the rise of the Wedza iron
trade, which was well established by 1857.[98] A recent study has shown
how the Njanja organized their labour, smelted and forged the iron, and
marketed the finished product. The Njanja did not make any major

innovations in either smelting or forging, but they did manage to increase production by bringing several forges together in one supra-village factory under the supervision of one expert, and by encouraging apprentices from other peoples to join them, supplying labour in return for training and, often, a daughter. In many ways their production techniques were very sophisticated. Their traders took hoes over a wide area, south-east as far as Bocha and the Ndau lands beyond the Sabi, south as far as Gutu and the Duma country, returning with cattle, goats, and ivory.[99]

What concerns us in this study is the importance of the Njanja iron industry and trade, both in terms of Shona history and to the Njanja themselves. The Njanja iron trade arose at a time when the last of the great Shona pre-colonial demographic movements was in progress. The eighteenth and nineteenth centuries saw a complete resettlement of the modern Karanga-speaking area by peoples from the north and east of the Shona country; no more than a few very small group identities survived from the earlier population. This major demographic expansion is comparable with that of south Russia in the sixteenth and seventeenth centuries, or of North America in the nineteenth century. Within a century, the migrating settlers in their new lands came to equal or surpass the population of their original homelands.[100] This involved the breaking of vast areas of new fields, and a consequent demand for many new hoes. It is thus hardly surprising that the Njanja iron industry developed when it did, nor that most of the lands to the south where this expansion was going on should have been supplied by the Njanja — while the much longer-settled lands to the north, where the demand was not so great, did not fall within the Njanja supply zone.

This does not explain why it was the Njanja and not the Hera or Mbire who benefited from this demand. Nor does it explain the Njanja trade to rather longer-established settlement areas, such as Buhera, Bocha, and the Ndau lands beyond the Sabi. The explanation lies in the excellent quality of Njanja hoes, which were preferred because they lasted for three to five years. Thus the hoes of the Dorowa area, which were full of phosphatic impurities and lasted no more than two years, were not sold outside northern Buhera.[101] But the fact that local industries such as those of Dorowa and the others cited above should have survived at all in the face of Njanja competition indicates the limitations of Njanja production and trade. In spite of the Njanja use of multiple forges and apprentices to maximize production and utilization of labour, there do not appear to have been sufficient Njanja available to market all their hoes. Although the Njanja could get a higher price (roughly a small goat for a small hoe and a big goat for a large and a small hoe) for their hoes in places farther away such as Bocha, Gutu, and Murwira (a ward of Buhera facing Gutu), they also sold at the forge site.[102] People from far away brought their goods to the Njanja, for prices of hoes dropped sharply close to Wedza, ten hoes being equal to a big goat; five for a small one and one for a chicken in upper Buhera,[103]

and three to five for a goat in south Maungwe and the upper Hunyani.[104]
This practice, the practice of the Mbire and Hera of taking Wedza ore
for their own forges, and the fact that the Njanja were never able to
control Wedza itself, prevented the Njanja from creating a trading
monopoly, which was important in an economy where hoes were so
badly needed that some of the poorer people of Bocha and Duma had to
revert to the neolithic digging-stick.[105]
    There is no doubt that the Njanja benefited considerably from their
iron industry and trade: it brought them cattle, goats, salt, and ivory in
some quantities. But did this mean that their political and economic
strength lay in the iron trade? The Njanja today tend to believe that it
did. They are today known as having been the ironworkers *par
excellence* of the southern Zezuru and northern Karanga areas, and
some Njanja even claim that they used to spend little time in growing
crops.[106] This is simply not supported by the documents of the 1890s,
which show that the Charter district close to the main road, which was
largely Njanja country, was one of the major suppliers of grain to
European traders before the 1896 Rising, and that trading centres for
grain were established at the villages of Ranga and Chivese, two of the
Njanja rulers.[107] The 1895 census, for all its faults, showed exactly the
same ratio of croplands to people among the Njanja as among the other
groups, and in fact they were not as well off proportionally in terms of
stock.[108] Even though the much more accurate survey of 1899 shows
that the Njanja were slightly better off than their neighbours in terms of
cattle and much better off in terms of goats, this can be accounted for by
the fact that their lands were not fought over in 1896, and by their
continuing sales of grain to the Europeans during the Risings.[109] If
there are only about four documentary references to the Njanja iron
trade in the 1890s,[110] this is surely due to the fact that in their economy
the ordinary economic activity of agriculture was of paramount
importance. The Njanja claim that their political power rested on the
wealth acquired by their rulers from the iron trade must be put into the
context of the overall demographic movement mentioned earlier.[111]
Under these conditions other Shona peoples who were not characterized as ironworkers achieved a political and demographic expansion equal to or surpassing that of the Njanja— the Rufura of the Gutu,
Ndanga, and Belingwe districts, the Mhari of the Lundi and Tokwe
valleys, and the entire Duma confederacy all expanded in a similar way
to the Njanja.[112] In short, the Njanja provide a classic example of the
dangers for the historian in ignoring the ideological superstructure of a
mode of production in the examination of its economic base, and vice
versa.
    Although the Njanja had their economy firmly rooted in agriculture,
it does not follow that they corresponded exactly to the model
proposed by Gray and Birmingham of a subsistence-oriented trading
group.[113] Nor indeed does any known Shona economy approximate to
Meillassoux's model of a subsistence economy in which trade goods
had only a conventional, social value and not a universal, monetary

value.[114] The inequalities of the Shona environment in climate, land, and natural resources saw to it that there was a clearly understood relationship between the values of externally imported goods as well as between salt-cakes and hoes, and foodstuffs and stock. The Njanja can be shown to have organized their production and trade with an eye to market forces. They had neither a monopoly of an iron-making technique, nor of iron ore. They were not forced into iron production by an especially hostile environment, nor were their customers forced to buy from them. By increasing production of high-quality hoes, they were able to be fairly sure of selling hoes that had been specifically ordered. This would qualify them as people who had made the 'transition' from subsistence to market-oriented trade,[115] but it has yet to be proven that any Njanja community relied largely upon its iron trade for either economic or political support. The Njanja were only just 'transitional' from the subsistence-oriented trade of their neighbours.

All other Shona groups involved with internal trade were clearly subsistence-oriented in that their trade was small scale, and primarily intended to offset the problem of an agricultural failure by allowing for a build-up of stock. All the other iron industries mentioned, the salt trade, trade in gunpowder, copperwork, pots, cloth, musical instruments, and other articles all followed this pattern. The Shangwe tobacco trade, to take a final example, shows how a basically agricultural people sought to guard against *shangwa* by growing and selling tobacco. The study of this trade shows how, after a concentration on the purchase of blankets and other trade goods in the early 1900s, the Shangwe used their tobacco to trade for small stock; and, given the problems of grain storage mentioned above, it seems likely that this had been the case in the nineteenth century. Yet the figures supplied by Kosmin in Chapter 11 clearly show that the total amount of tobacco grown in any year of the twentieth century was far outweighed by the grain grown. The suggestion by an early European official that the nineteenth-century Shangwe grew no grain is highly improbable, and probably reflects the ideology of the Shangwe rather than their economy.[116]

## External production and trade

Obviously, external trade from the Shona region was market-oriented trade, since it was linked to the demand of the world in general and India in particular for gold, ivory, and copper, these being the main products that were exported. Thanks to the scholarly attention focused on the stone buildings of the Zimbabwe-Khami culture and the activities of the Portuguese in southern Zambezia, the general outline and nature of this trade is fairly well known.[117] What is not so well known is the relative volume of the trade internally and its effect on the Shona communities concerned.

The development of the Shona culture in southern Zambezia saw a great increase in external trade, compared with that of its Early Iron Age predecessors. Although there is no proof that any of the Early Iron Age people carried out reef-mining, the import of a very limited amount of beads and references to a gold trade from Sofala in the tenth century suggest that some gold-washing had been carried on.[118] The arrival of the Later Iron Age coincided with the development of reef-mining,[119] and the thirteenth and fourteenth centuries saw the establishment of a trade between the Shona and India. Shona miners mined, washed, and milled the gold, and while Shona traders took it to the coastal ports, Muslim African traders came inland to buy. The gold was then taken in Muslim vessels to India. The goods imported were mainly cloth, beads, and ceramics, the first two being dominant.[120] Two major political and social developments followed the rise of this trade: firstly the rise of a Shona state at Zimbabwe some time after 1200, with its peak in the late fourteenth century and its fall by 1500, as well as its northern and southern successor-states of Mutapa, Torwa, and Changamire; and secondly the rise of the Muslim coastal cities which acted as middlemen in the trade, being succeeded after 1500 by the Portuguese *conquista* based on Mozambique.[121] The developments in the politics, society, and architecture of these Shona, Muslim, and Portuguese organizations are too well known to require detailed analysis here.[122] What is of crucial importance is the position of this mining industry and trade in the Shona economy.

The Shona miners were efficient prospectors and good miners, who exploited a difficult geological situation to the limits imposed by their technological ability to pump water and provide ventilation. Within these limits they worked out very nearly all of the payable reef gold by the beginning of the nineteenth century, so that by the time the Ndebele occupied the south-west in the 1840s and the Europeans the north-east in the 1890s it was nearly all gone. Their gold-washing rather than mining has continued into recent times. Their milling of the ore was rather less effective, and perhaps 40 per cent of the gold mined was left unrefined at this stage. The gold-mining and washing process was nearly always seasonal and carried out in the 'slack' period of the agricultural cycle, to which it was definitely subordinate.[123] There is no reliable evidence that any Shona goldfield was not primarily an agricultural area.[124]

The uneven distribution of the gold-bearing areas meant that very many of the Shona people were never involved with the gold industry in any way.[125] The gold export figures of Sofala give some idea of the size of the industry in the early sixteenth century, when Zimbabwe had already declined, but when the successor-state of Torwa was flourishing at Khami, and the Mutapa state was powerful in the Zambezi valley.[126] The Portuguese trade of Sofala was then being partly bypassed by Muslim traders using the Zambezi,[127] there was certainly unofficial trade that was not recorded, and the records themselves are incomplete.[128] But Sofala was receiving some of the trade of the Mutapa state,[129] and was well sited to receive at least some of the gold trade of Torwa and Manyika.[130] In a twenty-year period, with fluctuations ranging from 25,028 *miticals* in 1513–14 to 552½ in eight months of 1518–19, Sofala officially received round about 5,580 *miticals* or about 930 ounces of gold a year.[131] Given a number of factors, this was only 60 per sent of the gold yield of the ore mined;[132] an ounce of gold to a ton of ore as a fair yield;[133] Sofala was receiving only one-third, say, of the total gold trade of southern Zambezia;[134] a team of six people could mine about a ton of rock a day;[135] and there were two such teams to a village working only one of the two main months in which gold was traditionally extracted[136] — then at a time only a century after the height of Zimbabwe's power, perhaps eighty villages in the whole of southern Zambezia were mining gold. Since these figures obviously err very much on the side of caution, the figure of about a thousand Shona digging for gold in the early sixteenth century is rather a high estimate. As is well known, the Portuguese efforts to control the Shona gold mines and trade led, if anything, to the decline of the industry in the Mutapa state in the seventeenth century.[137] In the Changamire state, whose goldfields in the seventeenth century under the Torwa had been known as the *mae d'ouro*, the mother of gold, the output of gold in the middle of the eighteenth century through the Zambezi was about 60 *pastas* (990 ounces) a year. The evidence for this relates to a single year, 1762, and may have been exceptional, but the Changamire goldfields had less than eighty years of active life ahead of them.[138]

The export of copper was worth only a fraction of the trade in gold, and copper mines were relatively rare.[139] The second major item in Shona external trade was ivory. Elephants had always offered a great deal of meat to the more daring hunters, and according to Santos they were mainly killed for their meat by men who dug pit-traps near Sofala in the 1590s.[140] Another method used was the spearing of elephants by men in overhanging trees.[141] But the method remembered in traditions was one that let the hunter pick out the tusker he considered to be the best. It was first recorded among the Shona of Inhambane in the 1560s.[142] Approaching the elephant from downwind or through a specially prepared cloud of medicine-dust that hid his smell, the hunter struck at its hamstring with a big axe. The helpless elephant could then be killed with a large spear. This demanded skill and luck: if the wind changed or the hunter made a noise, if he hit the wrong place or not hard enough, the corps of hunters would be reduced by one.[143] Individual enterprise brought an individual reward: the ruler usually took one tusk, the meat was distributed to the community, but the hunter kept the tusk that protruded uppermost from the dead beast. The hunter and the ruler faced the same problems in disposing of the ivory. Locally, a tusk would pay the bride-price of a wife, thus allowing more croplands to be opened up and planted by the addition of her labour to the family. Alternatively, an area poor in iron such as Bocha might use the tusk to buy good iron ore from places such as Wedza.[144] But ultimately ivory, like gold, went to the coast.

The Shona owner of gold and ivory faced much the same problems from the very earliest years of the export trade down to the nineteenth century. If the goods were taken to the coast they would command a higher price than that offered by a trader from the coast, whether *mwenye*, Muslim, or *zungu*, 'Portuguese'. On the other hand the long journey to the coast took a man away from his fields and herds and exposed him to robbery and hardship. Naturally, it was the rulers who found it easier to organize and finance convoys to the sea,[145] but individuals did make the journey. People in Bocha and Gutu used to go to the ports of Chiluane and nearby Buene, while the people of Buhera could choose between Buene and faraway Sena.[146] The traders reached at least as far as Zimbabwe and Khami, Muslim traders up to the seventeenth century and African *vashambadzi*, pedlars, acting on behalf of the Portuguese, in the eighteenth and nineteenth centuries.[147] Manoel António de Sousa, holder of the *prazo* of Gorongosa from the 1860s, was so well known in the interior that his Shona name, 'Kuveya', became a synonym for all *zungu* traders of the time.[148] The importance of this trade in gold and ivory was that the communications network gave the Shona in their villages right across the country a very clear idea of the state of the economy over a very wide area indeed, as we shall see below in the context of migrant labour.

The volume of the ivory trade appears to have risen as that of the gold trade fell. The records of Sofala for the early sixteenth century, subjected to the same caveats as those for gold, and even less comprehensive, show that $488^1/_2$ *quintals* of ivory were traded between 1506 and 1519, probably averaging about 60 *quintals* a year if full records had survived.[149] This annual rate was equivalent to about 7,680 lb, or about 71 elephants at 40 lb a tusk.[150] Santos, writing of Sofala after the Portuguese had brought the Zambezi leak in the trade under their control, thought that 3,000 *arrobas* or 97,020 lb of ivory left the coast every year: i.e. 1,212 elephants at the rate given above.[151] In 1762 the total export of ivory from the rivers of Sena, Sofala, and Inhambane, drawn from a hinterland that included the north bank of the Zambezi, and much of the Tsonga country south-east of the Shona, was 130 *bares*, or 69,381 lb: i.e. 867 elephants.[152] Unfortunately, these latter two references are isolated estimates, and even the Sofala figures for ivory are less reliable than those for gold. Putting these very unsatisfactory figures into human terms and assuming for argument's sake that the average specialist hunter killed three elephants a year, this gives us about 404 hunters operating in the 1590s and about 289 in the 1760s. Once more, we can see that the external trade of the Shona, no matter how important it was to entrepreneurs such as the Muslims and the Portuguese — or even to the Shona rulers of the Zimbabwe, Torwa, Mutapa, and Changamire states — was only peripheral to the economy of the great bulk of the Shona people. Yet, if the total volume of Shona industry and trade was so small, this does not reduce its value in the eyes of the people. Far from it. This historical record shows an extraordinarily rapid response to economic opportunities of all kinds, ranging from the Mutapa's rapid approach to the Portuguese after they took Sofala to the individual man's sale of vegetables to the incoming British in 1890.[153] The task of the economic historian is to get a more accurate picture of the nature of the Shona economy than can be given by a simple list of branches of production. One of the factors that must be taken into account, even before we have an analysis of relations of production, is that of relative wealth and poverty.

## Wealth and poverty

We have already seen that in the economic history of the Shona, not all the people have shared the same degree of prosperity or poverty. Partly, this was a question of space: some areas were too dry, too sandy, too alkaline in their soil structure to support an agriculture as flourishing as that of other areas. Some areas were affected by tsetse fly which prevented them from building up herds of cattle.[154] Others were deficient in minerals, iron and salt, gold and copper. A second kind of difference involved time: not only were there short-term changes in the economic state of the country caused by droughts, wars, or locust plagues, but there were much more gradual changes. Goldfields were worked out; there may have been long-term climatic changes. To take one area, Buhera, which has been occupied as far back as traditions go by the *shava* Hera people: at some time between *c*. 1400 aand *c*. 1700, this area was wealthy enough to finance the construction of several stone *zimbabwes,* even though there was no gold in the area.[155] Yet by the nineteenth century Buhera, even though affected only briefly by raids in the 1860s,[156] was clearly at a lower economic level than in the past, and the Hera were generally much poorer than they had been two or three centuries earlier.[157]

A third difference involved the people within a single community at a single time. The archaeology of the Shona people at Zimbabwe shows that there was a wealthy class of people there who could afford elaborate stone walls around their well-built huts, and who used a specialized pottery for liquids, their cooking being done away from their own huts. At the same time there were poorer people whose huts and pots were less elaborate.[158] In the Mutapa state there was a clear distinction between the court of the Mutapa, rich in cloth obtained from taxation, and the ordinary people. The situation in Teve was the same, and the use of cloth as a currency by the Portuguese up to the nineteenth century as well as the production of excellent but expensive (because time-consuming) cloth by the Shona shows that in the earlier centuries the amount of cloth owned was an index of wealth.[159]

In the later centuries, with the help of oral traditions, it becomes easier to distinguish the poor than the rich. There were four groups of people whose low social position was linked to a lower level of economic power and wealth: women, children, slaves, and bondsmen. Both women and children played a considerable part in the running of the economy, yet they were legally classed as minors and received little

more than the food for which they worked, their wealth being limited to
a few immediate belongings and, very rarely, a few beasts.[160] In the
Zambezi valley before the Portuguese came, there were two kinds of
*akaporo:* slaves who were captured in war or sold by their home
community in times of drought, and bondsmen who sold themselves
under similar circumstances.[161] Shona communities were generally
better off than the Tonga peoples of the drought-prone valley, and were
keen to acquire extra members. Men from Manyika went to Sena and
Tete on the Zambezi with hoes, goats, gold, and skins to buy women
and small boys.[162] Sena traders sold people for ivory near Zimbabwe
and in Chwaya,[163] and famine-stricken Sena people exchanged women
for grain in Mbire.[164] Male slaves 'were given any kind of work, and
they had no voice to complain or report anywhere'.[165] Slaves could be
bought and sold: Mangwende Mungati bought one for his son
Muchemwa, the 1896 Rising leader.[166] Slaves were not very common,[167] but bondsmen, *varanda,* were. Poverty led a *muranda* to sell
himself to his father-in-law in return for a wife — an extension of the
idea of uxorilocal marriage extended to a lifetime! A *muranda* 'is not a
free man. He can be sent anywhere . . . his chief work was to do difficult
work and to do all the home work. He would plough . . . .' Both slaves
and *varanda* were unfree for life, but their children were free.[168] There
was no theoretical bar to the acquisition of wealth by such people, but it
was difficult: often a slave could not afford to marry.[169]

   This kind of differentiation between wealth and poverty, between
the extremes of the rulers of Zimbabwe and the *varanda* of the
nineteenth century, was both an end product of the entire economic
process and a cause of the remarkable efforts made by the Shona to
develop their economy in all directions. It is one of the major
underlying factors in the Shona response to the situation created by the
onset of the capitalist economy in the nineteenth and twentieth
centuries.

## Pre-colonial peasantries and migrant labour

The date of the onset of colonial rule over the Shona ranges from 1894,
when the British South Africa Company began to collect tax, to 1903,
when some of the people of the north-east were still refusing to
recognize the Native Department as anything but a raiding force.[170]
Some writers prefer to concentrate on the onset of the capitalist
economy, but this too is a variable date. In either case, Shona
peasantries and migrant labourers are recorded at very early dates —
'peasant' being defined for the moment as an independent agriculturalist who plants in the hope of profit.

   For a long time, until they established the *prazos da corôa* at the
beginning of the seventeenth century, the Portuguese on the coast
relied upon African growers for their food. In December 1506 a Shona
ruler in the hinterland of Sofala informed the Portuguese that he had
brought peace to the land in order that he might send them food

supplies, and in about May 1507 he himself arrived to meet them.[171] If this commerce in food was in the prerogative of the ruler, other such trades were not, and by the 1590s Sofala was reliant upon the vegetables grown by the people both near Sofala and at the mouth of the Sabi.[172] Thus, where a mercantile economy was unable to supply its own food, an African peasantry arose to supply that need. When a capitalist economy appeared and had the same need, there was the same response, before any governmental pressures were applied. From 1890 to 1894, before the Native Department began to levy tax, the Shona rapidly expanded their acreages and diversified into growing maize as a staple crop for sale to the mines, as described above in connection with the Njanja, and subsequently in Chapters 9 and 10.

Given that capitalism frequently entails a situation in which a man sells his labour for money, then capitalism can be seen to have been affecting the Shona by the early 1870s. We have already seen that the gold and ivory trade, in which Shona traders travelled long distances to the ports, encouraged a very shrewd appreciation of market opportunities of all kinds. This extended to the south as well as to the east. There are traditions of eighteenth-century Shona economic contacts with the Nguni (Zulu, etc.),[173] and in the nineteenth century men such as Karemba, one of Selous's men who was hired in Klerksdorp on the Vaal in 1884 and who had contacts in the Shona south-east as well as in Chivero's country on the Umfuli, must have done much to spread news of opportunities.[174] The Kimberley diamond mines began to employ African labour on a significant scale in 1869–70, and by 1873 at least one Shona from near Zimbabwe was *returning* from work there.[175] By 1883, over twenty-five Shona from the Duma country were returning from Kimberley.[176] By 1890 many people near Zimbabwe had been to Kimberley,[177] and in 1895 much of the hut tax was paid in gold coins earned at Johannesburg and Kimberley.[178]

Migrant labour also appeared at Rhodesian mines before 1894. There were relatively few cases of labour enforcement by the British South Africa Company before the Native Department began this practice on a large scale in 1894.[179] The wage offered for a Shona labourer — 15 shillings a month in the Hartley district in 1895[180] — was not an attractive one, and in the circumstances it is surprising that any Shona people at all cared to work for the mines, yet this seems to have been the case. In June 1893 'a good many' Shona from Lomagundi as well as 'Shangaans' (Tsonga and Chopi — see next chapter) arrived at Hartley, and some at least of the labour force at Victoria at the same time seems to have been Shona.[181] Since the Europeans, in the fond belief that race determined achievement, paid 'Shangaan' labourers more than Shona, many of the 'Shangaans' who were employed on the mines before 1894 may have been Shona, especially from the Ndau-speaking areas.[182] One group from Bikita set out to look for work in Salisbury in 1893.[183]

Most of the income from early peasant sales and migrant labour went into purchasing trade goods, some of which could be exchanged

against stock as the traditional bulwark against *shangwa,* and in many
cases firearms were acquired, which offered several methods of
economic advancement from raiding to elephant-hunting. But it is
interesting to note that by 1895 coin was being used directly to buy food
by the people of Lomagundi, whose crops had been ruined by the
locusts,[184] and by 1897 a great deal of the tax paid in Bocha was in
Portuguese coin, which also implies a wide, and possibly early,
movement of labourers and crops to Portuguese Manyika.[185]

The very brief account given here of the transition from the
'traditional' economy to the capitalist economy shows how rapid was
the response of the Shona to changing conditions. The rapid expansion
of Shona agriculture to meet the opportunities offered by the
mercantilist economy by the sixteenth century and the capitalist
economy in the nineteenth was dramatic enough. The speed of the
Shona response to the opening of Kimberley was also rapid. Since we
are reliant at present upon only scattered missionary reports for the
period before 1890, there were certainly other Shona migrant labour
movements that went unrecorded. But the truly surprising thing is that
anyone cared to become a migrant labourer, either to Kimberley and
the Rand before 1890 or to the Rhodesian mines after then, until
compelled to do so by the Native Department's demands for tax and
labour. Labour conditions in South Africa were not princely, and in
Rhodesia they were much worse.[186] Most goods, including firearms,
were anyway available in the Shona country from *zungu* and Venda
traders. The conclusion seems to be that in the era before colonial
pressures, there were other pressures within the Shona economy and
society that forced people to go to considerable lengths to acquire
wealth of some kind.

## Conclusion

The picture given here of the Shona economy stresses the importance
of agriculture as its base, and points out the limitations of other
branches of production, ranging from hunting to gold-mining, in terms
of relative value, even though in some cases these branches of
production involved very sophisticated techniques. Yet the agricultural base itself is shown to have suffered from a serious weakness, in
that longer periods of prosperity in farming were followed by short but
weakening periods of disaster, *shangwa,* against which the Shona were
not able to devise an absolutely reliable defence. It seems likely that the
root of the problem lay in a range of crops and storage methods that did
not stand up to the demands of the harsh environment. Since the
agricultural base was not completely secure, livestock, and especially
cattle, assumed a special importance as an emergency food supply and
as a self-perpetuating form of wealth. Mining, manufacturing, and
trade were developed as far as possible, but for a variety of reasons
were not able totally to offset the limitations of agriculture. Consequently, there was not only a rapid response to mercantilist and

capitalist market opportunities in the form of peasant production of crops, but there was even a certain amount of migrant labour towards the generally uninviting mine compounds before colonial government compulsion began at the end of the nineteenth century. Indeed the inherent fragility of the economy explains the speed with which the Shona reacted to the opportunity presented of becoming peasant producers. It also shows that this opportunity gave the Shona the chance of achieving better economic security through agriculture, the one field in which all the people could participate. The crippling of Shona agriculture in the early twentieth century after a few years of prosperity was thus especially tragic, since it forestalled the achievement of the kind of economic and social stability in the rural areas sought after in developing nations today.


## NOTES

1.   The identification of 'southern Zambezia' as an economic zone cuts off many of the peoples mentioned from greater numbers of them to the north and south.
2.   P.S. Harris, *Black Industrial Workers in Rhodesia* (Gwelo, 1974).
3.   G. Arrighi, 'Labour Supplies in Historical Perspective: A Study of the Proletarianization of the African Peasantry in Rhodesia', *Journal of Development Studies*, 6, 1970, 197–234; Chapter 10, I.R. Phimister, 'Peasant Production and Underdevelopment in Southern Rhodesia, 1890–1914, with particular reference to the Victoria District'; Chapter 9, R.H. Palmer, 'The Agricultural History of Rhodesia'.
4.   R. Summers, *Ancient Mining in Rhodesia*, National Museums of Rhodesia Memoir No. 3 (Salisbury, 1969); N. Sutherland-Harris, 'Trade and the Rozwi Mambo', in R. Gray and D. Birmingham (eds), *Pre-Colonial African Trade* (London, 1970), 243–64.
5.   R.M.G. Mtetwa, 'A Dynamic Precolonial Economy: The Duma Case, *1720–1900', unpublished, Salisbury, 1974.
6.   The main exception being the Manyika: see H.H.K. Bhila, 'The Manyika and the Portuguese, 1575–1863', PhD thesis, University of London, 1971.
7.   For example, Sutherland-Harris, 'Trade', 243.
8.   C. Meillassoux, 'From Reproduction to Production: A Marxist Approach to Economic Anthropology', *Economy and Society, 1*, 1972, 93–8, 103; E. Terray, *Marxism and 'Primitive' Societies* (New York, 1972), 95, 183–4.
9.   Terray, *Marxism*, 97–8.
10.   Terray, *Marxism*, 99.
11.   University of Rhodesia, History Department Text 93 Gta. [Henceforth URHD Text(s).]
12.   National Archives of Rhodesia, N 9/2/2, Report of the N/C Hartley for the half-year ending September 1898. *Note:* unless otherwise stated, all archival references are to the National Archives of Rhodesia.
13.   Chapter 11, B.A. Kosmin, 'The Inyoka Tobacco Industry of the Shangwe People: The Displacement of a Pre-Colonial Economy in Southern Rhodesia, 1898–1938'.
14.   J.M. Mackenzie, 'A Pre-Colonial Industry: The Njanja and the Iron Trade', *NADA, 11*, 2, 1975, 200–20, J.M. Mackenzie, 'Iron Workers and the Iron Trade in Southern Zambezia', unpublished, Salisbury, 1974.
15.   C. Meillassoux, 'The Social Organisation of the Peasantry: The Economic Base of Kinship', *Journal of Peasant Studies, 1*, 1973, 83; Meillassoux, 'Reproduction', 99–100.

16. Terray, *Marxism*, 108, 115–18, 138, 157, 160.
17. Terray, *Marxism*, 109–11; Meillassoux, 'Reproduction', 99.
18. This is a very tentative dating. Pottery, and hence almost certainly agriculture, has been dated to about 1500 BC in the neolithic Kintampo culture of Ghana, while the use of iron was well established in Nigeria by 200–300 BC and in South Africa by the third century AD. P.L. Shinnie (ed.), *The African Iron Age* (London, 1971), 39, 12.
19. M. Gelfand, *Diet and Tradition in an African Culture* (Edinburgh, 1971), 134–41; W. Roder, *The Sabi Valley Irrigation Projects*, University of Chicago, Department of Geography, Research Paper No. 99 (Chicago, 1965), 63–5.
20. URHD Texts 79–86 Bha; 'T.E.', 'The Origin of the Name "Makoni" ', *NADA*, *14*, 1937, 77; N 3/33/8, N/C Umtali to CNC Mashonaland, 19 January 1904.
21. Mtetwa, 'Precolonial Economy'; H.N. Hemans, 'History of the Abenanzwa Tribe', *Proceedings and Transactions of the Rhodesia Scientific Association*, *12*, 1913, 85–7.
22. N 1/1/11, N/C Umtali to CNC Mashonaland, 21 December 1896 and 22 February 1897.
23. E.E. Burke (ed.), *The Journal of Carl Mauch 1869–1872* (Salisbury, 1969), 159–63.
24. Burke, *Mauch Journal*, 159–63; URHD Text 58 Hty; N 1/1/6, N/C Mazoe to CNC Mashonaland, 30 October 1897; J.T. Bent, *The Ruined Cities of Mashonaland* (London, 1892), 265–6.
25. P.S. Garlake, *Great Zimbabwe* (London, 1973), 159–60.
26. Personal communication from Dr T.N. Huffman.
27. URHD Texts [numbers not yet allocated: questionnaire answers, 1970] Bwe.
28. W.M. Kerr, *The Far Interior, Vol. 1* (London, 1887), 44.
29. NB 1/1/2, Assistant N/C Mpateni to N/C Belingwe, 16 December 1897.
30. M. Wilson, 'The Hunters and Herders', in M. Wilson and L. Thompson (eds), *The Oxford History of South Africa, Vol. 1, South Africa to 1870* (Oxford, 1969), 48.
31. Gelfand, *Diet*, 100–1, 105–12.
32. N 3/1/5, N/C Charter to CNC Mashonaland, 5 December 1899 and 26 August 1903.
33. Shinnie, *The African Iron Age*.
34. D.N. Beach, *An Outline of Shona History* (forthcoming), Chapter 1.
35. Beach, *Shona History*, Chapters 2, 4–6.
36. W. Roder, 'The Division of Land Resources in Southern Rhodesia', *Annals of the Association of American Geographers*, *54*, 1964, 41–58; R.H. Palmer, 'Red Soils in Rhodesia', *African Social Research*, *10*, 1970, 747–58; J.M. Mackenzie, 'Red Soils in Mashonaland: A Re-assessment', *Rhodesian History*, *5*, 1974, 81–8.
37. URHD Texts 87 Gtu, 98–9, 102 Gzi, 105 Wza.
38. URHD Texts 71–3 Uti, 82–3 Bha, 87, 89 Gtu, 97–9 Gzi, 105 Wza; Gelfand, *Diet*, 73–80; Roder, *Sabi Valley*, 56.
39. J. dos Santos, 'Ethiopia Oriental', in G.M. Theal (ed.), *Records of South Eastern Africa, Vol. 7* (Cape Town, 1898–1903), 186.
40. Gelfand, *Diet*, 74.
41. URHD Text 83 Bha; personal communication from F. du Toit, Department of Conservation and Extension, Salisbury; N 9/1/5, Report of the N/C Charter for the year ending March 1899; N 1/1/9, N/C Salisbury to CNC Mashonaland, 24 November 1895; W.F. Rea, 'The Missions as an Economic Factor on the Zambezi, 1580–1759', PhD thesis, University of London, 1974, 27 n. 4.
42. I am indebted to F. du Toit and Dr G. Smith, Department of Education, University of Rhodesia, for their help on the question of grain storage. The final conclusions, however, are my own responsibility.
43. Personal communication from R.M.G. Mtetwa, who comes from a dry, *mapfunde*-growing area; Gelfand, *Diet*, 74.
44. URHD Texts 82–3 Bha, 87, 89 Gtu.
45. M.O. Collins (ed.), *Rhodesia: Its Natural Resources and Economic Development* (Salisbury, 1965), 26.

46.   M.W. Murphree, *Christianity and the Shona* (London, 1969), 45; M.L. Daneel, *Old and New in Southern Shona Independent Churches, Vol. 1* (The Hague, 1971), 550.
47.   URHD Text 88 Gtu; A. Livneh, 'Some Notes on Drought... in Rhodesia', SOAS/ICS African History Seminar, 1974.
48.   N 3/33/8, N/C Marandellas to CNC Mashonaland, 1 January 1904.
49.   N 1/1/5, N/C Lomagundi to CNC Mashonaland, 26 September 1895.
50.   N 9/1/7, Report of the N/C Charter for the year ending March 1901.
51.   F.H. Ferrao, 'Account of the Portuguese Possessions within the Captaincy of Rios de Sena' (c. 1810), in Theal, *Records, Vol. 7*, 372.
52.   URHD Texts 82−3 Bha, 87, 89 Gtu.
53.   N 9/4/5, Report of the N/C Charter for the month December 1899; N 3/1/5, N/C Charter to CNC Mashonaland, 5 December 1899.
54.   N 9/4/5, Report of the N/C Charter for the month December 1899; N 3/1/5, N/C Charter to CNC Mashonaland, 5 December 1899; Chapter 10, Phimister, 'Peasant Production'.
55.   N 1/1/9, N/C Salisbury to CNC Mashonaland, 22 July, 24 November 1895.
56.   N 1/1/6, N/C Mazoe to CNC Mashonaland, 30 October 1897.
57.   N 1/1/11, N/C Umtali to CNC Mashonaland, 21 December 1896.
58.   URHD Text 103 Mds.
59.   Hist. MSS WI 8/1/1, Account by Nkani, 1−2.
60.   J.P.R. Wallis (ed.), *The Matabele Journals of Robert Moffat, 1829−1860, Vol. 1* (London, 1954), 214−15, 224, 265.
61.   Arrighi, 'Labour Supplies', 202.
62.   T.N. Huffman, 'Test Excavations at Makuru, Rhodesia', *Arnoldia, 5,* 39, 1973, 1−21.
63.   F 4/1/1, Secretary, Native Department, to Statist, BSA Company, 21 September 1895.
64.   URHD Texts 71−2 Uti; N 1/1/11, Assistant N/C Umtali to N/C Umtali, 22 December 1896.
65.   F 4/1/1, Report of the N/C Umtali, 4 July 1895.
66.   E.A. Nobbs, 'The Native Cattle of Southern Rhodesia', *South African Journal of Science, 24,* 1927, 333.
67.   'Viagem que fez o padre Antonio Gomes' (1648), *Studia, 3,* 1959, 196−8.
68.   D. Kousu, 'An Account of the Livestock Proper', in G. Fortune (ed.), *Ndevo Yengombe Luvizho* (Cape Town, 1949), 17.
69.   Nobbs, 'Native Cattle', 336.
70.   Garlake, *Great Zimbabwe,* 156, 122; personal communication from Dr T.N. Huffman; J. de Barros, 'Da Asia', (1552), in Theal, *Records, Vol. 6,* 272; Fr. Monclarro, 'Account of the Journey... 1569', in Theal, *Records, Vol. 3,* 237; 'Antonio Gomes', 196−8; S.I. Mudenge, 'The Role of Foreign Trade in the Rozvi Empire: A Re-assessment', *Journal of African History, 15,* 1974, 389.
71.   J.R.D. Cobbing, 'The Ndebele under the Khumalos, 1820−96', PhD thesis, University of Lancaster, 1976.
72.   F 4/1/1, Report of the N/C Victoria, 1 July 1895.
73.   A 15/1/1, Hut tax return, 19 July 1895.
74.   Nobbs, 'Native Cattle', 331; Cobbing, 'The Ndebele',
75.   Kousu, 'An Account', 9.
76.   See, for example, J.F. Holleman, *Shona Customary Law* (Cape Town, 1952), 161−9.
77.   E.G. Howman and J.H.S. Adam, 'The Hand of Glory', *NADA, 6,* 1928, 32−3; H. Franklin, 'Nyaningwe', *NADA, 6,* 1928, 80.
78.   URHD Texts 87−8 Gtu, 94 Gta, 102 Gzi, 105 Wza.
79.   J.D. White, 'Some Notes on the History and Customs of the Urungwe District', *NADA, 10,* 3, 1970, 38.
80.   Dos Santos, 'Ethiopia', 265.

81. White, 'Some Notes', 38.
82. URHD Texts 93–4, 96 Gta.
83. EC 3/1/1, Executive Council Minute No. 124, 13 May 1899.
84. Roder, *Sabi Valley*, 68.
85. URHD Texts 72–4 Uti, 82–3, 85 Bha; N 1/1/11, Assistant N/C Umtali to N/C Umtali, 22 December 1896.
86. URHD Texts 72–4 Uti, 80–3, 85 Bha, 89 Gtu, 98–9, 102 Gzi, 103, 105 Wza.
87. Summers, *Ancient Mining*, 215; M.D. Prendergast, 'Research into the Ferrous Metallurgy of Rhodesian Iron Age Societies', *Journal of the South African Institute of Mining and Metallurgy, 74*, 1974, 225.
88. URHD Text 93 Gta.
89. URHD Texts 81–2 Bha.
90. J. Chidziwa, 'History of the va Shawasha', *NADA, 9,* 1, 1964, 17.
91. Prendergast, 'Research', 225.
92. I.C. Pereira, 'Mappa das minas conhecidas no distrito de Senna', 30 July 1857, and F. de P. Carvalho, 'Relaçao das minas conhecidas na provincia de Moçambique', 15 October 1879, in *Memoria e Documentos acerca dos Direitos de Portugal aos Territorios de Machona e Nyassa 1890* (Lisbon, 1890), 296–328.
93. Mackenzie, 'Iron Workers', 8.
94. URHD Texts 93 Gtu, 97 Gzi.
95. N 3/33/8, N/C Marandellas to CNC Mashonaland, 1 January 1904.
96. F.W.T. Posselt, *A Survey of the Native Tribes of Southern Rhodesia* (Salisbury, 1927), 21.
97. Beach, *Shona History,* Chapter 6.
98. Pereira, 'Mappa', 292.
99. Mackenzie, 'Pre-Colonial Industry', 200–20; URHD Texts 71 Uti, 89 Gtu; Mtetwa, 'Precolonial economy'.
100. Beach, *Shona History,* Chapter 6.
101. URHD Texts 81–2 Bha; personal communication from Dr C.A. Lee.
102. URHD Texts 71 Uti, 82 Bha, 88 Gtu.
103. URHD Text 80 Bha. This may be a depressed price due to the proximity of the Dorowa iron industry.
104. URHD Texts 98, 102 Czi, 107 Rse.
105. Mackenzie, 'Pre-Colonial Industry', 216; J.P.R. Wallis (ed.), *The Northern Goldfields Diaries of Thomas Baines, Vol. 3* (London, 1946), 787; URHD Text 74 Uti; R.M.G. Mtetwa, 'The Rise of the Duma Confederacy, *1700–1800', University of Rhodesia, Department of History, Henderson Seminar No. 23, 1973.
106. Mackenzie, 'Iron Workers', 6; Mackenzie, 'Pre-Colonial Industry', 208 n. 30.
107. Chapter 10, Phimister, 'Peasant Production'; N 1/1/2, N/C Charter to CNC Mashonaland, 17 July, 26 August 1895; N 1/1/2, Range Diary, 19, 20, 21, 25, 30 September, 1, 2, 13 October, 15, 27 November 1896; N 1/1/12, N/C Victoria to CNC Mashonaland, 12 June, 1 July 1895; in 1895 the trader H. Short moved from his trading station at Umniati in the Hera country to Altona near Ranga's, L 1/2/2, Surveyor General to E.E. Homan, 5 March 1895.
108. F 4/1/1, Report of the N/C Charter, 14 June 1895.
109. N 9/1/5, Report of the N/C Charter for the year ending March 1899.
110. Bent, *Ruined Cities,* 272; I. Shimmin, 'The Mashonaland Mission', *Work and Workers in the Mission Field, 3,* 18, 1893, 421; LO 5/2/41, Report of the N/C Marandellas, 31 December 1894; S.716, Range Diary, 27 June 1897, which mentions that the skinning of live goats for bellows was forbidden.
111. Mackenzie, 'Iron Workers', 6, 8, 16.
112. Beach, *Shona History,* Chapter 6. These are the most spectacular examples, but most Karanga groups and many Zezuru carried out remarkable demographic expansions at this time.
113. R. Gray and D. Birmingham, 'Some Economic and Political Consequences of Trade in Central and Eastern Africa in the Pre-Colonial Period', in Gray and Birming-

ham, *Pre-Colonial African Trade*, 3.
114.   C. Meillassoux, 'Essai d'interprétation du phénomène économique dans les sociétés traditionelles d'auto-subsistance', *Cahiers d'Etudes africaines*, 4, 1960, 38–67. Cited in Gray and Birmingham, *Pre-Colonial African Trade*, 3.
115.   Mackenzie, 'Pre-Colonial Industry', 206–14; Gray and Birmingham, *Pre-Colonial African Trade*, 3–10.
116.   Chapter 11, Kosmin, 'The Inyoka Tobacco Industry'.
117.   Mudenge, 'Foreign Trade', 373–91; Garlake, *Great Zimbabwe*, 131–5; T.N. Huffman, 'The Rise and Fall of Zimbabwe', *Journal of African History*, 13, 1972, 362–4.
118.   T.N. Huffman, 'Tafuna Hill', *South African Archaeological Bulletin*, 29, 1974, 65–6; G.S.P. Freeman-Grenville (ed.), *The East African Coast* (London, 1962), 15.
119.   Beach, *Shona History*, Chapter 1.
120.   Antonio da Silveira to the King (c. 1528), in A. da Silva Rego and T.W. Baxter (eds), *Documents on the Portuguese in Mozambique and in Central Africa, 1497–1840*, Vol. 5 (Lisbon and Salisbury, 1962–), 563.
121.   Beach, *Shona History*, Chapters 1–5.
122.   For example, M.D.D. Newitt, *Portuguese Settlement on the Zambezi* (London, 1973); W.G.L. Randles, *L'empire du Monomotapa du XVe au XIXe siècle* (Paris, 1975).
123.   I.R. Phimister, 'Pre-colonial Gold Mining in Southern Zambezia: A Reassessment', *African Social Research*, 21, 1976, 5, 9, 26–7. See also I.R. Phimister, 'Alluvial Gold Mining and Trade in Nineteenth-Century South Central Africa', *Journal of African History*, 15, 1974, 445-56.
124.   The main statement to the contrary, H.H.K. Bhila, 'Trade and the Survival of an African Polity: The External Relations of Manyika from the Sixteenth to the Early Nineteenth Century', *Rhodesian History*, 3, 1972, 11, relies upon C.A. Guerreiro, 'Inquerito em Mocambique no ano de 1573', *Studia*, 6, 1960, 12–18. This refers to the *moradores*, the Portuguese settlers, buying food from elsewhere, not the people of Manyika itself.
125.   See map 1.
126.   R.W. Dickinson, 'Sofala and the Rivers of Cuama: Crusade and Commerce in South East Africa, 1505–1595', MA thesis, University of Cape Town, 1971, 150; Beach, *Shona History*, Chapters 3–4.
127.   Notes of Gaspar Veloso (1512), in Rego and Baxter, *Documents, Vol. 3*, 187.
128.   Dickinson, 'Sofala', 150. The annual averages are computed on the basis of the monthly figures available.
129.   Pero de Anhaia to the King's Treasurers, 19 May 1506; Manuel Fernandes to the King's Treasurers, 21 October 1506, Rego and Baxter, *Documents, Vol. 1*, 507, 687.
130.   See map 1.
131.   Dickinson, 'Sofala', 150.
132.   Phimister, 'Pre-Colonial Gold Mining', 14–16.
133.   Phimister, 'Pre-Colonial Gold Mining', 15–16.
134.   Diogo de Alcaçova [to the King, 20 November 1506], in *Documents, Vol. 1*, 395, who otherwise greatly overestimated the bulk of the gold trade, thought that the Zambezi trade was only a fraction of that of Sofala. The Portuguese in their disappointment at the low return from Sofala in turn exaggerated the gold trade of the Zambezi, but when they finally came to control the trade in the 1540s it did not prove to be very great.
135.   H. Preston, 'Primitive Mining in Central Africa', *Chamber of Mines Journal*, 7, 2, 1965, 41. I am indebted to Ian Phimister for this reference.
136.   Phimister, 'Pre-Colonial Gold Mining', 5.
137.   It is obvious that estimates of this kind, based on so many variables, must be handled with care: if a ton of ore averaged only half an ounce, it could double the labour involved for the same amount of gold exported. But it is important to have some idea of economic activity in terms of human activity rather than in ounces or tons, which

convey little to most non-specialists.
138.   'Antonio Gomes', 197; Anon. (prob. R. de M. Pereira), 'Memorias da costa d'Africa Oriental e algumas reflexões uteis para estabelecer melhor, e fazer mais florente o seu commercio', (1762), in A.A. de Andrade (ed.), *Relações de Moçambique Setecentista* (Lisbon 1955), 219. A further 50 *pastas* of gold, some of it probably from the Changamire state, left through Sofala. An accurate summary of trade figures over the whole Portuguese period is long overdue: Marco Antonio de Montaury in the same year credited Zumbo alone with 300-400 *pastas* (5,775 ounces) of gold a year, Rea, 'The Missions', 163–4. At this late date in the Shona gold industry, the lower figure looks the more probable.
139.   Pereira, 'Mappa', 296.
140.   dos·Santos, 'Ethiopia', 321–2.
141.   Roder, *Sabi Valley,* 63.
142.   André Fernandes to Luis Frois, 25 June 1560, in *Documents, Vol. 7,* 483.
143.   URHD Texts 71, 74 Uti, 80–3, 85 Bha, 87 Gtu, 93 Gta.
144.   URHD Texts 71, 73–4 Uti, 80–3, 85 Bha, 87, 89 Gtu, 93–5 Gta, 98, 102 Gzi, 103 Mds.
145.   André Fernandes to Fr. Provincial, India, 24 June 1560, in Rego and Baxter, *Documents, Vol. 7,* 467.
146.   URHD Texts 73 Uti, 80, 83, 85 Bha, 87 Gtu.
147.   Garlake, *Great Zimbabwe,* 132; 'Antonio Gomes', 197; Mudenge, 'Foreign Trade', 373–91.
148.   URHD Texts 98 Gzi, 108 Rse, 109 Wza.
149.   Dickinson, 'Sofala', 153.
150.   The same *caveat* applies as at note 137.
151.   Dos Santos, 'Ethiopia', 321–2.
152.   Anon. (Pereira), 'Memorias', 212; Randles, *L'empire,* 113–15.
153.   Beach, *Shona History,* Chapter 2.
154.   R. Summers, 'Archaeological Distributions and a Tentative History of Tsetse Infestation in Rhodesia and the Northern Transvaal', *Arnoldia, 3,* 13, 1967, 1–18; J. Ford, *The Role of the Trypanosomiases in African Ecology* (Oxford, 1971), 327–39.
155.   P.S. Garlake, 'Rhodesian Ruins — a Preliminary Assessment of their Styles and Chronology', *Journal of African History, 11,* 1970, 510.
156.   D.N. Beach, 'Ndebele Raiders and Shona Power', *Journal of African History, 15,* 1974, 643–4.
157.   N 9/1/5, Report of the N/C Charter for the year ending March 1899.
158.   Personal communication from Dr T.N. Huffman. Work on the poorer parts of Zimbabwe is only now being developed.
159.   Duarte Barbosa, 'Description... ', in *Documents, Vol. 5,* 359; Barros, 'Da Asia', 270–1; T.N. Huffman, 'Cloth from the Iron Age in Rhodesia', *Arnoldia, 5,* 14, 1971, 1–19.
160.   Mtetwa, 'Pre-Colonial Economy'.
161.   A.F. Isaacman, *Mozambique: The Africanization of a European Institution: The Zambezi Prazos, 1750–1902* (Madison, 1972), 47–9.
162.   Hist. MSS MA 14/1/1, Draft book by J. Machiwenyika, Lesson 43.
163.   Burke, *Mauch Journal,* 213; URHD Texts 93–4 Gta.
164.   URHD Text 103 Mds.
165.   Hist. MSS MA 14/1/1, Draft book by J. Machiwenyika, Lesson 43.
166.   N 3/1/15, Evidence of Manando, Inquest at Matuniki's, 9 November 1898.
167.   C. Bullock, *The Mashona* (Cape Town, 1927), 66.
168.   URHD Texts 71 Uti, 82, 85 Bha, 87 Gtu, 97 Gzi.
169.   Hist, MSS MA 14/1/1, Draft book by J. Machiwenyika, Lesson 43.
170.   N 3/1/16, Acting N/C Mtoko to Acting N/C Salisbury, 24 April 1903.
171.   Manuel Fernandes to the King's Treasurers, 30 December 1506, in *Documents, Vol. 1,* 769; Martin Fernandez de Figueroa, 'Account, 1505–11', in *Documents, Vol. 3,* 612.

172.   Dos Santos, 'Ethiopia', 186; see also João Vaz de Almada to the King, 26 June 1516, in Rego and Baxter, *Documents, Vol. 4*, 283—5.
173.   Chidziwa, 'History', 17; H. von Sicard, 'Shaka and the North', *African Studies, 14*, 1955, 147.
174.   Kerr, *Far Interior, Vol. 1*, 99.
175.   H. von Sicard, *Zvakaitika kare zveKereke yamaLuthere munyika yeRhodesia* (Gwelo, 1972), 17. The response from Shona living under Ndebele rule was equally rapid, Cobbing, 'The Ndebele'.
176.   Hist. MSS BE 2/1/1, Half-yearly report, Tshakoma, 1st semester, 1883.
177.   Argief van die N.G. Kerk, Cape Town, Report of C.P. Helm, 1891, 28.
178.   N 1/1/12, Acting N/C Victoria to CNC Mashonaland, 3 February 1896. Similarly, Ndebele society also witnessed a significant degree of pre-colonial labour migration to Kimberley and the Rand. J. Cobbing, 'Historical Materialism and the Nineteenth Century Ndebele', University of Rhodesia, Political Economy Research Seminar No. 11, 1974, 10.
179.   T.O. Ranger, *Revolt in Southern Rhodesia, 1896—7* (London, 1967), 67, 72—3.
180.   DL 1/1/1, Report of the C/C Hartley, 23 April 1895.
181.   LO 5/2/28, Report of the N/C Umfuli, 30 June 1893, F.R. Harris to London Board of BSA Company, 26 July 1893; LO 5/2/29, L.S. Jameson to London Board, 24 August 1893 (Goldfields letter 131, Victoria).
182.   DL 1/1/1, Report of the C/C Hartley, 23 April 1895.
183.   W.R. Peaden, 'Nenguwo Training Institution and the First Shona Teachers', in A.J. Dachs (ed.), *Christianity South of the Zambezi* (Gwelo, 1973), 75.
184.   N 1/1/5, N/C Lomagundi to CNC Mashonaland, 26 September 1895.
185.   N 1/1/11, Report by Acting N/C Umtali, 9 December 1897.
186.   C. van Onselen, 'Black Workers in Central African Industry: A Critical Essay on the Historiography and Sociology of Rhodesia', *Journal of Southern African Studies, 1*, 1975, 228—46.

# CHAPTER 2

## Fertility and Famine: Women's Agricultural History in Southern Mozambique

## SHERILYNN YOUNG

### Introduction

Like belief in witchcraft, faith in a static Africa can evidently not be eliminated by a single submission to the ordeal of academic inquiry. Historians have demonstrated change in politics, in trade, and in war. But the great majority of Africans who are agriculturalists, and the majority who are women, have yet to be treated dynamically. 'Traditional agriculture' is the term all too frequently ascribed to whatever happened before the plough and outside the irrigation project. The study of women has suffered from this neglect of agricultural history since women are usually the main cultivators. But beyond this the study of women has suffered from its own static generalization: from the idea of the 'traditional woman', the idea of the essentially unchanging existence led by African women before or outside the transformations of Christianity and urbanization.

The social consequence of this concept of the 'traditional' agriculturalist has been the formulation of plans to replace him or her in order to achieve 'progress', which has proved not only economically unfeasible for many areas, but socially and ecologically disastrous. The image of the 'traditional' woman has obscured the realities of changing opportunities and thus denied women much chance to have a voice in creating the policies which affect them.

But this chapter is not a study of these contemporary consequences. It is rather an attempt to undercut the overgeneralized view of the past which has brought them into being, and to describe some of the many faces of 'traditional' agriculture and of women. It hopes to demonstrate, moreover, that understanding these aspects of African societies promises to provide a greater insight into the internal dynamics of the phenomena described in other kinds of African histories. Histories of migration, centralization, and political conflict, and of expansion of trade, should not be studied in isolation from the changes in products and modes of production that facilitate them and are affected by them. Neglect of production history is sometimes defended on the grounds that it is difficult to identify historically particular occupation groups. But this is not the case with women, whom both European and African observers have always been able to identify at any point in history, even if they have not so often deigned to do so. Since it has been women who have provided most of the labour for cultivation, who have prepared food and drink, and who have raised and provided for the young — then women as a group represent a fundamental division of labour and responsibility and can be studied as such.

This chapter is concerned to study women as a division of labour with different interests from other divisions of labour, and to analyse how this division has influenced their wider role in society. It attempts to do so over a long period of time, even though such a reconstruction must often be conjectural, because it is only in the perspective of a series of interactions and changes in the mode of production that its continuing dynamic and its influence in particular on the last hundred years can be demonstrated. Finally, in turning to the twentieth century, with its much richer data on ecological and economic flux as well as on social and ritual organization, I will attempt to demonstrate more specifically the close continuing dynamic between women's position in the economy and in their other social roles.

Southern Mozambique appears particularly appropriate for this purpose due to its combination of ecological features and two cultural-linguistic groups of people. The region is a low-lying coastal plain with sandy soils, in climate and vegetation distinct from the highlands of Swaziland and South Africa to the west, and from the wet tropical territories to the north of the Savé (Sabi) river. It contains some of the best cattle country in Mozambique, but cattle apparently never acquired the sustained economic and ritual importance that they did among the Nguni- and Sotho-speaking peoples to the south and west. This may have been due to the absence of good available groundwater farther inland where low rainfall makes cultivation least profitable, so that cattle-keeping has had to compete directly with cultivation for good land and water on the coastal belt. Moreover, between the lower Limpopo and Inhambane some areas are infested with tsetse fly, while in general the swamps and low altitudes have not proved consistently healthy for domestic animals. Thus two basic ways of producing food — agriculture and cattle-keeping — directly compete within the region. Similarly, there are two cultural-linguistic groups, which though closely related and interacting have maintained separate identities and taken different approaches to labour allocation and to women's roles in society. I shall refer to them as (a) the Chopi, including the dialects of Lenge, Chopi, and Gi-Tonga, and (b) the Tsonga, including speakers of the dialects called Ronga or Landim, Tsonga or Shangaan, and Tswa.[1]

Further characterization of the cultures in the region seems improper in the spirit of this chapter without turning to the dynamics of their historical development. I move first to a discussion of these societies in the period before 1800.

From the linguistic evidence and the archaeology of neighbouring regions, it appears that the proto-communities of the Tsonga and Chopi linguistic groups entered our region in the first half of the first millennium AD. An Early Iron Age site near Tzaneen in the north-eastern Transvaal (where Venda, Tsonga, and Sotho groups overlap) has been carbon-dated to the third to fourth century AD. Christopher Ehret and others have postulated that proto-Nguni, -Sotho, -Venda, -Tsonga, and -Chopi were originally five dialects of 'proto-South-East-Bantu' related to Shona, which split from each other in the present north-eastern Transvaal.[2] Their preceding linguistic affinities were with proto-communities of the Bantu groups now stretched across Central Africa to the north, in which primary food production is by cultivation, and cultivation is primarily by women. The importance of cultivation in early Tsonga and Chopi societies is evident in the cluster of reconstructable cultivation terminology and specifically the words for millet and sorghum. These two crops could be grown throughout the whole region[3] and continued to predominate as staples until at least the sixteenth century.[4]

Women's association with crops precedes men's role in cattle-keeping in Tsonga mythology. The first man is named 'the one who brings a glowing cinder', and the first woman, 'the one who grinds vegetables'.[5] This conceptualization of male and female contributions to society was practically attested in the patterns of ritual service and inheritance rights of uterine nephews and in some cases uterine nieces that persisted into the late nineteenth and early twentieth centuries.[6] The case of the nieces seems particularly relevant in demonstrating the responsibility of women for contacting spirits for the ecological welfare of the community and in acts associated with cultivation and food preparation. On the other hand Rita-Ferreira has suggested that agriculture was left to women because weeding was easy in the loose soils and wild crops were abundant in the coastal sandy belt — a situation reinforced by the later successful adaption to the soil of imported high nutrition crops.[7] It is certain however that before the sixteenth century, when these societies were first described by outside observers, economic changes had taken place which resulted in men playing a more influential role in the economy. Hunting was probably always important, both as a source of food and of male prestige. The main factor of economic change was the increasing importance of cattle.

This began in the period of initial proto-South-East-Bantu dialect expansion, but linguistic evidence shows cattle did not attain their full significance in any of the groups until further innovations were made as they developed in separate homelands. It is even possible that male dominance was not firmly established until men found ways to supplement their cattle through importation. Thus the rise of external trade assumes considerable importance.

## The sixteenth century

The evidence available from the sixteenth century onwards outlines the economic conditions internally and the relations between the sexes in a period in which regular economic exchanges with other South African regions and with extra-African trade were established, but during which their volume was relatively limited.

The evidence begins in the mid-sixteenth century. At this time a ship from Sofala to Inhambane annually exported ivory, beeswax, copper, and slaves from Chopi territories, demonstrating not only their seaborne trade but their contacts with the highlands to the north-west, from which they obtained the copper.[8] An annual ship was also expected at Delagoa Bay, while chiefs there imported additional foodwealth into the region by their cattle raids on societies to the south.[9]

Food production was observed to be limited and regular seasons of hunger were expected. The missionaries reported that millet and sorghum were grown everywhere between the lower Limpopo and Inhambane, along with peas, a large variety of beans, and some type of root crop which the Europeans called 'potatoes'. They claimed that women provided all the food, and that no men of any rank would turn their hand to work. The priests themselves undertook some cultivation and thus became convinced after their travails that women of this region worked harder than did Portuguese men.[10]

Despite the central role played by women in production, the priests perceived them to be little respected in the society. As usual this is difficult to assess. In ritual the ancestors — then as in the nineteenth century — were the most powerful legitimate spiritual forces,[11] and diviners were charged with discovering their wishes and 'smelling out' witches, who were people who used spiritual powers in 'evil' ways.[12] However in that period observers did not identify diviners by sex. Women were said to be particularly associated with the mystical forces carrying sickness and death and thus were often accused of witchcraft and named in cases of contamination.[13] While some commentators have concluded from this that women were particularly despised, the two most specific examples given in reference to them were that a woman was blamed for the death of her child if she had separated from her husband, and that women brought contamination through adultery.[14] In fact both issues directly identify tension over the failure of males to control women. In one widespread folktale that Junod collected among the Tsonga, the rightful return of a woman and her children to her parents when the husband had failed to share his hunting meat properly was the key theme.[15] Thus a woman's continued security in her own family may have provided an opportunity for her to leave an undesirable man, whose only recourse was to await a subsequent misfortune, such as the death of a child, and attempt to discredit her through accusations of witchcraft.

There were disadvantageous results for women of the division of labour between sexes. When disputes between clans occurred in which settlement involved transferring a member of one clan to the other as compensation, women were more commonly transferred. As one priest observed, 'Commonly these pagans do not accept males because they are costly and the females work'.[16]

However, it should also be acknowledged that the priests were predisposed to be critical of 'pagans', and in their short stay they may have not had an opportunity to appreciate balances in the society. Women did have a legal voice and could bring a case to court,[17] and the cases recorded of witchcraft accusations demonstrate that men were accused of the same crime. In the Delagoa Bay region women were reported to hold political power as sub-chiefs in their brothers' realms as well. But by the end of the nineteenth century we have no records of them in such positions, although women still occasionally headed governments, as illustrated by the case of Zambi, powerful Queen Mother of Maputo.

Even if sixteenth-century European observers were critical of the subordination of women, therefore, we have reason to suppose that this period forms an intermediary stage between earlier relatively equal distributions of economic responsibility and rights in the society, and the more complete dominance by men which characterized the nineteenth century. There were in fact both economic and political changes taking place between the sixteenth and nineteenth century which probably affected the position of women, and we will summarize these now.

## Developments between the sixteenth and nineteenth centuries

As previously stated, we have regrettably little direct information on women in this period, but in their role as agriculturalists it is possible to identify some of the innovations that they made and how these affected their position in society. Furthermore the expansion of trade in this period appears to have benefited the society as a whole, but the position of males in particular, in ways that the nineteenth-century developments undercut, thereby affecting the way these societies entered the twentieth-century economy.

In the seventeenth century Portuguese ships came only semi-annually, but trade with English factors supplemented extra-African economic interchanges.[18] Regular exports of ivory, rhino horn, and amber brought beads and cloth to the region and probably facilitated inter-African trade relationships. A key change in male-female opportunities can be asserted as a result. The complementary relationship in sharing products resulting from an equal division of labour, with men providing meat through hunting and herding and women providing grain crops and vegetables from cultivation, was fundamentally altered as a result of trade. For from this point onwards men's hunting activities no longer yielded purely internally shared and consumed products, but produced ivory and horns of value in trade which could produce additional prestige goods and investment in cattle. These could be further reinvested in more wives and thus supply men with cumulative wealth and power which women could not gain from subsistence food production through cultivation.

The opportunity provided for inland trade is evident in the continued coastal export of copper, now by the British from the Limpopo-Inhambane region,[19] while Dutch traders in the early eighteenth century noted seasonal overland trade between Delagoa Bay and Inhambane in which Tsonga obtained hoes, axes, and assegais, some of which may have been produced by Chopi iron-workers. At least by the second half of the eighteenth century this region was interacting with the whole South African trading network. Beads and cloth were exported to the Venda, Pedi, and Nguni; while ivory, copper, and hoes were imported from the Venda; ivory, horns, and cattle from the Pedi (further connecting them with Tswana and Sotho cattle and trade), and ivory and cattle from the Nguni.[20] Some copper was retained in the region, and was a prestigious item of adornment, particularly useful to men in gaining the favour of, and rights to, existing and promised wives. Both copper and ivory were exported overseas. The great profit to the region of this trade appears primarily to have been in agricultural implements, which it had been the duty of men to provide, and in considerable numbers of cattle. All this certainly enhanced male power but it would be wrong to conclude that women had lost their initiative or the capacity to precipitate economic development.

There is no published information on whether women were traders or porters in these ventures, but they certainly continued to be the bulk of the cultivators. In this role they were active in adopting new crops, especially maize, cassava, and South American groundnuts by the end of the eighteenth century.[21] They had to be primarily responsible for determining the seasonal and soil adaptability of each of these crops to each part of the region. By the nineteenth century they had also rendered cashew nuts edible and prepared alcoholic beverages from both cashews and maize. These innovations permitted increased yields from each unit of labour, thus increasing the ability of the society, and of the individual families, to subsist primarily from the products of female cultivation. Their increasing capacity in this production was perhaps coupled with the prestige and profits which males could obtain from hunting and trading, to produce an *ideal* for males of long-distance travel and employment in hunting and trading activities, while their wives looked after the home. Herding may also have been included in this ideal lifestyle but, by the end of the nineteenth century, the ideal had become a social duty for every young man, as well as a means of his gaining wives and children who made the man stout and important among his peers.

If there had been any residual matrilocality the increased prosperity of male economic activities in this period must have eradicated it. However Junod's folktales, such as the one already referred to, indicate the persistence of inherent rights of women which continued to be perceived by the community, both to reasonable treatment by her husband, and to recourse to her own parental family if he failed to provide. It is within this context that we can view the societies of southern Mozambique as they entered the nineteenth century.

## The nineteenth century: the Nguni impact

The Nguni incursions of the 1820s mark a major watershed in Tsonga and Chopi economic history. Prior to this the evidence for the early nineteenth century suggests the continuing prosperity of external trade and of cattle-keeping. After Nguni rule was established both trade and cattle-keeping were greatly disrupted, placing severe strain on the Chopi and Tsonga economies as a whole and in particular compelling a redirection of male energies, which helps to explain the subsequent movement of Tsonga and Chopi men in migrant labour. [22]

Two details in particular emerge for the early nineteenth century. First there was extensive employment in external trade, over which Tsonga chiefs never managed to exercise a monopoly. [23] Secondly the regional economy was dependent on considerable imports of cattle from external sources, important both in providing food and as a means of obtaining rights over women and children.

In the period from the establishment of Nguni rule until the 1860s, we know little of the details of economic change but certain major trends can be seen. First, Alan Smith has argued with some force that one of the primary motivations of Nguni incursion into this area was to obtain direct control of trade, eliminating Tsonga profiteering, and that under Nguni rule, trade, particularly in ivory, was a monopoly of the Gaza rulers. [24] Thus even assuming some continued Tsonga and Chopi activity in trade after Nguni rule was established, a substantial reduction occurred in the distribution of its profits. Secondly, that trade, formerly bringing cattle from Nguni territories and the west, was increasingly disrupted both by the wider effects of Nguni expansion and by Afrikaner and British intervention in the source areas. Thirdly, Tsonga and Chopi regions not subject to Nguni rule were vigorously raided for cattle and slaves, reducing normal male activities in the economy and food supplies, as well as producing considerable general dislocation. Fourthly, large numbers of males in subject territories were incorporated into the Nguni military, while non-subject territories engaged their men in opposing military activities, thus further removing them from primary production. And fifthly, in the mid-nineteenth century, Portuguese and Asian traders began to control export and internal trade in the immediate vicinities of the ports.

In part the Nguni may have hoped to cause little disruption to basic food production, so they could utilize it for their own benefit. Their imposition of kingship ceremonies on existing 'first fruits' ceremonies may be seen as one attempt to come to terms with the cultivators and general populace. [25] Furthermore it would be a mistake to assume that they generated no loyalty, since their power and prestige gained many adherents. But the economic dislocation is evident on a general level from the shifting of *lobolo* from cattle to hoes in this period. [26] Both reduction in cattle and increasingly heavy demands for ivory were producing further change in the ecology of the region. By the end of the nineteenth century not only had the elephants been destroyed for what might be termed 'cash-cropping', but antelopes and wildebeest, which were mainly 'subsistence crops' of hunting, were seriously depleted, while giraffe and zebra were said to have fled inland.[27]

Perhaps a strain on food supplies coupled with vastly extended external contacts served to bring on epidemics. An epidemic of smallpox, remembered by some as the first and by all as the worst in history, visited sometime between 1859 and 1862, for it is remembered as the 'smallpox of Mawewo'.[28] Dysentery, typhoid, and blackwater fever also took their toll.[29]

Periodization of these trends is not yet precise, but they give much more internal logic to the beginning of Tsonga and Chopi labour migration which took place before colonial control was effective. Several hundred workers were contracting their services in Natal in the 1860s on sugar plantations, while in the 1870s several thousand were known to be at work on alluvial goldfields elsewhere in South Africa and in Natal, and the pound sterling began to replace hoes as *lobolo*.[30] In the 1880s the Cape Colony joined in recruiting for farms and public works, and Natal railways and farms employed another thousand, as did diamond-mining; and then the Witwatersrand was proclaimed a gold-bearing area and economic opportunity for thousands more was offered. The difficulty of obtaining local labour in Southern Africa for periods of more than three to four months made the 'Shangaans' of southern Mozambique particularly valued and sought after, for they remained on the job for two- to three-year stretches. By 1890 the mines employed 14,000; by the end of the decade their total working force was 97,000,[31] of which the mine employers estimated two-thirds to three-quarters were from Portuguese East Africa, the overwhelming majority of whom were from south of the Savé river.[32]

## The position of women at the end of the nineteenth century

Our particular interest in women and agriculture can be more fully satisfied in the last part of the nineteenth century. It is possible to identify both what their economic responsibilities were and what their roles in other aspects of communal life were like. At this point some comparisons between Tsonga and Chopi societies can be made.

Although Marvin Harris's informants claimed Tsonga men had once had felling and burning responsibilities, by the 1890s women performed these tasks.[33] While in folklore men were depicted as assisting in planting, field-watching, and harvesting, these too had become solely women's occupations by the turn of the century. Junod noted that husbands might keep a small garden, but the wife's fields and gardens fed the family while the man's were for his own disposal or particularly for tobacco. And Rita-Ferreira added that in contrast to elsewhere in Southern Africa, where the adoption of the plough intensified male participation in agriculture, no such effect was evident among the Tsonga where the plough was essentially unsuitable for sandy soils.[34]

On the other hand among the Chopi, where population was much more densely settled, the men were said to work as much as the women. They were supposed to do all work requiring metal tools,[35] and so were reported 'supervising' cutting and burning at the beginning of the planting season.[36] Men might have their own fields, but the women weeded and assisted in the harvest of these,[37] and while the women's fields fed the family, created a famine reserve, and provided future seed, the products of the men's fields were for their own disposal.[38]

Given the absence of important deities in this period, we should note the ways in which women and women's ancestors were recognized in ancestral worship. Among the Chopi some recognition of women appeared in this regard. The names of great wives were sometimes included in the calling of praise-names of the ancestors;[39] at field openings and fertility rituals the headmen offered the sacrificial mealies to both his mother's and father's lineages;[40] and the *nyanga* (diviner), in diagnosing the cause of barrenness of a woman or the sickness of a child, consulted the ancestors of both lineages.[41] The great wife of the chief of the village was further required to be present at all sacrifices her husband made, and it was she who was at the head of the hierarchy of the women of the village.[42] Yet clearly the rituals as a whole were controlled by male diviners, male chiefs, and male ancestors, even if they were of a woman's lineage.

Among the Tsonga too some ritual importance was accorded to women. The importance of the uterine niece in the northern clans has already been referred to. In some ceremonies a woman might be the one to take the clan heir into the sacred forests and assist him in the rituals. However this position was accorded her only if she were the oldest member of the lineage and might as easily be held by a man.[43]

Some more general contrasts between women's positions in the two societies have been made. Junod held there was a greater respect for women among Chopi/Gi-Tonga communities than among Tsonga.[44] Women, he said, are not so despised among the Chopi: they eat in the presence of men, and families may be seen walking on public roads with the husband carrying a child while the wife and children walk with him. On the other hand illegitimate births were acceptable in Tsonga families, while among the Chopi fear of a husband's anger was given as a cause for the practice of abortion and contraception.[45] However the most interesting contrasts between the Tsonga and the Chopi, and the area which seems most to evidence consciousness of women among the Chopi, appeared in their initiation rituals.

While one cannot avoid seeing in these ceremonies specific instruction in the need for solidarity of women in their common situation, it is difficult to determine at this point whether this consciousness and these ceremonies led to common actions by women to secure their rights, or served more as a means of preparing them to submit to the rigours of the life they would have to lead as women and subordinate to their new husbands. During the twentieth century these initiation rites appear to have lost some of their cohesion in formulation of the instructions and in their communally based execution. However they were also suppressed by Portuguese authorities and suffered from competition with Christianity. On the other hand new forms of women's ritual activity were devised.

## The twentieth century

At the beginning of the twentieth century the African women of southern Mozambique were facing a series of difficult situations in which their economic obligations and expectations in the community were to alter substantially. Labour migration and internal forced labour of men kept more than half of the adult males away from home at most times. Drought and flood brought frequent famines, while Portuguese alienation of land and imposition of taxes placed unusual demands on cultivators. One could hardly have expected the position of 'traditional women' to have remained unchanged and it did not. Nor were such women merely passive victims in the process.

In the first decade of the century, with the population of the region between half and three-quarters of a million, the annual number of men legally at work in the South African mines was 50,000–60,000, while a third as many again are believed to have worked illegally outside Mozambique, and thousands more were conscripted for work on *colono* farms and government military and public works. Of those registered as legally entering and returning from South Africa between 1905 and 1912, some 87,000 failed to return at all.[46] Those that did brought with them not only cloth, blankets, and oil, but venereal disease and accusations of adultery to their women. Elders' accounts of birth and death rates among children born in their families during this period vary from 15 to 50 per cent.[47] Cattle had been decimated by rinderpest and east coast fever in the last decade of the nineteenth century, and showed remarkably little recovery in their numbers during this period — reaching only 50,000 by 1913.[48]

Women were thus increasingly being expected to fulfil all home duties and supply food without the assistance of men, and with increasing uncertainty as to whether their men would in fact ever return or what the men would do to their women when they did. In the Maputo (formerly Lourenço Marques) and Inhambane districts large plantation schemes had expropriated literally hundreds of square kilometres of prime farmland and the owners then demanded local labour to develop it at the rate of 6—8 cents a day for women, 8—10 cents a day for men.[49]

In 1908 the maize crop failed and only the women's ability to procure edible wild roots and leaves prevented large numbers of Africans from starving.[50] In 1912 drought turned them again to famine crops which were said to have sustained thousands. but hundreds more died within the areas under mission observation.[51] Some women by this time were gathering the *mafura* fruits (which yielded oil) for sale, and 6,000–7,000 tons were exported in 1912 and again in 1913, but the returns to each gatherer were so small that it hardly increased their ability to buy food. In 1913 famine struck again.[52]

In such circumstances of ecological disaster, women took ritual initiatives. Efforts to cleanse their societies and restore fertility were observed by the Rev. Haley as he scouted for future mission sites between Manjacaze and Inharrimo. The women assembled in quasi-military manner and, brandishing assegais, threatened the evil spirits from the huts of each village as well as from the Reverend. In the north, near the Savé river, a different approach was initiated by the Hlengwe (Tsonga) clans which had a wider effect on women's positions.[53]

Messengers were sent into Rhodesia to visit *Mwari*. They were well received by the high god and given cleansing instructions and sacred tobacco, which they were to mix with nasal mucus and the soils of their fields to restore fertility. In 1915, the heaviest rainy season in twenty years brought floods and devastation through the Limpopo valley and the rite of *mourimi*, as it was known, spread into that vicinity.[54] The disaster was attributable to the anger of *Doumapansi* (a Tsonga praise-name used in reference to *Mwari* as a god beneath the earth) at the removal of the Nguni king Gungunyana in 1895. This connection with the institution of Portuguese authority led officials to attempt to suppress what they perceived as a subversive movement, imprisoning the *mourimi* messengers. They failed; the movement continued to spread for a least another year, promising not only fertility but a millennial era of unlimited food and the end of death.

Acceptance of the *mourimi* cleansing ritual reasserted the importance of the chiefs[55] and the process was in the first instance one of confession and eradication of witchcraft. But it also asserted a new importance for a high god in whose name women took direct responsibility for the rituals and fertility of their fields and villages.[56] Men who had been absent at the mines were forbidden from entering their homes until they had undergone the cleansing period and taken the *mourimi* tobacco, and the provision of food or assistance in labour to any uninitiated person was forbidden.[57]

Rebinding the community in crisis was clearly only one aspect of this movement. It was also a direct demonstration of purely 'traditional' means of responding to ecological disaster and of reorganizing communal ritual responsibilities in keeping with new economic factors and the dominant role of women in agricultural and communal responsibilities. It provided a ritual means of relieving some of the pressure caused by the return of males from the mines. Its success in resolving the ecological problems was less impressive.

In 1917 torrential rains again destroyed crops: one bushel of groundnuts was said to have been gathered where a thousand were expected.[58] Imported food prices had been inflated 150 per cent by the war and little was available even at those prices.[59] Cattle and goats died by the thousand, and in both 1917 and 1918 measles, dysentery, pneumonia, and smallpox were each said to have taken hundreds, and in some cases thousands, of human lives.[60]

The extent to which these climatic irregularities, and the insecurities they brought, promoted labour migration is not clear. However, the migrants are known to have assisted home communities in need. Another severe famine struck in 1922, in which a third of the population was said to have died in some sub-districts.[61] But missionaries also reported that during the famine mineworkers sent 'vast sums of money home'.[62]

Despite such devastating experiences, women who were 'traditional' both ritually and agriculturally were experimenting with the cultivation of new crops and the sale of their produce. Sisal production, which had been encouraged among *colonos* during the First World War, began to be grown by women.[63] In addition they gathered cashews, peddling roasted nuts on public roads and selling them to exporters, and they expanded their production of groundnuts. Initial exchanges in some areas were for cloth and clothes, but increasingly the women demanded cash rather than accept the cheap goods of Indian traders.[64] The extent of their expansion is evident in the export figures for groundnuts, which were principally African produced. Production reached 11,429 tons in 1925, doubled to 22,096 in 1926, and then climbed to 37,604 in 1936.[65] Cotton production in this period grew rather slowly, but the seed and marketing rights were allocated by the government to the *colonos*. Not until they failed in this task did the government turn in the Second World War to reliance on African growers. Women were then required to work in the cotton fields four days a week under male supervisors, clearing land, cultivating, destroying the insects, harvesting, and marketing the cotton. Initially the prices were not sufficient to compensate for the food crops they might otherwise have produced and they suffered until the government reduced cotton requirements and encouraged cassava expansion. The success of the women's response was evident in the 1951–2 reports that in Chopi territory families sold an average of $120 worth of cotton, produced sufficient staples for themselves, and could also market some cassava.[66]

Women were not only capable of economic adaptation and expansion, but they asserted themselves in formerly male dominions of social organization. The practice of ancestral rites under male control began to lapse, and diviners complained that they were being neglected. Possession cults — largely led by female mediums and priestesses, whose first roles had been in placating and exorcising spirits — gradually turned to modifications of practices connected with ancestral rites. Reference to the ancestral relationship became omitted in many cases, and cult practitioners also took up herbal medicines and other remedial practices formerly associated with *nyanga* men. Spirit possession, which had first been by Nguni and Ndau spirits, came also to be by Indian merchants, Jewish storekeepers, Portuguese farmers, and Roman Catholic priests. The cults extended to feature dramatizations of the sins committed by men at the mines, sometimes naming the man, and they dramatized the roles of the housewife, the chief, the gold-miner, and the pedlar.

The direct relationship of cults to agricultural practices was also evident. A medium was reported to dance with her hoe 'dramatizing modern agricultural practice' while her chorus sang: 'If you neglect to hoe your family will be hungry'. Songs varied from indigenous tunes to modern lyrics urging the destruction of flies and mosquitoes. One powerful medium, who persuaded eight wives and a number of husbands to serve her, performed fertility and agricultural rituals nearly identical with those the chief used to perform. She 'compelled' all her patients to join her in making a sacrifice to the spirits before they began their gardening.

Men, on the whole, did not join these cults: a great many were Christianized, and Christians had their own agricultural rituals while non-Christian men made little attempt to become cultivators. Not all 'traditionalists' were dependent on ritual for new attitudes towards cultivation processes either. One non-Christian woman claimed the best 'medicine' for a field was rotted grass and manure!

The Gwambi Chopi, whose experiences have been most fully recorded on the latter period of change, feel that the division of sexes increased when men began working on the mines. Women became virtually rulers of the home and much more economically independent. Their understanding of the men's life experiences and the demands men have made on them increasingly deteriorated. Men came to express their own independence by keeping their savings to themselves, selling their own crops, and living independently in the towns.[67]

At this point it is difficult to assess the changes as for better or for worse, but the evidence emphatically denies that conditions have remained, or ever were, static.

## Conclusion

This twentieth-century experience of Tsonga and Chopi women differs from the generalizations which have been made about women in agriculture in the colonial period. In this case the development of cash crops and of new agricultural techniques did not result in male dominance of modern agriculture. Instead women took over cash crop production as well as continuing to expand food production. Their income in crop sales gave them substantial independence. Their participation in spirit possession cults cannot be interpreted as in the Interlacustrine area of Middle Africa and elsewhere in terms of compensation for deprived status. Rather it was a mechanism for asserting control over community ritual, commensurate with increased female importance in community life and in the economy.

Nor can we explain the difference between this situation and the generalized picture presented by Boserup[68] merely in terms of the particular policies of Portuguese administrators. The Portuguese merely built upon and intensified the situation of labour division they found.

Though the colonial period did witness rapid and far-reaching change, this was not a unique phenomenon, to be contrasted with 'traditional' agriculture or the experiences of 'traditional' women. Generations of Tsonga and Chopi men and women had experienced economic change which redefined the relationships between them and the history of their societies. The redefinition of labour divisions in the twentieth century was merely the latest of a series of such realignments, and it cannot be properly understood without reference to its precedents. But it will certainly not be the last, for both the important role played by women in the recent war of liberation against the Portuguese and the composition of the 1975 Frelimo government suggest that women in independent Mozambique are likely to play a much more radical and assertive role than in neighbouring countries, where political independence was achieved through the ballot box.

## NOTES

1. For a discussion of the competition between cultivation and cattle-keeping in current times, see J.M. da Silva, 'Panorâmica da nossa pecuária', *Boletin da Sociedade de Estudos de Moçambique, 34*, 1965, 69. Smith supports H.A. Junod's division of the peoples of southern Mozambique into Tsonga, Chopi, and Tonga *ethnic* groups in a recent article, in which he argues that they emerged by the eighteenth century from a series of interactions, including Shona and Sotho (Pedi) population infiltrations. A.K. Smith, 'The Peoples of Southern Mozambique: An Historical Survey', *Journal of African History, 14*, 1973, 565–80. 'Chopi' and 'Gi-Tonga' may today  be considered as separate languages; however, basic vocabulary analysis shows that they derive from what was a single common parent language in the first half of the second millennium AD, and that this common parent 'proto-Chopi' belonged to the 'proto-South-East-Bantu' during the first millennium. The differentiation between Ronga, Tsonga, and Tswa is much less distinct.
   The author wishes to emphasize that this essay was written early in her research project, before commencing fieldwork in southern Mozambique.
2. R.J. Mason *et al.*, 'Early Iron Age Settlement of Southern Africa', *South African Journal of Science, 69*, 1973, 324; C. Ehret *et al.*, 'Outlining Southern African History: A Re-evaluation, AD 100–1500', *Ufahamu, 3*, 1, 1972, 9–27.
3. Carvalho discusses the requirements (especially climatic) for the staple cultigens of Mozambique and the areas in which they are now predominant. Sorghum and millet are still predominant in the interior, since maize, cassava, and groundnuts require higher rainfall. M. de Carvalho, *A Agricultura Tradicional de Moçambique* (Lourenço Marques, 1969).
4. The Portuguese terms for grains in this area are discussed in H.A. Junod, 'The Condition of the Natives of South-East Africa in the Sixteenth Century, According to the Early Portuguese Documents', *Report of the South African Association for the Advancement of Science, 10*, 1913, 155–6. Fuller claims maize in the area, but without referring to the term he has translated as such. The Portuguese term for maize, which is now *milho*, has apparently undergone the same shift as the English term 'corn' has in America. Furthermore, Fuller discusses porridge made from *mexoeira* as 'corn meal mush'; the Portuguese *mexoeira* however most consistently refers to pearl (or bulrush) millet. C.E. Fuller, 'An Ethnohistoric Study of Continuity and Change in Gwambe Culture', PhD thesis, Northwestern University, 1955, 45.
5. H.A. Junod, *The Life of a South African Tribe, Vol. 1, Social Life* (London, 1927), 21.
6. Junod, *The Life, Vol. 1*, 269.

7.   A. Rita-Ferreira, 'Labour Emigration Among the Moçambique Thonga: Comments on a Study by Marvin Harris', *Africa, 30*, 1960, 143.

8.   A. Smith, 'Delagoa Bay and the Trade of South-Eastern Africa', in R. Gray and D. Birmingham (eds), *Pre-Colonial African Trade* (London, 1970), 270.

9.   Junod, 'The Condition of the Natives', 140.

10.  Fuller, 'Gwambe Culture', 30, 45. Compare this with Rita-Ferreira's remarks above on the 'easiness' of cultivation. See also A. da Silva Rego and T.W. Baxter (eds), *Documents on the Portuguese in Mozambique and in Central Africa, 1497–1840, Vol.* 7 (Lisbon and Salisbury, 1971), 468–517.

11.  Junod, 'The Condition of the Natives', 160.

12.  Fuller, 'Gwambe Culture', 64.

13.  Fuller, 'Gwambe Culture', 67.

14.  Fuller, 'Gwambe Culture', 57.

15.  H.A. Junod, *The Life of a South African Tribe, Vol. 2, Mental Life* (London, 1927), 246–8.

16.  Fuller, 'Gwambe Culture', 69.

17.  Fuller, 'Gwambe Culture', 58.

18.  Smith, 'Delagoa Bay', 270.

19.  Smith, 'Delagoa Bay', 270.

20.  A. Smith. 'The Trade of Delagoa Bay as a Factor in Nguni Politics 1750–1835', in L. Thompson (ed.), *African Societies in Southern Africa* (London, 1969), 183.

21.  A. Lobato, *História do Presídio de Lourenço Marques, Vol. 2, 1787–1799* (Lisbon, 1960), 22.

22.  Prior to the results of my own fieldwork, this essay is not the place for me to enter the argument between Marvin Harris and A. Rita-Ferreira conducted in the pages of *Africa* (the journal of the International African Institute) during 1959–61. Harris explained the high rate of Tsonga labour migration from the later nineteenth century by reference to the social structure and alien oppression, while Rita-Ferreira suggested that local ecology and external market incentives were more important. See *Africa, 29,* 1959, 50—60; *30*, 1960, 141—52, 243—5; *31*, 1961, 75—7. See also M. Newitt, 'Migrant Labour and the Development of Mozambique', University of London, Institute of Commonwealth Studies, *Collected Seminar Papers on the Societies of Southern Africa in the 19th and 20th Centuries, Vol. 4* (London, 1974), 67–76; M.D.D. Newitt, 'Land and Labour in Early Twentieth-Century Moçambique', *Iberian Studies, 1, 2,* 1972, 45–52.

23.  Smith, 'The Trade', 183.

24.  Smith, 'The Trade,' 180–9.

25.  C. Montez, 'Kossi N'quaio!', *Moçambique, 4*, 1935, 10–15.

26.  Junod, *The Life, Vol. 1*, 276.

27.  Fuller, 'Gwambe Culture', 75. In 1898 the Transvaal proclaimed part of its border area with southern Mozambique a game reserve, which was expanded into the Kruger National Park in 1926.

28.  H.A. Junod, 'Native Customs in Relation to Small-Pox Amongst the Ba-Ronga', *Report of the South African Association for the Advancement of Science, 15*, 1918, 696. Mawewe, the son of Soshangane (Manikusi), ruled the lower Limpopo from 1859 to 1862.

29.  Fuller, 'Gwambe Culture', 76. These diseases may well have occurred before this period as well.

30.  Figures are to be found in A. Rita-Ferreira, *O Movimento Migratório de Trabalhadores Entre Moçambique e a Africa do Sul* (Lisbon, 1963); S.T. van der Horst, *Native Labour in South Africa* (Cape Town, 1942), 216–21. On *lobolo* prices, see Junod, *The Life, Vol. 1*, 276.

31.  van der Horst, *Native Labour*, 218–19; M. Harris, 'Labour Emigration Among the Moçambique Tsonga: Cultural and Political Factors', *Africa, 29*, 1959, 50–60.

32.  Great Britain, Naval Intelligence Division, *Manual of Portuguese East Africa* (London 1920).

33.  Harris, 'Labour Emigration', 58; Junod, *The Life*, Vol. 2, 23–4.
34.  Junod, *The Life*, Vol. 1, 337–8, Vol. 2, 14–15; Rita-Ferreira, 'Labour Emigration', 143.
35.  J. Nunes, 'Apontamentos Sôbre a Tribu du Ba-Thonga', *Boletin de Estudos Moçambique, 3,* 1932, 32–3; Fuller, 'Gwambe Culture', 93.
36.  Fuller, 'Gwambe Culture', 79.
37.  Fuller, 'Gwambe Culture', 80.
38.  Fuller, 'Gwambe Culture', 81.
39.  Fuller, 'Gwambe Culture', 112.
40.  E.D. Earthy, 'Notes on some Agricultural Rites Practised by the VaLenge and VaChopi (Portuguese East Africa)', *Bantu Notes, 2.* 8, 1925, 194.
41.  E.D. Earthy, *Valenge Women* (London, 1933), 61.
42.  Earthy, *Valenge Women,* 115.
43.  A.D. Clerc, *Chitlangou, Son of a Chief* (London, 1950), 34–5.
44.  H.P. Junod, 'Chopi', in A.M. Duggan-Cronin (ed.), *Bantu Tribes of South Africa: Reproductions of Photographic Studies, Vol. 1* (Cambridge, 1938).
45.  Earthy, *Valenge Women,* 64.
46.  *Manual of Portuguese East Africa,* 17.
47.  Fuller, 'Gwambe Culture', 74.
48.  R.N. Lynes, 'The Agriculture of Moçambique', *Bulletin of the Imperial Institute, 9,* 1913, 102–10.
49.  The 1913 annual mission report gives 8 cents for women, 10 cents for men; Haley 6 cents for women, 8 cents for men. *Annual Report for the Board of Foreign Missions of the Methodist Episcopal Church* (New York, 1913), 470; J.W. Haley, *Life in Moçambique and South Africa* (Chicago, 1926), 92.
50.  *Methodist Episcopal Church Annual Report 1908,* 67–9.
51.  *Methodist Episcopal Church Annual Report 1912,* 328; Methodist Episcopal Church Report Book Africa D–29, meeting of 17 December 1912.
52.  Methodist Episcopal Archives, New York, Missionary Correspondence, 1912–49, Film no. 71, Drawer 54, File 15, Bishop J.C. Hartzell to North Inhambane, 7 October 1913.
53.  Haley, *Life in Moçambique,* 58.
54.  The principal sources for this movement are M. Guye, 'Recrudescence paienne — Le Culte de Mourimi', *Mission Swisse Bulletin,* 1916, 165–71; H.A. Junod, 'Le Mouvement Mourimi: un reveil au sein de l'animisme Thonga', *Journal de Psychologie normale et pathologique, 21,* 1924, 865–82; J.K. Rennie, 'Some Revitalization Movements among the Ndau and Inhambane Thonga 1915–1935', Paper for the Conference on the History of Central African Religious Systems, Lusaka, 1972, 15–20.
55.  Junod, 'Le Mouvement Mourimi', 869; Methodist Episcopal Archives, 71/54/16, Hartzell to 'Dear ones at Home', February 1915.
56.  Junod, 'Le Mouvement Mourimi', 870, 872.
57.  Junod, 'Le Mouvement Mourimi', 875–7.
58.  *Methodist Episcopal Church Annual Report 1917,* 424.
59.  *Methodist Episcopal Church Annual Report 1918,* 421.
60.  *Methodist Episcopal Church Annual Report 1917,* 346; Nunes, 'Apontamentos'; Junod, 'Native Customs'.
61.  Methodist Episcopal Archives, 66/49, Sauffer to Richards, 1922.
62.  *Methodist Episcopal Church Annual Report 1923,* 413.
63,  Clerc, *Chitlangou,* 11.
64.  Clerc, *Chitlangou,* 40–4.
65.  A. Pimenta, 'Subsidios para a estudo dos Amendoims de Moçambique', *Moçambique, 17,* 1939.
66.  Fuller, 'Gwambe Culture', 151.
67.  The evidence for these paragraphs is derived from Fuller, 'Gwambe Culture', 151, 154, 180–1, 191, 203–4, 244–5.
68.  E. Boserup, *Women's Role in Economic Development* (London, 1970).

# CHAPTER 3

## Trade and Dependency in Central Angola: the Ovimbundu in the Nineteenth Century

### FOLA SOREMEKUN

### Introduction

In a recent study of the impact of mercantilism on East Central Africa, Edward Alpers has demonstrated that the original cause of modern underdevelopment is to be found in the *pre*-colonial period.[1] The point is well taken as a counterbalance against simplistic explanations of African poverty which attribute all evil to colonialism sweeping away the virtues of a static 'traditional' Africa. But in his revisionist enthusiasm, Alpers leaps into that camp of political economists for whom no good can come out of Africa, decrying all attempts at African development until world capitalism magically melts itself. Alpers argues that external African trade and its internal supply routes between the thirteenth and nineteenth centuries 'did nothing to promote either economic development or social equality', and in fact the opposite was inevitable because of overseas market controls and wealth-grabbing local rulers.[2] Africa and Africans, it appears, were — as they are — helpless victims of historical inevitability.

It is not the purpose of this chapter to deny the validity of the general historical processes identified by Alpers, but rather to underline their subtleties in response to local conditions and human initiative in West Central Africa. Furthermore, we need to re-emphasize the political and thus economic contrast between the mercantile and colonial periods otherwise blurred by Alper's analysis. Can one equate mercantile dependence on Europe, leading to underdevelopment of local production and social distortion, with later colonial dependence? Or did colonial rule, with its direct European control of the means of production in Africa itself, constitute a new economic as well as political order? With trading contracts spread far and wide in West Central Africa, the Ovimbundu of central Angola in the nineteenth century are a major illustration of how African people experienced the transformation of mercantile dependency into colonialism.

### The Ovimbundu of Central Angola

The Ovimbundu of the Benguela Highlands were popularly known as the 'Mambari' to the rest of West Central Africa in the nineteenth century.[3] Reaching as far east as southern Zaïre and western Zambia, travellers attested to their keenness as traders.[4] Numbering perhaps over a million people, the Ovimbundu at home were grouped into twenty-two states, of which two, the kingdoms of Bailundu and Bié, were much larger than the rest.[5] Through their area passed goods such as firearms, cloth, and liquor into the interior in return for ivory, slaves, wax, and eventually rubber exported at the coast.

Ranging in height from 1,000 to 1,500 metres above sea level, the Benguela Highlands is a great catchment area from which flow the major rivers of Angola — the Kwanza (Cuanza), the Kuve (Cuve), the Kunene (Cunene), and the Okavango (Cubango). The Bié Plateau on the eastern part of the Highlands faces out towards the Kasaï and the Lungwebungu tributary of the Zambezi. The Benguela Highlands are thus strategically placed to dominate the communications of West Central Africa running along the line of rivers or of watersheds. The focal position of the Highlands for communication between the interior and the coast is complemented by their potential for productive agriculture. The soils are of modest fertility, and the climate is comparatively temperate, with rainfall varying between 1,000 and 1,500 mm per year, making the Benguela Highlands comparable to the Kikuyu Highlands of Kenya in relation to surrounding humid or dry lowlands.

Under the agriculture and industry of the emergent Ovimbundu over the centuries, the Benguela Highlands realized their potential in supporting a heavy population and an internal system of production and trade. Agricultural practices such as terracing and irrigation made their mark, and Ovimbundu blacksmiths were famous for the quality of the hoes they manufactured from local ores.[6] Ovimbundu trade with their neighbours became well established, importing barkcloth and salt, and exporting hoes and goods acquired from Portuguese on the coast, with whom contact had first been made in the year 1600.[7] The Portuguese founded the port of Benguela on the coast in 1617, in the country of the Ndombe, and by 1681 Ovimbundu from the Highlands were familiar traders at the port — the Ngola kingdom of the Ovimbundu being six to seven days' walk inland.[8] From the later seventeenth century, Portuguese mercantilism was dominated by Brazilian capital, and slaves for trans-Atlantic export became its major demand on the Angolan interior. The Ovimbundu responded by organizing a system of long-distance trading based on royal caravans, omaka, and complex trading and political alliances between their states on the Highlands. By the 1770s, when the Portuguese set up isolated trading posts on the Highlands, it is evident that the kingdoms of Bié and Bailundu had emerged as real powers over other Ovimbundu states. The Portuguese, with their local Ovimbundu agents, pombeiros or 'barefoot traders', became embroiled in the flurry of trade expansion in the late eighteenth century. They succeeded in defeating Bailundu, which thereafter regained its independence and tended to be hostile, and placed a political agent at the heart of Bié, which thereafter tended to be an ally of the Portuguese.[9] Trading contacts with the coast, in a wide range of commodities but specializing in slaves, was now institutionalized among the Ovimbundu states. The Portuguese had found it necessary to intervene politically in order to establish the principle of economic dependency on coastal trade, but they did not consider it necessary or expedient to maintain that principle with political power.

## Ovimbundu trade in the nineteenth century

The nineteenth century saw a great expansion of Ovimbundu trade, over routes already operated by their northern neighbours and over new routes to the south-east. The official banning of the slave trade by the Portuguese government in 1836, and the consequent decline of the Kassanje to Luanda route, which had been the major slave route since the sixteenth century, led to a focusing of trading attention upon the Ovimbundu and the Bié to Benguela route. The effects of the change from the slave trade to 'legitimate' trade were probably minimal for the Ovimbundu, for the lifting of the Portuguese government's monopoly over the trade in ivory opened up fresh avenues for those Ovimbundu located close to the Chokwe, the great elephant-hunters, to become middlemen in the ivory trade. The fifty years between 1840 and 1890 were in fact the great age of Ovimbundu trade, in which they dominated the exchange of goods between the interior and the coast.

Ovimbundu pre-eminence as long-distance traders, however, has tended to obscure the importance of internal, or home-based, trade. As middlemen between the coastal trade and trade to the east and north-east, most of their preparations for trading in both directions had to take place at home. If goods came from the coast, they had to be assembled on the Highlands; some of them would be sold or exchanged for local products, and the rest would then be sent eastwards. If goods came from the east, they also had to be assembled again on the Highlands before being sent towards the coast.

Beeswax and cattle provide two examples of the relationship between internal and external trade. Cikuma, in Ovimbundu country, was generally unable to supply sufficient beeswax to meet the demands of the coastal traders. Thus the Ovimbundu obtained more beeswax from the Chokwe, but the Chokwe in turn demanded tobacco from Mdulu in exchange. Thus the Ovimbundu trader was obliged to establish a complex network of trade connections within his own country in order to satisfy the demands of both the coastal traders and the Chokwe. Secondly, a devastating cattle disease of c. 1870, which destroyed large numbers of Ovimbundu stock, forced the Ovimbundu to buy a great deal of cattle from the Lozi,[10] with whom they had trading connections, in order to protect their home-based economy in which cattle played a crucial role.

Another major factor which strengthened the home base was the double descent kinship system. This widened the Ovimbundu range of human connections; their wives, children, or parents could be left at home under the general care of relatives, while Ovimbundu traders and travellers went about their business for months, or even years, without fear of what might happen to their families. The same kinship system made it possible for a trading caravan to be comprised of groups of people who were related to one another and could thus work together with a minimum of friction.

As part of the conduct of internal trade, the arts of haggling and bargaining were developed to a fine degree. Trading transactions were generally open, rather than secret, in order to have witnesses in the event of disputes. When debts were contracted, pawning was used, consisting of slaves, cattle, or capable bailsmen. There were contracts to buy or to sell. The proof of such contracts lay in an adequate down payment. If, after an object was paid for, the seller then fraudulently sold the same object to someone else, he was obliged not only to restore the amount paid by the original purchaser, but also to pay him an indemnity.[11] Because business by its very nature tends to strain people's morals, the Ovimbundu had to devise such regulations for the conduct of trade.

Trading also helped to foster the concept of 'indebtedness' in the business sense, as distinct from normal tribal obligations. Debt was sacred and one could not avoid paying it. Indeed a creditor could, in the last resort, enslave a debtor who was unable to repay him. By the nineteenth century the Ovimbundu had become attached to the idea that business ran on credit. This may have been inspired by the Portuguese *negocio de banzo*, 'trust trade'.[12] Although business could be conducted in a humane manner, Ovimbundu businessmen were capable of being quite hard-headed, as illustrated in the saying *Kiolombongo japali usitive*, money and relatives don't mix. The Ovimbundu also believed that money should not be tied up, but put to work, *Olombongo vilala k'ekumbi*.[13]

The ability to keep the rates and items of exchange clearly in mind was remarkable among the Ovimbundu, who, unlike the people of the Guinea Coast, had no single currency of exchange. By the late nineteenth century, rubber and cloth had become the effective Ovimbundu currencies. Cloth was usually cut into pieces of eight, four, or two yards. One load of rubber, weighing 25 kg, was called *ochirira*, and it was used to pay fines. Adultery, according to Malheiro, was worth three loads of rubber, rape six, and forced impregnation twelve.[14] In order to deal with the problem of small transactions, such as buying a drink or some salt, the Ovimbundu created a unit called the *mutali*. A *mutali* consisted of five small rubber balls joined together.[15]

The hallmark of the Ovimbundu was indeed long-distance trade, information about which comes both from oral tradition and travellers' reports. Long-distance caravan trade was a very serious affair in which nothing was left to chance. According to the traditions of Bailundu and Huambo,[16] there were certain definite steps which had to be taken before a caravan set out. Preparations began when the *Ekope*, big merchant, announced that he was assembling people for a journey. There was a general willingness to go. Serpa Pinto recorded that

> They are brought up to wandering from their very infancy, and all caravans carry innumerable children, who, with loads proportionate to their strength, accompany their parents or relatives on the longest journeys; hence, it is no uncommon thing to find a young fellow of five-and-twenty who has travelled in Matianvo [Lunda], Niangué [in Tipu Tib's empire], Luapula, Zambesi, and Mucusso districts, having commenced his peregrinations at the age of nine years.[17]

While the people were being summoned, the *Ekope* would go to consult his ancestors. He would go to the ancestral shrine, *etambo,* to ask for their blessing. If he was not to lead the caravan himself, the *Ekope* would recruit a *seculo,* an old caravan hand, to do so, and would appoint a *pombeiro* usually from among his own relatives to be the recorder and accountant of the caravan. Once the *seculo* had gone to the diviner to get advice on the best road to take, all was ready for the departure. On the morning of the departure, each man was allotted a load weighing between 30 and 36 kilos, which he had to attach to his *olomango,* wooden fork. Sometimes the men would be given a shot of *aguardente* to keep out the morning chill of April (the beginning of the dry season). Some *Ekopes* would pay the men in trade goods before starting, while others would wait until the caravan had returned. In the 1870s a carrier from Bié to Luapula used to receive twelve pieces of trade cloth worth 12s, and for the return journey a piece of ivory worth about 20s, making some 32s for the round trip.[18] This was without food, which it was the *seculo's* duty to provide.

As the *seculo* shouted *kwacha!,* it's dawn, the village camp, which had been a hive of activity, would see one more outburst of apparent confusion as each man rushed to his *olomango* and loaded up. With the *seculo* in the lead, the caravan was on its way. The men would break spontaneously into song, usually descriptive of the journey ahead. The caravans must have been impressive sights. The largest one ever recorded in East and Central Africa left Bié for the coast in 1873, comprising some 20,000 people.[19] The normal caravan, however, was about fifty people, with the larger ones containing up to two hundred. Cameron, for example, noted in November 1875 that on his way to Benguela he met ten caravans, numbering on average between seventy and eighty men.[20]

For the typical caravan, the journey from Bié to Benguela took about sixty days, including two or three days' rest at the coast.[21] After 1870, the journey back eastwards had become routine, except for occasional difficulties with highway robbers in the area around Kiyaka and Ganda. It was the journey eastwards away from the Highlands that was the most testing. Men on these journeys were sometimes away for as long as two years.[22] The crucial geographical point was Bié. Travellers going into the interior had to pass through Bié, 'on account of the roads which open from it in every direction.

The Cassongo [in Tipu Tib's empire], the T'chiboco [Chokwe], the Garanganja [Msiri's], the Catanga [Katanga], the Canunguessa [Lunda of Kanongesha], the Gengi [Losi], the Bucusso [Mbukushu] are all connected with the Bihé by commercial tracks.'[23] While we do not know for certain when the Ovimbundu first entered each area, we know from Livingstone's account that they did not begin active trading in Bulozi (then under the Kololo) until 1853—4. Prior to that, in about 1840, they had approached the Lozi king, Mulambwa, asking for slaves, but had been refused.[24] But by 1870 Ovimbundu trade to all the areas mentioned above had become routine.

Ovimbundu caravans were armed with both guns and medicine, but usually were able to rely on persuasion rather than force. On the journey eastwards, the *seculos* knew every village elder on the route and as the caravan approached, songs would be sung to flatter and befriend the chief and his people, and make them well disposed towards the approaching Ovimbundu. On arrival at the village, the first order of business was to provide suitable gifts for the chief. Then they would settle down to trade, a process which might take weeks, or even months. This enabled the Ovimbundu to plant crops and build huts. In 1854, Livingstone noted that 'when they mean to trade with a town, they deliberately begin the affair by building huts, as if they knew that little business could be transacted without a liberal allowance of time for palaver'.[25] Such huts became trade bases. Capello and Ivens, passing through Chokwe country in 1878, observed 'the encampments of Bihénos, in search of wax, are dispersed through the dense woods of the country'.[26]

It would seem in fact that the Ovimbundu and the Chokwe worked out what amounted to a trading alliance. As a result of trading with the Ovimbundu, the Chokwe, from about 1840, were able to expand their own trade, and their empire, into the interior.[27] It was from the Ovimbundu that the Chokwe got most of their guns and gunpowder for elephant-hunting, ivory being the main item of their trade. Chokwe caravan methods were also based on those of the Ovimbundu, and by the late nineteenth century the development of the Chokwe empire led to an even greater demand for Ovimbundu middlemen, since the Chokwe had no access to the coast. After 1875 a number of new routes into the interior were opened up.

The trading relations between the Ovimbundu and other peoples varied a great deal. The peoples of the interior naturally wanted the goods of the coast, cloth, gunpowder, salt, etc., which the Ovimbundu could supply. In January 1854, Livingstone noted in his journal that 'their visits explain why Sekelenke [an Mbunda headman] kept his tusks so carefully'.[28] In 1875, an Ovimbundu caravan visiting Katanga complied with Msiri's order to adopt local tribal marks 'to curry favour with him'.[29] But they were also ready to use their guns when the occasion demanded. They nearly raised Mpepe to succeed Sebetwane in the Kololo kingdom. Mpepe, jealous of the power of Sekeletu, made an alliance with the Ovimbundu. They were allowed to buy slaves in

Toka and Ila country in return for giving Mpepe a blunderbuss mounted
as a canon. But the plot was uncovered and Mpepe was executed in
June 1853.[30]

The basic concern of the Ovimbundu was to maintain their trade
links at all costs. They were therefore not above cheating. Even today
many Lozi firmly believe that the Ovimbundu were cheats, though
they admit that the Ovimbundu brought 'a lot of interesting things into
the country', such as cloth, forks, saucers, and *monare,* a type of red
maize.[31] In order to preserve their trade monopoly, it was in the
interests of the Ovimbundu to intimidate others from going coastwards
with trade goods. Livingstone relates how Ovimbundu traders
attempted to scare off the Kololo from going to the coast with their own
version of the 'silent trade' myth:

> The Mambari repeated the tale of the mode in which the white men are said
> to trade. 'The ivory is left on the shore in the evening, and next morning the
> seller finds a quantity of goods placed there in its stead by the white men who
> live in the sea.' 'Now,' added they to my men, 'how can you Makololo trade
> with these 'Mermen'? Can you enter into the sea, and tell them to come
> ashore?'[32]

The return of a caravan from the interior was always an occasion for
jubilation, especially if all went well. If the journey had been
successful, the *Ekope* would give thanks once more to his ancestors.
Special praise and worship would also be given to the gods of
prosperity, *Kandundu* and *Otjipuku,* and liberal libations of *aguardente* would be made at their shrines.[33]

Bastos, writing in 1912, tells us a great deal about Ovimbundu trade
with the coast in the nineteenth century, especially with the towns of
Catumbela and Benguela. By about 1840 Catumbela was being built up
by Portuguese traders on the coast because the Ovimbundu liked to
stop there on their way to Benguela. In the period 1836–46 it was
moved from one side of the river to the other, a move determined
through the affluence of the Bihenos and Bailundos with their trade for
which they either go to Benguela or remain in Catumbella'.[34]

Portuguese traders did all they could to make the coastal entrepôts
attractive to the Ovimbundu. *Aguardente* (rum) breweries were set up,
Ovimbundu traders were deferred to, and in the years 1856–64 the
products of the interior — wax, ivory, guns, hides, and slaves —
poured into the towns. The slaves were designated as *servicães,*
servants, or *contractos,* contract workers, to circumvent the anti-
slavery laws. These slaves were usually sent on to São Tomé and
Principe islands, though some remained in Catumbela and Benguela,
nominally as servants. During the decade 1864–74, large numbers of
slaves continued to reach the coast, 'brought in by bands from the
territories of Bie, Ganguela and Lunda'. These 'cheap' slaves cost
from 5 to 20 reis. A 'servant' was usually bartered for a *lazarina,* trade
gun. The cheapness of slaves did not, however, undermine the value of

other trade items, for wax and ivory continued to be in high demand at the coast. These years indeed witnessed 'a new era of unfolding prosperity and riches',[35] no doubt in response to increased European trading demands in the wake of the Industrial Revolution.

But from 1850 onwards, some of the Ovimbundu peoples of the middle regions, anxious to get their share of this growing prosperity, began plundering the caravans. The worst-hit areas were in Nganda, Kivula, and Kiyaka. This led to a reorganization of the caravan trade by the bié and Bailundu dominant trading groups, who increased the size of the bands and worked out what amounted to a convoy system, in which the caravans flowed into Catumbela at regular intervals of six, eight, and ten days. Another technique was to avoid the affected areas by taking the 'new road' allegedly pioneered by Silva Porto, who lived in Bié from about 1845 onwards.[36]

More research must be conducted in Angola itself today, among the various groups of the Ovimbundu and their neighbours, before we can answer with certainty the question of the effects of trade in enriching or impoverishing different sections of society. The tendency of Ovimbundu *sobas*, kings or paramounts, to exact fines on the rich acted as a form of taxation and as a check on the abuse of power by the rich, which if unchecked could threaten the authority of the *soba* himself. There appears to be a correlation in the later nineteenth century between growing wealth among the Ovimbundu and an increasing rate of fines exacted by the *sobas*. And of course within the families of rich trade principals, there were the economic obligations between kin which tended to spread the wealth of the principal through the extended family. The *soba* on his part was checked from accumulating wealth by political as well as kinship reciprocities of allegiance in return for patronage.

The rapid increase in the level of Ovimbundu trade in the second half of the century swamped out European competitors from the Highlands, so that by the 1870s Capello and Ivens noted:

Nowadays the travellers or *aviados* of European houses are few. The death of some, the flight of others, have so disenchanted the merchants on the coast with the system of sending goods into the interior, that they have given it up almost entirely, so that the trade at this present time is almost exclusively carried on by the natives themselves, working on their own account.

While at the coast:

The life of a European in Benguella is purely and exclusively a commercial one. The caravans which come in . . . the products that are brought forward, the prices made through the competition of others, and his negotiations with the natives absorb every moment of daylight. It is no uncommon thing for the latter, after haggling for two or three hours with a merchant, suddenly to break away and carry the rest of the troop with them, to seek a more liberal

purchase elsewhere. . . . These men know how to drive very hard bargains,
and having learned how much is to be gained by competition among the
Europeans, they have gone on constantly raising the standard of value.[37]

The period after the 1870s was increasingly one of trade in wild
rubber, followed in importance by that in ivory and wax, with some
slaves still being offered but no longer as a major trade commodity.
After 1886 the collection of wild rubber assumed particular importance
because of the voracious demands of secondary industry in Europe
using rubber for a number of products, notably electrical goods. The
rubber delirium, *delirio de borracha*,[38] witnessed the last burst of
Ovimbundu trading superiority in the interior, and became the 'Red
Rubber' scandal of the Congo Basin under European exploitation in
the early twentieth century. Phenomenally high prices were being paid
for this rubber, and the American Board Congregationalist missionaries, then pioneering in Bié and Bailundu, reported major
setbacks in their work. It was said that 'Let us go to the Nganguela' was
on everyone's lips. And, in their paternalistic fashion, the missionaries
set up Christian caravans to rival the trading caravans, where, they
feared, the people were drinking rum and being de-Christianized.[39]

## Colonization and impoverishment

While the Ovimbundu controlled the trade between the interior and the
coast, they did not control the forces shaping the world trade in which
their own trade was inextricably tied up. While the end of the
Ovimbundu trading system did not become manifest until about 1900,
when the Belgians and Portuguese divided the spoils among themselves, there were already at work, as far back as 1876, forces destined
to affect the Ovimbundu in all spheres of their lives. From that date,
outside forces were beginning to force the Portuguese to claim
sovereignty over their 'colony' of Angola. There were more frequent
criticisms in Europe of the failure of the Portuguese to stamp out the
slave trade in Angola. There were numerous debates, both in Portugal
and in Angola, on whether the 'colony' was worth hanging on to, with
a conflict of views emerging. An International Geographical Conference on Africa was held in Brussels, to which Portugal was not
invited. Piqued by this and other snubs, the Portuguese sent out their
*Expidicao Africa Portuguesa,* one of whose aims was to control the
road to the coast via Bié.[40]

To the many travellers who began infiltrating their country, the
Ovimbundu displayed purely commercial attitudes, perhaps because
by this time they had no other frame of reference. In 1884, *Soba*
Ekuikui of Bailundu was reported to have sworn an oath of loyalty to
the Portuguese crown.[41] In reality, being involved in a trade war with
Bié at the time, he merely sought the traditional help of a patron in his
struggle with a rival *soba*. American board missionaries who wanted
to enter Bié were stopped in Bailundu by Ekuikui, who feared that

they might help the Biéans against himself. According to the missionary leader,

> He [Ekuikui] fears to do anything that will injure the trade of his people in Catumbella. He also feared lest the missionaries write to their country where cloth is made and tell the people 'Don't send any more to Bié', which would, of course, cut him and his people off.[42]

This trade war, which started in 1880, meant that the two most powerful Ovimbundu kingdoms had become rivals at the precise time when the Portuguese were pushing their way up on to the Highlands. Thus, when Paiva Couceiro was on his way to co-ordinate the Portuguese conquest of Bié, Ekuikui allowed him to pass through Bailundu and helped him with food and carriers. Bié was then crushed and occupied and Portuguese traders began entering the Highlands. With the support of the Portuguese government, many of these adventurers began oppressing the Ovimbundu. This, combined with the trade depression of 1900, led to the Bailundu revolt of 1902.[43]

For good or ill therefore, Ovimbundu trade brought the peoples of West Central Africa within the orbit of European mercantile capitalism. In Chapter 12, Jean-Luc Vellut shows how the Angolan trading frontier became subsumed within the 'wild capitalism' of the Congo Free State in the years between 1890 and 1910. The trade in rubber became wholesale plunder of natural resources and the pretext for massive repression and slaughter of human beings, to meet the demands of industrial capitalism overseas without the expense of administration or concern for long-term production. Then with the importation of industrial capital into Katanga (Shaba), a new political economy was instituted, with corresponding necessities for regular rural production and labour recruitment to service the copper industry. But in Angola ('Portuguese West Africa'), characterized by straight extraction of surplus from black peasants to white estates without substantial inflow of industrial capital, the characteristics of 'wild capitalism' were retained. Among African colonies, Basil Davidson remarked in 1955, 'Angola is peculiar because forced labour remains the flywheel of the country's whole economy'.[44] A bitter harvest indeed was to be reaped in the plantations and cantonments of central Angola.

## Conclusion

The rise of the Ovimbundu as long-distance traders was a triumph of human organization in a positive response to the opportunities presented by coastal mercantilism in pre-colonial times. Having been initiated into such trading by coastal contact with the Portuguese, the Ovimbundu developed ways and means to maintain the terms of trade to their economic and political advantage. But all this was only possible because of their internal economic and political potentials serving as the organizational base on which to build. Trading contact with the Portuguese was the key factor in accelerating the expansion and consolidation of the Ovimbundu kingdoms.

Though Ovimbundu and Portuguese were equal trading partners, the goods they exchanged were by no means of equal value. By no stretch of the imagination can cloth, guns, and rum be considered the equal of human beings in value. If moral censure is to be levelled in the matter of the slave trade, it must be shared between the Ovimbundu and Portuguese. If an economic judgement is to be made, then undoubtedly the Portuguese got the best of the bargain in obtaining labour with its own power of reproduction in exchange for consumer goods soon depleted and needing replacement. But a social and political judgement must also be made in terms of Ovimbundu society: external trade had become integral to its operation, and removal of that trade led to its collapse and subordination beneath Portuguese social and political supremacy.

So, undoubtedly, dependency on an externally controlled market, with increasingly unequal exchange of values, was the lot of Ovimbundu trade in West Central Africa. But simply to equate that 'dependency' with 'underdevelopment' is to fly in the face of historical evidence.

To claim that only the dominant trading aristocracy profited from Ovimbundu long-distance trade is to adopt a capitalist notion of profit inapposite for a pre-colonial society, as well as to ignore the role of trade as a social institution. The significance of trade to the Ovimbundu appears to have been centred more on the very acts of bargaining and travelling than on the profit that trade brought, though the profit was naturally important to them. This seemingly paradoxical statement should be understood in the light of trade being part of the very nature of Ovimbundu society and culture as it had historically developed. Trade operations rather than just profits reinforced the functions of the body politic of each Ovimbundu kingdom. And in economic terms, trade helped to raise the levels of production and consumption for the majority of the Ovimbundu through its 'multiplier' effect on demand for local produce and on the redistributive mechanisms of patronage in imported goods.

If the case for trade stimulating internal social repression among the Ovimbundu has yet to be established, the evidence of aggression against neighbours for commercial reasons is quite clear. But the Ovimbundu or 'Mambari' never attempted to build a vast empire around the Benguela Highlands, though they had the power to do so. As the earliest possessors of firearms in West Central Africa, and as jealous preservers of their trading monopoly and of the routes inland, the Ovimbundu could have deprived their neighbours of access to firearms and gunpowder. But this they did not do, and so we are forced to conclude that the Ovimbundu believed basically in trade (even if accompanied by occasional violence) rather than in political domination (expressed in a regular tribute system) over their eastern and southern neighbours. War, indeed, was limited to trading disputes between Ovimbundu kingdoms themselves — which was to prove the fatal flaw when colonialism intervened.

Mercantilism, it is true, imposed a deepening external dependency on African traders in the interior and bled the continent of its natural and human resources through the export of ivory and slaves on unfavourable terms of exchange. But the growth of external trade stimulated existing local trade and raised productive levels in exchange commodities such as salt and ironwork, and introduced new crops such as maize and cassava. And if the mercantilist boom aggravated socio-economic inequalities among some peoples (like the Lunda, as noted by Jean-Luc Vellut in Chapter 12), among other peoples it was checked by social mechanisms for the general redistribution of wealth. In other words, whatever distortions it entailed, mercantile contact with the world economy pressed forward the evolution of potentials within African economies. Colonialism on the other hand entailed the direct penetration of European capitalism to grasp the productive resources of the continent through maximum political control on the spot, whereas it had previously been content with a foothold in coastal outlets of trade with minimal political responsibilities. Though both were the expression of the demands of European capitalism in stages of its development, mercantilism and colonialism must be clearly distinguished in their impact on African societies. To do otherwise is to capitulate before a particularly vague economic determinism which denies the significance of politics in determining economics.

## NOTES

1.  E.A. Alpers, *Ivory and Slaves in East Central Africa* (London, 1975).
2.  Alpers, *Ivory and Slaves*, 266.
3.  The origin of the word 'Mambari' is in dispute, but probably derives from the term *quimbares,* used in old Portuguese documents to refer to armed bandits, whose main task was to stir up small wars so that captives could be taken to the Portuguese forts and sold as slaves. The Ovimbundu should not be confused with the Mbundu of northern Angola nor with the Ambunda or Mbunda of western Zambia. The warning is necessary because old Portuguese documents tended to refer to the Ovimbundu as 'Quimbundus' or 'Quimangolas'. See 'Recenseamento Geral do Populacao de Angola: Doutrina e interpretacão', *Boletin da Agencia Geral das Colonias, 184,* 1940, 36; M. Gluckman, *Economy of the Central Barotse Plain* (Manchester, 1968), 11 n. 2; G.M. Childs, *Umbundu Kinship and Character* (London, 1949), 19 n. 1; A. de A. Felner, *Angola: Apontamentos sôbre a colonisação dos planaltos e litoral do sul de Angola,* Vol. 1 (Lisbon, 1940), 123; A. de O. de Cadornega, *História Geral das Guerras Angolanas,* Vol. 3 (Lisbon, 1942); A Bastos, *Tracos Geráes sôbre a Ethnografia do Districto de Benguella* (Lisbon, 1909); M. McCulloch, *The Ovimbundu of Angola* (London, 1952), 1, 8.

My research for this chapter has been spread over many years. I have used the archives of the American Board Mission (Houghton Library, Harvard) and the United Church of Canada (Victoria University, Toronto). See my unpublished 1965 PhD for

Northwestern University, 'A History of the American Board Missions in Angola, 1880–1940'. Since joining the University of Zambia in 1967, I have been able to interview a number of Angolan refugees, notably Neo Gil (died 1972), Mario Wandundu, and Samuel Chitunda. Thanks are due to MPLA, for putting me in touch with informants, to Mariano Matsinha, for keeping my Portuguese in good shape, to Isaac Masumba, a university student, for information on the Chokwe, to Njekwa Simakando and Martin Kamwengo, now both teachers, and to the Kenneth Kaunda Foundation and the UNESCO Oral History Project for information on the Lozi.
4.   D. Livingstone, *Missionary Travels and Researches in South Africa* (London, 1857), 91, 271, 483; V.L. Cameron, *Across Africa, Vol. 2* (London, 1877), 222, 248, 251; A.A. da R. de Serpa Pinto, *How I Crossed Africa, Vol. 1* (London, 1881), 36, 160–6; F.S. Arnot, *Garenganze or Seven Years' Pioneer Mission Work in Central Africa* (London, 1889), 97–102, 114.
5.   The twenty-two Ovimbundu kingdoms were: Bailundu, Bié, Wambu, Kiyaka, Ngalangi, Kivula, Ndulu, Kingolo, Kalukembe, Sambu, Ekekete, Kakonda, Kitata, Kasongi, Ngalanga, Civanda, Namba, Sanga, Cenge, Kipeyo, Mbongo, and Elende.
6.   J.T. Tucker, *Angola: The Land of the Blacksmith Prince* (London, 1933); L. Magyar, *Reisen in Süd-Afrika in den Jahren 1849 bis 1857* (Pest and Leipzig, 1859), 297, 391; D. Waln, 'The Economic Life of the Ovimbundu', MA thesis, Kennedy School of Missions, Hartford, Conn., 1941, Chapter 1; Childs, *Umbundu Kinship*, 24, 165–7.
7.   For a general history of early Portuguese involvement in Angola, see J. Duffy, *Portuguese Africa* (Cambridge, Mass., 1959), 49–78.
8.   Cadornega, *História, Vol. 3*, 168, 171, 177 n. 90.
9.   Childs, *Umbundu Kinship*, 197–8; A. Edwards, *The Ovimbundu under Two Sovereignties* (London, 1962), 18.
10.   Cameron, *Across Africa, Vol. 2*, 199–200.
11.   Bastos, *Tracos*, 32, 42.
12.   A. Malheiro, *Chronicas do Bihe* (Lisbon, 1903), 154, Chapter 9.
13.   P.J.F. Valente, *Seleccão de Proverbios e A Divinhas em Umbundu* (Oporto, 1964), 85.
14.   Bastos, *Tracos*, 42; Malheiro, *Chronicas*, 169.
15.   Malheiro, *Chronicas*, 155. See also J.C. Miller, 'Chokwe Trade and Conquest in the Nineteenth Century', in R. Gray and D. Birmingham (eds), *Pre-Colonial African Trade* (London, 1970), 185.
16.   Where points are not documented, I have relied on oral traditions relating to Ovimbunda trade.
17.   Serpa Pinto, *How I Crossed Africa, Vol. 1*, 163–4.
18.   Serpa Pinto, *How I Crossed Africa, Vol. 1*, 164–6.
19.   A. Bastos, *Monographia de Catumbella* (Lisbon, 1912), 19. The largest recorded for the Nyamwezi was said to be three or four thousand. J.L. Krapf, *Travels and Missionary Labours in East Africa* (London, 1860), 421.
20.   Cameron, *Across Africa, Vol. 2*, 251.
21.   Malheiro, *Chronicas*, 160.
22.   Cameron, *Across Africa, Vol. 2*, 201–2.
23.   H. Capello and R. Ivens, *From Benguella to the Territory of the Yacca, Vol. 1* (London, 1882), 102.
24.   Livingstone, *Missionary Travels*, 217n. See also E. Flint, 'Trade and Politics in Barotseland during the Kololo Period', *Journal of African History, 11*, 1970, 71–86; A.D. Roberts, 'Pre-Colonial Trade in Zambia', *African Social Research, 10*, 1970, 731–4.
25.   Livingstone, *Missionary Travels*, 271.
26.   Capello and Ivens, *From Benguella, Vol. 1*, 197.
27.   Miller, 'Chokwe Trade', 175–201. The Chokwe and Ovimbundu also developed a joking relationship. Personal communication from Chokwe informants.
28.   Livingstone, *Missionary Travels*, 271.
29.   Cameron, *Across Africa, Vol. 2*, 208.

30.   Livingstone, *Missionary Travels*, 216.
31.   Interview at the Lozi *Kuta* (Litunga's Council), Limulunga, May 1973; Livingstone, *Missionary Travels*, 483.
32.   Livingstone, *Missionary Travels*, 384; Cameron, *Across Africa, Vol. 2*, 179; P.F. de Moraes Farias, 'Silent Trade: Myth and Historical Evidence', *History in Africa. A Journal of Method, 1*, 1974, 9—24.
33.   Edwards, *The Ovimbundu*, 10.
34.   Bastos, *Monographia*, 7, 10.
35.   Bastos, *Monographia*, 13, 18.
36.   Childs has challenged the novelty of Silva Porto's 'new road', pointing out that it was new only at the point where it made its final ascent on to the Highlands and in the section crossing Ovimbundu country, but not in the sections crossing Cisangi and in the final descent to the coast, where it followed the long-established Ovimbundu slave route. Childs, *Umbundu Kinship*, 201.
37.   Capello and Ivens, *From Benguella, Vol. 1*, 19, 15–16.
38.   Bastos, *Monographia*, 27–8.
39.   F. Soremekun, 'Religion and Politics in Angola', *Cahiers d' Etudes africaines, 11*, 1971, 354.
40.   *Diario de Noticias*, Lisbon, 21 November, 29 December 1877. See also J.R. Dias, 'Black Chiefs, White Traders and Colonial Policy near the Kwanza: Kabuku Kambilo and the Portuguese, 1873–1896', *Journal of African History, 17*, 1976, 245–65.
41.   P. Couceiro, *Relatorio de Viagem entre Bailundo E as Terras Mucusso* (Lisbon, 1892), 21.
42.   American Board Archives, Sanders to Means, 11 October 1881, encl. 24.
43.   F. Soremekun, 'The Bailundu Revolt in Angola, 1902', *African Social Research, 16*, 1973, 447–71; J. Duffy, *A Question of Slavery* (Oxford, 1967), 78–83, 96–101, 168–210.
44.   B. Davidson, *The African Awakening* (London, 1955), 197.

# CHAPTER 4

## Underdevelopment and Class Formation in Ovamboland, 1844–1917

### GERVASE CLARENCE-SMITH
### AND RICHARD MOORSOM

### Introduction

Much work has recently been done, in this collection and elsewhere, on the processes of underdevelopment and class formation in Southern Africa during the nineteenth and twentieth centuries. Mostly it has focused on agricultural societies in close and direct conflict with white settler or company agriculture, under the shadow of the colonial state. The purpose of this chapter is to look instead at a peripheral African society in a period when contacts with white settlers, companies, or colonial officials were reduced or non-existent. Even in these conditions Ovambo and Nkhumbi society underwent a process of underdevelopment essentially similar to that of other African peoples who have become impoverished labour-exporting peasantries. Articulation with European capitalist societies was characterized by an initial productive boom, followed by a slow decline into rural stagnation.[1]

### Ecology and pre-colonial agriculture

The lands of the Ovambo and Nkhumbi form an isolated area of dense population in the wide expanses of the northern Kalahari.[2] The Nkhumbi inhabit the flood plain of the middle Kunene, which spreads out on the western bank of the river. The Ovambo, linguistically and culturally closely related to the Nkhumbi, inhabit a flat sandy plain immediately to the south-east, normally flooded by a wet-season river, the Kuvelai, which has its source to the north. The floodwaters of the Kuvelai and a few smaller streams filter through Ovamboland in an intricate maze of broad and shallow channels, with some surplus water occasionally reaching the Etosha Pan. All around this island of fertile flooded land lie vast areas of thorn bush and meagre pastures, which support only sparse groups of hunter-gatherers and cattle nomads. The traveller Galton, who reached Ovamboland from the south in 1851 after a weary journey through the thornveld, was struck by the sudden appearance of cultivated land: 'Fine, dense timber trees, and innumerable palms of all sizes were scattered over it. Part was bare of pasturage, part was thickly covered in high corn stubble; palisadings, each of which enclosed a homestead, were scattered everywhere over the country. The general appearance was that of most abundant fertility.'[3]

The similarities with the ecological conditions prevailing in Barotseland (see Chapter 6) spring immediately to mind. Like the Lozi, the
Ovambo and Nkhumbi combined fairly permanent settled agriculture
with cattle-herding. However there were a number of important
differences. The characteristic Lozi mounds did not exist in Ovamboland, and the population lived on sandy ridges which were not normally
flooded. The land was less fertile, and only a very little maize was
grown in the most manured areas close to the homesteads. Cassava
was extremely rare. Some sorghum, generally used for making beer,
was planted along the clay-covered margins of the flooded areas, but
the staple crop was drought-resistant pearl (bulrush) millet, grown in
the sandy soils of the ridges. Pasture for cattle was provided as the
floods receded, and water remained in small pools for a considerable
time. At the height of the dry season the Kunene provided a permanent
source of water, and the surrounding bush alternative forms of pasture.
As among the Lozi, fishing was a very important subsidiary source of
food, and it was supplemented by hunting and gathering.[4]

The basic unit of production was the family, and homesteads were
isolated in the middle of family fields. Fields were cultivated for four to
eight years, and settlements were even more permanent, remaining in
one location for up to forty years. Polygamy was widely practised and
young men remained unmarried until fairly late. A typical household
would thus have consisted of the family head, his wives and children,
and his married or unmarried adult sons. Division of labour within the
family was according to sex, the women being responsible for hoe
agriculture and the men for the care of livestock. Specialization of
labour within the society as a whole was limited to two crafts,
iron-smithery and medicine. All other activities, such as pottery or
trading, were carried out in the spare time allowed by the prior
demands of the agricultural cycle.

The efficient exploitation of varied local resources made possible the
production of a certain surplus over and above subsistence needs, and
by the mid-nineteenth century had allowed the development of two
phenomena that will be of particular concern to us—vigorous local
trade and strong centralized kingdoms. Taking kingship first, it is
difficult to assess how far state and class formation had proceeded.
European explorers at the time, and ethnographers since, have painted
a stark picture of absolute tyranny, but this is suspect because it is so
often used to justify European conquest and acculturation, and it is
contradicted by some accounts.[5] The first thing to note is that there was
no single political authority over the whole area, although there is a
possibility that in the eighteenth century the Nkhumbi kings of Humbe
may have exercised some form of hegemony in the population cluster.[6]
In the mid-nineteenth century the Kwanyama kings of north-eastern
Ovamboland were the most powerful, and the Kwanyama are still the
most populous by far of the peoples of the area, but every kingdom was
completely independent. In addition the tendency seems to have been

towards increased fragmentation, as kingdoms on several occasions split in two as the result of a contested succession, although most of these splits did not prove permanent.[7]

## The powers of kingship

Within each kingdom the powers of the kings were great by the standards of South-Western Africa, and were often commented on by travellers. But society was still essentially structured on a kinship basis, with dispersed matrilineal clans. The royal clan does not appear to have been structurally different in any respect from the other clans, and was in many ways only *prima inter pares*. Indeed a cluster of very small Ovambo and Nkhumbi states living close to the westward bend of the Kunene had not developed the institution of kingship at all, and their Mbalantu neighbours were reputed to have had a king once but to have dispensed with him.[8] Royal power was based in part on classic co-ordinating and arbitrating functions. The king exacted regular military service for raiding, although he was personally forbidden to leave home territory and thus could not act as war-leader. Supreme administrative and judicial power was exercised by him, but under the supervision of a powerful council of commoners. District headmen were appointed and revocable at will by the king, but in fact exercised considerable local power. Headmen of the royal clan were particularly independent and often much resented by the people of their districts, and they provided a constant focus for intrigue and even separatist tendencies.

The powers that were vested specifically in the king's person were intimately linked to ecological conditions. In ideological terms this was expressed in the belief that the king's greatest power was the magical one of making the rains fall, and it is significant that almost all reported cases of dethroning were justified by the inability of the monarch to perform this vital function.[9] In practical terms it was the king who organized *corvée* labour to dig the large reservoirs to store the floodwaters,[10] and it was he who had to take the difficult decision of when to start planting, judging whether the rainy season had started in earnest. It was the king who strictly preserved the fruit trees and checked excessive deforestation. In an area where climatic conditions were so precarious, these activities were essential for the survival of the whole community and legitimated a certain degree of centralization. Another source of royal power was control of land, all of which was ultimately the 'property' of the king, although strict rights of usufruct and the extended permanence of settlements limited this in practice. Land was still in some sense an open resource, in that large swathes of uncultivated land separated the kingdoms from one another and have only recently been entirely brought under cultivation, but the dependence on floodwaters made for competition for privileged locations close to the major channels, and thus contributed to royal power.

The formal political powers of the king do not, however, in themselves give any precise indication on the extent of state and class formation. The crucial element is rather the extent of surplus appropriation, which in the mid-nineteenth century seems to have been little developed. Tribute was in kind and irregular. The king received half the cattle and captives taken on raiding expeditions, but these were still small-scale affairs, limited to the population cluster. *Corvée* labour was only demanded for limited work in the king's field and for moving the royal homestead, apart from the reservoir digging mentioned above. The king exercised a right of ritual seizure of young girls to be his wives, which made his homestead the largest and the most agriculturally productive in the land, and helped to spread his network of clientship. All this did not add up to very much, and the circulation of goods and services which centred on the royal court was still largely in the form of reciprocal gifts.

Nor can one speak of any form of 'feudal aristocracy' in the mid-nineteenth century. There was no private property of land, and the king had very few permanent dependants living at his court. The formation of bodies of armed men living permanently at the royal court clearly seems to have been an innovation of the late nineteenth century.[11] It was almost impossible for any restricted kin group to build up and transmit to other generations a substantial amount of movable property, particularly cattle, for inheritance of such property was matrilineal and extended to the whole kin group, whereas residence was patrilocal. Thus at the death of a particularly wealthy family head, his herds of cattle would be redistributed throughout the land to all his distant matrilineal relatives. There was therefore in operation a powerful mechanism of social redistribution, which precluded the emergence of a permanently wealthy group, although it should be noted that certain clans were reputed to be more wealthy than others. Nor did this system stop the temporary accumulation of large herds in one man's hands, and particularly in the hands of older men.

## Local and external trade

So far only directly productive activities have been considered, but surplus generated in the process of exchange must also be taken into account. Ovambo and Nkhumbi kings managed to exert a remarkably thorough control of the whole trading process, and a system of compulsory 'gifts' meant that in effect the surplus generated in trade tended to accumulate in royal hands. The limitation of possible trade routes in a semi-desert environment was probably an important factor facilitating this royal control, particularly with regard to long-distance trade. As this phenomenon was to be of the utmost importance in the period of contact with European imperialism, it is worth trying to sketch out the patterns of pre-colonial trade, as they emerge from the nineteenth-century sources and the ethnographic material.[12]

Local trade was varied, but rested on three staple commodities, iron and copper artefacts, and salt. Iron ore came from the area of the present Kassinga mines of southern Angola, and was worked chiefly by the northern Ovambo. At some point before the mid-nineteenth century the Kwanyama kings managed to impose a monopoly over the sources of ore. Copper ore came from the area of the modern Otavi-Tsumeb mining complex in northern Namibia, and seems always to have been a monopoly of the Ndonga, the second largest Ovambo group who lived in the south-eastern part of the country. Salt was to be found in many places, but the principal sources were to the north of the Etosha Pan, and the southern Ovambo were its main purveyors. One of these southern Ovambo peoples, the Ngandjera, made a speciality of trading, both at the regional and long-distance level, but their predominant position was broken in the 1860s.

Long-distance trade was in slaves and ivory to the north, sold directly or indirectly to the Portuguese traders of Benguela, and in metal artefacts to the east and south, sold to the peoples of the Okavango and the Herero. The Ovambo and Nkhumbi organized their own caravans, but were also visited by their neighbours, particularly the Ovimbundu or 'Mambari' (see Chapter 3) and the Bergdama. However long-distance trade was of subordinate importance in the mid-nineteenth century, particularly as the Nkhumbi kings completely forbade the entry of Portuguese traders into their lands. It must also be repeated that there were no full-time traders as such among the Ovambo and Nkhumbi, although it would seem that itinerant smiths along the Okavango and in Hereroland may have formed the nucleus of such a group.[13] There was no organized system of markets, and exchange was by barter, although tendencies to use certain commodities as currency were apparent. Surplus from exchange was to a large extent appropriated by the kings, and the system of widely dispersed matrilineal inheritance acted as an effective barrier to long-term private accumulation of capital.

European traders were from the first subjected to the same rigorous controls, and had to pay heavy 'gifts' to enter or leave the country, to trade, or to hunt. Royal officials watched over every move made by the traders, and reported regularly to the king. Bernardino Brochado, who managed to enter Nkhumbi territory in 1844, could only do so at the price of wearing a skirt, and the ban on trousers was periodically enforced by some Nkhumbi and Ovambo kings as late as the 1870s. In later years European missionaries, officials, and labour recruiters were constantly to come up against the same pervasive royal control of their activities. This meant that the new wealth and learning brought by the whites were first and foremost appropriated by the kings, and were used to distort the old social equilibrium in their favour.

Three phases in this process stand out clearly. From the mid-1840s to the mid-1880s trade relations were dominated by the growing European demand for ivory, but there were few formal attempts by the Europeans at colonization in the whole South-West African region. From the mid-1880s to about 1900 cattle replaced ivory as the principal export commodity, while the Portuguese and the Germans imposed their control over the highland areas to the north and south. The final phase, which ended with the complete colonial conquest of the whole area in 1917, witnessed the decline of the cattle trade and the development of the migrant labour system. We shall attempt to show that the initial increase in the productive capacity of Ovamboland proved to be highly illusory, and led only to a slow decline into a rural backwater providing cheap unskilled labour for the colonial heartlands.

## 1844 –85: ivory trading

Portuguese traders from Mossamedes and 'Cape' traders from Walvis Bay both began to reach the Ovambo-Nkhumbi population cluster around the middle of the nineteenth century. The Portuguese traders arrived earlier and were more numerous until the 1860s, at which point the 'Cape' traders, more highly capitalized and equipped with horses and ox-wagons, began to supplant them. In both cases it was the search for ivory, already depleted in the areas closer to the home ports, which drove the traders ever farther into the interior. Slaves in the north, ostrich feathers in the south, and cattle throughout the area supplemented the trade in ivory, but were no more than subsidiary items. The white traders brought beads and other forms of ornaments as well as clothes, alcohol, and horses, but one item stands out as being of critical importance—firearms. When the Europeans first reached the area the Ovambo and Nkhumbi possessed no firearms, and for a brief period in the late 1850s and early 1860s they suffered severely as a result. Between 1859 and 1863 the Portuguese made a short-lived attempt at the conquest of the interior, and although the Nkhumbi and Kwanyama had by then acquired a few firearms, they were deeply impressed by the effects of Portuguese weapons.[14] In the south the introduction to firearms was even more dramatic, for the Ndonga were completely unable to resist the onslaught of the Nama overlord, Jonker Afrikaner, who ravaged the southern peoples with peculiar ferocity in 1860.

The Nkhumbi and Ovambo thus learnt the bitter lesson that firearms had become a new necessity for a people who wished to preserve their independence. And since local technology was generally incapable of producing firearms, external trade became essential for survival.[15] The long-term success of this strategy was crucially dependent on the terms of trade, and here the Ovambo and Nkhumbi possessed a certain number of advantages. The traders came up against strong trading partners in the kings, who exercised close control over the whole trading process, and who from 1870 began to have missionary advisers to inform them of the values of commodities on the world markets. The substantial 'gifts' levied by the kings acted as a form of customs duty. At the same time the rivalry between the Portuguese and 'Cape' traders was skilfully exploited. The kings of the Kwanyama were particularly well placed for this, for the fluctuating trade frontier between the hinterlands of Mossamedes and Walvis Bay usually passed through their territory. The white traders undoubtedly made considerable profits from their trade in the area, but it is not possible to assess the rate of unequal exchange simply on the basis of exchange values in world markets. It is also essential to see the impact of the trade on the productive base of the African economy) In a sense this impact was very positive, for firearms were not simple objects of consumption, but rather productive investments, in that they markedly increased the efficiency of hunting and raiding] At the same time ivory had not been exploited traditionally, and was therefore a new resource. But this increase in productivity could only be temporary, for the prevailing ecological equilibrium was rapidly upset and elephants were all but shot out in the space of three decades. And the period of prosperity had brought the Africans no further towards being able to produce their own firearms, while leaving them dependent on importing new and increasingly expensive rifles and ammunition.

## 1885 –1900: cattle raiding

However there remained one way in which to 'invest' the accumulated stocks of firearms, the intensification between about 1885 and 1900 in the scope and scale of traditional raiding activities.[16] The southern slopes of the Bié highlands of Angola became the scene of annual raids, in which the horses and firearms acquired during the ivory boom gave the Ovambo and Nkhumbi a decided advantage over the fragmented and ill-armed Ngangela and southern Ovimbundu, The raiders seized mainly cattle and people, the former to sell to the European traders, the latter to ransom, sell to the Portuguese, or incorporate into their own lineages. The slaves who remained within Ovambo and Nkhumbi society were used to increase agricultural production, and the Nkhumbi today say that their fields were much larger when they had slaves.[17] There was little resistance to the raiders from the Portuguese, who were crippled by a severe financial crisis during the 1890s. A slightly earlier attempt to conquer the Nkhumbi between 1886 and 1891 ended in a partial and very insecure victory for the Portuguese, but the garrison in Humbe was practically impotent. Not until 1905 did the Portuguese complete the conquest of the entire Nkhumbi area, and push their frontier definitively to the Kunene.

The Ovambo and Nkhumbi were also able to find ready markets for the fruits of their raiding. Slaves were sold to Portuguese and Ovimbundu traders from Kakonda, in spite of occasional attempts by the Portuguese authorities to stamp out this illegal traffic. The slave market was particularly buoyant, for the Ovimbundu needed planta-tion slaves to work their farms whilst they mounted long-distance rubber caravans, and also ran a lucrative trade with the Portuguese on the coast, who 'redeemed' the slaves and packed them off as indentured labourers to the cocoa islands of São Tomé and Principe. In return the Kakonda traders brought the Ovambo and Nkhumbi alcohol and smuggled firearms.[18]

But the major commodity in the trade of the Ovambo–Nkhumbi area was now cattle. Most of these were still exported through Mossamedes, but restrictions on arms sales after 1887 made this market less attractive. An important trade developed with the areas to the south-east of the Kalahari, to which over 4,000 head of cattle were exported from U-Kwanyama alone between 1885 and 1895, according to Portuguese estimates.[19] The demand on this market may be explained by the boom along the 'missionary road' of Botswana before and during the construction of the railway to the north which is discussed by Neil Parsons in the next chapter.[20] The route from Botswana to southern Angola had been pioneered by the 'Thirstland Trekkers' from the Transvaal in 1875–81, and had remained a minor trade route ever since.[21] The advantage of this market also lay in the fact that the Transvaal constituted a major loop-hole in British measures to prevent arms sales to Africans.[22] Indeed there is evidence to suggest that the terms of trade were becoming generally more favourable to the Ovambo; in 1891 a modern rifle was said to cost twelve head of cattle in U-Kwanyama, whereas in 1895 the price was quoted as seven head of cattle.[23]

However pressure on the cattle resources of the Ovambo and Nkhumbi was growing in spite of raiding, resulting in some social tension. As early as the 1870s the king of the Kwambi, a southern Ovambo people, had considerably reduced the cattle population of his kingdom by ruthless taxation and extravagant spending on luxury goods (from fiddles to wagons), although his successor had restored the situation.[24] In the 1890s similar pressures on the cattle population of U-Kwanyama began to appear, and the king made up for the shortfall in cattle by seizing that of his subjects. The traditional seizure of cattle for the king's court (*okasava*) slowly developed into a regular form of taxation. Some Kwanyama began to emigrate permanently or to seek temporary employment with the Portuguese and the Germans, although this process remained fairly limited during the 1890s.[25]

Natural disasters and increasing Portuguese intervention brought the period of prosperous cattle-trading to an end at the turn of the century. Rinderpest broke out in Botswana in 1896, and the economic boom on the 'missionary road' collapsed.[26] The disease reached Ovamboland from the Okavango in 1897, and in the space of a few devastating months destroyed over 90 per cent of the cattle herds. This disaster was followed by a long series of drought years, interspersed with floods and plagues of locusts, which culminated in the terrible famines of 1911 and 1915.[27] The Ovambo and Nkhumbi attempted to recoup their losses by intensifying raiding, but they found other areas as badly hit as they were. And under the pressure of raids and natural disasters the Ngangela and southern Ovimbundu drifted ever farther north, or sought refuge in mission stations and in mountain hide-outs.[28]

Raiding also became increasingly hazardous after the turn of the century, because of more effective Portuguese resistance. The Portuguese financial crisis was at last resolved in 1902, and measures were taken to strengthen garrisons and equip them better. At the same time it was decided to conquer the whole of the Ovambo–Nkhumbi population cluster within the Portuguese sphere of influence, partly in order to put an end to raiding once and for all. A first expedition in 1904 was crushingly defeated by the Mbadya, the Ovambo people living closest to the Kunene, but between 1905 and 1907 this defeat was avenged and a chain of forts was set up in Mbadya territory. In 1908 and 1910 three other small Ovambo kingdoms were occupied without bloodshed by the Portuguese, and a chain of forts was set up along the Okavango river.[29] The Kwanyama remained independent, but they were surrounded to the north and raiding became more difficult. Both the Portuguese and the Germans imposed strict regulations on trade, going so far as to ban it altogether in order to deprive the Ovambo of arms. Although raiding continued, and although the traders still managed to smuggle in arms from both sides of the frontier, there can be no doubt that the terms of trade were now heavily loaded against the Ovambo.[30]

## Pauperization and labour migration

In this critical situation the Ovambo and Nkhumbi kings fell into ever-increasing debt with the traders, and the only solution left open to them was to intensify pressure on local cattle resources, which made it impossible for Ovambo and Nkhumbi society ever to recover fully from rinderpest. However this pressure was not evenly distributed in social terms. The kings did not pay the traders from their own herds, but turned to internal taxation in order to maintain both the European standard of living to which they had become accustomed and sufficient patronage to retain the loyalty of their followers. The increase in raiding had led to the formation at court of a permanent group of war-leaders, the *lenga,* each of whom received a horse and a number of rifles from the king and led a body of about a hundred men on raiding expeditions. The *lenga* now become tax collectors, and the traditional seizure of cattle for the king's court, *okasava,* became a harsh and arbitrary tax, which fell mainly on the most vulnerable members of society.[31] The polarization of the traditional stable social order had begun, and incipient classes were entering into increasingly unequal and antagonistic relationships. In the long term the rules of dispersed matrilineal inheritance could have evened out this tendency, but the pace of social change was now outrunning the traditional capacity for surplus redistribution.

The ravages of consecutive years of natural disasters and the growing weight of internal taxation combined to produce, at the opposite end of the spectrum from the *lenga,* a new social stratum: men without cattle. To be sure, the agricultural production of their wives was scarcely influenced by taxation, or by the pressures of external trade. Millet was of little interest to the *lenga* or traders, and the Ovambo continued to make their own hoes until the 1920s, thus insulating the agricultural cycle of production from external pressures.[32] But drought, flood, and locusts between 1900 and 1916 followed in an almost uninterrupted sequence, reducing agricultural production severely, and both the Portuguese and the Germans sent in relief supplies of grain.[33] And even when a family's agricultural production was substantial, it should be stressed that the loss of cattle constituted a severe social disaster, in view of the importance attached to the possession of cattle.[34] A complex process of pauperization was thus set in motion, which the compensatory mechanisms of traditional society were incapable of entirely relieving.

There were several possible courses of action left open to this new group of pauperized men: they could attach themselves as clients to the *lenga,* join the Christian settlements of the missionaries, set themselves up as bandits in outlying areas, or emigrate permanently to other regions. But the major response to pauperization was the development of migrant labour. The survival of kinship structures and of crop cultivation within the family unit, the distances to the centres of employment, and the controls imposed by both traditional and colonial authorities on migrant labourers combined to restrict the form of proletarianization to recurrent migrancy, rather than permanent settlement in mining and urban centres. There was little or no attempt within the colonial economies at stabilizing the workforce, for recurrent migrancy provided the type of labour most required by the large-scale employers, that is, substantial quantities of cheap unskilled labour for mining and infrastructural works.[35]

The growth of pauperization in the Ovambo–Nkhumbi population cluster coincided with a sudden expansion in the demand for labour in the colonial economies. In Angola this was due to the building of the Mossamedes and Benguela railways from 1904 and to a permanent shortage of labour in the plantations and fisheries of the coast, especially after the abolition of servile labour in 1911.[36] Ovambo and Nkhumbi labour was especially important in railway building, for they generally refused to work in plantations and fisheries, but there are unfortunately no detailed statistics. It would appear that the numbers rarely exceeded 2,000 per annum in the period under consideration. It should also be noted that much of this labour was obtained through the imposition of hut tax after 1907 on the Nkhumbi and Ovambo conquered by the Portuguese.[37]

The flow of labour to the south was on a larger scale, and can be fairly accurately charted.[38] Before 1908 it was under 2,000 per annum, but between 1910 and 1914 it averaged 10,000 per annum. In the year 1910–11 it was even estimated that over 5 per cent of the total Ndonga population was away working in Namibia, which may have meant as much as a third of the able-bodied adult males. Percentages for other kingdoms were however lower, and it should be remembered that this was a year of terrible famine in the area.[39] This expansion of migrant labour to central and southern Namibia was due to the fact that the Germans were struggling with a permanent and growing labour crisis from the outbreak of the Herero Revolt in 1904. The war of extermination waged against the Herero and Nama drastically reduced the local supply of labour, while increasing the acreage given over to white farmers, thus intensifying the agricultural demand for labour. The almost simultaneous opening up of the Otavi copper mines (1906) and the Lüderitz diamond fields (1908) created overnight an acute shortfall in the labour supply. An accelerated programme of railway and harbour construction and the generally buoyant state of the colonial economy rendered the crisis even more desperate. The German response was to segment the sources of labour supply. The forced labour regime instituted in 1907 bound the Herero and Nama to the farms and towns. Employers in construction and mining were thus forced to seek their supplies of labour elsewhere. Since foreign contract workers, principally from South Africa, proved expensive both in wages and in transport costs, it was to Ovamboland that the Germans turned their attention.[40]

They did not follow the Portuguese example of conquest and taxation, although Governor Leutwein had contemplated this before the Herero Revolt, but preferred the methods of indirect pressure. The expense and dangers of conquest had been clearly demonstrated by the Portuguese campaigns of 1904–7, and as the Ovambo were not raiding to the south there was no pressing need for military occupation. After the traumatic events of the Herero Revolt, the German *Reichstag* was firmly opposed to any further military action in the colony, particularly in the far north where there were neither minerals nor lands suited to white settlement. In addition, the Portuguese victory over the Mbadya in 1907 had impressed the other Ovambo kings, and had made them far more amenable to German pressure. The spread of mission stations provided the Germans with excellent intermediaries. By 1909 the German and Finnish Lutherans had stations amongst all the Ovambo states in German territory which had kings. With the help of the missionaries, protection treaties were signed with all these kings in 1908, and constant contact was maintained with them to persuade them to send as much labour as possible to the south.[41] In this the Germans were favoured by the dual process of natural disasters and pauperization that we have outlined above.

## Migrant labour and the loss of independence

The origins of the migrant labour syndrome may thus fundamentally be related to the process of pauperization in the Ovambo–Nkhumbi homelands, combined with a severe labour shortfall in the colonial economies. However two other less specific factors should also be considered. The most difficult factor to handle concerns cultural adaptability to migrant labour. Colonial officials had an obvious interest in stressing this point, and its exact value remains in doubt. One can tentatively say that labour migration reveals many structural similarities with raiding and long-distance trading. In all three cases the men had to cross long distances through inhospitable country in order to bring back specific material prizes. As raiding and trading were increasingly curtailed by the expansion of the colonial system, it would appear that there occurred a form of culture transfer in favour of migrant labour.[42] It should however be pointed out that whereas raiding exalted a feeling of self-confidence and pride in one's own society, migrant labour seems in the long term to have had an exactly contrary effect.

The other factor to take into account is that during the period under consideration the permanent shortage of labour in Angola and Namibia offered some relative advantages to Ovambo and Nkhumbi labour. Although the German authorities attempted to apportion labour on their own terms, the migrant labourers could in effect exercise a certain amount of choice. Groups of Ovambo refused to be broken up, and rejected offers of work on farms, where conditions were worst. The copper mines at Otavi tended to be used as a staging post on the way to the diamond fields, where conditions were bad, but wages were higher.[43] And the Ovambo and Nkhumbi retained the possibility of playing off the Portuguese against the Germans in order to secure better terms. The Kwanyama were visited by rival groups of Portuguese and German officials, who used all kinds of blandishments to entice labour into their economies. In general, the Kwanyama (and also a few Mbadya and Nkhumbi) preferred to go to central and southern Namibia. King Nande explained to the Portuguese envoys in 1909 that this was because they received better terms from the Germans.[44]

The Ovambo kings never seriously opposed the growth of the migrant labour system, but tried to make maximum profit out of it, while limiting its disruptive effects as far as possible. Workers were only allowed to leave for periods of six months, and at times when the annual cycle of subsistence activities required the least labour. Workers left in structured groups, under a leader, and remained together during the period of employment, thus maintaining cohesion and discipline on lines reminiscent of the raiding parties. 'Gifts' had to be made to the kings on return, a system reminiscent in form and intention to earlier taxation of long-distance traders and of raiding parties.[45]

Although the degree of royal control maintained over the process is a striking tribute to the resilience of African institutions, royal control was by no means absolute. German statistics show constant surpluses of departures over returns, partly due to the high death rates, but mostly to the setting up of Ovambo settlements in the towns of the 'Police Zone' formed in 1911 (see map 6).[46] Similar settlements also sprang up in the highlands of Angola.[47] Both within their home country and at their places of work the migrant labourers came increasingly under the influence of the missions, with all that this implied in the way of subversion of older institutions such as matrilineal kinship, polygamy, and kingship. This cultural mutation was most advanced among the Ndonga by 1915, for they were most profoundly affected by all aspects of European intrusion from the earliest date. It is significant that the last independent king of the Ndonga was the first Ovambo or Nkhumbi king to be converted to Christianity; and the colonial conquest of the whole area in 1915–17 was followed by a general increase in conversions.[48]

Early in 1915 a power vacuum was suddenly created for a brief period throughout the Ovambo–Nkhumbi population cluster. The Portuguese were defeated in a border skirmish with German forces, related to the outbreak of war in Europe, and retreated to the highlands. The Germans were unable to follow up this victory, for they had to retire to combat the invading South African forces. The last Kwanyama king, Mandume, made an attempt to impose his paramountcy over the whole area, and as Portuguese troops closed in on Ovamboland towards the end of the year he became the symbol of resistance. With Mandume's defeat at the hands of the Portuguese in 1915 and his death at the hands of South African troops in 1917, the era of complete colonial domination had begun.[49]

## Underdevelopment and class formation

Colonial strategy in the Ovambo–Nkhumbi area was essentially restricted to the maintenance of an effectively functioning pool of migrant labour, particularly in the sector controlled by South Africa. The general implications of this policy were that levels of production for the mass of the population should be kept below consumption needs, but sufficiently high to bear the costs of reproducing and servicing the migrant labour force.[50] The incipient class differentiation noted above was more or less frozen, the *lenga* becoming a largely hereditary collaborating group, and becoming the direct representatives of colonial administrations in those kingdoms, such as that of the Kwanyama, where the kingship was abolished. The rest of the population sank to a generalized level of pauperization, although upward social mobility was by no means impossible. The pressures of an ever-expanding population on extremely limited resources have been particularly important in this process, and by the mid-twentieth century land shortage and deforestation had become acute problems.[51] The intensification of migrant labour was the only solution to these pressures. The stagnation of the economy of southern Angola up to the late 1960s meant that the mines of Namibia became the chief centre of employment for the whole population cluster, and indeed labour migration to Namibia or the Rand spread slowly to cover a very wide area of southern Angola.[52] The particular form of underdevelopment that affects Ovambo and Nkhumbi society has thus been integrated into the classic Southern

African pattern of the creation and artificial maintenance of labour-exporting peasantries. This raises a difficult theoretical problem as to the precise class position of the migrant labourer. Recent discussion of the peasants of Africa has defined them as a social stratum 'whose ultimate security and subsistence lies in [its] having certain rights in land and in the labour of family members on the land, but [which is] involved, through rights and obligations, in a wider economic system which includes the participation of non-peasants'.[53] Labour-exporting peasantries are then defined as a specific sub-type.

But there is a qualitative difference in terms of the objective relations of production between peasants, who own the product of their labour up to the moment of exchange, and wage-labourers, who sell their labour-time to the owners of the means of production. The family units of migrant labourers are systematically involved in both relations of production, which renders their class position genuinely indeterminate. Normally it would also be transitional, but in this case non-economic forces are used to endow it with an abnormal degree of permanence. The definition of the class position of a migrant labourer must therefore rest, in the last instance, in the distribution of his own and his family's labour time between peasant production and wage-labour, and in the tendency for one or other to become increasingly dominant. The 1971 Ovambo strike in Namibia is an indication that in this instance the process of proletarianization has now reached an advanced stage.[54]

## NOTES

1. A seminal work in this field is G. Arrighi, 'Labour Supplies in Historical Perspective: A Study of the Proletarianization of the African Peasantry in Rhodesia', *Journal of Development Studies*, 6, 1970, 197–234. See also C. Bundy, 'The Emergence and Decline of a South African Peasantry', *African Affairs*, 71, 285, 1972, 369–88; and many of the chapters in this book. This essay is the fruit of research by Gervase Clarence-Smith on southern Angola and by Richard Moorsom on Namibia, and has involved the use of three major archival sources on the Portuguese side: the Arquivo Histórico Ultramarino (AHU) in Lisbon, the Arquivo Histórico de Angola (AHA) in Luanda, and the Archives Générales de la Congrégation du Saint-Esprit (AGCSSp) in Paris.
2. The ecological and ethnographic conditions described in these opening paragraphs are taken from the following: C. Estermann, *Etnografia do Sudoeste de Angola*, Vol. 1 (Lisbon, 1956); C. Estermann, 'Les Bantous du Sud-Ouest de l'Angola', *Anthropos*, 59, 1964, 20–74; T. Delachaux, *Ethnographie de la région du Cunène* (Neuchâtel, 1948); A. Urquhart, *Patterns of Settlement and Subsistence in South-West Angola* (Washington, 1963); E.C. de Carvalho and J.V. da Silva, 'The Cunene Region — Ecological Analysis of an African Agropastoral System', in F. Heimer (ed.), *Social Change in Angola* (Munich, 1973); J.P. Neto, *O Baixo Cunene* (Lisbon, 1963); E. Loeb, *In Feudal Africa*, published as an annex to *International Journal of American Linguistics*, 28, 1962; C. Mittelberger, 'Entre os Cuanhamas', *Estudos Ultramarinos*, 6, 1956, 131–72; G. Nitsche, *Ovamboland* (Kiel, 1913); F.R. Lehmann, 'Die anthropogeographischen Verhältnisse des Ambolandes im nördlichen Südwestafrika', *Zeitschrift für Ethnologie*, 79, 1954, 8–58; H. Tönjes, *Ovamboland* (Berlin, 1911); V. Lebzelter, *Eingeborenenkulturen in Südwest- und Südafrika* (Leipzig, 1934), 188–254; C.H.L.

110     GERVASE CLARENCE-SMITH AND RICHARD MOORSOM

Hahn, H. Vedder and L. Fourie, *The Native Tribes of South West Africa* (Cape Town, 1928), 1–36; J. Wellington, 'The Cunene River and the Etosha Plain', *South African Geographical Journal, 20,* 1938, 21–32.
3.   F. Galton, *Narrative of an Explorer in Tropical South Africa* (London, 1853), 125.
4.   This and the following paragraph are written in an 'ethnographic past tense', which excludes modern activities and gives a picture of what conditions were probably like in the mid-nineteenth century. For the Lozi see M. Gluckman, *Economy of the Central Barotse Plain* (Manchester, 1968); Chapter 6, L. van Horn, 'The Agricultural History of Barotseland, 1840–1964'. The best work on the Ovambo and Nkhumbi from this angle is Urquhart, *Patterns of Settlement.*
5.   A. Nogueira, *A Raça Negra* (Lisbon, 1880), 253–311; H. Hahn, 'Neueste deutsche Forschungen in Südafrika', *Petermann's Mitteilungen, 12,* 1867, 290. Nogueira's testimony is particularly valuable as he was a mulatto trader who lived for many years in the 1850s among the Nkhumbi and spoke their language fluently.
6.   Loeb, *In Feudal Africa,* 49–50.
7.   For the splitting and reunification of Ndonga, see F.R. Lehmann, 'Die politische und soziale Stellung der Häuptlinge im Ovamboland...', *Tribus, 4–5,* 1954–5, 269–79.
8.   For the Mbalantu see Hahn, Vedder, and Fourie, *The Native Tribes,* 8–9; P. Serton (ed.), *The Narrative and Journal of Gerald McKiernan in South-West Africa* (Cape Town, 1954), 107; C. Duparquet, 'Voyage en Cimbébasie', *Missions Catholiques,* 1880, 429, 1881, 514.
9.   For the dethroning of the king of Humbe in 1891, see J.P. do Nascimento, *Da Huila as terras do Humbe* (Huila, 1891), Prologue; not all kings were credited with the same power to make the rain fall.
10.   AGCSSp 465–III, Duparquet, Notes sur les différentes tribus des rives du Cunène, and 478–B–II, Duparquet, 25 July 1883; Urquhart, *Patterns of Settlement,* 40; J.V. de Castro, *A Campanha do Cuamato em 1907* (Luanda, 1908), 185–6. This important point only rarely gets the attention it deserves in view of the intimate relations between this kind of activity and the rise of despotic state systems in Asia.
11.   Hahn, 'Neueste deutsche Forschungen', 292–3; AGCSSp 478–B–III, Duparquet, 26 March 1885.
12.   For nineteenth-century trading patterns before and during the ivory boom, see notes 2, 3, 5, and 8, and the following: B. Brochado, 'Descripçao das terras do Humbe, Camba, Mulondo, Quanhama e outras...', *Annaes do Conselho Ultramarino,* Parte nao-oficial, *Serie 1,* 1855, 187–97, 203–8; J.L. da Silva and A. Franco, 'Annaes do Municipio de Mossamedes', *Annaes do Conselho Ultramarino,* 1858, 483–90; J.L. de Lima, *Ensaios sôbre a estatistica das possessoes Portuguezas, Vol. 3* (Lisbon, 1846), Part 2 and map; L. Magyar, *Reisen in Süd-Afrika in den Jahren 1849 bis 1857* (Pest and Leipzig, 1859), 298–9; C. Duparquet, *Viagens na Cimbébasia* (Luanda, 1953); J. Chapman, *Travels in the Interior of South Africa* (London, 1868), 1; C. Andersson, *Lake Ngami* (London, 1856); C. Andersson, *The Okavango River* (London, 1861); C. Andersson, *Notes of Travel in South Africa* (London, 1875); *Report of Mr. Palgrave* (Pretoria, 1969 edn, 1st edn 1877), 46–50; *Petermann's Mitteilungen,* 1859, 295–303, 1867, 8–12, 281–311.
13.   Serton, *Narrative,* 74; Lebzelter, *Eingeborenenkulturen,* 203–4. Archaeological evidence of iron-smelting along the Okavango is discussed in B.H. Sandelowsky, 'Prehistoric Metal-Working in South West Africa', *Journal of the South African Institute of Mining and Metallurgy, 74,* 1974, 363–6. See also B.H. Sandelowsky, 'The Iron Age in South West Africa and Damara Pot Making', *African Studies, 30,* 1971, 3–14.
14.   N. da Matta, 'Relatorio', *Boletin Oficial de Angola,* 28 July 1860, 3–8, and supplement to 17 June 1867, 267–89.
15.   H. Vedder, *South West Africa in Early Times* (London, 1938), 269–71, is always quoted on this, but he is confusing and contradictory. Preferable sources are Andersson, *Okavango River,* 105, 139–40, 231–3, 239–40; Andersson, *Notes of Travel,*

216—17. There is however evidence of the smiths of king Mandume having manufactured a breech-lock for an imported canon, Hahn, Vedder, and Fourie, *The Native Tribes*, 35—6.
16. For raiding from the Ovambo point of view, see Estermann, *Etnografia, Vol. 1*, 141—6. For Portuguese action, see R. Pélissier, 'Campagnes militaires au Sud-Angola, 1885—1915', *Cahiers d'Etudes Africaines, 9*, 1969, 65—82. Vast amounts of detailed information on the raids are contained in AHU, AHA, and AGCSSp.
17. Urquhart, *Patterns of Settlement*, 88.
18. AHU—1R—15P, Governor General, 15 January 1895 and others; *Le Philafricain* [Swiss Mission Journal], *Série 1*, Rapport 4, 9.
19. AHU-Companhia de Mossamedes-9 Chefe Humbe, 5 January 1896.
20. Chapter 5, N. Parsons, 'The Economic History of Khama's Country in Botswana, 1844—1930'.
21. D. Postma, *Einige schetsen voor eene geschiedenis van de trekboeren* (Amsterdam and Pretoria, 1897); F. Seiner, *Ergebnisse einer Berichtung des Gebiets zwischen Okawango und Sambesi* (Berlin, 1909), 106 and maps.
22. S. Miers, 'Notes on the Arms Trade and Government Policy in Southern Africa between 1870 and 1890', *Journal of African History, 12*, 1971, 577.
23. AHU—2R—15P, Relatorio Ramalho, 20 June 1891; AHU-Companhia de Mossamedes-9 Chefe Humbe, 5 January 1896. Unfortunately it is not clear whether these two figures are strictly comparable.
24. Serton, *Narrative*, 103—4.
25. For migrant labour, see Loeb, *In Feudal Africa*, 29—32; Estermann, *Etnografia, Vol. 1*, 146. For emigration as a result of 'vexations' practised by the king and his followers, see AHU-Companhia de Mossamedes-9 Chefe Humbe, 5 January 1896.
26. Chapter 5, Parsons, 'Economic History'; C. van Onselen, 'Reactions to Rinderpest in Southern Africa, 1896—97', *Journal of African History, 13*, 1972, 473—88.
27. For the rinderpest, see G.S. Dias (ed.), *Artur de Paiva, Vol. 2* (Lisbon, 1938), 97—105. For the drought, see W.G. Clarence-Smith, 'Drought in Southern Angola and Northern Namibia 1837—1945', SOAS/ICS African History Seminar, 1974.
28. AGCSSp 476—B—II, Lecomte, 1 September 1899; AHU—1R—21P, Projecto de reorganisação, 9 December 1901; *Le Philafricain, Série 1*, Rapport 11, 7.
29. Pélissier, 'Campagnes militaires', 78—96.
30. Nitsche, *Ovamboland*, 147; C.M. Braz, *Districto da Huila* (Coimbra, 1918), 14.
31. Loeb, *In Feudal Africa*, 29—32; Estermann, *Etnografia, Vol. 1*, 141—2; *Bulletin Général de la Congrégation du Saint-Esprit*, 1908, 455—6.
32. Urquhart, *Patterns of Settlement*, 126—7.
33. E. Stals, 'Die aanraking tussen Blankes en Ovambo's in Suidwes-Afrika, 1850—1915', *Archives Yearbook for South African History, 31*, 1968, Part 2, 334; J. de Almeida, *Sul d'Angola* (Lisbon, 1912), 153.
34. Estermann, 'Les Bantous', 53—6.
35. H. Bley, *South-West Africa under German Rule, 1894—1914* (London, 1971), 198, 272—3. For a detailed treatment, see R. Moorsom, 'Underdevelopment and the Formation of the Namibian Working Class', MA thesis, University of Sussex, 1973.
36. Almeida, *Sul d'Angola*, 389—90; S. Katzenellenbogen, *Railways and the Copper Mines of Katanga* (Oxford, 1973), 54—7; J. de O.F. Diniz, *Negocios Indigenas, Relatorio do ano de 1913* (Luanda, 1914), 61, 81—3.
37. Almeida, *Sul d'Angola*, 289, 389—90, 519; R. Hutchinson and G. Martelli, *Robert's People* (London, 1971), 180—2; *Le Philafricain, Série 2*, 2, 32; AHA Avulsos 41—83—7, Relatorio, 30 September 1912.
38. Detailed monthly statistics are given by Stals, 'Die aanraking', 333. For earlier years, see Nitsche, *Ovamboland*, 130—9.
39. Nitsche, *Ovamboland*, 134. For the famine, see Lehmann, 'Die politische', 289.
40. Moorsom, 'Underdevelopment'; Nitsche, *Ovamboland*, 130—9; Bley, *South-West Africa*, 170—3, 180—1, 198, 259—60, 272—3.
41. T. Leutwein, *Elf Jahre Gouverneur in Deutsch-Südwestafrika* (Berlin, 1908),

174–7, 191–2; Lehmann, 'Die politische', 270–95; H. Driessler, *Die Rheinische Mission in Südwestafrika* (Gütersloh, 1932), 249; Tönjes, *Ovamboland*, 250; N. Mossolow, *Die Verhaal van Namutoni* (Windhoek, 1971), 45–7.
42.   Estermann, *Etnografia, Vol. 1*, 146–7; C. Estermann, *A vida economica dos Bantos do Sudoeste de Angola* (Luanda, 1971), 36.
43.   Stals, 'Die aanraking', 343; Nitsche, *Ovamboland*, 130–9; A. Calvert, *South-West Africa During the German Occupation, 1884–1914* (London, 1915), 23; Foreign Office, *South-West Africa*, Handbook 112 (London, 1920), 43; Moorsom, 'Underdevelopment'.
44.   AHA Avulsos, 31–9–4, Relatorios of Moraes, 27 February 1909, and Lobo, 1 March 1909; Nitsche, *Ovamboland*, 130–9.
45.   Estermann, *Etnografia, Vol. 1*, 146; Nitsche, *Ovamboland*, 130—9; Driessler, *Die Rheinische Mission*, 260–1; Tönjes, *Ovamboland*, 88–9; C. Schlettwein, *Der Farmer in Deutsch Südwestafrika* (Wismar, 1907), 183.
46.   Stals, 'Die aanraking', 333, 338–9; O. Köhler, *District of Karibibib*, Union of South Africa, Department of Native Affairs, Ethnological Publications No. 40, (Pretoria, 1958), 83.
47.   *Bulletin Général de la Congrégation du Saint-Esprit*, 1913, 255–6; AGCSSp 477–A–X, Rapport Steinmetz, 1917.
48.   Driessler, *Die Rheinische Mission*, 260–3; Loeb, *In Feudal Africa*, 33–8. The contrast in attitude between the kings of the two largest Ovambo peoples is striking. Mandume of the Kwanyama did his best to oppose these tendencies, whereas Martin of the Ndonga encouraged them. See Lehmann, 'Die politische', 277–9, 290; L. Keiling, *Quarenta Anos de Africa* (Braga, 1934), 173–4.
49.   Pélissier, 'Campagnes militaires', 96–111; P. de Eça, *Campanha do sul de Angola em 1915* (Lisbon, 1921); S. Pritchard, *Report by the officer in charge of native affairs on his tour of Ovamboland* (Cape Town, 1915); E. Gorges and M. de Jager, *Report on the conduct of the Ovakuanyama chief Mandume and on the military operations conducted against him in Ovamboland* (Cape Town, 1917).
50.   H. Wolpe, 'Capitalism and Cheap Labour-Power in South Africa: From Segregation to Apartheid', *Economy and Society, 1*, 1972, 437, 439.
51.   Moorsom, 'Underdevelopment'; I. Goldblatt, *History of South West Africa* (Cape Town, 1971), 214–15, 227–8 [the date given for Mandume's death is incorrect]. For deforestation, see Lebzelter, *Eingeborenenkulturen*, 189; J. Wellington, *South West Africa and its Human Issues* (Oxford, 1967); deforestation gets progressively worse from north to south.
52.   A. Valente, 'Problemas da emigração de trabalhadores rurais . . . ', *Trabalho, 18*, 1967, 133–40.
53.   J.S. Saul and R. Woods, 'African Peasantries', in T. Shanin (ed.), *Peasants and Peasant Societies* (Harmondsworth, 1971), 105.
54.   For details of the strike, see *The Observer*, 6 February 1972.

# CHAPTER 5

## The Economic History of Khama's Country in Botswana, 1844–1930

### NEIL PARSONS

*His political and economic views were narrow and stern; for he had not been schooled in sociology and had to handle crude and refractory material. Professor W.C. Willoughby on Khama, 1924.*[1]

*Lately he had been regulating Bamangwato commerce in a spirit that reminds one of early Tudor statutes; is it a phase growing nations go through? Mrs. Laura Knight-Bruce on Khama, 1889.*[2]

## Introduction

For the last quarter of the nineteenth century Khama's Country was the crossroads between Central and Southern Africa—the Missionaries' Road, the 'Suez Canal' of colonialism, the bottle-neck and 'bowling alley' of Rhodes-ians, the Road to the North for capital and to the South for labour.[3] Situated in east-central Botswana on the high dry lands that span the South African and Zimbabwean plateaux, nipped between the Kalahari thirstlands and the tsetse-infested Limpopo valley, Khama's Country was the focus of the wagon routes that splayed out north and south to Zambezia and the Cape.[4] Maps published at the time of the scramble for Africa mark Khama's Country as stretching from the Limpopo to the Boteti (Botletle) and even to the Chobe and the Zambezi as far east as the Gwai. 'Khama's Country' was the synonym for the kingdom of the BamaNgwato under the rule of Khama III (c. 1835–1923), who reigned vigorously for forty-eight years after 1875, until his death at Serowe around ninety years of age. This chapter seeks to reconstruct the general economic history of his territory from before Khama's accession, through the apparent boom of the 1890s, into the demise of 'structural underdevelopment' within early colonial Southern and Southern-Central Africa.[5] Wider reference is made to the economic inheritance of the kingdom from earlier times and to the economic heritage left by Khama's rule to the middle colonial period. An essay published elsewhere deals with Khama's attempt to resist 'underdevelopment' with his own brand of state capitalism between 1910 and 1916.[6]

There are an increasing number of historical studies of the 'development of underdevelopment' in Africa, which take as their base-line the development of pre-colonial economies through the period of colonial change. For Eastern and Southern Africa these

113

studies have concentrated on the stimulation, then strangulation, of peasant production under early colonial capitalism.[7] There has been little publication, as yet, on the economic development of pre-colonial African polities, of the type pioneered by K. Onwuka Dike in his *Trade and Politics in the Niger Delta 1830—1885*, published in 1956, and synthesized more recently by Samir Amin for Western and Northern Africa.[8] This chapter links elements of both historiographies—to show how an African state developing towards a 'colonial trade economy' on the West African model was reduced to a labour reserve within the orbit of South African regional colonialism.

## The foundations of the Ngwato economic system

The Ngwato kingdom which Khama violently inherited from his father was comparatively new as a sovereign state, having emerged in the 1840s from the disruption of the *Mfecane* period in eastern Botswana. But the kingdom had strong institutional links with the pre-*Mfecane* Ngwato chiefdom that had split off from the Kwena cluster of chiefdoms in the Tswana heartland (western Transvaal) sometime in the last half of the eighteenth century.[9] The Ngwato chiefdom moved north from the vicinity of modern Gaborone across the intrusive thirstland sands of the Serurume plain into the statuesque Shoshong Hills, where it probably already possessed cattle-posts on the trade route to the Boteti river and the Zimbabwean plateau. In the Shoshong Hills the Ngwato chiefdom immediately split again. A major section moved off via the Boteti to the far north-west, to the cattle and possibly to the mining of Ngamiland, where it consolidated itself as the Tawana kingdom. The remnant Ngwato chiefdom contented itself with dry but extensive grazing grounds, until its chief Kgari (ruled *c.* 1817—1826/8) temporarily extended it during the great 1826—8 drought into the richer agricultural lands northwards beyond the iron-rich Tswapong Hills. He was killed and his people dispersed by a Kalanga counter-attack in the Matopos Hills.[10]

Kgari is credited with creating or rationalising the system of socio-economic stratification that tied together the political structure of the Ngwato state. It was based on the *mafisa* system characteristic of Tswana and Sotho societies, whereby the ruling class farmed out cattle to client clans or families, who became herdsmen holding royal property in a sort of feudal system. *Mafisa* cattle formed the contractural basis of political relations between the rulers and the ruled.[11] Kgari then appointed senior commoners as hereditary vassals, *batlhanka*, in the charge of specified royal herds which had been appropriated from conquered or voluntarily amalgamated 'settlers', *bafaladi* (lit. refugees), within the kingdom. The tribute of the *batlhanka* to the king was symbolic in the form of an occasional milk-pail, *kgamelo*, from the herd; the real obligation of the *batlhanka* was to provide unswerving support for the king against all comers, notably against the king's uncles and brothers, the royalty or aristocracy, *dikgosana*. In addition Kgari and his successors used the royal wards—formed in the reigns of four previous Ngwato rulers to 'look after' their heirs—as the lynchpins of four 'sections', *ditlhase,* which clustered together the wards of commoners and 'settlers' multiplying as the state incorporated more population.[12] Given the fact that all subjects underwent common initiation into age-regiments, the 'section' system allowed ethnically diverse groups to retain their peculiarities of language, law, and culture while identifying with the larger whole of the state. However, 'serfs', *malata,* from incorporated acephalous societies, like Khoisan hunters and herders and Tswapong cultivators and miners, were not granted such civil rights until much later.

A state structure was thereby evolved which Fortes and Evans-Pritchard, in the Introduction to their classic *African Political Systems,* thought closely resembled 'the pattern with which we are familiar in the modern nation-state'.[13] Kgari, like the founder of any dynasty, had to institutionalize himself in power and perpetuate the succession of his descendants. From an economic point of view, Kgari's reforms can be seen as an adjustment of the socio-political formation to fit in with the changes in what Samir Amin calls the 'tributary mode of production'[14]—no longer based on mining and herding in the well-populated Tswana heartland, but on herding and hunting on the extensive margins of the Kalahari.

The next stage of development was to use the possibilities inherent in the state structure and the economic system to build up a kingdom covering extensive territory with a sovereign government and secure sources of revenue and allegiance. This stage was not possible until the late 1830s under Kgari's son Sekgoma I, when the Kololo and Ndebele armies from the south had swept far enough up the north-western and north-eastern trade routes to the Zambezi and Zimbabwe. Even then, the consolidation of a kingdom was to take decades to achieve, costing kings a string of *coups* and counter-*coups*—the scoreboard reading like this: Sekgoma I ruled 1834–57/8, Macheng 1857/8–9, Sekgoma again 1859–66, Macheng again 1866–72, Khama III 1872–3, Sekgoma yet again 1873–5, and Khama finally 1875–1923.

The territorial expansion of Ngwato state sovereignty corresponded with the concentric zonage of Tswana land-usage. At the centre there was the settlement nucleus of the capital town, its wards grouped around the great Kgotla, forum of the king, where all royals or aristocrats, commoners and 'settlers', plus a few personal serfs, had permanent (or *de jure*) households, thereby literally establishing their citizenship of the state. At the town edge there began the garden lands of the agricultural zone, ideally within a couple of hours' walk; the cattle-posts of the pastoral zone were within a few days' walk; and the wide open spaces of the hunting zone within a few weeks' walk. All these zones increased in scale as the state expanded. By 1842 Sekgoma had built up a capital town of 600 households, with another 200 adjacent in a 'settler'-cum-serf village.[15] By 1866 the capital town, Shoshong,

had reached its maximum size to accommodate a *de jure* population of
up to 30,000 people.[16] The agricultural zone was determined by
available soils and by prevailing technology: on the one hand,
cultivation around the town had to 'shift' farther and farther out;
on the other, subsidiary pockets of agricultural production could be
incorporated by wagon transport within the expanding northern frontiers. But it was cattle rather than grain which was the initial dynamic
of territorial expansion to Ngamiland and the Zimbabwean plateau
along routes where the Kololo and Ndebele had led. By 1863 the
farthest Ngwato cattle-posts stood along the Boteti river in the
north-west and along the Motloutse (Macloutsie) river to the north
and some way down the Limpopo to the north-east.[17] The pastoral
zone constituted the hard edge of the political frontier zone—to the
north against the Ndebele kingdom and to the south against the
Kwena kingdom of Sechele I. In the west and north-west the few
inhabitants of the thirstland only accepted Ngwato sovereignty according to the frequency of hunting parties into the Kalahari and up to
the Chobe and Zambezi.

## The Ngwato kingdom as a trading state, 1844–75

There were therefore comparatively sound organizational possibilities for the expansion of the Ngwato kingdom. But two main
factors remain to be accounted for in the period before the accession
of Khama—political instability at the centre and the vigour of expansion from the 1840s.

The military threat from the north of the Ndebele kingdom, established on the Zimbabwean plateau by 1840, was not an effective stop
to Ngwato expansion. Annual Ndebele raids on the Shoshong Hills
ceased in 1842; and after 1844, when Sekgoma executed the Ndebele
tax collectors, the Ngwato were not troubled by the Ndebele until
1863, when it was Mzilikazi who felt threatened by Sekgoma, whose
cattle-posts were drawing up to the Motloutse and Shashe rivers. The
brief 1863 Ndebele–Ngwato War was a symbolic victory for the
horses and firearms used by the Ngwato.[18] The two powers did not,
despite warlike noises, go to war again until 1893 when the Ngwato
joined the British against the Ndebele.

It was the competition for economic resources from the south with
the Kgabo-Kwena kingdom of Sechele (as later with the Afrikaner
republic of the Transvaal), which was the more effective external
threat to the Ngwato kingdom, since it endangered internal stability.

> The Bakwena taking the precedence of the Bamangwato as to rank, it has
> been the life-long endeavour of Sechele to obtain such influence in the town
> of the Bamangwato as would enable him to secure some of the treasures of
> ivory and ostrich feathers and furs which are brought from its extensive
> hunting grounds, extending northwards to the Zambese.[19]

It was Sechele who deposed Sekgoma in 1857/8 by getting the

Ndebele kindly to return the 'true heir' Macheng to take over the Ngwato kingship. It was Sechele who first deposed Macheng in 1859 and then granted him refuge. It was Sechele who encouraged young Khama to lead Christian agitation against his father, 'solved' by the substitution of Macheng once again as king in 1866. It was Sechele who assisted in Khama's first *coup* of 1872, etc.[20]

Another threat, part internal and part external, to the stability of the kingship was that of the 'settler' groups voluntarily or involuntarily incorporated into the Ngwato kingdom, but this affected the periphery rather than the centre. At the centre 'settler' headmen could become *batlhanka* vassals, i.e. obtain the status of Ngwato commoners. At the periphery, 'settler' grievance and revolt was promoted by seizure or tribute of property by the king in the form of all their livestock (though it might be returned in *mafisa*) and some of their grain, hoes, etc.

The main internal threat to the stability of the kingship lay in the relationship to the king of the royals or aristocrats and of the leading vassals who held cattle in feud. Whose property were the cattle? Kgari's reforms had made moves towards 'private' ownership for a few notables. But Macheng attempted to apply the Ndebele model of indiscriminate royal ownership of all cattle. He thereby, according to young Khama's reckoning, precipitated his own downfall at the hands of a small group of large cattle-holders in 1859.[21] It was a similar question of ownership of cattle, royal or personal, that led to the final *coup* by Khama against his father in February 1875.[22] Khama diagnosed the ills of royal claims to cattle ownership that had torn his father's rule apart: 'This custom also interfered to a very large extent with the people's freedom, and at times when the Chief was not liberal in his dealings with his people, a bitter feeling generally existed between himself and his people which resulted in civil wars waged in order to have him deposed.'[23]

So much for political instability at the centre: what of the dynamics of expansion of the kingdom? In political terms this can be seen as the success of an organized group under forceful leadership with a state structure capable of incorporating diverse ethnic loyalties, filling up the power vacuum left in the wake of the Kololo and the Ndebele armies. In economic terms the initial dynamic no doubt repeated pre-*Mfecane* desire for the cattle, grain, and ironwork of the Boteti and Tswapong areas. But the continuing economic dynamic for expansion of territorial control was the increasing demand for 'the treasures of ivory and ostrich feathers and furs' by the mercantile capitalism of the Cape.

The first white trader of significance to reach the Ngwato kingdom was Gordon Cumming, an adventurous laird weary of deer-stalking in Scotland, who pioneered elephant-hunting with horse, kilt, and musket. However, like subsequent authors who presented themselves as great 'hunters', Cumming obtained most of his ivory by trade and not by hunting. He reached the Ngwato capital in the Shoshong Hills in July 1844, and returned to those parts from the Cape for five successive years before retiring to his Scottish estates to live on the proceeds and write his memoirs. On his first visit, Cumming took the advantage of novelty to dictate price levels, gaining three male tusks of ivory for each musket he offered.

> Although I voted these matters an immense bore, it was nevertheless well worth a little time and inconvenience, on account of the enormous profit I should realise; I had paid £16 for a case containing twenty muskets, while the value of the ivory I demanded for each firelock was upward of £30, being about 3,000 per cent., which I am informed is reckoned among mercantile men to be a very fair profit.[24]

Three days later the price had fallen to two tusks a musket, and by 1846 to one tusk. Cumming made enormous profits: his 1845–6 trip realized 'somewhere about £1,000' in the Grahamstown market of the Cape, and he relates with engaging candour the price calculations that flashed through his mind even while taking aim: 'Ah! a good bull; tusks at least fifty pounds; 4s 6d a pound; bring me in £22 10s. Capital day's work.'[25]

It is evident that Cumming penetrated an already existing trade network relaying ivory towards the Cape. The ivory that he obtained from Sekgoma in the Shoshong Hills had been transported from the Boteti by the porterage of Kgalagadi serfs. The Tswana were exporting ivory, karosses, and ostrich feathers southwards in exchange for 'beads of all sizes and colours, brass and copper wire, knives and hatchets, clothing for both sexes, ammunition and guns, young cows and she-goats' (i.e. for breeding) obtained in the relay-trade of white, coloured, and other black groups.[26] The Ngwato themselves did not hunt the elephants of which they sold the ivory prior to 1844; Sekgoma bought the ivory with beads from skilled Khoisan hunters (Ura or Denassana) on the Boteti.[27] It was horses and guns, introduced and maintained by Cumming and his fellow Scotsmen like David Livingstone, which enabled the Ngwato and other Tswana themselves to maximize the production of ivory and feathers. Serf hunters armed with firearms were sent out by the king, or hired out to alien hunter-traders on payment of one musket to each hunter per trip.[28]

The old relay-trade, diffused in many directions and carrying varied commodities, was now transformed into long-distance trade of a sort of mono-economy based on hunting products funnelled towards the Cape. By 1849 Livingstone had opened the old route to Lake Ngami for wagon-borne trade and by 1851 to the Chobe. In 1851 no less than 100 wagons of the Griqua (Khoi-Dutch) opened up the trade from the Ngwato capital to the Ndebele capital; while by 1853 a joint Griqua and Tlhaping (southern Tswana) expedition had reached Lebebe on the Okavango river to link up with 'Portuguese' (no doubt Ovimbundu) from Angola.[29] Livingstone's companion on the 1849 Ngami venture, the trader J. H. Wilson (Sechele's son-in-law), is reported to have made

£500 profit on the trip, and others from the Cape were encouraged northward by such reports.[30]

Between the 1840s and the 1860s the capital of the Kwena of Sechele (shifting from Tshonwane to Kolobeng/Dimawe to Dithubaruba) was the most northerly entrepôt of the Grahamstown-based Cape trading network into the 'Far Interior'.[31] But Shoshong gradually rose to challenge Sechele's in the 1860s. The Ngwato and Kwena kingdoms expanded and competed on the dynamic of the demands of the growing mercantile economy of the Cape, itself a direct extension of the rapidly developing industrial economy of Europe. The Tswana economies were becoming a 'periphery to the periphery' of European capitalism: exactly *how* this process was to be ordered became a matter for political competition marked by the coming of colonialism.

## Khamaian reformation, 1875–87

It was the genius of Khama III that he recognized the economic roots of continuing political instability from internal and external threats. 'I thought a great deal' about such problems before coming to power, Khama later recalled.[32] And so he began a programme of reform in 1875 to bring the relations of production and trade in the state under royal authority.

His first action was to summon the Ngwato to the Shoshong Kgotla. To the royal headmen and to the *batlhanka* vassal headmen he renounced any royal rights to the ownership of the cattle that they held: the cattle (and therefore the serfs with them) were now 'private' property. To the 'settlers' Khama renounced taxation in the form of regular tribute, and allowed them property rights to their produce. As a result, Khama later claimed: 'I was left without any personal stock of my own . . . so far as prosperity was concerned, practically on the same footing as any individual member of the tribe, and like each of them I had to struggle hard for my subsistence; a matter unprecedented in the whole history of our tribe as well as of the other native tribes in general. . . .'[33]

But despite Khama's personal puritan-capitalist ethic, the liberalization of private property relations was a slow and cumulative process, dependent on the scale of productive opportunities in the market as well as upon the progressive extension of citizenship rights even to some serfs by 1911.[34] It was only the large cattle-owners and serf-employers who could obtain real benefits in cash value from the sale of cattle and hunting produce in exchange for imported goods in the long-distance wagon trade prior to the late 1880s. And Khama was the largest cattle-owner and serf-employer of all. He built up his own herds, seemingly from scratch, using them as his 'savings account'. 'My kingdom consists in my gun, my horses and my wagon', he had boasted as a young man proclaiming his ability to be independent of his father.[35] Now as king he was to put such principles into operation for the economic independence of kingship from the 'overmighty subjects'. He converted some of his cash income from traders back into breeding-stock, and obtained other cattle through royal dues and privileges such as *matimela*, 'waifs and strays'. He managed his far-flung cattle posts by regular personal supervision on horseback. By 1878 Khama had built up the numbers of his cattle to some seven or eight thousand.[36]

Though Khama looked upon his herds and other property as 'personal' in some respects, in fact he used them for purposes of state, so strong was his personal identification with the institutional role of kingship. His economic policies were quite literally paternalistic towards his people, at least towards those in the capital town: 'For the position of chief is that of a father over the tribe, who is expected to have enough of this world's goods to supply the needs of his children, as it is his duty to support the tribe as a whole or as individuals in times of exigencies or distress occasioned by famine or otherwise.'[37]

His paternalism towards his people included gifts, loans, credit, and the sale of goods to groups or individuals—notably firearms, ploughs, wagons, and horses to improve methods of production and transportation. In technology, as in education and religion, Khama was an enthusiast for things 'Western', but insisted on being the selective filter to his subjects.

Khama's income, now apparently freed from burdensome political reciprocities, came from his measure of monopolistic control over the market between internal and external trades at Shoshong. The income of the Ngwato king was estimated at £3,000 in 1874 and at £2,000 to £3,000 in 1877, though it is not clear whether this was in cash or cash value.[38] The cash income was due in large measure to predominant royal ownership of the means of production—the king 'owned' the land and the elephants and employed or hired out his serf hunters. He extracted a 50 per cent levy on ivory production—the 'ground tusk' of every elephant shot in his domains, a common and venerable royal prerogative in Southern-Central Africa.[39] Other controls over production included strict hunting regulations on diminishing species of wild life, and an embargo on the export of breeding-stock, whether of domestic or wild animals.[40] But these controls are hardly surprising when one considers that Khama had inherited a situation in the 1870s where actual hunting in his country was becoming severely limited. The elephant herds of the plateau in Khama's Country had been largely exterminated by the new firepower, and commercial ostrich farming in the Cape Colony was beginning to challenge the northern trade in ostrich feathers.[41] Khama was hard pressed to preserve the hunting resources of his kingdom, either for the royal exchequer in the case of large game, or for local consumption of meat and skins in the case of small.

Khama's accession to power in the 1870s coincided with Shoshong becoming the essential entrepôt between Southern and Central Africa alluded to at the beginning of this chapter. It was the strategic centre where all roads met. Khama allowed no bypass from Shoshong to travellers from south to north, though the difficult road pioneered by Baines in 1871, from Nylstroom in the Transvaal 'direct' to Tati via the middle Limpopo valley, was on occasions used until stopped in 1888.[42] (Tati had been set to become the nucleus of a white colony in 1869 by sub-equatorial Africa's first industrialized 'gold rush', but declined rapidly after 1871 and had little more effect than to soften the shatter-zone between the Ndebele and Ngwato kingdoms into a buffer-zone.) Shoshong itself had a white trader ward of forty-two, including six women and thirteen children, by 1878,[43] while it apppears that some black and coloured African traders from the south were incorporated into the Tshosa ward.[44] The white ward became institutionally established, with permanent trading stores replacing the royal Kgotla as the market-place, and it became the transit camp of itinerants between the Cape and Zambezia, a halfway rest and recreation centre.

Before the 'notable and sometimes naughty' firm of W. C. Francis and R. Clark was established in 1872 or so as the first fairly well-capitalized resident general merchants, Shoshong had had six stores. By 1878 it had nine stores and exported seventy-five tons of ivory culled from 12,000 elephants in the far north. An estimate of 1879 put Shoshong's average export of ivory at £30,000 worth per annum. Serpa Pinto attributed the success of British businessmen at Shoshong in sustaining African confidence to their use of *cash* rather than barter. The Shoshong traders must have been well capitalized to do so.[45]

The figure of £55,000 for the produce that passed southwards through Shoshong related by its traders to the British government in 1878,[46] and the figure of £200,000 value offered by an international capitalist who visited Shoshong as a tourist in 1878,[47] may reflect an increasing gap between colonial and metropolitan produce market prices, due to profit-taking by distributors in Europe and America. It is evident that between the 1860s and the 1870s there was a drop in Shoshong merchant profits. Tabler attributes this to increasing competition,[48] but one also suspects deliberate 'rationalization' by metropolitan business interests of the commodity markets for ivory and feathers. Suspicions are aroused by falling London market feather prices during the 1868–73 Euro-American boom and rising prices during the 1873–9 depression.[49]

In the 1880s it was scarcity of elephants (available in East Africa) and ostriches (available on Cape farms) which depleted Zambezian trading profits. But the export of cattle and small stock to Kimberley became increasingly important, and the growing general retail market in clothing/blankets ('softwares') and ironwares signified an emerging cash economy beyond Cape colonial borders. Old white traders in the Interior might look back to the 'good old days' when one might gross £6,000 to £9,000 on one annual trip, and measure profits in hundreds of per cent at the beginning of the 1870s.[50] But there was little real reason to complain. An apparently typical trip from Shoshong to the Cape in

1887 by Francis and Clark was grossing over £1,000 and making 'at least 40 per cent' in profit.[51]

How much influence did Khama have over terms of trade? One hesitates to reply 'none', because he, like metropolitan capitalism, used political power to manipulate the conditions of exchange while officially professing a policy of economic liberalism in the period before 1887. Khama controlled the land, labour, and much of the machinery of production, and between 1875 and 1878 brought the trading community under strict social control. In 1875 he isolated the white ward from the rest of Shoshong and acquired its well to sell its water to the traders.[52] In 1876 he affirmed the inalienability of land and water supplies by proclamation: thus making trading stands dependent on his will for security.[53] And in 1878 he expelled traders who defied his liquor ban.[54] He sat in judgement over both legal and commercial disputes between traders; and even at this juncture he probably allotted regions of operation within his kingdom for itinerant traders.[55] European traders were still guests dependent on their host's goodwill, much as others were with the coastal rulers of West Africa.

## The wagon trade boom, 1887–96

Liberal imperialism, in the form of a treaty of reciprocity between the British and the Ngwato in 1885, was soon overtaken by monopoly colonialism in the form of the British South Africa Company. This is the juncture at which parallels between Khama's Country and coastal West Africa part company. The Royal Niger Company was a very different kettle of fish from the BSA Company.[56] The BSA Company combined heavy backing from the financial institutions of London up to the level of royalty, overlapping ownership by its principals of the gold and diamond production of South Africa, and the energies of a vigorous class of adventurers and would-be settlers from Europe and elsewhere. Ironically Khama laid one of the foundation stones of the BSA Company with his first, last, and only mineral concession, given to an Englishman and an American on 16 April 1887. This concession and their Bechuanaland Exploration Company were incorporated into the BSA Company, chartered two years later.[57]

The increasing scale and politicization of trade in Khama's Country was reflected even prior to the 1889 formation of the BSA Company by a growing stream of white adventurers, some plotting war, and in Khama's own reactions as 'a Tudor monarch'[58] in regulating the terms of trade by law. By a Notice of 28 June 1888 (the British did not assume political sovereignty over the Bechuanaland Protectorate until 1891) Khama banned the giving of credit by traders to Ngwato on pain of expulsion from his Country. Also in 1888 he fixed the price for kaross-making at a guinea, the prices of goats at 10s, and sheep at 15s,[59] and gave a royal semi-franchise to the Exploration Company to form its Bechuanaland Trading Association (BTA). Frank Johnson of the Exploration Company later recalled:

The trading business was born out of a discussion of the price Khama's people had to pay for ploughs, blankets, etc., from itinerant traders, who periodically visited his country from the Transvaal. I said the prices were too high, and to prove it offered to get some samples at a much lower price. So pleased was the Chief at these importations that I soon found the Company involved in an ever-growing trading business, which interfered with its more legitimate work of mining and 'interior' politics. Consequently, at my suggestion, a subsidiary trading company was formed to take over and extend this business.[60]

The development of consumer demands in Khama's Country therefore brought in a highly capitalized trading company with monopolist tendencies. The BTA soon became part of the BSA Company group. It had been founded with £130,000 of the speculative capital available on the London money market for Rhodes-ian adventures.[61] It obtained a general trading monopoly (cigarettes 2s 6d for ten, etc.) on supplies to the 'Pioneer Column' entering Mashonaland in 1890.[62] (For its total operations in Bechuanaland and Rhodesia it made a £22,146 profit in 1895–6, 127 per cent more than in 1894–5.)[63] And though the BTA lost favour because of its close connection with the BSA Company, with Khama probably encouraging other traders to compete with it, the BTA remained the largest trading firm in Khama's Country until 1913.[64]

The 1887–96 period saw a new phase in the development of trade and production in Khama's Country created by British expansion into the 'Rhodesias'. Long-distance trade to remote markets was subsumed within a flourishing local market, the victualling trade to itinerants on the Road to the North. But royal control did not keep pace with the outburst of production of goods and services. On the one level this may be attributed to the success of previous royal economic paternalism—the previous credit or donation of firearms, wagons, ploughs, horses, seed, and breeding-stock which enabled Ngwato now to sell surplus production direct to traders and travellers. Three social groups may be mentioned as particularly benefiting from the demand of the Road to the North—the big cattle-owning royals or aristocrats who sold cattle on the hoof (for Kimberley) and for meat and hides, wagoners such as the Khurutshe, and cultivators like some Kalanga groups. Hoe cultivation had been dramatically superseded by the plough, which in a dry climate on sandy soils not only extended space but also *time* when cultivation was possible. As far back as 1878 there were said to be forty ploughs around Shoshong.[65] 1888–94 sales of grain to whites at the Ngwato capital (first Shoshong, then Phalapye) were at least a thousand bags, even though Khama restricted sales after poor harvests.[66] Contemporary and photographic evidence of the widespread adoption of Western dress[67] suggests that income from the Road extended to the broad masses—at least of the capital town—through piecework, provision of entertainment, and the sale of artefacts or 'curios', eggs, goat's milk, melons, sweet-reed, etc. The

lavish capital income of white transients was splashed on the Road to
the North. 'The new movement towards Mashonaland,' remarked a
Phalapye missionary in 1891, 'is like a flood rising rapidly. Probably no
movement in South Africa has ever approached it. Transport, drivers'
wages, wagons, oxen, everything is in an advancing market.'[68]

Khama himself was undoubtedly the most entrepreneurial of all
Ngwato. Besides his extensive sale, hire, and use of cattle, wagons,
and grain crops, he grew tobacco for the market (himself a non-smoker)
and bred bloodstock in horses as well as cattle.[69] As a businessman he
maintained a reputation that his word was his bond,[70] and invested
much of his income in the paternal duties of kingship to his people as
their provider in times of need, or reinvested it in production. His
personal consumption was modest, beyond a good taste in suits.[71] He
eschewed other Western patterns of living and absolutely abstained
from alcohol, but spent some hundreds of pounds on sending his son
and other close relatives to the Cape for education. He banked largely
with local traders but also used the Standard Bank for his son's
education. He could obviously raise cash with ease: he spent £559 on
his 1895 delegation to the Colonial Office in London. (That visit
included receptions by most major Chambers of Commerce and civic
authorities in England and Scotland.)[72]

The observant reader will have noted no mention of labour migration
as yet in this chapter. This is because, contrary to preconceptions of
more recent times that there was a 'traditional sector' paying tribute to
a 'modern sector', the drain of labour appears to have been of little
significance in Khama's Country until the twentieth century. Labour
migration did begin on a formal basis early in Khama's reign. In
response to the first outside labour recruiter of 1877 Khama apologeti-
cally sent 'only' 105 men to the diamond fields.[73] And no doubt labour
migration to Kimberley continued, probably mostly of serfs but also
including 'true' Ngwato (like the father of Professor Z. K. Matthews)[74]
who slipped away with or without the king's permission. Evidence
for the Tati mines suggests that the labour force was predominantly Zambezi-Tonga with some Lozi, rather than neighbouring
Kalanga.[75]

There was room for considerable employment of labour within
Khama's Country during the 1890–3 boom of the Road to the North.
Men were organized in their age-regiments, *mephato,* for occasional
tasks outside the agricultural season—notably for war or patrolling,
but also on cutting new roads, building new royal accommodation, etc.
This was the system of recruitment that Khama utilized when the BSA
Company used him as their labour agent in 'developing' the Road to the
North. But this recruitment could not be extended beyond seasonal
limits, as foreman Smith found in 1891 when the Ngwato construction
workers on the telegraph line went on strike at the beginning of the
ploughing season: 'It is all very well for Khama and you white men.
You have people who will till your lands, and take care of your crops
and families in your absence, but we have no one; and if we do not do it

ourselves, no one will do it for us, and our wives and children will starve and die.'[76]

When these telegraph workers, 'many hundreds', were paid off on 14 November 1891, their foremen/headmen were paid up to £150 each in cash—much of it being spent in the BTA store on ploughs, etc.[77] Once the infrastructure was established between the Cape and Zambezia, prosperity continued on the basis of victualling services to the transit trade. The first annual report of a British administrator in Khama's Country, for 1893–4, suggested that 'transport riding' for the Ngwato 'may settle into an industry, so long as there is no railway'.[78] And his second annual report, for 1894–5, opined: 'Commercially the year has been fairly prosperous. A large amount of money is being earned by the natives in the carrying trade between this place and Bulawayo.'[79] Khama himself painted an idyllic picture of agricultural change, particularly in respect of the role of women:

> It is a sure sign of advance when you see the men use the ploughs which have come to us from Sweden and America; the men are proud to drive two oxen in a plough. A little Bechuana boy is said to have described his home as a place where women work and men dress their hair and fight and talk; but this is no longer true. This generation of women can, many of them cut out dresses and sew for themselves, and sew for their husbands as well. . . . I wish they did learn more to spin and weave, but they mostly string beads . . . I have heard even missionaries say that it were better the women still worked in the field than be idle at home. There is much to be done yet for them.[80]

It would be idle to pretend that here was an economy with a solid productive base ready to take off into any 'self-sustained growth'. But during the 1887–96 period Khama's Country used a net inflow of capital to expand its productive capacity (namely, ploughs and wagons), as well as expenditure on consumer goods and a certain amount of cash hoarding. The terms of trade with alien itinerants (if not with resident retailers) for local goods, services, and labour, were favourable to the latter while Khama's Country remained a strategic centre for the expanding 'Rhodesian' political economy.

## Rinderpest, railway and war, 1896–1902

By 1902 Great Britain had destroyed the pre-colonial state system of Southern-Central Africa, upon which the strategic importance of Khama's Country depended. Furthermore in the period from 1896, when the old state system was being given its death blows from the crushing of its African and Afrikaner 'revolts', the transit victualling trade of the Road to the North was being removed by the railway, and Botswana experienced natural disasters of drought and disease, but the Ngwato temporarily experienced unparalleled prosperity. The period 1896–1902 saw the flower of past Ngwato development and the seeds of its future underdevelopment.

Between April and November 1896 most of the cattle in Khama's
Country were wiped out by the great rinderpest pandemic from the
north.[81] Current 'guestimates' were as high as 96 per cent bovine
mortality, though the absolute figure of 800,000 dead cattle in Khama's
Country alone must have been a gross exaggeration.[82] Anyway the
Road to the North ground almost to a halt: 'hundreds' of wagons were
abandoned with oxen rotting in their yokes—the value of goods
abandoned between Mafeking and Phalapye (a distance less than 400
km) was estimated at £25,000 in April 1896, consisting mostly of luxury
items (from ladies' stays to champagne) for the affluent 'frontier' of
White Rhodesia.[83] Khama himself lost 300 to 400 trained trek-oxen and
the cattle export market was obviously entirely stopped.

Rinderpest and drought gave rise to rampant inflation in April
—November 1896. Remaining cattle sold for as much as £30 each, at
which price Khama sold one or two hundred to traders. The demand for
small stock for meat and milk is not recorded, but must have been
correspondingly high. Mealies (per 200 lb bag) rose in price from 50s to
170s, and Kalanga around Phalapye sold perhaps a hundred bags to
traders. As consumers Ngwato suffered the same inflation; mealie-
meal (per 200 lb) rose from 200s to 400s, etc.[84] But 'in the midst of the
times of the greatest want the natives would eagerly flock to local stores
to secure meal at £10 a bag of 200 lb, sugar at 2s and 2s 6d per lb, and
sweets, jams and other luxuries at exorbitant rates.... The local
merchants have reaped a rich harvest.'[85]

One Phalapye trader found his cash receipts for September 1896
£2,000 in excess of any previous month.[86] Ngwato cash reserves,
accumulated since 1890, were truly remarkable. The situation was
compared to the 1870–1 siege of Paris: the entrepreneurial class
thrived while the servile masses outside the cash economy starved.
The 'Bechuana Relief Fund', formed by friends of Khama in London
and headed by the Duke of Westminster, raised £1,432. But Khama and
other Tswana chiefs rejected the aid as a colonial threat to economic
independence and royal prerogative in famine relief. Khama insisted
on his people paying at cost price in cash or labour for mealies bought to
Phalapye under the scheme.[87] But, as the missionary W. C. Willoughby cynically observed, Khama turned a blind eye to Ngwato who
mustered enough oxen to take a wagon south to Gaborone where the
mealies were free of charge—so relief from famine was available 'in
proportion to the cattle which a man still possesses'.[88]

The famine following the rinderpest in Southern Africa played to the
contemporary obsession of mining capitalists with the 'labour question'. The inventor of the closed compound system for migrant labour,
F. R. Thompson, expressed the wish that the 'rinderpest will drive the
natives into the labour market'.[89] But in Khama's Country this labour
market during 1896–7 was internal, consisting of the employment,
with 'very liberal rates of pay' in colonial eyes, of workers in
constructing the Mafeking–Bulawayo railway. And from 1897 onwards there was a ready market for wood collected by regimental

labour for export to Kimberley and to fuel the railway locomotives themselves.[90]

Khama was therefore able to show remarkable independence from any 'dual economy' being erected in Southern Africa. He turned down a request made obsequiously by Koffyfontein Mines (Orange Free State) in February 1896 for 1,000 men over twelve months at £3 to £5 per man per month, with a trades school and an instructor for Phalapye thrown into the bargain— it was too far from home and too long a time, interfering with agriculture, to be popular (sic) with so many men![91] This is the background against which Khama at first supplied 'a big party of about 150' to the Rand Native Labour (Supply) Association in 1896 or 1897, but then banned labour recruitment in his territory from 1898 until after the South African War. According to a district manager of the RNLA's 'Wenela' successor in 1904, Khama's ban was because of the high mortality rate among Ngwato workers on the Rand.[92]

Khama's Country emerged relatively unscathed from the rinderpest. It was spared the locusts of the south and the revolts of the north, and received better rains than its neighbours in the 1896−7 and 1897−8 seasons: in mid-1898 Phalapye was selling plentiful mealies at 20s per bag of 200 lb to buyers from abroad.[93] New breeding stock to build up the cattle herds was imported from Barotseland, as can be seen in correspondence between Khama and Lewanika in this period.[94]

During 1899−1901 Khama's Country housed garrisons of British/Rhodesian troops as well as itself participating in the war. Expenditure on military victualling created another inflationary boom in meat and meal, while the war destroyed Afrikaner agricultural competition in the Transvaal, where some Boers were eventually reduced to buying shirts off Africans' backs.[95] Cattle sold at prices not reached again for sixty years, at £25 to £30 each, and the military authorities purchased no less than £25,000 worth in Khama's Country. Sheep and goats, selling at between 50s and 60s were exported to Southern Rhodesia. The interruption of railway traffic as a result of the war revived the wagon trade for transportation of goods.[96]

Despite sky-high consumer prices, the Ngwato bought so many imported goods (foodstuffs, clothing, and blankets) that traders ran short of cash and offered concessions on bank notes and premiums of up to 15 per cent on silver and gold currency.[97] The cash reserves among Ngwato are reflected by the hut tax yield (see below), strict exaction of church membership dues, *phalalo*, without dissent, and the fines which Khama's son attempted to impose on offenders against his liquor prohibition—£80 for the richer, and £50 for the poorer.[98] When the sum of £1,728 was paid to the Maolola regiment by the British for military services, its commander rejoiced to Khama: 'Chief, I see that God has helped us wonderfully, for this war has not hurt us at all . . . no dead or wounded to lament, as in former wars. Instead we have made much money in this war.'[99]

The first exaction of hut tax on Khama's Country yielded £3,816 for 1899−1900. The tax had been pressed on the Colonial Office in 1895 by

Khama and his fellow delegates, to emphasize the reciprocity of the Tswana–Imperial relationship, and thereby to pre-empt Rhodesian attempts to relieve the burden of the Bechuanaland Protectorate from the shoulders of the Imperial administration. The hut tax stood at 10s and had, at Khama's insistence, to be paid in cash; and to it Khama added a tribal tax of 5s on men too young to be included in the regimental lists for the hut tax. The Assistant Comissioner for the Northern Protectorate, stationed at Phalapye, was amazed to find that yield exceeded estimate by £600 even on 1 July 1899, when £3,093 had been paid in. This was partially explainable by Khama's desire to receive the 10 per cent due to him on collection before that date. Another vital factor was ready collection via age-regiments and Tswana settlement nucleation. Phalapye's 30,000, perhaps half the total population of the territory of the Ngwato, paid up £3,725 of the total collection. But yet another factor was the special relationship of Khama and the Ngwato with the British to their economic and political advantage: total yields for 1899–1900 for Sebele's Country and Bathoen's Country to the south were £379 and £98 respectively. The tax yield of Khama's Country rose to £5,024 for 1900–1, and to £5,300 for 1901–2.[100]

## Deforestation and veld deterioration

It may be suggested that the 1896–1902 producer/consumer apparent 'boom' in Khama's Country was in fact eating into capital rather than experiencing real economic growth in the long run. The same point may certainly be made with regard to consumption of the ecological basis for production. The Road to the North developed in a period of remarkably good rains in Southern Africa from 1886 to 1895, broken by the 1897 drought, and thereafter succeeded by the 'normal' pattern of intermittent drought.[101] Holub in 1887 had noted how the 'considerable traffic' of the Road had thinned the woods of the Marico (Madikwe) valley of the upper Limpopo since his first visit of 1874.[102] What the 1886–95 pluvial period did was first to avert this process and then to give support to even more considerable traffic which further accelerated veld deterioration. Trees were felled by men, and grass was eaten by their cattle, and virtually any vegetation by their goats, with the result that woody plants or 'bush' encroached on the vigour of the grasslands, and erosion set in with the drying-up of surface waters.[103] Rinderpest in a sense was a blessing in disguise: by killing off so many cattle it relieved perhaps chronic overstocking, and by killing off the wildlife hosts ('reservoir of infection') of tsetse the rinderpest extended potential grazing land for the next generation of cattle.[104]

The consumption of grasslands and the destruction of forest in Khama's Country was most aggravated along the wagon routes of the Road to the North, and then along the railway. The former capital of Shoshong had been abandoned in 1889 partially because of the exhaustion of local alluvial soils by intensive plough-cultivation.[105]

The cycle of denudation was even more rapid at Phalapye, which was estimated to have a population of 37,000 Ngwato and 200 resident whites in 1896. On contemporary observation the veld around Phalapye was eaten bare, and the 'abundance of large and useful timber' on the plain in 1889 had disappeared by 1895.[106] By around 1900 the Photophoto waterfall at Phalapye was dry and water was being obtained in wells up to round 15m deep in the sand of the Lotsane river bed, and was reportedly sold by a headman to women for an equal amount of mealie-meal. The traditional answer to depletion of local natural resources was to move the settlement, but Phalapye represented so much capital investment in immovable property, like the church buildings valued at £4,000 (used as a fortress by the British army). From 1896 the population was dispersed to new regional towns[107] but the town then attracted new population by its prosperity, in the form of refugees from the Transvaal, and the South African War itself strategically delayed the decision to abandon the site. Serowe to the west was chosen as the new capital town site and the move was made in planned stages between February and August 1902—burning down the ruins of Old Phalapye, with the exception of the church buildings intended for an educational complex, and the government headquarters for the Northern Protectorate.[108] The sudden abandonment of Old Phalapye in 1902 for ecological reasons was maybe not so different from the avandonment of the site of Great Zimbabwe in the mid-fifteenth century.[109]

The rapid deforestation of the Botswana line-of-rail occurred from 1897 to about 1904, when Rhodesia Railways converted from wood-burning to coal-burning locomotives.[110] The greatest demand was from the 'ravenous maw' of the Kimberley mines, and it was rejoiced in 1897 that Khama's Country would not be exhausted of wood for fifteen years.[111] Government plans of promoting reafforestation were still-born.[112] The pattern had been set whereby Botswana was regarded as a human and natural resource to be indefinitely bled for the benefit of the large-scale 'modern' sector of South Africa.[113]

## Structure for underdevelopment, 1902–10

In the peaceful years that followed the South African War the colonial system contrived to extract the surplus, while the economy of the Ngwato Reserve gradually lost ground in production because of the restrictions of political boundaries and declining terms of trade. The way was laid for the politico-economic equation of 'development' with white control, institutionalized in the 1910–61 Union of South Africa and High Commission Territories relationship and in the 1910–69 South African Customs Union.

The colonial income from Ngwato hut tax grew steadily from its 1901–2 figure of £5,300. For 1903–4 it leapt 8·5 per cent over the previous year because the hut tax was effectively converted into a poll tax on all adult males. For 1907–8 and 1908–9 it leapt 12·3 per cent and 14·5 per cent to accommodate in its own mysterious way the increase of the tax from 15s to £1, to yield £13,225 for 1908–9. The government auditor was most impressed by Ngwato book-keeping: on the other hand it may well have been a reflection of continuing anxiousness not to prove a burden which would justify white settler takeover. In 1908 direct taxation of Africans accounted for 61 per cent of all government revenue and from 1911–12 until 1956 the Bechuanaland Protectorate revenue matched or exceeded expenditure.[114] In fact in 1908 the two largest items of the £75,801 government expenditure were 'police' (£39,559) and 'railway subsidy' (£8,333): 'district administration' was a poor fifth (£3,584), and African social services totalled a £500 subsidy to trades education.[115] There was minimal government spending even indirectly on the African population of a 'Native Territory'. The administrative capital was a white town, Mafeking, twenty-five kilometres outside the Protectorate; the Northern Administration including Khama's Country was based after 1903 in the white company village of Francistown. In fact most of the costs of administration were being carried by the tribal governments, and the 'chief business' of the colonial administration was 'to collect taxes, and receive salaries, a business which seems to exhaust the whole of its administrative energies'.[116]

The capital costs of the move from Phalapye to Serowe were undoubtedly heavy, and largely borne by 'Khama', i.e. by the Ngwato state exchequer. New wells at Serowe cost up to £250 each, and had to be provided for police and mission, and a well halfway along the road to Serowe from the railway station called 'Palapye Road' (now simply Palapye) cost over £800.[117] Regimental earnings from British military employment amounting to two or three thousand pounds were allotted to the establishment of elementary education at Serowe. But it was mostly spent on out-districts by the London Missionary Society which fell out of favour in a period of 'Ethiopianist' sentiment. The fate of the Old Phalapye church complex, valued at £4,000, hung in the balance as an educational institution to rival Lovedale, etc., and was never utilized before final demolition in 1918.[118] Enthusiasm for education waned, Khama declining to institute a 2s national educational levy suggested by the colonial government in 1905.[119] Plans for a new church at Serowe were disastrous. Between 1906 and 1907 £2,400 was collected with more promised from Khama, but a crooked architect in Kimberley appears to have creamed off £3,000 in consultancy fees, and the project was abandoned until 1911.[120]

The railway had well and truly come, and with it had disappeared the victualling trade of the Road to the North, both its social vices and economic virtues. The railway created minimal employment and demand for local produce: the 100-yard wide strip owned by Rhodesia Railways was quasi-legally part of Southern Rhodesia itself. But the economy of Khama's Country by no means collapsed; there were traders' stores in profusion and the widespread adoption of ploughing and wagoning served an internal market. Khama's Country, after all, covered 130,000 sq km, and had a developed infrastructure of wagon-roads—and more research needs to be done on this 'internal market' of yesterday and today.

Agricultural production between the South African War and Union was marked by the beginnings of a regime of falling prices combined with restrictions on external markets, made worse by drought and disease. The war price boom dropped away rapidly: the 1900 price of 50s to 60s for sheep and goats and £25 – £30 for cattle had dropped to 15s to 18s and £20 by the end of 1901. There was a sequence of crop failures in Khama's Country because of drought—by September 1904 water cost 1s a pot in the Shoshong gorge; 1905 and 1906 – 7 saw a partial recovery; 1907 was disastrous; 1908 had good rains at Serowe; 1909 – 10 and 1910 – 11 only harvested sorghum, not maize, the earlier crop. And 1911 – 12 saw dire drought continuing for a decade with the exception of 1914 – 15. As a result production of cereal crops in these years was cut even to a fifth. The most surplus-oriented producers were reduced to bare subsistence, and in 1904 for the first time in many years it was noted that Ngwato cash reserves were insufficient to tide over famine without widespread export of labour. The market for cattle absolutely collapsed between 1902 and 1910 – 11, through an embargo on all exports because of east coast and other fevers, with temporary respite of export in 1908 – 9 to the Transvaal. But in 1910 – 11 the Ngwato exported 2,500 slaughter stock to Southern Rhodesia at £4 a head, and within three months of the restricted opening of the Johannesburg abattoir in 1911 the Bechuanaland Protectorate exported 11,812 cattle at £5 a head.[121]

As a result the imported consumer goods market in the Bechuanaland Protectorate, and especially the Ngwato Reserve, recovered in 1911 – 12. The Ngwato had had a taste of the 'sub-subsistence' level already experienced by the southern Tswana: a depressed tribal economy exporting its productive labour to contribute only to white-controlled production, as a missionary observed of the Tswana in general in 1903.[122] In June of that year Khama was pressured to drop his ban on labour recruitment for the Rand, and as a result within a year 600 Ngwato were recruited through Khama to work on the mines, 'railways and the cantonments' of the Transvaal.[123] The continuing 'labour question' meant that Khama was treated with kid gloves. When Ngwato workers were ill-treated on railway construction, the general manager of Central South African Railways himself wrote to Khama to apologize in May 1904.[124]

Evidence suggests that the rate of labour migration from Khama's Country in this period was directly related to depressions in the internal economy. The period from 1910 to the Great War saw some revival of economic health. But the 1902 – 10 economic depression in a way remained with Botswana until 1969 in that it was institutionalized into the South African Customs Union. The Bechuanaland Protectorate was allotted a fixed percentage (0·27622 per cent) of the union's

total customs revenue based on its imports of the three years before
1910.[125]

## Underdevelopment within the South African colonial region

Khama responded to the conditions of the 1902—10 period by setting
up a state economic structure which he hoped to bequeath to his
successors. His attempts largely failed—because of political-
economic manoeuvring by white supremacist capitalism within the
framework of Southern Africa as a whole, and because of inefficien-
cies, impracticalities, and sheer bad luck. Khama's ideas at least
survived to be taken up by his sons and grandsons, and bore fruit in
somewhat paradoxical policies of state-directed self-help to provide
social services and retain labour and skills within the community.[126]
    But the colonial structure of the Southern African economy was
against such self-sufficiency: the Ngwato State was a Tribal Reserve
which *ipso facto* must subsidize the export of labour and other primary
produce, but must not challenge or isolate itself from the financial and
other institutions which affected market values.
    Khama's analysis of his Country's economic ills concerned itself
certainly with trade and probably also with employment. The story of
'Khama and Co.', his royal trading venture from 1910 to 1916, is told
elsewhere.[127] But some indication must be given of the contemporary
background to the trade and employment questions.
    It has been suggested that Khama disliked labour migration for its
disruptive social effects, and instead advocated a development policy
of modernizing the indigenous economy so that the labour force could
be employed at home.[128] There is no reason to reject this suggestion
simply for lack of an explicit self-conscious recorded statement by
Khama. It helps to explain Khama's retention of regimental labour on
'cathedral' building—a white critic called it 'a wanton waste of muscle'
that should have been exported[129]—at Serowe between 1911 and 1917.
It certainly appears that most of the migrant labour 'pushed' out by
drought in 1916 and 1922 came not from the capital but from the north of
Khama's Country; and Khama threatened to ban migration to the Rand
in 1918.[130] The more usual labour migrants to the Rand might have been
serfs pleased to gain in social and economic status, and 'target-
workers' out to earn a bicycle, etc.[131] Khama's Country actually
attracted migrants in search of work, and between 1909 and 1919, when
'Bushman Mine' was in operation, may have been a net *importer* of
labour (Lozi, Tonga and Subiya) at times. 'Bushman Mine' was a small
mine run by a BSA subsidiary which closed, after producing
ninety-four tons of copper, because of a slump. It paid Khama about
£1,500 in revenue and regularly bought cattle for slaughter.[132]
    The widest possibilities of employment in the internal economy lay
in surplus-oriented agriculture, but this depended on export markets,

natural conditions and agricultural practices. Ngwato had invested in imported technology during cash booms to boast the remarkable figures of 5,491 ploughs for cereal production and 1,025 wagons for transportation by 1921.[133] But the great drought and soil erosion practically wiped out cereal production for export. As for livestock, 'Khama and Co.', while it lasted, provided marketing, credit, and bloodstock facilities. But natural conditions led to the decline of Ngwato cattle quality: one source claims a decline from a 1900 average beast of 900 lb to one of 400 lb in 1914.[134] The limited Johannesburg market was closed in 1917 because of bovine pleuro-pneumonia and opened only to the southern Bechuanaland Protectorate in 1919, when prices began to drop dramatically to a mere 15s or £1 per head in 1922, and in 1924 South Africa imposed its notorious minimum weight restrictions: the real price level of 1910 was not reached again until 1942.[135] The northern Bechuanaland Protectorate, including Khama's Country, managed to export about 2,000 head per annum between 1912 and 1917 to Southern Rhodesia via the firm of Jas Haskins and Sons. However the Southern Rhodesian mutton market declined after anthrax in Khama's Country in the 1910s.[136] And markets lost in the 1910s could not be regained in the 1920s when white farmer settler power in South Africa and Southern Rhodesia (see Chapters 7 and 9) created its own protective barriers against black (and, even more, 'foreign' black) competition.[137]

The cornerstone of Khama's economic policy was the spreading of the cash nexus. He had this to add about his liberation of semi-servile groups to own property: 'These tribes became in the first instance [so] apprehensive of the declaration that at last I had to ask European traders to travel among them and sell goods.'[138]

His advocacy of cash led him to campaign against 'good-fors', the slips issued by traders for produce bought on credit for future purchases—a paper money which subsidized small traders' operations 'without possessing a farthing of capital'. Traders in the drought of the 1900s took advantage of colonial protection to revive such practices banned by Khama when he had independent power over them, despite warnings by Khama in 1905 and 1912 and a 'voluntary' ban in 1916.[139] The 1923 Credit Sales to Natives Proclamation stopped wholesale credit to African retailers, i.e. it put African traders out of business, in its attempt to limit white trader credit to African customers.[140]

I have not obtained figures of trade turnover among the Ngwato before 1930. But by 1915 there were at least twenty-one trading firms (plus a blacksmith/mechanic) with stores at eighteen or more locations, five firms having more than one branch, in Khama's Country. The smaller traders benefited from direct capital injection from 'Khama and Co.', i.e. state participation, and the white trading community was an integral part of Ngwato economy and society despite its racial identity with white supremacy elsewhere. Many were local born, many had local (white or black) wives. Some were more, some were less, 'white Bamangwato'. The only firm that attempted to work without royal patronage, the BTA, was finally forced to withdraw in 1916.[141] This patronage suited 'parallel rule', in that the chief carried the administrative burden of issuing cattle identity permits, etc.

It was the question of a repository for—and regeneration of— capital, now that cattle were a diminishing asset, that Khama himself pointed to as the most important reason for establishing 'a business in which I would invest my stock'.[142] (It may also have been the reason for his investigation of the overseas land market in 1912, in which he declined to buy property in the City of London or Brighton-Hove.)[143] Khama wanted a safe 'savings account' offering ready cash while gaining interest invested in productive activity. There is every reason to suppose that as a very old man Khama wished to ensure royal income and state expenditure for his successors. He was not content to bequeath a mere 'Native Reserve', but a territory with the qualities of statehood. It was to this end that expenditure on prestige projects was heavy after 'Khama & Co.' had apparently assured a considerable measure of economic self-sufficiency for Khama's Country. The 'cathedral' at Serowe built between 1911 and 1918 cost up to £10,000; in 1910 all the regiments were required to buy uniforms for ceremonial purposes; and up to 1918 hope was apparently not abandoned of turning the remains of Old Phalapye into an educational complex. 'Khama & Co.' was above all a mechanism of direct royal or state financial benefit from the circulation of goods and services in the country. Before setting up his own trading corporation Khama had to use the largest local traders as bankers—depositing between £5,000 and £12,000 with the BTA and drawing cash up to £2,500 from the account.[144] When forced to close 'Khama and Co.' in 1916, he resorted to a deposit account at the Standard Bank, Mafeking, from 1917, which reached £1,253 by April 1920, but thereafter never topped £500 before his death in 1923.[145]

The deliberate destruction of 'Khama and Co.' in 1916 by the British authorities, on behalf of the BTA's backers, removed Ngwato capacity to resist the downward spiral of 'structural underdevelopment' within the Southern African regional economic system. Damaged by drought and cut off from export markets for livestock, the colonial revenue from the Ngwato Reserve dropped from over £18,000 in 1918 to under £14,000 by 1922.[146] And thereafter, a missionary remarked, the colonial government had a propensity to heighten taxes 'in proportion to the deepening distress of the general public'.[147] Government promotion of economic development openly until 1930 (and more discreetly thereafter) was confined to BSA Company concessions and white settler production.[148] The white progressive view as expressed by Emmanuel Gluckmann (father of Max), in 1922 newspaper articles attacking Khama, was that: 'With the advent of the diamond-drill to overcome the scarcity of water, it is a country of great possibilities, but nothing can be done without the consent of the chiefs, and they pursue consistently a policy antagonistic to development, probably to discourage a greater influx of whites into their territory.'[149]

By 1930 the Ngwato Reserve had an unfavourable trade gap of £25,611 in traders' returns. *Exports* amounted to £55,072−£34,336 in cattle; £11,259 in cattle hides; £3,294 in karosses; and £3,184 in sheep and goats. *Imports* amounted to £82,683−£73,915 in general merchandise; £3,431 in mealies and meal; £2,272 in wheat and meal. Given additional outflow of £30,000 in taxes and levies, and the inability of migrant labour remittances to close the gap, Leonard Barnes, the Oxford socialist, still reckoned that 'the native community, even at present standards, is living beyond its income and eating into its capital'.[150]

The vital question that remains for future research is not so much whether there was general rural impoverishment in east-central Botswana, but how that poverty originated and how it was distributed. That there were structural changes in society related to labour migration was established in the 1930s and 1940s by Schapera's pioneering studies.[151] But not until the late 1960s did the significance of such changes for socio-economic stratification become clear. The 1967−8 Agricultural Census was in retrospect every bit as important for Botswana as the discovery of diamonds at Orapa at that time. It showed that fully 13 per cent of the rural population in Botswana derived their living from no crops or cattle at all, but survived on the income of absentee wage-earners; a further 31 per cent possessed no cattle at all; and among the remaining 56 per cent who did own cattle, some 12 per cent owned 60 per cent of all the cattle.[152] This completely undermined the conventional assumption at the heart of late colonial rural development policy in building up the cattle industry: that 'the great bulk of the population are self-employed, operating principally on a subsistence basis though obtaining a small cash income from the sale of cattle'.[153]

More recently it is suggested that this gap between rural wealth and poverty, in the supposedly communal rather than individual estate sector of agriculture, is ever-widening.[154] How far into the past then may its origins be projected? It cannot be simply equated with patron-client relations of the nineteenth century, based on economic and political reciprocities within the structure of the pre-colonial state. The general economic history of Khama's Country up to 1930 does however indicate guidelines for more intensive studies at the local and family level. Legal reform of property relations, combined with the spread of cash values and new obligations within the wider colonial state structure, produced new varieties of wealth and poverty. As Simon Ratshosa noted in the late 1920s and early 1930s, a 'neo-feudalism' had developed in Botswana in which royal wealth based on the customary dues of state was translated into chiefs' personal and family fortunes.[155] At the rank of aristocrat and commoner, the large cattle-owners and the serf-masters—'about a tenth of the Bamangwato', K.T. Motsete told the 'Masarwa Commission' of 1931—a parallel process was discernible. Serf labour liberated sons from cattle-herding and daughters from domestic duties, and enabled them to obtain the education and lifestyle of the 'new élite' that spanned Southern Africa.[156] Other witnesses to the 'Masarwa Commission', Gaofetoge Mathiba and John Ratshosa, indicated that client labour had recently entered a 'second servitude', to borrow the term applied to East Prussia under the Junkers, whereby masters under pressure of cash market conditions had intensified their use of serf labour, while the serfs themselves increasingly attempted to flee such oppression by becoming labour migrants to the mines.[157]

However, the main insights into the growth of rural poverty in the Central District of Botswana may well be obtained from neither the upper nor lower social strata, but from the 'settlers', 'refugees', or 'aliens', who constituted the majority of the 'Bamangwato'. Among these *bafaladi* groups may be found both 'peasantization', into dependence on production for the market, and 'proletarianization', into no crops/no cattle dependence on sale of labour elsewhere. The relationship between the two processes, if indeed they are useful concepts, remains to be elucidated. It appears that, as elsewhere, 'peasantization' gave way to 'proletarianization' as the dominant trend in the period between the two World Wars. In 1895 a missionary resident of Khama's Country reported, referring to *bafaladi* agricultural production: 'Indeed, there are those who prophesy that, very soon, the Makalaka [Kalanga] will become richer than the Bamangwato [nuclear clans].'[158] But by 1922 crop failure and market depression forced large numbers of Kalanga men, reportedly the majority, to go to the mines, and the women to scatter from the main concentrations of population along the Shashe river into the countryside.[159] Between 1923 and 1930 an average of 1,400 Kalanga were recruited annually for the diamond mines of South West Africa. By 1942–3 the rate of labour migration among Kalanga may be gauged from the absentee taxpayers (exclusive of those serving in the British army) in the Tati District round Francistown, an area of exclusive Kalanga and white farmer settlement, outside the Bamangwato Reserve: the rate was no less than 43.2 per cent.[160]

In the Bechuanaland Protectorate as a whole from 1924 onwards the Native Advisory Council (composed of chiefs and headmen) expressed growing concern over the rate of labour migration. But the post-1933 boom in gold pricing and then the maximizing of gold production during the Second World War saw a rapid increase in labour migration, while economic opportunities at home withered under the impact of cost inflation and markets limited by foreign competition.[161] No longer could it be claimed, even hypocritically, as Jousse had done in his attack on Khama published in 1914: 'The Bechuanas contribute but in a very small measure to the labour demands of South Africa. The masses are not to blame for this, and if they do not go to the mines or other work, like other tribes, it is because they have not the liberty of action that other natives have.'[162]

By 1945 it was accepted almost as a state of nature—certainly by the colonial authorities—that the Bechuanaland Protectorate should be a labour reserve for the needs of South Africa.

## Conclusion

The general economic history of Khama's Country in Botswana demonstrates how a vigorous African economy became subordinated to the special conditions of capitalist development in Southern Africa as a colonial economic region. The economy had been stimulated by mercantile .contacts with the world economy into a phase of productive growth, which reached its climax when Khama's Country serviced the Cape-to-Rhodesia wagon transit trade. But the railway removed this pole of growth, and the terms of trade turned against the local economy when British power succeeded in creating a Southern African political and economic region after 1902. Khama's Country then became a minor element in the periphery of a colonial system which had its regional centre in the Union of South Africa—dominated by the interests of the mining industry, increasingly those of Afrikaner estate agriculture, and eventually of manufacturing industry (see Chapter 7). By overt political controls, as well as through 'unseen' and natural factors affecting production and trade, these interest groups in South Africa restricted local production and manipulated the terms of trade to create a structure in which the black periphery paid invariable tribute to the white centre in capital funds and resources as well as labour. However, Khama's Country was not levelled out in the middle colonial period to the extent of other black 'homelands' in Southern Africa. The dynamics of its social structure meant that impoverishment was unequally distributed internally. So when the economy recovered and political self-determination was gradually regained, the gap between rural rich and rural poor was seen to be ever-widening.

In pre-colonial and early colonial times Khama's Country accommodated 'modern' services and industry within its economy. Today there is the Shashe mining complex (diamonds, copper/nickel, coal, etc.) within the Central District of Botswana, as Khama's Country is now called. Yesterday as today the economy had a flourishing cattle-market, copper-mining, and a measure of state participation. Today as yesterday this may lead to new patterns of dependence and domination.

## NOTES

1. W.C. Willoughby, 'Khama: A Bantu Reformer', *International Review of Missions*, 13, 1924, 83.
2. L. Knight-Bruce, 'Khamé', *Murray's Magazine*, 5, 1889, 461.
3. See A.J. Dachs, 'Missionary Imperialism—The Case of Bechuanaland', *Journal of*

*African History, 13,* 1972, 647–58; A. Sillery, *Botswana: A Short Political History* (London, 1974), 53–113; A. Holmberg, *African Tribes and European Agencies* (Goteborg, 1966), 24–147.

4.   E. Holub, 'The Past, Present, and Future Trade of the Cape Colonies with Central Africa', *Proceedings of the Royal Colonial Institute, 11,* 1879–80, 59–60.

5.   This chapter concentrates on the unfolding political economy of an area in regional context, rather than on 'agricultural history' *per se,* the econometrics of the 'New Economic History', or the perspectives of the ecological school of cultural evolutionists.

6.   N. Parsons,[6] "Khama & Co." and the Jousse Trouble, 1910–1916', *Journal of African History, 16,* 1975, 383–408.

7.   See especially Chapters 8 to 11 by Colin Bundy, Robin Palmer, Ian Phimister, and Barry Kosmin. Also H. Saker and J. Aldridge, 'The Origins of the Langeberg Rebellion', *Journal of African History, 12,* 1971, 299–317; E.S. Atieno-Odhiambo, 'The Rise and Decline of the Kenya Peasant, 1888–1922', *East Africa Journal, 9, 5,* 1972, 11–15.

8.   S. Amin, 'Underdevelopment and Dependence in Black Africa—Origins and Contemporary Forms', *Journal of Modern African Studies, 10,* 1972, 503–24.

9.   Neil Parsons, 'On the Origins of the Bamangwato', *Botswana Notes and Records, 5,* 1973, 82–103.

10.   Parsons, 'Origins', 82–103.

11.   I. Schapera, *A Handbook of Tswana Law and Custom* (London, 1955 edn), 246–8. Similar systems are evident elsewhere, for example the Shona *kuronzera*: S.I. Mudenge, 'The Role of Foreign Trade in the Rozvi Empire: A Reappraisal', *Journal of African History, 15,* 1974, 389–90 n. 105.

12.   Schapera, *Handbook,* 67–8, 248–50; T. Tlou, 'Melao yaga Kgama: Transformation in the Nineteenth Century Ngwato State', MA thesis, University of Wisconsin, 1968, 12; National Archives of Botswana, S.43/7, S. Ratshosa, 'Disclosing some of the Serious Facts for the First Time to the Administration of the Bechuanaland Protectorate: How the Masarwa Became Slaves and Why the Chief's Word is Law', 1926.

13.   M. Fortes and E.E. Evans-Pritchard (eds), *African Political Systems* (London, 1940), 6.

14.   Amin, 'Underdevelopment', 506–7.

15.   D. Livingstone (ed. I. Schapera), *Livingstone's Missionary Correspondence 1841–6* (London, 1961), 18, 43.

16.   W.D. Mackenzie, *John Mackenzie: South African Missionary and Statesman* (London, 1902), 108, citing Mackenzie to London Missionary Society, 19 March 1866.

17.   E.C. Tabler, *The Far Interior* (Cape Town, 1955), 23, 26–31, 41.

18.   J. Mackenzie, *Ten Years North of the Orange River* (Edinburgh, 1871), 359–61, 267–85.

19.   Mackenzie, *Ten Years,* 361.

20.   H. Bryden, 'A Friend of Livingstone' [Sechele], *Chamber's Journal,* 7 July 1894, 420–1.

21.   D. M'Intosh, *South Africa: Notes of Travel* (Glasgow, 1876), 102; National Archives of Botswana, J.978A, Khama to High Commissioner, 28 March 1916.

22.   J.D. Hepburn, *Twenty Years in Khama's Country* (London, 1895), 26–9.

23.   National Archives of Botswana, J.978A, Khama to High Commissioner, 28 March 1916.

24.   R.G. Cumming, *The Lion Hunter of South Africa* (London, 1904 edn, 1st edn 1850), 254.

25.   Cumming, *Lion Hunter,* 256, 351, 404, 434.

26.   Cumming, *Lion Hunter,* 7.

27.   Cumming, *Lion Hunter,* 254–5, 257; Parsons, 'Origins', 100–1 n. 62.

28.   See E.C. Tabler (ed.), *Zambesia and Matabeleland in the Seventies* (London and Livingstone, 1960), 16, 65, 99, etc.

29.   J. Chapman, *Travels in the Interior of South Africa 1849–1863* (Cape Town, 1971 edn, 1st edn 1868), 50, 102.

30.  A. Sillery, *Sechele: The Story of An African Chief* (Oxford, 1954), 125.
31.  See Tabler *omnia opera*, but especially *The Far Interior, Pioneers of Rhodesia* (Cape Town, 1966), and contributions to *Africana Notes and Records*.
32.  National Archives of Botswana, J.978A, Khama to High Commissioner, 28 March 1916. 'When I was still a lad, I used to think how I would govern my town, and what kind of a kingdom it would be.' Hepburn, *Twenty Years,* 140.
33.  National Archives of Botswana, J.978A, Khama to High Commissioner, 28 March 1916.
34.  I. Schapera, *Tribal Innovators: Tswana Chiefs and Social Change 1745–1940* (London, 1970), 89.
35.  Mackenzie, *Ten Years,* 446.
36.  Tabler, *The Far Interior,* 20.
37.  National Archives of Botswana, J.978A, Khama to High Commissioner, 28 March 1916.
38.  *C.2220, Further Correspondence Respecting the Affairs of South Africa* (London, 1878), 237–9.
39.  *C.2220,* 74–6. See also H.W. Langworthy, 'Chewa or Malawi Political Organization in the Pre-colonial era', in B. Pachai (ed.), *The Early History of Malawi* (London, 1972), 116.
40.  Tabler, *Zambesia,* 31, 65–6, 70; Schapera, *Tribal Innovators,* 245, 262.
41.  P. Gillmore, *The Great Thirstland* (London, 1879), 331–2; A. Douglass, *Ostrich Farming in South Africa* (London, 1881); W.P. Greswell, *Geography of Africa South of the Zambezi* (Oxford, 1892), 235; Tabler, *Zambesia,* 112; R. Sampson, *The Man with a Toothbrush in his Hat: The Story and Times of George Copp Westbeech* (Lusaka, 1972), 31*ff.*
42.  *C.5524,* Bechuanaland, *Further Correspondence Respecting the Affairs of Bechuanaland and Adjacent Territories* (London, 1888); *C.5918,* Bechuanaland, *Further Correspondence Respecting the Affairs of Bechuanaland and Adjacent Territories* (London, 1890).
43.  R.R. Patterson, 'On the Bamangwato Country', *Proceedings of the Royal Geographical Society, 1,* 1879, 241. The number had temporarily declined during the civil disturbances from its 1866 figure of forty-two. T. Tlou, 'Khama III—Great Reformer and Innovator', *Botswana Notes and Records, 2,* 1970, 102; Tabler, *The Far Interior,* 11.
44.  I. Schapera, *The Ethnic Composition of Tswana Tribes* (London, 1972), 84.
45.  Tabler, *The Far Interior,* 20; E. Holub, *Von der Capstadt ins Land der Maschukulumbwe* (Vienna, 1890), 498; A.A. da R. de Serpa Pinto, *How I Crossed Africa, Vol. 2* (London, 1881), 221–2.
46.  *C.2220,* 239.
47.  J.A.I. Agar-Hamilton, *The Road to the North 1852–1886* (London, 1937), 153. The capitalist was Richard Frewen, an Englishman, who later became a multi-million dollar speculator in cattle ranching in Wyoming, USA. Tabler, *Zambesia, 117–95,*
48.  Tabler, *Far Interior,* 20.
49.  See prices in F. Wilson, 'Farming, 1866–1966', in M. Wilson and L. Thompson (eds), *The Oxford History of South Africa, Vol. 2, South Africa 1870–1966* (Oxford, 1971), 116. In 1868 Natal/Cape exports of ivory were given at £40,000 per annum, and trade with Africans beyond colonial borders was guessed at £47,000 worth of ostrich feathers, £100,000 worth of cattle and small stock, and £10,000 worth of hides and skins. A. Hamilton, 'On the Trade with the Coloured Races of Africa', *Journal of the Statistical Society of London, 31,* 1868, 25–48.
50.  Sampson, *Man with a Toothbrush,* 37, 66, 121, 126.
51.  Holub, *Von der Capstadt,* 497–8.
52.  E. Holub, *Seven Years in South Africa, Vol. 2* (London, 1881), 41; Tabler, *Pioneers,* 55.
53.  *C.2220,* 54.
54.  Hepburn, *Twenty Years,* 141–52, gives an edited version of the events of October 1878.

55.   See Neil Parsons, 'Khama III, the Bamangwato, and the British, with Special Reference to 1895–1923', PhD thesis, University of Edinburgh, 1973, 36–41.
56.   It is hard to conceive of the BSA Company employing Mr Justice Sam Moore in one of its most senior positions, as did the Royal Niger Company. Moore, a lifelong friend of Marx and Engels, translated *The Communist Manifesto* and the first volume of *Capital* into English, and delivered Engels's funeral oration. *The Times*, 12 August 1895, 10.
57.   See F.W. Johnson, *Great Days* (London, 1940), 67–250; J.S. Galbraith, *Crown and Charter* (Berkeley, Los Angeles, and London, 1974).
58.   Knight-Bruce, 'Khamé', 461.
59.   Knight-Bruce, 'Khamé', 461.
60.   Johnson, *Great Days*, 71.
61.   E.P. Mathers, *Zambesia: England's Eldorado in Africa* (London, 1891), 460; G. Arrighi, 'Labour Supplies in Historical Perspective: A Study of the Proletarianization of the African Peasantry in Rhodesia', *Journal of Development Studies*, 6, 1970, 200; I.R. Phimister, 'Rhodes, Rhodesia and the Rand', *Journal of Southern African Studies*, 1, 1974, 74–90.
62.   A.G. Leonard, *How We Made Rhodesia* (London, 1896), 34.
63.   *African Review*, 9, 1896, 529.
64.   Parsons, ' "Khama & Co." ', 390.
65.   *C.2220*, 236.
66.   *Cape Times Weekly Edition*, letters to the Editor, 31 October 1894.
67.   'A fair proportion of the men and some of the women are adopting European costume' [1878], *C.2220*, 236. By 1890 such dress was widespread in the capital. See the much-reproduced photograph by W. Ellerton Fry of Khama trying prisoners: Schapera, *Tribal Innovators*, opp. 172; Mathers, *Zambesia*, 129.
68.   Hepburn, *Twenty Years*, 341.
69.   The weak point of Khama's character was said to be 'his jealousy of [other] men who are becoming rich and powerful'. But 'A love of money has never been a fault of his', though 'In business transactions he is keen, and anxious to get the best price'. E. Lloyd, *Three Great African Chiefs: Khâmé, Sebelé, and Bathoeng* (London, 1895), 83–5.
70.   See J.C. Robinson's tribute in *Outward Bound*, 3, 31, 1923, 485–6; E.A. Maund, 'Khama and a Diamond', *The Times*, 5 March 1923, 13.
71.   'The greater proportion of his income he administers as national revenue, buying therewith waggons, ploughs, hunting apparatus, &c.' *C.2220*, 238. Khama's one vanity, of dress, was often remarked on: 'He is a Christian and dresses as if to walk in Rotten Row.' N. Macleod, 1875, cited in E.C. Tabler (ed.), *Trade and Travel in Early Barotseland* (London, 1963), 108.
72.   See Parsons, 'Khama III', 142, 240, 339, etc.
73.   *C.2220*, 72.
74.   In apologizing for sending only 105 labourers in 1877, Khama explained that they were 'a very few Veldt people', i.e. *malata*, 'serfs', and not 'from my own town'. *C.2220*, 76.
75.   C.E. Fripp, 'Recent Travels in Rhodesia and British Bechuanaland', *Journal of the Society of Arts*, 45, 1897, 519.
76.   Leonard, *Rhodesia*, 16.
77.   R. Churchill, *Men, Mines and Animals in South Africa* (London, 1893), 319.
78.   *C.7629, Annual Report on British Bechuanaland for 1893–4* (London, 1895), 4–7.
79.   *C.7944, Annual Report on British Bechuanaland for 1894–5* (London, 1896), 52ff.
80.   'King Khama Interviewed by a Lady', *Christian World*, 12 September 1895.
81.   C. van Onselen, 'Reactions to Rinderpest in Southern Africa, 1896–97', *Journal of African History*, 13, 1972, 473–88.
82.   Parsons, 'Khama III', 153.

83. Parsons, 'Khama III', 154; R.S. Godley, *Khaki and Blue* (London, 1935), 33.
84. Parsons, 'Khama III', 155*ff*.
85. *C.8650, Annual Report on British Bechuanaland for 1896 – 7* (London, 1898), 14.
86. *Diamond Fields Advertiser,* 10 October 1896.
87. Parsons, 'Khama III', 157 – 63.
88. London Missionary Society [henceforth LMS] Archives, School of Oriental and African Studies, University of London, South Africa In-Letters [all subsequent LMS letters cited are in this series], W.C. Willoughby to LMS, 4, 12 October 1896.
89. *African Review, 9,* 1896, 555.
90. Neil Parsons, 'Railways and Underdevelopment: The Bechuanaland Case, 1895 – 1908', *Botswana Notes and Records,* in press.
91. Khama Family Papers, Serowe, file 'Receipts and Accounts'.
92. *Cd.1897,* Transvaal, *Further Correspondence Regarding the Transvaal Labour Question* (London, 1904), 194.
93. Parsons, 'Khama III', 155*ff*.
94. Khama Family Papers, Serowe; P.M. Clark, *The Autobiography of An Old Drifter* (London, 1936), 141.
95. National Archives of Botswana, RC 4/14.
96. Parsons, 'Khama III', 190 – 3.
97. LMS Archives, H. Williams to LMS, 27 May 1899, 11 January 1900.
98. Parsons, 'Khama III', 190 – 3.
99. LMS Archives, E. Lloyd to LMS, 20 August 1909, [recalling *c*.1902].
100. Parsons, 'Khama III', 125 – 6, 409.
101. F. Wilson, 'Farming, 1866 – 1966', 127.
102. Holub, *Von der Capstadt,* 496 – 7.
103 A.C. Campbell and G. Child, 'The Impact of Man on the Environment of Botswana', *Botswana Notes and Records, 3,* 1971, 91 – 110.
104. See J. Ford, *The Role of the Trypanosomiases in African Ecology* (Oxford, 1971).
105. H.A. Fosbrooke, 'Land and Population', *Botswana Notes and Records, 3,* 1971, 184.
106. Lloyd, *Three Great African Chiefs,* 111; H.M. Hole, *The Passing of the Black Kings* (London, 1932), 271.
107. Parsons, 'Khama III', 212 – 21.
108. Parsons, 'Khama III', 228, 302.
109. P.S. Garlake, *The Ruins of Zimbabwe,* Historical Association of Zambia Pamphlet No. 4 (Lusaka, 1974), 25 – 8.
110. B. Ronan, *Forty South African Years* (London, 1923), 211; L.H. Gann, *A History of Northern Rhodesia* (London, 1964), 125 – 6; A.H. Croxton, *Railways of Rhodesia* (Newton Abbot, 1973), 60 – 1, 76 – 7, 110.
111. *Bechuanaland News,* 23 October 1897, 4.
112. Public Record Office, London, CO 879/552.
113. Parsons, 'Railways', in press.
114. Q. Hermans, 'Towards Budgetary Independence: A Review of Botswana's Financial History, 1900 to 1973', *Botswana Notes and Records, 6,* 1974, 90 – 106; W.M. Hailey, *Native Administration in the British African Territories, Part V: The High Commission Territories, Basutoland, The Bechuanaland Protectorate and Swaziland* (London, 1953), 207.
115. National Archives of Botswana, S.294/7.
116. LMS Archives, R.H. Lewis to LMS, 27 August 1918.
117. LMS Archives, A.E. Jennings to LMS, 28 January, 30 March 1904.
118. Parsons, 'Khama III', 229 – 97.
119. LMS Archives, 'Report by Mr. E.B. Sargant on Education in Bechuanaland Protectorate 1905', 38.
120. LMS Archives, A.E. Jennings to LMS, 28 January, 30 March 1904.
121. Parsons, 'Khama III', 325 – 30.

122. R.W. Thompson, 'The Outlook in South Africa', *Chronicle of the London Missionary Society, 12,* 134, 1903, 45.

123. *Cd. 1897,* 193.

124. Khama Family Papers, Serowe, In-Letters 1903–5, General Manager, Central South African Railways, to Khama, 16 May 1904. CSAR was the state railway company set up by the British to take over the railway system of the former South African Republic [Transvaal] and Orange Free State.

125. P. Robson, 'Economic Integration in Southern Africa', *Journal of Modern African Studies, 5,* 1967, 474. In 1965 the British authorities adjusted Bechuanaland's share to 0.30971 per cent at the expense of Basutoland's. South Africa's share remained unchanged until 1969.

126. M. Scott, *A Time to Speak* (London, 1958), 208–12.

127. Parsons, ' "Khama & Co." ', 383–408.

128. Scott, *A Time to Speak,* 209.

129. P. Jousse [*pseud.* 'Inquisitor'], *Khama the King: Truth about the Bechuanas* (Johannesburg, 1914), 23–4.

130. Parsons, 'Khama III', 332–3. The 1913 ban on labour recruitment north of 22°S, which bisects Khama's Country, was only made effective, though even then not fully, by South African immigration and pass legislation in 1921–3.

131. For one early labour migrant, 'His next ambition was to buy a bicycle. ... This made him take a contract in 1905 and he worked at a mine in Benoni, Eastern Transvaal. But even before he could buy one, his ambition switched to a higher ideal—education.' K. Lebotse, 'Profile of a Pioneer—Mpubuli Matenge', *Kutlwano, 10,* 7, 1971, 28–30.

132. Parsons, 'Khama III', 333–5.

133. Bechuanaland Protectorate, *Census* [Abstract] (Mafeking, 1921). Compare this with the total of 22,746 ploughs for the whole of Northern Rhodesia in 1950, and 9,046 for its Eastern Province as late as 1962. J.A. Hellen, *Rural Economic Development in Zambia, 1890–1964* (Munich, London, and New York, 1968), 131, 190.

134. Jousse, *Khama the King,* 40–1.

135. The restrictions were introduced to protect South African cattle-ranchers from competition in the High Commission Territories, and the colonial authorities were obliged to accept them under the threat of a total embargo from South Africa. The minimum weight restrictions discriminated directly against African cattle-owners, since it was normally only the well-capitalized European cattle-owner who could meet them. As Hertzog, the South African Prime Minister, noted with satisfaction in 1924, the restrictions 'will no doubt materially further restrict the development of these territories' [Protectorates]. S. Ettinger, 'South Africa's Weight Restrictions on Cattle Exports from Bechuanaland, 1924–41', *Botswana Notes and Records, 4,* 1972, 21–9, 23.

136. Parsons, 'Khama III', 329–30.

137. Ettinger, 'South Africa's', 21–9.

138. National Archives of Botswana, J.978A, Khama to High Commissioner, 28 March 1916.

139. National Archives of Botswana, S.29/2.

140. *Cmd. 4368, Financial and Economic Position of the Bechuanaland Protectorate: Report of the Commission appointed by the Secretary of State for Dominion Affairs March, 1933* (London, 1933), 18.

141. Parsons, ' "Khama & Co." ', 400–3.

142. National Archives of Botswana, J.978A, Khama to High Commissioner, 28 March 1916.

143. Neil Parsons, *The World of Khama,* Historical Association of Zambia Pamphlet No. 2 (Lusaka, 1972), 16, 28 n. 35.

144. Parsons, 'Khama III', 336, 339.

145. Khama Family Papers, Serowe, Out-Letters 1923.

146. National Archives of Botswana, B.P.33/163.

147. LMS Archives, Annual Reports, Serowe Church Report for 1922.

148. Until the 1930s, the Bechuanaland government failed to enforce a licensing tax on joint stock companies, which was liable under Proclamation No. 14 of 1897. The loss in revenue for 1933–4 was estimated to be £98,215, and the total loss to revenue may be reckoned between thirty and fifty times that amount. *Cmd. 4368*, 49–50; National Archives of Botswana, S.262/3. In 1924 a deputation of ten Ngwato headmen protested against a 'new system of protecting traders' by the government, 'to monopolise the trade in Native Territories and to do as they like for their own interests'. This was a reference to the restriction on new trading licences and possibly to the 1923 Credit Sales to Natives Proclamation. National Archives of Botswana, S.7/1/2.

149. E. Gluckmann, *The Tragedy of the Ababirwas* (Johannesburg, 1922), 1. 'Development' in this context usually referred to an expansion of white estates: see Minutes of annual European Advisory Council, Bechuanaland Protectorate. But Paul Jousse and other trading interests referred to white traders as 'the real developers of the country': Jousse, *Khama the King*, 25.

150. L. Barnes, *The New Boer War* (London, 1932), 145–8.

151. I. Schapera, *Migrant Labour and Tribal Life* (London, 1947); I. Schapera, 'Economic Conditions in a Bechuanaland Native Reserve' [Kgatla], *South African Journal of Science, 30,* 1933, 633–55.

152. See especially P.M. Landell-Mills, 'Rural Incomes and Urban Wage Rates', *Botswana Notes and Records, 2,* 1970, 79–84. Schapera did note evidence of labour migrants coming from 'poorer and socially inferior sections of the community' in the Tswana, Ngwato, and Ngwaketse Reserves, where Koba, Sarwa, Tswapong, and Kgalagadi 'inferiors' migrated in large numbers. Among the south-eastern Reserves, excepting the Ngwaketse, even members of chiefly families migrated to the mines. Schapera, *Migrant Labour*, 42.

153. *The Development of the Bechuanaland Economy* (London and Gaborone, 1965), 6.

154. W. Tordoff, 'Local Administration in Botswana', *Journal of Administration Overseas, 12,* 1973, 172—83 and *13,* 1974, 293—304; H.A. Fosbrooke, 'An Assessment of the Importance of Institutions and Institutional Framework in Development', *Botswana Notes and Records, 5,* 1973, 28.

155. Neil Parsons, 'Shots for a Black Republic? Simon Ratshosa and Botswana Nationalism', *African Affairs, 73,* 293, 1974, 449–58.

156. For example, the title group of L. Kuper, *An African Bourgeoisie* (New Haven, 1965). See also A. Sillery, *The Bechuanaland Protectorate* (Cape Town, 1952), 208. The Khama family now fits into a marital network embracing the Gaseitsiwe, Molema, Moroka, Mbelle, Plaatje, Msimang, and many other prominent families. It should not however be assumed that the 'new élite' always lived a life of secure petty bourgeois affluence: see J. Hermans, 'Victoria Namane', *Kutlwano, 14,* 11, 1974, 3–7.

157. National Archives of Botswana, S.204/8, 61–2, 102–3, 118.

158 Lloyd, *Three Great African Chiefs,* 82.

159. LMS Archives, Annual Reports, Serowe Church Report for 1922.

160. Schapera, *Migrant Labour*, 28–9, 34–5.

161. Schapera, *Migrant Labour*, 30–2.

162. Jousse, *Khama the King*, 23–4.

# CHAPTER 6

## The Agricultural History of Barotseland, 1840–1964

### LAUREL VAN HORN

### Introduction

Hellen, Ranger, Kay, and others have attempted to explain why, in Ranger's terms, the recent agricultural history of Zambia has been characterized by 'stagnation, crisis and failure'.[1] The causal factors they delineate explain in part what has occurred in Barotseland, now the Western Province, where a viable mixed economy based on agriculture, herding, and fishing was centred on the Zambezi flood plain. Acclaimed by Livingstone in 1853 as a 'fruitful' and 'fertile' valley where 'the people never lack abundance of food',[2] by 1947 the central area around Mongu, the Lozi capital, faced a severe seasonal shortage, and Senanga and Sesheke in the south were threatened by famine conditions. In 1965 Gluckman described the central plain itself as 'notorious even beyond its borders as almost a permanent famine area'.[3] Despite the growth of governmental expenditure on infrastructure and agriculture since independence, the province in 1973 was still importing 75 per cent of its maize requirements.[4]

My intention in this chapter is to examine what led to this extreme deterioration in food production. Of the factors which may explain the decline, many are specific to the area because of the uniqueness of its environment and of the social and governmental systems of the Lozi people. Even under colonial rule the situation of the Lozi was rather singular, in that Barotseland was granted a 'protectorate' status which permitted the Lozi for a time to maintain part of their former empire. The essential conflict, however, between a pre-colonial African imperialism and the British imperialism which sought to supplant it was a drama also acted out in other parts of the former Northern Rhodesia.

### The Lozi economy and agriculture before 1880

Throughout his writings on the Lozi, Gluckman stresses the close correlation between the environment of the flood plain and the type of agricultural production and social organization which developed there. What was to become the Lozi state had its simple beginnings when the Luyana people,[5] grassland cultivators from the north, migrated to the Bulozi flood plain early in the seventeenth century. Bringing with them a limited number of cattle, they settled almost

144

exclusively on mounds in the plain, from which they could have access to garden sites, grazing areas, and fishing sites. Except for the brief move out of the plain during the annual high water season, the Luyana settlements could be permanent because the fertility of gardens was restored by the floods and by the use of manure. From three dispersed sub-groups and a small population, the Luyana in time coalesced into a centralized state under one king, or Litunga. As population increased and mound sites became relatively more scarce, a hierarchical structure emerged based on the ownership of these valuable raised areas in the plain. Not only kinship groupings but also governmental organization revolved around possession of these sites. The Litunga owned by far the most land, which he could use to attract the greatest number of followers. His relatives (royalty) and councillors or indunas (elected from among the commoners) had the next largest landholdings. Access to political office was in general linked to mound ownership and in turn each titled position brought with it the use of a specific piece of land, as well as additional followers and tribute. From these bands of followers, who were dependent for their land and livelihood on more wealthy kinsmen and on the fledgling aristocracy, originated the *makolo* system. Organized into sectors, each headed by an induna at the capital, the Litunga's subjects could be ordered to provide labour for a certain project or to perform a specific task, such as salt production or ironworking. They could also be called up for military purposes.[6]

The environment of the flood plain thus helped to differentiate the Luyana from the surrounding groups of forest dwellers, whose unlimited lands precluded the development of such a hierarchy. The Luyana rulers used their organizational ability to mobilize men and resources under the *makolo* system to subjugate neighbours increasingly far afield. Since their arrival in the plain they had been at the centre of a barter system because their products—fish, cattle, and, later, maize—were unique to the area. In addition, because river routes converged on the plain, the forest peoples had tended to trade with the Luyana rather than with each other.[7] The Luyana were thus able to establish their dominance over this exchange system: the sixth Litunga, Ngombela, regularized the flow of tribute goods by placing lower-level indunas, *lindumeleti,* among the conquered peoples. Also, under the institution of *maketiso,* young men and women were sent at given intervals to serve in central Bulozi.[8]

These various types of tribute were to assume greater importance as agricultural methods in and around the flood plain became increasingly complex. At first Luyana cultivation encompassed few crops and few types of gardens. Early staples included finger millet, sorghum, and several varieties of tubers. These were supplemented in the eighteenth century by flint maize and sweet potatoes, both New World crops introduced into Angola.[9] When Livingstone reached the area in the 1850s, he also found sugar cane, Egyptian arum, two types of cassava, pumpkins, melons, beans, and groundnuts.[10] This growth in the variety of crops was paralleled by an increase in the types of gardens being prepared. The Kwanga at the plain edge near Mongu developed the use of drained margin gardens. Their techniques were later taken up by the Mbunda, who migrated from Angola to settle east of the plain in the early nineteenth century. The Mbunda themselves brought from the west a method of bush cultivation and two staples, cassava and bulrush millet. Gardens outside the floor of the plain were not adopted by the Luyana to any degree, however, until after the Kololo occupation of c. 1840–64. The Kololo were a group of Sotho people who migrated northwards as a result of the *Mfecane*. Many Luyana fled into exile in the north and north-west, and it was during this period that they became familiar with the techniques of bush cultivation and learned of the advantages of cassava. Following their return to the plain after the defeat of the Kololo, a number of Lozi (Luyana) who lacked mound sites moved permanently to the margin of the flood plain, from where they exploited sites in the outer plain and the bush. More commonly, households remained in the plain but extended their cultivation to the margin and beyond.[11] These additional gardens were insurance against early and high floods—the greatest hazards to Lozi agriculture—while cassava was also resistant to drought and locusts, and thrived in poor soils.

Because of this settlement at the plain edge and the use of margin and bush sites by those who remained transhumant, local demands for labour increased. A man who had already worked several types of garden sites within the plain, grazed his cattle in a number of dispersed areas, and fished with a variety of methods in numerous places, might now have additional gardens and at a greater distance. Because plots were small—usually a quarter to half an acre—travel time consumed a greater percentage of working hours. To rationalize production it became more common for a household to maintain two sets of dwellings, but this too required extra labour. These new types of gardens also tended to need more time-consuming and strenuous preparation and therefore more men. *Sishanjo* gardens, of a very fertile, waterlogged peat soil, required the digging of a criss-crossed network of drainage ditches; while in bush cultivation, where it was necessary to cover the soil with a fertile layer of ash, large quantities of branches and small trees had to be hacked down and piled into heaps. Because soil in the bush became rapidly depleted of nutrients, the clearing of new gardens was an annual task.

The indunas and royalty, who were now given holdings outside the plain commensurate to their status, felt most strongly the need for a greater number of dependants for labour. The men already living in the area, occupied as they were year-round with herding, fishing, and, increasingly, gardening, were not available to meet the shortage; nor was the tribute labour of outlying groups sufficient. Thus in the 1880s the scope of forced immigration, a practice begun by earlier Luyana kings, increased. Langworthy argues that because the labour of these serfs captured in Lozi raids was needed by the ruling class, the Lozi never engaged to any degree in the export slave trade to the west coast.[12]

The complexity of Lozi agriculture was thus made possible, not only by the cultural diversity of the peoples in the restricted area of the flood plain, but also by the development of the wider Lozi state, which, as it expanded, made use of the labour and resources of those it conquered. While Gluckman is at pains to show how tribute benefited the common man, it is clear that such an outcome was incidental. The intention of the Lozi aristocracy was to appropriate the surplus and potential surplus of peoples and classes weaker than themselves, and not to redistribute otherwise unobtainable goods. Without tribute, public works such as the canals dug by the Litungas Sipopa and Lewanika could not have been undertaken, nor could agriculture in Bulozi have become so developed.

In addition to the circulation of goods within the state through tribute, bartering, and blood-brotherhood exchange, trade with the Ovimbundu and the Portuguese had taken place since at least the 1820s. The Lozi offered mainly ivory and cattle in return for cloth, while their neighbours to the north-west traded beeswax and rubber. George Westbeech provided the Lozi with an important trade link to the south via Botswana for seventeen years (1871–88). Although this external trade was later to have a great impact on the Lozi economy, prior to 1880 it had little effect on the volume of local exchange or on the pattern of distribution of goods; the Litunga shared out trade goods between himself and the aristocracy much as he had tribute.[13]

## Lewanika and the empire to 1890

On coming to power in 1878, the Litunga Lewanika faced a number of problems, not the least of which was to ensure his own political survival. Under the Kololo the indunas had gained in influence in relation to the king: restoring his former status would prove no easy matter, and Lewanika was in fact temporarily overthrown in 1884. In order to reassert his political authority, Lewanika sought to control tribute and free labour, and to gain also a monopoly over external trade. The tribute system, which had continued during Kololo rule, had however declined in regularity and the subject peoples were now less willing to meet Lewanika's demands.[14] With, in addition, an increase in the number and scale of public projects, the burden on the people approached the point at which they would soon have baulked. Of this potential crisis Mainga writes:

> Those sections of the tribute and labour paying groups who still remained under undisputed Lozi control were reduced almost to a status of serfdom.... The Ma Subiya for instance found themselves charged increasingly with duties which included 'cultivating the great fields of excellent soil belonging to the king.... They are also charged with

transporting travellers' canoes above the rapids.' All these duties were apparently done without any form of privilege or compensation in return. The cost of sustaining the grandeur of the revived Lozi State was beginning to affect even the Lozi themselves.[15]

As in the past, the people's continued support of the government was bought at the expense of outside groups, such as the Ila in the east, who were raided for both slaves and cattle in 1882 and 1888. According to Westbeech, some 20,000 cattle were brought back to Bulozi from Ila and Toka country in 1882. This stock, as well as the new supply of labour, may have helped sweeten the mood of the people under the Litunga's immediate control and thus avert the crisis predicted by the missionary Coillard. The labour situation remained healthy for some time after the 1888 raid, since groups of Ila, from fear of further reprisals, voluntarily offered up both tribute and men.[16]

The empire, then, was expanding at the end of the nineteenth century and was thereby providing Lewanika with the means to undertake further development. Coillard makes several references to the Litunga's canal-building in 1894 and 1895: 'Thanks to the thousands of hands which they command . . . the canal . . . drains the marshes, and has changed them into fertile fields.' 'Canals are in fashion: Lewanika is making them, and Mokwae also, in four or five parts of the Valley at once.'[17] In reference to what he calls 'the great canal', Coillard comments, 'The king had summoned the whole nation. Thousands of men worked at it for months and months. It was the same the following year, and yet it is not finished.'[18] He also takes note of the bountiful and varied tribute flowing into the capital. Lewanika was thus taking full advantage of the resources tradition-ally available to him. Cognizant of developments to the south, he now sought to maximize as well the benefit to himself and his class of the growing white presence.

Lewanika's strategy towards the Europeans seems to have been guided first by the insecurity of his position within Barotseland and second by the perceived threat of the Ndebele to the south and the Portuguese to the west. In seeking alliance with the whites, the Litunga was following the lead of Khama, with whom he was in direct correspondence, and whose country had become a British protect-orate in 1885 at his own request. It was Khama also who first sent Coillard to Barotseland in 1878.[19] Lewanika quickly perceived the advantages of missionaries such as Coillard and Arnot: first as diplomats, and secondly as repositories of European technology and skills, Arnot, a Plymouth Brethren missionary, found himself in 1882 teaching the three 'R's to a few royal sons—the fourth 'R', religion, being expressly forbidden[20]—while Coillard observed: 'Lewanika would gladly overwhelm us with apprentices, grown-up men, whom he would like to see learning in a couple of months or so to accomplish every possible handicraft of the whites.'[21]

Lewanika's aims in seeking British protectorate status can be seen in the terms of the Lochner Concession, which he granted to the British South Africa Company in 1890, more particularly in the copy given to Lewanika, which read:

> The Company further agrees that it will... aid and assist in... the education and civilization of the native subjects of the King, by the establishment, maintenance and endowment of such churches, schools and trading stations as may be from time to time mutually agreed upon by the King and the Resident.

The Litunga wanted modernization, but of a kind of his own choosing which would maintain the political and economic *status quo*. In the official copy, however, the final clause was deleted. Likewise, while Lewanika's copy gave assurance that his internal authority would not be broached—'The Company shall not be allowed or obliged to interfere in any matter concerning the King's power and authority over any of his own subjects'—the official document did not include the crucial word 'allowed'. In addition, the concession promised protection from external attack and £2,000 per annum in return for the mineral rights.[22] What must have seemed a personal triumph to Lewanika in 1890 was soon proved to be a well-executed swindle. No money was forthcoming for seven years, after which the BSA Company reduced its payment to £850;[23] no schools or 'industrial establishments' (promised in the official concession) were ever created with Company money; and the powers of the Litunga and his Kuta, council, were slapped down one by one by subsequent colonial legislation.

## The Lozi economy to 1915: dislocation and stimulation

The arrival of Europeans and the gradual incorporation of the Lozi economy into their economic system had a variety of effects, sometimes contradictory, upon land and labour in Barotseland. Alongside the initial stimulation provided by new markets, trade goods, and opportunities for wage employment, was laid the foundation for later economic stagnation. Even during this early period of growth, a range of positive and negative effects was evident. Wage labour and the growth of markets had a radically different impact on the indunas and royalty than on the Lozi commoners, on the Lozi than on the outlying subject peoples. For this reason, there was a varied response to the advent of white rule, the indunas fearing and resisting it most vigorously, and the serfs welcoming it as a salvation. On the arrival of Coryndon, the first British Resident, in 1897, the latter poured into the capital expecting an emancipation proclamation.[24] Ironically, it was the ruling class which reaped the greatest benefit prior to 1915, while the serfs, pressured by the hut tax—but also drawn by the promise of trade goods—died at an appalling rate in the mines of South Africa and Southern Rhodesia.[25]

In general, the trend during the colonial period was towards a widening the gap between the Lozi élite and commoners, and between the Lozi and the other peoples of Barotseland.

As in Bembaland, labour acquired new value and traditional systems of kinship labour assistance and political tribute labour were undermined. Lewanika recognized this danger, and advised Coillard in the 1880s not to pay the local people for porterage around the Ngonye Falls, as it would set a bad precedent.[26] But with increasing trade and the settlement of Coillard and other whites along the plain margin, the trend was unavoidable. While indunas and others of the cattle-holding class were able to raise the money to pay for services (and they were affected only after 1906, when slave labour was abolished), the average mound-owner could not, and was often forced to cut back on labour requirements. For this reason, some of the households with two sets of dwellings now moved permanently to the margin. Another possible result of the increased value of labour was the 'insurrection amongst the slaves of Sesheke against their chiefs' reported in October 1893. As mentioned earlier, the Lozi serf was bearing an increasing share of the burden of state development; if he now perceived that his poorly rewarded efforts could command material benefits on an open market, he might well have been motivated to revolt. Lewanika was forced to decree shortly thereafter that true Lozi could no longer be enslaved.[27]

Two other incidental developments also sped the decline of the tribute labour system. As with the Bemba and Ngoni of North-Eastern Rhodesia, the imposition of what Allan terms 'the peace of the suzerain powers'[28] spelled an end to raiding, although the immediate effect on the Lozi was not so drastic. Neither the Bemba nor the Ngoni were self-sufficient in agriculture: each depended on raids and the threat of violence to extract agricultural surpluses from their neighbours. The captives the Bemba took were not employed to develop their agricultural system, but were exchanged for goods with slave traders, while the Ngoni placed more captives in their military system than on the land. Thus, with the exception of the cattle captured by the Ngoni, most of the benefits these two groups derived from raiding came to an abrupt halt when the raiding itself ended. For the Lozi though, who used captive labour to build their state and incorporated these foreigners to a greater degree than did the Ngoni into their society, a significant internal source of labour remained available after the external one had been cut off. These people could not be called on indefinitely however. An additional setback for the aristocracy was the loss of approximately 52,000 sq. km of territory west of the Zambezi to the Portuguese in 1905. With further expansion and raiding closed to them, this reduction of the Lozi area of tributary serfdom was a severe blow.

While the simple interaction of the Lozi and capitalist economies would in time have led to the utter collapse of the tribute and serf labour system, the BSA Company was determined to expedite the process. Although a good number of Barotseland residents had been migrating to the Southern Rhodesian mines, many before the turn of the century,[29] the Company was not satisfied with the extent of the flow. Nor was it pleased with the amount of hut tax being collected. Slave labour, the Company reasoned, must be at fault: a man would be loath to undertake paid employment if his master was going to take his wages, nor could he travel south if he was required to work or fulfil other obligations within Barotseland. The Company, therefore, forced Lewanika in 1906 to issue his 'Proclamation of the Abolition of Slavery'. While the Litunga retained the right to twelve days of tribute labour from each subject for his own personal use, as well as for public works, the indunas and headmen were to utilize this labour only 'for the exclusive benefit of the Community or Kraal'.[30] For cultivating their own fields they would either have to hire labour or rely on dependants. In addition, a later ruling stipulated that a man could be required to work only a *total* of twelve days, the Litunga having the first call on his services.[31] The indunas, of course, felt that Lewanika had betrayed their interests, as indeed he had. By 1905, the Litunga's internal support had dwindled to such a degree that he remained in power only by the Company's backing. Recognizing this, he had no choice but to acquiesce in its demands.

In that year, in fact, unrest had reached such a level that the Company sent in forty police and a Maxim gun to Lealui in order to reinforce Lewanika's authority.[32] During the crisis, the Company took advantage of the Litunga's dependence to force him to agree to extend the ten shillings' hut tax, collected since 1904 in the Batoka and Falls districts, to his territory outside the Barotse valley in 1905 and to the valley itself the following year.[33] Lewanika was to receive 10 per cent of the tax: £1,200 payable to himself and the indunas, and the remainder to be placed in a 'development fund' for the Barotse people. With the decline of tribute following close on the imposition of the hut tax, and with the abolition of domestic slavery shortly thereafter, the indunas' share of the tax, in particular, proved grossly inadequate. Only by violating the Proclamation of 1906 or by selling their cattle could they obtain sufficient labour to cultivate their former acreages.

The end of free labour and the levying of the hut tax in place of tribute were not in themselves bad. But because the Lozi lacked the means to substitute an employer—employee relationship for the master—servant one, and because there were few opportunities available to earn one's hut tax within Barotseland, the economic system was destroyed rather than transformed. This process was delayed until after 1915 however.

Like labour, agricultural products had by the turn of the century begun to take on new value. Food could now be exchanged for trade goods such as cloth and beads. With the settlement of missionaries, administrators and traders along the plain margin, a constant market for fruit and vegetables opened up. By 1907 there were already fifty-seven whites around Mongu, the colonial headquarters.[34] From seeds imported by the missionaries, the local people were offering for sale in 1910–11 '1. Potatoes., Tomatoes., Cabbages., Lettuce., Onions., Turnips. 2. Pineapples., Pau-paus., Bananas., Peaches (very few)'.[35] There is no evidence that the indunas or royalty cornered this market, although, with larger holdings, they were in a better position to exploit it. The tendency to establish permanent dwellings at the margin, encouraged by population growth and labour considerations, was given new impetus by this market for garden crops. Fish, cattle, game (scarce by 1906), maize, and milk could also be traded or sold. With the latter, some interesting issues arose. The use of milk, which formerly had been the prerogative of the herder, now reverted to the cattle-owner, who wanted to realize this new possibility for profit himself. As labour became more expensive and thus more scarce for tasks like herding, especially after the complete abolition of tribute labour in 1925, the owner was in some cases forced to allow the herder the use of the milk. The understanding between the two took on more the nature of a contract.

The sale of milk provides an interesting example of how an agricultural system can be distorted by the introduction of a market for a specific product. Because milk which would once have gone to the calves could now be sold to pay, for example, a man's hut tax, an increasing number of calves either starved to death or, in a weakened condition, succumbed more easily to disease. The cows were also adversely affected during the flood season because they were now kept near to Mongu, the market, where grazing was poor. A short-term profit was thus gained at the expense of a greater long-term one. By contrast, in earlier trade with the Ovimbundu, a previous Litunga had ruled that only oxen could be exported from Barotseland, so that breeding stock would not be depleted.[36] The use of such foresight by the Lozi, pressured as they now were by European tax demands, became less and less possible.

A considerable market in grain, which opened up after 1903, when the Rhodesia Native Labour Bureau became active in the area, was supplied with maize meal from the flood plain and cassava meal from the bush surrounding the plain and from Balovale on the upper Zambezi.[37] After 1912, supplies were required not only for outgoing labour recruits but also for the employees of the Zambezi Sawmills. Although they may have been forced to reduce the types of crops under cultivation and concentrate on maize production, before 1915 the Lozi, and in particular the ruling class, could command enough labour to meet the demand for grain. Labour migration during this period affected mainly the subject peoples; once it included the Lozi as well, their ability to produce a grain surplus would obviously be impaired.

More important economically to the Lozi than the sale of grain was that of cattle. From Westbeech's early trade in cattle and guns, the business had grown in leaps and bounds. The Lozi, who had themselves imported cattle from the west, parted willingly with their beasts and welcomed the increased trade. Barotseland escaped the brunt of the 1896 rinderpest disease, and was able to supply breeding stock to replenish the devastated herds in Southern Rhodesia and in Khama's Country.[38] That cattle had increased in immediate economic importance to the Lozi royalty can be seen in Lewanika's efforts to brand his herds, reported in 1907.[39] According to Gluckman, his attempt to wrest control of his cattle from the people failed and 'almost precipitated a rebellion'. The Litunga Yeta, however, later succeeded where his father had failed.[40] There were 7,712 cattle sold in 1909–10, 8,108 in 1910–11 and 7,578 in 1911–12 at prices in the latter year of £1 to £8 for oxen, £2 10s to £4 10s for cows, and £2 to £3 for heifers, all above the average for the period.[41] The Bechuanaland Protectorate in the same year was exporting cattle to Johannesburg at £5 per head.[42] With cattle, as with any other commodity, the Lozi were disadvantaged because of their extreme distance from the market. Despite low prices, the sale of cattle did allow the indunas and royalty to pay their taxes and to hire labour. At a minimum per head of £2, the cattle sold in 1911–12 would have brought in £15,156, or about 85 per cent of the total revenue of Barotseland for that year.

## Lewanika and modernization

While commoners as well as indunas and royalty readily took advantage of the new opportunities for profit introduced by the Europeans, it was Lewanika himself, controlling as he did the bulk of the country's resources, who attempted the most ambitious profit-making schemes. These were intended not only to maximize his own wealth and that of the people around him, but also to make Barotseland economically viable within the capitalist economy. Ranger comments that 'as Lewanika came to understand more about the forces at work in the new Africa, so he came to set himself the goal of modernizing Barotseland, under the shelter of British protection and with the assistance of "those who understood the notion of progress", so that it could eventually stand on its own feet.'[43] Lewanika seems to have realized shortly after the turn of the century that neither the BSA Company nor the Paris Missionary Society were likely to be agents for modernization in Barotseland. With the latter he expressed his disappointment as follows: 'What are you good for then? What benefits do you bring us? What have I to do with a bible which gives me neither rifles nor powder, sugar, tea nor coffee, nor artisans to work for me—none of the advantages I had hoped for?'[44] In response to his complaint in 1906 that the BSA Company had carried out none of the obligations agreed to in the 1900 Coryndon Concession (which replaced the earlier Lochner Concession), the Company replied that it had established a postal service, constructed roads, and built 600 km of railway and telegraph lines.[45] That the

railway ran east of the Kafue river and completely bypassed
Barotseland, while clearly not an issue in the Company's mind, may
well have been the final blow to Lewanika's hopes for Company
assistance.

Even before 1906 though, the Litunga had seen the need to be ·
self-reliant. The Paris Missionary Society (PMS) having failed to meet
his educational demands, Lewanika turned in 1904 to Willie
Mokalapa, who had broken with the staid French mission and
founded a local branch of the African Methodist Episcopal Church.
Based in the black community in South Africa, the AME Church was
also attractive in that it promised to teach Lozi youths 'to read, write
and speak English in two or three months',[46] as well as to provide a
better and more diverse technical education. Determined to set up a
wagon road between Lealui and Kazungula, and having had no
response to his proposal from the district commissioner, Lewanika
asked Mokalapa to assist him. With £700 and instructions to buy '14
waggons, 3 or 4 boats, 3 carriages and a scotch cart', Willie set off for
Cape Town, where he was swindled out of the entire sum by
unscrupulous businessmen. The AME Church mission school closed
down in 1905 for lack of funds. While a humiliating and financially
disastrous episode for Lewanika himself, it did at least move the
administration to set up the Barotse National School in 1906. In
addition to this school, which was financed entirely by the Litunga's
share of the hut tax, the PMS also began to expand its school system,
using its own funds.[47]

Another transport scheme which Lewanika attempted to establish,
this time under a man named Simpson, also ended badly. The annual
report for 1911–12 mentioned that it had become a 'hopeless muddle'
and had finally come to an end. The main reason for Lewanika
wanting to establish a direct and inexpensive route to Livingstone
town was that he wished to market Lozi produce there. According to
Ranger, he was 'clamouring' to the administration in 1905 for
'experienced horticulturalists and gardeners to train Lozis in improved agricultural techniques', for 'high quality cotton, tobacco and
rice seed', and for 'good bulls and fowls to improve Lozi stock'.
Lewanika did realize his plan to raise fruit and vegetables for sale in
Livingstone, but how much of a success or failure it was is difficult to
determine. In his essay 'Lozi Land Tenure', Gluckman refers twice to
Lewanika's vegetable schemes. In the first instance he states that 'at
Sicili and Masese in the Sesheke District, Lewanika drained the river
valleys to provide gardens whose crops he sold'. His second
comment is more detailed:

> The paramounts *have* sold crops, on a large scale: Lewanika drained a
> river-valley in Sesheke District especially to provide gardens where he
> could grow crops to sell to a recruiting bureau. I am told he realized about
> £30 p.a. thus. But he gave part of the improved land to settling the
> labourers who drained the valley and worked his gardens.[48]

Ranger on the other hand, without providing any details, says 'Lewanika's agricultural enterprises failed through lack of support and because of poor communications'.[49] Whatever their outcome, Lewanika remained interested in agricultural development. It was reported in 1912 that rye wheat was being grown for him in two or three places in Mongu and Mankoya districts.[50] Six months before his death in 1916, he was negotiating through the Secretary for Native Affairs the purchase of two ploughs, one a three-furrow type and the other a three-blade Canadian disc plough costing £30.[51] In a letter to the resident magistrate in June 1915, Lewanika mentioned, with regard to two Ndebele ploughmen, that he had a sufficient number of his own; he must therefore have been using ploughs before this date. He also asked the R/M to notify him if he found 'a native gardener with knowledge of fruit and cabbage growing'.[52] Given this information, and the fact that in 1915 Lewanika was making money from transport wagons at Livingstone, it is probable that he was still marketing crops.[53] But, limited in scope and hampered by transport costs, Lewanika's vegetable scheme was no solution to Barotseland's larger economic problems. There is no evidence to suggest that it even continued under Yeta.

Lewanika's most valuable contribution to the development of agriculture in Barotseland was the digging of canals. Not only did they drain and make usable the most fertile soils available to the Lozi, but they also reduced the time and effort needed to transport crops to market. Equally important, the canals lowered the height of the flood and therefore its duration. Crops in the plain had barely enough time to mature between floods: any increase in the peak of the flood waters, and thereby in the length of time it took the flood to fall, might shorten their growing season and increase the probability that they would be drowned before they could be harvested. The canal digging observed by Coillard in the 1890s was continued by Lewanika beyond the turn of the century. In 1907 the D/C Barotse remarked that the largest of the canals, soon to be completed, would 'lead the water of the Leuna to join with that of the Namitome and enable boats to pass for twenty miles on the Eastern edge of the plain'.[54] After this time, however, it became increasingly difficult for even the Litunga to raise the numbers of labourers required for such projects.

During the period 1912–15 the Lozi economy was in a relatively strong position. The hut tax was yielding around £17,000 per annum, most of which was being earned locally through the sale of cattle. It was estimated that the herd now numbered about 120,000, though Lewanika refused to allow any official census to be taken. Slightly more than 2,000 people were employed within Barotseland while an estimated 8,000, roughly 29 per cent of the taxable males, found employment elsewhere. On labour migration the 1912–13 annual report commented, 'The Barotse natives do not go to work much they are too well off.' Indeed, although Lealui district had among the lowest number of migrants, it paid over one-third of the total tax for

Barotseland. The report went on to note that labour agents were
devoting their attention to greater effect to 'other tribes in the
different districts'. The number of traders had more than doubled
from the 1906 level to thirty-two in 1912, and African hawkers were
also on the increase. Of the twenty-eight stores doing business in
1912, most were concentrated in the area of the flood plain, although
a few more were located farther afield as labour migrants brought
money to outlying areas.[55]

## The collapse of 1915—16

In 1915 the economic self-reliance of the Lozi collapsed abruptly. An
epidemic of bovine pleuro-pneumonia reduced the herd to about
70,000, none of which could be sold outside the province after April.
This embargo, which remained in force until 1947, utterly destroyed
the basis of the Lozi economy. The number of cattle sold plummeted
from 6,346 in 1914—15 to 106 in 1915—16. The hut tax likewise fell
from £16,143 to £8,721. As the Resident Magistrate aptly commented,
the year was 'a very heavy one for the Barotse nation'. Foot and
mouth disease closed down the trade in hides. There was no flood at
all, the drought affecting the entire province. Food was most scarce in
Sesheke, where it was said that men had 'gone to look for food, rather
than tax'. In February 1916, Lewanika died. And just to add to the
general hardship, the colonial authorities demanded 2,000 carriers for
the war front in the Luapula. The annual report noted that the
situation 'has deeply affected the life of the natives around our
Station, as most of them have been compelled to leave their homes
and seek work in the South, in order to get money for their tax and for
their personal needs . . . even small boys have, in some instances, left
the country and deserted school to look for work.' It commented
further on the decrease in local employment: 'The openings for labour
have decreased very considerably owing to stoppage of the cattle
trade. I estimate that approximately 1000 natives cannot now find
work owing to this reason, these boys were previously engaged as
cattle herders, paddlers and carriers, store boys, and their services
are now dispensed with.'[56] In addition to the eight trading stores that
were put out of business, a transport service employing more than a
hundred men closed down. Thus, although it was the Lozi aristocracy
which lost the most in absolute terms because of the epidemic, the
Lozi commoner perhaps lost more because he had less to lose: it was
he who was forced to become a migrant labourer.

The number recruited by the Rhodesia Native Labour Bureau
(RNLB), 1,838, although trebled from the previous year, can only be
a small fraction of the total number which left Barotseland in search of
work. The breakdown by district is revealing, though. The increase in
the number recruited in the three districts in the flood plain and
Sesheke was 1,143, while that in the two non-cattle-owning districts
was only 103. Dependent as the agricultural system of Barotseland

was on as many hands as could be found, this beginning of a mass labour exodus could point only to its decline.

By 1917 the BSA Company was satisfied at the trend of events in Barotseland. Not only did it have Lozi labour for the mines and farms of Southern Rhodesia, but the hut tax had risen again to £16,138, just slightly short of the 1914–15 level. In the tax the annual report commented, 'very satisfactory when one takes into consideration . . . the cattle trade has been closed, and is due to the fact that the Barotse natives have turned out to work in large numbers for the first time'. The RNLB took 1,500 recruits in 1916–17, while the administration took 2,500 as war carriers, 1,000 less than it requested. Also recruiting in Barotseland was a representative of the Katanga mines, where the term of contract was a popular six months. Of the 2,300 who signed on, 500 deserted on hearing of or experiencing inhumane conditions in the compounds, and 130 died. A number of other repatriates were in such poor physical condition that they died after returning home. Whether labour migrants died or decided not to return, Barotseland's loss of human resources was often a permanent one.

Within Barotseland the white man's business was once again doing very well, largely because a system of deferred pay had been worked out with the RNLB and Robert Williams & Co. recruiting for Katanga. Twenty-eight stores were again open, the 'local natives . . . slowly realising the benefits that accrue to them by going out to work'.[57] While the specialized crafts practised by the mélange of peoples in Barotseland were never supplanted by trade goods to the same degree as in other parts of Zambia, the tendency was for the people to enter more into unequal and disadvantageous trade with the Europeans to the detriment of local exchange and industry. This was especially true after tribute was abolished, not only because craftsmen no longer had to make a certain number of items, but also because the subject peoples no longer had to provide the raw materials which the craftsmen required. Thus it was reported from Sesheke in 1928 that Totela ironworking was dying out because ore was no longer being sent from Nalolo.[58]

## Yeta and self-interest: the mid–1920s

One wish expressed time and time again by Lewanika and, after 1916, by his son Yeta III, was for Barotseland to come under the direct rule of the British Crown. Because the BSA Company was a commercial concern interested above all in maximizing its profits, it had done its best to break the grip of the Lozi ruling class on its subject peoples. The Lozi hope was that under a benevolent and economically disinterested government, 'they could hope to see the traditional rights and powers of the Lozi ruling class restored'.[59] When direct Crown rule did come in 1924, rather than regaining the unlimited free labour they had once enjoyed, the aristocracy lost their remaining twelve days of tribute labour. In its stead, the British administration offered the Litunga £500 per annum and the indunas £2,000. It also bought out for £1,000 the Litunga's share of the game licences and ivory outside the reserved area. In selling its remaining privileges, the ruling class had resigned itself to the idea that 'affluence would have to compensate for real power. Gradually but perceptibly over the next several years, incessant demands for more money for the ruling class came to replace those for modernizing Barotseland and reviving the authority of its elite therein.'[60] Rather than attempting to raise money from his considerable landholdings as his father had done, Yeta and the head indunas relied more and more for their living on concessions from the administration. The lesser indunas, however, could do little more with their subsidies than pay their hut tax. For fifty-five indunas in Kalabo district in 1926, the total subsidy was £80.[61] Although this was raised in 1928 to £223 for fifty-one indunas,[62] it was hardly adequate compensation for the tribute labour lost. It is little wonder that the indunas began to go on tour seeking fines in matrimonial cases.[63]

In giving up completely their right to raise labour for public works, the indunas and the Litunga effectively renounced all control over modernization. Yeta in his early years of rule had continued the building of new canals and the maintenance of older ones. In 1924 this essential work largely came to an end, either from mismanagement of funds or from a growing lack of concern. The canal at Lealui had become 'dangerously dirty' by 1926, while the others were 'silted a great deal'. Yet Yeta would contribute only £50 and the administration £100.[64] Except for maintenance work on this meaningless kind of level, the canals remained neglected and in many cases unusable until the late 1940s, when the administration did clear some of the channels. It was only then that the British recognized their importance even to subsistence agriculture.

Labour migration increased considerably after 1917: the report for 1924–5 described many villages as having 'no able-bodied men in them'. The RNLB recruited 4,719 on contract, while most of the men from Lealui, Mankoya, and Nalolo went out on their own. The effects on agriculture of the emigration would have been even more severe but for a massive immigration of 'Wiko' from Angola, starting in 1919 and continuing at a significant rate until 1934. As well as introducing bush cultivation to the plain dwellers for the first time on a large scale, they provided a cheap source of labour of particular benefit to the indunas. Wages were generally 5s per month, and the immigrants 'usually undertake casual employment merely for their food during the first year or so after their arrival'.[65] This was long enough, in other words, for their first crop of cassava to mature. During this period the indunas were also able to derive some profit from the sale of cattle to Angola through a number of local traders. But the traders preferred to pay in goods rather than cash, and during the 1930s, when it became much harder to earn one's hut tax locally, conflict over this issue grew quite heated, though the administration never intervened in the Lozi interest.

Under Colonial Office rule, as under the BSA Company, the people got very little in return for their money. Although the total revenue in Barotseland in 1925–6 was £22,083, the administration's expenditure was only £3,839.[66] Hall, the resident magistrate, who conducted an investigation into the economic resources of Barotseland in 1927, encountered the following criticism of governmental efforts:

> Since the Crown Government has succeeded the Chartered Company, we have seen no improvement worth mentioning. We hear no one speak of a railway to Barotseland or of cheaper transport. We have seen no work undertaken for the benefit of the country, or to help the people to earn money without going far away from their homes. What is our good trying to improve or increase the produce of our gardens? . . . Transport is so expensive that it does not pay to send anything to Livingstone for sale. Why should the government not help to transport our produce to Livingstone?[67]

The answer appeared in the Northern Rhodesian annual report on native affairs two years later, when it was explained very matter of factly that 'The Territory may be divided roughly into three zones: the mining areas, the farming areas and the labour supply areas.'[68] Barotseland, the Luapula, and various other backwaters would remain undeveloped so that they could continue to supply manpower to the more favoured areas. But the Barotse people were also providing some of the capital for the development of such areas. The revenue for Barotseland in 1929 was £26,601, the highest in the whole country; the second, Batoka, falling £1,600 short of this total. Under a quarter of the money raised locally was actually spent on administering and 'developing' Barotseland. If Yeta and the ruling class conceived of the masses, in the words of resident magistrate Hall, as just 'cattle whom they are no longer allowed to milk', they were merely following the British lead.

## The decline in agricultural production, I: the 1930s

The period from 1930 to 1937 was a terribly demoralizing one for the Lozi people. Although this time it was the capitalist economy which collapsed, the Barotse peoples had become sufficiently dependent on wage-labour to suffer the shock as well. What little had been rebuilt of local industries was again levelled by a series of natural disasters. Caplan describes the period thus:

> paid employment both in Barotseland and abroad became increasingly scarce—the recruiting agencies shut their doors in 1932—while floods, drought and locusts destroyed four successive crops, and pleuro-pneumonia, anthrax and foot-and-mouth disease terminated the remnants of the cattle trade and the small export trade in skins. Famine,

unemployment, and imprisonment or compulsory menial labour for non-payment of the poll tax characterized the life of the average inhabitant of Barotseland during most of the decade.[69]

In 1937 there were still 4,437 such tax-relief labourers, though this was a drop of 3,000 from the previous year.[70]

After 1935, when employment outside Barotseland again opened up, the rate of labour migration from the flood plain reached new heights. Government estimates of population and migration at the time were so haphazard that accurate calculations are impossible. The official figure of able-bodied male absentees was 45 per cent in 1935;[71] Gluckman and Peters computed a figure of 38 per cent for 1938. Mongu and Sesheke districts had the highest percentage of absentees, with Balovale among the lowest. This was because the people of Balovale were able to capitalize on the deficit of meal in the flood plain proper, especially around Lealui. Without the population pressures facing the Lozi, the Lunda were able to cultivate extensive bush gardens of cassava, which they then transported to the plain by canoe. In 1937 the cassava crop was said to have exceeded 20,000 tonnes, some 50 of which were exported outside the district.[72]

In Barotseland the women who remained on the land could cultivate the gardens in the plain, but they did not plough, prepare bush gardens for planting, or dig drainage ditches. With a growing number of men of the village away, they needed to cultivate less land, but at the same time, because of the scarcity of male labour, the women wanted to be assured that all their crops would survive. Crops normally grown in the plain, and which could easily be destroyed by flooding, were increasingly abandoned in favour of cassava, which had found widespread acceptance during the locust invasions, and was cultivated in the forest near the plain. The problem of finding labour to cut trees was solved, according to Gluckman, by the women calling the local men together to work, which was followed by a beer drink. As a result of the influx of 'Wiko', who traditionally cultivated such *matema* gardens, and of the Lozi substitution of bush for plain and *sishanjo* gardens, Trapnell and Clothier found in 1937 that the forests around the plain were suffering serious damage. Rather than shifting to a new site after five years of cultivation and allowing the soil a long period of regeneration, the people, because of the scarcity of land, were recultivating after four to seven years. Although the land would get a long period of rest after an additional two to five years of use, this system led to more permanent destruction of the bush and greater soil depletion.[73]

That *sishanjo* gardens, whose cultivation did not involve more risk, should decline in number was perhaps due to the amount of labour required for their drainage. Hermitte submits, however, that there were enough men to dig the small feeder ditches, especially since fewer gardens were needed to sustain the smaller remaining population. He also discounts the seriousness of the effect that the deterioration of the larger state canals was having on seepage soils.[74] But, given the declining productivity of *matema* gardens, one must ask why the Lozi were not employing these fertile seepage areas to their full potential. I would argue that it was because *sishanjo* gardens did require larger inputs of male labour, which were no longer available. Trapnell and Clothier also noted that *sitapa* gardens were not being cultivated to the extent that they should have been. Located in abandoned watercourses along the Zambezi, they were very susceptible to flooding: Peters estimated that an average 20 per cent of the crops in *sitapa* gardens were lost each year.[75] With the use of the plough, however, a larger expanse of ground could be prepared more quickly and therefore assure the maximum growing season. Although ploughs were relatively scarce during the 1930s, their owners often enhanced their investment by hiring them out. It would have been possible for a woman to hire both a plough and a ploughman, though such contracts were not legally enforceable.[76] These *sitapa* gardens though, despite their fertility and ease of preparation, were a great risk, proportionately greater now that labour was more scarce. The Lozi were probably rather more cautious also, having been through several famine periods in the previous twenty years. But in minimizing risk, they also minimized profit.

The Pim Report of 1938 estimated that while the current tax demand was for £25,000, the amount of revenue which could be derived from within Barotseland was only £4,400. With so few opportunities for wage-employment at home, the Lozi people had little choice but to go out to work in ever-increasing numbers. An agreement reached in 1936 granted the Witwatersrand Native Labour Association the right to recruit 3,500 men per annum for the South African gold mines.[77] A larger number were now moving to the Copperbelt, where a decade earlier only those from Balovale had made a significant showing.

## The decline in agricultural production, II: the 1940s

Gluckman and Peters are the main sources on the decline in food production in Barotseland during the 1940s, while Hermitte's recent thesis sheds new light on the situation. Until this period, although the amount of surplus produced locally had declined as labour migration increased, and although the staple cassava had come to occupy a greater portion of the Lozi diet, the people were in general able to grow enough to feed themselves. It is true that a significant amount of cassava was being brought down the Zambezi from Balovale, but perhaps an equal amount was being consumed by labour migrants and other rationed employees, as well as by recent repatriates. The Lozi were also producing for the local European market. With about 40 per cent of the taxable males away, Lozi agriculture was able to hold its own, and even to expand in a few isolated cases.[78]

Gluckman reports that in 1940 there was 'an abundance of grain, tubers, fish, milk, meat, chickens and eggs, wild-fowl, vegetables, and fruits'. In 1942, when he returned to the plain, he found shortages, which by 1947 had become severe.[79] Because labour migration had increased from 38 to 50 per cent during the course of the decade, Gluckman hypothesized that the lack of male labour had passed the critical point and was the main causal factor behind the drop in food production. Indeed, the ranks of the migrant labourers had been swelled by the numbers sent off to aid in the war effort, and by those who had gone to the Copperbelt, where the total number of Africans in employment leapt from approximately 23,000 in 1938 to 33,000 in 1948.[80] In 1947 an estimated 14,264 Barotse migrants had left the country, mostly for Southern Rhodesia and South Africa, while some 19,483 were employed elsewhere in Northern Rhodesia.[81]

Unlike Gluckman, Hermitte attributes the sharp decline in food production to a series of bad floods which destroyed crops on the margin as well as in the plain.[82] Coming at a time when the overcrowded and overworked land in the vicinity of the plain had already made the profitability of cash cropping a tenuous affair, these severe floods impelled the Lozi to seek a more secure return for their efforts through labour migration. Thus the decline in the productivity of agriculture led to a sharp increase in migrant labour, and not vice versa. However, this additional withdrawal of labour in turn led to a further deterioration in Lozi agriculture and pastoralism.

The colonial government, which since the Pim Report of 1938 had taken a more active concern in Barotseland, was shocked and puzzled by the drop in agricultural production among the Lozi, who had once provided one of the best examples of good native nutrition. In 1948 the administration sent in David Peters, Barotseland's first agricultural officer, to determine what had happened to the once-viable system. Peters found that there were only twelve to sixteen able-bodied men for each hundred residents in the average Lozi village, and that Lozi agriculture had been unable to adapt to such a drastic reduction in labour. He commented: 'like all other tribes, they have not proved capable of modifying their agriculture to take account of newly induced conditions such as the fall in rural male population, nor have they been able to provide for new wants while at the same time conserving the natural resources upon which agriculture is based.'[83]

While population density for Barotseland as a whole was six per square mile, on the plain margin it had increased to between 30 and 40 per square mile, far too high for an agricultural system which had become increasingly dependent on bush fallow.[84] Only 10 per cent of *sishanjo* soils in the plain were now being cultivated, and the use of *sitapa* gardens had continued to decline since the 1930s. This meant that the Lozi were attempting to grow an equal quantity of foodstuffs on much less fertile soil. As a result, the forest was becoming even more overcultivated: as cropping periods grew longer and fallow cycles recurred more frequently, fertility levels ceased to reach the maximum. Decreasing productivity of soils encouraged an expansion of the area under cultivation, which in turn reduced the fallow period and thus fertility. By about 1950 Peters estimated that there was an annual demand for 5,000 tonnes of maize and cassava. Although nutrition in the area remained generally good, there was now a definite hunger period in November and December. The 1950 annual report on African affairs made this comment on the Lozi situation:

> This realisation of capital by the sale of labour and cattle is bringing much money into the Province, but little real prosperity. Too little of the labour of men's hands has been devoted to the production of food and the drainage of swamps and the result is that meal costs up to £3 a bag for those who are fortunate to be able to buy it. Many are tasting the bitter-sweet of a jingling pocket and an empty belly.

Like the Bemba, the Lozi now 'bought clothes with hunger'.[85]

The shortage of labour in the area of the plain was having an adverse effect on cattle, as well as on food production. With approximately 80 per cent of Barotseland's cattle concentrated around the flood plain, finding sufficient grazing space outside the plain during high water had always been difficult. The herders had taken the animals long distances to the best grazing lands available, where they remained with them until the flood had subsided. Now that the floods were generally higher because of the neglect of drainage canals, headwaters where cattle had formerly grazed became waterlogged and unusable.[86] In addition to this scarcity of grazing sites, the Lozi, like the Ngoni and the Tonga, suffered from a growing shortage of herders. Tending cattle was a man's job, so that with labour migration and with an increasing number of boys in school, herders became more difficult to find. With young men being unwilling to spend such a long time away from the plain, cattle were no longer taken to the best sites. Many more animals starved or succumbed to disease, as grasses in the vicinity of the plain proved inadequate. Combining herds permitted the use of fewer herders, but, no longer as closely watched, more cattle were killed by predators. To illustrate how drastic this problem was during the flood season in 1951, 10,000 cattle died from malnutrition and its side-effects; 5,000 suffered the same fate in 1952; and in 1953, 8,000 died from insufficient grazing, 2,349 from disease, and 900 from predators.[87] It was an immense loss of capital. In contrast to the 26,249 which died accidentally during the period, only 9,490 were exported for slaughter.[88]

With the era of 'benevolent paternalism' under way,[89] in the 1950s the British, in addition to setting up the Namushakende Development Centre, did provide some funds for the clearing of drainage canals. According to Hellen, they spent £20,000 and employed 2,500 men in 1958 to reopen ninety-three km of canals and to clean an additional

fifty km miles of reconstructed canal. Ironically, they also encouraged the Barotse National Government's plan to reintroduce compulsory communal labour to maintain the drainage network.[90] The
efforts of the colonial authorities seem to have had little effect. Had
they considered the social and economic background to the difficulties confronting Lozi agriculture, the administrators would have
realized that clearing the silted canals could not in itself alter the
issues which lay behind the decline in production. Instead the
authorities saw the problem only in agricultural terms. Their
blindness to the plight of the Lozi labourer was revealed all too clearly
in their unrealistic endorsement of a return to tribute labour. The
same sort of criticism applies to colonial crop experiments in
Barotseland. Without first a solution to the transport problem, such
research was meaningless.

The benevolence of individual administrators aside, the British had
practical reasons for investing this money in Barotseland: for a trifling
sum they hoped to minimize future political and economic difficulties.
Unrest elsewhere in Africa, coincidental to the increasing dependence of Britain on her colonies, made it imperative that the British
presence in Central Africa remain unchallenged.[91] At a meeting in
1948, the Secretary for Native Affairs announced that 'it was
desirable from the political point of view that there should be at an
early stage some visible form of development in Barotseland'.[92] And
so the Barotse Development Centre came into being. Economically,
it was important that the decline in subsistence agriculture in
Barotseland be arrested as soon as possible. Hopefully, an immediate
investment of resources would prevent the province becoming a
heavy liability later on. For some years the administration had been
providing famine relief in Sesheke. A 1955 booklet, entitled *Barotseland Protectorate–Schemes of Development, 1955–1960*, stated:

> Agricultural policy is directed towards the production of sufficient food,
> and the right kind of food, with emphasis on proper land utilization and
> maintenance of soil fertility. As the subsistence level is gradually being
> reached, the emphasis is placed upon cash crops to be fitted into the
> agricultural pattern, so as to broaden the present exchange economy.[93]

The British intention was not to make Barotseland economically
viable. They preferred to concentrate spending on 'high potential'
areas, from which they could expect a good return: it was to this end
that Colonial Development and Welfare Funds were mainly expended.[94] The limited government effort had an equally limited effect
on Lozi agriculture, in part because of a large population increase in
Mongu district, which put additional strains on bush cultivation.[95]
At independence in 1964, the maize deficit in Barotseland had
reached 80,000 bags per annum.[96]

## Conclusion

The decline in the productivity of Lozi agriculture to the point at which it could no longer provide even subsistence living was thus the product of a number of forces, many of them at work also in other parts of Zambia. Natural disasters and ecological limitations played a major role. Had bovine pleuro-pneumonia not destroyed the only important source of Lozi income, developments in Barotseland might have taken a somewhat different course. Certain incidental effects of the British presence, such as the end to raiding and the creation of new boundaries, were also of consequence in limiting the pool of labour on which the Lozi could draw. Unlike the Ngoni, who were herded into 'native reserves', the Lozi population increase posed few problems, at least until the decline of the agricultural system in the 1940s. Although they lost control over and resources from a vast piece of territory, none of the Lozi homeland was ever alienated to Europeans, as was that of the Lamba and the Ngoni. Alternatively, the absence of settler farmers in Barotseland, as in northern Malawi, precluded a potential source of local employment.

The Lozi responded ambitiously to the opening of new markets for both cattle and produce. Had transport been less problematical, or had the BSA Company funded its development, the Lozi could have put more *sishanjo* soils into use to produce a larger cash crop. The Company, however, was interested in Barotseland only as a source of revenue and labour for Southern Rhodesia. Once the basis of the local economy had been destroyed and the master—servant bonds broken, the hut tax assured a flow of labour to the mines of the south and of money into the Company's coffers.

After tribute labour came to an end in 1925, the drainage network excavated by the Lozi state fell gradually into disrepair, and some of the most fertile soils available to the plain-dwellers became water-logged and unworkable. This was in part the fault of the aristocracy, who saw no reason to sacrifice their comfort to pay for the mainten-ance of canals while the Northern Rhodesian government was itself spending nothing on development. Only after the Second World War, when they felt compelled to do so, did the British contribute to what was by then the rescue of Lozi agriculture, but because their efforts made no attempt to alter the economic situation at the root of the Lozi difficulties, they had scant impact.

As labour migration increased during the 1930s, and as gardening shifted from the more fertile soils of the plain to those of the bush, the Lozi ability to feed themselves became more and more tenuous. Overcrowding in the forest near the plain can be seen from one angle as a consequence of the massive influx of 'Wiko', which began in the 1920s. On the other hand, the Lozi would not have been competing for these garden sites had a shortage of male labour not altered their system of grassland cultivation. Beginning in the late 1930s, an unusually long and destructive series of floods washed out crops and

soils, and with them the slim margin of profitability which had
remained to agriculture in Barotseland. As a result, the absentee rate
of taxable males jumped from 38 to 50 per cent during the 1940s, and
with this additional loss of labour, Lozi agriculture simply collapsed.

The deterioration in Lozi agriculture was perhaps more drastic than
for other groups such as the Lunda and Mambwe because it had been
particularly intricate. At its height it had required not only the
full-time, year-round effort of the local people, but also the
introduction of large amounts of labour from outside. Until 1940 the
Lozi were able to compensate for labour migration by simplifying
their patterns of agricultural production, but these adaptations were
destructive of the land and yielded diminishing returns. As earning
one's living through agriculture became less and less possible,
especially under adverse climatic conditions, more of the Lozi were
forced to turn to wage-labour for the Europeans. Given that the Lozi
were competing for those resources which the British themselves
were determined to control, the destruction of their economy was
inevitable. It was only a matter of time.

## NOTES

1.   J.A. Hellen, *Rural Economic Development in Zambia, 1890–1964* (Munich, London, and New York, 1968); T.O. Ranger, *The Agricultural History of Zambia*, Historical Association of Zambia Pamphlet No. 1 (Lusaka, 1971), 23; G. Kay, 'Agricultural
Progress in Zambia', in M.F. Thomas and G.W. Whittington (eds), *Environment and
Land Use in Africa* (London, 1969), 495–524.
2.   D. Livingstone, *Missionary Travels and Researches in South Africa* (London,
1857), 246, 254, 215.
3.   M. Gluckman, *Economy of the Central Barotse Plain* (Manchester, 1968), x.
4.   This is an estimate based on District Annual Reports for 1972–3 and on the
Provincial Annual Reports of the Ministry of Agriculture for 1969–70 and 1970–1.
5.   The people who originally migrated to the flood plain are known as the Luyana.
After the Kololo occupation and the adoption of the Sikololo language, the Luyana
came to be known as the Lozi.
6.   M. Mainga, *Bulozi under the Luyana Kings* (London, 1973), 58–60.
7.   H.W. Langworthy, *Zambia before 1890* (London, 1972), 50.
8.   Mainga, *Bulozi*, 58–60.
9.   C.G. Trapnell and J.N. Clothier, *The Soils, Vegetation and Agricultural Systems
of North Western Rhodesia* (Lusaka, 1937), 25–7.
10.   Livingstone, *Missionary Travels*, 220.
11.   Gluckman, *Economy*, 37–41.
12,   Langworthy, *Zambia*, 79, 101.
13.   Gluckman, *Economy*, 79–80. For Westbeech, see R. Sampson, *The Man with a
Toothbrush in his Hat: The Story and Times of George Copp Westbeech* (Lusaka,
1972).
14.   Mainga, *Bulozi*, Chapter 5.
15.   Mainga, *Bulozi*, 148–9.
16.   Mainga, *Bulozi*, 150.

17.  F. Coillard, *On the Threshold of Central Africa* (London, 1897), 515, 559.
18.  Coillard, *Threshold*, 601.
19.  G.L. Caplan, *The Elites of Barotseland* (London, 1970), 24.
20.  Caplan, *Elites*, 27.
21.  Coillard, *Threshold*, 262.
22.  Mainga, *Bulozi*, 174−5.
23.  Lewanika was apparently willing to have the subsidy dropped to £850 in exchange for 'recognition of an extensive area to be reserved from prospecting'. E. Stokes, 'Barotseland: The Survival of an African State', in E. Stokes and R. Brown (eds), *The Zambesian Past* (Manchester, 1966), 273.
24.  Mainga, *Bulozi*, 200.
25.  The death rate of Africans from North-Western Rhodesia in Southern Rhodesia was 42.68 per thousand in 1907−8 and 65.43 in 1912. L.H. Gann, *A History of Northern Rhodesia: Early Days to 1953* (London, 1963), 107. For conditions on the mines in Southern Rhodesia, see C. van Onselen, *Chibaro: African Mine Labour in Southern Rhodesia 1900−1933* (London, 1976).
26.  Gluckman, *Economy*, 81.
27.  Mainga, *Bulozi*, 199.
28.  W. Allan, *The African Husbandman* (Edinburgh and London, 1965), 335. Cited in Ranger, *Agricultural History*, 13.
29.  In fact, the Bulawayo Chamber of Mines had sent a recruiting agent named Bagley to the Barotse valley in 1895. Gelfand regards it as 'the first concerted effort by Southern Rhodesian mines to obtain labour'. M. Gelfand, 'Migration of African Labourers in Rhodesia and Nyasaland (1890−1914)', *Central African Journal of Medicine, 7*, 1961, 295.
30.  Barotse Proclamation of 1906. In M. Gluckman, *Essays on Lozi Land and Royal Property* (Livingstone, 1943), 83.
31.  According to the D/C Barotse, the twelve-day limit applied only when the men were called from their homes, and 'the usual work of the village for the Chief still has to be performed, whether it is paddle making, blacksmithing or other labour'. National Archives of Zambia, KDE 8/1/1, Report of the D/C Barotse for the year ending March 1907.
32.  Caplan, *Elites*, 89, 90.
33.  Stokes, 'Barotseland', 283.
34.  KDE 8/1/1, Report of the D/C Barotse for the year ending March 1907.
35.  KDE 8/1/2, Report of the D/C Barotse for the year ending March 1911.
36.  Gluckman, *Economy*, 77.
37.  Trapnell and Clothier, *The Soils,* 67.
38.  Chapter 9, R.H. Palmer, 'The Agricultural History of Rhodesia'; Chapter 5, Neil Parsons, 'The Economic History of Khama's Country in Botswana, 1844−1930'.
39.  KDE 8/1/1, Report of the D/C Barotse for the year ending March 1907.
40.  Gluckman, *Essays,* 74.
41.  KDE 8/1/2, Report of the D/C Barotse for the year ending March 1911; KDE 8/1/3, Report of the D/C Barotse for the year ending March 1912.
42.  Chapter 5, Parsons, 'Economic History'.
43.  T.O. Ranger, 'The "Ethiopian" Episode in Barotseland, 1900−1905', *Rhodes − Livingstone Journal, 37,* 19655, 28.
44.  Mainga, *Bulozi*, 190−1.
45.  Ranger, "Ethiopian Episode", 29.
46.  BS 2/195, Letter from F. Z. S. Peregrino, 23 January 1905.
47.  Mainga, *Bulozi*, 205−6.
48.  KDE 8/1/3, Report of the D/C Barotse for the year ending March 1912; Ranger, "Ethiopian Episode", 28−9; Gluckman, *Essays,* 16, 45.
49.  Ranger, *Agricultural History*, 21.
50.  KDE 8/1/3, Report of the D/C Mankoya for the year ending March 1912.
51.  KDE 2/1/1, Lewanika to Secretary for Native Affairs, September 1915.

52.  KDE 2/1/1, Lewanika to R/M Barotse, 9 June 1915.
53.  KDE 2/1/1, Lewanika to Assistant R/M Barotse, 20 September 1915.
54.  KDE 8/1/1, Report of the D/C Barotse for the year ending March 1907.
55.  KDE 8/1/7, Report of the R/M Barotse for the year ending March 1916; KDE 8/1/4, Report of the N/C Barotse for the year ending March 1913.
56.  KDE 8/1/7, Report of the R/M Barotse for the year ending March 1916; Report of the Acting A/M Sesheke for the year ending March 1916.
57.  KDE 8/1/8, Report of the R/M Barotse for the year ending March 1917.
58.  KDE 8/1/20, Report of the A/M Sesheke for the year 1928.
59.  Caplan, *Elites*, 122–3.
60.  Caplan, *Elites*, 134.
61.  KDE 8/1/18, Report of the A/M Kalabo for the year 1926.
62.  KDE 8/1/20, Report of the A/M Kalabo for the year 1928.
63.  KDE 8/1/20, Report of the R/M Barotse for the year 1928.
64.  KDE 2/9/1, correspondence on canals, December 1928 to August 1929.
65.  KDE 8/1/16, Report of the Acting R/M Barotse for the year ending March 1925; KDE 8/1/21, Report of the D/C Nalolo for the year 1929.
66.  KDE 10/2, Barotse Provincial Notebook.
67.  Caplan, *Elites*, 144–5.
68.  *Annual Report upon Native Affairs for the year 1929* (Livingstone, 1930), 16.
69.  Caplan, *Elites*, 145–6.
70.  *Native Affairs Annual Report for the year 1937* (Lusaka, 1938), 101, 103.
71.  *Native Affairs Annual Report for the year 1935* (Lusaka, 1936), 6.
72.  *Native Affairs Annual Report for the year 1937* (Lusaka, 1938), 96.
73.  Trapnell and Clothier, *The Soils*, 59–64.
74.  E.L. Hermitte, 'An Economic History of Barotseland, 1800–1940', PhD thesis, Northwestern University, 1973, 276.
75.  D.U. Peters, *Land Usage in Barotseland* (Lusaka, 1960), 41.
76.  W. Allan and M. Gluckman, 'Preface' to Peters, *Land Usage*, xiii.
77.  *Report of the Commission appointed to Enquire into the Financial and Economic Position of Northern Rhodesia*, Colonial No.145, (London, 1938), 119; R.S. Kapaale, 'A Survey of Wenela in Barotseland', in R.H. Palmer (ed.), *Zambian Land and Labour Studies, Vol. 3*, National Archives of Zambia Occasional Paper 4 (Lusaka, 1977), 75–120.
78.  Hermitte, 'Economic History', 275.
79.  Gluckman, *Economy*, x; Allan and Gluckman, 'Preface' to Peters, *Land Usage*, ix–x.
80.  I. Henderson, 'The Economic Origins of Decolonisation in Zambia, 1940–1945', *Rhodesian History, 5*, 1974, 64.
81.  *African Affairs Annual Report for the Year 1947* (Lusaka, 1948), 77.
82.  Hermitte, 'Economic History', 278.
83.  Peters, *Land Usage*, 57.
84.  Peters, *Land Usage*, 54.
85.  *African Affairs Annual Report for the Year 1950* (Lusaka, 1951), 96; G. Wilson, *An Essay on the Economics of Detribalization in Northern Rhodesia, Part I* (Livingstone, 1941).
86.  W.C. Verboom and M.A. Brunt, *An Ecological Survey of Western Province, Zambia, with Special Reference to the Fodder Resources, Vol. 2* (Tolworth, 1970), 30.
87.  Hellen, *Rural Economic Development*, 246.
88.  Ministry of Agriculture, Provincial Annual Report for Barotseland, 1965–6.
89.  Term used by Kay to designate the period 1946–64. Kay, 'Agricultural Progress in Zambia', 509.
90.  Hellen, *Rural Economic Development*, 247; *African Affairs Annual Report for the Year 1950* (Lusaka, 1951), 94.
91.  R. Gray, *The Two Nations* (London, 1960), 197–200.
92.  SEC/DEV/13, Minutes of a meeting held in the Central Offices on 11 October 1948

93. *Barotseland Protectorate–Schemes of Development, 1955–1960* (Lusaka, 1955), 5.
94. Gray, *Two Nations*, 198–9.
95. Gluckman, *Economy*, xi.
96. H.A.M. Maclean, *An Agricultural Stocktaking of Barotseland* (Lusaka, 1965), 17.

# PART II

*The Growth of Southern Africa*

Having considered the local and regional impact of mercantilism and early colonialism on economic systems associated with pre-colonial states, we turn in the second part of the book to an examination of the characteristics of rural life under the new colonial states within the Southern African regional economy.

The driving force behind Southern African regionalism has been the political power wielded by an alliance of capitalist mine and farm interests ('Gold' and 'Maize') in what became the Union of South Africa. In Chapter 7, Martin Legassick demonstrates how the evolution of this alliance has been related to international capital outside Africa and to techniques of labour coercion on mine and farm which have been adapted to the challenge of manufacturing industry within South Africa. Colin Bundy, in Chapter 8, then takes up the theme of a colonial black peasantry in the Transkei being integrated into the rising capitalist market to the stage of dependency, when decline in market terms under settler controls produced automatic impoverishment and structural underdevelopment. The Transkei peasantry were one of the first in Southern Africa to undergo this process.

Southern Rhodesia, as outlined in Chapter 9 by Robin Palmer, followed a variant of the South African model, with white enclave development and the related underdevelopment of black reserves, achieved by similar legal and market mechanisms. Palmer's chapter takes up questions raised by David Beach in Chapter 1 and leads into two case studies by Ian Phimister and Barry Kosmin. In Chapter 10, Phimister traces the initial rise of an African peasantry under the primary stimulus of expanding produce markets, and the role of traders in minimizing the returns from these markets to peasants. In the case of the Victoria district, peasant prosperity was undermined when new railways bypassed the district and permitted the importation of cheaper grain to the mines, thereby enabling local traders to peg prices lower. In Chapter 11, Barry Kosmin investigates the fate of tobacco production among the Shangwe people of Inyoka, just south of the Zambezi. Inyoka tobacco, traded in pre-colonial times, found a ready market among early colonial mineworkers, but the trade was destroyed in the 1930s when, following the loss of overseas markets, Rhodesian tobacco manufacturers in alliance with settler growers captured the local African market. Thus the Shangwe provide one of the latest examples of delayed proletarianization south of the

173

Zambezi, and of a peasant economy being eventually strangled by the capitalist market forces which had previously fattened it.

## The contributors

Martin Legassick was born in Britain and grew up in South Africa. He studied natural sciences at the Universities of Cape Town and Oxford. After a year at the University of Legon, Ghana, he obtained his doctorate on early nineteenth century Griqua history at the University of California at Los Angeles in 1969. He has taught at the University of California, Santa Barbara, and the University of Sussex. After three years as interdisciplinary research fellow at the Centre for International and Area Studies, University of London, he became a lecturer in sociology at the University of Warwick in 1974. He has written widely on different periods of South African history and politics, with a recent concentration on the post-1910 era.

Colin Bundy was born in South Africa, in Vryburg in the Northern Cape, and grew up in the Transkei and the Eastern Cape. He took his first degrees at the Universities of Natal, Witwatersrand, and Oxford, and since 1973 has held a lectureship at Manchester Polytechnic. In 1976 he completed his doctorate for Oxford University on the peasantry in South Africa, 1870—1913.

Robin Palmer is co-editor of this volume. He was born in Britain, and like Barry Kosmin went to the University (College) of Rhodesia as an undergraduate. He took his first degree there and wrote a 1968 doctorate on Rhodesian land policies at the University of London. From 1969 to 1971 he lectured at the University of Malawi, and since 1971 has held a lectureship at the University of Zambia. He has written widely on land and labour problems in Rhodesia, Malawi, and Zambia, has edited three volumes of student research essays, *Zambian Land and Labour Studies,* and has just completed a major monograph, *Land and Racial Domination in Rhodesia* (London, 1977).

Ian Phimister took up a lectureship at the University of Zambia in 1975, having completed a doctorate on pre-colonial and colonial mining in Rhodesia. He was born and grew up on the Zambian Copperbelt, and took his first degree at the University of Nottingham. He has published widely on Rhodesian mining history.

Barry Kosmin was born in Britain, went to Rhodesia as an undergraduate, and has taken degrees at the Universities of Rhodesia, London, and McMaster. His 1974 doctorate was a socio-historical study of the Asian, Hellenic, and Jewish populations of Rhodesia, 1898–1945. Since 1974 he has been Director of the Social Research Unit of the Board of Deputies of British Jews in London.

# CHAPTER 7

## Gold, Agriculture, and Secondary Industry in South Africa, 1885–1970: from Periphery to Sub-Metropole as a Forced Labour System[1]

## MARTIN LEGASSICK

### Introduction

The discovery of diamonds and gold in South Africa in the last part of the nineteenth century set in motion changes which had a profound and qualitative effect over the whole of the Southern African sub-continent. A region comparatively marginal to the world economy became transformed into the supplier of that economy's money commodity—gold. An area of the world where capital accumulation, though slow and small in quantity, was local, became rapidly dominated by metropolitan capital, which has continued to play an important rôle to this day. The whole tempo of economic change accelerated, reaching its peak in the South African heartland between the 1930s and 1960s; and it was change which proceeded on the basis of institutions of forced labour, already in existence in agriculture, but qualitatively transformed to meet new circumstances. The labour needs of gold-mining, of commercial/capitalist agriculture, and of secondary industry, were the basis on which emerged new social institutions and structures, new classes, new ideologies. Moreover growth in the South African heartland was accompanied by and caused stagnation or decay in the peripheries. In a parallel process to the international dialectic of metropole and satellite, Southern Africa proceeded from *un*development to the development of *under*development.[2] With mining and secondary industry came the growth of cities. The Witwatersrand (the Reef, 'Goli') became the economic, social, and ideological focus of a sub-continent. But alongside, in the African 'reserves', in Mozambique or Malawi, wherever the imperatives of the growing South African economy penetrated, there were also changes, and these changes were usually in the direction of rural underdevelopment, economic decay, and pauperization. In South Africa itself, moreover, the entrenchment of racialism in the institutions of the society meant the correlation of development with whiteness, and of underdevelopment with blackness. The correlation was not, and is not, complete, but it is cruelly strong. Thus, over a hundred years, South Africa changed from a peripheral part of the world economic system to a developed sub-metropole, generating underdevelopment and exploitation in its own periphery.

## Southern Africa and the world commodity market, 1652–1880³

By the mid-nineteenth century Southern and Central Africa had been extensively penetrated by the world commodity market: the tentacles of trade in a variety of goods carried by a variety of middlemen criss-crossed the interior, linked to Europe (and elsewhere) through the Swahili and Portuguese settlements of the east and west coasts, and through the mercantile houses of the South African ports. Such a network of relationships, their character, their geographical extension, and social deepening, affected the forms of economic, political, and social differentiation in African societies.

In South Africa the extension of economic exchange relationships was intimately linked, though by no means identical, with the spread of a colony of white settlement. Khoisan and Bantu speakers, with redistributive forms of social organization, were linked indirectly with external transoceanic markets, prior to the establishment of a Dutch colony at the Cape of Good Hope. They began to participate in the Cape colonial economy through trading cattle and the products of hunting. In itself this trade tended to sap the productive capacities of the indigenous societies, and this impact increased to the extent that white colonists used coercion and raiding to supplement trade, hunted on their own account, and brought indigenous land under the system of colonial private property relations. Through these means, class differentiation between rich and poor within indigenous societies was encouraged, while the regional transfer of surplus promoted underdevelopment, and was often accompanied or followed by political and cultural domination of the indigenous societies by colonial forces. This, of course, is a vast generalization. The processes at work differed in each particular case according to the length and intensity of colonial penetration and its character, and according to the character and dynamics of the indigenous grouping.

At the same time in South Africa the establishment of a coastal colony meant the emergence of new forms of production, in particular in the organization of agriculture for export. It is important to realize that in large part, prior to the development of mining, the labour force for such activities was drawn from outside the Cape Colonial social formation. Until the early nineteenth century, production of wheat and wine was carried out by slaves, imported from the East Indies, Mozambique, and Madagascar. By the time slavery was gradually abolished in Cape Colony in the early nineteenth century, the ex-slaves could be supplemented by a proletarianized Khoisan population, deprived by colonization of land and cattle, who together formed the 'Cape Coloured' people. Coercive measures such as making breach of labour contract a criminal offence, vagrancy, and pass laws (the 1890 'Caledon Code' etc.), replaced the coercion of slavery. Equally when the viability of sugar production in Natal was discovered, the labour force was imported from India on five-year indenture—or, in other words, temporary slavery. Such non-indigenous labour was used where agricultural production was to be intensive rather than extensive. Where production was not such, or could not be made so, the indigenous population might be subject to surplus extraction from colonists by other means: labour service, sharecropping, rent. Such a system was quasi-feudal rather than quasi-slave in character, though colonists might attempt, through intensifying coercion and confiscating means of subsistence in the hands of the indigenous population, to turn those they had already made serfs into coerced proletarians or even slaves. Yet by the 1880s such a process had not been completed even on the land within the colonial frontiers, that is, land within the system of private property relations. Still less was it true where the indigenous population had retained control of its land and formal political autonomy.

Politically, South Africa was controlled by the Netherlands for 150 years after the establishment of a colony by the Dutch East India Company. In the early nineteenth century control passed to Britain. Under the metropolitan umbrella there emerged to social dominance a *comprador* class of import-export merchants acting on behalf of metropolitan capital, who were the inheritors of political authority in the Cape Colony as Britain delegated formal power to it in the form of self-government in 1854. Within the Cape, the merchants governed in unstable and asymmetrical alliance with colonial farmers, while they also dominated economically the (Afrikaner) colonial and (African) indigenous polities which adjoined the Cape Colony to the north.

## South Africa in the mining era, 1885–1924: gold, maize, and segregation

The rivalry between imperialist powers in the era of monopoly capitalism—spurred on by the challenge to British nineteenth century 'free trade imperialism' of rival European states come late to industrialization—led to the scramble for African territory in the years after 1884: the political domination by European colonial powers of the African continent. This partition of Africa coincided with the discovery of gold in South Africa. British imperial power and metropolitan capital was used not simply to annex territory, but to assist in the transformation of social relationships. As a result of the mining of gold (dominated by metropolitan capital) the South African ruling alliance of merchants and farmers was transformed into what Stanley Trapido has termed the alliance of 'gold and maize'—the Chamber of Mines and the emerging class of capitalist farmers in the *highveld*.[4] Simultaneously the centre of gravity of South Africa, economic, political, and cultural, shifted from the Cape to the Transvaal. The new circumstances required new institutions—and hence the Anglo–Boer War, the assumption of British hegemony over South Africa, and the creation of the unified South African state—and new policies. In particular, new policies were required for the mobilization and control of black labour, policies which can be lumped under the general name of 'segregation'.

Both mineowners and potential (or actual) commercial farmers demanded a qualitatively increased supply of labour, and a supply that was cheap, under conditions where the majority of the potential black labour force retained its access to independent subsistence in rural 'reserves'. In mining, the problem of black labour costs was supreme. Technical and geological problems had produced, both in diamonds and gold, an industrial structure whose ownership was highly concentrated in the pockets of a few magnates, and which required large-scale investment of metropolitan capital. Gold sold at a fixed price in the world market, and diamond prices could be stabilized by a monopoly cartel. Through *direct* taxation, railway rating policy, and state monopolies to tax the importation of mining equipment and supplies, the Transvaal state took its share of the mining surplus for the benefit of farmers. The mineowners had to pay their skilled (and white) workers high wages to attract them to South Africa from overseas. And the white farming community, till then geared to production for European markets, to a very limited local market, or to subsistence, suddenly found themselves unable to compete with the American grain that was carried from the ports to the new urban mining centres along new rail-lines that bypassed them. Moreover in the production of such foodstuffs as maize, the small emerging group of African farmers producing for the market, with their better knowledge of local conditions, intensive cultivation of small holdings, more frugal living, use of kin rather than coerced workers as a labour force, presented a potential economic threat to white farmers.

At the point of production, mineowners rapidly instituted forms of labour coercion. From almost the earliest days of large-scale diamond-mining, the non-white workforce of Kimberley was housed in closed compounds, barracks which subjected the worker during his term of employment to well-nigh total regimentation. Ostensibly to prevent diamond theft, the compounds operated to impede the labour force from organizing, bargaining, striking, or desertion. In 1889 the few gold-mining houses of the Witwatersrand came together to form the Chamber of Mines. 'Its major objective was to reduce the mining industry's labour cost':[5] and this it tried to achieve by eliminating competition between mines over wages and working conditions, centralizing the control over recruitment of the labour force, and in general establishing a monopsonistic policy towards labour. Yet this was not in itself enough. If it controlled—as on export-oriented farms—the labour force which existed, it did not generate a sufficient supply of labour from elsewhere at the wages which mineowners were prepared to pay. Between 1890 and 1910, indeed, the major additions to the gold-mining labour force came from Portuguese East Africa, and between 1902 and 1906 indentured Chinese labour was introduced. This was the old pattern of imported semi-slave labour, seized from beyond the limits of the South African political economy—it was not a proletariat generated by processes within South Africa itself.

The diamond mines had been able to attract a workforce since the 1870s without recourse to direct coercion. From those African areas on the peripheries of colonial settlement which had retained their political autonomy, people came to work to buy guns with which to defend themselves against further losses of land or against loss of autonomy. In such 'rural' areas, already penetrated by the mercantile network, storekeepers might recruit labour among the poorer or landless by advancing goods against prospective mining wages, and so Africans came to the mines—and then to the towns—as migrants. There was class differentiation in these rural areas which sharpened as their connections to the capitalist economy grew, causing their impoverishment and underdevelopment. Yet it was in these areas, where there had been successful resistance to expropriation of land and loss of sovereignty, that Africans retained their cultural and economic roots. But in some cases poor or landless Africans deserted such areas permanently for the towns. Other Africans, Coloureds, or Indians, escaped from their positions as quasi-slaves or quasi-feudal tenants in the colonial farming sector to move to where railways and harbours, public works, domestic service, transport riding, and petty production provided expanding avenues of employment.

Yet these economic processes, the slow unfolding of the dynamics of the existing political economy, were not sufficient to meet the new external economic and political pressures.[6] Those blacks who moved permanently to the towns were competed for by employers and tended to drive up wages, while farmers could not intensify exploitation without losing labourers. The supply of migrant workers from the autonomous African areas was insufficient. In this sector, as in the case of tenants or sharecroppers on white-owned land, the 'opportunity cost' to a small-scale cultivator of production for subsistence or a market was lower than taking employment on mines or on commercial farms.

The first step towards a solution of the labour problem brought on by diamond- and gold-mining was taken by completing the process of conquest. In the last quarter of the nineteenth century those African areas which had remained politically autonomous both inside and outside official colonial borders were brought under white rule, either by the exertion of British imperial military power or by Afrikaner and other settler colonial commandos strengthened by the booming economy. Economically weakened, losing their political autonomy, Africans were now disarmed: until they could regain their guns, they would be compelled to seek redress within the white-controlled political system. Taxation was imposed to ensure that no African remained outside the imperatives of the cash economy. Britain, already exerting her hegemony over the Cape Colony and Natal, went to war against the politically independent Orange Free State and

Transvaal republics in 1899 and annexed them in the following year. It seems probable that this extension of British hegemony was stimulated by, as much as anything, the need to establish in these areas an administrative system more efficient and powerful than that of the settler republics.[7] Under British hegemony, four white-ruled colonies and most of the recently-conquered African areas[8] were constituted into the Union of South Africa of 1910. The growing economic interdependence of white capital and coerced black labour was crystallized in this political unity: the political unity from the coastal ports to the mining heartland augmented state power to continue to control the forms of economic interdependence. In 1910 Britain returned state power to the alliance of 'gold and maize'.

The major task of this alliance was to increase the supply of black labour under conditions which would allow both mineowners and farmers to perpetuate their coercion of the workforce. As an early economic historian of South Africa wrote in 1924, 'Until comparatively recent years the only important labour problem in South Africa was how to secure an adequate supply of labour.'[9] In 1911 the Native Labour Regulation Act extended to the mines the criminal sanctions against contract-breaking (strikes) provided elsewhere by the Masters and Servants Acts. Two years later the Natives Land Act tackled the problem of a coerced labour supply more directly. A recent commentator writes,

> It is possible to regard the 1913 Land Act as being an act of collusion amongst the hirers of farm labour not to give remuneration above a certain level. At the same time as the land legislation was being discussed and passed, mine owners were working out, not for the first time, an agreement whereby the average wage of blacks on any mine would not exceed a certain maximum, and there is a sense in which the Land Act was, for farmers, what the maximum-permissible-average agreement was for the mining magnates.[10]

As with other measures before and since, it was a major aim of the Land Act to redistribute more evenly the labour supply on white-owned land, and to eliminate the quasi-feudal forms of rent or tribute payment or sharecropping by Africans to be replaced by either labour tenancy or wage-labouring. Its initial application was in the Orange Free State, where settler farmers wished to convert to maize-growing and yet could not intensify the exploitation of their workforce so long as more favourable opportunities of occupation were open to available labourers on other white-owned land. The Land Act's territorial enforcement has been gradually extended, along with other measures stiffening criminal sanctions on contract-breaking and inhibiting movement of labour from farms to towns. In consequence, on the farms as well as on the mines, the absolute real wages of the labour force have remained stationary or declined from 1910 to the present day.[11]

Yet neither farmers nor landowners wanted this transformation of the relations of production in the rural areas to proceed too far. Even if Africans were prevented from sharecropping or rent payment on white-owned land, they still owned land themselves, either as individuals, as groups, through third parties, or in the recently conquered areas. What they had lost through the exertion of white political power and colonial conquest, some of them could still recover in the market. The retention of a free market in land, in other words, would have continued the process of class differentiation in the African community between the growing group of market-farmers, potentially competitive with whites, and the vast majority of Africans who would have become permanently landless. Flocking to the towns, such Africans would have increased the pulls away from the rural coerced labour sector, as well as constituting a serious urban political threat to the system of white control.[12] Moreover, the mineowners were well satisfied with the system of migrant labour and closed compounds which had developed in the late nineteenth century, since this allowed them to pay wages at the level appropriate for a temporary single worker, rather than for a salaried worker with a family.[13]

Hence the consolidation of the forced labour economy of gold and maize required the abolition of a free market in transfer of land between white and non-white, and at the same time restrictions on the permanent urbanization of a potential non-white proletariat. The 1913 Natives Land Act, as amended in 1936, achieved the first of these tasks. The second aspect, though it had half-heartedly characterized earlier policy, was systematized in the Native (Urban Areas) Act of 1923 and its periodic amendments at later times. The premise of this legislation was that 'the town is a European area in which there is no place for the redundant Native, who neither works [for the white man] nor serves his or her people',[14] and its instrument was, and remains, the *pass*. All African men from that time, and subsequently all adult Africans, had to carry with them at all times a pass, containing details of their life-history and employment, and hence of their 'right' to be where they are. Clearly the pass provides a fundamental instrument of labour regulation, allowing the state to channel and distribute labour between farms and towns, among different capitalist sectors, or—when it is not needed—to remove it from white-controlled sectors of the economy. Moreover in periods of particular rural labour shortage the numerous Africans convicted under the pass laws are directly channelled to jails on white farms where they serve their sentence as convict labour.

Under the 1913 Land Act African occupation of territory was restricted to some 13 per cent of the area of the Union of South Africa, as well as to Swaziland, Basutoland, and Bechuanaland Protectorate, which had remained under direct British control. It was from these areas—the 'reserves' as they were termed—that migrant labour was to come to the towns. It was to these areas that rent-paying or sharecropping Africans on white-owned land refusing to re-engage themselves as mere labourers were to go. It was in these areas that the families of migrants were supposed to earn that subsistence that was not paid to the migrant on the mines. It was in these areas that children were to be raised, the sick and disabled were to be nursed, and old men were to die. Thus was the white-controlled state of South Africa to be spared, in large measure, the welfare costs of housing, pensions, social facilities, and amenities for the non-white majority of the workforce. If during the nineteenth century the tendency of the colonial political economy had been towards the expropriation of African land and the encouragement of class differentiation among the African population, now these processes were halted. What remained of the indigenous African economy was to be frozen in a static form and harnessed to the needs of white development. And not only social services, but social control, were to be exerted through traditional indigenous institutions. The chiefs, whose powers had generally been undermined in the nineteenth century, found their authority resurrected but in subordination to the administrative arm of the white state: indeed the South African Governor-General (now State President) was given the rank of Supreme Chief of the African population. The corollary to such 'tribalism' was that no African, or blacks as a whole, should be permitted political rights in the central white-controlled institutions, either parliamentary or trade-unionist. The resurrection and consolidation of 'traditional authority' can be traced from the Native Affairs Act (1920) and the Native Administration Act (1927) to the Bantu Authorities Act (1951) and the Promotion of Bantu Self-Government Act (1959). The 'reserves' have now become *Bantustans:* their economic and political functions remain unchanged. Conversely such political rights as non-whites had managed to win during the nineteenth century were gradually whittled away from the 1920s, so that today the South African Parliament contains no direct or indirect representatives of any black peoples.

This policy—restrictions on permanent urbanization, territorial separation of landownership, the use of 'traditional' institutions in the rural reserves as providers of social services and means of social control—was originally termed segregation. It was not, as many commentators have argued, a policy produced by the imposition of earlier social attitudes on the new conditions of South African industrialization: nor were its proponents the more conservative of the white rural population. Its major theoreticians and ideologists in the inter-war period, General Smuts, General Hertzog, and Heaton Nicholls, spoke for other supposedly progressive groups, essentially for the alliance of gold and maize.[15] Along with other mechanisms of labour coercion, segregation created and perpetuated the system of migrant labour which has characterized South Africa's road to industrialization. After the Second World War segregation was continued—its premises unchanged—as *apartheid* or 'separate development'.

The final achievement of the alliance of gold and maize was the encouragement—through the state—of white capitalist farming at the expense of any potential African peasant production for the market, and in the face of competition from foreign sources. If segregation was one side of the weapon to be used, the other was direct and indirect state subsidization of white farming. Already by 1907 one commentator was able to write that 'it is probable that during the last twenty years more money per head of the rural population has been devoted to the relief of the farmers in South Africa than in any country in the world':[16] mainly as the result of diversion of surplus from mining. This policy was intensified after Union: between 1910 and 1935 alone, eighty-seven Bills relating to the land were enacted by the white Parliament. The rating policies of the state-owned railway system favoured agricultural products at the expense of materials needed by the mines. New railway branch lines were constructed largely for the benefit of farmers, particularly maize farmers who were able to restore South Africa's food-importing condition to one of export by the end of the First World War. White farmers were provided with technical assistance and agricultural research by the state. Irrigation and land settlement schemes were funded by the state. And, most important of all, the Land Bank established in 1912, two years after Union as the result of an election pledge, provided both short-term loans against crop harvesting and long-term loans for capital improvement. By the inter-war period South Africa was an increasing exporter of maize, dairy products, meat, and fruit in addition to the old-established crops of wool and sugar. In this field the state again came to the assistance of the farmer, controlling the quality of produce, and then protecting him against both external competition and the fluctuations of prices characteristic of agricultural raw materials in the capitalist world market. The culmination of this policy was the Marketing Act of 1937, by which the marketing of the bulk of South Africa's farm produce came under the control of a series of produce boards, set up by the state but controlled by white farmer producers.

Thus, between the two World Wars there were two sectors in the South African economy: the white capitalist farming sector with its coerced labour force, and the mining economy with its migrant force recruited in the African 'reserves'. The process of development and underdevelopment continued, and mineowners, capitalist farmers, and white workers were reaping the benefits. Those Africans who had retained access to the rural means of production in the nineteenth century were squeezed off white-owned land into the territorially restricted and increasingly overcrowded reserves, and squeezed out of marketing the produce of their own land by the pressures of population, segregation, and subsidization of white agriculture. Perhaps by 1900 in some areas—and certainly by the 1920s and 1930s—the African reserves had been reduced from production of a surplus to sub-subsistence, i.e. they were unable to meet even their bare subsistence needs. Yet restrictions on permanent urbanization, and the mechanisms of labour coercion which inhibited African organization and strikes, inhibited the process of proletarianization and struggling for a better standard of living in the urban areas. Real wages for blacks were, in other words, by and large static or declining in the white-controlled economy; while the possibilities for supplementing such wages by productive activity in the reserves fell steadily. Indeed while white capitalist agriculture produced vast subsidized surpluses for export, the marketing board policy kept domestic prices high and in the reserves African malnutrition and starvation increased.

## The mining economy, secondary industrialization, and the white worker, 1910–40

The mining of gold, it has been argued by many commentators on South Africa, was the motor of economic transformation and industrialization: the goldmines were 'perhaps the single most important factor determining the rate of economic growth of South Africa then and now'.[17] Yet the mineowners themselves were not responsible for this internal structural growth of the economy. It was through the state that a part of the mining surplus was diverted to finance commercial agricultural development. It was because of state-imposed tariffs, etc. that a certain amount of industrial development in support-industry for mining (e.g. explosives) took place, rather than continued importation of foreign products by the mines. Apart from such support industries for mining, the only manufacturing developments prior to the 1940s were in 'easy import substitution' light industries, probably financed by commercial capital. With such an economy based on mining, export agriculture, and light industry, South Africa remained in the 1920s a colony of international capital.

Indeed the fact that many mineowners resided in South Africa itself did give them a certain 'national' as well as 'international' interest. But by and large their capital was reinvested in mining and not diversified: their interests spread geographically rather than structurally. Between the wars the most notable example was the Anglo-American Corporation, founded by Sir Ernest Oppenheimer. Partly with American capital, Anglo-American gained control of diamond production in South Africa itself, South West Africa, Angola, Tanganyika, and eventually on a world scale. Similarly it was a major investor in the Northern Rhodesian copper mines when these were developed in the late 1920s.[18] As with capital, so with labour: mineowners pressed continually to be allowed to use black labour drawn from tropical Africa.

Such geographical expansion of mining at the expense of structural change in the South African economy found its political expression. The 'alliance of gold and maize' supported the incorporation of South

West Africa as a 'mandated colony' of the Union after the First World War, and was anxious for the transfer of the High Commission Territories from British to South African rule,[19] but it was predominantly the mining interest that wished for further political expansion. Spurred on by his experience in East Africa in the World War, General Smuts was the chief spokesman for such views. 'All the highlands of East Africa from the Union to Abyssinia are healthy for Europeans and can be made a great European state or system of states.... It is one of the richest parts of the world and only wants white brains and capital to become enormously productive' he wrote in 1924[20] and, by intriguing for the incorporation of Southern Rhodesia in the Union, and by pressuring the British Colonial Office, this remained his policy until the 1940s. 'From every previous war South Africa has emerged a greater country and this war will prove no exception' he told departing South African troops in the Second World War, and in the context 'greater' clearly is geographic in its meaning.[21]

Such a lack of interest in developing South Africa itself was not shared by commercial farmers. The ban by the South African government on the introduction of mining labour from north of 22°S latitude between 1913 and 1933 might well be explained in terms of the farmers' desire to turn mineowners' energies to the conversion of the African population within South Africa into a suitable labour force. And when Smuts's programme for expansion was attacked in 1929 as a desire to create 'a black Kaffir state extending from the Cape to Egypt',[22] his white opponents like Hertzog were deploring his inadequate attention to industrial development in South Africa. Commercial farmers—a national rural bourgeoisie—would benefit from the expanded urban markets for their produce consequent on industrialization. And, as agriculturalists who had no principled objections to a state role in the promotion of industry and indeed had practical reasons in favour, they were able in the 1920s to win the support of two other sections of the white community—workers and 'poor whites'—and to modify and enlarge the scope of the policy of 'segregation'.[23]

The first of these was the organized white working class, especially in mining, which was skilled and paid high wages. Over time, a proportion of such white mineworkers had become overseers of black labour, and blacks sometimes moved from unskilled to more skilled jobs, though at paltry wages. Nevertheless the 'job colour bar'—division of labour in the form skilled white v. unskilled black—provided a justification for the coercion of black labour while itself being dependent on this forced labour system. As such the colour bar's overall premises of inequality were supported both by the mineowners and the white workers.[24] In the years immediately after the First World War, however, mineowners were faced with a falling rate of profit, and therefore sought to lower their costs by displacing higher-paid whites in borderline occupations by lower-paid

Africans—'raising', in other words, the level at which the job colour bar operated.[25] White workers, able to organize in trade unions, and with access to state power through political organization and voting, defended their monopoly of skills and level of wages. In fact, denouncing the 'semi-slavery system' of coercion of black labour · practised by the mineowners, white workers sometimes advocated total segregation without any black labour at all, in a totally white workforce on the mines.[26] White workers recognized quite correctly that their own relationship to the means of production was different from that of black workers. And, believing that mineowners might in time try to use state power to impose similar disabilities on them, white workers took industrial action, culminating in 1922 in the 'Rand Revolt'. A general strike here escalated into near-insurrection, with the South African government calling out the army to break the resistance of white worker commandos. It was South Africa's most violent labour struggle up to that time. But, in its wake, white workers turned to state power for an entrenchment of their position.

The dissatisfaction of the white working class, which by this time had become predominantly Afrikaans-speaking, coincided with the grievances of another largely Afrikaner group. Resistance by African societies, the freezing of the free market in land, the commercialization of agriculture, meant that an increasing number of rural whites were reduced first to the status of landless *bywoners,* squatters, and were then displaced from the land to the cities.[27] Characteristically in a colonial economy, jobs did not expand in number as fast as the demand for them, leading to white unemployment and destitution. In the South African context this was exacerbated by the forced labour system for blacks which reduced prevailing wages in less skilled jobs below what whites were prepared to accept. Such 'poor whites' began to demand of the state both industrialization to create employment, and an assurance that they would not be paid wages at the level of the forced labour system.

These groups—commercial farmers, organized white workers, and the newly urbanized 'poor whites'—were the basis of the Nationalist –Labour Pact government which came to power in 1924. Against the protests of mining capital, but in line with the requirements for development in a colonial economy, this government used state capital (the surplus acquired from mining) to create South Africa's first heavy industry, an iron and steel plant (ISCOR). Since that time state industry, or state capital as a catalyst of private industry, has been an important lever in South Africa's industrial growth. Of ISCOR itself one commentator has written, 'There is hardly a sector in the country's economy which its activities do not permeate and influence to a greater or lesser extent.'[28] The state-run Industrial Development Corporation (IDC), founded in 1940 under wartime conditions, has since that time stimulated other industrial 'growth poles'—SASOL, for example, producing oil from coal, and laying the basis for petrochemicals, or FOSKOR, producing fertilizers.[29]

Other legislation in the 1920s entrenched the job colour bar in mining to the satisfaction of white workers. Over the wider industrial field, entry to skilled trades was stringently limited on racial grounds through regulation of apprenticeship. A structure of collective bargaining between employers and white workers was established which—at least under conditions of economic growth—ensures that the white working class, like white farmers, receives a proportion of the surplus generated by the forced labour economy. As a consequence industrial peace between white workers and their employers has reigned in South Africa since the 1920s on a scale unmatched in any advanced capitalist society. The final achievement of the period before the 1920s was legislation securing the preferential employment of the 'poor whites' at suitable wages: the so-called 'civilized labour policy'. In the public sector (railways, harbours, ISCOR, postal services, etc.) this was made compulsory, resulting particularly in the displacement of Indians and Coloureds who had moved into such jobs out of the agricultural forced labour sector. In private industry as it developed—footwear and clothing, food industries, motor assembly—tariff policy encouraged the employment of 'civilized labour', i.e. whites only.

Much attention has been paid by analysts of South Africa to the job colour bar: this, above all, it is argued, is the product of white *racial* attitudes. As racist rural whites moved to town, it is claimed, they found themselves in competition with black workers and demanded an entrenchment of their position which—by preventing 'least-cost substitution' of labour at the lowest wages—has subsequently hindered South Africa's economic growth. This is an absurd argument. The job colour bar is the product of two processes: (a) the imposition of a system of forced labour on blacks which, reducing their freedom and bargaining ability, meant that at no time were they directly in competition with white workers; (b) the access of white workers to state power, a consequence of the colonial economy of South Africa and of the justification of the forced labour system in terms of a racist ideology by the alliance of gold and maize. In short, the job colour bar is merely a special aspect in a total system, a system which has indeed promoted South African economic growth. The job colour bar is the means by which white workers have placed themselves on the favourable side of South Africa's unfolding dynamic of development and underdevelopment.

## Secondary industrialization in a forced labour economy, 1945–70

The degree of state power in the hands of South African 'national' interests rather than international-imperial capital was able to ensure the establishment of an infrastructure for industrialization in South Africa, and to prevent accumulated capital from being eaten away in inflation or drained out of the country. But the rapid development of manufacturing industry itself, in a situation where the internal market was small and the income distribution of the population was grossly skewed, required stimuli from outside the society. The first such stimulus came as a result of the world capitalist Depression in 1929. Britain and other countries went off the gold-standard, and after initial hesitations South Africa followed suit, resulting in the increase of earnings for her gold exports from 85s per fine ounce in 1925–32 to 125s in 1933, levelling off at 168s in 1940–5. The outbreak of the Second World War not only stimulated military manufacture but necessitated import substitution for goods no longer available in wartime trade conditions. Such enforced isolation from overseas imports was encouraged after 1948 by exchange controls, while stimulus for export production came into agriculture in the early 1950s as the result of the (Korean-war-induced) price inflation of raw materials. Meanwhile the opening of the Orange Free State gold mines from 1946 and the extraction of uranium content from the residual of gold-bearing ores after 1949 tests gave a fresh lease of life to the mining industry. And, from 1960, South Africa's determination to eliminate her vulnerability to international sanctions and to build up a self-sufficient military machine has provided further stimuli to industry. Since 1933, in fact, South Africa's rate of economic growth has been steady and high.

Under South African conditions, and with these external stimuli, the rate of capital accumulation is hardly surprising. What the economists euphemistically disguise as 'self-financing', 'high rates of profit retention', represents the reinvestment of capital accumulated from the forced labour economy. What available evidence makes harder to discern is the precise structure of capital control in manufacturing industry. To some extent it has been mining capital, responding to indirect pressures from the state, which has diversified into control of sectors of manufacturing. Particularly in the consumer goods area—in wholesaling and retailing as well as manufacture—it has been commercial capital which has extended its control, with country storekeepers and *emigrés* from Hitler's Europe joining the existing merchant class. And state capital has played a crucial role both in totally financing key industries and in providing catalystic finance in others in partnership with private capital. Beyond this, there exist two further important elements in the control of South African industry: foreign capital and agriculturally based capital.

British capital was already involved in South Africa through commerce and land speculation from the early nineteenth century, and through diamond- and gold-mining from the century's end. United States capital partnered South African in the Anglo-American Corporation (1917), and financed motor assembly plants from the 1920s. After 1933 there was renewed foreign investment in mining, and to some extent in manufacturing; from after the Second World War such foreign capital moved increasingly into manufacturing industry. Until the 1960s the bulk of this foreign capital was British, but in the last decade the contributions from the United States and Western Europe have been increasing rapidly. From the point of view of the investors the major attraction has been, of course, the high profits generated by the forced labour economy. For South Africa the advantages have been not so much quantitative as qualitative. If there is debate on the precise significance of foreign capital in South Africa for rate of economic growth or balance of payments, its contribution to industrial sophistication is undoubted. South African industrialization has depended on employment of more and more capital-intensive and 'modern' methods in a succession of industrial sectors. And in each case, it would appear, it has been foreign capital which has financed the purchasing of the requisite machinery, and it has been foreign firms which have imported the expertise to initiate the handling of such machines.

In the early stages of industrialization, then, it was foreign, mining, and commercial capital that reaped the greatest benefits. Capital based in agriculture which, as suggested, had played a major political role in guiding the economic structure towards secondary industrialization, found itself unable in a 'free market' situation to diversify into manufacturing, commerce, or mining—the commanding heights of the economy. Moreover as petty commerce and production were abandoned by capital-accumulating whites, their places were taken by Indians, and, to a lesser extent, by Coloureds, who by operating on small profit margins and working long hours, impeded other aspirant whites from entry to such fields. Hence from the 1930s agriculturally based capital began to mobilize to gain entry to these areas. Earlier than that rural co-operatives and separate financial institutions for white agriculturalists had provided means for capital accumulation on the farms of the surplus diverted from mining by the state. Now aspirant rural entrepreneurs began to mobilize those whites whose material prosperity had been entrenched by job colour bars and by the civilized labour policy. In the late nineteenth century Afrikaner nationalism had been the weapon of 'maize' in its formation of an alliance with commercial capital and then mining capital. In the 1920s 'maize' had used Afrikaner nationalism to gain the power to lay the infrastructure for industry. Now Afrikaner nationalism was used to mobilize white savings and consumption patterns in the interest of agricultural entrepreneurs. This can clearly be seen in the fate of the 1938 fund set up to alleviate the situation of the remaining 'poor whites'. When, in the following year, a so-called People's Economic Congress was held to determine the use of the fund, the conference decisions reflected 'carefully-prepared schemes, radically different from the simple act of salvation to rescue poor white Afrikaners from poverty,' which adopted 'the premise that the main cause of poor-whiteism was the Afrikaners' negligible share in commerce and industry'.[30] Save Afrikaans, Buy Afrikaans: these were the initial means by which agriculturally-based capitalists accumulated and entered commerce and industry.

The accession of the Nationalist Party to government in 1948, based on a political mobilization of these same groups, was followed by increasing use of state power to assist agriculturally-based entrepreneurs. More than ever before, a systematic assault on the economic and political position of Indians and Coloureds was launched through the Population Registration Act, the Group Areas Act, and the removal of Coloureds from the common voters role: they were not to be permitted to compete with whites for petty-bourgeois roles in the white-dominated economy.[31] Moreover, by co-operation between agriculturally based capital and the Industrial Development Corporation, by relocation of industry, through the allocation of building and liquor licences by political authorities, 'national' agricultural capital increased its proportional economic share at the expense of 'foreign connected capital'. By 1963 agriculturally-based capital controlled one mining house; and foreign connected mining and industrial capital had well-nigh capitulated to the assault—agriculturally connected entrepreneurs were being invited on to their boards of directors.[32] This use of self-mobilizing techniques and political power by agricultural Afrikaner capital was analogous to the methods of Italian-Americans and Irish-Americans in the United States. And by the 1960s the goals had been achieved: *Verligte*, 'enlightened', Afrikaner capitalists and their erstwhile 'foreign connected' English and Jewish competitors showed remarkable agreement over the continued dynamics of the South African forced labour economy.

White agricultural capital had found its remedy against decline in the increasing use of state power. Africans in the 'reserve' agricultural section were, conversely, forced even more imperatively into the labour-coercive economy from the time of the Great Depression. But the rapid expansion of secondary industry, and its changing structure during the Second World War, meant that demand for labour began to give bargaining power to blacks in the 1940s. Increased capital-intensity, increased mechanization, meant that the old labour structure of skilled whites and unskilled blacks began to be replaced by a division between supervisors (white) and semi-skilled machine operatives. Increasingly during the wartime years manufacturers employed blacks in such operative positions because they could be paid lower wages than whites. Increasingly during this period the segregationist structures of labour control, in particular the restrictions on African movement to the towns, were undermined by the needs of industry. Temporarily, indeed, Africans found themselves in a stronger bargaining position in the 1940s and, although strikes in manufacturing industry were banned, trade union organizing and collective bargaining among non-whites was more effective than ever before or (probably) since. For the only time in South African history African wages in the manufacturing sector increased faster than whites' between 1936 and 1948.[33]

As in the mining industry in the 1920s, such a situation—in which white workers saw potential or actual deterioration in their material position, in which manufacturing industry was depending on the racial income inequalities of the forced labour economy to substitute black for white labour—led to renewed tensions between industrial capital and the white labour force. The white working class, as in the 1920s, looked to the state to provide entrenchment of its position and hitched its wagon to the force of Afrikaner nationalism being mobilized by agricultural entrepreneurs.[34] Manufacturing capital and the wartime government began tentatively to question the relevance of the inherited structure of labour coercion to the situation of a booming secondary industry. Did not secondary industry, with its use of semi-skilled operatives, require training of workers? Did not trained workers mean that the labour force must be permanent rather than migrant? Must permanent urbanization of Africans not be accepted, and housing and social services oriented to that situation? On the academic peripheries, a few whites went further: if industrialization meant permanent urbanization, did not permanent urbanization mean that political rights would have to be extended to representatives of the urban masses in the central institutions of government, as had happened with industrialization in Europe?[35]

Yet such arguments combined wishful thinking by liberals with woolly, short-sighted, or hypocritical argument by manufacturers. Not only would permitting permanent urbanization have slowly undermined the labour controls and controls on peasant production upon which white mining and agriculture relied, but it would in the long run have undermined the position of manufacturers themselves. Their desire for black rather than white labour depended on the cheapness of the former; and that was dependent on the maintenance of the ban on black trade union organizing, on the unwanted labour-pool function performed by the rural 'reserves', on restricted entry to towns and on the social control and social service functions performed by the maintenance of African 'tribal' structures. Nor would it be easy to allow *some* permanent urbanization, *some* relaxation of controls without threat to the whole system. Indeed manufacturing interests were chiefly concerned about continued economic growth and continued profit, and would be content if this could be achieved through elaboration of the existing system.

This elaboration of the existing system in the context of the new situation of secondary industrialization was one major task performed by the Nationalist government after its accession to power in 1948. *Apartheid,* or 'separate development', has meant merely tightening the loopholes, ironing out the informalities, eliminating the evasions, modernizing and rationalizing the previous inter-war structures of 'segregationist' labour control. Or, to put it in another way, *apartheid* has meant an extension to the manufacturing economic growth and continued profit, and would be content if this all remnants of African land and property ownership have been removed, and a massive building programme of so-called 'locations' or 'townships' around the cities now means that the African workforce is housed in carefully segregated and police-controlled areas that resemble the old mining compounds on a much larger scale. All the terms on which Africans could have the right to reside permanently in the towns have been whittled away, so that today no African, no matter his place of birth or that of his parents, no matter where he has lived before, has the right to a permanent residence anywhere except in the 'reserve'—or, as they are now termed, *Bantustans* or 'homelands'—allotted to him by authority. Taking over the monopsonistic functions of the mining recruiting organizations, the state has instituted a system of labour bureaux which are the only means by which Africans can obtain contracts of employment; i.e. it is the state which totally regulates the distribution of labour. In the white-occupied rural areas, those Africans who had managed to retain tenure, even if under white ownership, have been evicted. These, and the Africans from towns regarded as 'surplus' labour units, have been relocated in either the 'homelands' or in so-called 'resettlement camps' from where they can contract out to labour if, when, and where it is needed.[36]

Mining and farming, whose requirements are basically unskilled labour, have since the 1950s increasingly drawn their labour from outside the borders of South Africa. The structure of control by the state within South Africa is now designed more particularly for manufacturing industry and the contemporary situation. For this reason the state also assumed control from 1953 of the black educational system which had previously been in the hands of missionaries. A new curriculum was devised with two purposes. First, to provide for the mass of Africans the minimum of educational skills necessary for participation in semi-skilled positions in the forced labour economy. Secondly, to attempt to train a small African élite who would seek their economic and political outlets not within the central white-controlled state but in the 'homelands'. Thus the old segregationist structures of social control would be perpetuated and modernized, and from the late 1950s partly-elected institutions of government have been created to supplement the role of chiefs in the *Bantustans,* where such an élite could take its place.

To modernize the protection of the white working class, 'job reservation' was legislated in 1956. The purpose of this legislation was to provide a systematic classification of the kinds of semi-skilled positions in each industrial sector, and to ensure that white workers received a sufficient allocation of these to secure full employment.[37] The legislation itself was much less specific than the entrenchment of the job colour bar in mining in the 1920s, indicating a recognition of the need for flexibility and re-negotiation of the 'levels' at which the white/non-white divide should come. For, given the small numbers of the white workforce in conditions of an expanding economy, rigid demarcation of 'levels' would rapidly produce labour shortages in the legislated white positions. In recent years there has been a gradual job reclassification, at first covert but now more openly espoused, so that white workers move upwards into more skilled or supervisory posts, while the jobs they vacate are 'diluted' into a larger number of less-skilled tasks and filled by black workers at lower wages.

This process of reclassification has often been termed by commentators the 'breakdown of job reservation', and is argued to indicate an erosion of racism or *apartheid*. This is not correct. Like the job colour bar in mining, 'job reservation' was a consequence of the forced labour economy, by which the white workers used the state to protect themselves from being supplanted by non-whites whose cheapness as a labour force was conditioned by the state. This job reclassification simply represents a means of dynamically modifying the system of racial differentiation in changing economic conditions. Non-whites may indeed move into more jobs, into more skilled jobs in manufacturing industry, and may receive marginally increased wages. But the whites move upwards even farther. Nor can an attempt to pay equal wages for equal work—as some American and British companies have proclaimed an intention to do—have any greater effect in isolation from change in the system as a whole. This will simply produce greater mechanization and fewer employees— with non-whites rather than whites fired. It is the role of the state in regulating the non-white labour force, the institutional inhibitions on African bargaining power, the differential access to education, which are at the heart of the system of racial differentiation. So long as these institutions exist, the gap between white and black wages even in manufacturing industry is likely to increase. And, still more starkly, the gap between white prosperity and the low real wages, malnutrition, poverty, starvation of Africans on the mines, on white farms, and in the reserves, will grow apace. Increasing development under the forced labour economy produced increasing underdevelopment.[38]

## Development and underdevelopment in Southern Africa: South Africa as a sub-imperialist power

Since the inception of colonization, South Africa has contained an expansionist society, acting in the interest of expanding the world capitalist economic system. At the same time state power and ideology have been used by white groups within the colonial economy to wrest a share of economic surplus from the metropole of world capitalism, by further exploitation of the indigenous inhabitants. This can be seen in the cattle trade, in the development of commercial farming, in the entrenchment of the position of white workers in mining and manufacturing, and in the establishment of secondary industry. In terms of the importation of labour and the export of capital for investment, this economic expansionism was not contained within the borders of South Africa as constituted at the start of the twentieth century, and with it went an impetus towards political expansion. Previously resisted by groups concerned with internal structural change in South Africa—notably those associated with Afrikaner nationalism—this political and economic expansionism acquired a new momentum during the 1960s.

The momentum of the 1960s resulted from the exigencies of continued economic growth in a forced labour economy. The low wages of blacks make South Africa's domestic market comparatively small, so that capital seeking to reinvest must either move itself outside South Africa or must develop an export market large enough to produce economies of scale. For minerals and raw materials Europe provided the markets, but in the manufacturing sphere the metropolitan market is hard to penetrate. (Though South African-made trousers may now be bought in Britain.) For South African capital it is tropical Africa, with its colonially distorted economies, which is South Africa's 'natural' outlet.

The value of penetration of the continental African market had been emphasized by white South Africans as early as the 1920s, but it has only been over the last two decades or so that it has been a conscious aim of policy. And, significantly, this has been in the context of increasing penetration of overseas capital with domestic capital in South Africa, and hence a growing congruence of interests. In 1958 the Viljoen Commission argued for the encouragement of 'overseas firms that at present export to African territories to establish their factories in the Union, in order to be in closer proximity to their markets'.[39] The events of Sharpeville in 1960 and their national and international repercussions delayed implementation to some extent, but by 1965–6 the South African government was beginning to embark on an 'outward-looking' policy: careful cultivation of allies elsewhere in Africa was designed to destroy the united front of sanctions against South Africa which newly independent African countries were erecting. The current phase of this policy in the 1970s involves the extension of economic, inducing infrastructural, relationships throughout Southern Africa. The extent to which South African political and economic expansionism furthers the interests of multinational corporations is shown in the remarks of American businessmen who were hoping 'to be in on the ground floor when the political climate eases and South African exports can move freely in Africa'.[40]

The consequences of this South African economic expansionism can be assessed in the light of the history of South Africa. Economic growth brought a concentration of industrial activity around limited geographical areas: the Witwatersrand, Durban, Cape Town, and Port Elizabeth/East London. Both inside and outside the formal borders of South Africa, other areas became peripheral satellites of these growth poles, supplying to them labour (or at most primary commodities such as cattle),[41] under coercive conditions which maintained that labour cheap. Within South Africa itself it was the machinery of the state, spurred by the alliance of gold and maize, which instituted the forced labour economy. In Angola, Botswana, Lesotho, Malawi, Mozambique, Swaziland, and Zambia the impetus to labour migration was the political economy of European colonialism. The dynamics of this simultaneous development and underdevelopment have created a situation where South Africa seeks outlets for capital and manufactures, while the peripheral areas are dependent on exports of labour, or food, or raw materials, and on imports of manufactures and investment goods. Even without extension of white rule, even without exportation of the full thrust of South Africa's mechanisms of political and ideological coercion, the 'satellites' are ripe for plucking.

Within the political limits of South Africa itself, the current trend is towards decentralization of industry. The *Bantustans,* pools of unfree labour, are to have manufacturing industry situated adjacent to them in so-called 'border areas'. In this way the traditional structures continue to reduce 'welfare' and 'social control' costs to the South African state, the benefits of migrancy are retained, and large concentrations of Africans in major industrial centres are avoided. The state, with its wide powers over wage determination, has authorized lower wages to the workforce in such areas. Significantly, among the first of such border industries was a textile plant jointly financed by the South African IDC and British interests already operating cheap labour plants in Java and India: 'they found that their plans fitted in very well with ours' said the chairman of the IDC.[42] This pattern continues in Lesotho, Swaziland, Botswana, Namibia and Malawi, and did until recently in Angola and Mozambique. South African capital thrusts 'outward' to organize primary production, establishes facilities for processing food or raw materials or producing inexpensive consumer goods: capital goods or more sophisticated manufactures are supplied by South Africa.

In the long run South Africa's plans are more ambitious: the establishment of a common market in Southern Africa presumably involving common decisions on tariffs, investment, currency, and so on. Beyond this region South African goods already penetrate the black African boycott through Mauritius and other states, and rumours have circulated of loans to or trade agreements with the Ivory Coast, Gabon, Ghana, Senegal, Zambia, the Central African Empire and Kenya. The economic imperatives of such expansion are reinforced by the messianic vision which has informed white supremacy in South Africa from Cecil Rhodes and Ian Smuts to the present. As former Prime Minister Strijdom wrote, South Africa's aims are 'what we believe God has put us here for – our influence to spread right through Africa'.[43] Clearly such economic expansion, supported and promoted by South Africa's current economic, political, and military predominance, would place economic change in African countries under South African control and perpetuate the development of the white South African centre and the underdevelopment of the African peripheries.

The South African policy of 'détente', pursued with increasing intensity in the late 1960s and early 1970s, was intended to open the way for this economic expansion. It was believed that the African boycott could be undermined by giving *apartheid* internationally some fresh cosmetics. Backing the carrots of 'aid' were the sticks of military force. South African air bases in the Caprivi Strip in north-east Namibia gave her, and continue to give her, strike power over most of tropical Africa. South African military forces in Rhodesia participate in border incursions into Zambia, and probably covertly in sabotage and other forms of manipulation. But the political and military terms on which 'détente' could be pursued were fundamentally altered by the Portuguese coup in April 1974, stimulated by the increasing victories of the liberation movements in Mozambique and Angola, and resulting in the accession to power of Frelimo and the MPLA. In the early 1960s white South African mercenaries operated in Zaire to suppress an anti-imperialist move-ment. In 1975 the South African state over-exposed its 'big stick' by intervening in Angola in an attempt forcibly to replace the MPLA government with a pro-imperialist regime. The attempt was unsuc-cessful, thanks to the resistance of the MPLA forces and those who came to their assistance. In early 1976 the policy of 'détente' appeared to lie in ruins.

The stake of international imperialism in South Africa was, however, too great for this situation to persist. Not only were the Frelimo and MPLA victories a setback to the plans of American and South African capital for economic expansion in Africa, they also posed a direct threat to the continued dependence of Namibia and Zimbabwe on the South African system, and an indirect challenge to white supremacy and capitalism in South Africa itself. The American response was rapid: the Kissinger mission, as an attempt to restore a 'détente' between South Africa and African states on the basis of controlled transition from white minority rule to black neo-colonial rule in Zimbabwe. The domination of South African capitalism over any commitment to preserving 'white rule' *per se* has become evident: it is economic expansion, and consequent political hegemony, rather than a 'kith and kin' commitment to white settlerdom, which is informing current South African, British, and American policy. At the moment of writing, the immediate outcome of the current feverish diplomacy is uncertain. But the long-term alternatives are clear. South Africa's transition from an underde-veloped periphery of the world economic system to an expansionist sub-metropole is complete: given her way, South Africa intends to dominate Africa's southern parts 'to the same, if not greater, extent than the United States enjoys pre-eminence in the Americas'.[44] The only alternative is the continued development of people's war, as fought in Mozambique and Angola, merging with other forms of struggle within South Africa itself, until the economic and political basis on which South African expansionism and internal domination is built has been finally defeated.

## Conclusion

The establishment of a colony of white settlement on the South African coast in the mid-seventeenth century initiated the exploitation of the indigenous peoples as well as of imported bondsmen. In the next 200 years colonial economic relationships, reinforced by political coercion and racist ideology, spread to embrace almost all the peoples of the area which became the Union of South Africa. Unequal trade and the use of black labour extracted a surplus which became divided between the colonial (white) ruling class and the overseas metropolis of the world economy; increasing white material privilege and extended white control reinforced one another. At the end of the nineteenth century the imperial imperatives of new metropolitan investment in mining and the interests of emergent white commercial farmers led to the establishment of full local white control over South Africa through the deployment of British political-military power. Within a unified South African state, white control used political devices to secure a black labour supply and to distribute it, while perpetuating the 'reserves' to which African polities had been reduced as a labour pool in which the costs of social welfare and social control of workers could be minimized. Political power and racial ideology (Afrikaner nationalism) was similarly used in the struggle to divert the mining surplus from metropolitan appropriation to develop white farming, to secure material privileges for white workers, and to establish growth poles for the transformation of the South African heartland into an industrial economy.

> The energy of the enormous labour pool gradually changed South Africa. The whites become rich and the Africans remained poor. The meaning of white supremacy today is to be found not only in the ability of one race to control other races but also in the incredible differences of wealth and opportunity which separate the races.[45]

Whatever the form, in substance racialism persists in the perpetuation of white privilege and power, and in the processes which sustain the development of the South African heartland alongside the underdevelopment of its periphery.

## NOTES

1. This essay is a further development of areas presented in R. Harris (ed.), *The Political Economy of Africa* (Boston, 1975, 229-70). For criticisms, see, for example, H. Wolpe, 'Capitalism and Cheap Labour-Power in South Africa: From Segregation to Apartheid', *Economy and Society, 1,* 1972, 425–56; N. Bromberger, 'Economic

Growth and Political Change in South Africa', in A. Leftwich (ed.), *South Africa: Economic Growth and Political Change* (London, 1974), 61–123; M. Lipton, 'White Farming: A Case Study of Change in South Africa', *Journal of Commonwealth and Comparative Politics, 12,* 1974, 42–61. My own views have also been modified, by theoretical criticism, by new research, and by the pattern of subsequent events, though not all the modifications are reflected in this text. See M. Legassick, 'South Africa: Capital Accumulation and Violence', *Economy and Society, 3,* 1974, 253–91; M. Legassick, 'Legislation, Ideology and Economy in Post – 1948 South Africa', *Journal of Southern African Studies, 1,* 1974, 5–35.

2.   Cf. A.G. Frank, *Capitalism and Underdevelopment in Latin America* (New York and London, 1969), and the application of this to South Africa in M. Legassick, 'Development and Underdevelopment in South Africa', unpublished, London, 1971. Apart from Frank, the main theoretical influences on this piece are H.J. Nieboer, Barrington Moore, and John Rex, in addition to such Marxist writers as Maurice Dobb, Paul Baran, Ernest Mandel, E. Genovese, and Giovanni Arrighi. I should also acknowledge my debt to discussions with, *inter alia,* Tony Atmore, Rick Johnstone, Ben Magubane, Shula Marks, Bob Sutcliffe, Stan Trapido, and Harold Wolpe.

3.   For more detail, see Legassick, 'South Africa: Forced Labour'. Since 1971, there has begun to appear further work on relations of production in the pre-mining South African economy, for example C. Bundy, 'The Emergence and Decline of a South African Peasantry', *African Affairs, 71, 285,* 1972, 369–88; and other unpublished papers by, *inter alia,* Bundy, Stanley Trapido, Henry Slater.

4.   S. Trapido, 'South Africa in a Comparative Study of Industrialization', *Journal of Development Studies, 7,* 1971, 309–20.

5.   R. Horwitz, *The Political Economy of South Africa* (London, 1967), 26.

6.   Because of our inadequate understanding of precolonial 'redistributive' economies, the processes within such economies as a result of new external economic and politically coercive pressures are not well understood. One analysis of this, introducing the ideas of 'disguised unemployment' and 'necessary and discretionary income', is made in G. Arrighi, 'Labour Supplies in Historical Perspective: A Study of the Proletarianization of the African Peasantry in Rhodesia', *Journal of Development Studies, 6,* 1970, 197–234. Clearly the 'cultural' assault waged by the missionaries was also important.

7.   See Trapido, 'South Africa'; and also G. Blainey, 'Lost Causes of the Jameson Raid', *Economic History Review, 18,* 1965, 350–66; D. Denoon, ' "Capitalist Influence" and the Transvaal Government during the Crown Colony Period, 1900–1906', *Historical Journal, 11,* 1968, 301–31.

8.   The areas of Botswana, Lesotho, and Swaziland remained under British 'protection'. However their economies were integrated into that of South Africa. Apart from a white capitalist agricultural sector in Swaziland (and to some extent in Botswana) and some African production of cattle in Botswana (and to a lesser extent Swaziland), their main export to South Africa was labour, their main revenue a share of customs duties on foreign imports to their countries. See Introduction and Chapter 5, Neil Parsons, 'The Economic History of Khama's Country in Botswana, 1844–1930'.

9.   M.H. de Kock, *Selected Subjects in the Economic History of South Africa* (Cape Town, 1924), 434.

10.   F. Wilson, 'Farming, 1866–1966', in M. Wilson and L. Thompson (eds), *The Oxford History of South Africa, Vol. 2, South Africa 1870–1966* (Oxford, 1971), 128. See also 117–18, 127.

11.   Among such measures were the Masters and Servants Amendment Act of 1926, the Native (Urban Areas) Amendment Acts of 1930 and 1937, and the Native Service Contract Act of 1932. On the level of real wages, see Wilson, 'Farming', 158–62; F. Wilson, *Labour in the South African Gold Mines, 1911–1969* (Cambridge, 1972), 60–7; M. Legassick, 'Race, Industrialization and Social Change in South Africa: The case of R.F.A. Hoernle', *African Affairs, 75, 299,* 1976, 224 n. 2.

12.   The imperatives of social control in white policy-making are stressed by H.J.

Simons, *African Women: Their Legal Status in South Africa* (London, 1968), 42*ff.*; H.J. and R.E. Simons, *Class and Colour in South Africa* (Harmondsworth, 1969), 345; P. van den Berghe, *South Africa: A Study in Conflict* (Middletown, Conn., 1966), 79, 150; D. Welsh, 'The Growth of Towns', in Wilson and Thompson, *Oxford History, Vol. 2*, 184—96.
13.   Welsh, 'Growth of Towns', 195; Arrighi, 'Labour Supplies', 200, 223. As Rex argues, 'the compound system in conjunction with the reserves system involves a kind of exploitation unknown to the plantations. For while the plantation owner had a perpetual responsibility for the upkeep of his slave, the mineowner . . . has no responsibility to his worker beyond the nine-month period.' J. Rex, *Race Relations in Sociological Theory* (London, 1970), 56. See also C. van Onselen, *Chibaro: African Mine Labour in Southern Rhodesia 1900—1933* (London, 1976), 128—57.
14.   Union of South Africa, *Report of the Native Affairs Commission, "Israelites" at Bulhoek and Occurrences in May 1921* (Cape Town, 1921), 25—7; cf. Province of Transvaal, *Report of the Local Government Commission* (Pretoria, 1922).
15.   See particularly, J.C. Smuts, 'Problems in South Africa', *Journal of the African Society, 16*, 1917, 273—82; J.C. Smuts, *Africa and some World Problems* (London, 1930); 'Racial Separation: A View Taken in 1936' [by G. Heaton Nicholls], *African Studies, 26*, 1967, 95—105. The academic commentators include Horwitz, *Political Economy;* van den Berghe, *South Africa;* S.T. van der Horst, *Native Labour in South Africa* (Cape Town, 1942).
16.   F.B. Smith, *Some Observations upon the Probable Effect of the Closer Union of South Africa upon Agriculture* (Pretoria, 1908).
17.   Horwitz, *Political Economy,* 53; cf. de Kock, *Selected Subjects,* 238; D.H. Houghton, *The South African Economy* (Cape Town, 1967), 104*ff.*
18.   See particularly T. Gregory, *Ernest Oppenheimer and the Economic Development of Southern Africa* (Oxford, 1962).
19.   There were also pressures from South Africa towards the annexation of Delagoa Bay and southern Mozambique from Portugal, providing an additional port and control over the labour supply from this area.
20.   Smuts to Amery, November 1924. Quoted in W.K. Hancock, *Smuts, II. The Fields of Force* (Cambridge, 1968), 223.
21.   J.C. Smuts, *Greater South Africa: Plans for a Better World* (Johannesburg, 1940), Chapter 17.
22.   The attack came from General Hertzog. Hancock, *Smuts, II,* 218.
23.   On the nature of the 'national interest' of commercial farmers, see G. Arrighi, *The Political Economy of Rhodesia* (The Hague, 1967), 20, 23—4; Simons, *Class and Colour,* 347.
24.   This argument is developed in F.A. Johnstone, *Class, Race and Gold* (London, 1976).
25.   However, significantly, the mineowners initially made approaches to the British money-market for the raising of the gold price. See de Kock, *Selected Subjects.*
26.   See, for example, Simons, *Class and Colour,* 95, 128—30, 142, 146, 155, 162.
27.   In other words, there was a trend not only of concentration of landownership in white hands, but of concentration of ownership *within* the white community, although the huge tracts owned by land speculators appear to have been subdivided by this time. Much research is needed on the structure of landownership within the white community.
28.   A.J. Norval, *A Quarter of a Century of Industrial Progress in South Africa* (Cape Town, 1962), 31. See also Houghton, *South African Economy,* 101, 115—16, 122, 195.
29.   On the role of the Industrial Development Corporation, see, *inter alia,* H.J. van Eck, *Some Aspects of the South African Industrial Revolution* (Johannesburg 1953); G.S.J. Kuschke, *South Africa: The Basic Philosophy on Which her Economy Has Been Built* (Johannesburg, 1966).
30.   A. Hepple, *Verwoerd* (London, 1967), 60—2.
31.   As a result of pressure from white Natalians, the assault on the Indians was in fact

initiated by the Smuts government in the 1943–8 period.

32.   For some of these points, see Trapido, 'South Africa'. Some research needs to be done on the connections between the opening of a money-market in South Africa, as opposed to London, by Oppenheimer in 1955–7, the move into the South African field of the American Charles Engelhard (Rand Mines 1957, American-South African Investment Corporation 1958), the moves by Federale Mynbou, and the raging controversy among Afrikaners in 1955–8 over the value of foreign capital in the economy.

33.   Evidence on this question was drawn together by J.G.B. Maree in an unpublished paper at the University of Sussex in 1971.

34.   In particular, in crucial trade unions there was a struggle between Afrikaner nationalist organizers, spearheaded by Albert Hertzog, and those who believed in the illusory possibility of non-racial trade unionism as a 'progressive' political force.

35.   This argument, proved empirically false by twenty years of subsequent South African development, has so permeated commentary and analysis on South Africa that it is hard to document its origins and social base. Landmarks in party political thinking were Smuts's speech to the Institute of Race Relations in early 1942; Union of South Africa, *Report of the Native Laws Commission, 1946–8* (Cape Town, 1948); the statement of United Party policy in November 1954; and the formation of the Progressive Party in 1959, which clearly indicates a *decline* in the political acceptability of this argument despite its continuous promulgation by academics. See, *inter alia*, Hancock, *Smuts, II*, 481–504; Welsh, 'Growth of Towns', 189–91, 198–9; J. Robertson, *Liberalism in South Africa, 1948–1963* (Oxford, 1971).

36.   The literature on these constantly modified and strengthened labour controls is vast, but a useful introduction is A. Hepple, *South Africa: Workers under Apartheid* (London, 1969). On rural resettlement, see C. Desmond, *The Discarded People* (Harmondsworth, 1971). For an account of a recent urban resettlement to a compound-like 'homeland township', from which workers will migrate/commute, see P. Mayer, *Townsmen or Tribesmen* (Cape Town, 1971), 294–318.

37.   The 1944 Apprenticeship Act had already ensured that skilled artisanal work in industry was restricted to whites.

38.   See the important article, F.A. Johnstone, 'White Prosperity and White Supremacy in South Africa Today', *African Affairs, 69*, 275, 1970, 124–40.

39.   Union of South Africa, *Report of the Commission of Enquiry into Policy Relating to the Protection of Industries* (Cape Town, 1958), 6. See also, for example, J. Hofmeyr (ed.), *Coming of Age* (Cape Town, 1930), 100, 109.

40.   *US News and World Report,* 22 April 1968. Among the immediate stimuli to the outward policy were the forthcoming political independence of the High Commission Territories, UDI in Rhodesia, the unfavourable World Court decision on Namibia in 1966, and the successful repression of internal non-white protest. See S.C. Nolutshungu, *South Africa in Africa* (Manchester, 1975).

41.   See the comment above, in note 35.

42.   Van Eck, *Some Aspects,* 19–28.

43.   Quoted in S. Patterson, *The Last Trek* (London, 1957), 128. Cf. Prime Minister Vorster in November 1968: 'We are of Africa and our destiny *lies in Africa*. . . . It is our challenge and we dare not fail in our mission.'

44.   N.J. Rhoodie, quoted in S. Gervasi, 'South Africa's Economic Expansionism', *Sechaba, 5,* 6, 1971, 21. On South African expansion, see also R. Molteno, 'South Africa's Drive to the North', University of Zambia, *Zambia and the World* (Lusaka, 1970), 33–58.

45.   United Nations, Unit on Apartheid, *Industrialization, Foreign Capital and Forced Labour in South Africa* (New York, 1970), 26.

# CHAPTER 8

## The Transkei Peasantry, c.1890–1914: 'Passing through a Period of Stress'

### COLIN BUNDY

### Introduction

This chapter discusses certain features of the Transkeian economy in the first quarter-century after the discovery of gold in the Witwatersrand. The period must loom large in any history of South Africa: the Raid, Rhodes, railways, the influx of capital and consolidation of the mining companies, Kruger, Milner, war, reconstruction, convention, and Union—the barest recital reminds one how momentous were these years, pivoting neatly about the turn of the century. Less spectacularly, the same period was a crucial one in the history of the Transkei peasantry: between about 1890 and 1914, limits were prescribed for the growth and development of that peasantry within the emerging capitalist economy; the peasant's relations *vis-à-vis* the wielders of political and economic power were restructured, and his role in the political economy was defined.

In the pages that follow, some of the changing conditions of life in the Transkei will be outlined, and an attempt made to relate these to certain specific features of the South African economy as a whole. It will be proposed that:

(i)   Between the discovery of gold and the First World War, the quickening economic pace and modernization of South Africa produced qualitative changes in the economy of the Transkei.

(ii)   Some peasants were able to consolidate, and others to enjoy for the first time, modest economic success, as they grasped opportunities for profit, improved their agricultural techniques, and produced a surplus for sale.

(iii)   At the same time, there was an acute rise in social and economic pressures; these had their origins in physical/demographic/natural causes; in aspects of the internal economy of the Transkei—especially peasant/trader relations, debt, and stratification; and in aspects of the 'external' Southern African economy—market prices, transport costs, the commercialization of white farming, the increased demand for labour, and the legislative and recruiting practices this gave rise to.

(iv)   Substantial numbers of Transkei peasants lost the measure of economic independence they had enjoyed at the beginning of the period under review—i.e. they lost the ability to meet their subsistence requirements through pastoral and agricultural pursuits as they became separated from the means of production (although without experiencing the full geographical and social departure that this 'normally' entails).

(v) By 1914, a growing number of individual peasants had become proletarianized; the peasant community as a whole was less economically resilient and increasingly less self-sufficient; the peasant sector was in the process of becoming underdeveloped. The Transkei had become a structurally underdeveloped region within the developing economic system of Southern Africa.

## 'Passing through a period of stress'

The Transkei is a roughly oblong portion of land, 16,000 square miles (41,000 sq. km) in extent, lying on South Africa's east coast (see map 9). The most densely populated rural area in South Africa, it remained in the late nineteenth century almost exclusively inhabited by various South Nguni peoples; to its south and north, respectively, lay the settler colonies of the Cape and Natal. Between its natural boundaries of the Drakensberg mountains and the Indian Ocean, the Transkei comprises a narrow, thinly settled coastal belt, a fertile and favoured interior plateau, and a series of ridges and valleys where half a dozen rivers etch parallel lines between escarpment and coast. The Transkei lies to the east of the 20-inch isohyet, so that it receives a fair, and, by South African standards, reliable rainfall.

At the beginning of the 1890s the great majority of the Transkei's peasant families raised enough food to feed themselves; many could satisfy their cash needs (for taxes and other fees, and for the purchase of traders' goods) through the production of an agricultural surplus or through selective acceptance of wage-labour. Certain areas of the Transkeian territories—notably Fingoland, Emigrant Tembuland,[1] and East Griqualand—had responded vigorously to market opportunities that accompanied the diamond boom, and peasants in these districts exported significant quantities of wool, grain, hides, and cattle, while a few sold vegetables, fruit and dairy produce to local towns and villages. About 20,000 young men sought work annually, at the gold mines, on road and railway works, and in the north-east Cape and Orange Free State at reaping and shearing seasons; this labour supply was sensitive in marked degree to alterations in wages and working conditions.

Although the land area of the Transkei was limited, and despite the low levels of accumulation and technology prevailing there, certain social and economic circumstances enabled African peasants to participate in the produce and labour markets on terms not wholly unfavourable. Apart from his specialized knowledge of local conditions, the peasant's relatively low consumption costs and his use of pre-capitalist forms of labour (chiefly that of his kinfolk, but also that of communal work parties) meant that production of a modest surplus—the sale of a few bags of grain or a bale of wool—enabled him to participate in the exchange economy largely on the terms of his own choosing and without the surrender of his land, security, or cultural identity. These factors might operate at one end of the peasant continuum in favour of the large-peasant or small-scale commercial farmer, enabling him to diversify and improve his agriculture and to compete successfully with white agriculturists. At the other end, the same factors could just tilt the balance for the small or marginal peasant, permitting him to retain access to the means of production—his plot of land and livestock—and to withstand the demands being made for cheap labour by white employers.

There is considerable evidence, often provided by would-be employers, that white colonists were aware of the extent of the African peasant's economic independence. The Cape Labour Commission of 1893–4 was told by several witnesses of the difficulty of obtaining sufficient agricultural labour at the low wages being offered; when asked 'Is there any reason you can give for this want of labour with such a labour supply as we have in this colony?' one George Warren replied succinctly that 'The natives are independent. They have land and grow what they choose, and their wants are extremely small.'[2] The commissioners themselves were obviously impressed with the evidence on this topic, for they concluded that the shortfall of labour arose from the conditions of life of the Africans:

> The mere necessities of life are few, and are obtainable with little effort. These people do not therefore feel impelled to work. . . . A cause of the insufficiency may also be found in the fact that some natives are in some sense land or rather lease-holders . . . on shares as it is called. . . . The natives are also in another sense landholders, where they cultivate their own fields in the parts of the country called Native Locations or Reserves, in what was known as the Eastern Province and in what may be called generally the Transkeian Territories.[3]

Other potential employers arrived at similar conclusions: mine-owners on the Rand knew that 'sufficient' labour at the rates they offered would not be forthcoming while the African peasant enjoyed access to his lands and the ability to produce enough agricultural surplus to meet his cash requirements. The President of the Chamber of Mines explained:

> The tendency of the native is to be an agriculturist, who reluctantly offers himself or one of his family as an industrial worker for just so long as the hut tax can be earned, and expects the industrial demand to expand to give him work when his crops are bad. He cares nothing if industries pine for want of labour when his crops and home-brewed drink are plentiful.[4]

In the Transkei, the four magisterial districts of Fingoland had been among the foremost areas of African response and prosperity during the 1870s and 1880s. Travellers, magistrates, and missionaries penned encomiums upon the hard-headed, hard-working Mfengu peasantry, who had subscribed thousands of pounds to the building of schools and roads, raising much of the money through their transport riding and sales of wool, grains, and vegetables. Another area singled out for particular mention was Emigrant Tembuland (Xalanga and St Mark's districts), where similar reports of industry and progress were the rule rather than the exception in the twenty years before 1890. The prosperity enjoyed by the substantial peasants in these districts was in some respects more firmly based than that of their counterparts in the Ciskei. The Transkei was far less penetrated by white settlers, so better land and more land was available; the region was better watered, and the population density lower.

As these factors would suggest, the 1890s saw continued instances of enterprise and economic reward in Fingoland and Emigrant Tembuland. African peasants still disposed of surplus grain and wool; there was 'an enormously increased trade' in the Territories, wrote the Chief Magistrate after the good harvests of 1892.[5] African farmers near the Mbashe river experimented with coffee; in Emigrant Tembuland thousands of fruit trees were planted in a cash venture; in Xalanga 4,000 bags of wheat were threshed by machinery and 'the prize wheats of the last show were pronounced by competent judges to have been equal to the best grown in the colony'. In the same district, 125 houses valued at from £20 to £600 were built by African farmers, and the Cala and Indwe markets were supplied with the vegetables they grew.[6]

Yet at the same time, and from the same districts, another note was being sounded. In tones varying from puzzled regret to impatient scorn, magistrates and others remarked upon arrested progress and signs of economic hardship. Agriculture, they noticed, showed seemingly contradictory features of advance and degeneration; class formation and stratification were permitting simultaneous gains and losses by different individuals. In the context of what has been said of these areas during the phase of prosperity engendered by the diamond boom, it is noteworthy that several officials described what was taking place specifically in terms of a comparison with the recent past. Thus, graphically, the magistrate of Tsomo recounted that:

> There are headmen and others who fifteen years ago had fine square houses, fine enclosed gardens with fruit trees.... Today ... you will find the square houses dilapidated and the roofs falling in. You will find the men living in the huts, the garden wall has fallen down, and the trees eaten down by the goats. Fingoland has gone back tremendously in the last four or five years. It is not in the progressive state in which it was 15 or 20 years ago.[7]

In neighbouring Nqamakwe, the magistrate noted that the agricultural shows once held there had fallen away; some years earlier 'the enthusiasm of the Fingoes was more easily aroused than at present ... agriculture and stock farming have attained to no higher order of merit now than they possessed then'.[8] Another long-serving magistrate was equally gloomy about Fingoland. Once, he said, the inhabitants had prospered and built Blythswood, but 'at the present moment these men are far worse off and not so loyal as they were twenty years ago'.[9] In Emigrant Tembuland the municipal chairman of Cala told the 1893–4 Commission: 'There is no question about it. In this district they are becoming poorer than they were',[10] and in Xalanga the magistrate said, 'During the past 25 years I think degeneration has taken place.... The natives as a body are growing poorer.'[11] In sum, although it was obviously exaggeration for a magistrate to speak of 'indications of retrogression and a rapid relapse into barbarism', there is no denying the worried conclusion of a missionary who wrote in the same year that 'just now we are passing through a period of stress'.[12]

In the late 1890s, the peasant economy of the Transkei was jolted by a sudden and severe setback, in the shape of the rinderpest epidemic. The political and social consequences of the disease have been described by van Onselen;[13] those that affect the analysis to follow are recapitulated here. For countless Africans the disease which destroyed 80 to 90 per cent of the cattle in the Transkei was an economic disaster; it liquidated much of the peasant's capital, adversely affected his credit-worthiness, made ploughing more difficult and transport facilities rarer and dearer. The immediate effect was to impoverish thousands of peasants and to force Transkeians onto the wage-labour market in considerably greater numbers than before (see Table 1). Rumours circulated that rinderpest was deliberately spread by whites to induce poverty and compel Africans 'to work for very low wages'.[14] Such tales had no factual basis, but possessed a symbolic truth; the cattle scourge brought about several results long advocated by the stern logic of nineteenth-century liberalism; the rumours accurately reflected motives, if not means. Missionary reports of 1898–9 contained several accounts like that of Charles Taberer, who felt the disease was 'not altogether an unmixed evil' as

with the natives, the possession of great numbers of cattle is as a rule conducive to idleness. After the fields are planted, they have little to do until harvest time if they have plenty of milk and a supply of grain on hand from the previous season's crops. Now however, we have them going off in all directions to earn money to provide for their families.[15]

With uncomplicated satisfaction the magistrate of Kentani observed that the peasants no longer held cattle like 'fixed deposits', and concluded that the loss of this security had 'left the native less independent, more inclined to work, less impudent, and generally better in every way than he was before'.[16]

The impoverishment of the peasants was not necessarily long term;

numbers of them demonstrated that they had accumulated sufficient resources to begin rebuilding their herds almost at once, and even greater numbers took to labour with the immediate and limited objective of replacing their cattle. The disease was a far more serious blow to the small or marginal peasant than it was to the relatively well-off peasant; the former was less resilient, possessed fewer resources, and would find it more difficult to produce a surplus through extra exertion on his own land. Put simply, the wealthy peasant who lost, say, forty of his fifty beasts could employ the

## Table 1: Patterns of Labour Migration, 1893–1916

| Year | Total numbers leaving Transkeian Territories | Numbers going to Transvaal gold mines | Numbers supplied by 7 Pondoland districts |
|------|------|------|------|
| 1893 | 27,511 | 8,500 (Transvaal) | |
| 1894 | 38,582 | 16,800 (Transvaal) | |
| 1895 | 40,000* | 18,000* (Transvaal) | 961 |
| 1896 | 38,400 | 15,491 (Transvaal) | 1,983 |
| 1897 | 45,000* | 22,120 (Transvaal) | 1,722 |
| 1898 | 61,033 | 18,302 (Transvaal) | 4,127 |
| 1899 | 45,000* | 7,105 (Transvaal) | 2,081 |
| 1900 | ? | | 3,473 |
| 1901 | 50,000 | | 5,388 |
| 1903 | 76,556 | 14,806 (mines) | 12,000 |
| 1905 | 48,000* | | |
| 1906 | 56,066 | | |
| 1907 | 63,149 | | |
| 1908 | 67,825 | 25,000* (mines) | |
| 1909 | 63,802 | | |
| 1910 | 79,377 | 50,886 (mines) | |
| 1911 | 79,839 | 51,000* (mines) | |
| 1912 | 96,667 | 63,000 (mines) | |
| 1916 | 90,000* | 60,390** (mines) | |

Note: In the third column, I have indicated whether the total is for all employment in the Transvaal, or merely for gold-mining. Indications are that during the 1890s the proportions of those working in the Transvaal actually on the gold mines was quite low—perhaps about half the total.

* These are estimated figures based on faulty statistics (not all districts giving figures in annual reports, etc.) and educated guesses. Statisticians please forgive—but they do serve as a crude guide.

** This figure of 60,390 if for all Cape Africans at the mines; the Transkei total would be perhaps 50,000.

remainder to plough his lands (of which more had been released from grazing needs) and sow a larger crop than usual, with the grain fetching enhanced prices because of the demand. The small peasant, with a proportionate loss of four out of five cattle, could look to the survivor neither for ploughing nor for reproduction.

No totting up of profit and loss to individual peasants conveys the overall impact of rinderpest upon the peasant economy; the topic is one that awaits detailed economic analysis. Tentatively, it will be suggested here that one result was to promote differentiation and the unequal distribution of resources; and that another was to intensify the structural inferiority of the peasant economy *vis-à-vis* the capitalist sector. Bishop Key suggested one element in this—the dilution of the peasant community's social and cultural integrity:

> The rinderpest has done a great deal to wean the people from their old traditions of heathenism, as cattle have always been the foundation of their whole system, social, political, and to a great extent religious; and although they are rapidly collecting cattle again . . . they will never be to them what they were in the past.[17]

Bley, in his study of South West Africa, provides a different emphasis. He indicates the manner in which rinderpest sapped the economic base of the peasantry while at the same time offering certain advantages to the wielders of social and economic power:

> In rebuilding the herds, European agricultural superiority was more widely accepted, because for the first time European cattle breeders found a large enough market. If it was true that the Hereros' large cattle herds had previously acted as a sufficient counter-balance to European industriousness, then it was now true that every European thrust forward—for instance, in the sphere of trade on credit—threatened the economic base of the tribe.[18]

The impact of the South African War on the peasant agriculture of the Transkei was more ambiguous. The loss of wages on the gold mines must have thwarted the aspirations of many who were still seeking to recover from the rinderpest reversal; we learn that 'many of the few cattle that survived . . . found their way into the hands of the traders in exchange for grain'.[19] In some districts large sections of the population were forced into desperate straits and had to live on roots. Yet other peasants were able to turn to gain the exigencies of war. Wherever troops were quartered and fed, prices for agricultural produce and stock rose steeply. Those peasants in the vicinity of troop concentrations—as in Tembuland and East Griqualand—as well as those who could arrange or afford the transport farther afield, prospered in consequence; grain and other foods were sold at 'remunerative prices' while thousands of horses were sold to the remount officers.[20] Other Transkeians willingly accepted work at the inflated wages available in military employment; and after the war was over, Transkei peasants sold 24,000 sheep to the Orange Free State in the administration's efforts to restock the ex-Boer republics.[21]

Thus far, the chronological outline has concentrated upon those nine or ten of the Transkei's two dozen magisterial districts that contemporaries would have called the 'most advanced'. Mention must now be made of the extent to which different districts displayed levels of development/underdevelopment. This was particularly evident in the decade after the war. In Pondoland, 1894–1910 has been described as 'the high point in the peasant response';[22] with annexation and the imposition of taxes, the Mpondo invested in agricultural implements and sheep, and exported wool, grain, cattle, and tobacco. There were indications, wrote a magistrate early in the century, that 'Western Pondoland will soon vie with many of the older districts in these territories', and he added significantly that the labour recruiters could attract hardly any migrant workmen from the district.[23] Why should we work', asked the Mpondo peasant, 'is not the country ours, and have we not lots of land and many women and children to cultivate it? We prefer to remain as we are.'[24]

To remain as they were, however, meant that they had to change, to adapt, and this they did. There had been only six trading stores in Bizana at the time of annexation; but ten years later there were fifteen,

> and the largest shop among these fifteen does, I should estimate [wrote the magistrate] far more business than the whole six did [in 1894]. In the old days there was not much encouragement to grow much more grain than they required for their own use, as there were no regular markets, and the producer usually obtained about half a crown a bag. Now there is a steady demand and prices range . . . from 5/- to 15/- . . . there is quite three times as much ground cultivated as there was ten years ago.[25]

In other similarly 'less civilized', 'Red',[26] or 'more tribal' districts, peasant agriculture continued to respond dynamically, while labour agents made thin pickings. The 1893–4 Commission had commented on this phenomenon: 'These [Transkeian] Territories appear to produce labour for work outside them somewhat in proportion to the length of time their inhabitants have enjoyed good government.'[27] To anticipate, for a moment, the analysis that follows this chronological sketch, the Commissioners' findings might be rephrased thus: that the territories produced wage-labourers somewhat in proportion to the extent that structural underdevelopment had been induced by the penetration of colonial rule and capitalist economic relations. The more it was integrated into the advanced economy, the greater tended to be social stratification and proletarianization within it. Such a formulation proceeds from the concept of underdevelopment that has emerged as an alternative explanation for regional or national inequalities to those that rely on 'stages of growth' or 'dual economy' models.[28]

If one's gaze shifts from Pondoland after the South African War to Fingoland, Emigrant Tembuland, Gcalekaland, and parts of East Griqualand (Umzimkulu and Matatiele districts), a different picture is revealed. Those ten (out of twenty-seven districts) magistracies, although they contained less than 40 per cent of the total African population of the territories, continued to supply the majority of migrant labourers (63 per cent in 1894, and perhaps 66 per cent in 1905). The total number of wage-labourers who left the Transkei continued to rise year by year (see Table 1) with an exceptional exodus in 1903, a year of drought and crop failure. It reached about 80,000 in 1910 and 1911, and then increased by over 20 per cent in 1912 as a consequence of east coast fever. This disease, like rinderpest, decimated herds and pauperized families—and its effects seem to have been less rapidly offset than those of the earlier epidemic. In part, this was due to the lingering nature of the disease, and the manner in which it could reinfect a 'clean' district; but there were also certain long-term economic aspects.[29] One was that the increased incidence of debt amongst the peasantry by 1910 made the repurchase of cattle very difficult, and meant that recourse to wage-labour was necessary for greater numbers for longer periods. Secondly, the regulations imposed for the control of east coast fever made it almost impossible for an African peasant to sell his cattle to any purchaser other than the local trader, whose response to this monopoly was to offer the peasant very low prices. This contributed to the overstocking deplored by so many observers, as well as to the 'irrational' and 'uneconomic' attitudes that Africans were said to hold towards their stock (see Introduction). Not until 1930, during the Depression, was there a relaxation of the regulations, when (commented a senior civil servant) 'Quite a number of Native stock-owners took advantage of this opportunity to dispose of some of their surplus stock. . . . [Since the imposition of the restrictions] there had been no outlet . . . for Natives to get rid of their surplus stock'.[30]

The number of labourers who registered for passes in 1912 was just under 100,000. The 1911 census gave the total of males between the ages of twenty and seventy, plus two-fifths of those between fifteen and nineteen (a formula used to calculate the potential labour force) as 172,562. The chief magistrate in his report for 1912, while expressing reservations about the accuracy of the pass statistics, wrote that it was becoming 'usual rather than rare' for men 'to go out regularly each year', and that thousands went twice a year.[31] In particular, Transkei migrants became a regular and major supply of labour on the gold mines (an account of links between mine recruiting and the plight of the peasantry follows later): from having supplied less than 10 per cent of the total workforce on the Rand in 1896, the Cape's share rose to 13.7 per cent in 1906 and then swelled to nearly 40 per cent in 1912, levelling out at 33 per cent in 1916. It was to remain a more or less steady supply after 1912; fifty or sixty thousand Transkei peasants turned goldminer each year—an enormous rural-based workforce composed of individuals with no land, or too little land, or insufficiently productive land, who could not subsist without wage-labour. It was, moreover, a stream of labour that was forthcoming despite 'a massive drop in the real value of the wages of African mine workers in this [1911–19] period',[32] a phenomenon in contradistinction to the responsivity to wage rates demonstrated by Transkei workers in the 1890s and even immediately after the South African War.

Another indication of the intensified agricultural degeneration of the Transkei between about 1900 and 1914 was the increasing inability of the Territories—and especially of certain districts—to produce enough grain to feed its population. Grain was imported, either from other parts of South Africa or from the American prairies, into some districts in almost every year between 1902 and 1914; in a year of poor harvests like 1903 the Transkei as a whole depended on imported food. The next section will show how, in the same period, the pressure upon the competition for available land intensified; it is during these years that Transkei magistrates (notably in districts where Glen Grey surveys and titles were introduced) came increasingly to sound like their fellow-officers in the acutely crowded African areas of the Ciskei, with refrains of 'the rising generation will have no land for allotment' and 'the land is already becoming exhausted'.

## Underdevelopment and stratification

In the chronological sketch above, it has been asserted that peasant production in parts of the Transkei showed signs of strain and weakness in the 1890s, and that these grew more pronounced after 1900, causing increasing numbers of peasants to accept wage-labour, even when the rise in supply was not matched by any rise in attractiveness of employment. Some peasants left the land completely, taking their families with them or founding new ones; they settled in the 'locations' of Johannesburg, East London, or Port Elizabeth, or they entered domestic or agricultural service in the villages and towns of the Transkei (there were 17,000 whites in the Transkei by 1911). The majority of the wage-labourers retained their foothold in the 'reserves', a destination reinforced both by post-Union urban policy and by the preference of peasant-migrants for the world they knew best. They lived in an underdeveloped rural region; and this obviated the need for employers to pay individual 'units of labour' the wages necessary to support a family; it meant that the state need not house or police a large urban population, nor be menaced by an organized proletariat. They lived, explained a Cape liberal, in a reserve which was 'a sanatorium where they can recuperate; if they are disabled they remain there. Their own tribal system keeps them under discipline, and if they become criminals there is not the slightest difficulty in bringing them to justice. All this absolutely without expense to the white community.... '[33] A more explicit statement of the benefits to the developed economy of its relationship with an underdeveloped region could scarcely be wished for; in this paper, it remains to explain how the symptoms of underdevelopment came to be embedded in the Transkei after 1890.

One set of factors operating to make more costly a continued existence within a peasant mode of production was the toll wrought by geophysical, demographic, and natural phenomena. It is impossible to provide precise population statistics for the Transkei territories, but the following figures provide a rough guide: 1891, 640,000; 1898, 770,000; 1904, 800,000; 1911, 870,000.[34] Natural population increase was augmented throughout this period by the influx of peasants pushed off the land elsewhere in the Cape, especially by the Location Acts of 1892, 1899, and 1909, and more generally by the propensity of commercializing white agriculturists to dispense with the quasi-feudal relations that had previously afforded thousands of Africans access to lands owned but not occupied by whites. In 1893 (several magistrates were startled by the 1891 census figures) the chief magistrate posed the problem in simple terms: 'Year by year, the territories are becoming more thickly populated, and the question arises, what is to be done with a population that promises to be too numerous to be supported in the land under the existing conditions?'[35]

Population increase was closely related to the physical deterioration of the land; the available area was required to bear more people and more stock than it had hitherto been accustomed to. The accumulation of cattle, as well as the major technological adaptation of the late nineteenth century—the use of the ox-drawn plough—were both forms of surplus absorption, Arrighi has argued, with a 'land-consuming bias': i.e. they tended to eliminate the 'traditional' abundance of land and to promote an actual shortage.[36] Additional garden plots were hacked out of fallow bush that was undergoing natural regeneration; trees and shrubs were cleared to create more grazing or sowing space, loosening the sandy topsoil and baring it to erosion by wind and water; the sharp rise in the number of sheep owned by Transkei peasants represented another potent agency for the destruction of natural flora. Peasants were compelled to exist on a smaller total arable area, so that despite adaptations such as irrigation or fertilizing that might stabilize or increase production on individual peasant holdings, in overall terms normal rotation was disrupted, fertility lessened, erosion hastened, and returns diminished. 'Compared with 25 or 30 years ago', wrote an administrator who had lived all his life in the Transkei, 'the desiccation of the country in many parts is clearly apparent.'[37]

The role played by droughts and animal diseases in weakening the peasant's ability to produce an agricultural surplus needs no further stress. The situation of increasing land scarcity and of falling returns bred competition for resources. Within the traditional redistributive tenets of Nguni society, such competition might have been cushioned or contained; in conditions of increasing stratification its effects were given freer rein. Resources were not only becoming scarcer, they were also becoming more unevenly distributed; Scully wrote in 1894 from Nqamakwe that

> there is far more poverty among the Natives than is generally supposed, or would be inferred from the amount of live stock that one sees in passing through the country. The property is very unevenly distributed. Some natives own thousands of sheep and hundreds of cattle ... while others—and these forming far the larger proportion—own very little, if any, stock. A large number of men are absent at work in the different mines.

From Griqualand East came equally pointed evidence:

> In marked contrast with the farm servants or squatters, or inhabitants of the locations are the few natives who own land. There are about a dozen in this happy position. They are well housed, well clad, and well fed, in fact they have become a sort of aristocracy among the other natives.[38]

In Emigrant Tembuland some members of this 'aristocracy' gave notice of their intention to defend their elevation against 'commoners'. Sixty-two landowning Africans petitioned the magistrate in these words:

> When we were allowed to come and take possession of these morgen we were strictly told that the Government wanted only civilized natives. Now some of these natives who were dressed up have pulled off their breeches and turned out to be Red Kaffirs....[39]

The general council and district council administrative system gave the upper stratum of peasants institutional form: in its membership one finds a class of headman/bureaucrat/farmer keenly aware of its place in a stratified society. When a credit system on the lines of a Land Bank was discussed during the 1909 session of the Transkeian Territories General Council (TTGC), a Councillor Nkala

> quite approved of the introduction of the land bank system because it appeared it would not help every one. Poor people would not reap any advantage from it. It would only raise those who already had property ... It was good that men who desired to improve their position should be given an opportunity to do so.[40]

A generation later, a survey of the Transkei found that about 33 per cent of all the cattle were in the hands of 5 per cent of the people, including many of the Bunga members. In one location, three out of a thousand stockowners held 70 per cent of the sheep and 50 per cent of the cattle. Some of the councillors had as many as 3,000 sheep and most had 200 sheep and 50 cattle.[41] Stratification is not peculiar to underdeveloped regions, but it does have the characteristic of bearing particularly heavily upon the 'have nots' where the general level of economic activity is low. Each stock disease or drought could have provided a Transkei missionary with a sermon on the text that ends 'But from him that hath not shall be taken away even that which he hath'.

Another set of factors that raised the cost of peasant existence, and that derived directly from the penetration of the Transkei by market relations, was the whole complex of peasant/trader dealings. The traders, backed by merchants in the Cape and Natal, who entered the region, built their stores and plied their business, were the most important single agents of economic change, the influential envoys of the advanced economy. The relationship was, from the outset, a major means of the appropriation of the peasant community's surplus. In exchanges between peasant and trader, the terms of trade were against the contractually inferior peasant consumer/producer. In the trader's hands were concentrated the several economic functions of purchaser of agricultural produce, purveyor of manufactured goods, and supplier of credit. The trader's control of these functions meant that agricultural surpluses tended to be absorbed in the form of his profits rather than made available for reinvestment by the peasantry.[42] Trader and peasant enacted in microcosm the adverse terms of trade of a colonial relationship.

The African peasant was disadvantaged as a consumer in several respects. He could do little more to affect the prices of the manufactured articles that the trader sold than to travel to more than one trading store, and it is clear that, buttressed as they were against untoward competition by the five-mile law, there was little tendency amongst traders to undercut one another's prices.[43] The goods that passed from trader to peasant were not only retailed at a profitable margin over their wholesale price, but also tended to carry substantial duties; 'loading' articles that were clearly destined for 'native trade' was a popular resort of politicians. A magistrate calculated in 1906 that a Transkei peasant paid an average 20 per cent customs duty on the goods he purchased.[44]

He suffered as a producer inasmuch as the trader was able to buy his grain and animal products cheaply, precisely because of 'the lack of development of the market—the inability of the producers to effect an exchange of their products on any more than a parochial scale'.[45] The peasant in need of cash for taxes, debts, or consumption wants, had little bargaining power, and had to accept depressed prices for his products, especially when good seasons meant that he had more to sell. The adverse trade terms encountered by the peasant as consumer and producer were summed up by the 1932 Economic

Commission: 'The Native, particularly in the rural areas, has to pay more for the same article than would a European, while for the same class of goods of the same quality he would receive less than a European.'[46]

It was, however, in the system of credit that the trader/peasant relationship was most heavily slanted against the petty consumer/ producer. The extension of credit involved peasants in costly repayments, and the spread of debt in the peasant economy was one of the most striking features of the post-1890 years. The trader advanced goods on credit, commonly upon the security of stock possessed by the buyer. If payment was not forthcoming, the sheep or cow would be forfeited, and in these cases (one learns without great surprise) the trader made 'a huge profit'.[47] Inflated profits were his, too, if the peasant made a prompt payment, for goods sold on credit were far more expensive than the same items in a cash transaction. This feature prevailed throughout our period, and twenty years later a study of Transkei trading practices found that goods were sold on credit at double the market price. This was particularly true in the sale of grain.[48] A second form of credit extended by the trader was the cash advance: apart from the cash that flowed back to the trader in purchases, these debts commonly bore punitive interest rates.[49]

The practice of cash advances, and the provision of commodities on credit both developed enormously in the 1890s as a result of recruiting procedures adopted by the gold mines: procedures that operated as systematic debt inducement. Labour agents received a capitation fee per every recruit that they 'signed up', and the majority of traders took out licences as agents. Labour agents were empowered to make a cash advance—commonly £5— to the labourer, to be repaid by remittance or upon return from the mines. Indebtedness—either as 'instant debt' on receipt of the agent's advance, or in long-term endemic form—became the crucial device in separating Transkei peasants from the means of production.[50] Quite apart from the fees they received for migrants formally recruited, it was in general terms in the trader's interest to offer credit upon a scale which was likely to be recoverable only through wage-labour. As A.W.G. Champion told the Mining Industry Board in 1922,

> The native is induced and encouraged to take as much in the way of goods as he likes although he has no cash to pay for them. Then his crop fails and he finds that he cannot pay, and the trader comes along and says 'If you do not join I will run you in, and you will have to pay all the costs. I will take out a civil action and annex your cattle'.[51]

Indebtedness spread enormously. By 1904, it was estimated that the sixty-four traders in a single district were owed £100,000; another magistrate wrote in 1906 that 'I am convinced that a large proportion of the Natives in this and other districts are virtually insolvent'.[52] Two of the traders who showed Haines their account books had, respectively, made cash advances of £10,500 in eight years, and sold goods on credit worth over £18,000 in a nine-year span.[53] Debts became most burdensome at those times the peasants were least well off; the growing integration of the Transkei's economy with the national (and international) economy was clearly demonstrated in times of recession. As in the depression of 1908, traders would refuse to allow the normal terms, would press for payment, or foreclose on outstanding accounts, while such crop surpluses that were raised realized depressed prices.[54]

A further aspect of the peasant/trader nexus emerged in the 1890s: an increasing reluctance by traders to buy African-grown grains, or an insistence on paying for them in kind, not cash. Behind this lay the trader's growing difficulty in disposing of grain profitably at market towns like Queenstown, Kingwilliamstown, or East London. In the 1870s and 1880s, the grain he transported thence competed with maize or wheat grown elsewhere in the hinterland, also transported by ox-wagon. Now it would suffer in competition with cereals brought to the towns by rail—or even by steamship and rail from the American mid-west.

For this reason, the reports of the period are dotted with comments upon the new reluctance of Africans to raise grain that they would not be able to sell; in a confidential report for the Cape government in 1905 it was stated that between the Kei and Umtata rivers underproduction for want of access to markets was the great drawback.[55] As Stanford, the Chief Magistrate, put it in 1908: 'The easy access to the labour market contrasts with the difficulty or absolute lack of transport for agricultural produce.'[56] The 'difficulty' of transport costs was spelled out by the magistrate of Umtata: the prevailing transport system, he said, operated

> very unfavourably on the price of mealies. In fruitful seasons when growers wish to sell, it does not pay to export, the cost of transport being too great. In seasons of scarcity, when consumers wish to buy, the cost of transport again enhances the price of grain; a few months ago when mealies were selling at Butterworth at 12/6 per muid,[57] they sere selling here at 18−20s, the difference being due to the fact that, at Butterworth, dealers were able to import by rail from the Free State, while at Umtata they had to depend on local supplies or to import by wagon.[58]

Perhaps the most important variable introduced into structural relations between the white agricultural sector and the African peasantry after the mineral discoveries was the relative ease of access to markets for farmers in each sector. Macmillan has pointed out that 'to locate the native reserves it is no bad rule . . . to look for the areas circumvented or entirely missed, by even branch railway lines'.[59]

While the 'difficulty of transport' cut down the amount of grain that the trader would purchase, it certainly did not abolish trade in crops, for the good reason that a limited local trade in grain was one of the largest sources of a trader's annual income. Grain was sold by peasants immediately after harvest, to be resold later in the season, at handsome profits.[60] Probably no other item of African economic behaviour elicited the scorn of white observers as regularly as this 'fecklessness', 'improvidence', or 'stupidity'. Yet examination shows that the seemingly irrational behaviour was in itself an indication of the pressures to which the peasants were being subjected. The sales after the harvest took place because cash or goods were needed—to pay debts, to meet taxes or rents, or simply because of consumer demands that had become imperative. Storage facilities were inadequate to allow 'banking' the grain until it could be off-loaded at more favourable rates, while more sophisticated storage or marketing devices were ruled out even for substantial peasants by the dearth of private or public investment in the region, and the growing inability of peasants to accumulate capital.[61]

For one must bear in mind that ultimately any production of agricultural surplus by the peasantry would involve competition with white agriculturists; at the same time that changes in the internal economy of the Transkei were restricting the surplus-generating capacity of African peasants, the commercialization of white agriculture began to be aided by a massive programme of subsidies, grants, and other assistance. As early as 1908, with the floodgates of interest politics not yet fully raised, it was remarked that 'it is probable that during the last twenty years more money per head of the rural population has been devoted to the relief of the farmers in South Africa than in any other country in the world'.[62] The peasant's ability to participate in the produce market was being weakened at the same time as the competitive position of white farmers was being shored up by state aid and by modernization. Once capitalist agriculture 'has overcome the initial difficulties related to its competitive weakness in the produce market . . . market forces themselves tend to widen the gap between productivities in peasant and capitalist agriculture'.[63] Between 1929 and 1939, the production of maize and sorghum in the Transkei declined by about 25 per cent, while that of white farmers rose by 40 per cent.[64]

## Conclusion

In conclusion, it must be mentioned that the picture of a Transkei economy already underdeveloped before 1914, with the symptoms and the agents of underdevelopment prevalent throughout the years 1890–1914, is somewhat at variance with other historical assessments. The broadly current version is stated most strongly by Brookes who fifty years ago celebrated the Transkei peasant as 'the most prosperous, the most advanced. and (with the exception of the Natal tribal native) the most contented Native in South Africa today'. This was so because of a 'unique progressive policy', a 'coherent, intelligible, progressive and conscious evolution' from Blyth through

Rhodes to the workings of the TTGC under the paternal eyes of white magistrates. The Transkei entered the twentieth century 'in a state of great tranquillity and prosperity', and under the Glen Grey system stood 'alone' in its 'remarkable progress'. De Kiewiet also stressed the 1894 Act, and said that the Transkei thereafter showed 'distinct elements of success'.[65] More recently (and in the context of the chapter in which it appears, more surprisingly) Monica Wilson has written that agriculture declined in the Transkei only 'after 1930'.[66]

Those favourable judgements seem to have arisen in large part because the historians concerned have taken the proceedings of the TTGC (with its expenditure on agricultural schools and improvements, its debates on stock breeding and on soil conservation) as evidence of agricultural innovation and material well-being. And so they are—but, crucially, the enterprise and well-being that they reflect belong to a specific class that had emerged and was even then consolidating its position in the society. The Glen Grey Act contributed to the definition of that class: to the overlapping of the categories of bureaucrat and well-to-do peasant, to the enjoyment by the headmen and their favourites of the choice land, to the circulation of funds and skills at the upper strata, and to the heightened pressure on the young and the landless to sell their labour. (Symbolically, the general council's first agricultural school, in Tsolo, stood alongside the educational institution for chiefs' sons!) Like the kulaks in the Russian countryside, who 'had the great advantage' of being 'members, very important members, of the village commune', the most prosperous peasants in the Transkei were also able to use 'political power' in their own interests.[67] As has already been argued, the success of a large stratum of peasants is not only compatible with, but is a predictable feature of, the underdevelopment of a peasant society as a whole.

Viewed structurally, the workings of the internal economy of the Transkei as well as the subordination of the regional economy to the capitalist economy make it clear that underdevelopment and not progress was the distinctive feature of peasant production in our period. The daily existence of the peasant was increasingly influenced by economic disabilities beyond his control; their effects were cumulative and mutually reinforcing. From the rising cost of a peasant mode of production there stemmed the Transkei's peculiar form of proletarianization: the creation of proletarians who retained the semblance of access to the means of production, but who had to sell their labour power in order to subsist.

# NOTES

1.   'Emigrant Tembuland' was the name given to those lands occupied by the four Tembu chiefs and their followers who emigrated from the Cape (in the vicinity of Queenstown) in the late 1860s. After several changes of boundary and name, the area was divided in 1884 into the magisterial districts of Xalanga and St Mark's.
2.   Cape Printed Papers [henceforth CPP], G.3–'94, *Report of Commission on Labour Supply* [henceforth *Labour Commission*], *Vol. 3* (Cape Town, 1894), 57. For similar evidence see 57–8, 136, 174 *et passim*.
3.   *Labour Commission, Vol. 3, 5.*
4.   Speech by President, Johannesburg Chamber of Mines, 1911. Cited in F.A. Johnstone, *Class, Race and Gold* (London, 1976), 27.
5.   CPP, G.7–'92, *Blue Book on Native Affairs* (Cape Town, 1892), 31.
6.   CPP, G.4–'93, *Blue Book on Native Affairs* (Cape Town, 1893), 61, 63; CPP, G.8–'95, *Blue Book on Native Affairs* (Cape Town, 1895), 81; CPP, G.19–'97, *Blue Book on Native Affairs* (Cape Town, 1897), 108.
7.   *Labour Commission, Vol. 3, 110.*
8.   *Labour Commission, Vol. 3, 54.*
9.   *Labour Commission, Vol. 3, 76.*
10.   *Labour Commission, Vol. 3, 71.*
11.   CPP, G.9–'94, *Blue Book on Native Affairs* (Cape Town, 1894), 63.
12.   CPP, G.9–'94, *Blue Book on Native Affairs* (Cape Town, 1894), 56; United Society for the Propagation of the Gospel [henceforth USPG] Archives, London, E.MSS, 1894, E. Coakes, St Mark's Mission, 30 September 1894.
13.   C. van Onselen, 'Reactions to Rinderpest in Southern Africa, 1896–97', *Journal of African History, 13*, 1972, 473–88.
14.   CPP, G.42–'98, *Blue Book on Native Affairs* (Cape Town, 1898), 76. See van Onselen, 'Reactions to Rinderpest', 477, for prevalence of this belief and other examples.
15.   USPG Archives, E.MSS, 1898, Volume 2. See also van Onselen, 'Reactions to Rinderpest', 487.
16.   CPP, G.31–'99, *Blue Book on Native Affairs* (Cape Town, 1899), 81.
17.   USPG Archives, CLR Series, Kaffraria 1874–1927, Vol. 2, Bishop Key, 20 January 1900.
18.   H. Bley, 'Social Discord in South West Africa 1894–1904', in P. Gifford and W.R. Louis (eds), *Britain and Germany in Africa* (New Haven, 1967), 627–8.
19.   CPP, G.25–'02, *Blue Book on Native Affairs* (Cape Town, 1902), 8.
20.   CPP, G.25–'02, *Blue Book on Native Affairs* (Cape Town, 1902), 8.
21.   CPP, G.37–'03, *Sheep Inspector's Report for 1903* (Cape Town, 1903), 44–5.
22.   W. Beinart, 'Peasant Production, Underdevelopment, and the Traditionalist Response: Pondoland, *c.*1880–1930', MA thesis, University of London, 1973, 11.
23.   CPP, G.25–'02, *Blue Book on Native Affairs* (Cape Town, 1902), 37.
24.   CPP, G.42–'98, *Blue Book on Native Affairs* (Cape Town, 1898), 111.
25.   CPP, G.12*–'04, *Blue Book on Native Affairs* (Cape Town, 1904), 57.
26.   'Red' was the name given to the 'pagan' or 'conservative' element in the Eastern Cape and Transkei; the term derives from the use of red ochre or clay. See M. Wilson, 'The Growth of Peasant Communities', in M. Wilson and L. Thompson (eds), *The Oxford History of South Africa, Vol. 2, South Africa 1870–1966* (Oxford, 1971), 74–6.
27.   *Labour Commission, Vol. 3, 5.*
28.   With desperate brevity: underdevelopment is not a necessary stage in the formation of modern capitalist economies. Rather, it is a special process due to the penetration of capitalist enterprises and relationships into archaic or pre-capitalist structures, a 'discrete historical process through which economies that have already achieved a high level of development have not necessarily passed'. The underdevelopment of any region is historically determined by the process of capitalist development in another region: 'development and underdevelopment are structurally different from, yet

caused by [the] relation [of each] with, the other'. The relation between the two is complex, and involves the several ways in which the developed country/region exerts economic superiority over the underdeveloped. For the moment we need mention only (i) that the underdeveloped economy is looked to for the provision of materials and labour, and for the consumption of goods manufactured in the developed economy; (ii) that certain of the economic relations and features of the capitalist economy/region are replicated in the underdeveloped economy/region, albeit in attenuated or distorted form because of the very different historical conditions prevailing in the two sectors. In particular, the appearance in underdeveloped regions of class stratification, the cash nexus, and social relations deriving from these is crucial in restructuring the internal economy of the underdeveloped region. C. Furtado, *Development and Underdevelopment* (Berkeley, 1971), 129; A.G. Frank, *Capitalism and Underdevelopment in Latin America* (New York and London, 1969), 9.

29. J.R.L. Kingon, 'The Economic Consequences of East Coast Fever', *Christian Express*, 45, 1915, 46, 1916 (Nos. 539–42).

30. J.T. Kenyon, *An Address on the General Council System of the Transkeian Territories* (Umtata, 1932), 64.

31. U.G.33–'13, *Native Affairs Department Report for 1912* (Cape Town, 1913), 14.

32. Johnstone, *Class, Race and Gold*, 181. The average earnings per shift for African workers barely fluctuated between 1911 and 1919; the lowest average was 1s 11d and the highest 2s 0d, yet between 1910 and 1920 the wholesale price index rose from 1,000 to 2,512.

33. Evidence of Howard Pim to *Cd. 7707, Royal Commission on the Natural Resources, Trade, and Legislation of Certain of His Majesty's Dominions* (London, 1914), 111.

34. Figures are for the African population of the Transkei. They are based on the census reports of 1891, 1904 and 1911, with considerable reliance on informed guesswork to supplement the 1891 figures, which did not include Pondoland.

35. CPP, G.9–'94, *Blue Book on Native Affairs* (Cape Town, 1894), 52.

36. G. Arrighi, 'Labour Supplies in Historical Perspective: A Study of the Proletarianization of the African Peasantry in Rhodesia', *Journal of Development Studies*, 6, 1970, 214.

37. CPP, G.12–'04, *Blue Book on Native Affairs* (Cape Town, 1904), 40. The administrator was W.E. Stanford, Chief Magistrate in 1904.

38. CPP, G.5–'96, *Blue Book on Native Affairs* (Cape Town, 1896), 92; CPP, G.19–'97, *Blue Book on Native Affairs* (Cape Town, 1897), 141.

39. CPP, G.25–'02, *Blue Book on Native Affairs* (Cape Town, 1902), 31.

40. Transkeian Territories General Council, *Proceedings and Reports*, Session 1909 (Umtata, 1909), lxiii.

41. P.G.J. Koornhof, 'The Drift from the Reserves among the South African Bantu', PhD thesis, Oxford University, 1953, 268.

42. A. Pearse, 'Metropolis and Peasant: The Expansion of the Urban-Industrial Complex and the Changing Rural Structure', in T. Shanin (ed.), *Peasants and Peasant Societies* (Harmondsworth, 1971), 73.

43. 'Cash commodity prices... do not show very great variation from trader to trader.' E.S. Haines, 'The Transkei Trader', *South African Journal of Economics, 1*, 1933, 203. Licences for new stores were only granted if they were at least five miles away from existing stores.

44. CPP, G.46–'06, *Blue Book on Native Affairs* (Cape Town, 1906), 48.

45. M. Dobb, *Studies in the Development of Capitalism* (London, 1946), 89. Cited also in Chapter 10, I.R. Phimister, 'Peasant Production and Underdevelopment in Southern Rhodesia, 1890–1914, with Particular Reference to the Victoria District'.

46. U.G.22–'32, *Report of Native Economic Commission 1930–1932* (Cape Town, 1932), 137. Cf. Phimister's suggestion, 'So it would seem in many respects that traders represented institutionalized "raiding" of the peasant produce surplus for the ultimate benefit of the capitalist sector.' Chapter 10, Phimister, 'Peasant Production'.

47.  U.G.17–'11, *Blue Book on Native Affairs* (Cape Town, 1911), 180.

48.  Haines, 'The Transkei Trader', 208.

49.  Interest rates varied enormously, especially before the Cape's Usury Act of 1908. A common rate of interest in the Transkei was one shilling per pound per month—60 per cent per annum. Instances were quoted of interest at 100 per cent and more.

50.  Cf. the situation in nineteenth-century Russia, where poorer peasants 'tended to sink progressively into dependence, until burdened by debt and taxation and no longer able to maintain themselves on their meagre holdings, as whole families they joined the ranks of the rural proletariat, or at least supplied part of the family as semi-proletarians to eke out the income from the family holding by wage-employment in . . . mines or factory towns'. Dobb, *Studies,* 253.

51.  Cited in Johnstone, *Class, Race and Gold,* 28.

52.  CPP, G.12*–'04, *Blue Book on Native Affairs* (Cape Town, 1904), 14; CPP, G.46–'06, *Blue Book on Native Affairs* (Cape Town, 1906), 63.

53.  Haines, 'The Transkei Trader', 206.

54.  CPP, A.2–'09, *Select Committee on Native Affairs* (Cape Town, 1909), 233.

55.  CPP, G.22–'05, *Report on Trade with Native Territories* (Cape Town, 1905), 7–8.

56.  CPP, G.24–'08, *Blue Book on Native Affairs* (Cape Town, 1908), 24.

57.  One Cape muid was the equivalent of three bushels, or about 109 litres. In late nineteenth century South Africa, the average bag of maize was reckoned as a three-bushel bag.

58.  U.G.17–'11, *Blue Book on Native Affairs* (Cape Town), 1911), 142.

59.  W.M. Macmillan, *Complex South Africa* (London, 1930), 212.

60.  'As a general rule it is probably safe to reckon the trader's purchase price as about 50% of his [cash] selling price in the following summer.' Haines, 'The Transkei Trader', 206.

61.  Transkeian Territories General Council, *Proceedings and Reports,* Session 1909 (Umtata, 1909), xxxvii. A co-operative storage and marketing scheme was proposed, but fell away because it would have been too expensive to institute.

62.  F.B. Smith, *Some Observations upon the Probable Effect of the Closer Union of South Africa upon Agriculture* (Pretoria, 1908). Cited also in Chapter 7, M. Legassick, 'Gold, Agriculture, and Secondary Industry in South Africa, 1885–1970: From Periphery to Sub-Metropole as a Forced Labour System'.

63.  Arrighi, 'Labour Supplies', 221.

64.  Koornhof, 'The Drift', 233.

65.  E.H. Brookes, *The History of Native Policy in South Africa, 1830 to the present day* (Cape Town, 1924), 108, 115, 386; C.W. de Kiewiet, *A History of South Africa: Social and Economic* (London, 1941), 199.

66.  Wilson, 'Peasant Communities', 56.

67.  S. Stepniak, *The Russian Peasantry* (London, 1888), 55. Cited in Dobb, *Studies,* 252.

# CHAPTER 9

## The Agricultural History of Rhodesia

### ROBIN PALMER

### Introduction

Agricultural history has become decidedly trendy. In 1971–3 general histories of Tanzania, Kenya, Zambia, Malawi, and South Africa were published,[1] while more recently a number of regional studies have appeared, some of which are to be found in this book. This paper endeavours to provide a comparable general study for Rhodesia which may serve, as Ranger's pamphlet on Zambia has done, as a stimulus to further research, particularly at the local level. It is encouraging to note the excellent start already made in this direction in the chapters by Ian Phimister and Barry Kosmin, which immediately follow this one.

The dominant theme of Rhodesian agricultural history is surely the triumph of European over African farmers, and it is with this theme that I shall be principally concerned. The chapter begins with a brief geographical introduction, it goes on to examine the agricultural systems of the Shona and Ndebele of Rhodesia and that of the Europeans of South Africa (which was imported into Rhodesia after 1890), it looks at early African economic responses to the coming of colonial rule, and finally concentrates on the expansion of European agriculture and the decline of African agriculture, and shows how the two were intimately related.[2]

Rhodesia (formerly Southern Rhodesia) is a landlocked country, approximately 450 miles (725 km) long and 520 miles (835 km) wide, covering an area of about 150,000 square miles (389,000 sq. km), or some 96 million acres. It is therefore about half the size of Zambia and one-third that of South Africa. Under the 1969 Land Tenure Act, the land is divided equally between Europeans and Africans, though the latter outnumber the former by some 20:1.

Geographically, Rhodesia is divided into three main regions. Running approximately north-east to south-west through the middle of the country, with an offshoot to the north-west of Salisbury, is the predominantly flat *highveld,* land over 4,000 feet (1,220 m), which forms the watershed between the Zambezi, Limpopo, and Sabi rivers, and comprises some 25 per cent of the country. This is a cool, well-watered, and fertile area which attracted first the Ndebele and later the European settlers. To the west and to the east the land falls away to form the *middle-veld,* between 3,000 and 4,000 feet (915 and

1,220 m), which covers about 40 per cent of the country. This is a more dissected, undulating area than the subdued *highveld*, though in the west it flattens out and becomes remarkably featureless, to the extent that the Victoria Falls railway runs for seventy miles from Gwai to Dett in a perfectly straight line. Many of the 'native reserves' (now 'tribal trust lands') are situated within the *middle-veld*. Finally, beyond the *middle-veld* lies the hot, dry *lowveld,* land below 3,000 feet (915 m), mostly in the Sabi-Limpopo and Zambezi valleys, which constitutes the remaining 35 per cent of Rhodesia. In the Sabi-Limpopo the country is extremely flat, while in the Zambezi it is much more broken and rugged, with precipitous slopes along the escarpment. Neither valley has proved attractive to human settlement and their present sparse populations were probably at one time pushed there by stronger peoples who dominated the *middle-* and *highvelds.* The tsetse fly has been confined to the two *lowveld* valleys and today affects only 10–12 per cent of the country, though in the past it was far more widespread.[3]

The climatic feature which most influences farming in Rhodesia is of course that of rainfall. For over half the year, from April to October, there is virtually no rain throughout the country. Towards the end of the dry season the weather becomes progressively more humid and oppressive until the rains eventually break with devastating force in November. The rain, however, is fickle and deceptive. Only about one-third of Rhodesia enjoys an average annual rainfall of over 28 inches (712 mm), while approximately half the country has between 20 and 28 inches (508 and 712 mm). In general, as one moves from north to south and from east to west, so the annual average decreases, though there are very great regional and annual variations. But the rain tends to come in torrents: 'Over a period of 10 years at both Salisbury and Bulawayo, more than 30% of the total annual rainfall fell at rates exceeding 1 inch per hour. 4 to 5 inch falls during a single storm are not uncommon.'[4] Consequently a great deal of Rhodesia's rainfall—Kay suggests as much as 65 per cent[5]—is wasted in runoff. Some years however the rains fail altogether, drought conditions ensue, church leaders and traditional rain-makers alike pray for rain, and everyone suffers. In other years there is too much rain, and crops are washed away or severely damaged. Farming in Rhodesia is thus a hazardous occupation for everyone; as one European farmer of the 1930s testified with feeling, 'In England there is no real parallel to the ruin that can be caused in Africa by a black drought, or a plague of locusts, or cloud bursts. And when the main crop is a leaf crop, like tobacco, and so exceptionally susceptible, there are occasions when a year's hard work can be wiped out in twenty minutes, as I've reason to know.'[6]

## The nineteenth century

A striking feature of many travellers' accounts of East and Central

Africa in the nineteenth century is the evident agricultural prosperity of many—though not all—of its peoples and the great variety of produce grown, together with the volume of local, regional, and long-distance trade and the emergence of a wide range of entre-preneurs. An equally striking feature of accounts written in the 1920s and 1930s is the picture of widespread stagnation and decay which emerges, with a greatly reduced number of crops being grown, with an almost complete cessation of inter-African trade, and with an increasing cycle of rural poverty driving more and more people away to the towns.[7] By 1939 virtually all vestiges of African economic independence have been shattered, African cultivators have become tied to a world market over which they have no control, and a pattern of underdevelopment has been firmly established. Rhodesia is no exception to this general trend.

Three different agricultural systems ultimately came into collision in Rhodesia; those of the Shona, who now comprise nearly 80 per cent of the total population, the Ndebele, who number about 15 per cent, and the European settlers, whose numerical insignificance, at 5 per cent of the population, has been more than compensated for by their economic and political dominance. Each of these systems is examined in turn.

Though there were naturally great regional variations, the Shona were in general skilled agriculturalists, who enjoyed a degree of prosperity which belies the standard, though palpably false, picture of a people utterly demoralized by Ndebele raids. However, Shona agriculture was never entirely secure; it was vulnerable, as David Beach shows in Chapter 1, to *shangwa*, droughts or disasters, which periodically ravaged the country, and against which there was no assured defence, since it was not possible to store surplus grain for more than two to three years. Both their agricultural skill, and their vulnerability in the face of a harsh environment, explain the eagerness and rapidity with which the Shona availed themselves of the opportunity to become peasant producers at the end of the nineteenth century.

'In my opinion', wrote the N/C Umtali in 1897, 'the Mashona works his lands better than any other native tribe I know.'[8] Certainly nineteenth-century Shona farmers produced a wide variety of crops. The basic grain staples were finger millet (*Eleusine coracana*), known as *rapoko* or *rukweza,* and bulrush millet (*Pennisetum typhoideum*), or *mhunga*. Also widely grown were sorghum, *mapfunde* or 'kaffir corn' in white Southern African terminology, especially in the drier areas, and maize, *magwere* or *chibagwe,* which became very popular in the twentieth century. In the wetter eastern districts in particular, rice was grown by the Ndau group of Shona-speakers, though it could also be grown on a small scale in any *vlei*.[9] These staples were supplemented by a variety of fruits, such as pineapples, lemons, and pawpaws, by vegetables, like peas, beans, sweet potatoes, and tomatoes, and by cucurbits, such as pumpkins, marrows, melons, and cucumbers. In various parts of the country tobacco, cotton, groundnuts, yams, cassava, and sugar were also produced. Further variety was provided by game and fish, and the Shona were excellent hunters and fishermen. Numerous wild foodstuffs were also collected from the plant and insect life. Livestock, an important insurance against *shangwa,* included cattle, goats, sheep, dogs, and fowl. Other activities included the working of iron for agricultural tools and weapons, pottery, wood-carving and the making of cloth, baskets, nets, and mats. Gold had been mined and traded extensively with the east coast in previous centuries, notably between the twelfth and fifteenth, and even though the volume of this trade had declined, the washing of alluvial gold continued and copper was also mined in small quantities.[10]

Long-distance trade routes, while used less extensively than in the days of the powerful Shona states, continued to run north-eastwards towards Tete and the other Portuguese settlements on the Zambezi, and many Shona felt aggrieved when British occupation gradually brought an end to the gold trade with that area. There was also a very great deal of local trade, for example in the Melsetter area between the people of the drought-ridden Sabi valley, who in bad years exchanged salt, dried fish, palm wine, mats, baskets, and cloth for grain and tobacco from the people of the more favoured uplands. Iron tools and pots were bartered throughout the Shona country, and the early Europeans, like modern tourists, were beseiged by people offering them a wide range of goods.[11] In short, within the limitations of the prevailing technology, the Shona made intelligent use of their harsh environment, though they never entirely mastered it, and consequently were very responsive to the new markets created by the arrival of the Europeans.[12]

The Ndebele, on the other hand, have usually been categorized as pastoralists, and cattle undoubtedly played an important role in their society. In fact the Ndebele probably elected to settle on the Matabeleland *highveld* precisely because it was free of tsetse fly and was ideal cattle country, and by 1890 they had built up an enormous herd of something in the region of a quarter of a million head. But the Ndebele were not beef-eaters—cattle were killed mainly on cere-monial occasions—and though milk was readily available, this was not in itself an adequate diet.

Thus the Ndebele were in fact, like the Shona, basically agricul-turalists.[13] This is scarcely surprising in view of the fact that the Ndebele state was 'a successor to the Shona-speaking Changamire Rozvi state, which influenced it in many ways',[14] and that much of the agricultural work was performed by the incorporated Shona—the so-called *holi.* In a society in which socio–economic differentiation was increasing as a result of contacts with Western capitalism, all the larger villages contained 'a royal field and granary to supply the king with food whenever he visited', while the *holi* 'had to hoe in the king's fields before they were allowed to start on their own'.[15] The missionary T.M. Thomas, who spent the years 1859–70 vainly endeavouring to convert the Ndebele to Christianity, wrote glowingly of 'gardens full of ripe maize, and various indigenous grains', of 'extensive fields of Indian corn and other cereals', and of some valleys 'converted into the most fruitful gardens'. He also mentioned that in some areas cotton was grown, from which the Ndebele made durable garments, and that he knew of no village without its tobacco garden. In addition to this, the Ndebele evolved a system of underground granaries—later raided by the Europeans—which were well disguised, water- and air-tight, and in which 'corn is preserved sometimes for many years; and in this way the natives have occasionally stored up food enough to keep themselves active during years of scarcity'.[16] One European looter estimated that each granary could hold some thirty 200-lb bags of grain.[17] In October 1887, the concession-hunter 'Matabele' Wilson noted in his Bulawayo diary that 'there is more stuff about the place in the shape of cattle, sheep, goats, eggs, potatoes, rice, groundnuts, sweet potatoes, Indian corn and millet, poultry by the dozen, and milk and beer which the natives bring round to the white men's wagons for sale'.[18]

There is clear evidence too that the Ndebele were not plunderers and economic parasites, but rather were involved in a good deal of regional trade. They provided the main market for the thriving tobacco industry of the Shangwe (Shona-speaking) people of Inyoka, near Gokwe, for instance,[19] they obtained grain from the Ngwato and copper from the Lemba, and also 'had considerable traffic with the Amasili/Masarwa of the edge of the Kalahari, exchanging iron, dagga, spears, hoes, and knives for ostrich-egg-shell beads, ivory and feathers, horns, and skins'.[20] Bhebe observes that 'Periodic droughts were among the most powerful forces that drove the Ndebele into trade relations with their neighbours', and at such times cattle, goats, and beads were sold to the Shona in return for grain.[21] In the early days of Ndebele settlement at Bulawayo, cattle were apparently traded out to the Rozvi in return for young people who were promptly incorporated into Ndebele society.[22] Cattle were also sold to white missionaries, traders, and, after 1890, to the newly arrived settlers.[23]

It was not until twenty years after the white occupation of Rhodesia in 1890 that European farming began to offer any serious threat to African cultivators. In part this was because most Europeans were obsessed with the notion of finding a 'Second Rand', and their energies were directed almost exclusively towards mining; as the *Bulawayo Sketch* put it in 1895, the 'main reason we are all here is to make money and lose no time about it'.[24] Though European farming was slow to develop in Rhodesia, it did however inherit a number of characteristics from South Africa, since the vast majority of the settlers were either South African born, or had spent some time 'down south'. It is therefore worth examining briefly some of the main features of European farming as it grew up in South Africa.

In 1654 the first land grants were made to settlers near Cape Town to encourage vegetable-growing, and under the Cape Dutch system of land tenure which subsequently emerged, Europeans were virtually given a free hand to peg out their own farms. A tradition quickly grew up whereby when they managed to defeat Africans in warfare, they were allowed to parcel out the lands of the conquered among themselves. The farther north white settlement extended, the larger the European farms became, partly because so much of the land was suitable only for ranching, and a general lack of water necessitated extensive farms if ranching was to be successful. Thus in the Cape interior during the seventeenth and eighteenth centuries, 'It became an established custom that a man could possess all the land within half an hour's ride, at walking-pace, from his house on the centre of his farm. Thus farms could be spaced out at an hour's ride from one another. The area involved was 3,000 morgen [6,350 acres][25] per farm. . . . In time the term "farm" and 3,000 morgen of land became synonymous.' In the Transvaal in the nineteenth century, however, square 4,000-morgen farms were found to be more economical than the circular 3,000-morgen farms of the Cape, though here 'horses were sometimes ridden at speeds greater than walking-pace and farms of up to 6,000 morgen were not uncommon'. Such expansiveness was further enhanced by the very African tradition that 'each member of the family was entitled to a farm and a farm was regarded as the birthright of every man'.[26] Afrikaners believed in having large families.

So the white frontier moved northwards, but eventually the seemingly inexhaustible supply of land began to run out and wars were waged on African societies specifically for land. During the 1880s small Afrikaner 'republics' were carved out of Bechuanaland, Zululand, and Swaziland, while new settlements were founded in South West Africa and Angola. Hence it is not surprising that the European pioneers who entered Mashonaland in 1890 were each promised farms of 1,500 morgen, which they were 'to be allowed to "ride off" ' . . . in the Boer manner', [27] or that the trekkers from the depressed and land-short Orange Free State, whom Dunbar Moodie led to Melsetter in 1892–3, were given farms of 3,000 morgen, as were those Europeans who volunteered to invade Matabeleland in 1893. The 1893 invaders in fact refused to fight for the British South Africa Company, though they were under a legal obligation to do so, until they had been promised land and mineral concessions and a share of the Ndebele cattle.

Before the mineral revolution of the late nineteenth century, 'land was all that South Africa had to offer the prospective colonist',[28] but on that land, to which he had helped himself so liberally, he was as yet by no means the master. Both Bundy and Denoon have clearly shown how, in all four provinces of South Africa, some African cultivators seized avidly the economic opportunities afforded by the expansion of the white frontier and became peasant farmers, producing a wide variety of crops, competing successfully with European farmers, and winning prizes in competition with them at agricultural shows.[29] As Denoon rightly says, until the early twentieth century 'African peasants were more efficient and productive than white farmers'.[30] They were able to be so despite being dispossessed of much of their land. Some simply bought the land back, others farmed as rent-paying squatters on the millions of acres held by absentee landlords and land companies, while others again, largely in the Orange Free State and the Eastern Cape, became sharecroppers, surrendering half of their crop in return for seed and the use of the land. In the end it was the mineral revolution, which dramatically increased the demand for African labour and offered substantial incentives to European commercial farmers, combined with 'a sustained, several-pronged offensive ... launched by white legislators and administrators ... against the self-reliance and independence of the peasantry',[31] which ultimately put an end to African agricultural prosperity in South Africa.

## The era of peasant prosperity, 1890–1908

Europeans helped themselves liberally to land in Rhodesia. Under the benevolent gaze of Leander Starr Jameson, one-sixth of the entire country, or some 15¾ million acres, passed nominally into European hands during 'the age of the fortune hunters' in the 1890s. Much of this was simply paper alienation, with European 'farms' existing only on the surveyor-general's maps, while nearly two-thirds of this land was in the hands of the same kind of speculative companies which had earlier taken such a stranglehold over Natal. The value of land, it was hoped, would rise as the new colony became more firmly established. Nevertheless the land which the Europeans acquired, but did not immediately occupy, contained a very high proportion of the best land in the country, situated, as most of it was, on the fertile highveld.[32]

These 'conquest lands', on which European farming later established itself, were acquired without any regard whatsoever for existing African rights. Virtually the entire Ndebele homeland was expropriated following the defeat of Lobengula in 1893, and because the British South Africa Company assumed, for its own purposes, that Lobengula controlled the whole country, the Shona chiefs were denied the customary privilege of being offered a crate of whisky or champagne and perhaps a small stipend in return for signing away their ancestral lands. It was only after the 1896–7 Shona and Ndebele Risings, and in response to British pressure, that 'native reserves'—another import from South Africa—were assigned throughout the country. The reserves, totalling some 20 million acres, were chosen in an exceedingly haphazard manner, but they could not include any of the conquest lands, nor any land near the existing or projected railways, or lying on the 'Gold Belt'.[33]

There were at this stage numerous obstacles to the development of

European commercial farming: the lack of capital, equipment, and a regular supply of labour, the rinderpest and later the east coast fever which decimated the cattle, and the locusts and drought which preceded the Risings. Moreover, with no mining boom and no railway until the turn of the century,[34] and consequently with a highly limited internal, and a non-existent external, market, the early European farmers were 'subsistence cultivators indistinguishable (by style of life, techniques of production, and crops cultivated) from the African peasantry'.[35] This is nicely illustrated in a report of the Civil Commissioner, Bulawayo, for March 1895, in which he says that only 'about 150' of the 1,070 white farms in his area were occupied and that the white farmers were cultivating only 'about 900 acres', or 6 acres per farm.[36] As one white settler wrote of the 1890s, 'In those days . . . no farmers grew grain, it being cheaper to trade the country's requirements from the natives.'[37]

Early European agriculture was thus little more than market gardening for Salisbury and Bulawayo and the small mining centres. Most 'farmers' were primarily transport riders, storekeepers or traders, who bought—and sometimes stole—food from their African neighbours, while even 'the most elaborate farm consisted of little more than a collection of thatched huts and up to ten ploughed acres of land'. Moreover, not only were the early settlers 'completely ignorant of local conditions and potential for agriculture—but few of [them] had much agricultural background and experience in a practical sense. Even the Dutch Boer trekkers were to experience new hazards and many of them were content to live a semi-subsistence existence rather than actually develop their farms.'[38] Thus in the Fort Victoria district, which was one of the most important European centres in Mashonaland, out of a total of seventy registered farms in 1897, '20 are now more or less occupied being used by traders for grazing purposes and on a few of these 5 or 6 acres of land have been ploughed up', while 'the land owned by Companies is not occupied at all'.[39]

While European farming, such as it was, remained at a subsistence level, African farmers in Rhodesia, notably the Shona, were able to seize the opportunities afforded by the opening of new markets, and to set off 'on the high road to prosperity'[40] and in search of an agricultural security hitherto denied them by *shangwa*. The labour once employed in maintaining defensive positions against raiders could now be turned to agricultural production, while Shona manpower was no longer abducted for incorporation into the Ndebele state. Thus the Shona immediately began producing surplus crops[41] for sale to the Europeans, who numbered some 11,100 in 1901, compared to only 304 in Nyasaland the same year and about 850 in Northern Rhodesia in 1904. Hence it proved possible, and obviously preferable, for the Shona to meet their tax commitments through the sale of foodstuffs and cattle rather than by becoming migrant labourers. Indeed, as Phimister has argued, such was the viability of the peasant sector at this time that mine wages were forced up from between 5s and 10s per month in 1896 to between 30s and 80s in 1903.[42] As Lawrence Vambe puts it, 'Now that my people were under foreign rule, they believed even more firmly than they had before that self-sufficiency in their own food supplies was essential to their limited freedom. As long as they grew enough food for themselves they were spared the humiliation of working for white men',[43] who had, it should be remembered, so recently crushed the Shona Rising with appalling brutality. This conscious withholding of labour meant that Rhodesian employers were obliged to rely heavily on *chibaro* migrant labour from the north.

So we find that in 1903 African sales of grain and stock, some of which was exported, fetched c.£350,000, while in the same year African wage-earnings amounted to only c. £100,000–£150,000. In other words, agricultural sales comprised some 70 per cent of all African cash-earnings. An indication of the extent to which the Shona were responsible for this situation can be deduced from the fact that in 1902 only an estimated 13 per cent of able-bodied Shona men worked for three months for a white employer, compared to 48 per cent of the Ndebele, and in the following year the figure was c. 20 per cent for the Shona and c. 50 per cent for the Ndebele.[44] The main reason for this difference was that the economy of the Ndebele had been shattered in the 1890s. Their cattle had been destroyed, their land expropriated, and their raiding brought to an end, and hence they were obliged to become wage-earners far earlier than the Shona in order to meet the demands of both tax and rent, which was sometimes as high as £3 per annum. An additional factor was that wages tended to be higher in Matabeleland than in Mashonaland.

Shona prosperity was made possible by a combination of factors. At this time many Shona were still living on the *highveld* within easy access of the main European markets and the line of rail, the population was small, and hence there was no pressure on the land.[45] In addition the opening of numerous small mines provided an increasing demand for food and beer for the mineworkers—mostly foreign migrants forced to come to Rhodesia by the lack of markets and employment opportunities at home—which the Shona were able to meet, and which resulted in increased prices for their produce— bags of maize fetching 30s to 40s at the turn of the century. Also the number of African-owned cattle rose rapidly from an estimated 43,926 in 1901 to 195,837 in 1908, and many people found in the stock trade an easy way of meeting their financial obligations. Thus something of a minor agricultural revolution took place, mirroring exactly the earlier South African experience, with new crops such as market vegetables being grown as the demand arose. Hence 'the Shona responded to the new dietary regulations for the mines introduced in 1907 by growing and marketing more beans and monkey nuts',[46] while the VaShawasha people, helped by the Jesuit fathers of Chisawasha Mission, were 'able to supply Salisbury with maize, cement, beef, timber and a certain amount of wheat, barley and grapes'.[47] Indeed, some Shona near Salisbury were at this time employing other Africans as wage-labourers for 10s per month, while many of those previously involved in the working of alluvial gold abandoned this 'in favour of meeting the more lucrative demands of an expanding produce market'.[48] In general, native commissioners displayed remarkably little enthusiasm for all this activity, largely because it reduced the labour supply,[49] but perhaps also because, like their counterparts in Nyasaland and elsewhere, they 'preferred the warlike noble savage to the passive unmanly farmers'.[50]

Even the doubling of the hut tax from 10s to 20s in 1904,[51] while it meant that the African contribution to the revenue increased from 27 per cent to 41 per cent, failed to curb this expansion.[52] This was certainly facilitated by the fact that the Shona faced no real competition as yet from European farmers. Arrighi estimates that in the 1903–4 season, European holdings 'accounted for approximately 5 per cent of the total acreage under cultivation and for less than 10 per cent of the total marketed output'.[53] Most European farmers found it far more profitable to trade in African produce than become producers themselves and, in the Marandellas district at least, they relied upon their tenants to grow sufficient maize to feed their 'foreign' labour force.[54] All this explains why the BSA Company and the white landlords, bona fide and absentee, were perfectly happy to allow the Shona to remain where they were, and why there was no concerted attempt to push them into the 'native reserves'.[55] After 1908, however, things began to change.

## The white agricultural policy, 1908–14

In South Africa, it was the mineral revolution which ultimately led to the impoverishment of the African peasantry. In Rhodesia, paradoxically, it was the absence of such a revolution which had much the same effect. In 1907 a party of BSA Company Directors came to Rhodesia,[56] toured the country, and decided that the time had come to put an end to the myth of the 'Second Rand'. The myth had persisted for so long partly because mineral exploitation had been severly hindered by the Risings of 1896–7 and by the South African War of 1899–1902, which had cut Rhodesia's rail links to the south.[57] The end of that war was followed by a brief mining boom, but this collapsed in the financial crisis of 1903–4. The Company then made tentative inquiries into land settlement schemes elsewhere in the empire, and set up its own Land Settlement Committee in 1905, before sending out its directors two years later. The directors, no doubt influenced by contemporary imperial policies in Kenya, concluded that it was essential to diversify the economy, and that the best way of doing this was to encourage European farming, thereby promoting greater economic self-sufficiency, cutting the import bill and raising the value of land and providing more traffic for the railway, both of which, at the time, were owned by the Company. This 'white agricultural policy', as it was called, which began in 1908, was ultimately to affect radically the position of Africans on the land.

There were various aspects of the new policy. To begin with, an Estates Department was set up in 1908, designed specifically to promote European settlement and deal with all applications for land, while an information office, under a superintendent of emigration, was opened in London with a branch in Glasgow, and two agents were sent to South Africa to publicize Rhodesia at the leading agricultural shows there. The Estates Department 'possessed a fairly numerous staff, including an engineer, a citrus adviser and land inspectors'.[58] The type of immigrants it sought were people 'endowed with capital and experienced in farming on the African highveld. In addition they had to be loyal to the British connection.'[59]

Also in 1908 the Department of Agriculture was reorganized and a first director of agriculture appointed. He was Dr E.A. Nobbs, a trained scientist from the Cape—previous officials had been amateurs—and he was responsible for stimulating a great deal of agricultural research, much of which was published in the pages of the *Rhodesia Agricultural Journal*. A number of specialists were appointed to the Department, including a botanist, an entomologist, a chemist, an agriculturist, an irrigation engineer, and a tobacco expert. An experimental station and farm were opened near Salisbury, and a bevy of visiting experts were encouraged to come and offer their advice. The Department was thus in a position to place a wide range of extension facilities at the disposal of the new European farmer, and in 1910 it took over the grading of maize for export, a job previously undertaken by railway officials. Some idea of the extended scope of the Department may be gauged from the fact that its annual average expenditure rose from £10,065 in the years 1903–4 to 1908–9, to £22,476 in the period 1909–10 to 1913–14.[60]

The BSA Company itself began to develop an interest in tobacco and citrus, and in ranching. It used its Central Farms, near Bulawayo, Gwelo, Marandellas, Sinoia, and Umtali, to familiarize new immigrants from Britain, who had to possess a minimum of £700 capital, with the problems of farming on the Rhodesian *highveld*. A Land Bank was set up in 1912 with a share capital of £250,000, to make credit facilities 'available for persons of European descent only'.[61] The Bank gave loans of up to £2,000 for the purchase of farms, livestock, and agricultural equipment, and for improvements such as fencing, irrigation works, etc. The loans had to be repaid, at 6 per cent interest, within ten years. The Bank was of crucial importance in helping new European farmers to establish themselves on the land. Its success led white farmers elsewhere, notably in Kenya, where one was not established until 1930,[62] to demand something comparable. Such facilities were not available to African farmers in Rhodesia until 1945.

In addition, the minimum price of ranching land was reduced, until

1912, to about 8¹/₂d per acre, while agricultural land was reduced to 3s 9d. This compares with the 1904 average prices of 34s 4d in the Orange Free State, 33s in the Cape, 28s 6d in the Transvaal, and 25s in Natal,[63] while land along the Northern Rhodesian line of rail was fetching between 3d and 8d per acre at this time.[64] Also a much simpler form of land title was issued, rebates of between 20 and 30 per cent on the purchase price were granted in the event of positive improvements being made to the land, a concession claimed in practice by an 'infinitesimal' number of farmers,[65] and the Mines and Minerals Ordinance was revised so as to restrict the privileges of prospectors on occupied farms,[66] an interesting comment on the state of the mining industry.

From the Company's point of view, the results of the white agricultural policy were quite encouraging. In the years 1908–14 over 5¹/₂ million acres of land were sold, and the 1911 census revealed a total of 1,324 European farmers, compared to only 545 in 1904, while the number of occupied farms rose from 301 in 1904 to 2,042 in 1914, when some 183,407 acres were said to be under crops. By 1912, according to van Onselen, 'commercial agriculture was sufficiently profitable to draw capital previously employed in mining', while 'after 1912 most of the mines' food requirements were met by European commercial agriculture'.[67] For the most part, the new European farmers concentrated on the production of maize and tobacco, and on cattle-ranching.

Initially the Europeans obtained maize seeds from African farmers, and soon they were growing maize throughout much of Mashonaland 'with some success, but in a primitive and extensive fashion, so that the European yields were little better than those of the African peasant farmers'.[68] In particular the 'Gold Belt' areas, which were opened up to white farmers in 1903, were used for maize production. Maize was initially grown, by African labour rather than machinery, to feed African labourers at the mines, but it began to be exported in quantity for the first time in 1909. Production rose dramatically from 45,815 (203 lb) bags in 1903–4 to about 180,000 bags in 1906–7 to 634,133 bags in 1913–14. Exports, mostly to Britain, rose from 11,442 (200 lb) bags in 1909 to 202,105 bags in 1914, and some indication of the extent to which it 'caught on' can be gauged from the fact that an estimated 78 per cent of European land under cultivation in 1924 was devoted to maize.

Tobacco, which was ultimately to develop into 'the mainstay of European farming and a major support of the Rhodesian economy', was, like maize, widely grown by Africans before the European occupation. It had the attraction of offering a quick return for capital invested—a necessity if new immigrants were to be attracted to Rhodesia—and of being best grown in the previously neglected sandy soils, so that 'the Company would now be able to sell many farms which had hitherto attracted few buyers'.[69] The BSA Company did a great deal to stimulate its production. It appointed a tobacco expert,

G.M. Odlum, to the Department of Agriculture and sent him off to study tobacco-growing in America, Turkey, and Greece, whence he returned with fourteen Greeks, who were to assist in the development of turkish tobacco.[70] European farmers began to grow the crop avidly, especially in Mashonaland, and production rose swiftly from 132,210 lb in 1909–10 to about 2,240,000 lb in 1912–13. The following year, when 3,061,750 lb were grown, 'over-production brought chaos to the industry and for several years it floundered'.[71]

Cattle-ranching, which began to expand over much of the Matabeleland *highveld,* also owed its origin to African initiative, though in this case the Europeans simply stole the bulk of the Ndebele cattle after the war of 1893, and subsequently added to this haul by acquiring much of the herd looted from Mpezeni's Ngoni in Northern Rhodesia in 1899.[72] The 'indigenous' cattle were, according to a visiting professor from Edinburgh University, 'remarkable for their hardiness and ability to keep their flesh during the long dry season when pasturage is poor, but are very small in carcase'.[73] This was confirmed in the drought of 1912, when, as the CNC Mashonaland noted, 'the superiority of the condition of the native stock, as compared with the better breed animals owned by Europeans, was most marked'.[74] The local cattle were in fact upgraded by crossing with bulls imported from Northern Rhodesia, Nyasaland, and South Africa, which helped to add weight and quality to the existing durability.[75] Some 33,000 head of cattle were imported in the years 1909–13, and the number of European-owned cattle rose sharply from 38,611 in 1907 to 341,878 in 1914. Experts came from Texas, and a number of ranching companies began operating on a large scale, for, as the handbook for prospective settlers put it, 'while 15,000 acres is taken as the minimum area suitable for ranching, opportunities exist for the establishment of large ranching concerns (involving 50,000 acres and upwards) for those possessed of the necessary means'.[76]

All this activity inevitably gave rise to conflict and competition between European farmers and the Shona and Ndebele. European maize production posed an obvious threat to African peasant farmers, and European tobacco was grown predominantly on the sandy soils which the Shona had long favoured.[77] Indeed, in 1908 the CNC Matabeleland noted of new settlers, 'In selecting their land they have naturally been guided by the number of natives located thereon, whose knowledge of the productive powers of the soil must necessarily be the best guide.'[78] Similarly, as the number of African-owned cattle more than doubled, from 195,837 in 1908 to 406,180 in 1914, this led to tremendous competition for grazing lands with the Europeans, whose own cattle were increasing even more rapidly and whose number exceeded the number of African cattle for the first time in 1919. This competition was especially fierce in Matabeleland, where the land was drier, and the European farms larger, than in Mashonaland. Thus Europeans began to challenge Africans for markets,[79] for cattle and for land; the BSA Company was at this time endeavouring to extract the choicest pieces of land from the 'native reserves' and make them available to incoming settlers.[80] So began what Marshall Hole aptly called 'the squeezing-out process'.[81]

Prior to this rapid expansion of European farming, white land-owners had very little reason to turn Africans off their land, since they could extract from them crops, rents, or labour, as desired, and since African farmers were playing such a vital role in food production. But by 1914 the situation had begun to change. Because European agriculture was labour- rather than capital-intensive,[82] and because 'the sight of white men, and even more so white women, performing heavy, unskilled manual labour is one that is generally repugnant to most Rhodesians and South Africans',[83] the white farmers needed black labour. Here they came into competition with the mines, which were also labour-intensive, and which could generally afford to pay higher wages. The demand for labour indeed grew very rapidly. 'In 1905, it was calculated that Southern Rhodesia needed no more than 25,000 labourers all told,' writes Philip Mason, but 'by 1910, the mines alone wanted 39,000 and the farmers another 23,000.'[84] The white farmers needed large supplies of seasonal labour—at precisely the time when local Africans needed to tend to their own crops. They thus found themselves in much the same position as white farmers elsewhere in Africa, heavily reliant on migrant labour from depressed areas, and demanding a reduction of African land holdings and a tax mechanism which would effectively compel local Africans to work on their farms.[85] This was not going to be easy, for the Shona 'developed an almost universal anti-farming mentality which considered that a Shona... had sunk very low, socially and economically, if he worked for a white farmer'.[86] In response to this refusal to work, and in order to reduce the competitiveness of African farmers and cattle-owners, the European farmers began to impose high rents and other burdens such as dipping fees, and to evict Africans from their farms and push them into the reserves, which were situated farther away from the main markets.[87]

Thus in 1909 the BSA Company, in the teeth of Native Department opposition, imposed a £1 rent on unalienated land; in 1910 landlords, when obliged under the Private Locations Ordinance to pay a licence for each of their adult male tenants, promptly raised their rents; in 1912 a number of Matabeleland ranching companies subjected their tenants to grazing fees; in the same year, when an outbreak of east coast fever imposed restrictions on the movement of cattle, some landowners raised their rents, and others, rather than pay for dipping tanks, ordered African cattle-owners to quit, which was an impossible demand at such a time; in 1913 some European farmers refused to allow Africans who had been evicted from other farms to move cattle across their land, so that the Africans were obliged to sell for whatever they were offered; and finally, in 1914, compulsory dipping at 1–2s per head, could be 'applied in any area where this was the wish of the majority of farmers'.[88] By 1923 three-quarters of all African cattle was being compulsorily dipped. This plethora of impositions naturally provoked hostility. The rent on unalienated land caused 'great dissatisfaction' and was 'extremely unpopular' in Melsetter,[89] while in Bubi news of the grazing fees was greeted 'with a storm of protest and angry feelings', and the people complained eloquently that the landowners 'will be taking money from the flies in our kraals next; better be dead than pay such demands'.[90] But this was just the beginning.

## The economic triumph of European agriculture, 1915–25

A major concomitant of the expansion of European farming was the growing clamour for 'segregation' which arose in the decade 1915–25, a clamour in which the European farmers assumed the dominant role. The question hinged on the old Cape clause, introduced into Rhodesia at British insistence in 1894, which stipulated: 'A native may acquire, hold, encumber and dispose of land on the same conditions as a person who is not a native.' The law was not at all popular with white Rhodesians, and the Company managed to prevent it becoming effective through the simple expedient of refusing to sell land to Africans, and the vast majority of European farmers did the same. The result was that by 1925 only fourteen farms, totalling 46,966 acres, had been sold, seven to black Rhodesians and seven to black South Africans, mostly at inflated prices.[91]

The kind of segregation which the European farmers wanted was of a limited nature, confined to the *ownership* of land, for, as one of the country's leading white farmers put it, 'wholesale segregation of natives was an impossible proposition, because it would affect the labour supply and labour was essential for the development of the country'.[92] European farmers were strongly opposed to the emergence of an independent African landowning class of commercial farmers for two basic reasons. In the first place they objected to Africans as neighbours. As labourers or rent-paying tenants they were of course welcome, for they were beholden to the European farmer and could be evicted by him at will, but as landowners they would have to be treated, legally at any rate, as equals, and this was something which would cut right across Southern African racial prejudices.[93] Perhaps more important, if Africans 'invaded' the European farming areas, they would, by and large, be tilling the better soils and have equal access to markets, and hence be in a strong position to compete with European farmers. Indeed the white farmers were afraid that as the African earning capacity increased, so more and more Africans would be in a position to buy land, and they wanted the law changed before this could happen.[94] On the other hand, the Native Department and the missionaries were afraid that the existing trend would continue and that Africans would ultimately be left with no land at all outside the reserves. These conflicting fears for the future helped bring about a divergence of opposites, the end result being the Land Apportionment Act of 1930 which set aside 7¹/₂ million acres of 'native purchase areas', within which Africans alone could purchase land, with the *quid pro quo* that they could no longer buy land in the better-situated European areas.[95]

The decade of the segregation debate witnessed a further expansion of European farming and a not unconnected dramatic decline in African agriculture. Though European production fell during the First World War, when many farmers were on active service,[96] there was a post-war boom as new settlers arrived and an increase in mining activity created a larger internal market for agricultural commodities. Then came the recession of 1921–3, caused by a combination of external and local factors, which hit Africans far harder than Europeans, but this was followed by a period of renewed expansion as the new settler government, which took over from the BSA Company in 1923, did all it could to encourage the further development of European agriculture.

Thus the average annual expenditure of the Department of Agriculture rose from £33,468 in the years 1918–19 to 1922–3, to £75,636 in the period 1923–4 to 1928–9. The number of European farmers increased from 1,324 in 1911 to 2,355 in 1921, while altogether some 8¹/₂ million acres were alienated to Europeans in the period 1915–25, which brought the total European area up to just over 31 million acres, or a third of the entire country. This was sometimes very striking, as at Lomagundi in 1920, when the native commissioner reported: 'Land has been taken up in all directions and the European population has practically doubled itself.'[97] The price of land rose to an average of 7s per acre in 1920, and some of the absentee landlords took advantage of this and began to subdivide their huge estates and to sell off parts to the new immigrants. Finally, the new government greatly increased the amount of money devoted to road building and maintenance in the major white farming areas, in an endeavour to expand the existing infrastructure.

European agriculture continued to be dominated by maize, tobacco, and cattle. Maize production fluctuated a good deal, rising from 914,926 (203-lb) bags in 1914–15 to a peak of 1,505,580 bags in 1922–3 and then falling to 1,068,904 bags in 1924–5. Maize exports rose from 346,855 (200-lb) bags in 1915 to a peak of 774,449 bags in 1923 and then dropped to 383,338 bags in 1925. After the collapse of tobacco through overproduction in 1913–14, the industry slowly recovered and production rose from 426,423 lb in 1914–15 to a record 5,659,809 lb in 1925–6. The number of European-owned cattle continued to rise sharply, from 394,856 in 1915 to 1,006,086 in 1925, while African-owned cattle increased similarly from 445,795 to 1,095,841 in the same period. This twofold increase naturally intensified the racial competition for grazing lands. An export market was opened up to Johannesburg in 1916, and cattle exports rose from 12,928 in that year to 72,738 in 1926, by which time Southern

Rhodesia was exporting to South Africa, the Belgian Congo, Mozambique, Britain, Germany, and Northern Rhodesia, with South Africa taking some 80 per cent of the total. Exports at this time were greatly helped by the low railway rates prevailing as a result of the shipment of substantial quantities of Katangan copper to Beira over the Rhodesian railways.[98]

Thus European farming emerged from its pioneer period to a position in which it was firmly established as a central sector of the Rhodesian economy, with its members occupying strategic positions in government and in parliament.[99] As might be expected, this increasing success gave rise to a good deal of aggression towards Africans living on European land. The British High Commissioner for South Africa, Athlone, who visited Rhodesia in 1926, noted that the great majority of European farmers demanded excessive grazing fees and 'made considerable profit out of the unfortunate natives'. He observed that as dipping was compulsory, 'the temptation to make exorbitant profits in this way must be difficult to resist'.[100]

Relations were particularly bad in the Insiza district, between Bulawayo and Gwelo. In 1918 the local native commissioner remarked that 'The eagerness of some land owners to make a profit out of the [Compulsory Dipping] Ordinance—either by charging high dipping fees or by increasing the rent charges to cover the cost of constructing tanks, has left a very bad impression on the natives.' The following year he mentioned the case of one farmer who 'captured 70 head of native cattle . . . trespassing on his farm[101] (not on cultivated land) and charged the owners of the cattle an ox valued at £5 and £4 in cash'. The N/C commented, 'When farmers descend to such contemptible methods of enriching themselves at the expense of ignorant natives, it is not surprising if the natives do retaliate by burning farms out, but unfortunately decent farmers suffer in the process of retaliation, as when once a grass fire is started there is no saying where it will end.'[102] In the face of such evidence it is scarcely surprising that most Africans should feel that 'the white Rhodesian farmer . . . represented the worst in European racial feelings. . . . He was harsh, domineering, unfair, inhuman and took the law into his own hands when dealing with Africans, some of whom felt that they were placed in the same class as the cattle or even lower.'[103]

It is against such a background of racial hostility that one needs to look at the impoverishment of the African peasantry in Rhodesia. The remarkable prosperity enjoyed by many Shona farmers in the early years of the century was brought to an end by a combination of factors. Primarily, African farmers faced the full blast of competition from heavily subsidized European farmers while simultaneously being pushed away from easy access to markets, a process greatly facilitated by the work of the 1914–15 Native Reserves Commission, which reduced the reserves by a million acres and took from them much of the best land within easy reach of the main centres.[104] In addition, Africans were confronted with an ever-increasing number

of costly dues—taxes, rents, dipping and grazing fees, etc.—at a time
when their own appetite for consumer goods was on the increase. The
end result was that when they were no longer able to sustain
themselves and purchase their requirements from the sale of their
agricultural produce, they would be forced to ˙become wage-
labourers.

It was inevitable that European and African farmers would come
into open conflict, and the conflict would probably have occurred
earlier than it did but for the intervention of the First World War,
which led many Europeans to abandon their farms and presented
Africans with an opportunity to sell maize and cattle at rising prices.
This situation lasted until 1920. Then came the slump of 1921–3,
which, in Arrighi's words, 'radically altered the position of the
African peasantry in the structure of the Rhodesian economy'. In
1920, Africans sold some 198,000 bags of maize at 10s per bag; in 1921
they sold 43,600 bags at 5s—a drop in earnings from about £100,000 to
under £10,000. Similarly, in 1919 they sold some 20,000 head of cattle
at £7 to £8 each, while in 1922 they sold practically none.[105] On top of
all this, prices were rising fast. Between 1914 and 1920 the cost of ten
types of goods widely purchased by Africans rose on average by 165
per cent, while African wages went up by only 13 per cent in the same
period.[106]

Thus Africans were forced out on to the labour market, and many
employers, especially the farmers, took advantage of the situation to
reduce wages, in some districts to as low as 5s. Many tenants could no
longer afford to pay the rents and other fees demanded by their
landlords, and since the price of maize and cattle had fallen so low,
there was far less incentive to remain close to the main markets.
Hence there was, in the Chief Native Commissioner's words, 'a
continual stream' into the reserves,[107] with probably over 60,000
moving in the period 1915–25; and 'Once the migration had taken
place, the future ability of Africans who had migrated to obtain their
cash requirements through the sale of produce was, of course,
jeopardized.'[108] This was because of the greater cost, and difficulty,
of marketing their produce from the 'native reserves',[109] which by
now were beginning to show distinct signs of overcrowding.

The movement of thousands of Africans into the reserves obviously aroused a great deal of resentment. The situation was
particularly critical in Matabeleland, where, as Governor Chancellor
confessed, 'there is undoubtedly cause for complaint'.[110] To be
turned off a farm in central Matabeleland often entailed a trek of fifty
to a hundred miles to the nearest reserve, which was usually deficient
in water supplies, and many Ndebele whose homes were on the
*highveld* succumbed to malaria when they moved to the lower,
fever-stricken areas.[111] It was in such circumstances that Nyamanda,
the eldest son of Lobengula, and his cousin Madhloli Kumalo, who
had both been evicted several times from farms in the past, gained
considerable support in their campaign to restore the Ndebele

monarchy and establish a 'National Home', where all the Ndebele might settle and be free from the exactions of European farmers, who, as one Minister of Agriculture had the grace to admit, 'have ever so much more land than they ... can profitably make use of'.[112]

## The political triumph of European agriculture, 1926–36

In the period 1926–36 European agriculture was remarkable more for its political than its economic successes. The momentum of previous years was not maintained, and the great Depression of the early 1930s, which drove many white farmers off the land in Kenya, Nyasaland, and Northern Rhodesia, threatened the political and economic hegemony of the white Southern Rhodesian farmers and workers, and produced a series of demands for total segregation and non-competition between whites and blacks, which the new Huggins government of 1933 did its best to meet. The Depression indeed left a deep scar on the consciousness of European farmers, for it was they who provided the largest single group amongst the ranks of the unemployed whites,[113] and many more were only rescued from this fate by a combination of loans from the Land Bank—amounting to over one million pounds in 1934—and a three-year moratorium in 1933 on all instalment payments for farms.

The comparatively static nature of European agriculture in this period is illustrated by the number of Europeans employed in the industry, which rose from 3,995 in 1926 to 4,172 in 1931, and then dropped to 4,009 in 1936. This was in spite of an increase in the annual expenditure of the Department of Agriculture from £91,874 in 1928–9 to £262,957 in 1936–7. Tobacco enjoyed another brief boom, following an increase in imperial preference, and production soared from 5,659,809 lb in 1925–6 to over 19 million lb the following year and 24,943,044 lb in 1927–8. But once again, as in 1913–14, Rhodesian tobacco growers had over-reached themselves, for the overseas market was saturated, vast unsaleable stocks accumulated in British warehouses, the order books were closed and a great many tobacco farms were abandoned, with some 700 producers, three-quarters of the total, eliminated. As the official history of the industry puts it, 'Nearly all the progress of the previous ten years was wiped out in one season.'[114] In response to this collapse, cigarette manufacturers began making a determined, and successful, attempt to penetrate the local African market, to the exclusion of the traditional 'Inyoka' tobacco. But immediately there followed a slowing down of mining and industrial activity within the country, and in 1930 South Africa decided to impose a quota system on duty-free tobacco from Rhodesia. These factors, plus the coming of the Depression, resulted in production dropping to 8,644,390 lb in 1930–1, before picking up again to 22,401,707 lb in 1935–6. In 1936 the Tobacco Marketing Act introduced greater government control over the industry, with the compulsory registration of all growers, and by giving the minister powers to fix minimum prices, to regulate production, and control exports.

A similar pattern can be observed in regard to the maize industry, where production rose from 1,393,654 (203-lb) bags in 1925−6 to 1,985,848 bags in 1935−6, and exports rose from 434,592 (200-lb) bags in 1926 to 745,010 bags in 1930. But by the beginning of 1931, with the export price falling from 11s to 3s 4d, most European maize-growers were facing bankruptcy.[115] Many increased their acreages in an attempt to offset falling prices, but this led to rampant soil erosion, while their economic plight was worsened by increasing competition from African growers. The government promptly came to their rescue with the Maize Control Acts of 1931 and 1934, which will be examined shortly, but whose main effect was to keep European maize-growers on the land, though prices remained low. In 1936 maize exports totalled 396,000 bags.

Though the numbers of African-owned cattle continued to increase, from 1,197,466 in 1926 to 1,547,623 in 1936, European-owned cattle showed a decrease for the first time, dropping from 991,216 to 753,419 in the same period, as many white ranchers attempted to jump on to the tobacco boom, or switched to dairying or cotton-growing. In 1930 an export market to Britain of chilled and frozen meat was made possible by Rhodesia Railways' acquisition of nine refrigerator wagons,[116] but almost immediately an outbreak of foot-and-mouth disease resulted in a two-year embargo on all agricultural exports, with the exception of tobacco and citrus. All in all, 'the early thirties were years of severe stress and strain for the hard-pressed Rhodesian farmer'.[117]

How did the white Rhodesian farmers react to such stresses and strains? As one might expect, they called upon the government to bale them out and to assist them 'to achieve a return large enough for them to continue farming and live according to "civilized standards" '.[118] Such standards could only be maintained in normal times by paying extremely low wages, and during the Depression many farmers simply stopped paying their African workers altogether.[119] Like European farmers elsewhere at this time, they raised the spectre of African competition,[120] and feared that unless they were protected from such unfair competition, the country would 'surely revert to a native State, as is happening in Nyasaland'.[121] That such fears were taken seriously even at the Colonial Office can be seen from a decision in 1933 to forbid the British Central Africa Company to grow maize in Nyasaland in case this should result in competition for the tottering maize industries of Southern Rhodesia and Kenya.[122] So the European farmers, whose 'methods of cultivation remained inefficient' according to Gann,[123] demanded greater government participation in production and marketing, which resulted in the setting up of Tobacco and Dairy Control Boards and the passing of Maize Control Acts. Moreover, like the Kenya settlers, they resented the very limited attempts by government to encourage African agriculture.[124]

In 1934, for example, they successfully campaigned for a reduction in the number of African agricultural demonstrators being trained—for a short while the government imposed a complete standstill on training—and in Fort Victoria, where the demonstrators had helped African farmers to grow maize successfully for the first time, E.D. Alvord, the American ex-missionary who was in charge of the demonstration work, was shunned and treated as a pariah by the Europeans whenever he went to town.[125] Alvord took the view, in words which were neatly excised from one of his annual reports, that European farmers who could not stand African competition 'would do the most good for Rhodesia by moving out'.[126]

Perhaps the best illustration of the way in which European farmers sought to protect themselves is provided by the Maize Control Amendment Act in 1934. The Act was highly complex, but broadly speaking it 'discriminated in favour of the small white as against both the larger white and the African grower'.[127] It proved in fact to be a good deal more detrimental to African farmers than similar, and contemporary, pieces of legislation in Kenya and Northern Rhodesia.[128] The pro-settler Governor, Sir Herbert Stanley, pronounced himself 'not a devotee of the principle of maize control, but I regard its introduction . . . as a necessity if European maize farmers . . . are to be kept on the land'.[129] The African maize-growers of the Belingwe district found, however, that whereas they had previously managed to sell some 10,000 bags a year, after the Act they were able to sell none at all.[130] In Mazoe, Africans had once sold maize locally at 6s to 7s per bag; after the Act they were obliged to carry it long distances and sell at 2s to 2s 6d. Not surprisingly, a meeting of the Mazoe Native Board in 1934 expressed its 'grave dissatisfaction' and even became 'somewhat unruly'. One speaker asked, 'Why does the Government do everything to help the white farmer and nothing to help us? . . . The Government is killing us by this Act which we do not understand. It is made to do good to the white man and harm to us. . . . Why are not our Native Commissioners consulted before things like this happen and why are we also not consulted? This thing is not fair. It is put on us by force.'[131] The local N/C wrote that 'never before during my 30 years service in this Department have I heard natives express themselves so strongly or so openly display a spirit of antagonism to any law as they did to the Maize Control and Cattle Levy Acts'.[132] The antagonism was clearly justified, for even the ultra-conservative Chief Native Commissioner, C.L. Carbutt, who wanted to dispatch all 'advanced natives' to Northern Rhodesia, concluded that 'it is quite impossible for Natives to benefit in any way' from the Act,[133] while his successor, Charles Bullock, made it clear to Stanley that 'he disagreed entirely with the principle of maize control, and that he had no confidence in the fairmindedness of the Maize Control Board'.[134] A Government report of 1944 was even more scathing:

It is difficult to conceive of a principle more inequitable or dangerous than that of deliberately paying to the better-off producers of a State more for a product than is paid to less well-off people in the same State for the identical product. It is the antithesis of assistance according to need and of the universally acclaimed principle of raising rather than depressing the lower classes.[135]

Maize Control was perhaps the most vivid example of the impact of the Depression on African peasant farmers, though the Europeans also successfully pressed the government 'to decrease the Native production of wheat'.[136] Rather more sober, but none the less revealing, is Arrighi's estimate that whereas in 1903 some 70 per cent of African cash-earnings had come from the sale of agricultural produce, by 1932 the proportion had slumped to below 20 per cent.[137] As Carbutt put it, 'From the Natives' personal point of view, the situation is very harassing: he cannot sell cattle: he cannot get cash for his maize . . . and he has great difficulty in obtaining employment, and when he does get it, it is at a reduced rate of pay.'[138] Increasingly, Africans sought refuge in the reserves, whence they were 'encouraged' to move by the Land Apportionment Act, which envisaged that, with certain minor exceptions, only labour tenants would be allowed to remain on European land after 1937, and by the attitude of most European farmers, who, with their farms at a standstill, often changed labour into rent agreements in search of easy cash but in contradiction of the aims of the Act, and who also demanded that Africans be evicted from unalienated land to make way for future settlers. What was particularly galling about such evictions was the tiny proportion of European land which was actually being put to good use[139]—14 out of the 31 million acres of European land in 1925 were lying unoccupied—and the fact that so much of the land from which Africans were moved lay idle and unused, as happened also in Northern Rhodesia during the 1930s.[140] Thus, in the Mtoko district, 'covetous eyes are always cast on the mile after mile of vacant land from which the Natives have been turned off in the past'.[141]

But the reserves were no escape, even though one did not have to pay rents or grazing fees, for, as Alvord put it,

the greatest handicap to our efforts to introduce better methods of tillage among reserve Natives is the lack of marketing facilities. In many areas it is impossible for Natives to sell for cash, and they are forced to take salt or cloth for their grain, or they cannot sell it at all . . . [this] imposes a hand to mouth existence upon him under which he cannot progress.[142]

At least 50,000 people were moved into the reserves in the 1930s, with the result that they became increasingly overcrowded and overstocked—in some districts of Matabeleland in particular there was an acute shortage of land—and since it was no longer possible in many areas to live off the land, people were forced to turn to wage labour, and by 1932 over 80 per cent of African cash-earnings was coming from this source. Thus a process of involution, of gradually falling productivity, modelled closely on the South African pattern, was set in motion. The government's attempts to 'develop' the reserves could do little to alleviate the situation.[143] Even when the demonstrators achieved successes, there were problems. Thus in Fort Victoria, prior to Maize Control, 'the demonstration work was really going ahead in leaps and bounds, and in certain areas the demonstrators were unable to cope with the large numbers of Natives interested in the better methods of farming'. But after the Act all this stopped, and the people asked 'Why should we grow crops and sell them at less than we used to?', and complained, 'Yes, we told you when you first brought demonstrators on to the reserves that they had come to try out the land, and later the Government would either take it or our crops.'[144] An identical feeling was expressed at Matobo where, as a result of the Act, Africans could no longer sell their surplus maize, and the Native Board 'wanted to know why Native Demonstrators had been sent into the Native Reserves to teach them modern methods of growing maize'.[145] It cannot have been an easy question to answer.

## Conclusion

Thus, by the end of the 1930s, the agricultural economy of the Shona and the Ndebele, like that of the Kikuyu and most South African peoples, had been destroyed. The struggle between 'the European farmer seeking to reduce the African to a proletarian and the African seeking to retain the maximum amount of economic independence'[146] had been won conclusively by the Europeans. Even the 'native purchase areas', supposedly set aside for the benefit of 'progressive' African commercial farmers, revealed a picture of utter stagnation, as the majority of farmholdings passed into the hands of urban workers, who simply followed the European tradition of buying land for their retirement, and were therefore little more than 'weekend farmers' at best.

The reasons for the European triumph fall into three broad categories. In the first place, after 1908 European agriculture was heavily subsidized while African agriculture was utterly neglected.[147] Potential European farmers were wooed in Britain and South Africa, were offered training on arrival, received Land Bank loans to help establish themselves, and had a wide range of extension facilities placed at their disposal. Moreover, with control over the land came, in varying degree, control over labour, and the ability, after 1920, to rely on cheap supplies of labour was a fundamental prerequisite for the success of European agriculture.[148] Shona farmers, who had clearly demonstrated their potential in the early colonial period, were afforded no such assistance. A Rhodesian governor of the 1940s admitted that 'insufficient money is spent in the Reserves', and that the number of Europeans attached to Alvord's staff before 1939 had been 'almost ludicrously insufficient'.[149] In the financial year 1940−1, £14,107 was voted for the 'development of agriculture in native areas and reserves', a sum which, as Lord Hailey observed, 'seems somewhat exiguous compared with the £208,217 provided in the Vote for European agriculture'.[150] After the Second World War, Africans received a slightly larger slice of the cake, but the £2 million spent on African agriculture in the years 1945−6 to 1953−4 pales into insignificance beside the £12 million voted to the European sector.[151]

Secondly, the competitiveness of the African peasantry was reduced by increasingly forcing them off European land, either by direct eviction or by imposing such a battery of financial and other burdens that they elected to go. Once settled in the reserves they could aspire to be little more than subsistence cultivators[152]—and migrant labourers, prepared to work for the prevailing low wages. Those who remained on European farms, as either labour- or rent-paying tenants, were obviously in no position to compete with their landlords. Thirdly, as if the earlier financial discrimination were not enough, came the repressive legislation of the 1930s, born of a fear of competition. The Land Apportionment Act of 1930 legally demarcated the European area for the first time—the Europeans got 48½ million acres, or half the country—confined African purchasers to separate and largely non-productive areas, and endeavoured to pack as many Africans as possible into the reserves, leaving behind only labour tenants.[153] The Maize Control Amendment Act of 1934 discriminated blatantly against African maize-growers and effectively undermined the work of the agricultural demonstrators. Finally, the Industrial Conciliation Act of 1934 most skilfully imposed an industrial colour bar in the towns, and so placed yet another obstacle in the path of African advancement. The white farmers and workers, having obtained this position of strength, concentrated thereafter on maintaining it at all costs.

Thus the marked European prosperity of the post-1945 period was achieved, as in South Africa, as a direct result of African poverty.[154] In the years 1937−58 the volume of European agricultural output increased by 259 per cent and its value, thanks almost entirely to tobacco,[155] by over 1,000 per cent,[156] and the industry, now at last highly capitalized, appeared to have reached the stage of self-sustained growth, only to be hit drastically by the international sanctions imposed since Rhodesia's illegal declaration of independence in 1965. African productivity meanwhile limped behind, barely able to provide for the rapidly growing population, which was eking out a living on increasingly overcrowded and deteriorating reserves,[157] and being forced to seek work in the towns, where they were harried by the notorious pass laws, paid, housed, and fed as single men, and denied the opportunity to lead a normal family life—the social costs of urban development being borne by the rural areas. For black Rhodesians, therefore, the essential reality of Huggins's 'two pyramids'[158] consisted of rural poverty and urban insecurity. This position still obtains in September 1976, though there are at last clear signs that the period of European dominance is drawing to a close.

## NOTES

1.  J. Iliffe, *Agricultural Change in Modern Tanganyika*, Historical Association of Tanzania Paper No. 10 (Nairobi, 1971); R. van Zwanenberg, *The Agricultural History of Kenya to 1939*, Historical Association of Kenya Paper No. 1 (Nairobi, 1972); T.O. Ranger, *The Agricultural History of Zambia*, Historical Association of Zambia Pamphlet No. 1 (Lusaka, 1971); M. Chanock, 'Notes for an Agricultural History of Malawi', *Rural Africana, 20*, 1973, 27–35 [revised for this volume]; C. Bundy, 'The Emergence and Decline of a South African Peasantry', *African Affairs, 71*, 285, 1972, 369–88.
2.  I am greatly indebted to, and have borrowed much from, the oft-cited G. Arrighi, 'Labour Supplies in Historical Perspective: A Study of the Proletarianization of the African Peasantry in Rhodesia', *Journal of Development Studies, 6*, 1970, 197–234.
3.  J. Ford, *The Role of the Trypanosomiases in African Ecology* (Oxford, 1971), 283–366.
4.  B.N. Floyd, *Changing Patterns of African Land Use in Southern Rhodesia* (Lusaka, 1961), 43.
5.  G. Kay, *Rhodesia: A Human Geography* (London, 1970), 16–17.
6.  L. Hastings, *Dragons Are Extra* (Harmondsworth, 1947), 129. A contemporary agreed that 'within a few minutes a valuable crop of tobacco may be destroyed by wind and hail'. R. Hoare, *Rhodesian Mosaic* (London, 1934), 92. The agricultural economist Yudelman noted that 'in common with many other parts of Southern, Central and East Africa, Southern Rhodesia does not have a well-endowed agricultural resource base. More than 75 per cent of the country is subject to conditions that make crop production a risky venture.' M. Yudelman, *Africans on the Land* (Cambridge, Mass., 1964), 34.
7.  See, for example, Iliffe, *Agricultural Change*, 33; W. Rodney, *How Europe Underdeveloped Africa* (London and Dar es Salaam, 1972); and also many of the chapters in this book.
8.  National Archives of Rhodesia, N 9/1/3, Report of the N/C Umtali for the year ending March 1897. *Note:* all archival sources refer either to the National Archives of Rhodesia or to the Public Record Office, London. The PRO files contain the prefix CO or DO and consist of original correspondence belonging to the former Colonial and Dominions Offices.
9.  The much travelled F.C. Selous wrote of Chief Mtoko's area in north-eastern Mashonaland, 'His people are wonderfully well supplied with all kinds of vegetable food and in no part of the country have I seen such fine rice as is here grown of very large grain and beautifully white.' Hist. MSS SE 1/1/1, Selous to Colquhoun, 25 January 1891.
10.  R. Summers, *Ancient Mining in Rhodesia*, National Museums of Rhodesia Memoir No. 3 (Salisbury, 1969); I.R. Phimister, 'Alluvial Gold Mining and Trade in Nineteenth-Century South Central Africa', *Journal of African History, 15*, 1974, 445–56; I.R. Phimister, 'Pre-Colonial Gold Mining in Southern Zambezia: A Reassessment', *African Social Research, 21*, 1976, 1–30.
11.  See Chapter 10, I.R. Phimister, 'Peasant Production and Underdevelopment in Southern Rhodesia, 1890–1914, with Particular Reference to the Victoria District'.
12.  This account is based on a number of sources, the most important of which are: Chapter 1, D.N. Beach, 'The Shona Economy: Branches of Production'; J.K. Rennie,

'Christianity, Colonialism and the Origins of Nationalism among the Ndau of Southern Rhodesia, 1890–1935', PhD thesis, Northwestern University, 1973, 46–54; W. Roder, *The Sabi Valley Irrigation Projects*, University of Chicago, Department of Geography, Research Paper No. 99 (Chicago, 1965), 42–72; H. Kuper, A.J.B. Hughes, and J. van Velsen, *The Shona and Ndebele of Southern Rhodesia* (London, 1954), 24–8.

13. For a recent reassessment of the Ndebele, see J. Cobbing, 'The Evolution of Ndebele Amabutho', *Journal of African History, 15*, 1974, 607–31; J. Cobbing, 'Historical Materialism and the Nineteenth Century Ndebele', University of Rhodesia, Political Economy Research Seminar No. 11, 1974.

14. D.N. Beach, 'Ndebele Raiders and Shona Power', *Journal of African History, 15*, 1974, 634.

15. Kuper, Hughes, and van Velsen, *The Shona and Ndebele*, 56.

16. T.M. Thomas, *Eleven Years in Central South Africa* (London, 1873), 81, 84–5, 92, 180, 189–90.

17. N. Jones, *Rhodesian Genesis* (Bulawayo, 1953), 116–17. Interestingly, in 1912–13 the new Bulawayo railway station was built 'on the site of the kraal of one of Lobengula's crack regiments and underground storage bins for their grain were found when the foundations were being excavated'. A.H. Croxton, *Railways of Rhodesia* (Newton Abbot, 1973), 115.

18. Jones, *Rhodesian Genesis*, 23.

19. See Chapter 11, B.A. Kosmin, 'The Inyoka Tobacco Industry of the Shangwe People: the Displacement of a Pre-Colonial Economy in Southern Rhodesia, 1898–1938'.

20. Cobbing, 'Historical Materialism', 8; N. Sutherland-Harris, 'Trade and the Rozwi Mambo', in R. Gray and D. Birmingham (eds), *Pre-Colonial African Trade* (London, 1970), 253–4.

21. N.M.B. Bhebe, 'Ndebele Trade in the Nineteenth Century', *Journal of African Studies, 1*, 1974, 89.

22. Beach, 'Ndebele Raiders', 638.

23. P. Stigger, 'Volunteers and the Profit Motive in the Anglo–Ndebele War, 1893', *Rhodesian History, 2*, 1971, 15–17.

24. *Bulawayo Sketch*, 20 July 1895. Quoted in H.A.C. Cairns, *Prelude to Imperialism* (London, 1965), 228.

25. One Cape morgen equals 2.11654 acres.

26. A.J. Christopher, 'Land Policy in Southern Africa During the Nineteenth Century', *Zambezia, 2*, 1971, 3, 4. See also A.J. Christopher, 'Government Land Policies in Southern Africa', in R.G. Ironside (ed.), *Frontier Settlement* (Edmonton, 1974), 208–25; W.K. Hancock, 'Trek', *Economic History Review, 10*, 1958, 331–9.

27. A 1/2/4, Harris to Colquhoun, 20 September 1890.

28. Christopher, 'Land Policy', 7.

29. Bundy, 'The Emergence', 372–86; Chapter 8, C. Bundy, 'The Transkei Peasantry, c.890–1914: "Passing through a Period of Stress" '; D. Denoon, *Southern Africa since 1800* (London, 1972), 128–35.

30. Denoon, *Southern Africa*, 61. Dr E.A. Nobbs, Rhodesia's first Director of Agriculture, 'held the opinion that the native methods of cultivation were frequently of a high order, and enabled a crop to be produced under drought conditions when a large European acreage would have failed', while two vastly experienced native commissioners, J.W. Posselt and 'Wiri' Edwards, believed that 'as far as their own crops are concerned, I do not think we can teach the Natives anything. The excellence of their crops around tree stumps is indisputable', and while 'Native methods of agriculture may be primitive in our eyes... we must remember that they are the results of many generations of experience gained by their forefathers in agriculture, with the implements at their command'. F 35/2(25), Memo by Jennings, 1927; S 138/10, N/C Charter to CNC, 23 September 1925; S 235/503, Report of the N/C Mrewa for the year 1925.

31. Bundy, 'The Emergence', 383.

32.  R.H. Palmer, 'War and Land in Rhodesia in the 1890s', in B.A. Ogot (ed.), *War and Society in Africa* (London, 1972), 85–107; R.H. Palmer, 'Johnston and Jameson: A Comparative Study in the Imposition of Colonial Rule', in B. Pachai (ed.), *The Early History of Malawi* (London, 1972), 293–322.

33.  Palmer, 'War and Land', 97–102. Two totally inadequate reserves, the Gwaai and Shangani, were assigned to the Ndebele in 1894, following their military defeat. For this and other aspects of land policy, see R.H. Palmer, *Land and Racial Domination in Rhodesia* (London, 1977).

34.  Bulawayo was linked by rail to South Africa in 1897, Salisbury to Beira in 1899, Bulawayo to Salisbury in 1902, and Bulawayo to Victoria Falls in 1904. See Croxton, *Railways*.

35.  Arrighi, 'Labour Supplies', 209.

36.  British South Africa Company, *Report on the Company's Proceedings and the Condition of the Territories within the Sphere of its Operations, 1894–5* (London, 1896), 67; Stigger, 'Volunteers', 14.

37.  Jones, *Rhodesian Genesis*, 116. A government report of 1961 noted that 'Native agriculture was of great importance to the European settlers at this early stage, as the Natives supplied them with their grain and vegetable requirements for much of the year, and, in addition, native cattle formed the basis of many new European-owned cattle.' Federation of Rhodesia and Nyasaland, *An Agricultural Survey of Southern Rhodesia, Part II, Agro-Economic Survey* (Salisbury, 1961), 14.

38.  D.N. Beach, 'The Rising in South-Western Mashonaland, 1896–7', PhD thesis, University of London, 1971, 291; M.G.B. Rooney, 'European Agriculture in the History of Rhodesia, 1890–1907', MA thesis, University of South Africa, 1968, 73. 'The majority of the so-called early "farmers" were employed solely in transport-riding—their farms merely serving as bases where they maintained a rough homestead and kept a few spare oxen.' Rooney, 'European Agriculture', 70.

39.  DO 119/520, Gazeteer by the C/C Victoria, 11 November 1897; DO 119/586, Report of the N/C Victoria for the year ending June 1900.

40.  British South Africa Company, *Reports on the Administration of Rhodesia, 1898–1900* (London, 1901), 199. Cited also in Chapter 10, Phimister, 'Peasant Production'.

41.  In 1903, the missionary A.S. Cripps noted that Shona farmers would 'produce in good seasons a great surplus of grain for trading'. South Africa, *South African Native Affairs Commission, 1903–5, Vol. V* (Cape Town, 1905), Written reply by A.S. Cripps, 1903, 320.

42.  Chapter 10, Phimister, 'Peasant Production'; Arrighi, 'Labour Supplies', 228 n. 14.

43.  L. Vambe, *An Ill-Fated People* (London, 1972), 176. Even the BSA Company, noting that the acreage under cultivation in Mashonaland in 1898–9 was estimated to be 542,700, compared to 236,186 the previous year, observed 'It is obvious that the natives now plant crops for sale, and are not content, as formerly, to grow merely sufficient for their own consumption.' British South Africa Company, *Reports, 1898–1900*, 179.

44.  Arrighi, 'Labour Supplies', 229 nn. 30 and 31.

45.  In 1903 the N/C Lomagundi noted that 'The native by having a sufficient area of land to raise more than sufficient crops for his own consumption, absolutely free of all rent or tax on it, is in the position of an independent landed class', while in the same year the N/C Makoni observed that 'at present the Natives living in these Reserves cultivate as much ground as they please, the products of which are in excess of their consumption and the large remaining surplus they sell to the traders in order to meet their Hut Tax and by this mode of living the average Mashona does not require to look for work'. N 3/6/3, N/Cs Lomagundi and Makoni to CNC Mashonaland, November 1903.

46.  J.M. Mackenzie, 'African Labour in South Central Africa, 1890–1914 and Nineteenth Century Colonial Labour Theory', PhD thesis, University of British Col-

umbia, 1969, 208. 'Between 1890 and 1912 much, if not most, of the fresh produce requirements of Rhodesian mines was supplied by the competitive local black peasantry.' C. van Onselen,, *Chibaro: African Mine Labour in Southern Rhodesia 1900–1933,* (London, 1976), 42.

47.   Vambe, *An Ill-Fated People,* 149. Mission stations not infrequently acted as a stimulus to agricultural innovation.

48.   Phimister, 'Alluvial Gold Mining', 454.

49.   'The natives today are cultivating twice the amount they did when we came to the country', wrote 'Wiri' Edwards in 1906, 'and so long as the land is unlimited and they have a market for their produce, will the labour supply suffer.' In 1898 the N/C Malema welcomed a swarm of locusts as 'not an unmitigated evil, for a really abundant harvest of kaffir corn and mealies would probably have the effect of reducing the number of Native labourers 50 per cent'. N 9/4/19, Report of the N/C Mrewa for the month June 1906; NB 6/4/2, Report of the N/C Malema for the month November 1898.

50.   M.L. Chanock, 'The Political Economy of Independent Agriculture in Colonial Malawi: The Great War to the Great Depression', *Journal of Social Science, 1,* 1972, 117.

51.   'At present the paltry sum of 10s per hut is so easily earned it will never induce them to work', wrote the N/C Makoni in 1903. N 9/1/8, Report of the N/C Makoni for the year ending March 1903. The BSA Company had wanted the tax increased to £2, while some white employers thought £4 would be a more suitable amount, but the British Resident Commissioner vetoed these proposals.

52.   Hut tax receipts rose as follows: 1897–8, £35,638; 1898–9, £73,122; 1901–2, £92,415; 1904–5, £176,538. The £200,000 level was reached in 1909–10, £300,000 in 1925–6, and £400,000 in 1937–8.

53.   Arrighi, 'Labour Supplies', 209.

54.   R. Hodder-Williams, 'The Development of Social, Economic and Political Attitudes in a European Community, 1890–1968' (draft thesis).

55.   The N/C Victoria noted in 1899 that 'this district is very much depended on for grain and if the natives were shifted into Reserves from farms whenever the farmers were unreasonable the supply would be greatly interfered with'. N 9/4/4, Report of the N/C Victoria for the month July 1899. Cited also in Chapter 10, Phimister, 'Peasant Production'.

56.   They came to Rhodesia partly in response to settler complaints that the administration was favouring the miners against the farmers unduly, and that land settlement was being discouraged by the high price of land.

57.   Phimister makes the point that by 1894–5 Rhodes, at least, was under no illusion about Rhodesia's mineral potential, and that the Jameson Raid and the other political disturbances which followed 'were in a number of respects a direct consequence of the failure of the "Second Rand" to materialize between the Limpopo and the Zambezi'. I.R. Phimister, 'Rhodes, Rhodesia and the Rand', *Journal of Southern African Studies, 1,* 1974, 75.

58.   V.W. Hiller (ed.), *A Guide to the Public Records of Southern Rhodesia under the Regime of the British South Africa Company, 1890–1923* (Cape Town, 1956), 224.

59.   R. Hodder-Williams, 'Afrikaners in Rhodesia: A Partial Portrait', *African Social Research, 18,* 1974, 616.

60.   The various statistics dotted about the rest of this paper have been taken largely from official sources; I shall not reference each statistic. See Southern Rhodesia, *Official Year Book of the Colony of Southern Rhodesia,* Nos. 1–4 (Salisbury, 1924, 1930, 1932, 1952); Southern Rhodesia, *Handbook for the Use of Prospective Settlers on the Land* (London and Ipswich, 1924); H. Weinmann, *Agricultural Research and Development in Southern Rhodesia, 1890–1923,* University of Rhodesia, Department of Agriculture, Occasional Paper No. 4 (Salisbury, 1972); H. Weinmann, *Agricultural Research and Development in Southern Rhodesia, 1924–1950,* University of Rhodesia, Series in Science 2 (Salisbury, 1975); Kay, *Rhodesia.*

61.   S 138/21, Manager, Land Bank, to CNC, 3 September 1926.

62.  R.M.A. van Zwanenberg with A. King, *An Economic History of Kenya and Uganda 1800–1970* (Dar es Salaam, 1975), 209, 288–9; R.M.A. van Zwanenberg, *Colonial Capitalism and Labour in Kenya 1919–1939* (Dar es Salaam, 1975), 20–6.

63.  R. Hodder-Williams, 'The British South Africa Company in Marandellas: Some Extra-Institutional Constraints on Government', *Rhodesian History*, 2, 1971, 56 n. 85.

64.  R.H. Palmer, 'Land in Zambia', in Palmer (ed.), *Zambian Land and Labour Studies, Vol. 1*, National Archives of Zambia Occasional Paper 2 (Lusaka, 1973), 57.

65.  Department of Lands, Memorandum on Land Settlement Policy (mimeo., 1925), 9.

66.  P.F. Hone, *Southern Rhodesia* (London, 1909), 290–7.

67.  van Onselen, *Chibaro*, 41–2.

68.  F. Clements and E. Harben, *Leaf of Gold: The Story of Rhodesian Tobacco* (London, 1962), 51.

69.  Kay, *Rhodesia*, 113; Hodder-Williams, 'The British South Africa Company', 51.

70.  In connection with the Greeks, Odlum cabled the Director of Land Settlement, 'Kindly request that farmers and others treat them with consideration, for they are not quite Barbarians, many of them being very nice people. None of them speak any language other than Greek, but they have books and will soon learn.' Hodder-Williams, 'The British South Africa Company', 52.

71.  Kay, *Rhodesia*, 46.

72.  As the official handbook for prospective settlers nicely observed, the large number of African cattle existing in 1890 'was reduced to a small fraction' by 'lungsickness, rinderpest and war', adding that 'the great bulk of our European-owned cattle is derived from native breeds'. *Handbook, 1924*, 30.

73.  Weinmann, *Agricultural Research, 1890–1923*, 108.

74.  *Report of the Chief Native Commissioner Mashonaland for the Year 1912* (Salisbury, 1913), 3.

75.  As one white Rhodesian rancher recalled, 'My scheme was to start with native stock, acclimatized to local conditions, and cross them with fairly decent bulls; and later to cross the progeny with first-class Aberdeen-Angus beasts. It was a slow way of beginning, but the only sound one. By the third or fourth generation the herds would be fully graded up to type, yet retain the indigenous stamina; and the grazing of their forebears would "tame" the land into fit conditions to carry good stuff.' W. Robertson, *Rhodesian Rancher* (London and Glasgow, 1935), 13.

76.  *Handbook, 1924*, 14.

77.  R.H. Palmer, 'Red Soils in Rhodesia', *African Social Research*, 10, 1970, 747–58.

78.  NB 6/4/9, Report of the CNC Matabeleland for the month September 1908. Cited also in Chapter 11, Kosmin, 'The Inyoka Tobacco Industry'.

79.  Chapter 11, Kosmin, 'The Inyoka Tobacco Industry'.

80.  Palmer, *Land and Racial Domination*, 83–7.

81.  A 3/15/11, Hole to Milton, 26 November 1909.

82.  Hodder-Williams notes that 'The survey of farmers in the Marandellas District carried out by Company officials in 1914 makes abundantly clear the poverty of capital assets. A single wagon and a couple of ploughs, normally only single disc ones, represents the average; a maize shelter, some oxen and a few milking cows, tack for the oxen and a collection of small tools made up the inventory. This meant that most of the cultivation was done by hand'. Hodder-Williams, 'The Development'.

83.  L.H. Gann, *The Birth of a Plural Society* (Manchester, 1958), 141.

84.  P. Mason, *The Birth of a Dilemma* (London, 1958), 225. For two sharply differing discussions of the labour question at this time, see J.M. Mackenzie, 'African Labour in the Chartered Company Period', *Rhodesian History*, 1, 1970, 43–58; C. van Onselen, 'Black Workers in Central African Industry: A Critical Essay on the Historiography and Sociology of Rhodesia', *Journal of Southern African Studies*, 1, 1975, 228–46.

85.  In Nyasaland between 1901 and 1921 Africans who did not work one month in the

year for a white employer were taxed at double the rate of those who did, a measure introduced at the insistence of the white planters of the Shire Highlands, who habitually paid very low wages.

In Matabeleland in 1912, the Rhodesian Landowners' and Farmers' Association passed a resolution pointing out that 'the present system of exploiting natives squatting on private lands for an annual rental per head is the principal cause of the labour trouble', and demanding that the Private Locations Ordinance be amended so that all African tenants should show that they were 'contributing towards the economic development of the State by working for an employer for at least six months in every year'. *Bulawayo Chronicle*, 2 February 1912.

86.   Vambe, *An Ill-Fated People*, 219.
87.   One white farmer acknowledged that the reserves 'did not offer the same facilities for getting rich rapidly that much private land offered. They were mostly so situate that grain would have a smaller value, and the opportunities for selling beer—a very important source of income—would be much curtailed.' *Bulawayo Chronicle*, 2 February 1912.
88.   Weinmann, *Agricultural Research, 1890–1923*, 111.
89.   N 9/1/12, Report of the Acting N/C Melsetter for the year 1909.
90.   A 3/15/12, N/C Bubi to CNC Matabeleland, 13 November 1912.
91.   Palmer, *Land and Racial Domination*, 279–82. Compare this figure with the 1,548 registered African landowners holding 191,466 acres in Natal in 1907, and the paltry 4,383 acres held in freehold and 1,180 acres held in leasehold by Africans in Nyasaland in 1925.
92.   R.A. Fletcher, in *Bulawayo Chronicle*, 7 October 1910.
93.   'Segregation is necessary because fundamental race difference exists; and herein lies the core of the matter', wrote Sybil Bowker in 1920. S. Bowker, 'A Scheme for Segregation Areas', *Contemporary Review, 117*, 1920, 548.
94.   In Natal, writes Welsh, 'It is clear that the colonists favoured segregationist ideas not because Africans were "barbarous", "primitive", or "savage" but because a significant group of Africans no longer conformed to those stereotypes and claimed admission into the upper caste.' D. Welsh, *The Roots of Segregation* (Cape Town, 1971), 321.
95.   Palmer, *Land and Racial Domination*, 131–94.
96.   An estimated 64 per cent of European men between the ages of fifteen and forty-four were away on military service, with the result that many farms were temporarily abandoned.
97.   N 9/1/23, Report of the N/C Lomagundi for the year 1920.
98.   S. Katzenellenbogen, 'Zambia and Rhodesia: Prisoners of the Past. A Note on the History of Railway Politics in Central Africa', *African Affairs, 73*, 290, 1974, 65.
99.   In 1930, thirteen of the thirty members of the Legislative Assembly were, or had been, farmers, while all Rhodesian Prime Ministers with the exception of the first, Coghlan (1923–7), and the majority of cabinet ministers, have been farmers. The Rhodesia Agricultural Union, which by 1918 embraced 46 affiliated associations with some 1,200 members, held annual congresses which were well attended by government ministers, and whose resolutions carried considerable weight. M.C. Steele, 'The Foundations of a "Native" Policy in Southern Rhodesia, 1923–33', PhD thesis, Simon Fraser University, 1972, 35; E. Mlambo, *Rhodesia: The Struggle for a Birthright* (London, 1972), 20, 41 n. 1; D.J. Murray, *The Governmental System in Southern Rhodesia* (Oxford, 1970), 63.
100.  DO 9/3, Athlone to Amery, 15 October 1926. The following year, the N/C Umtali cited the case of a white farmer who had built a dipping tank for his tenants' cattle in 1918, charged 3s 6d per head per annum compared to 1s in the reserves, and 'today he owns 200 head, all of which he got from the natives for fees, with the exception of 18 head'. F 35/26(5), N/C Umtali to CNC, 1 February 1927.
101.  In 1914 the N/C Bulalima-Mangwe wrote that 'the excessive fining of natives for trespass is a common practice in this District, and a source of considerable revenue to

many of the white inhabitants.... It seems that natives are afraid of many people here, and are very chary of bringing cases against white people, however much their rights are infringed.... Much of the trouble arising from alleged trespass is due to the fact that landowners do not take any steps to demarcate their boundaries, so that neither natives, nor anyone else knows where they are. It is thus possible for unscrupulous persons to make a living out of the trespass laws, and instead of their being a protection, they become an instrument of extortion.' N 3/7/2, N/C Bulalima-Mangwe to CNC, 14 January, 11 February 1914.

102. N 9/1/21, Report of the N/C Insiza for the year 1918; N 9/4/37, Report of the N/C Insiza for the month September 1919.

103. Vambe, *An Ill-Fated People*, 219. Even Gann and Duignan admit that 'the frontier farmer's racial outlook was usually of the harshest.... The pioneering period saw a great deal of cruelty, for on the farms and in the mining camps the white boss was usually a law unto himself. Insults and beatings went unpunished; manslaughter or even murder earned derisory penalties. White juries were notoriously unwilling to convict whites for crimes committed against blacks.' L.H. Gann and P. Duignan, 'Changing Patterns of a White Elite: Rhodesian and Other Settlers', in Gann and Duignan (eds), *Colonialism in Africa, 1870–1960, Vol. 2: The History and Politics of Colonialism, 1914–1960* (Cambridge, 1970), 108.

104. Palmer, *Land and Racial Domination*, 104–30. Thus, for example, Msana reserve in the Salisbury district, which the Commission reduced by half, was said to be 'ideal farming country as there is plenty of water and rich red soil also a good class of sand soil'. Hist. MSS HO 7/2/1, Holland's Diary, 21 May 1915, 4.

105. Arrighi, 'Labour Supplies', 216. In Gwanda, where Africans owned some 30,000–40,000 head of cattle, this was 'their principal source of income, hence their chief means of paying rent and taxes, and for purchasing supplies'. L 2/2/122, N/C Gwanda to S/N Bulawayo, 22 July 1919.

106. *Report of the Chief Native Commissioner for the Year 1920* (Salisbury, 1921), 5.

107. N 3/24/36, CNC to Secretary, Department of Administrator, 22 March 1923.

108. Arrighi, 'Labour Supplies', 217.

109. Arrighi points out that 'it was generally recognized that grain crops could not bear the cost of more than 15 miles of ox-wagon transport when railway costs were to be added'. Arrighi, 'Labour Supplies', 215.

110. CO 767/2, Chancellor to Thomas, 24 September 1924.

111. ZAH 1/1/4, Evidence of C. Bullock to Land Commission, 17 June 1925, 1407–13.

112. Hist. MSS NE 1/1/2, Downie to Newton, 2 November 1925.

113. 'In Salisbury to-day', wrote Rawdon Hoare in 1934, 'the majority of [African] hotel and household servants can be seen riding expensive bicycles, dressed in attire of the latest fashion, while many white men, on account largely of the tobacco slump, plough their way on foot along the dusty roads.' Hoare, *Rhodesian Mosaic*, 65–6.

114. Clements and Harben, *Leaf of Gold*, 114. Hoare, passing through Headlands, between Salisbury and Umtali, in the early 1930s, noted 'On either side stretched abandoned lands, cultivated and prosperous before the tobacco slump four years before. Here and there among the kopjes stood houses, fallen and decayed, once the homes of planters who had left them to the mercy of the elements. No sounds of life could be heard, the gay prattle of native labourers having long since departed from those melancholy fields.' Hoare, *Rhodesian Mosaic*, 130.

115. In 1934 Hoare wrote that 'Maize land had always been considered a good investment, so the slump of 1930 was a great shock to the country as a whole. £3 and £5 an acre had been paid for a maize farm in the past; today, even at 30s an acre, they would prove difficult to sell.' Hoare, *Rhodesian Mosaic*, 55–6.

116. Croxton, *Railways*, 172.

117. *Agro-Economic Survey*, 17. One positive development at this time however was the introduction by Rhodesia Railways of a road motor service. The first, in June 1927, ran 'from Sinoia to Miami, seventy-two miles away, the centre of the mica mining

district. Within two years no less than fifteen road services to feed the railway had been
started, of which eight were subsidised by the government to serve developing areas.
Motor lorry services were a completely new feature of life in Rhodesia and quickly
proved of immense value in helping farmers to market their produce and obtain their
supplies.... The Road Motor Services played a very important role in opening up
promising farming country and in providing cheap transport for both agricultural and
mining produce, so bringing extra traffic to the rail system.' The mileage of these
services rose from 266 in 1927 to 1,626 in 1937. Croxton, *Railways*, 158–9.
118.  Murray, *Governmental System*, 80.
119.  In 1931 there were 357 convictions of Europeans for this crime, compared to 217
in 1913, B.A. Kosmin, 'Ethnic and Commercial Relations in Southern Rhodesia: A
Socio-Historical Study of the Asian, Hellenic and Jewish populations, 1898–1943',
PhD thesis, University of Rhodesia, 1974, 120.
120.  As Jack Woddis has observed of European farmers in general, 'Even with the
best lands in their possession they have had to be constantly subsidised and aided by
governments, and "protected" against African competition by the introduction of
various restrictions or limitations on African agriculture, and by the introduction of
various discriminatory measures in favour of the European farmer.' J. Woddis, *Africa:
The Roots of Revolt* (London, 1960), 8. Similarly, Barber concludes that in Rhodesia
'European agriculture has... been made a sheltered industry'. W.J. Barber, *The
Economy of British Central Africa* (London, 1961), 24.
121.  Southern Rhodesia, *Report of the Committee of Enquiry into the Economic
Position of the Agricultural Industry of Southern Rhodesia* (Salisbury, 1934), 30.
Evidence submitted to the Committee demanded that 'all natives farming in
European areas should be removed to the native areas at once; that no native-pro-
duced article should be sold in the European areas and *vice versa* except under permit'.
*Report*, 27.
122.  CO 525/147, Minute by Shirkdale, 20 January 1933. In Kenya in the 1930s the
colonial government 'used every possible means at its disposal to maintain European
farming in existence'. van Zwanenberg with King, *Economic History*, 209.
123.  Gann, *The Birth*, 149. This was confirmed by Governor Rodwell, who wrote in
1930 that many European farmers were 'at last awakening to the necessity of proper
methods of fertility, rotation and green manuring, but the awakening has come too late.
Thousands of acres of the best soil in the Colony have been robbed of their productivity
and the owners cannot face the expenditure necessary to restore it.' This was especially so since many maize farmers 'are at the end of their resources and are being
carried by the Bank'. DO 35/370, Rodwell to Thomas, 17 October 1930.
124.  M.P.K. Sorrenson, *Origins of European Settlement in Kenya* (Nairobi, 1968),
236.
125.  E.D. Alvord, 'Development of Native Agriculture and Land Tenure in Southern
Rhodesia' (unpublished, 1958), 20, 27.
126.  S 138/72, Alvord to CNC, Draft Annual Report for 1928, 14 January 1929.
127.  L.H. Gann, *A History of Southern Rhodesia* (London, 1965), 298. For a detailed
study, see C.F. Keyter, 'Maize Control in Southern Rhodesia 1931–1939: The African
Contribution to White Survival', MA thesis, University of Rhodesia, 1974.
128.  van Zwanenberg, *Agricultural History*, 21; K. Vickery, 'Aspects of Plateau
Tonga Economic History', in R.H. Palmer (ed.), *Zambian Land and Labour Studies*,
Vol. 3, National Archives of Zambia Occasional Paper 4 (Lusaka, 1977), 70.
129.  DO 35/842, Stanley to Macdonald, 6 April 1937.
130.  S 1542/N2, Report of the Belingwe Native Board Meeting, 13 May 1937.
131.  S 1542/N2, Report of the Mazoe Native Board Meeting, 12, 19 June 1934.
132.  S 1542/N2, N/C Mazoe to CNC, 12 July 1934. The Cattle Levy Act increased
slaughter fees from 2s 6d to 10s which, in conjunction with low prices, acted as a strong
deterrent against Africans selling their stock.
133.  S 1542/M2, CNC to Huggins, 7 February 1935.
134.  DO 35/842, Stanley to Harding, 21 July 1937.

135.  Southern Rhodesia, *Report of Native Production and Trade 1944* (Salisbury, 1945), 62.
136.  S 1542/A4, Secretary, Rhodesian Wheat Growers' Association, to Director of Native Development, 4 June 1935.
137.  Arrighi, 'Labour Supplies', 216. Ranger writes that 'The 1920s saw the triumph of European agriculture over African.' T.O. Ranger, *The African Voice in Southern Rhodesia* (Nairobi, 1970), 112.
138.  S 1561/38, CNC to Secretary to Premier, 2 September 1931.
139.  The 1934 Committee was 'satisfied that one of the major causes of the position of the industry is the ownership of land heavily mortgaged and greatly in excess of what the farmer can productively use'. *Report* [on] *the Economic Position of the Agricultural Industry*, 25. This was especially the case in Insiza, where the N/C regretted that 'Large tracts of land are held by Europeans but nothing is being done with it. . . . It seems to me', he added, 'that some of the land now held by Europeans should be given to the natives who will use it, whereas the Europeans have held the land for years without making any use of it.' Hist. MSS AT 1/2/1/11/4, N/C Insiza to S/N Bulawayo, 19 May 1936.
140.  Palmer, 'Land in Zambia', 60–2.
141.  S 235/514, Report of the N/C Mtoko for the year 1935.
142.  'Report of the Agriculturist, Native Department, for the Year 1934', in *Report of the Chief Native Commissioner for the Year 1934* (Salisbury, 1935), 18.
143.  As the Official Year Book was careful to point out, 'The aim of farming demonstration on native reserves is not to stimulate high production of staple cash crops, but to teach the native farmer how to get good returns from his labour. . . . No individual can be permitted to go extensively into the production of money crops, wear out the land and crowd out other individuals who have a right to an equal share of the land.' *Official Year Book, 1932*, 674.
144.  S 1542/M2, Assistant Agriculturist to CNC, 19 January 1935.
145.  S 1542/N2, Report of the Matobo Native Board Meeting, 14 June 1937.
146.  Iliffe, *Agricultural Change*, 13.
147.  It is true that in the 1920s the BSA Company grudgingly condescended to sink a few boreholes in some of the more arid reserves. It had declined to do so earlier on the grounds that Africans in the vicinity should bear the cost, a somewhat curious attitude to adopt since the basic idea was to open up uninhabited areas for settlement.
148.  'The difference between the cost of production and the yield of our maize crop is well known to be small', wrote the Auditor General in 1927. 'Without our native labourer is it not probable that the wealth produced by the maize farmer would not have been produced at all? And though the margin of profit in regard to Tobacco is far higher, would it not be most seriously affected by the substitution of white for native labour if indeed it would be possible to grow the crop at all?' S 480/148, Auditor General to Colonial Secretary, 3 January 1927. I am indebted to Ian Phimister for this reference.
149.  DO 35/1169, Baring to Machtig, 15 June 1943; DO 35/1162, Baring to Machtig, 21 October 1944.
150.  DO 35/825, Draft Confidential Report by Lord Hailey on Southern Rhodesia, August 1941.
151.  H. Dunlop, *The Development of European Agriculture in Rhodesia, 1945–1965*, University of Rhodesia, Department of Economics, Occasional Paper No. 5 (Salisbury, 1971), 59. The discrepancy in Land Bank loans was much greater. In 1945–55, the first decade in which Africans were able to get loans, less than seventy farmers received a total of under £6,000; in 1958 outstanding Land Bank loans to European farmers totalled nearly £6 million. Yudelman, *Africans on the Land*, 102, 158.
152.  For an interesting example of Rhodesian African farmers dramatically increasing their production by leaving the crowded reserves and moving to Northern Rhodesia, see R.J. Mutsau, 'The Shona and Ndebele Settlements in Kabwe Rural Area, 1953–63', in Palmer (ed.), *Zambian Land and Labour Studies, Vol. 1*, 41–7.
153.  In 1936 Huggins told the Legislative Assembly that 'If eventually it is found that

there are so many natives and so little water and we cannot pack the natives into the area set aside under the Land Apportionment Act, it will have to be amended' and a little more land provided. Southern Rhodesia, *Legislative Assembly Debates, 16,* 28 May 1936, col. 2428.

154.   Bundy concludes that 'the emergence and decline of the peasantry was a necessary component of, and not separate from, the process of capitalist development in South Africa—that the structural underdevelopment of the peasant sector was the other side of the coin of capitalist development in South Africa'. Bundy, 'The Emergence', 388.

155.   The value of Rhodesia's tobacco sales rose from £3.9 million in 1945 to £29.5 million in 1960.

156.   Yudelman, *Africans on the Land,* 90.

157.   So much so that by 1968 only an estimated 13 per cent of African agricultural production found its way into the money economy, compared to 92 per cent of European production. A.J. Christopher, 'Land Tenure in Rhodesia', *South African Geographical Journal, 53,* 1971, 47–8.

158.   Huggins's two-pyramid policy envisaged that in the 'African areas' the African 'must be allowed to rise to any position to which he was capable of climbing . . . every step of the industrial and social pyramid must be opened to him except only—and always—the very top'. In the 'European areas' however, the African should 'merely assist, and not compete with' the European. Thus 'The interests of each race would be paramount in its own sphere.' Huggins, quoted in R. Gray, *The Two Nations* (London, 1960), 152.

# CHAPTER 10

## Peasant Production and Underdevelopment in Southern Rhodesia, 1890–1914, with Particular Reference to the Victoria District

### IAN PHIMISTER

### Introduction

When outlining some of the characteristics of the structural under-development of colonial Tanganyika, Iliffe emphasized the 'development within the country itself of a pattern of regional inequality which became relatively fixed and rigid'.[1] In Tanganyika this occurred during the 1930s, but in Southern Rhodesia a similar pattern was already largely determined in the second decade of this century and was confirmed by the Land Apportionment Act of 1930. As in Tanganyika, three broad economic sectors can be identified in Southern Rhodesia in this period: (1) that sector or regions specializing in production for export—for example, mines and, increasingly, certain capitalist farms and company-owned plantations; (2) a sector supplying the export-producing regions with food and services; and (3) a third category which consisted of 'peripheral regions which either supplied migrant labour or stagnated in near-isolation from the territorial economy'.[2]

In Southern Rhodesia this second sector was primarily in the hands of peasant[3] producers until shortly after the First World War, although their position was steadily undermined from roughly 1908 onwards. The establishment and expansion of the mining industry without an accompanying capitalist farming sector initially created favourable market opportunities for the emergence of an African peasantry in significant numbers.[4] But because the general profitability of the first sector, particularly in terms of minimization of wage costs, depended largely on the size and exploitability of the labour pool in the third category, it was vital that capitalist agriculture should dominate the second sector.

A report at the turn of the century described Africans as 'agriculturalists . . . [who] do not view the prospect of becoming miners with any enthusiasm. Their present occupation . . . pays better, and is a more pleasant life';[5] and this revealed an unsatisfactory situation from the viewpoint of the developing capitalist sector. One solution suggested was that the mining companies should produce their own grain, thereby depriving the peasant of his market and causing him 'in order to pay his taxes and meet his other requirements, to bring into bearing his only other source of income, that is his own labour'.[6] The essence of the situation was that if the

255

peasant could 'work for himself to a great profit he [was] not likely to work for the white settler for wages',[7] or at least not for wages compatible with settler profitability imperatives. Once the conflict within the second category was resolved in favour of capitalist farming, however, it led more or less directly to the relegation of peasant producers to Iliffe's third category and, perhaps, ultimately to proletarianization.

More broadly, the creation of African peasantries, as well as the subsequent differentiation among them, was '*primarily* the result of the interaction between an international capitalist economic system and traditional socio-economic systems'. As capitalism has further developed, it 'has begun to phase out the very peasantry at first defined and created'.[8] The basic validity of this concept has been demonstrated for South Africa by Bundy, and is central to Arrighi's analysis of the proletarianization of the African peasantry in Southern Rhodesia.[9] But it is important to remember the *caveat,* entered by Gray and Birmingham, that

> economic development in Africa has often been seen as an encounter
> between two extremes: self-sufficient homesteads, the inward-looking
> units of a subsistence economy, have been confronted by a vigorous,
> world-wide, alien industrial economy... [but such an] abrupt di-
> chotomy . . . nevertheless obscures and distorts out understanding of the
> earlier, pre-colonial period.[10]

Without this *caveat,* not only the 'earlier pre-colonial period', but also the beginnings of the colonial era are likely to be misunderstood. The word '*primarily*' in the earlier quoted explanation is of great importance, because it is very probable that the emergence of African peasantries following interaction between international capitalism and at least some 'traditional socio-economic systems' was one of scale rather than innovation. Although capitalism undoubtedly redefined the structural position of such peasantries and greatly enlarged their scale, future research might be usefully employed in examining this field.

The purpose of this chapter is to indicate certain modifications to Arrighi's analysis, to examine briefly the interaction between traders and peasant producers, and to illustrate at 'ground level' an aspect of the process of structural underdevelopment by providing a case study of the Victoria district.

## Mining development and peasant production

Because of the extensive experience by the Shona and Ndebele in pre-colonial trade, even Arrighi's cautious observation that in the 1890s Africans may have displayed some unfamiliarity to market opportunities is largely unwarranted.[11] The violence and dislocations associated with early white penetration, together with the African

Risings of 1896–7, naturally complicate the task of probing African appreciation of, and responses to, market opportunities. However, what evidence does exist indicates a swift awareness and exploitation of such opportunities. In September and October 1890 some Shona were already selling a variety of produce, including grain, sweet potatoes, pumpkins, and groundnuts, to the 'pioneers'—as, indeed, villagers had done to earlier white travellers before 1890. The Shona were soon appreciated as being 'close dealers'; in Manicaland, for example, it was said that

> [the] native does not show the whole of his wares at once, he keeps his best things hidden in the back, a few hundred yards from the camp. If he finds there is a lively demand for food and milk, he will return to the bush, call his caretaker from his hiding place and part with all he has. If his supply is greater than our demands, he will go home and consume his produce in his own house, returning with more when the milk and mealie market improves.[12]

The following year, Percy Fitzpatrick found the Shona 'anxious to barter and quicker to trade and more eager for business than any native I have yet seen. So keen are they on business', he added, 'and so quick to perceive an opening, that they have broken up fresh ground, and planted double crops this year, in order to supply the rush of the white men.'[13] This trend was sustained in 1892, by which time prices had risen near the towns where the demand for produce was greater.[14] The Shona were not alone in this perception of market opportunities. In 1891, the trader Dawson, acting for Lobengula of the Ndebele, was anxious to sell cattle and sheep to the whites in Mashonaland.[15] By 1895 the dependence of the mines on peasant produce had increased to the extent that the Wedza district normally exported large quantities of grain to the mines in Matabeleland. A partial crop failure the same year caused prices to rise and consequently forced the temporary closure of many mining activities.[16]

The basic components of this situation survived the 1896–7 Risings unaltered, and in fact the favourable 'terms of trade' enjoyed by the peasant *vis-à-vis* the capitalist sector enabled the former to recoup certain of their losses in a relatively short time. In Matabeleland at least one district planted a variety of crops 'considerably in excess of their own requirements, with the express intention of trading', while in Mashonaland the price of some peasant produce took cognizance of high transport costs: 'One native asked the other day 7s. for a small calabash of very bad honey weighing about $1^{1}/_{2}$ lbs. Perhaps the transport rates have got something to do with the Mashona's idea of coin. He could do little with a shilling in a store here at present.'[17] Even Cecil Rhodes was startled by the extensive acreage cultivated by Africans. When confronted with a report which claimed that the estimated African population of 500,000 worked over 600,000 acres,

Rhodes could 'hardly believe this possible. It seems such an enormous extent of land for the number of people . . . if true, it shows what an important asset the native is.'[18]

The scattered extent of the Southern Rhodesian mining industry provided the African peasantry with widespread markets for its produce, and in the period under discussion such markets, although of differing size and duration, expanded constantly as more mines were actively developed and brought into production. The proliferation of small workings after the beginning made to the restructuring of the mining industry in 1903 greatly increased the number of markets likely to depend on peasant produce. Two effects can be distinguished here. At the level of individual mines, grain could often be purchased more cheaply locally from peasant producers than from larger centres where high transport rates were an important cost factor.[19] But as regards the overall cost structure of the mining industry, wage reductions were of far greater importance in ensuring its profitability and such cost minimization was related to underdevelopment of the peasant sector.

During the boom of the regional mining economy between 1894 and 1895, average mine wages in Southern Rhodesia were relatively high,[20] but were still insufficiently attractive to bring forth labour in the required numbers. In the less-favoured province of Mashonaland where wages were lower than in Matabeleland one native commissioner observed that:

> 10s. a month is a ridiculously low wage for a native at the present price of food and am not at all surprised at them being unwilling to work for it. After working 30 days a native gets 10s. for which he can only buy 24 lbs of meat at 5d. per lb, this is just enough food for an adult native for 12 days, so that if his family consisted of two only, they would starve on his earnings.[21]

In both provinces the resultant gap between the supply and demand of labour was customarily closed by the device of forced labour. The N/C Hartley frankly reported that he was 'forcing the natives of this district to work sorely against their will', a practice which was later revealed, by their own admission, to number at least half of the Native Department amongst its adherents.[22] However, even this mechanism was hindered in its operation by the viability of the peasant sector: 'Should the Mashonas be compelled just now to leave their cultivation, the bad effects would be felt later on, thereby entailing much expense etc., on Syndicates, Prospectors, etc, as they would have to procure grain down Country.'[23]

The rise in cash wages on the mines between 1899 and 1902 was itself in part a direct reflection of the viability of the peasant sector and not, as Arrighi has claimed, due to mining companies working gold deposits 'irrespective of the costs involved'.[24] Even as the mining industry was beginning a phase of modest expansion, the outbreak of the South African War thrust it back into increased dependency on peasant grain production. Completion of railway communication with the south at the end of 1897 had allowed some of the larger companies to import food supplies, but this partial independence from the peasant sector was ended when hostilities cut the rail link. The Chief Native Commissioner for Matabeleland noted that owing to 'the interruption of railway communication with the South, and the high price of grain occasioned by the war, the natives have been able to trade their grain at a considerable profit'.[25] Peasant prosperity aggravated the 'uncertainty' of labour supplies and increased mining costs, particularly wages. Later wage reductions on the mines were largely successful because of the increasing number of foreign Africans (that is, Africans from outside Southern Rhodesia) recruited for mine labour, but were also related to the progressive underdevelopment of the peasant sector.

A suggested limiting factor on peasant responses to market opportunities is the extent to which this can be done 'without threatening the security of minimal subsistence production'.[26] For various reasons this calculation was probably central to Southern Rhodesian peasant responses, which largely consisted of increased production of 'traditional' crops or the sale of livestock. There were, however, important exceptions, sometimes associated with the move of African entrepreneurs to commercial agriculture.[27] Increased production of 'traditional' crops was nevertheless eminently suited to the demands of the various markets provided by the mines. The one which affected the largest number of peasant producers, and which was most important, was the demand for labourers' rations which, before the promulgation of the 1908 Diet Regulations (and to a certain extent, afterwards) consisted mostly of mealie meal occasionally supplemented with meat. The cornering of this market by capitalist agriculture was central to the subsequent underdevelopment of the peasant sector, and the broad features of this process have been well described by Arrighi.

A further dimension to the markets provided by the mines was the 'private' demand of labourers for extra foodstuffs to supplement their inadequate rations. Associated with this was the supply of beer to mine compounds by surrounding villages, and also the sale of food to migrant labourers travelling to and from the mines. The benefits of such a market were obviously limited to villages within a reasonable distance of mines and to those favourably sited on labour routes, but the small-scale, individual nature of such transactions did have the merit of having little attraction for capitalist farming.[28] In 1906, for example, a native commissioner observed 'gangs of native women taking beer to the mines for sale', and so remunerative was this market that 'all the natives living within 20 miles of the mines [were] able to make sufficient out of the trade to cover their liabilities to the Government and private individuals'.[29] Similarly, in the Belingwe district, where foreign Africans working on the mines earned a combined total of approximately £600 per month, 'nearly every penny was spent on beer, women and meat', with the result that neighbouring villagers were able to obtain 'all the money they require[d] by the sale of grain, beer, small stock, and fowls'.[30] Sale of grain to mine labourers for beer-making purposes realized far higher prices than those paid by traders, and when combined with prostitution was especially profitable:

> An old man and two or three youths with say six or seven women and girls go to the vicinity of some mine where they have a relation or friend working. They all carry grain and often already malted grain. A camp is made in the bush, while the women brew and the men tout for customers at the mines, and beer selling and prostitution by some of the women is carried on until they have sufficient money, they often returning with £7 or £8, and goods, blankets, hoes etc. purchased at the stores.[31]

Even this lucrative peasant activity suffered the fate of the general grain trade. The sale of beer was gradually curtailed following the implementation in 1912 of the Kaffir Beer Ordinance, and although the 'private' market on the mines continued to provide a small-scale outlet for peasant produce,[32] its absolute importance appears to have steadily declined, primarily because of the falling real wages of mine-labourers.

## Peasants and traders

Much of the surplus generated by peasant production was 'appropriated by Europeans in the form of labour-services, taxes, rents, etc', and it also 'became customary for European landowners to market their tenants' produce, and often that of neighbouring peasants as well, a practice that must have effectively prevented Africans, or traders on their behalf, from underselling European producers.'[33] To this extent traders were in conflict with capitalist agriculture, but the long-term effect of their operations was to limit the absolute amount of money available for reinvestment and innovation in the peasant sector. Although the expansion of trading stores throughout many parts of the rural areas did provide otherwise unobtainable 'markets' for peasant surpluses, the bulk of the profits accrued to the traders themselves. A close parallel is found in Latin American experience, where it has been observed that a

> further obstacle to the commercial development of the smallholders' economy is the marketing mechanism. On account of the contractual inferiority of the peasant, and the usual concentration of three commercial functions in the hands of single individuals (purchaser of produce, supplier of credit[34] and vendor of consumptions goods), any surpluses developed by the little economy tend to be transferred to the middleman rather than remain available for reinvestment.[35]

In the period under discussion, the bulk marketing of peasant produce remained firmly under the control of traders, leaving only the 'private' market of the mines directly in the hands of peasant producers. This pattern appears to have corresponded closely to the classic patterns of exploitation followed by an earlier merchant capital in Europe; traders were able to buy produce as cheaply as possible from peasants precisely because of the 'lack of development of the market' and utilized their access to transport to exploit the 'co-existence of local gluts and local famines'.[36] In the Victoria district grain was traded from peasants at 12s a bag, resold at approximately 25s in the township itself, and by the time it reached the mines at Selukwe, cost between 50s and 60s, although this latter price does partly reflect high transport rates. At a time when the local market value of grain was 20s a bag, traders in the Charter area bought it at 10s, before reselling it in Salisbury and Hartley at 37s 6d per bag.[37] One way of extracting the maximum profit from peasants was to offer only trade goods and refuse to pay cash for produce. Some traders even forced peasants to pay the costs of transporting grain to the various markets:

> A native is handicapped to a considerable extent in the sale of his produce: not having as yet adopted any other means of transport than the old fashioned 'pakamisa' [i.e. carrying], they are obliged to sell their grain to traders who make a double profit, viz:—on the goods and on the grain, and have also to pay transport to the place of consumption.[38]

These practices were resisted by peasants, but often their only alternative was to refuse to sell their grain surpluses. In 1898 the N/C Belingwe noted that 'Natives are already bringing grain in for sale but refuse to accept anything but cash. I am afraid they will have some difficulty in selling their grain as storekeepers and traders will only trade and refuse to pay even 10s a bag in cash.' In a neighbouring district peasants flatly refused to sell their grain because only trading goods were offered in return.[39] Such payments, of course, served a further purpose in the colonial political economy; they meant that peasants were forced into wage-labour in order to obtain cash to satisfy certain of their own needs and tax obligations to the government.[40] The persistence of this practice—for different lengths of time in the various districts—is shown by the request in 1916 of peasants in the Makoni area for a store which, it was emphasized, should pay cash for grain.[41] Peasants could attempt to bypass traders and deal directly with the mines and other markets,[42] but this was generally a difficult option to exercise because of remoteness from markets and organizational and transport problems. So it would seem in many respects that traders represented institutionalized 'raiding' of the peasant produce surplus for the ultimate benefit of the capitalist sector, or as one African expressed it: 'The result is this, that the storeman has highly improved his living conditions while the producer (African) remains poor in every branch of life.'[43]

## The case of Victoria district

Certain of these features and aspects of structural underdevelopment are further illustrated by a brief case study of the Victoria district. The district was comparatively heavily populated, suitable for extensive grain production and was ideally situated to take advantage of the market opened when mines in the Selukwe area began production in 1898. Local Africans initially serviced the Selukwe mines both as wage-labourers and especially as peasant producers, but this latter alternative was increasingly denied them. As in other parts of the territory, stores were established in various parts of the district and grain was bartered or bought from peasants. It was sent to Victoria township, and from there conveyed to the Selukwe mines by wagon.[44] At first the general terms of trade were firmly in favour of the peasant sector: 'the Native Makalaka has prospered, the Traders here consider them to be marvellously acute in business and they have traded all their surplus grain at considerable advantage to themselves... [and] have done very well with their sheep and cattle.'[45] So dependent was the district on peasant production at this time, that when local white farmers wanted to charge their tenants a high rent, the native commissioner had to dissuade them as 'this district is very much depended on for grain, and if the Natives were shifted into Reserves from Farms whenever the Farmers were unreasonable the supply would be greatly interfered with'.[46]

The expanding demand for grain at the Selukwe mines was readily met by the Victoria peasantry and this was 'gradually having the effect of placing the natives... on the high road to prosperity'.[47] This prosperity adversely affected the labour supply from the district, a phenomenon interpreted by the Acting Administrator in the usual terms of settler ideology: 'In Victoria there is a huge Native population of which only a very small proportion ever work at all. They are a contemptible race of men, weak, cowardly and indolent, relying on their wives to till their fields, gather their crops, and earn for them the hut tax which they are too lazy to earn for themselves.'[48]

The opening of the Gwelo–Salisbury railway in 1902, with a branch line between Gwelo and Selukwe in 1903, was the most important single element affecting the subsequent underdevelopment of the peasant sector in the Victoria district, for the district was completely bypassed by the new line. It meant that it would be possible in future to send grain from Salisbury and the Charter district, for example, to the Selukwe mines at prices considerably below those which had previously ruled. For the local traders, the only profit-maximizing solution to the problem seemed to lie in considerably reducing 'the prices at which they have hitherto purchased grain from natives, and further to abandon the practice of paying for grain in cash'.[49] But even so, a considerable amount of peasant grain went unsold in the 1902–3 season because the Selukwe mines could now draw on cheaper sources of supply.[50] By 1905, the market price of grain at Gwelo and Selukwe was 'guided very largely by the conditions ruling in Salisbury and Bulawayo, and as during the year Mashonaland figured as the largest producer of grain local prices were maintained at about Salisbury market price plus railage'.[51]

The consequences of this were significant; within two years the price of grain at Selukwe and Gwelo had dropped by 50 per cent, and in Victoria the number of trading stations declined as the local grain traders were undersold at Selukwe by peasant farmers near Salisbury who had the advantage of being situated near the railway.[52] The stock trade however, less susceptible to transport rates, expanded considerably in this period. Most of the cattle and sheep required for slaughter purposes at Gwelo and Selukwe were obtained from the Victoria district. In 1908 the local native commissioner observed that 'large numbers of cattle have been sold by the natives, and [the fact] . . . that cattle have risen in value, naturally affects the labour supply . . . The majority of peasants are not anxious to leave their homes and prefer selling their stock.'[53] The following year peasants were no longer producing grain in any significant quantities for the market, the price having dropped too low. In fact, many were purchasing grain from Europeans with the profits they had won from the sale of livestock.[54]

By 1910 a number of features were evident; the collapse of the grain trade left local Africans with two alternatives, migrant wage labour on the mines and settler farms, or continued sale of livestock. The latter was only a short-term alternative in the face of the accelerating development of capitalist agriculture through public sector subsidization. For the reasons outlined above, the cultivation of grain by peasants was substantially reduced in the Victoria district, and the sector's underdevelopment was symbolized in 1911, when, following a poor season, 'it was found necessary to import mealies . . . from other districts . . ., probably for the first time in the history of the country.'[55]

In the Victoria district lack of rail transport was vital in bringing about the underdevelopment of the peasant sector but, as Arrighi has demonstrated for the territory as a whole, it was the interaction of this factor with others such as land tenure and a variety of politico-economic mechanisms which raised the 'effort-price' of peasant participation in the produce market to the ultimate benefit of commercial farming and the capitalist sector in general. It was those factors which effectively prevented any significant resurgence of peasant productivity once Victoria was in a position to take advantage of the 'Blinkwater' railway extension, built between Umvuma and Fort Victoria in 1911–14.

By the beginning of the century most of the land within forty miles

of Fort Victoria itself had been alienated, leaving as reserves for
Africans areas which were described as largely 'rocky and unfit for
cultivation'.[56] Many Africans at first were allowed to remain on
alienated lands, subject to various rents, fees, and/or labour services,
and in 1903 only some 10 per cent of the population of the district lived
in the reserves. By 1913 this proportion has risen to over 40 per cent,
following the imposition of further rents and the growing occupation
of farms by white settlers.[57] As a result of the Native Reserves
Commission of 1914–15 the Victoria reserves were slightly increased, but were pushed farther from the town and, where
practicable, from the railway. There is no reason to doubt that the
general opinion expressed by Inskipp, the Acting Director of the
Estates Department, was equally applicable to the Victoria district:

> It is disappointing that it has been found necessary to recommend the
> assignment of so much new land; at the same time the greater part of the
> land so recommended is of inferior quality and therefore more suited for
> native than for European occupation; further it is hoped that the native
> reserve land to be returned to the Company will prove of . . . superior
> quality to that for which application has been made.[58]

In such ways was the 'effort-price' of peasant participation in the
produce market raised.

It should further be noted that when capitalist agriculture in the
Victoria district began to develop, it initially shared certain of the
problems experienced by the peasant sector as regards rail transportation to markets. But for the peasant sector this factor played a major
part in precipitating an 'irreversible' change 'in the sense that
subsequent recoveries could not restore the previous position of the
African peasantry *vis-à-vis* the capitalist economy'.[59] Settler farmers,
on the other hand, were able to exploit their favourable class position
to consolidate their hold on the best land and gain access to the
agricultural loan bank. For Southern Rhodesia, as in South Africa,
'the structural underdevelopment of the peasant sector was the other
side of the coin of capitalist development'.[60]

## Conclusion

This chapter, then, has attempted to trace the initial rise of an African
peasantry in Southern Rhodesia under the primary stimulus of
expanding produce markets, and the role of traders in minimizing the
returns from these markets to peasants. In addition, the development
and operation of both of these features have been further examined
through a case study of the Victoria district. Here, the absence of
railway transportation became central to the ultimate underdevelopment of the peasant sector, and this factor combined with land
alienation, taxes, and rents to reduce African peasants to the marginal
and dependent cultivators they are today.[61]

## NOTES

1.   J. Iliffe, *Agricultural Change in Modern Tanganyika,* Historical Association of Tanzania Paper No. 10 (Nairobi, 1971), 30. For Southern Africa it is often more useful to examine underdevelopment in terms of the regional economy: for example, see B.S. Krishnamurthy, 'Economic Policy, Land and Labour in Nyasaland, 1890–1914', in B. Pachai (ed.), *The Early History of Malawi* (London, 1972), 398–9.

2.   Iliffe, *Agricultural Change,* 30. Where this category allows the migrant labour access to means of subsistence outside the capitalist sector, it performs the vital function of enabling 'capital . . . to pay the worker *below* the cost of his reproduction'. See H. Wolpe, 'Capitalism and Cheap Labour-Power in South Africa: From Segregation to Apartheid', *Economy and Society, 1,* 1972, 425–56.

3.   'Peasants are those whose ultimate security and subsistence lies in their having certain rights in land and in the labour of family members on the land, but who are involved, through rights and obligations, in a wider economic system which includes the participation of non-peasants.' J.S. Saul and R. Woods, 'African Peasantries', in T. Shanin (ed.), *Peasants and Peasant Societies* (Harmondsworth, 1971), 105.

4.   G. Arrighi, 'Labour Supplies in Historical Perspective: A Study of the Proletarianization of the African Peasantry in Rhodesia', *Journal of Development Studies, 6,* 1970, 207. For discussion of peasantries differentiated according to locality, see Saul and Woods, 'African Peasantries', 109, and J.M. Mackenzie, 'African Labour in South Central Africa, 1890–1914 and Nineteenth Century Colonial Labour Theory', PhD thesis, University of British Columbia, 1969, Chapters 4 and 5.

5.   National Archives of Rhodesia, NBE 1/1/2, Report of the N/C Matobo-Mawabeni and Malema for the year ending March 1901. Note: all archival sources refer to the National Archives of Rhodesia.

6.   NB 6/4/17, Report of the Compound Inspector, Selukwe, for the month October 1902.

7.   Hist. MSS EY 1/1/1, Notes of proceedings at interview with Lord Selborne held at Salisbury, 12 October 1906.

8.   Saul and Woods, 'African Peasantries', 106, 107.

9.   C. Bundy, 'The Emergence and Decline of a South African Peasantry', *African Affairs, 71,* 285, 1972, 369–88; Chapter 8, C. Bundy, 'The Transkei Peasantry, *c.* 1890–1914: "Passing through a Period of Stress" '; Arrighi, 'Labour Supplies', 197–234.

10.   R. Gray and D. Birmingham, 'Some Economic and Political Consequences of Trade in Central and Eastern Africa in the Pre-Colonial Period', in Gray and Birmingham (eds.), *Pre-Colonial African Trade* (London, 1970), 1.

11.   Arrighi, 'Labour Supplies', 201. African sale of 'labour-time' in the early 1890s was equally discerning.

12.   A 2/1/1, P. Cambell, camp Mt Hampden, to *Cape Times,* 12 October 1890; LO 5/2/3, Pennefather to Harris, 17 September 1890; Hist. MSS WI 2/1/1, Hugh Williams letters, 14 October 1891.

13.   J.P. Fitzpatrick, *Through Mashonaland with Pick and Pen* (1892), edited by A.P. Cartwright (Johannesburg, 1973), 45.

14.   Hist. MSS DA 6/3/3, 'Mashonaland as a Field for Colonization', 1 July 1892.

15.   Hist. MSS US 1/1/1, Dawson to Lobengula, 13 November 1891.

16.   A 15/1/1, Statist. Record Office, to Acting Administrator, 23 March 1895; *Rhodesia Herald,* 11 September 1895.

17.   NB 6/1/2, Statistical Report for the Insiza District for the half-year ending September 1897; *Rhodesia Herald,* 27 October 1897.

18.   Hist. MSS MI 1/1/1, Rhodes to Milton, 5 December 1901. Both this statement and, for example, H. Wilson Fox's *Memorandum on Problems of Development and Policy* (London, 1910), indicate the need for examination of the (changing) imperatives of the various components broadly referred to as 'the capitalist sector'. The BSA Company certainly toyed at various times with the idea of encouraging peasant production.

19.   See, for example, British South Africa Company, *Mining in Rhodesia* (London, 1900), 163. I am grateful to Charles van Onselen for drawing my attention to this point. For more detailed discussion of the mining industry, see C. van Onselen, *Chibaro: African Mine Labour in Southern Rhodesia 1900–1933* (London, 1976); I. R. Phimister, 'History of Mining in Southern Rhodesia to 1953', PhD thesis, University of Rhodesia, 1975.

20.   I.R. Phimister, 'Rhodes, Rhodesia and the Rand', *Journal of Southern African Studies, 1,* 1974, 74–90.

21.   N 1/1/3, Report of the N/C Hartley Hills for the half-year ending December 1895.

22.   N 1/2/2, N/C Hartley to CNC Mashonaland, 30 November 1895; *C.8547, Report by Sir R.E.R. Martin on the Native Administration of the British South Africa Company* (London, 1897).

23.   N 1/1/5, N/C Lomagundi to CNC Mashonaland, 7 January 1895.

24.   Arrighi, 'Labour Supplies', 200.

25.   NB 6/1/3, Report of the CNC Matabeleland for the year ending March 1901.

26.   Saul and Woods, 'African Peasantries', 109.

27.   Arrighi, 'Labour Supplies', 201.

28.   But in the Mazoe district some white farmers even supplied the mines with 'tobacco made up in balls or cones in correct native style', N 9/1/13, Report of the N/C Mazoe for the year 1910.

29.   NB 6/4/7, Report of the N/C Gwelo for the month July 1906.

30.   NB 3/1/15, N/C Belingwe to S/N Gwelo, 12 December 1908.

31.   N 9/1/15, Report of the N/C Goromonzi for the year 1912; N 9/4/23, Report of the Acting N/C Chilimanzi for the month August 1910.

32.   S 235/517, Report of the N/C Mashaba for the year 1939.

33.   Arrighi, 'Labour Supplies', 213–14, 209.

34.   Credit was rarely offered to peasants by traders in Southern Rhodesia; personal communication from Barry Kosmin.

35.   A. Pearse, 'Metropolis and Peasant: The Expansion of the Urban-Industrial Complex and the Changing Rural Structure', in Shanin, *Peasants and Peasant Societies,* 73.

36.   M. Dobb, *Studies in the Development of Capitalism* (London, 1946), 89. See especially ZBJ 1/2/1, evidence of J.H. Farquar to the Commission on Native Production and Trade: 'The method of trading in Native Stores is a sordid relic of the system that produced the merchant princes.'

37.   NB 6/4/2, Report of the N/C Selukwe for the month January 1898; N 9/4/3, Report of the N/C Charter for the month May 1899.

38.   N 9/4/20, Report of the N/C Umtali for the month November 1907. For a particularly colourful description of the methods employed by white traders, see S.P. Hyatt, *The Old Transport Road* (London, 1914), 90, 107–8.

39.   NB 6/4/2, Report of the N/C Belingwe for the month March 1898; NB 6/4/3, Report of the N/C Bulalima-Mangwe for the month December 1899.

40.   See, for example, N 9/4/4, Report of the N/C Mrewa for the month May 1899.

41.   N 9/4/30, Report of the N/C Makoni for the month June 1916. This practice reappeared during the Depression, see S 138/22, Assistant CNC to CNC, 3 October 1931.

42.   *Report of the Secretary for Agriculture for the Year 1909* (Salisbury, 1910).

43.   ZBJ 1/1/1, evidence of Andrew Midzi to Commission on Native Production and Trade, 13 June 1944.

44.   LO 4/1/20, Agricultural Report of the C/C Victoria for the year ending March 1905.

45.   LO 4/1/3, Report of the C/C Victoria for the year ending March 1898.

46.   N 9/4/4, Report of the N/C Victoria for the month July 1899.

47.   British South Africa Company, *Reports on the Administration of Rhodesia, 1898–1900* (London, 1901), 199.

48.   LO 4/1/6, Captain Lawley's Report (1899–1900), Bulawayo, April 1900.

49.  LO 4/1/12, Report of the C/C Victoria for the year ending March 1902.
50.  N 9/4/14, Report of the N/C Victoria for the month February 1903.
51.  LO 4/1/20, Report of the C/C Gwelo for the year ending March 1905.
52.  LO 4/1/25, Reports of the C/Cs Gwelo and Victoria for the year ending March 1907.
53.  LO 4/1/20, Report of the C/C Victoria for the year ending March 1905; N 9/1/11, Report of the N/C Victoria for the year 1908.
54.  LO 4/1/29, Report of the C/C Victoria for the year 1909.
55.  A 8/1/6, Report of the C/C Victoria for the year 1911.
56.  R.H. Palmer, *Land and Racial Domination in Rhodesia* (London, 1977), 267–8.
57.  Arrighi, 'Labour Supplies', 208; Mackenzie, 'African Labour', 190.
58.  Palmer, *Land and Racial Domination,* 121, 268.
59.  Arrighi, 'Labour Supplies', 216.
60.  Bundy, 'The Emergence', 388.
61.  For a contemporary description of the Victoria district, see A.K.H. Weinrich, *African Farmers in Rhodesia* (London, 1975).

# CHAPTER 11

## The Inyoka Tobacco Industry of the Shangwe People: the Displacement of a Pre-Colonial Economy in Southern Rhodesia, 1898–1938

## BARRY KOSMIN

### Introduction: the Arrighi thesis

Recently a new historiography has arisen for Southern Africa which attempts to explain afresh the proletarianization of the indigenous African population—that is, their transition from their pre-colonial existence as 'pastoralist cultivators' to their contemporary status: that of sub-subsistence rural dwellers, manifestly unable to support themselves by agriculture and dependent for survival upon wages earned in 'white' industrial regions or on 'white' farms.[1] Earlier writers had seen the underdevelopment of the African peoples as an original state which was being eliminated by market forces and beneficial and rationalizing influences concomitant with the development of the capitalist sector of the economy. Economists especially propounded this view from the belief that in the subsistence sector there was a great deal of disguised unemployment among the male population.

This thesis was attacked by Arrighi for its anti-historical bias. He demonstrated that unlimited supplies of labour were gained by political rather than market mechanisms, which created in turn an ever-widening gap between the peasant and capitalist sectors of the economy. Moreover he showed that there was a transition period between the pre-colonial stage and the contemporary situation which was marked by the creation of a viable African peasant economy. This process was previously overlooked by persons who imagined that the frailty of the peasant sector and of the subsistence economy was due solely to unscientific and wasteful agriculture, ignorance and neglect. They overlooked the prosperity in the reserves during the early period of colonial rule in which traditional subsistence methods were adapted for a new situation, the production of cash crops, so as to avoid wage labour on the white colonists' terms. This was part of the resistance to the qualitative change in African social relations which the migrant labour system threatened. Arrighi, Palmer and Phimister in Rhodesia, Bundy in South Africa, and Chanock among the Chewa and Mang'anja of Malawi have all shown a similar reaction whereby peasants attempted to meet the demands of colonial governments for tax by seeking to earn money in the ways of which they were masters. This necessitated in turn discrimination and coercive measures being introduced by the wielders of economic and political power to undermine the viability of the peasant sector and so create an expanding labour supply.

Arrighi saw the mechanism whereby this came about as dependent on the concept of 'effort-price'—'the quantity of labour-time given to drudgery necessary to obtain a unit (measured in real terms) of cash income'—as seen in the contest between the effort-price of cash income obtainable through the sale of labour-time and through the production and sale of crops.[2] In Rhodesia the effort price of participation in the produce market was constantly rising because of the imposition of poll tax, dog tax, rents, dipping fees, and so on. To these were added land pressure and declining produce prices as the capitalist sector became self-contained with investment in plantation agriculture. Thus by the 1920s the capitalist sector was self-contained, and peasant independence of wage employment irreversibly undermined.

Arrighi estimated that at the beginning of the century 70 per cent of African cash earnings came from produce sales but in 1932 only 20 per cent.[3] An indication of the profit peasant production at one time yielded can be ascertained from the amount of specie withdrawn from circulation and which government officials considered was hoarded by Africans. In 1913, a year of bad harvests, the amount of specie withdrawn was £27,771, or £138,753 less than the average for the previous five years.[4] Admittedly there was a decline in mining development; nevertheless there was a drop of only 1,200 in the number of mining employees compared with the previous year. It is therefore probably safe to assume that after all expenses well over £100,000 a year was retained by the peasant sector during the most profitable years of peasant production. It is an irony that this period of prosperity created a dependence on importations and luxuries, thus increasing 'necessary' requirements, which in turn made participation in employment more indispensable later.

With this background in mind it should be of some interest to test the general hypotheses on the process of proletarianization put forward by Arrighi by a specific study tracing the fortunes of peasant production over a long period among a distinct community.

## The Inyoka country

The Inyoka country is an isolated area lying north of the Mafungabusi plateau between the Umniati and Sengwe rivers in the present-day Gokwe district of Southern Rhodesia. It is the traditional tribal area or *nyika* of the Shangwe people under Chiefs Nemangwe, Neganda, Nebire, and their paramount, Chireya, who holds the title *Inyoka*. The Shangwe claim a Rozvi origin and speak a Korekore dialect of Shona. In the nineteenth century Chireya was said to control all the area between the above-mentioned rivers down to the Zambezi, but the Shangwe inhabited only the area up to the Matusadona mountains. Below this the Zambezi valley was occupied by Tonga. There are a number of explanations for the name Shangwe. According to a history of 1906 the name was given to the people by the Rozvi Mambos, *Abashankwe,* meaning 'the people who live alone', an apt description of a people cut off from the south by large areas of uninhabited country.[5] Chireya, however, claimed that the area was known as Shangwe prior to his people's arrival and that they merely took over the name.[6] If this has connotations with the Shona word *Shangwa,* famine or misery, it is also appropriate for this inhospitable region, with its endemic malaria and sleeping sickness. Nevertheless the area was long famous for its tobacco culture and manufacture in a territory where tobacco was 'universally cultivated by Africans' prior to the European occupation.[7]

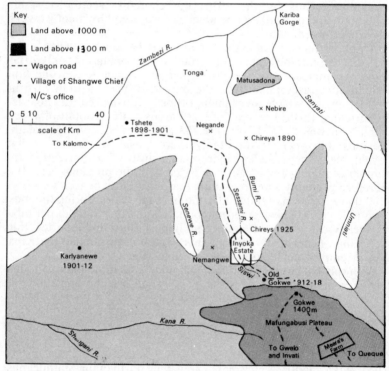

Sketch map of Sebungwe–Mafungabusi district, showing names and areas mentioned

Geographically the area falls into the northern *lowveld* region of Southern Rhodesia. It lies below 3,000 feet and consists mainly of rocky, broken country interspersed with *mopani* veld with an average rainfall of 24–8 inches. The soils consist of slightly acid sandy loams and soft, granular reddish-brown clays. Where the external drainage is reduced, *vlei*-like black clays or black turf soils result. The broken nature of the country causes the rivers to carry high floods in the rainy season and to have extensive areas of alluvial soils on their banks.[8]

From the agricultural point of view, the rich alluvial soils are suitable for the production of grain crops such as millet, sorghum, maize, and cucurbits like melons and pumpkins. However, the erratic nature of the rainfall—14 inches was recorded in 1924 and 60 inches in 1925—complicates riverine agriculture. Subsistence crops must be planted close to the river in order to get moisture if it is a drought year; on the other hand, they are open to inundation and being swept away in a very wet season. To a lesser extent these same problems also occur in the slightly less fertile *vlei* areas. Besides this hazard there is the destruction of crops by animals such as hippopotami and elephants which use the river banks, as well as wild pigs and baboons.

An *Agricultural Survey of Southern Rhodesia* suggested livestock production for this region. However, prior to the eradication campaign of the 1950s, except for a short period following the rinderpest outbreak of 1896, the area was subject to tsetse fly, thus precluding cattle-holding. Moreover, the *mopani* forest inhibits grass cover, which causes grazing problems, particularly in winter. Small stock, sheep and goats, could exist in the area but they were subject to scab and of no great trade value. Thus a rational exploitation of this region in order to gain a constant grain supply, and the hoes, cloth, and other necessities of life, would appear to necessitate the exploitation of the non-riverine soils in the *mopani* forests. The agricultural experts suggested that marginal areas could be used for turkish tobacco. This had been the decision of the Shangwe several generations earlier; in fact the indigenous dark tobacco leaf is very similar to turkish varieties. In addition tobacco was a much easier crop to grow. Statistics indicate that tobacco failed only half as often as grain crops in the harvests between 1898 and 1938. In fact in the years 1908, 1920 and 1936, when there was complete failure of grain crops, 'good' tobacco crops were harvested. On only two occasions in forty years—1925, when there was too much rain, and 1926, when the weather was too hot while the young plants were at a critical stage—were there good grain harvests in contrast with poor tobacco crops.

## Inyoka tobacco: the pre-colonial period

Rather than being content with crop specialization alone the Shangwe went further and specialized in the processing and manufacture of a special type of tobacco product. After the leaf was picked, from February to April, depending on the season, it was hung and air-cured. When the leaf was ready it was placed in wooden mortars, then mixed with ashes of wild aloe, damped with water, and thoroughly pounded. The resultant mixture was kneaded while damp into loaves or cones, and then placed on platforms to dry. The cones varied in weight from one to five lb, but about three lb appears to have been average. The cones were then tied on to reed trays ready for transportation. When wanted the cones were broken into pieces and allowed to dry out, before the very strong and pungent product was smoked in pipes or ground into snuff.[9]

Thomas mentions the fact that in the 1870s the Ndebele grew large quantities of tobacco and smoked it in pipes,[10] but it would appear that Inyoka tobacco was superior and its manufacture different in some way.[11] Despite their own large supply from the Gwai river and Bubi districts, the Ndebele prized the Inyoka variety and definitely imported it. That it was unique in some way is corroborated by the request of a European tobacco farmer at Figtree, who in 1913 wished to employ a Shangwe 'tobacco expert' to process his tobacco into 'the lumps', as 'none of our local boys can make them.'[12]

Mzilikazi is said to have raided the Shangwe on two occasions, but under Lobengula the relationship was friendly, and they were accepted as 'subjects . . . on payment of tribute consisting of tobacco'.[13]

The Mafungabusi district, or *Kwa Nyoka*, fell under the adminis- tration of the induna Tshoko, who lived north of Inyati. Each year he collected tribute at 'Nyoka's kraal' near the headwaters of the Sessami river. There is no direct evidence that the Shangwe traded with the Ndebele prior to 1893, but if the early reports that Chireya grew no grain are even partially accurate, some measure of trade must have taken place for the Shangwe to have survived.[14] This trade could also perhaps explain where the supposedly large quantities of grain went which were gained in Ndebele raids to the north and east. The Ndebele were definitely regular users of tobacco both for pipes and for snuff, which they took on all social occasions and usually carried with them in horn containers as part of their apparel.[15] This trade route from Inyati north-east to Mafungabusi was well known, for it was the route taken by Carbutt, Native Commissioner (N/C), Bubi, who in company with Tshoko first brought the British South Africa Company's presence to the Inyoka country as late as September 1898. At first the Company's Native Department copied Ndebele practice and attempted to administer the area from Inyati, but in 1899 a separate district of Sebungwe–Mafungabusi was established, centred on Tshete. There is a suggestion that the Shangwe probably traded in Matabeleland prior to 1893, since Carbutt mentioned that hawkers from the Inyoka country were in the Bubi district in 1898. The N/C Bulawayo district also reported in the same year that 'Nyokas' were in his area selling tobacco.[16] It is a salient point that the hawking was not remarked on as an unusual occurrence.

This route from Inyati to Gokwe was of some importance prior to the Ndebele intrusion, for there is mention in 1784 that the Rozvi trade route from Changamire, presumably in the vicinity of Thaba- zi-ka-Mambo (Manyanga) or Dhlo-Dhlo (Danangombi), to Zumbo had been redirected and 'started passing through "Chereye's" land'.[17] The impression that the industry was of long standing is also emphasized by its involvement in time-honoured ritual. When a new Chireya is selected the *mhondoro* Nyadati, who resides near Sinoia, is consulted, and a messenger is sent 'with a small quantity of tobacco snuff'; if he accepts the choice a messenger returns with a 'small quantity of other snuff'.[18]

Unfortunately the Native Affairs Department (NAD) officials who were posted to Sebungwe between 1898 and 1938 recorded little of what they saw which was not related to the collection of revenue or the recruitment of labour, except in the case of H. N. Hemans, who had a passion for big game hunting. Thus there is little evidence about the agricultural methods used for Inyoka tobacco culture. However, what information there is suggests that the 'weed' was so well adapted to its environment that it needed less cultivation than maize. If, unlike European-grown tobacco, its value and uniqueness lay in the processing method and not in producing a long, thin leaf of the correct colour, with the transplanting, topping, and other procedures Europeans found necessary to effect this result, this relative neglect of the culture side is understandable. Throughout the period the native commissioners commented on the lack of modernizing effort involved in Shangwe agriculture; the lack of draught animals, due to the tsetse fly danger, meant that the Shangwe never adopted the plough, and throughout the period under discussion the old short-handled hoe was used almost exclusively.[19] This in itself was not an undue hardship, since the hand hoe, which only penetrated six inches or so into the soil, and hand-planting provide a better germination rate and the small ridges better soil conservation than deep tillage (see Introduction). There is reference to hand-irrigation of small patches of tobacco in 1903.[20] However, this practice does not seem to have been general and was probably only carried out at crucial times in bad seasons. The NAD development schemes which were adopted in the inter-war years had not reached the Sebungwe district prior to 1939. So the district was not affected by the ideas or methods of agricultural demonstrators, nor by the irrigation works, afforestation projects, or other modernizing influences.[21] One may assume that agricultural methods and practice remained unaltered in the period and were firmly wedded to pre-colonial forms; any changes in the industry sprang from other sources.

There is no information on the volume of trade or production prior to the establishment of the Company administration, but all the early native commissioners remarked that they were surprised at the extent of tobacco production in the area. The rinderpest epidemic and the raids of rebellious Ndebele in 1896 had depleted the herds of small stock, but in the early years of the century a new prosperity had come to the area. By 1899 European traders were coming to buy small stock to resell to the mines, and others passed through the area on their way to North-Western Rhodesia along the wagon road to Kalomo.[22] Prior to the opening up of the Wankie coalfield it was even planned to run the Cape-to-Cairo railway through the district.

## Inyoka tobacco: expansion, 1898–1921

Unfortunately there are no data solely on the Shangwe, but most officials agreed they made up about 35–40 per cent of the population of Sebungwe–Mafungabusi district. Nevertheless the growth in the relative prosperity of the whole district up to the beginning of the First World War is apparent from Table 1. The native commissioners' reports also reflect this process among the Shangwe, for in 1900 they owned few blankets, but by 1903 most possessed them. It was a time of good tobacco harvests, and prior to 1916 the only setback was the poor crop of 1908. After the early acquisition of blankets the Shangwe began to invest in 'small stock rather than clothes or ornaments'.[23] There was a noticeable increase in their herds by 1910, while by 1914, where possible, in fly-free areas, they were investing in cattle.

The acreage under tobacco had increased markedly by 1903, and European traders were now coming to the area to buy it, 'The price obtained on sale being apparently sufficiently remunerative to justify the long distance over which it had to be transported'.[24] The good price and the ready sale among the Ndebele meant that the Shangwe had little reason to turn out to work in large numbers. It would seem that they could easily raise a great deal of their tax bill of approximately £1,200[25] from tobacco sales. Val Gielgud, the N/C in 1906, was the only official prior to the 1930s to take any interest in the industry. Three traders had now established themselves at the old Ndebele collection point near the headwaters of the Sessami. On patrol in that year Gielgud met one trader 'coming down with 30 carriers and four donkeys all loaded with tobacco from the Inyoka country', while another trader 'had paid one kraal alone for tobacco over £20 in cash, representing half a ton in weight'.[26] This represents a price of about 6d a pound, while in the same year European growers 'were advised not to grow the dark African type of leaf due to overproduction' and it sold for only 3d a pound on the Salisbury auction floors.[27] The value of £20 to a 'kraal' (village) is of interest. 'Native tax' had in practice been doubled in 1904, when it was converted from a hut tax to a poll tax which levied £1 on each male over the age of fourteen and £1 for each wife in excess of one. According to official statistics there were 740 villages in the whole Sebungwe district and the tax receipts were just over £6,000.[28] Thus the average village paid under £9 in tax, and for this specific village the remainder was surplus. This situation led to a marked increase in the standard of living, with the purchase of 'considerable quantities of clothing, blankets, beads and enamel ware'.[29] By 1914 it was considered that there was a large growth of capital in the district from tobacco, stock, and labour. 'Half-caste and native traders' also began to visit the district to purchase tobacco, and in 1915 'one European

**Table 1: Development of African Areas of Southern Rhodesia 1903–38**

| Year | Estimated population | Tax assessment (£) | Goats | Sheep | Cattle | Donkeys | Ploughs | Cultivated acreage | 200-lb bags of grain harvested |
|---|---|---|---|---|---|---|---|---|---|
| 1903 | 563,119 | 108,000 | 237,000 | 75,000 | 64,000 | n.a. | n.a. | 557,000 | 1,272,000 |
| 1938 | 1,185,000 | 443,000 | 744,000 | 133,000 | 1,555,000 | 79,000 | 93,938 | 1,614,000 | 2,935,000 |
| Development of Sebungwe–Mafungabusi District | | | | | | | | | |
| 1903 | 19,100 | 3,300 | 11,000 | 3,000 | 16 | 0 | 0 | 11,000 | 67,000 |
| 1906 | 23,000 | 6,700 | 13,500 | 4,000 | 50 | 0 | 0 | 10,000 | 46,000 |
| 1909 | 24,600 | 6,900 | 15,000 | 8,000 | 100 | 1 | 0 | 16,000 | 60,000 |
| 1912 | 25,800 | 6,800 | 20,000 | 10,000 | 175 | 0 | 0 | 16,500 | 25,000 |
| 1915 | 19,800† | 6,900 | 32,000 | 14,000 | 375 | 4 | 1 | 16,000 | 24,000 |
| 1918 | 20,319 | 6,700 | 28,000 | 20,000 | 837 | 52 | 12 | 16,800 | 12,000 |
| 1921* | 18,056 | 6,200 | 29,500 | 20,000 | 1,097 | 105 | 17 | 12,800 | 35,000 |
| 1924 | 19,122 | 5,700 | 34,000 | 22,500 | 1,910 | 250 | 18 | 13,000 | 13,000 |
| 1927 | 20,387 | 5,900 | 40,500 | 28,000 | 3,018 | 355 | 30 | 20,000 | 35,000 |
| 1930 | 22,627 | 6,500 | 40,000 | 28,500 | 3,800 | 412 | 60 | 24,000 | 60,000 |
| 1933 | 23,791 | 6,400 | 41,000 | 29,500 | 4,400 | 508 | 96 | 28,000 | 39,000 |
| 1936 | 22,111 | 6,700 | 47,000 | 30,500 | 3,100 | 615 | 109 | 26,700 | 47,000 |
| 1938 | 26,719‡ | 6,900 | 49,000 | 31,500 | 3,500 | 575 | 114 | 27,300 | 47,000 |

* 1919 boundary with Wankie district changed.
† New system of computation = number of males on tax register × 3.5.
‡ New system of computation = number of males on tax register × 4.33.
Source: CNC's annual reports.

trader alone had to fill a contract to supply 17,000 pounds, which he was able to do with no difficulty'.[30] Besides this upturn in local sales, increasing numbers of Shangwe tobacco-growers were now spending most of the winter months hawking tobacco in Matabeleland. In one month in 1906 Gielgud issued over a hundred passes for this purpose, mostly for journeys to the mines of the neighbouring Gwelo and Bubi districts.

Given this comparatively buoyant economic picture, it is not surprising that Europeans began to take an interest in the Inyoka country. It has been seen that traders had penetrated the marketing side and were helping to supply the increased market in the towns and mines which had been created by European economic development of the country. Much of this market of African workers was not Ndebele but the labour migrants to Matabeleland, who seemed to have adopted their tastes, and if the trend had continued a constantly expanding market would have been assured in line with economic development and the concomitant immigration of alien labourers. However, against this background must be set the early failures of speculative mining and other projects by the European settlers. With this in mind it is not difficult to see why Gielgud's contacts with the Department of Agriculture to obtain better tobacco seed and his attempts to improve Shangwe methods and send 'some extremely intelligent men' for training in curing methods were received so coldly by the Department. He even went so far as to suggest that the training expenses of these men should be borne by the government, and to encourage the industry it should guarantee to take all tobacco prepared in the new improved method at 7d a pound. 'In making these suggestions I am, I own, not so much influenced by any wish to procure the natives a higher price. . . . But it appeared to me that the quantity and quality of Nyoka tobacco had perhaps been overlooked, and that we were possibly passing by a source of wealth to the country.'[31]

Even Gielgud's apologetic tone could not persuade a Company administration, which had yet to pay a dividend and had failed to secure large-scale investment to forgo overseas investment opportunities in order to subsidize local Africans to grow cash crops. Rhodesia was not the Gold Coast. The Chief Secretary was not interested, and suggested that the best way for the Shangwe to learn was to take service with European tobacco-growers and pick up knowledge while working for them. Farm labour was not exactly the technical training Gielgud envisaged. Instead the Company published his remarks on the progress of the Inyoka country in the Director of Agriculture's report and suggested that here was an area ripe for exploitation by European growers.[32] This episode may be one of the earliest indications, especially in view of the collapse of mining speculations in the following year, that the Company was becoming increasingly dependent on white settlers for the economic development of the territory.

During 1906 the Inyoka Rhodesia Tobacco Company was formed in London, with Frank Johnson of Pioneer Column fame as its chairman. Encouraged by the favourable publicity, by August 1907 it had bought 20,000 acres around the confluence of the Siswi and the Sessami rivers on the condition that at least £4,000 was spent on developing the estate. The company planned to grow turkish tobacco for export, and initially brought out an expert, Mr X. Dardagan, and two other Ottoman Greeks from Smyrna.[33] The idea of trying to develop an estate from nothing in hot malarial country 140 miles from a railhead and with only a rough wagon road for communication, which became impassable during the rains, sounds economically absurd even in present-day conditions. However, it followed an established white Rhodesian speculative practice of attempting to exploit previous African economic initiatives. When mines were prospected in the 1890s no scientific methods were used; the pioneers merely sought out old African workings. When the Moodie trek arrived at Melsetter they took the land with the heaviest African population. And in Matabeleland as the Chief Native Commissioner observed in 1908, the settlers 'in selecting their land have naturally been guided by the number of natives located thereon, whose knowledge of the productive powers of the soil must of necessity be the best guide'.[34] This is, of course, less than flattering to the image of the European settler, who was normally portrayed as bringing rational economic development and expertise to the wilderness.

Once the Inyoka Company had established itself in the area it found that its curing barns, houses, and fields lay outside its boundaries, to the south of the marker beacons. The next few years were spent trying to buy another 30,000 acres to the south at 2s an acre, but the BSA Company was unwilling to sell because 'The Board understands that the Inyoka district is likely to prove one of the most valuable tobacco growing centres in the country, and it is thought that it should be carefully inspected before any further large areas are disposed of.'[35] This was to be done without reference to the present occupants, who were beneficially occupying the land for the same purpose envisaged for European settlers. It was only when the government tobacco expert, G. M. Odlum, inspected the property in August 1908 that the reason for the 'oversight'—almost certainly a 'deliberate' mistake—over the beacons was apparent. On the southern boundary were a number of Shangwe villages, and they had cleared some of the *mopani* veld. Possession of this land would add known producing tobacco land to the estate and, if the Africans wished to remain, either gain them labour or provide income from rents. This land was particularly valuable in view of the fact that it was costing £10 an acre to clear the bush, as mechanical means could not be introduced owing to transport problems.

Odlum found five Greek men, a Greek woman, and seventy Africans supposedly working on the estate. Sixty acres of land had been cleared but only twelve were under tobacco. One year's crop

had produced 8,000 lb of tobacco worth 2s a pound on the South
African market. The expert considered the white staff was now
sufficient for two hundred acres of tobacco and suggested that 'a
strong hand' was necessary with the Greeks 'to make them efficient
labourers'; also that irrigation and efficient management were
necessary for commercial success. Dardagan, however, who became
an important owner of African stores in the 1920s, with an eye on the
prosperous Shangwe market was already diversifying the operation
into less exhausting fields and had established a trading store
on the property with £500 worth of stock. Odlum was concerned
that 'this should not be regarded as one of the company's main
activities'.[36]

The Inyoka Company carried on growing small amounts of tobacco
until it became insolvent in the tobacco slump of 1914, but it was
never a success and by 1911 had cut its European staff to three men.
In 1909 it was agreed that it should get a 3,000 acre strip to the south
where it had strayed over its borders, but this policy does not seem to
have secured a labour supply, for it was reported in 1912 that the
Company was having difficulty getting the Shangwe to work for it,
and labour was being brought in from outside the area.[37] For the
venture to have succeeded would have required a massive injection of
capital, as the distance from the railway and the thickly wooded
nature of the country were great handicaps. Given the situation, the
Shangwe, with their low overheads, small, hand-worked acreages,
and personal hawking, while only requiring a low profit margin, were
a more efficient and rational economic unit than the plantation
system.

Thus by 1914 the attempt to exploit the Inyoka country had failed
and was not to be repeated on any scale. Yet if the area could not be
exploited by Europeans perhaps the product could. When W. M.
Wood of Figtree applied to get a Shangwe expert in 1913 his anxiety to
obtain such a man was obvious from his rather revealing letter, which
did not reflect the normal farmer's attitude to African labour. He
offered a choice of either a monthly wage or piecework: 'in the latter
case I will pay threepence per 3/4 lb weight. I will also pay all expenses
attendant on sending him down. I will take him for any period he likes
to stay. If he wants to bring down his wives to help him, I am quite
agreeable, and can give them all quarters in the compound.'[38] Wood
had made a similar arrangement before, and both sides were said to
have been pleased with the result. There is another letter extant from
a Salisbury grower in 1916 in which he applied to two experts, but the
N/C thought he would have difficulty getting them and insisted on rail
fares in advance for any he might recruit. Not for the 'tobacco
experts', the long walk to work normally associated with migrant
labourers at this time. However, it would appear that the demand for
their services, which the Shangwe were anyway reluctant to meet,
slackened off by the 1920s, when export markets were opened up for
virginia leaf, while at home, as will be shown, the Europeans decided

to subvert the tastes of the internal market rather than compete with the Shangwe.

After the departure of the European growers and the end of the threat to the Shangwe land, all seemed well in the Inyoka country, but the dangers of the heavy reliance placed on tobacco to get money for tax and grain were shown in the bad harvest of the drought year of 1916. The crop 'was a practical failure and traders were able to purchase but a very small quantity'.[39] This meant that cash was scarce, and what money was gained from other sources, such as sale of stock or labour, went to purchase food. The Shangwe were 'unable to buy the clothing or luxuries, or increase their stock, the new necessary requirements', to which they had become accustomed.[40] In 1917 there was a good demand for tobacco and the beginning of an improvement in the transport position, which aided marketing. Europeans had used donkeys for some years, since no permit was required to take them out of a tsetse fly or east coast fever area. Donkeys did eventually succumb to fly, but not before they had more than earned their keep. The Shangwe now began to purchase them as pack animals for transporting tobacco to the southern markets. The large increase in the number of these animals shown in Table 1 demonstrates the increase in the volume of the hawking trade until the 1930s. Prior to this a hawker-grower could carry only some 50–70 lb with him, but now this load was increased several times.

The years of prosperity, apart from a setback in 1919 when the harvest was so great that it could not all be sold, continued until 1922. In 1918 the chiefs gave generously to War Fund contributions, Chireya providing '£3/18/6, 21 native made mats, 30 cakes of Inyoka tobacco'.[41] It is interesting that the paramount, alone of the chiefs, gave a tobacco gift to the Ndebele's successors. The prosperity was such that it was estimated that only 10 per cent of the Shangwe men turned out for wage-labour, for which they had to journey outside the district, as there was no local employment.[42] The great famine and drought season of 1921–2 affected the Inyoka country as badly as any other area, and famine relief was necessary. The Shangwe made desperate attempts to relieve the position, and tried to grow tobacco during the winter in the *vlei* lands. This season saw the final demise on the Inyoka Estate of Europeans, who had opened up again on a small scale in 1919, and the land reverted to the government.

## Inyoka tobacco: decline, 1922–38

In the 1922–3 season, perhaps in expectation of another bad grain harvest, there was a tremendous growth in the tobacco acreage, and the Tonga now participated. According to the N/C, this was an attempt by the Tonga, who lived along the flood plain of the Zambezi valley to the north of the Shangwe and beyond the Matusadona Range, to copy the Shangwe and get tax money without selling their labour outside the district. It may well have been a reaction to the fall in wages and the oversupply of labour the previous year. Nevertheless, as the N/C remarked in his report:

> Cultivation of tobacco has increased to an enormous extent and the amount harvested this year has increased in proportion. Whereas in former years the Batonka grew little beyond their own needs, they now grow for the market... the prices realised by the sale of tobacco have fallen far below those fetched in former years and it has been usual for natives who have left the district carrying a full load of 50–70 lbs to return with 10–15s as proceeds of the sales. Even now natives are still away trying to find a market and others are still proceeding out of the district to hawk their tobacco.[43]

The tremendous crop grown is shown in Table 2. No information is available on yields per acre, but the early European yields prior to scientific farming were about 200 lb to the acre. Using this figure it would appear that about 1,500 acres in the Sebungwe district were under tobacco in 1923. This overproduction was the beginning of the downturn in the industry; 1924 was another bad year, this time owing to a small crop, and the older men, who relied entirely upon their sales of tobacco as a source of income, had to obtain grain on credit, otherwise 'their plight would have been a sorry one'. Half the Shangwe men had to go out to work, for which they searched throughout the colony; some even travelling to Messina in the Transvaal.[44] The bad harvests continued until 1927, and the Inyoka country entered the Depression years after a decade of disappointment in which the local economy had received rather a battering. Nevertheless tobacco was still 'the financial mainstay of a district with practically no cattle, and no market for ordinary crops'.[45]

Before reviewing the comparatively well-documented economic picture of the 1930s in the Inyoka country, it is advisable to study the tsetse fly position, because the general stagnation of the region after 1930, shown in Table 1, was due in no small way to this factor, which altered the geographical situation, helping to create an artificial land shortage. It has been noted that in 1896 the fly had retreated from a great deal of the region, and Chireya, who in earlier times lived on the upper Sessami, was found at the confluence of the Sessami and Bumi rivers in 1899. He was taking advantage of the opportunity to exploit new grazing areas for his small stock and to open up new agricultural land. The large grain yields of the early years of the century, though probably over-estimated at six bags to the acre in 1903, testify to the success of this policy. Prior to 1906 less than 25 per cent of the Sebungwe–Mafungabusi district was infested by tsetse fly. However, for the first time in 1913 five thousand Africans were moved north and south of the fly belt, and Chief Chireya himself was moved. The fly belt had spread about thirty miles in the direction of the Bumi from the east in two years. In 1916 there was an outbreak of trypanosomiasis on the Que Que to Gokwe road at Meara's Farm. By

## Table 2: Inyoka Tobacco Sales

| Year | | Weight (lb) | £ | Approximate price per lb (pence) |
|------|------|------|------|------|
| 1906 | Purchased by traders | 13,100 | 325 | 6.0 |
|      | Hawked by growers | 12,000 | 500 | 10.0 |
|      | Total | 25,100 | 825 | |
| 1923 | Traders | 72,500 | 460 | 1.5 |
|      | Hawkers | 227,500 | 1,890 | 2.0 |
|      | Total | 300,000 | 2,350 | |
| 1931 | Traders | 13,590 | 453 | 8.0 |
|      | Hawkers | 31,480 | 2,200 | 16.8 |
|      | Total | 45,070 | 2,653 | |
| 1932 | Traders | 24,000 | 800 | 8.0 |
|      | Hawkers | 43,000 | 2,200 | 10.0 |
|      | Total | 67,000 | 3,000 | |
| 1933 | Traders | 6,750 | 185 | 6.6 |
|      | Hawkers | 28,000 | 1,500 | 10.7 |
|      | Total | 34,750 | 1,685 | |
| 1934 | Traders | 7,980 | 234 | 7.0 |
|      | Hawkers | 26,220 | 1,190 | 9.0 |
|      | Total | 34,200 | 1,424 | |
| 1935 | Traders | 11,693 | 174 | 3.5 |
|      | Hawkers | 28,640 | 717 | 6.0 |
|      | Total | 40,333 | 891 | |
| 1936 | Traders | 30,000 | 550 | 4.4 |
|      | Hawkers | 64,000 | 1,550 | 6.0 |
|      | Total | 94,000 | 2,100 | |
| 1937 | Traders | 4,000 | 54 | 3.1 |
|      | Hawkers | 66,200 | 1,425 | 5.8 |
|      | Total | 70,200 | 1,479 | |
| 1938 | Traders | 560 | 8 | 3.4 |
|      | Hawkers | 51,000 | 1,083 | 5.5 |
|      | Total | 51,560 | 1,091 | |

These are the only years for which figures are available. 1906 estimate based on monthly reports; other years N/Cs' estimates in annual report.

1933 and 1934: poor crops due to drought; 1935 sales low due to drought and a reduced market. These figures do not include barter sales with other tribes in the district, and it is impossible to arrive at a production figure.

1926 the fly was reported on the old Inyoka Estate, and 75 per cent of the district was now infested.[46] NAD policy was to move people out of affected areas, and undoubtedly those like Chireya, who now owned some cattle, were in favour of this. The movement of the N/C's office reflects a similar policy with regard to their own personnel. The result of the policy was that the population was concentrated into a smaller area, and in practice shifting cultivation was prevented. On the other hand, no attempt was made to provide the new techniques and fertilizers which the shift to a sedentary system demanded. On the livestock side this constriction in area led to more frequent outbreaks of scab. With no virgin land available, the soil was soon drained of its nutriment. This is apparent from two references. When the main tobacco crop of 1927 failed, the Shangwe were forced to replant on old lands, though they did reap surprisingly good crops.[47] In 1928 a winter crop of tobacco was grown on the river banks, which twenty years earlier Odlum had regarded as 'too rich for tobacco'.[48] If one recalls that the Inyoka tobacco was easier to grow than grain crops, the importance of the following statement will be apparent. 'It is significant that although many reports of shortage of food have been made by natives in this district, the proportion of arable riparian land under tobacco is larger than grain crops.'[49]

Initially the European occupation aided the Inyoka tobacco trade, as it increased the market on the periphery of Matabeleland as farms and mines were established in Wankie, Bubi, Gwelo, and Hartley districts. Tobacco was now easier to sell, since money was available, whereas before presumably the Shangwe relied on a barter system. It has been seen how the number of traders coming to the area increased rapidly, but already by the mid-1920s the 'half-caste and native traders' were beginning to drop out of the picture. An increase in grower-hawker marketing with newly acquired donkeys hid this slow decline in popularity for a time, but by 1930 all but three traders had dropped out; by 1938 only one remained, and he would only take the tobacco in payment of bad debts or as credit for old customers.[50] The fall in price is clearly shown in Table 2. The surprisingly rapid decline of the industry, the reasons for which are discussed later, would appear to have been quite inexplicable to the Shangwe.

The data in Table 2 are based on the N/C's observations. The figures for European traders are probably quite correct, for they were asked directly the quantity bought and the price paid. For the grower-hawkers the figures were based upon an estimate that 90 per cent of them visited Gokwe to get passes, where they declared the weight they carried. 'The value for the tobacco sold outside the district is that placed on it by the Native growers, i.e. the amount they anticipate they will realise at the mines, etc. when they sell it.'[51]

Because their tobacco was consumed locally the Shangwe were not adversely affected by the second tobacco slump of 1928, which ruined many European growers and which was due to export marketing difficulties. In 1932 'the Natives had no difficulty in disposing of this tobacco amongst their usual native customers at the work centres', and the prevailing Depression did not appear to have adversely affected this industry.[52] In August alone 466 passes were issued to hawk tobacco, and the N/C was gratified to know that there was 'at least one form of lucrative agriculture open to the Native in which apprehension has not been expressed, so far, as to competition with the European'.[53] The 1932 crop, however, was the last which managed to meet the Shangwe tax bill of about £2,500; 1933 saw a bad crop and in 1934 the Shangwe were beginning to have trouble selling their product. As late as October so many hawkers were still away that it was impossible to collect tax in two valleys. By November 1934 the N/C was able to report that 'the local Natives are at last awakening to the fact that, their tobacco not having the same value as heretofore, they must look for work in order to find the balance of their tax'.[54] Other avenues were also affected as the market for small stock disappeared with the end of the foot-and-mouth epidemic of 1931–2.

The rapid dislocation of the economy caused the N/C to investigate the position to try and find the reasons behind it. The prime reason appeared to be that 'the Natives in working centres are acquiring a taste for manufactured tobacco which is put in attractive packets'.[55] In the late 1920s, following the tobacco slump and the loss of overseas markets, there was a determined attempt by manufacturers to penetrate the African market. A Salisbury firm began to produce cigarettes at ten for a penny, packed in brightly coloured packets with a crocodile or lion on the wrapping.[56] Glickman, the local storekeeper at Gokwe, agreed that the real trouble was 'that the younger generation prefer packets and tins of tobacco' and also now rolled their own cigarettes.[57] Moreover snuff-taking had practically died out except among the old men in the Ndebele villages. The other major reason was a decline in quality and an adulteration of the Inyoka product which was described as 'cunning commercialism' but was more probably a measure of desperation. On a cone being opened, stones were often discovered inside or the interiors were 'found to be quite mildewed and rotten and consisting of leaf other than tobacco'.[58] The storekeeper agreed that the product 'was not properly worked as it used to be'. According to him, good cones could still be sold but few of them could be bought. The N/C decided to tell 'the chiefs and their followers to stop the adulteration for their own good'.[59] He suggested that as they had returned with half their stock a better and surer marketing policy would be to work on the mines they visited to sell to their workmates. 'However, they prefer to come back resigned to fate that they cannot sell tobacco which is the only method of obtaining money to which they have become accustomed.'[60] There was a bad harvest in 1935 owing to drought and locusts, and 1936 saw a recurrence of the yaws epidemic which had begun in 1929. In 1936 there was a slight revival and a poor grain harvest in contrast with a good tobacco crop. The reason for this anomaly was 'that from weakness caused by their privation they were unable to cope with the larger acreage required for maize and the more intensive cultivation, that is, compared with tobacco'.[61] By 1938 it was remarked that there was no sale for Inyoka tobacco in the towns, and its value was diminishing every year, while the N/C's annual report for 1939 failed even to mention the crop.

What, then, were the causes of this situation? Undoubtedly the change in smoking habits among the traditional African market was significant. The Shangwe suffered from the effects of the Westernizing process, which was transforming the lifestyle of the African population and which was symbolized in this instance by the move away from pipes and snuff to factory-produced cigarettes. On the question of the decline in quality and adulteration of the product, the large crops of the 1920s, especially in 1923, probably led to disease. In fact the 1923 season encouraged bacterial and fungus disease among European tobacco crops, which were particularly affected by 'white rust' or mildew.[62] The European grower had all the facilities of a research station, established in 1924, and modern chemical aids to help him against the many tobacco diseases, such as rust, mosaic, angular spot, and wild fire. On the other hand, after Gielgud's efforts in 1906 no attempt was made by the NAD to try and aid the African sector of the industry in any way, either in agricultural demonstration, new seed, fertilizers, insecticides, marketing aids, or even advice. This *laissez-faire* policy is in contrast with that adopted in Nyasaland, where African tobacco growers on native trust land were encouraged and helped. In 1926 a Native Tobacco Board was appointed, and it worked to eradicate the adulteration and nefarious practices which were increasing in the Inyoka country under the pressure of the 1930s. In Nyasaland Africans were even trained in fire-cured methods, as Chanock has shown,[63] while in Rhodesia NAD help, which anyhow was almost entirely maize-oriented, was only given if Africans directly requested it.

If one accepts that in Southern Rhodesia the administrators were primarily interested in inducing Africans to go out to work for Europeans, their attitude is understandable. The success of the Inyoka tobacco economy restricted the labour supply and disappointed the officials. In March 1913 the N/C lamented that the Shangwe 'as a factor in the labour problem... can scarcely be counted at all. So far this year not a single pass has been issued to any Mshankwe Native to seek work.'[64] Even at the end of the period, when about half the adult males were working outside the district, the N/C admitted that remitting tax to his office was often their only link with the area.

## Conclusion

By the 1960s all trace of the Inyoka tobacco industry had disappeared,[65] and the Shangwe *nyika* was regarded as one of the most backward of the 'tribal trust lands'. Furthermore, as the tsetse fly was slowly driven back north the Gokwe district became a major resettlement area, and over 100,000 strangers were settled on the traditional lands of the Shangwe. If a balance sheet is produced for the effect of European contact with the Shangwe it can be seen that the effect was detrimental. The population increase was slow and did not match the territorial average increase shown in Table 1, which suggests a high infant mortality rate, the effect of disease, and the general lack of medical facilities. In purely financial terms approximately £90,000 was paid in direct tax by a community of between 8,000 and 10,000 people in the period 1898–1938, which at a conservative estimate amounts to £300,000 in present-day values.[66] For this outflow of capital they received 'administration and justice', an unsuccessful tsetse fly eradication campaign, the establishment of a temporary clinic in the dry seasons of 1929 and 1930 during the yaws epidemic,[67] the distribution of some stock medicines, and famine relief on credit when it was necessary. It has been seen that the 'uncompromising character of the country, the Tsetse Fly and the distance from markets . . . precluded the inauguration of progressive schemes',[68] such as agricultural demonstrators, irrigation, clinics, or even schools. The Ndebele overlords had been content with a smaller tribute and had at least provided a market which had encouraged the Shangwe regional specialization. In general the Company and settler governments had seen the problem of African areas as a choice between 'whether Africans should be allowed to stagnate in reserves or turned out to work', and later of whether they should produce cash crops in competition with whites or 'remain labour reservoirs self-sufficient in food crops, and refuges for the old and refractory'.[69] The Inyoka country, with its regional specialization geared to an African market and lack of European settlement, was atypical of this pattern, and it suffered neglect and decay which led to economic and social displacement.

In the light of the Arrighi thesis it would appear that this is a case of delayed proletarianization in which a peasant economy is first fed then later strangled by capitalism. The Shangwe love of independence and their unwillingness to turn out to work for Europeans led the authorities, whose prime concern in the inter-war years was to increase labour supplies, to regard the Shangwe as lazy and backward, but their desire not to enter into a hostile and complex new world when they could meet their cash needs in a familiar environment is very understandable and natural. They were able to withhold their labour because they were less integrated into the capitalist economy than other peasants. However, it would appear that holding out against the historical trend did not help them in the long run, and they were eventually forced into the vicious circle which drained their local capital in terms of migrant labour without any repayment by social investment in terms of health, welfare, and education. This was a direct result of the responsiveness of the state to the needs of white farmers, that is, political rather than market forces. Thus this study demonstrates the validity of the Arrighi thesis and shows it would be wrong to imagine that the peasant sector of the Rhodesian economy was inherently unable to respond to economic challenge.

# 286

BARRY KOSMIN

## NOTES

1.  C. Bundy, 'The Emergence and Decline of a South African Peasantry', *African Affairs, 71*, 285, 1972, 369.
2.  G. Arrighi, 'Labour Supplies in Historical Perspective: A Study of the Proletarianization of the African Peasantry in Rhodesia', *Journal of Development Studies, 6*, 1970, 229.
3.  Arrighi, 'Labour Supplies', 216.
4.  National Archives of Rhodesia, K 5/1/3, Report of the Controller of Customs for the year 1913. Note: all archival sources refer to the National Archives of Rhodesia.
5.  A 3/18/28, tribal histories: Sebungwe District by W.E. Farrar, 21 February 1906.
6.  S 1542/A2/10, ethnological and administrative classifications: Sebungwe District. R.L.D. Herbert, report on tribal structure, 18 October 1937.
7.  H. Weinmann, *Agricultural Research and Development in Southern Rhodesia, 1890–1923*, University of Rhodesia, Department of Agriculture Occasional Paper 4 (Salisbury, 1972), 12.
8.  Federation of Rhodesia and Nyasaland, *An Agricultural Survey of Southern Rhodesia, Part I: Agro-Ecological Survey* (Salisbury, 1961), 88, 109, 110. According to this survey, which is based on correlations of climate, soil, and vegetation, apart from a narrow strip along the northern edge of the plateau, the area falls into Natural Region IV. This region is described as suitable for semi-intensive livestock production and drought-resistant crops. The small belt on the upper Sessami and Bumi falls into Natural Region IIIA and is suitable for semi-intensive mixed farming with drought-resistant grain and cash crops.
9.  H.N. Hemans, *The Log of a Native Commissioner* (London, 1935), 130.
10.  T.M. Thomas, *Eleven Years in Central South Africa* (London, 1873), 180–1.
11.  Unfortunately, nothing specific is known of the actual differences in the manufacturing process.
12.  NGB 2/3/1, W.M. Wood, Figtree, to N/C Bulawayo, 25 March 1913.
13.  A 3/18/28, tribal histories: Sebungwe District by W.E. Farrar, 21 February 1906.
14.  NB 6/4/3, Report of the N/C Sebungwe–Mafungabusi for the month September 1899.
15.  Thomas, *Eleven Years*, 179–80.
16.  NB 6/1/2, Reports of the N/Cs Bubi and Bulawayo for the year 1898.
17.  N. Sutherland-Harris, 'Trade and the Rozvi Mambo', in R. Gray and D. Birmingham (eds), *Pre-Colonial African Trade* (London, 1970), 257.
18.  F. Marr, 'Some Notes on Chief Sebiya', *NADA, 39*, 1962, 81.
19.  There is no evidence that the Shangwe ever adopted the longer-handled hoe of European manufacture.
20.  NB 6/1/5, Report of the N/C Sebungwe–Mafungabusi for the year 1903.
21.  The best account of the agricultural and development policy of the Native Affairs Department is found in M.C. Steele, 'The Foundations of a "Native" Policy in Southern Rhodesia, 1923–33', PhD thesis, Simon Fraser University, 1972, 353–93.
22.  NB 6/1/2–3, Reports of the N/C Bubi for the years 1898 and 1899. The stock depredations in the Sebungwe district after the Risings are described in V. Gielgud, 'A Pioneer in Rhodesia: The Capture of Mpotshwana', *State, 3*, 1910, 292–303, 483–91. Since there appears to have been contact with northern Zambezia, and the Tonga people had a supposedly tributary relationship to the Shangwe, stock were probably imported from the north. This would explain the rapid build-up of stock in 1896–9.
23.  NB 6/1/11, Report of the N/C Sebungwe for the year 1910.
24.  NB 6/1/5, Report of the N/C Sebungwe–Mafungabusi for the year 1903.
25.  This figure is based on the common estimate that the Shangwe composed approximately 35 per cent of the district's population.
26.  NB 6/4/7, Report of the N/C Sebungwe for the months January and July 1906.
27.  'Pioneers of Rhodesian Tobacco', *Rhodesian Tobacco Journal, 5*, 12, 1953, 79.
28.  *Report of the Chief Native Commissioner Matabeleland for the Year Ended 31st March, 1907* (Salisbury, 1907), Tables 9 and 11.

29.  N 9/1/17, Report of the N/C Sebungwe for the year 1914.
30.  N 9/1/18, Report of the N/C Sebungwe for the year 1915.
31.  NGB 2/3/1, N/C Sebungwe to CNC Matabeleland, 8 September 1906.
32.  *Report of the Department of Agriculture for the Year Ended 31st March, 1906* (Salisbury, 1906), 8.
33.  L 2/1/114, general correspondence in Lands Department file on the Company.
34.  NB 6/4/9, Report of the CNC Matabeleland for the month September 1908. There was some rationality in this approach from the point of view of labour supplies.
35.  L 2/1/114, Memo on the Inyoka Rhodesia Tobacco Co. Ltd by Assistant Secretary, BSA Company London, 23 November 1907.
36.  L 2/1/114, Confidential Report on the Inyoka Tobacco Estate by G.M. Odlum, 4 July 1908.
37.  NB 6/4/12, Report of the N/C Sebungwe for the month January 1912.
38.  NGB 2/3/1, W.M. Wood, Figtree, to N/C Bulawayo, 25 March 1913.
39.  NGB 2/3/1, Acting N/C Sebungwe to J.W. Dunlop, Salisbury, 6 January 1916.
40.  N 9/1/19, Report of the N/C Sebungwe for the year 1916.
41.  N 9/1/21, Report of the N/C Sebungwe for the year 1918.
42.  N 9/1/22, Report of the N/C Sebungwe for the year 1919.
43.  N 9/1/26, Report of the N/C Sebungwe for the year 1923.
44.  S 235/502, Report of the N/C Sebungwe for the year 1924.
45.  S 235/509, Report of the N/C Sebungwe for the year 1931.
46.  NGB 2/6/1, Tsetse fly, Sebungwe District. This file gives detailed reports of the spread of this scourge over more than twenty years.
47.  S 235/505, Report of the N/C Sebungwe for the year 1927.
48.  L 2/1/114, Confidential Report on the Inyoka Tobacco Estate by G.M. Odlum, 4 July 1908.
49.  S 235/522, Report of the N/C Sebungwe for the month June 1928.
50.  S 235/516, Report of the N/C Sebungwe for the year 1938.
51.  S 235/509, Report of the N/C Sebungwe for the year 1931.
52.  S 235/510, Report of the N/C Sebungwe for the year 1932.
53.  S 235/510, Report of the N/C Sebungwe for the year 1932. The growing trend towards racial discrimination in the marketing of crops would have cut off the markets even if the Shangwe had survived the Depression successfully. Section 3(b) of the Tobacco Marketing Act of 1936, which established a quota system, threatened African tobacco-growers, who could at any time be brought under the system and forced to sell on auction floors.
54.  S 235/527, Report of the N/C Sebungwe for the month November 1934.
55.  S 235/512, Report of the N/C Sebungwe for the year 1934.
56.  Personal communication from T. Spengler, a smallworker in Matabeleland during the period. He corroborated the change in African tastes and habits among his labour force.
57.  S 235/512, Report of the N/C Sebungwe for the year 1934.
58.  S 235/512, Report of the N/C Sebungwe for the year 1934.
59.  S 235/513, Report of the N/C Sebungwe for the year 1935.
60.  S 235/512, Report of the N/C Sebungwe for the year 1934.
61.  S 235/515, Report of the N/C Sebungwe for the year 1936.
62.  Weinmann, *Agricultural Research,* 44. The attempt to grow two crops a year would aggravate the pest problem.
63.  M.L. Chanock, 'The Political Economy of Independent Agriculture in Colonial Malawi: The Great War to the Great Depression', *Journal of Social Science, 1,* 1972, 120.
64.  NGB 2/6/1, Acting N/C Sebungwe to CNC Matabeleland, 23 March 1915.
65.  Personal communication from the Rev. R. Peaden, formerly a missionary in Gokwe district. The author has approached the present district commissioner, but he had no records or knowledge of the tobacco industry.
66.  About £32,000 wàs paid in pre-1914 sterling and a further £42,500 in pre-1931

devaluation sterling.
67.   The clinic was discontinued in 1931 'through lack of funds'. S 1542/D5, N/C
Sebungwe to S/N Bulawayo, 23 February 1934.
68.   S 235/513, Report of the N/C Sebungwe for the year 1935.
69.   Steele, 'Foundations of a "Native" Policy', 379.

# PART III

---

*Development and Underdevelopment in Central Africa*

---

In the third and final part of this book we move northwards into Central Africa, tracing the varying paths to underdevelopment in Zaïre, Zambia, and Malawi. Though Central Africa is much less of a coherent economic region than Southern Africa, many of the same themes recur, with colonial governments—and indeed their post-colonial successors—tending to favour estate rather then peasant agriculture where possible. Thus peasant producers, as in the south, found themselves confronted with land alienation and compulsory cultivation of crops, with price-fixing and violent price fluctuations stemming from metropolitan conditions, with declining terms of trade, and with the rewards of cash-cropping deliberately pegged below those of wage-labour, while in turn diminishing peasant returns allowed industrial wages to be kept low until the Second World War.

In the first of two essays on southern Zaïre, Jean-Luc Vellut focuses in Chapter 12 on the changing connotations of 'rural poverty' in western Shaba (Katanga) from the period of dominance by Lunda and Luba aristocracies, through the extension of the Angolan trading network and the 'red rubber' collection of the Congo Free State, into the 1930s, by which time the area had become a 'frozen' rural periphery, compelled to yield up its productive resources to the core towns of the Katanga copperbelt. Vellut's essay is complemented by Chapter 13, in which Bogumil Jewsiewicki discusses the various contortions of colonial policy-making with regard to food production for Upper Industrial Katanga. He concentrates particularly on the impact of the Depression, which allowed the state effectively to dictate to peasants for the first time, and to place peasant agriculture—and compulsory cultivation and low food prices—at the disposal of capitalist industry in Zaïre and in Belgium. The 'unequal development' of southern Zaïre was matched by what Maud Muntemba, in Chapter 14, terms the 'thwarted development' of central Zambia—the Kabwe Rural district. Despite comparatively favoured access to growing urban markets, 'development' in the area was uneven, with peasant agriculture being generally subordinated to the paramount interests of the mining industry and of settler estate agriculture, which took the best land, and the best market terms and communications.

In Chapter 15, Leroy Vail directs our attention away from the local African level to the machinations of railway promoters in Europe, arguing with some force that Malawi (Nyasaland) became an 'imperial

292

slum' precisely because it had become a colony of the railways. He touches on the question of Malawi exporting her people to the mines and farms of the south, as does Martin Chanock in Chapter 16. Chanock deliberately sets out to provoke and stimulate future agricultural historians, and, like Fola Soremekun in Chapter 3, discusses the links between modern underdevelopment and the nineteenth-century trade in ivory and slaves.

## The contributors

Jean-Luc Vellut was born in Belguim, took his first degree at the Université Catholique de Louvain and his 1968 doctorate on Pacific history at the Australian National University. From 1964 to 1971 he lectured at the former Université Lovanium de Kinshasa, and since 1971 has held joint posts at the Université Nationale du Zaïre, Lubumbashi, and at the Université Catholique de Louvain. He is editor of the journal *Etudes d'Histoire africaine,* and has published widely (in French) on the pre-colonial and colonial history of Zaïre, especially the Shaba region.

Bogumil Jewsiewicki was born in Poland, where he took his first degree and his 1968 doctorate on Polish rural history at the University of Lodz. From 1968 to 1969 he lectured at the Institut Pédagogique Supérieur de Mbandaka, Zaïre, from 1969 to 1971 at the former Université Lovanium de Kinshasa, and since 1971 he has held a post at the Université Nationale du Zaïre, Lubumbashi. He has written widely (in French and in Polish) on the colonial socio-economic history of southern Zaïre.

Maud Muntemba was born and grew up in Zambia, and took her first degree at the University of Nottingham. From 1967 to 1973 she was Keeper of History at the National Museum in Livingstone, and wrote a 1973 MA for the University of Zambia on the evolution of political systems in south central Zambia. She is currently a doctoral candidate at the University of California at Los Angeles. As in the case of Sherilynn Young, it should be noted that her paper was largely written before she commenced fieldwork in central Zambia towards the end of 1974.

Leroy Vail was born in America, took his first degree at Boston College and his 1972 doctorate on Tumbuka linguistics at the University of Wisconsin. From 1967 to 1971 he lectured at the University of Malawi, and since 1973 has held a lectureship at the University of Zambia. He has conducted extensive field and archival research into the pre-colonial history of northern Malawi and eastern Zambia, and more recently has been working on underdevelopment in Malawi and Mozambique. He has published a number of articles on these topics and on Bantu linguistics.

Martin Chanock was born and grew up in South Africa. He took first degrees in law and in history at the University of Witwatersrand, and wrote a 1968 doctorate at the University of Cambridge on British and South African policies in Central Africa, shortly to be published as *Unconsummated Union*. From 1969 to 1973 he lectured at the University of Malawi, and from 1973 to 1974 at Ahmadu Bello University, Nigeria. Currently he holds a post at the University of Texas at Austin. He has written a number of papers on the peasantry in colonial Malawi, and together with Leroy Vail and Robin Palmer contributed to B. Pachai's *The Early History of Malawi* (London, 1972).

Ann Seidman (the author of the Postscript) was born in America, took her first degree at Smith College and Columbia University and her doctorate at the University of Wisconsin. She has taught in Africa for over ten years at the Universities of Ghana, Dar es Salaam, and Zambia (1972−4). Currently she is director of a project at Wellesley College on women's unemployment, and lectures on international relations and social change at Clark University. She is a distinguished economist, whose books include (with R.H. Green) *Unity or Poverty?: the Economics of Pan-Africanism* (Harmondsworth, 1968); *An Economics Textbook for Africa* (London, 1969); *Comparative Development Strategies in East Africa* (Nairobi, 1972); and *Planning for Development in Sub-Saharan Africa* (New York and Dar es Salaam, 1974).

# CHAPTER 12

## Rural Poverty in Western Shaba, c.1890–1930

### JEAN-LUC VELLUT

## Introduction

This chapter discusses some historical dimensions of rural poverty in south-western Zaïre. Using the modern term Shaba rather than 'Katanga', western Shaba may be defined as an area circumscribed in the west by the upper Kasaï and in the east by the upper Lualaba. The Zaïre–Zambezi watershed marks the southern limits of our region. Western Shaba as defined here is limited in the north by an area (approximately 8°30′S) where the South Central African or Zambezian ecosystem meets and gradually merges into Guinean grasslands. Most parts of our region are covered with *miombo* woodland, often on sandy soils. There are, however, wide stretches of mostly Zambezian grassland, with strips of dense thicket alongside streams. These streams run from south to north, being tributaries of the Kasaï river system, or of the Lualaba farther east. Marshes and open *dambos* form a discontinuous belt in the upper reaches of these two river systems.[1]

What is the connotation carried by 'rural poverty' in the history of this region? 'Rural' in its commonest acceptance indicates the existence of territory of different characteristics to some parallel urban area. We will use 'rural' in a wider meaning, connoting the relationship which links a core-area with its periphery within a particular historical context, or 'historical bloc'.[2] The modern rural–urban dichotomy is thus paralleled by other oppositions, depending on the historical context. Central African history in the eighteenth and nineteenth centuries shows that such oppositions existed between the courts of military aristocracies and their peripheries, or between the centres of trade which, in the course of the nineteenth century, developed a social and economic hegemony over their hinterland.

'Poverty' implies living conditions very close to bare subsistence. This sort of poverty has been rampant in our region. With the exception of some well-watered areas, where population was denser, human occupation seems to have been thin on the ground. Western Shaba was a region where two systems of extensive or 'shifting' agriculture met. Both, however, tackled the poor sandy soils with the tools of a simple technology. In large areas cultivation was not in fact really well established, at least not in the eyes of travellers of the latter part of the nineteenth century.[3] At that time, the population was subsisting on a diet of cereals along the watershed and in the Sanga (southern Luba) region, and a diet of cassava, cereals and groundnuts among the Lunda.[4] All indications are that surplus was not produced on any significant scale outside some settled areas, which were few and far between.

More generally, however, poverty is defined 'according to the conventions of the society in which it occurs'.[5] This poverty is not only economic but social. It was very much in evidence in the Lunda states of the nineteenth century. Pogge, who spent some months in 1875–6 at the Lunda capital, the *mussumba*, set up by each successive Mwant Yav (king), noted the discrimination in clothing, housing, eating habits, etc., which separated the rich from the poor. The poor 'class' was then largely composed of slaves and women; they were the 'hewers of wood and drawers of water'.

Such social distinctions were to lead to speculations by European observers on the conquering ('oriental' or 'hamitic') despotism of the state society which overlaid basically agricultural communities. Baumann deluded himself that he was actually perceiving physiological and religious differences between the Lunda *staatsvolk* and their subjects.[6] While these theories are discredited today, it remains true that state-building in the area met with opposition from within and from without. Internally, the state did not overcome all traces of rural autonomy in its peripheries, as was shown by persistent regionalism and by lack of correlation between landownership and political power. From without, the state was to be confronted by new economic and social formations. New dominant core-areas were to give fresh meanings to 'rural poverty' in western Shaba.

# I   A periphery of world commercial capitalism, c.1800–1920

Two phases should be distinguished in western Shaba's becoming a periphery of the world economy. In the first stage, western Shaba was introduced into the Angolan-based trading network. Absorbing previous political and cultural areas, the Luso–African frontier progressively integrated the western and south-western part of present Zaïre into one economic region.[7] This first phase extends in time from the latter part of the eighteenth century till the beginning of the twentieth century. By the end of the nineteenth century, so far as Shaba is concerned, the frontier extended from the ports of trade on the Atlantic seaboard to the Lufira–Lualaba Basin. In the second stage, a trading network based on Belgian and other trading stations gradually superseded the old Angolan frontier zone till it was itself supplanted in the early 1920s by further social and economic developments, linked this time with the mines of industrial capitalism.

We will examine in turn these two stages of western Shaba's

insertion into the periphery of world commercial capitalism, with a
view to analysing the changing meanings assumed by 'rural poverty'
in such a context.

## The Angolan trading frontier

Lwena traders may have been among the first to 'open' the
Zaïre–Zambezi watershed to trade financed by Atlantic commercial
capital. Beginning with the late eighteenth century, written documents describe the trade in this area as well as in the southern Luba,
Kaonde, Ndembu, and other regions farther off. Various stages can
be distinguished in the gradual expansion of the Angolan trading
frontier. Depending on the type of goods traded, one may see several
trading cycles—slaves through most of the period; ivory and wax; a
twenty-year rubber cycle; and later a lasting foodstuff cycle. One may
also distinguish geographical stages by plotting the locations of
trading stations, which moved by degree from the Benguela Highlands to upper Kasaï and upper Zambezi, or the routes of the main
trading caravans. Several overlapping trade networks functioned, in
some cases bulwarked by migrations of people—for example the
Chokwe, Ndembu, and Lwena. The high mark of Angolan trade was
reached with the rubber boom of the late nineteenth and early
twentieth centuries. By that time, the Atlantic coast was linked with
the Zaïre–Zambezi watershed even by ox-drawn wagons of the
South African type. Ovimbundu roads, enabling travellers to walk
twelve abreast, are shown on early twentieth-century maps of
southern Zaïre.[8]

Apart from the slave-worked plantations in the hinterland of
Benguela and the network of trading posts, the Angolan trading zone
invested in no other fixed property. Its social and economic effects
were, however, far-reaching. It widened the 'customary' sector of the
local African economy at the expense of its 'command' branch.[9] A
new society began to emerge which tended to hinge on trading posts
rather than on old military courts. Trade and personal initiative
tended to supplant tribute and aristocratic authority. More so perhaps
than in the old kingdoms, war and violence seem to have pervaded
this mercantile period: the trader often walked hand in hand with the
warrior. Armed bands were the main initial suppliers of slaves. Some
of these bands were placed at the service of traders by chiefs; some
newcomers, such as Msiri, took advantage of the troubled times to
launch the basis of new states. Some bands were recruited outside
any form of government and constituted troops of private mercenaries. Among the more famous of the latter, we should mention
the remnants of the so-called 'Tetela' mutineers of 1895 and 1898,
These former soldiers of the Force Publique of the Congo Free State,
regularly reinforced by new recruits, roamed the area west of the
Lualaba till their final defeat at the hands of colonial troops in 1908.
The links of these 'rebels' (variously called *Valessi, Tambeshi,* etc.)
with Bié traders from Angola were vital. For twelve years, the latter

supplied the breech-loading rifles (of Martini-Henry pattern) which, together with European-type strategy, enabled the 'Tetela' to repel successfully several European-led colonial columns.

It was also to be violence which blazed the trail of the new Congo Free State colonial trading frontier.

## Early colonial trading frontiers

The early Congo Free State (EIC = Etat Indépendant du Congo) colonial occupation of southern Zaïre hardly encroached upon the greater part of western Shaba. The first colonial stations and lines of communication were in fact established on the eastern and southern rim of today's Shaba Province, known to the Belgians as Katanga.

Belgian penetration into Katanga followed at first a south-easterly direction from Lusambo on the Sankuru. Occupation of Katanga for ten years after 1892 was limited to a few isolated strongholds east of the Lufira and along the Tanganyika–Mweru–Luapula border. From 1897, that part of colonial Katanga was attached to the 'Zone du Tanganika': communications were then organized through the agency of the African Lakes Company of Nyasaland. It is interesting to note that the EIC station of Lofoi communicated with its headquarters at Boma on the mouth of the Zaïre river through Bié traders.[10] To the south, on the plateau, Robert Williams's mineral prospectors, and later those of Tanganyika Concessions Limited (TCL), took advantage of southern lines of access through the Rhodesias. From 1902, they began operating west of the Lualaba.

On the whole, therefore, EIC colonial operations left the Luba–Hemba heartland, as well as the area west of the Lufira and north of the mining district, largely alone until the 1910s. Western Shaba still wholly belonged during those years to the Angolan economic sphere. From North-Eastern Rhodesia (now the eastern half of Zambia), some adventurous traders, such as Rabinek, tried to penetrate the area from the east, but they were few and far between. The region was, however, the scene of fierce fighting between colonial and 'native' armed bands. Shaba proved no exception to the thread of violence running through the early colonial history of Zaïre. At stake was the creation from scratch of an economic sphere to be carved out of the existing trading frontier zones—Swahili and Arab north and east of the Zaïre Basin, and Angolan on its western reaches.

The first clashes between EIC colonial troops and Angolan traders are recorded in the early 1890s near Lake Kisale on the Lualaba and in Kasaï. The following years saw a succession of raids and counter-raids which, though adding up to a war of attrition, passed with less notice into colonial annals than the shorter and more spectacular 'Arab' wars.

On the upper Kasaï and upper Zambezi confines, the Angolan trading frontier came under three-pronged British, Portuguese, and Belgian assault. To limit ourselves to the Congo Free State side, the Belgians had, since 1896, found allies among some factions at the

Lunda court, which was being threatened by Chokwe expansion. In the following years, the Belgians sent deep forays into this remote part of the territory claimed by the EIC. Their armed columns usually operated from two main bases. One Belgian thrust was directed south-south-west from Lusambo: it resulted in the construction of a colonial fortress at Dilolo in 1903. Other columns operated after 1901 in a south-westerly direction from the Lualaba lakes region. These columns hunted down Angolan traders and their allies (euphemistically referred to as 'mutineers', 'rebel chiefs', etc.) to the west and south of the Lunda heartland.

The years 1890–1910 were therefore years of ruthless warfare. Tactics were similar on both sides: building earthworks, striking terror in surrounding areas (there were 'cannibal soldiers' among both the Force Publique and the 'Tetela' mutineers), raiding stockaded villages, pillaging fields and cattle, and attempting to administer the country through trusted *nyamparas* or *sentinelles*. In western Shaba, the case of the twin Portuguese and Belgian forts of Dilolo is particularly well documented. On each side of the border, the forts served as rallying points for fugitives, deserters, armed bands, etc., who lived off the land.[11] On the Congo side, local government practice was overhauled in 1912 when this area was removed from Kasaï district and came under Katanga provincial administration. 'J'instaure une politique d'apaisement', wrote district commissioner Gosme in 1912. Administrative occupation became more systematic, and by 1920 warlike operations had become exceptional. North of Lunda country, however, the Force Publique did not penetrate the Kete country until 1925, while on the other side of the border the Portuguese only completed their occupation of the Lunda district in 1925–6. In Luba country, the last stockaded villages disappeared in 1921–2.[12]

The expansion of administration in the EIC often went hand in hand with the expansion of trading. By virtue of the 1891 regulations which had introduced taxes in labour and in kind, and of the 30 October 1892 decree which reserved large concession areas for the collection of rubber and ivory to the Free State, the economic exploitation of the Lualaba basin was in practice left to a state monopoly. In the 1890s, raiding for ivory was carried out on a large scale by the EIC *boma* at Lofoi, particularly under Capitaine Brasseur. He adopted the *nyampara* system left over by Msiri, the former ruler of the area. Yeke *nyamparas* were put in charge of villages, and were held responsible for forwarding food and ivory to the colonial *boma*.[13]

The Congo Free State itself was, however, only one part of the total colonial system. In 1900, a chartered company called the Comité Spécial du Katanga (CSK) was established and given full responsibility over Katanga east of 23°54'E. The CSK inherited the Free State's thin network of *bomas* and it soon engaged in rubber-trading. The area west of CSK territory fell in 1901 under another concessionary company, the Compagnie du Kasaï (CK). The CK held the rubber and ivory trading concession in most of the western Congo. Its first *bomas* appeared in western Shaba from 1905. This was the remotest *secteur* of its concession, deep in the Angolan trading sphere.

Both the CK and the CSK were closely associated with the Free State, and indeed were partly owned by it. The CSK could collect tax in kind from 1903, and in practice the CK held similar privileges in its concession.[14] Trading privileges in Katanga were withdrawn in 1910, but old practices were slow to disappear from the remote upper Kasaï region.

## Trading frontiers: economic changes

Behind its facade of violence, the growth of the trading economy entailed deep economic and social changes. Angolan trading was mostly concerned with a collecting economy. Rubber, ivory, wax, and, in sinister ways, slaves, were all collected. But agriculture was also affected. The traders purchased food (root crops, dried fish, etc.), or planted their own crops. Luvale people practised the damming of rivers and developed a prosperous trade in fish with passing caravans. In upper Kasaï, around the main refreshment stops where the caravans rested after crossing the 'hunger country' of Moxico, there were large plantations by 1900.[15] Bié traders used to establish their own fields around the temporary villages, *otjivango,* where they settled for up to eighteen months when trading in the Luba country. Lwena traders also obtained permission from Luba or Lunda chiefs to plant and harvest while they were busy collecting rubber. Such practices certainly hastened the introduction of new crop varieties and stimulated agricultural change.

Early colonial trading further quickened the pace of the growing market economy. It brought in large quantities of trading goods and rapidly opened up exports of rubber and ivory.[16] So traditionally collected products, which had previously been traded with Angola, still constituted the staples of western Shaba trade with the new colonial centres of the EIC. These commodities included ivory, rubber, and 'redeemed slaves'. Colonial trading at this stage can thus be analysed in terms of the general context of much older trading frontiers in the area. Similarities in aims and tactics should not, however, be allowed to obscure some important differences.

In the late nineteenth and early twentieth centuries, new forms of European capitalist enterprise intervened to deprive African producers of direct access to their market. This was particularly true whenever large concessionary companies were allowed to monopolize trading. CK practice may serve as a case in point, although we are unable to isolate its activities within western Shaba alone. Instead of paying the market price to the producer of rubber, the Company actually paid what came to be regarded as a rural wage. Throughout the boom years from 1903 to 1911 it bought rubber at an average price of only 2·4 francs per kilo, but 1.4 francs of this was withheld from the producers by African *capitas,* European trading station managers, etc. Despite this, the profits declared by the Company on the rubber it exported at Antwerp averaged 80 per cent of the cost price.[17]

On the whole, however, Belgian efforts to monopolize rubber-trading in western Shaba were largely unsuccessful. 'Contraband' trading with Angola or the Rhodesias continued to operate, far from the grasp of any effective Belgian control. After the abolition of trading privileges in Shaba in 1910, the CK continued to purchase rubber, but a parallel trade developed with Elisabethville (Lubum-bashi) mainly in the hands of Portuguese trading station managers, who in 1911 had moved from Kayanda (their stronghold in Angola, next to the border) and had settled at Sokele in upper Lubudi.[18]

For all practical purposes, the trade in men continued under early colonialism. It was now designed to supply the emerging labour markets in the mining areas, and around the first European settlements, missions, etc. The techniques had hardly changed from the slaving days. There is abundant information on the raids on unarmed villages carried out by the new traders in men, *soko muntu,* before the First World War.[19] The excesses of this early recruiting were later harped upon by the representatives of large enterprises when they tried to rationalize an orderly labour market out of the rough and ready practices typical of the 'wild capitalism' era.

Agricultural produce also entered the early colonial market economy. In some cases trading in foodstuffs was actually an expansion of former regional bartering. For example the trade in palm oil, which by 1905 had made the fortune of Chief Lumpungu, had linked for many years the oil-consuming and fish-producing areas of the Lualaba with the complementary economies of the Luba–Songe country farther north. But alongside such already established traffic, the new colonial poles of economic growth provided new outlets for surplus production of foodstuffs. In the immediate neighbourhood of European settlements, administrative and military coercion played some part in bringing agricultural produce to the market, but at least by the 1910s small-scale private entrepreneurs were playing a more important role. African and European petty traders, recruiters, sub-contractors, etc., roamed villages to purchase foodstuffs and to entice men to seek employment with Europeans.

Within Katanga, all regions were not drawn into the colonial market economy at the same pace or to the same degree. For example, the Katanga 'pedicle' (jutting into Northern Rhodesia) and the Luapula–Mweru region were within easier reach of the growing mining and industrial sites of Katanga, and they were quick in bringing cereals, fish, etc. to the market.[20] The early 1910s were thus decisive for the introduction of cash into the rural economy. Western Shaba for its part was more remote and more deeply ensconced in the Angolan sphere, but its eastern confines were drawn into the influence of the western group of mines—Busanga and Ruwe—which required foodstuffs. Recruiting raids for labour are recorded at Kinda among the Ndembu in 1913, and at Dilolo in 1917, but they seem to have been the exception so far west of the mining districts.

Despite the unequal pace at which the extension of the market was taking place, there are a few landmarks in time which affected *all* rural areas of southern Zaïre under early colonial rule. First, mention should be made of the fluctuating rates for commodities on the world market. This holds true in particular for rubber, the main trading asset of western Shaba and central Angola. Selling rates for rubber at Antwerp[21] fluctuated as follows (1886 = 100):

    1890: 102 (+2)        1895: 113 (+11)       1900: 171 (+58)
    1905: 205 (+34)       1910: 341 (+136)      1913: 76 (−265).

Rates for ivory and wax were temporarily more stable. After the rubber boom had subsided, ivory, wax, and the growing market for foodstuffs were the only substitutes for the rubber base in western Shaba and central Angola. In both regions, food requirements grew with the construction of railway lines and towns as well as with the sudden demand generated by the First World War.

A major landmark in the social and economic history of southern Zaïre was the introduction of poll tax in 1911; a measure which gave further impetus to the introduction of the cash economy in rural Shaba. But it was only in 1913 that the poll tax was introduced west of the Lufupa. This followed an administrative measure which marked a turning point for western Shaba. In 1912, a large area west of the Lufupa (a right bank tributary of the Lualaba) up to the Angolan border was carved out of Kasaï district and incorporated as the District de la Lulua into the Vice-Gouvernement général du Katanga. Instructions to the officer in charge of occupying the new district read that he should suppress slave-trading and arms-running, block all illegitimate trade, and open the district to recruiting of manpower for Industrial Upper Katanga, Haut-Katanga Industriel (HKI). This incorporation within Katanga meant that, in the view of the colonial authorities, the Lulua would become a 'granary' of manpower for the mines and industries of the Congolese copperbelt. As will be seen, it soon became apparent however that there were conflicting colonial strategies for the development (or underdevelopment) of Lulua.

## Trading frontiers and rural poverty

The military empires of the eighteenth and nineteenth centuries had seemed to herald the advent of a society where a warrior ruling 'class' would eventually confront a collectively poor peasantry. Trading frontiers called a final stop to this prospect. Social change is indeed the hallmark of the expanding Angolan frontier. Long adventurous journeys, new settlements, commerce with the trading stations, etc., held out the chance of acquiring riches while bypassing the claims to monopoly of the old aristocracies. Political authorities could only maintain their credibility insofar as they kept abreast of the changes made by commercialization in the collecting and agricultural economies. A telling illustration of changing social values is given by comparing the motto of the alleged founder of the Mwine Samba dynasty, east of the upper Lubilash: 'My country belongs to the carrier of the bow, the spear, and the shield', implying scorn for agriculture, with the praise-name of the later nineteenth-century chief of Samba who had become a 'good friend' of Lwena traders, a name which connoted foreign wealth: 'He who warms himself with gunpowder'.[22]

Rural poverty in this period must realistically be defined in terms of the accrued violence as well as commercialization of men and goods which accompanied the trading frontiers.

We have already mentioned the raids and punitive expeditions which befell cultivators. Women paid a heavy price for these as they were enslaved in large numbers, by the Chokwe in particular, for their child-bearing potential but also for collecting or preparing rubber. Chokwe rubber-traders were able to raise a mortgage on their slaves from colonial trading managers.[23] Freer access to prestige goods entailed the devaluation of dowry, increasingly regarded as the purchasing price for a woman. This in turn degraded women to the level of mere chattels, a process further hastened with the introduction of cash values.

The degradation of the status of the women must, however, be qualified. In some areas, where they kept control over their harvests, women were among the first to commercialize agricultural production.[24] Indeed, trading by women could also offer some relief from poverty and oppression. It enabled individuals of low status to flee oppressive chiefs or elders. A case may be made that trading societies such as the western Lwena, Chokwe, Ndembu, etc. challenged the old order as more egalitarian versions of traditional social life. The old order was, however, rescued in part by the colonial rulers when they set out to give an 'African' image to imposed institutions of their own making.

Rural poverty in the early twentieth century was still shaped by the ecological and economic constraints which had long burdened agriculture in the area. The conservative character of agricultural techniques led, on several occasions, to regional shortages of food whenever pressure was exerted on rural communities to dispose of their surplus reserves.[25] Rural conditions further suffered from the violence which prevailed throughout a large part of the period and which may have inflicted lasting ecological damage in the destruction of natural resources, importation of cattle epidemics, neglect of land which had formerly been cultivated, etc. In the short term at least, colonial conditions imposed upon African cultivators may have led to an overall impoverishment. It is significant that Europeans quickly expropriated African capital assets such as salt works, cattle, and of course the copper mines in southern Katanga.

Social and economic exploitation and limited productive capacity were the two main keys to African rural poverty, and were still very much to the fore in western Shaba during the more mature period of colonial rule which opened in the 1920s.

## II Towards the hegemony of industrial capitalism, 1920–30

The economic history of western Shaba in the 1920s is one of stagnation and impoverishment, in line with an overall colonial strategy which aimed at encouraging migration to the mining industrial sites of HKI. It is against this background that colonial state-building took place in the area. In this process, conflicting strategies emerged concerning the colonial development of western Shaba. After examining these points in turn, we will try to define the main components of rural poverty in this new phase of colonial history.

### Western Shaba: an outline of economic history in the 1920s[26]

Several factors combined in this period to render a deadly blow to the African trading economy of western Shaba. The decline of trading in products of the old collecting economy should be analysed in terms of conditions in world markets as well as of measures taken by colonial authorities with a view to encouraging recruitment for the mining industry.

The deterioration in terms of trade is well documented for the Belgian Congo as a whole.[27] It was a long-term tendency (1914–44), marked by two short periods of rapid deterioration, 1920–2 and 1930–3. In the early 1920s, the slump in world markets hit agricultural products harder than mineral goods. Rubber particularly suffered. Up to 1920 for all practical purposes it had been the only source of cash income for the Lunda region, but the price paid to the producer by the CK factory at Ngoie had dwindled to 0.95 francs per kilo in 1921, a heavy reduction on *real* prices paid in the heyday of the Angolan trade. The Compagnie could only find rubber at this price by resorting to the old practice of terror or compulsion, with the occasional help of the Mwant Yav (Lunda king) and sometimes the connivance of the *Administrateur*.[28]

Other products traditionally traded in the area, such as wax— collected by the Chokwe and Lwena, but not by the Lunda—never replaced rubber in importance. Here again, in any case, the producer received less: wax fetched 2 francs per kilo in 1916, and 1 franc in 1923. When account is taken of money depreciation, this represents a deterioration of 81 per cent in real terms.

Throughout the area, in Angola as well as in the Congo, the African trading economy also suffered from political measures. The Belgian government decision to align the Congolese franc with the Belgian franc and thus depreciate its value by 20 per cent in 1919 compounded the deterioration in terms of trade for products of the collecting economy. In the following years, the Congolese franc, henceforth linked with the Belgian currency, further slipped from 44 to 174 against the pound sterling in 1920–6, a 73 per cent loss in value.[29]

In fact, the 1920–2 crisis hit African producers doubly as their products tended to suffer most from the slump, and as they had to pay more for foreign goods: a deterioration in terms of trade which was particularly felt for imports paid in sterling. This held especially true for Katanga.[30] The early 1920s may thus be seen as a period of forced accumulation, largely to the benefit of Katanga's mining industry. In Lulua by 1921, the deterioration of living standards was striking. In the words of the district commissioner, 'les indigènes ne peuvent plus se payer le luxe d'une étoffe; ils vont vêtus de peaux de bêtes'.[31]

Other political measures tended to freeze trade, in particular the regulations forbidding the extension of credit to Africans, as well as a decree which, from 1925, imposed multiple restrictions on the granting of trading licences to Africans.[32]

These restrictions certainly drove many African producers back from gaining direct access to market prices. But the restrictions did not prevent the commercialization of cassava, groundnuts, etc., from gradually becoming one of the main resources of the area. Some of this trade was of ancient origin, such as the trade in dried fish (from the upper Lulua), in palm oil (brought by the Kete to the *mussumba*), and in cattle and smaller livestock from the Dilolo region. In the 1920s, however, food trading in the Lulua took on a new character. Above all, in the absence of any commercial alternative, it represented the best available insurance against deteriorating living conditions. On a Congo-wide, long-term basis, real income from food trading fell more slowly than from other cash crops, or from the rural and industrial wage sectors.[33] (For full details, see the next chapter by Bogumil Jewsiewicki.)

It is thus not surprising that food trading should have developed with the new colonial centres. By 1931, for example, the Kanda-Kanda area in north-western Katanga benefited from remitted wages and savings from HKI to the amount of an estimated 2 million francs, but its revenue from food trading was estimated at 30 million.[34] In western Shaba, it was noted in 1924 that 'on native markets' prices were fixed on the basis of imported indigo drill fabric.[35] One is nevertheless struck by the small scale of the nascent cash sector in Lulua. A few examples will suffice. The Lunda of western Shaba took food to the Angolan mining district where they purchased cloth to be sold on the return journey to the Congo. But imports of cloth from Angola were estimated at only 7,000 francs (£69) for the first half of 1925. In western Shaba the main consumer markets for foodstuffs were the small townships and government and mission stations, but their population was small. Sandoa, the district headquarters, was 'a village' in the early 1920s with a population of retired military and Lwena porters settled next to a few trading posts.[36] In the Kapanga market established by the administration, 1 tonne of flour was sold per month in 1920. Food for the western mines (Busanga, Musonoie) was purchased in larger quantities at Kayoyo by traders of European or 'Rhodesia–Nyasaland' origin (2 to 4 tonnes per week in 1922). In 1924 there were eleven registered African traders in the Kinda area, many of 'Rhodesian' origin.[37]

For the same period, we have gross estimates which all tend to show that the introduction of a cash economy in the Lulua District was very slow. An estimate of 1902 put regional food trading at 300 tonnes of flour, 60 tonnes of groundnuts, and 21 tonnes of dried fish. In 1924, the district commissioner estimated the revenue which accrued to African producers of hides and wax at 125,000 francs (£1,300)—14 per cent of the price these products fetched on the Antwerp market.[38] Foodstuffs were sold that year for 270,620 francs (£2,815). In 1923 Kayoyo and Kinda had supplied foodstuffs to the western mines to the value of an estimated 358,700 francs (£4,053).

The years 1926–8 may have represented a turning point for the monetization of Katanga as a whole, as indicated by the growth of revenue from the poll tax:

$$(1915 = 100)$$

|  | Standard francs | Gold francs |
|---|---|---|
| 1926 | 538 (+438) | 87 (−13) |
| 1927 | 712 (+174) | 103 (+16) |
| 1928 | 980 (+268) | 142 (+39) |
| 1929 | 1566 (+586) | 226 (+84) |

Source: Computed from information found in the Rapport aux Chambres

In 1924–8, the construction of the Chemin du fer de Bas-Congo au Katanga (BCK) railway line from Bukama to Kasaï provided fresh outlets for food-trading in western Shaba: many Lunda from the Kapanga area went to the line of rail in order to sell their produce. The construction of the Tenke–Dilolo link with the Benguela Railway (1928–31) gave a new and lasting impetus to food-trading in the district. By 1932, however, the Lulua district contributed only 4.29 per cent of the food requirements of HKI.[39]

Lack of communication links with this remote district certainly played a part in this slow start. In fact, the Lulua district remained largely a backwater. By 1928, it represented 16.6 per cent of registered population in Katanga, but contributed only 8.7 per cent of the provincial poll tax revenue. Apart from food production for the market, there were no agricultural opportunities open for western Shaba. African cattle herds were practically wiped out in the early 1920s by administrative measures which aimed at concentrating cattle-raising into European hands. A proposal by Texaf (Société Textile Africaine) to introduce cotton-growing in Lulua was rejected by the administration in order to keep the region open to labour recruiting.[40]

With the imposition of the poll tax, the major alternatives to food-trading were either local employment or migration to HKI. Local employment remained minimal under the no-development conditions experienced by Lulua: in 1927 there were only 931 locally employed wage-earners. On the other hand, the backward economy of the area meant that many people became porters: in 1922 2,000 porters were permanently employed on the main arterial road of the district (Bukama – Kafakumba – Sandoa – Kapanga). Four years later, it was estimated that 4,000 porters were continuously at work in the district. The lack of worthwhile local opportunities explains the large-scale migration to industrial centres in the 1920s.

During that period, the Katanga Labour Bureau, Bourse du Travail du Katanga (BTK)[41] sent 12,442 men from the Lulua for temporary employment in HKI. This represented about 17 per cent of the labour force it recruited in the Province of Katanga as a whole, a figure consistent with Lulua district's proportion of the total population of the province. The BTK was however unable to impose its monopoly, despite the support it received from the administration. Smaller, independent labour recruiters were also at work, and it was not uncommon for Lunda to avoid HKI and seek employment in Angola or in Kasaï. In 1927, a general survey revealed that 75.6 per cent of Lulua district wage-earners were employed at a great distance from their homes: this contrasts with figures obtaining in other districts of Katanga where local employment was often far more easily obtainable.[42] This survey showed that the no-development policy pursued in Lulua had imprinted a particularly backward character on the economy of the region, and that it had effectively served the interests of the mining industry, more than was indicated by BTK returns. It should be noted, however, that recruitment seems to have affected various regions of the District de la Lulua unevenly. By 1924, two-thirds of BTK recruits in the district were Chokwe, with Lunda accounting for 15 per cent: 'nos efforts doivent surtout porter à entraîner la population Kaluunda au travail', wrote the district commissioner. On occasion, the administration sought to prevent Lunda from seeking employment in Angola.[43]

Within the colonial hierarchy there was, however, no general agreement on the policy of large-scale labour emigration. This was made clear in the process of colonial state-building in the area.

## Colonial state-building: conflicting strategies

State investment in transport, infrastructure, etc., but *not* in agriculture; mobilization of labour through taxation and various forms of direct or disguised compulsion; overall supervision of the allocation of social and economic resources to large, mostly Belgian, enterprises—these were the main guidelines of colonial government policies in the Belgian Congo during the 1920s. This was a period of state-building, of implanting an organization able to plan social and economic development effectively.

In western Shaba state investment was kept at a minimum, with the exception of the financial guarantee extended by the state in 1927 to the proprietary company of the Dilolo railway line (Léokadi). The impact of the colonial state on the landscape was limited to the creation of small administrative stations, the headquarters of the district and its six *territoires*, and to the opening of a road network. In each case, the main investment was human. Road-building and porterage brought many people into effective contact with the colonial state for the first time. The programme of public works entailed arduous contributions from villagers, particularly in regions where embankments had to be built over wide marshes and *dambos*. The construction of the Kinda – Kafakumba – Sandoa – Kapanga road was completed in 1922, bringing about a severe food shortage since too many men and women had been kept away from the fields.

The administration sought to regroup the rural population along the axes of the new infrastructure, but for a long time its success was limited. Colonial centres of settlement were carefully planned, particularly in the eastern part of the district where the CSK possessed authority to make leases of land. The blueprint for Kayoyo in 1924 gives a good example of colonial planning for a small township; it reflects colonial concern to enforce residential racial segregation, in life as well as in death, to limit opportunities for African traders, and to open the way for future European traders who might want to settle.[44]

In the overall colonial strategy for Katanga, the local administration in Lulua had to pursue two objectives: to incorporate the male population into the modern labour market, mainly as temporary migrants to HKI, and at the same time to extract the surplus from rural communities. The poll tax played a key role in achieving both these objectives, as well as contributing in no small way to colonial revenue.[45] But compulsory labour and commandeered deliveries of produce also played an important part.[46] Even though these pressed taxes were paid, they certainly went a long way towards depressing rural incomes and commodity prices.

In some areas, recognized chiefs played an essential role in co-opting African rural communities into the colonial structure— chiefs gave colonial rule its African mask. This was especially the case at the court of Mwant Yav. Under the influence of the official doctrine of 'indirect rule' propounded in the 1920s,[47] local Belgian officials were tempted to strengthen the power of Lunda titles, to the extent of creating new titles—the *sous-chefs* or sub-chiefs—in the outlying areas of the 'empire'. It is significant that former *capitas* of Mwant Yav Muteb, who had made their fortunes in rubber trading on behalf of the CK, were among the *sous-chefs* who were installed in the Sandoa *territoire*. In other regions, the colonial state tried to impose chiefs on societies which had directly challenged the old military aristocracies. This was the case of the Chokwe, Lwena, and Ndembu immigrants into south-western Shaba. Attempts to cast these societies into a spurious 'traditional' mould amounted in practice to trying to set the clock back. It is not surprising that 'indirect rule' met with failure among the Chokwe.[48] Among the south-western Luba too, it proved a chimera. Local administrators noted with despair that by the late 1920s the Luba *mulopwe* titles had become monopolized by wealthy men.[49]

To some degree, the Christian missions provided the only local alternative to rule by the hierarchy of colonial officials, from *Administrateurs* and chiefs to messengers and *capitas*. At the same time, the missions introduced Africans to the market economy. In the words of J.M. Springer, a representative of the Methodist Episcopal Church, 'civilized and educated natives are more efficient workmen and are more likely to be continually employed in the general industries of the country, and they purchase more of the taxable commodities of commerce ... than is the case with uncivilized and unchristianized natives'.[50]

Among the main mission centres in western Shaba, Dr Piper's Methodist Mission was established at the *mussumba* in 1913. In the following years, it rallied a number of settlers to its stations—Lunda (some of them from Angola), Luba, etc. The first Roman Catholic mission was at Kanzenze, west of Musonoie. It had been created by Scheut missionaries in 1910, but its real development dates from the arrival of the Franciscans in 1923. By 1931 there were an estimated 1,000 settlers on the concession, mostly Angolan immigrants (Ndembu and Lwena). They were contracted to the mission: each family had to plant one hectare (2.5 acres) of cassava each year per adult male. The mission bought and thus commercialized harvests, 'presque dans l'entier bénéfice des agriculteurs eux-mêmes'. According to its Superior, the mission aimed at 'stabilizing' the peasant families on whom it would exercise its religious influence.[51]

Kanzenze provided an example of linked agricultural and social change. Unfortunately, we lack detailed studies of change in the rural societies of western Shaba. In the 1920s glimpses may, however, be culled from official reports dealing with the extension of cultivation under administrative pressure and the control of African agriculture by the introduction of new crop varieties, the spread of cassava at the expense of cereals, etc. Technological change seems to have been slow, increased production being obtained by the occupation of poorer soils, often at some distance from villages and roads, rather than by improved agricultural techniques.

Local district development under 'indirect rule' ran contrary in part to the official philosophy prevailing at Elisabethville, the provincial capital, which favoured recruitment for large-scale European-owned enterprises. Conflicts arose on several occasions, such as the decision to expropriate African cattle in Lulua which district authorities at Sandoa tried to resist.

There were two conflicting development strategies at stake. The first model advised a stronger emphasis on African agriculture together with the slowing-down of industrial development. These views were generally linked with support for 'indirect rule' and for an 'association' between African planters and European processing interests. As a first step in that direction, a Brussels-based Commission de la Main-d'Oeuvre tried to slow down recruiting by setting limits on the number of men who could be withdrawn from any rural community.[52] In 1928, the Commission imposed fresh restrictions on labour recruiting. *Zones économiques* were created which tended to restrict the influence of industrial core-areas and to give priority instead to local agricultural needs. In the Lulua district, for example, new European enterprises could not be established for a period of five years, with the exception of a 30 kilometre-wide strip on each side of the Tenke-Dilolo railway line then under construction. There, food-growing could be encouraged on European initiative.[53]

In the late 1920s the mining interests of HKI proposed an alternative model of development to that of restricting labour recruitment. By 1927, the Union Minière du Haut-Katanga (UMHK) was contemplating extending its mining operations to the western part of its concession, in the Fungurume–Musonoie area, provided local manpower could be recruited. With this in mind, on 23 September 1927, UMHK proposed to the government a plan to 'stabilize' labour both on the industrial sites and in neighbouring rural areas. This latter aspect of the programme was essential: it was thought that a settled agricultural population could, in the future, meet both the food supply and manpower needs of the mining centres. Long-term plans, advanced by Dr Mottoulle, in charge of the Département de la Main-d'Oeuvre Indigène of UMHK, foresaw settling 200,000 African planters alongside major lines of communication, including the BCK and Dilolo railways.[54] As a first step, in 1929, UMHK concluded an agreement with the Kanzenze mission in order to settle immigrants there from Ruanda and Urundi.[55]

The crisis between alternative development strategies provided an opportunity for stock-taking among colonial interests in Belgium. An address by Prince Léopold to the Belgian Senate on 25 July 1933 seems to have tipped the balance in favour of agricultural against further industrial development. The controversy which raged at the time allows us to gain an insight into some aspects of the colonial system. Supporters of the development of an inexpensive African agriculture were prone to denounce rough recruiting practices, poor wages, and the bad treatment meted out to Africans in the European sector; Prince Léopold spoke of the degradation of the African to the status of an *outil de production*.[56] Industrialists, for their part, stressed the tyrannical aspects of the rule exercised by petty rural oligarchies, pointing in particular to the abuses linked with the compulsory growing of cash crops.[57] In this debate, the advocates of a strong African productive sector 'associated' with European processors seem to have appealed to anti-capitalist sentiment in Belgium. Indeed, when the colonial state decided to back the development of African agriculture, it wrecked a scheme which had aimed at incorporating rural areas totally into capitalist development under the supervision of large enterprises. Instead the basis of a 'dualistic economy' was laid.

## New meanings of rural poverty

It has been seen that rural conditions in western Shaba deteriorated after the First World War. The region was remote from the new industrial core-areas, and was hard hit by the deterioration in the terms of trade, the absence of alternatives to recruitment for HKI, and the weight of colonial state-building. Poverty then began taking on new meanings. In some instances it meant that people were barely able to live at subsistence level. This was reflected in the high incidence of labour recruits from western Shaba who failed to pass the physical tests for recruitment demanded by the mines. It can furthermore be argued that poverty appeared as a general condition, shared by both African rural and urban populations in the 1920s. Poor living conditions in rural areas, such as Lulua, depressed industrial wages in the towns. In the Belgian Congo of the 1920s, the attitude prevailed among Europeans that living conditions for recruited African workers should approximate to those they knew in their home areas.[58] The reduction in real terms of rural income was thus compounded in some measure by the lower industrial wages (in real terms) which were enforced by the mining industry in the same period. It was increased rural poverty, and not any objective factor such as productivity, which arbitrarily served as the measure of urban poverty.

Poverty can also be defined by reference to the wealth enjoyed by the new European rulers and, to a lesser degree, by their African subordinates. With the exception of a few traders, official chiefs were among the few Africans who could, within strictly defined limits, overcome poverty. For many years, under the overall supervision of the local administration, they received fees for recruiting and for levying poll tax, and they were also in a position to extract tribute from their subjects. In 1918, for example, the Mwant Yav was able to confiscate cattle in the Chokwe region when travelling with an *Administrateur* who wished to build up Lunda influence in the area.[59]

In the late 1920s, the colonial administration became loath to tolerate administrative excesses on the part of the chiefs. Above all, with the passing of time, chiefly interference over recruitment was abolished, at least in law. In some cases, among the Lunda for example, chiefs had refused to co-operate with BTK recruiters.

Local colonial officials were often reluctant to act as the managers of a society which seemed doomed to impoverishment for lack of viable alternatives to long-distance labour recruiting. Their views in favour of local development 'in association with Europeans' prevailed in the early 1930s when cotton was introduced as a compulsory cash crop into the Lulua district.

There were however social causes for rural poverty which could not be allayed by the introduction of compulsory cotton-growing. 'Indirect rule' implied in fact the rule of small groups of African and foreign notables: it therefore carried petty oppression in its wake. The world economic Depression of the early 1930s temporarily rescued the rural regime which had been threatened by the growth of the capitalist economy. Western Shaba continued as an isolated area—a periphery dependent on the core-towns of Katanga, and yet isolated from their influence. Rural poverty thus increasingly appeared to be linked with isolation and backwardness.

It is important to realize that backwardness was a necessary component of the 'dualistic' system. It has been seen that access to the market had been deliberately limited, lest the 'native' should become cupid. Private ownership of land was also kept out of reach of Africans, either by formal regulations or by informal practices.[60] The Depression years of 1930–3 did show that resistance to oppression in the rural areas was widespread and varied. We should now, however, consider tentative conclusions on the question of rural poverty in the period before the wide-ranging overhaul of colonialism in the Congo brought about by the Depression.

## Conclusion

Historians are anxious to discover the historical continuities which are obscured behind major turning-points such as the introduction of capitalism into Africa. The tendency in African historiography has been to discuss exploitation in broad theoretical terms, generally within models of pre-capitalist economic formations.[61] Although the concept of 'poverty' does not seem to have been specifically used, pre-capitalist exploitation has been shown to have existed between elders and younger members of a community, or between states and (generally alien) tributary communities. But in the grasslands of Central Africa we find pre-capitalist formations which do not easily fit within the theoretical models often based on material from West or Equatorial Africa. The mercantile economy in West Central Africa does not seem to have had the effect of strengthening the exploitation of 'alien' peoples by monopolist traders or by tribute-based states. In fact, it seems to have stimulated the growth of new versions of society which challenged the power of the elders and of the military oligarchies from without and within. However the new trading frontiers introduced new forms of rural oppression through the more widespread use of slaves, the exploitation of women, rampant violence, and uneven distribution of the benefits of the trading economy.

As Jewsiewicki argues in the next chapter, rural poverty today appears to be closely linked with unequal development. Capitalism, it has been suggested, has tended to develop some core-areas while freezing their peripheries. This theme of stagnation and underdevelopment has been popularized in broad surveys of the world economy and of some major regions of the world.[62] More detailed studies show, however, that rural poverty may take many forms under conditions of capitalist development. The example of western Shaba has shown that there were several possible ways in which African rural communities could be incorporated into the peripheries of capitalist enclaves in southern Central Africa. Even universal phenomena—such as the deterioration in terms of trade, the development of labour markets, and the succession of world booms and crises—are not followed by identical effects. Within a large country like colonial Zaïre, there was scope for varied responses to world developments. Western Shaba may be typical of linked industrial polarization and rural underdevelopment, but it is neither representative of Zaïre as a whole, nor did the policies pursued in the District de la Lulua go unchallenged from colonial interests themselves. By the end of the 1920s, after a period of forced accumulation or 'wild capitalism', Belgian colonial interests felt that the time was ripe for 'rural development', either in the way of cash-crop extension in 'association' with European companies, or of foodstuff production under the overall influence of urban capitalism. Only as a result of more detailed studies will we be able to establish a complete typology of basic forms of association between rural poverty and capitalist development in Africa.

## NOTES

1. J. Lhoas, *Monographie forestière de la province du Katanga* (Brussels, 1957); W. Mullenders, *La végétation de Kaniama (Entre-Lubishi,Lubilash, Congo Belge)* (Brussels, 1954).
2. For the concepts of core-area and periphery, see M. Santos, 'Sous-développement et pôles de croissance économique et sociale', *Tiers-Monde, 15,* 58, 1974, 271–86. Historical bloc: I use the term as defined by A. Gramsci, *Selections from the Prison Notebooks of Antonio Gramsci* (ed. and trans. by Q. Hoare and G.N. Smith), (London, 1971), 366.
3. 'The greater part of the country is still primeval forest', remarked Cameron of the eastern Lunda country. When reaching the upper Lufira, Capello and Ivens had not seen flour or beans 'for weeks'. In 1886, west of Nana Kandundu, Arnot noted 'remains of former towns and large cultivated fields, now all weeds, exist on all sides. War parties from the Lovale have wrought these devastations.' V.L. Cameron, *Across Africa, Vol. 2* (London, 1877), 153; H. Capello and R. Ivens, *De Angola á Contracosta, Vol. 2* (Lisbon, 1886), 17–19; F.S. Arnot, *Garenganze or Seven Years' Pioneer Mission Work in Central Africa* (London, 1889), 165.
4. The most complete descriptions of Lunda agriculture are: H.A.D. de Carvalho, *Methodo pratico para fallar a lingua da Lunda* (Lisbon, 1890), 351–62. H. Baumann, *Lunda: bei Bauern und Jägern in Inner-Angola* (Berlin, 1935), 49–60. See also J. Wilmet, *Systèmes agraires et techniques agricoles au Katanga* (Brussels, 1963).
5. E.J. Hobsbawm, 'Poverty,' *International Encyclopedia of the Social Sciences, 12,* (New York, 1968), 398–404.
6. Baumann, *Lunda,* 11–12.

7.   J.-L. Vellut, 'Notes sur le Lunda et la frontière luso-africaine, 1700–1900', *Etudes d'Histoire africaine, 3,* 1972, 61–166.

8.   In 1901, a Belgian officer estimated that in one year seven large Ovimbundu caravans, of up to 5,000 members each, had traded in the Lunda country. *Archives du Comité Spécial du Katanga* [CSK], Dossier Révoltés, microfilm.

9.   I have borrowed these terms from J. Hicks, *A Theory of Economic History* (Oxford, 1969), 9–24.

10.   They sent the letter to its destination via Benguela. E. Verdick, *Les premiers jours au Katanga (1890–1903)* (Brussels, 1952), 63.

11.   *Archives régionales du Shaba, Affaires Politiques,* Lubumbashi, A24, and reference to Angolan and Belgian archives in Vellut, 'Notes', 131.

12.   *Archives régionales du Shaba, Affaires Politiques,* Lubumbashi, Dossier Kasongo–Nyembo. See also D. Campbell, *Wanderings in Central Africa* (London, 1929), Chapter 2; A. de A. Teixeira, *Lunda: Sua organização e ocupação* (Lisbon, 1948) for Portuguese operations in Lunda country in the 1920s.

13.   This system was abolished by Malfeyt in the Luba country in 1901: *Archives du CSK.* For a documented account of the workings of the system under Free State and Yeke partnership, see D. Campbell in E.D. Morel, *King Leopold's Rule in Africa* (New York, 1905), Appendix.

14.   In the CK concession, the state levied taxes in copper ingots, *croisettes,* which the CK alone could import. CK *capitas* were often accused of enforcing the compulsory collection of rubber. The best accounts are in: L. Frobenius, *Im Schatten des Kongostaates* (Berlin 1907); E. Vandervelde, *La Belgique et le Congo* (Paris, 1911).

15.   C. Lemaire, 'Les Wamboundous. Les Colporteurs noirs', *Revue de Géographie,* 1902–3. This account contrasts with the destruction later wrought by the Portuguese and Belgian forts in the neighbourhood of Lake Dilolo.

16.   For the Congo as a whole, the value of exports rose from index 100 in 1887 to 3,363 in 1910, 86 per cent of which consisted of rubber and ivory.

17.   Figures computed on the basis of information found in H. Waltz, *Das Konzessionswesen im Belgischen Kongo, Vol. 1* (Jena, 1917), 244–9.

18.   *Archives Zone de Sandoa,* Shaba. Letters from the Sokele firms were answered in Elisabethville by Teixeira de Matos, who by then had become the main rubber-dealer in the town. Teixeira's name appears frequently in both contemporary archives and literature. In 1902, as a trader in Blantyre, he had alerted Morel to the arrest of Rabinek at Pweto. In 1907 he was in Katanga, 'opening up food trading' west of the Lualaba. In fact he soon engaged in rubber-trading there; as Thornhill tersely commented, 'the Belgians soon found a way of getting Teixeira out of the country'. Morel, *King Leopold,* 261; J.B. Thornhill, *Adventures in Africa under the British, Belgian, and Portuguese Flags* (London, 1915), 164, 199.

19.   See, for example, F. Dellicour, 'Les premières années de la Cour d'Appel d'Elisabethville, 1910–1923', *Les Propos d'un Colonial belge* (Brussels, n.d.), 19. West of the Lualaba, in the Kafakumba region, state officials imposed a labour tax of one year at the *boma* on up to ten men per village in 1913. *Archives du Parquet d'Elisabethville,* Lubumbashi, Dossier Divers, Report to the *Procureur du Roi,* 12 September 1913.

20.   By the end of the First World War, each young boy in the Luapula region had made at least one trip to Elisabethville. *Archives Zone de Pweto,* Shaba, Registre des Rapports sur l'Administration générale, Territoire de Kilwa, 1923–8. For evidence of early food-trading in western Shaba, see *Archives Zone de Sandoa.*

21.   Figures computed on the basis of Waltz, *Das Konzessionswesen, Vol. 1,* 8, 249.

22.   B. Makonga, 'Samba-a-kya-buta', *Bulletin des Juridictions Indigènes et du Droit coutumier congolais, 10,* 1947, 304–16 and *11,* 1948, 321–45.

23.   *Archives de la Compagnie du Kasaï,* Dima, Rapport Frausto, 1905.

24.   *Archives Zone Sakania,* Shaba, Registre des Rapports sur l'Administration générale, Territoire de Sakania, 1916–28.

25. There was famine in upper Shaba in 1913, and a magistrate laid the blame on over-recruitment: 'Les Européens ont introduit chez le noir, au moins par période, le régime de la faim'. *Archives du Parquet d'Elisabethville*, Lubumbashi, Dossier Divers, Rapport Hoornaert, 1913. On that famine, and earlier ones, see L. Mottoulle, *L'alimentation des indigènes au Congo Belge* (Rome, 1939).

26. The main sources for this section are the published *Bulletins des Renseignements de l'Office Colonial* (Brussels, 1910—), the *Archives régionales du Shaba* at Lubumbashi, and local *Archives* at Kamina, Kapanga, Kolwezi, and Sandoa.

27. The best short analysis is G. Eyskens, 'Les indices de la conjoncture économique du Congo Belge dupuis la guerre, de 1919 à 1933', *Bulletin de l'Institut des Sciences Economiques*, 1933. The analysis is carried down to 1960 in J.Ph. Peemans, *Congo-Belgique, 1900—1960. Diffusion du Progrès et Convergence des Prix* (Louvain and Paris, 1970). See also the well-documented G. Vandewalle, *De conjoncturele Evolutie in Kongo en Ruanda-Urundi van 1920 tot 1939, en van 1949 tot 1958* (Ghent, 1966).

28. At Kapanga in 1917, 'la région, victime des exploits du Mwata Yamvo, est terrorisée', while in 1920 'Les indigènes sont terrorisés par les agissements des capitas de la CK'. Five had been brought to trial. In 1919—20, the *Administrateur* at Kapanga compelled men to seek rubber for the CK in order to pay their poll tax. 'The native is unable to gather enough rubber to pay for one *brasse* of cloth.' *Archives Zone de Kapanga*, Shaba, Registre des Rapports sur l'Administration générale, Territoire de la Kasangeshi, 1916—27. In 1921 the CK closed its factory at Ngoie.

29. The importance of this devaluation is not sufficiently recognized in the literature. The 1919 decision seems to have been taken in order to encourage Belgian investments in the Congo. It was only in 1925 that members of the Congrès Colonial regretfully noted that devaluation had had an adverse effect on internal trade in the Congo, but had been very beneficial to the Belgian currency. M.L. Gerard, 'Note sommaire sur le change', *La politique financière au Congo* (Brussels, 1925). See also 'L'évolution historique du franc congolais dans ses rapports avec le franc belge', *Bulletin de la Banque Centrale du Congo Belge et du Ruanda-Urundi*, November 1957, 437—54. In Angola, the exchange rate for the *conto* fell by 83 per cent from 1919 to 1924.

30. From 1915—20 the convertibility of the Congolese franc was suspended in the Congo, with the exception of Katanga, where prices and wages were in fact pegged to sterling.

31. On the use of bark cloth and hides, see the Commissaire Général's speech to the Comité Régional in Elisabethville in 1921.

32. On credit, see the ordinance of 12 July 1917, and on 'coloured traders' see the decree of 9 December 1925, and accompanying comment. *Recueil à l'usage des fonctionnaires et des agents du service territorial* (Brussels, 1930), 423—6; *Bulletin officiel*, 1926, 4.

33. Peemans, *Congo-Belgique*, 233. Asmis comments on the stability in real terms of food produce in Katanga: R.A.A.W. Asmis, *Der belgische Kongo nach dem Weltkriege* (Leipzig, 1920), 62.

34. *Problème de la Main-d'Oeuvre au Congo Belge. Rapport de la Commission de la Main d'Oeuvre indigène 1930—1931, Province du Katanga* (Brussels, 1931), 122.

35. *Bulletin des Renseignements de l'Office Colonial*, 1926, 461—5.

36. In 1923 Sandoa had a population of about 700 Africans and 30 Europeans.

37. Food-trading in the 1920s retained some of the characteristics of the earlier trading frontiers: it was still largely in the hands of small traders, *capitas*, etc. The 1925 decree hindered African trade with a view to inducing traders, porters, etc. to seek employment with Europeans. On African traders in western Shaba, see T. Kayombo and J.-L. Vellut, 'Commerçants africains de la Lulua, 1920—30', *Likundoli—Archives et Documents, 1—2*, 1974, 186—98.

38. For comparative estimates of various cash crops, see Peemans, *Congo-Belgique*, 277.

39. *Rapport aux Chambres*, 1932, 225. In 1929 dowry in the Kinda area included 100 francs in cash, an interesting feature for a region where, a few years earlier, factories

generally used barter rather than payment in specie. *Archives Collectivité locale de Kinda*, Shaba.

40. The Governor of Katanga feared that cotton-growing might retain in Lulua manpower required for HKI. Governor, Katanga, to Director, Texaf, Elisabethville, 13 June 1927. For the full text, see C. Bashizi, *Les Migrations de travailleurs dans le contexte de l'Histoire sociale et économique de l'ancien District de la Lulua, 1920–1940* (Lubumbashi, 1974), Appendix.

41. The BTK functioned as a recruiting organization financed by the large enterprises of HKI.

42. Wage-earners employed at a long distance from their homes (as a percentage of the total population of wage-earners): Lomami 58, Tanganika-Moëro 39, Haut-Luapula 37. Derived from *Rapport aux Chambres*, 1927, 10–11.

43. In the early 1920s. the *Administrateur* at Kapanga arrested men trying to reach Angola.

44. In 1928, the *Administrateur* at Kayoyo wrote to the CSK about the 'situation anormale' of the African trader, James Kawimbi, who had settled on a plot reserved for Europeans. Allocations were of 1,250 square metres for 'native traders' and 5,000 square metres for Europeans. *Archives des Titres Fonciers du Shaba*, Kayoyo O.G., 1924–8.

45. The poll tax totalled 11 per cent of the total Congo revenue in 1928. A high proportion of the duty on imported goods was also paid by the African population.

46. In 1920, forced labour was still the rule in the vicinity of government stations. In the Lulua district there were then 8,245 conscripts for non-payment of tax, i.e. 24.4 per cent of the total registered male population. *Rapport sur l'administration générale, District de la Lulua*, 1920, cited in Bashizi, *Les Migrations*, 79. The regulations provided for 60 days' labour per annum for 'educative work' (compulsory cultivation, for the benefit of the chiefs); twenty-five days could be commandeered for porterage, and work on the roads could also be imposed. *Recueil à l'usage*, 307–8, 354–8.

47. 'We do not want to make black Belgians, but better Congolese, that is to say, strong, healthy, hard-working Negroes who will be proud of their good work, proud of their people and race.' L. Franck, *Belgisch Kongo* (Antwerp, 1930), 102.

48. In the 1920s, the local administration repeatedly tried to extend the authority of the Mwant Yav to the Chokwe, but from 1922 this was always resisted by the provincial administration at Elisabethville.

49. For some social and economic implications of 'indirect rule', see J.-L. Vellut, *Guide de l'étudiant en Histoire du Zaïre* (Kinshasa and Lubumbashi, 1974) 130–7. Examples are taken from the Luba–Lunda region.

50. *Archives des Titres Fonciers du Shaba*, Mission Méthodiste du Sud-Congo, Springer to CSK, Elisabethville, 12 January 1915.

51. *Archives des Titres Fonciers du Shaba*, Mission Méthodiste de Kanzenze.

52. In Katanga, there prevailed a 'broad interpretation' of the regulations set forth by the Commission. *Rapport aux Chambres*, 1927, 9–11. In 1925–8 there were however several temporary prohibitions on labour recruitment in the Lulua district. For a general discussion, see Bashizi, *Les Migrations*, 118–30. In an effort to preserve manpower, porterage was severely restricted from 1926, a measure which temporarily brought to a halt all food-trading in the Lulua district. M.S. Inwen, *La suppression du portage au Katanga, 1925–1930* (Lubumbashi, 1974), 132–3.

53. *Problème de la Main-d'Oeuvre*, 69ff. In the course of discussions on the creation of *zones économiques*, representatives from HKI argued that 'local needs' should never prevent recruitment of 5 per cent of the adult male population for work in HKI.

54. Dr Mottoulle had been impressed by the example of Forminière settling workers in the neighbourhood of its mining sites in Kasaï. He wanted to duplicate this experiment, but on a larger scale. His report of 21 September 1927 explains at length the urban *and* rural aspects of 'stabilization'; the rural dimension has frequently been ignored in the literature. A copy of Mottoulle's report and of UMHK's correspondence with the

316 JEAN-LUC VELLUT

Prime Minister are to be found in the *Archives des Titres Fonciers du Shaba,* Mission Méthodiste de Kanzenze.

55. In part this was a move designed to offset possible missionary objections to large-scale settlement schemes.

56. On several occasions his speech was interrupted by applause from the left-wing benches. Royaume de Belgique, *Annales Parlementaires (Sénat),* 1932–3, 586–8.

57. Strythagen, Director of OCTK, the successor to BTK, strongly condemned compulsory cotton-growing as tyrannical and unpopular: 'le régime du coton, avec tout ce qu'il comporte d'aide de l'Etat, de pression de la part des moniteurs agricoles, de sanctions qui frappent l'indigène pour négligence ou infraction au décret contonnier de 1921, est très mal vu de l'indigène'. *Comité Régional du Katanga,* 1930, 102.

58. The Commission de la Main-d'Oeuvre, however, believed that wages should enable the worker to rise above his original standard of living. *Problème de la Main-d'Oeuvre,* 31.

59. J. Vandermissen, 'Essais d'introduction de matériel de culture à traction animale dans la région de Sandoa', *Bulletin Agricole du Congo Belge,* 1944, 201–13.

60. In the area controlled by the CSK, land grants to Africans were made at rates two to three times higher than the purchasing price paid by the Comité itself, 'pour obliger l'indigène à attacher une valeur à la terre'. Outside the CSK concession, private landownership was in practice out of the reach of Africans.

61. I. Sellnow, 'Vorkapitalistische Produktionsweisen und die Periodisierung des Geschichte altafrikanischen Staaeten', *Ethnographisch-Archäologische Zeitschrift, 14,* 1973, 501–36; C. Coquery-Vidrovitch and H. Moniot, *L'Afrique noire de 1800 à nos jours* (Paris, 1974), 283–5.

62. See the works cited in notes 8, 9, and 10 of the Introduction to this book.

# CHAPTER 13

## Unequal Development: Capitalism and the Katanga Economy, 1919–40

### BOGUMIL JEWSIEWICKI

## Introduction

The aim of this chapter is to examine the impact of colonial economic policies upon the integration of African farmers into the capitalist market for food crops. The underproduction, and indeed the underdevelopment, of certain 'national' agricultural economies in Africa appears to be a direct consequence of the 'rationalization' of food markets for the benefit of the development sectors of the capitalist economy, situated either in the metropoles or in the colonies themselves. Today many African governments continue to apply the same policy of rationalization in the interests of the export trade and of selected internal 'development areas'.

In the period 1919–40 Haut-Katanga Industriel (HKI), Upper Industrial Katanga, in the Belgian Congo, now part of the Shaba Province of Zaïre, constitutes an excellent area for such a study. The mining industry of HKI wielded great influence. By the end of the First World War Katanga copper accounted for between 30 and 50 per cent of the total values of Congolese exports.[1] Copper was exploited by a single company, Union Minière du Haut-Katanga (UMHK), which dominated the economic life of HKI. To a somewhat lesser though still significant extent, Géomines monopolized the exploitation of tin. Such a situation makes an analysis of the reciprocal relationships between agricultural production and the industrial sector easier to undertake. Finally the authoritarian tendencies of the Belgian colonial administration and its aspiration to become the enlightened arbiter between the interests of the 'European economy' and African peasant societies makes Katanga something of a laboratory for this type of analysis.

The period between the two World Wars has been chosen deliberately because it illustrates the role of the Great Depression in determining the model of development finally chosen for the Congolese colonial economy. The pre-Depression period was characterized by a certain degree of economic liberalism in which the administration, though striving to assert its authority over the food and labour markets, did not attempt to assume direct control over the capitalist economy. After the period of Franck's ministry (1918–24), it was generally agreed that the free play of economic mechanisms was the most effective stimulant to development. Considerable

317

efforts were made to free the labour market from administrative constraints and to replace these with economic ones. From 1928 freedom of movement was curtailed by the policy of *zones économiques,* the first statutory check on unstructured development. However, within these zones the administration, in conformity with the recommendations of certain consultative bodies which it had set up, preferred to give free rein to the mechanisms of the capitalist economy rather than use direct compulsion, and on the eve of the Depression this had increasingly become the policy of the big companies such as UMHK. Then the Depression suddenly gave the administration an unparalleled importance in the planning and control of the economy, for it was forced to rescue the capitalist economy and its various interests or risk making colonialism appear unprofitable to the metropole. In the course of this rescue operation, the burden of the Depression was placed squarely upon the non-capitalist African economy, that is, upon African agriculture.[2]

## Geographical location and communication problems

In Katanga, environmental factors impose certain constraints on the development of agriculture in those regions where the demand for food is greatest. The mining area of HKI, situated almost entirely on the very old peneplain[3] of southern Katanga, is a high plateau area (1,200 to 1,800 metres), with a climate characterized by a long dry season of six to seven months and by great variations in temperature. There is a daily range of between 15° and 22°C in the dry season, though the mean temperature is quite high. The soils of the peneplain tend to be sandy, heavily leached, and worn out. Often affected by laterization, they do not generally offer favourable conditions for agriculture. Nor are the *dambos,* with their greyish-black soils, good for agriculture. They often require draining before they can be used for cultivation, and their soil is deficient in calcium and in the phosphates indispensable for plant growth.

However, though Katanga does not possess large stretches of fertile land, it does contain several small strips of such land dotted about the sparse forests. In such areas, where hard rock complexes come to the surface, the surrounding soil, enriched by the results of recent erosion, is often fertile. In the southern Katanga area the relief of tight folding also contributes to the formation of strips of fertile land here and there; for example, in the Mufufya–Lufira–Luembe and Kando–Kazembe alluvial valleys. Southern Katanga is thus characterized by small pockets of fertile land, a near-absence of extensive areas capable of supporting large-scale mechanized agriculture, and by consequent competition for the best land resources.[4]

Given the great demand for food from the mining centres which grew up in HKI, it became imperative to enlarge the scale of the potential food-supplying areas. In fact to the north, north-east and west of Upper Katanga there were large alluvial plains capable of supporting a considerable expansion of agricultural production. The 'natural' granaries of the mining area were the Kamalondo plain in the north along the Lualaba river, with its recent alluvial formations from the lower Lufira river,[5] and the Luapula—Moëro [Mweru] plain in the north-east. The fertile, moist soils of these alluvial plains provided favourable conditions for large-scale agricultural production, thanks to a shallow water-bearing stratum as well as a warmer climate and good rainfall distribution. In addition outside Katanga, in Kasaï, in Maniema, and in nearby Northern Rhodesia, there were either immediate or potential possibilities of obtaining food supplies.

In the light of the above, and in view of the constantly growing demand for food on the part of the mining centres (see Figure 1), it is clear that the food market for HKI was going to be intimately linked to the development of a modern network of transport. Situated in an area of high plateaux, Upper Katanga lacks adequate river routes. It also possessed a very sparse population, as a result both of environmental factors and of the political situation prevailing during the second half of the nineteenth century. The area was thus incapable of providing porterage on a large scale, and in any event labour was reserved for the needs of the mines and subsistence agriculture.

In such a context, a railway might hope to provide HKI with food from the *zones de production,* which both the administration and the commercial sector were anxious to create. But Northern Rhodesia, which organized its own food and labour markets during the 1900s, aspired to embrace the Katanga mines within its economic orbit. The geographical 'liberation' of Katanga, inspired more by political than economic considerations, would thus be dependent upon the development of a transport network linking HKI to the Atlantic Ocean and thereby assuring it of easy and inexpensive access to those areas in the Congo which would supply food crops and labourers. The political and economic occupation of parts of the Congo, achieved during the first quarter of the twentieth century, thus paved the way for the incorporation of local peasant societies into the now dominant capitalist system.

HKI was in fact first linked to the coast by the 'Cape to Cairo' railway from Northern Rhodesia in 1910. In the same year the Chemin de fer des Grands Lacs Africains (CFL) brought a railway from Kindu on the Lualaba to Kongolo farther south along the river, making it possible to transport goods along the Congo—Lualaba as far as Bukama, near the Katanga copper mines, after reaches of the Lualaba and Lake Kisale south of Kongolo had been made navigable. The completion of the Kabalo—Albertville railway from Lake Tanganyika to the Lualaba in 1915, and the construction of a line from Kambove, in the copper mines, to Bukama in 1918 meant that the Lomami and Tanganika districts as well as eastern Katanga were now opened up to HKI. There were no further extensions for ten years, until 1928 when

the Chemin de fer du Bas-Congo au Katanga (BCK) linked Bukama
with Ilebo in the north-west, thereby opening up Kasaï. Finally in
1931, the Tenke–Dilolo line linked the Elisabethville–Bukama route
to the Benguela Railway of Portuguese Angola, and hence opened up
Upper Lulua.[6] It is important to note that the 1928 and 1931 railway
extensions virtually coincided with the Depression, while the earlier
phase of construction had taken place in what, in terms of both mining
production and employment, had been a boom period.[7]

## I: Regional origins of food supplies to HKI

There is a close parallel between the volume of food supplies
imported into HKI and the number of industrial workers employed in
the region (see Figure 1). In 1917–19 food consumption in HKI was
around 8,000 to 10,000 tonnes,[8] of which probably 40 to 50 per cent
was produced locally, the remainder being imported, principally from
the Rhodesias.[9] Consumption then rose from about 20,000 tonnes in
1924 to 35,000 tonnes in 1929, of which only between 10 and 20 per
cent was produced locally. The structure of food imports was
naturally connected closely with the development of the railway
system.

### Katanga

In 1919 the districts of Upper Katanga produced the following
amounts of foodstuffs: Sakania 1,500 tonnes, Kambove 600 tonnes,
Etoile 500 tonnes, and Nasandoie (Musonoie) 150 tonnes, while in
southern Katanga European farmers produced 1,000 tonnes.[10] This
geographical distribution was subsequently maintained, with southern Katanga, using the railway from Northern Rhodesia, being the
largest local producer of food for HKI.[11] European farmers settled in
this region, and near the mining centres, and in response to rising
maize prices devoted large areas of land to this crop.[12] The distinction
between European and African farmers as such has little importance
in this analysis, since there was open competition between the two in
commercial agriculture and there was no attempt to impose crop
restrictions in the period before the Depression.

Although the figures for commercialized production in Katanga are
incomplete, it is possible to discern general tendencies whilst ignoring
small annual variations.[13] Production in Upper Katanga rose from
(approximately) 3,000–4,000 tonnes in 1917–20 (40 per cent produced by Europeans) to 7,000–8,000 tonnes by the end of the 1920s
(75 per cent produced by Europeans),[14] while European production in
southern Katanga rose from 1,000 tonnes in 1917 to 7,500 tonnes in
1929. The relative importance of local production declined. Whereas
in 1916 it had comprised some 40 to 50 per cent of HKI's total
consumption, by 1920 the proportion had dropped to about 25 per
cent and by 1927 to less than 15 per cent.

We have every reason to believe that during this period there was a continuing expansion of food production on the part of European farmers.[15] By comparison African production appears stagnant and even in decline, which may partly be explained by the counter-attraction of work in the towns, and by labour recruitment which was far from voluntary. The increase in European production, on the other hand, was only made possible by a combination of very high maize prices and the semi-forced recruitment of workers for European farmers who, like their counterparts elsewhere in Central and Southern Africa, were renowned for paying very low wages and for being extremely harsh employers. Once prices began falling during the Depression however, the administration immediately wanted European farmers to abandon food production, thereby underlining the fact that they were inherently ill-prepared to meet African competition.[16]

## The Rhodesias and Angola

The initial policy of encouraging the development of European agriculture in order to ensure the necessary food supplies, while at the same time attracting Africans from Upper Katanga to the urban centres as wage-earners, was not successful.[17] European agriculture failed to fulfil these hopes, and the lack of adequate transportation, coupled with connections with British capital, meant that a great deal of labour was recruited from Northern Rhodesia.[18] Indeed, Robert Williams and Co. supplied more than half of the required workforce for UMHK from Northern Rhodesia. At the same time, agreements were reached with the British South Africa Company to buy food from the south; before 1918 it had been impossible to do otherwise, given the existing transportation system. Also maize from the south was cheaper than local maize, thanks partly to low tariffs by Rhodesia Railways designed to facilitate exports. Local producers frequently found it difficult to compete with imported maize,[19] and a close link was established between the extent of imports from the south and the annual price of maize in Katanga.

Maize imports were also closely connected with labour recruit-ment. Following the drying-up of local supplies of labour and recruitment difficulties in Northern Rhodesia, as a result of the development of the Copperbelt there, the Katanga Labour Bureau contemplated recruiting from Angola, and the same bargaining counter was used—workers for maize.[20] Commercial interests in Katanga did everything possible to obtain customs protection for local maize, but competition from the Rhodesias and Angola proved too severe—even after the opening up of Kasaï by the railway.[21] In any event, the Conventions of Luanda and Saint Germain-en-Laye between the Belgian and Portuguese authorities expressly prohibited the use of protective tariffs. The problem eventually resolved itself when local demand in Katanga began falling off because of the Depression, while at the same time demand increased rapidly in Northern Rhodesia as a result of the expansion of the Copperbelt.[22]

Northern Rhodesia thus had less food to spare for export, and indeed in 1934 Katanga was able to export 359 tonnes of maize and meal to the south, though this was very much a flash in the pan.[23]

## The northern railway areas

The constant increase in the demand for food during the 1920s and the desire to make the Katanga economy less dependent on the south forced HKI to search for supplies in the areas opened up by the CFL and Kambove−Bukama railways: Lomami, Tanganika−Moëro, Orientale Province, and Ruanda−Urundi. In the period 1921−5 supplies from these areas increased by 18 per cent. Tanganika district then declined in relative importance against the other regions as a result of increasing local consumption following the development of the tin industry by Géomines.[24] Similarly, supplies from Lomami and Orientale Province showed a marked expansion in the early 1920s, but slowed down later as a result of increasing local needs connected with BCK railway construction and the start of mining development in Maniema. However the BCK (1928) and Tenke−Dilolo (1931) railways enabled Kasaï and Lulua respectively to send foodstuffs to HKI for the first time. Supplies from Kasaï increased from 250 tonnes in 1928 to 6,200 tonnes in 1931, while Lulua exports rose from 530 tonnes in 1932 to 1,521 tonnes the following year.

### Regional supplies: a conclusion

Figure 5 illustrates the regional distribution of food supplies to HKI. One should note an overall increase of 25 per cent in the volume of supplies in the period 1921−5, and of 40 per cent in 1925−8. Supplies from the south increased in these years by 45 and 47 per cent respectively. The Depression year 1931 saw a total drop of 30 per cent on the 1928 level, with imports from abroad falling by 30 per cent as well, but supplies from within Belgian possessions declining by only 5 per cent. By 1933 total supplies had dropped a further 29 per cent from the 1931 level. In the face of this falling demand, and in response to the expansion of Kasaï and Lulua exports, imports from the south had fallen to virtually nothing by 1933. After 1933 about half of the maize requirements of the urban population of HKI were met from Kasaï and Lomami, now united in the Lusambo Province in an administrative reshuffle which also saw Katanga Province emerge with new boundaries.[25]

## II: Colonial policy towards African cultivators

The Belgian colonial administration recognized from the very beginning the key role of local agriculture in supplying foodstuffs to the mining centres, but early policy suffered from a belief in the ultimate supremacy of European agriculture—a belief not dissimilar to Northern Rhodesia's 'settler dream'.[26] Rapid development through white—preferably Belgian—colonization was the prevailing belief in Brussels as well as locally, and generous credit facilities were made available first through a private company and then by the state.[27] But the belief was based on an overestimation of African soil fertility, especially that of the Upper Katanga area. In 1913 Leplae, Director of the Department of Agriculture, reported that good soils were rare and were already being cultivated by Africans. The solution, he felt, was to intensify African methods of cultivation, so as to make room for European settler farmers on the better land.[28]

The attempt during the 1910s to build up a substantial European farming community was a complete failure. The result was that the Department of Agriculture resorted to imposing compulsory cultivation on African producers. This was especially the case, as it was also across the border in Northern Rhodesia,[29] during the First World War, when food was urgently required for the troops in the East African campaign. Compulsory cultivation as an official policy gradually gained ground until by the early 1920s it was commonplace throughout the Congo, though with great regional variations.[30] By this time the official encouragement of European settlement had been suspended. In 1923 the Comité Spécial du Katanga (CSK), inquiring into the failure of the earlier policy, reported that European farmers were small in number and low in productivity. Among the main reasons adduced were the high cost of farm machinery, the inability to use draught animals because of the tsetse fly, and the relatively high level of industrial wages which made it impossible for the European farmers to procure adequate labour supplies at a cost they could afford.[31]

## Patterns of African development in Katanga

During the 1920s an attempt was made to separate the world of mining from the world of agriculture by introducing the Southern African system of 'native reserves'. With the aim of promoting rapid agricultural settlement, the provincial government in 1921 set up a commission of inquiry into the availability of vacant land in the outskirts of Elisabethville. As the Governor of Katanga reported, 'It was necessary to stop the blacks from settling anywhere they wanted and from moving whenever they felt like it. Land was required to establish agricultural settlements. . . . The increasing needs of European agricultural settlement persuaded the Katanga Government to pass several laws creating native reserves.'[32] At the same time it was agreed that 'The territorial authority will be careful to limit its economic penetration to these reserves in such a way as to guide the natives very gradually. It will carry out the necessary work to improve public health and will closely supervise the creation and building of new villages.'[33]

The reserves policy came under attack however. The Bishop of Katanga, Mgr de Hemptinne, an opponent of 'indirect rule' and advocate of African agricultural development, had more 'progressive' views, in line with those of big business, and led a frontal attack on the concept of reserves, which he considered, rightly, to be straightforward plundering of the African for the direct benefit of European agriculture and industry. He feared a profound social and demographic crisis in a society already buffeted on all sides and now being forced into a wholly artificial living space.[34] De Hemptinne found support for his views from Councillors Louwers and Bertrand in the Colonial Council in Brussels, as well as from the Attorney-General of Katanga.[35] In 1926 the second Colonial Congress, under the impression that the colony was being depopulated, concerned itself with the question of African population growth. It advocated a rational organization of labour recruitment, the development of African agriculture—delegates were no longer in favour of European agriculture in Upper Katanga—and an overall plan of economic development.

From these recommendations was born the 1928 metropolitan Consultative Committee on Indigenous Labour (MOI) and the policy of *zones économiques*.[36] Under pressure from the opposition of de Hemptinne was others, Bureau, the Governor of Katanga, who had hitherto defended the policy of 'native reserves', now conceded that the creation of urban centres for Africans was viable only within the *zones industrielles*. And in 1926 he outlined a tentative proposal for the replacement of reserves, 'in order for native society to continue living on the land deemed necessary for its existence, groups of natives, if UMHK agrees, will now be allowed to live in close proximity to white settlement and will derive the benefits which this will bring.'[37] This modernizing approach was carried further in 1928 when Heenen, the originator of the idea of *zones industrielles* and *communes indigènes,* become Governor of Katanga.[38] He organized and divided Katanga into *zones économiques* designed to facilitate rational development within the province, giving first priority to the urgent problem of food supplies and to African, rather than European, agriculture.[39] The concept of *zones industrielles* around the major centres, free of any 'traditional' rights, was in many ways the direct antithesis of the 'native reserve'. Unlike reserves, such zones would be open to all outside influences like any normal urban ward anywhere in the world.

As part of this new approach, African market gardens around Elisabethville, Jadotville, Lubudi, Albertville, and Sakania were developed under the patronage of the CSK, despite protests from European settlers who resented competition from African-grown vegetables.[40] Heenen, and indeed the big companies in Katanga, wanted to lower the cost of living, and especially the total costs of the MOI, by a general lowering of agricultural prices and by offering high industrial wages which would produce a supply of labour greater than the demand.[41] In this way, the development of African market gardening, the first supplies of foodstuffs from Kasaï, and the attempts to recruit in Angola all went hand in hand with the special labour-recruiting missions of UMHK and the policy of labour stabilization.

Heenen's old idea, from the time he had been District Commissioner for Lomami, of a modern type of African farming settlement, was now revived on a larger scale in plans by UMHK and the Franciscan mission at Kanzenze to establish settlements of Ruandan immigrants.[42] Heenen had sought to establish first nuclei and later islands of African commercial farming on capitalist lines, by setting up ex-soldiers in designated plots in model villages along roads on the Bukama–Kasaï axis, and by contemplating private ownership of land and the creation of a savings bank and a mutual aid society.[43] Following the example of the missionaries, UMHK in Kanzenze foresaw the creation of a food and labour reserve through the distribution of plots of land to selected Ruandan workers after their first contract on the mines. Lacking any traditional attachments to the area, such people would comprise a self-perpetuating source of food and labour for the industrial regions.[44] 'We hope to see native agriculturalists gradually establishing themselves around the mining centres', said Dr Mottoulle on behalf of UMHK.[45] Ruandan colonization in the UMHK concession at Kanzenze was only the forerunner of a scheme, proposed by Mottoulle, for the settlement of some 200,000 Africans along the main lines of communication, which would allow intensive commercial agriculture to take root while the surplus labour power would be absorbed into industry.[46]

The desire to integrate at least part of African society more fully into the industrial world was however somewhat thwarted by subsequent events. During the Depression a government decree of 1931 did recognize the existence of an African working class and its future need to develop outside the confines of 'traditional' society, but the new agricultural policies decided at that time, coupled with the maintenance of 'indirect rule' and the consequent strengthening of 'traditional' institutions, effectively maintained the division of Africans into two worlds, urban and rural, and brought about, as we shall see, rural stagnation in Katanga.

## The impact of the Depression

The Depression put an end to the ambitious schemes of Mottoulle. The only project to survive was in fact the most modest of all—market gardening, which had received a somewhat surprising stimulus from the Depression.[47] The African unemployed who either did not want to return to their villages, or no longer had any to return to, fell back upon the urban centres. A scheme was even conceived, and partially put into effect in Jadotville, to grant plots of land to unemployed Africans who did not wish to be repatriated; the same scheme was also attempted for Europeans, but proved a total failure.[48]

After 1929 Kasaï became a major source of food supplies to HKI. A commercial firm quickly established a monopoly there and complained that:

The Governor [Heenen] begrudges the inflated prices paid to our natives. The Government's action in this regard is ineffectual and the system of fixed market prices has proved a fiasco everywhere. It is obvious however that the prices paid to the natives have become excessive.... But it is up to the buyers to come to an understanding on this. As for the natives, they must submit to a moderate and gradual reduction in the purchase price, and in general they are sufficiently advanced now to understand the fluctuations of the market.[49]

In 1930 representatives of the big commercial companies were already asking that an attempt be made to 'stabilize' African production and prices, with the aim of removing Africans from the direct influence of the capitalist market.[50] They were agreed that in the new market conditions prevailing, European agriculture would never be able to stand competition from the food prices offered by Africans. Moreover, they even questioned whether African agriculture in Katanga would be capable of producing food at the same price levels as that sent down from Kasaï.[51] It was thus felt necessary—and this was partially achieved during the Depression—to reorient European agriculture towards dairy-cattle rearing, pork and poultry production, and market gardening. The companies wondered whether it would be necessary to eliminate competition from African market gardeners by directing them towards maize production, but the CSK opted instead for the solution that Europeans should produce choice vegetables and Africans basic vegetables.

The decisive turning-point in both agricultural and 'native' policy occurred in 1934 in a series of decisions from the newly created Katanga Economics Office.[52] Two important choices appear to have been made. First, there was broad acceptance of the principle that the economy should now be managed by the state. In his memo on the setting up of an economic programme for the Province of Elisabethville, Cloquet, President of the Katanga Chamber of Commerce, observed: 'We think it falls to the Government to bring its support and enlightened direction to the activities of the country; to suggest settlements; to control prices (by legislation for example); to limit production; to instigate discussions between traders engaged in the same activity with a view to establishing durable and recognized settlements.'[53] Secondly, it was agreed to organize food production and the social reproduction of the labour force within the 'traditional' village structure, planned and strictly controlled by an 'enlightened' administration. The whole of the province was divided into two *zones agricoles* (Tanganika and Upper Katanga), which replaced the former *zones économiques* of 1928. These new zones were in turn sub-divided into *régions économiques,* forming bands 50 km across on both sides of arterial routes within the zone, and designated as producers of food for the urban centres. In theory, the Tanganika zone was to be self-sufficient while the Upper Katanga zone would continue to be supplied from Kasaï and Lomami.[54] It was even hoped to export food from Kasaï to the Rhodesias. Outside Region A (the food supply *régions économiques*), B Regions would be created in areas farther than 50 km away from lines of communication, where food production would not be urged but export crops would be encouraged. Very detailed tables projected the production levels of each region, taking into account the number of able-bodied men and women in the villages and the nutritional needs of village populations and urban workers. An annual area of about 1.5 hectares (3.7 acres) under cultivation was presumed for each able-bodied man, and an annual clearing of 0.85 hectares (2.1 acres). High production targets were set in the hopes of obtaining between 750 and 1,000 kilograms of maize meal per hectare, and between 1,500 and 2,000 kilograms of cassava meal.[55]

In 1934, during a sitting of the Provincial Council, the Provincial Commissioner (formerly Governor) rejected the notion that administrative pressure would be applied in order to maintain production levels. He said that production was not to be a matter of forced extraction, and that traders should not go and establish themselves in the interior unless they were sure that production levels would warrant it.[56] However, a generalized system of compulsion did emerge. The Economics Office fixed purchase prices, estimating that 20 centimes per kilo bag of maize within the *régions économiques* would ensure a 'just' return to producers, and expressed the hope that the cultivators in the zones would obtain an annual income of 3,600 francs (£29). The Governor hoped that the new system would make Katanga self-sufficient in food supplies: 'I must at all costs ensure supplies for the population of Katanga. It is logical that we should produce as near as possible to the centres of consumption.'[57] The political implications of these economic choices were not yet apparent.

The inherent conflict between major industrial concerns, such as UMHK, and commerce and transport, with their interests in the food trade, came to the surface with the setting up of the Economics Office in 1933.[58] The representatives of the major commercial and transport companies were strongly opposed to the idea of self-sufficiency in food for Katanga, to the administration fixing minimum food purchase prices, and accordingly to the UMHK scheme, mentioned above, propounded by Mottoulle. In a note to the Economics Office, BCK, the railway company which brought Kasaï food into Katanga, described the UMHK scheme as 'a policy of absolute provincial particularism'. Katanga, BCK insisted, 'must be above all an industrial area with a European population. If the land does not suit the natives, it will certainly suit the setting up of European farms.'[59]

## Compulsory cultivation

Local cultivators living near centres already integrated into the capitalist market system posed a real threat to the food collection monopolies. The Depression and the fear of political upheaval[60] led to a recognition of the need 'to maintain productive activity in good order, and to avoid stagnation liable to bring about discouragement and disturbances of the peace, giving rise to pessimism and anxiety, whose ultimate repercussions it would be difficult to calculate'.[61]

The choice adopted in 1931–3 under the pressure of the prevailing political mood—that Africans must carry on farming at all costs in order to maintain the economic activity of the colony—found legal enforcement in a government decree of 1933 which brought the question of compulsory cultivation to the fore once again.[62] Political and economic interests pushed for the abandonment of the idea of free market agricultural production by Africans in Katanga in favour of compulsion, which would allow the retention of low prices and ensure supplies where the European economy most needed them.[63] Compulsory cultivation would thus act as a regulator for controlling the prices paid to the producer.

In the official correspondence there was a certain reticence to use the word 'compulsion' which, until 1935 at least, was mostly reserved for the cotton-producing zones.[64] Thus the 'Agri Decree' of 25 November 1935 mentions only 'mobilization of food supplies', though for Tanganika district there was the more explicit 'campaign of persuasion, supported by a distribution of seeds'.[65] Yet a month earlier, in a decree of 29 October, the Provincial Commissioner had prescribed the cultivation of cassava, maize, and groundnuts in certain regions of the Upper Katanga district in which cotton production was not compulsory.[66] In 1936 the Provincial Council of Katanga, having rejected the idea three years earlier, now gave its blessing to the wish of the Council of Government to have the maximum of all compulsory labour raised from sixty to a hundred days per year, of which a maximum of fifteen days were to be spent on public works and the remainder on compulsory cultivation. In defence of the proposed change, it was argued:

> It appears justified today, because we have come to realize that it was impossible to pursue the educative effect of the programme in such a short space of time. There is a particularly strong case for the cultivation of cotton, which in itself absorbs about 35 days for an area of 3,000 sq. metres. Our goal is not so much to increase production, but to educate the natives by inculcating in them rational methods of cultivation and by teaching them how to grow new crops.[67]

In practice, however, because of the lack of agricultural staff and administrative preoccupations elsewhere, such 'education' was in fact limited to compulsory cultivation and, on occasion, seed distribution.

If the system of compulsory cultivation was in itself nothing new, its emphasis certainly shifted in an important way. From an essentially free-market, food-producing agriculture—with compulsion of an 'educative' nature, concerned for example with the introduction of new crops, and covering a total area of only 1,000 sq. metres (excluding cotton at Lomami)—one moves in 1935 to an essentially rationalized agriculture, in which compulsory cultivation was of the order of 4,000 to 6,000 sq. metres a year, with the ceiling of sixty days' forced labour practically always reached. Indeed in 1938 the Governor of Katanga observed that the ceiling could be ignored in the case of food crops. A report of 1939 on the state of compulsory cultivation in Katanga Province revealed that 180,000 men had been forced into the system—which represented the entire non-wage-earning able-bodied male population.[68] The fear of legal punishment seems to have been a sufficient incentive to labour in view of the fact that only 2.2 per cent of all criminal cases were concerned with the non-fulfilment of forced labour obligations. Finally, one should note that even outside the area of compulsory cultivation, the peasant farmer was not always free to grow the crops he wanted: cotton, for example, could only be grown in the designated cotton areas.[69] Compulsory cultivation thus entailed the manipulation of African agriculture to the will of European economic interests, since an important sector of agricultural endeavour was detached from market influences and submitted to arbitrary decisions which, from an agricultural point of view, were often economically unwise.

## III: Prices and incomes in the rural areas

While the Belgian colonial administration had from the start attempted to control labour recruitment through the Katanga Labour Bureau, it had been content to leave the buying and transporting of foodstuffs in the hands of European private enterprise,[70] though it often assisted food-buyers even when the food was not all destined for state employees.[71] The Interfina Company was the largest buyer of African produce, but there was also a network of small traders who obtained food crops with trinkets and engaged in secret labour recruiting.[72] However it was the colonial administration itself which organized and supervised the markets at which food was sold, and which operated a system of bonuses for African producers. It was the colonial administration which forbade trading outside designated market-places, and which fixed maximum prices in order to keep down the cost of living in the mining centres.[73] Commercialized peasant production reached its peak around 1925, but it must be remembered that rural society had simultaneously to provide its productive labour for the mines while being expected to increase production at home.[74]

### Food prices

The demand for food rose constantly and prices tended to favour producers. Figures 2A and 2B show that the gap between wholesale and purchase prices was smallest between 1925 and 1928. The improvement in the terms of trade led producers to become increasingly integrated into the commercial economy of Katanga. But such favourable conditions existed only in those limited areas sufficiently close to the railway network to make porterage viable. Road transport, either by wagon or truck, was virtually non-existent,[75] and beyond a certain distance from main lines of communication, the effort-price of porterage became higher than that of farming itself for producers, and uneconomic for commercial traders.

In such a context it is easy to understand why the administration's 1925 ban on porterage and its restriction of small traders were considered necessary. The continual rise in food prices was increasing the cost of labour for employers. For example, during the first six months of 1924 the weekly cost of supplying food rations to a worker in Elisabethville rose from 11.76 to 17.04 francs, an increase of 45 per cent.[76] In part such rises were attributable to commercial speculation: the maximum market prices introduced in 1918 proving a dead letter, since many inspectors favoured a free play of supply and demand.[77] In addition, traders were able to bypass the official markets and buy direct from the villages.[78]

The food trade was extremely profitable despite high transport costs. Figures 3A and 3B show the difference between wholesale prices in Elisabethville and purchase prices paid to producers in the official markets. The gap was most marked at the beginning of the 1920s, but narrowed in 1925 due to competition between traders and to heavy maize imports from the south. In 1926 wholesale prices returned to their normal rhythm and profit margins increased accordingly: it is possible that the 1925 restrictions on small traders helped bring about the fall in producer prices. The constant increase in the size of the industrial workforce also ensured a rapid return to the dominant tendency in the wholesale price curve. An analysis of Figures 2A and 2B reveals a steady rise up to 1925 followed first by a stabilization and later, from 1928 to 1930, by a fall which is far worse for producer than for wholesale prices. A stabilization of wholesale prices is confirmed by the analysis in Figure 4 of a triennial model of mean wholesale prices computed in real terms.

Until the Depression neither the administration nor the big capitalist enterprises had been able to dominate the food and labour markets effectively. The development of HKI had been extensive, rather than intensive, and had resulted in an uncontrolled rise in food prices and thus in a similar rise in cost price to the capitalist economy, as well as to a depletion of available resources within the structure of the extensive economy. But during and after the Depression the monopoly of the large commercial companies at last made itself felt.[79] The opening up of the important food market in Kasaï offered new possibilities for large-scale capital investment. At the same time, the Depression caused a considerable number of small traders to go out of business—the number of trading stores in Katanga fell from 2,390 in 1930 to 1,169 in 1933—and finally eliminated the production of 'native' foodstuffs by European farmers and food imports from the south. The Interfina and Amato Companies thus found themselves in a monopoly position in which they could dictate purchase prices to African producers living in the compulsory food-producing zones.[80] Hence the average prices in 1933–5 were some 20 per cent below those prevailing in 1928. The economic policies pursued in the 1930s tended to reduce the gap between maximum and minimum prices paid to the producers (see Figures 3A and 3B). The big commercial companies could now lower food prices in the urban markets of Katanga, from which the small traders had been practically eliminated. Such a monopoly was easy to establish since the main buyers of maize and cassava, such as Amato, were often financially linked to the big commercial companies. Such links were both illustrated and solidified with the creation by UMHK of the Katanga Flour Mills in 1930, which consumed the bulk of locally produced maize.[81] Imports of maize and maize meal from the south constituted the only remaining competition of real substance, but these were effectively brought to an end by the development of the Northern Rhodesian Copperbelt after 1930.

## Peasant incomes

During the 1920s the main areas involved in the commercial production of food appear to have enjoyed a modest prosperity. For example, an economic report from the Tanganika–Moëro district in 1921 noted that 'the necessity of offering higher and higher prices in order to obtain foodstuffs has meant that the buyers—traders established along the Lualaba—have had to increase excessively the purchase price they offer to the natives'. Three years later, it was observed that 'in view of the high prices paid, the farmers in this district presently enjoy a life of ease', while in 1925,' the agricultural population enjoys great profit from its crops; [industrial] workers' incomes are far inferior to the profits earned by villagers'.[82] Similarly in Pweto, an area which only began to export food in 1925–6 after the setting up of water transport on Lake Mweru and the Luapula, and where prices were relatively low, the local administrator estimated that the average annual income for a farmer was 300 francs (£3) in the years prior to the Depression.[83] In comparison, the 1929 monthly income of a worker in Albertville was 60 francs (90 including rations), and with UMHK from 90 to 120 francs (excluding rations).[84] Given that rations were provided only for the worker himself, and not his family, and taking into account the very high price of food in the urban centres, it can be argued that the normal income of an African family head in the food-producing regions was comparable to that of an urban dweller. Yet it is important to stress that peasant incomes were derisory in terms of the effort required, and that cultivation was often carried on only under the threat of administrative action.[85]

The low food prices which prevailed in the Depression were maintained during the subsequent recovery (see Figures 2A and 2B,

3A and 3B). In such circumstances the development of African commercial agriculture was impossible without significant changes in agricultural technology. But though the question of individual ownership of land was raised once again in 1936, it did not get beyond the discussion stage.[86] Agricultural incomes were in fact so low that they positively encouraged the exodus towards industrial centres rather than any increase in crop yields. The following figures from the Tanganika district, which from 1932 was subjected to the compulsory cultivation of both food and cotton, depict estimated annual incomes.[87]

|  | 1933 | 1934 | 1935 | 1936 | 1937 | 1938 | 1939 |
|---|---|---|---|---|---|---|---|
| Standard | 97 | 97 | 91 | 146 | 201 | 220 | 247 |
| francs |  | (+0) | (−6) | (+55) | (+55) | (+19) | (+27) |
| 1931 | 126 | 138 | 115 | 165 | 211 | 201 | 227 |
| francs |  | (+12) | (−23) | (+50) | (+46) | (−10) | (+26) |

One should remember that the pre-Depression annual income in Pweto had been about 300 (1931) francs. By comparison, the monthly wage in 1932 of workers from Tanganika district was between 45 and 48 francs in most urban centres, and from 60 to 100 francs in Elisabethville. In 1936 the average worker for UMHK was getting 100 francs per month.[88] The gap between rural and urban incomes had thus widened considerably in favour of the town worker.

Thus the abandonment of the agricultural settlement schemes of the 1920s locked the African farmer ever more firmly within the confines of 'traditional' society, with its various social pressures, and kept him at a frozen level in terms of technology and in relation to the ownership of the means of production and redistribution. The development of profitable commercial agriculture within such a framework was impossible without recourse to compulsory cultivation.

## Conclusion

The various figures which accompany this chapter together with the short analysis of rural incomes reveal a positive upward swing during the period 1919–29. This fact had important consequences for the economic position of Katanga industries. The rise in the price of food resulting from the pressures of demand—in itself a consequence of the extensive nature of economic development in Katanga—and also from very heavy transport costs, produced an increase in the cost price of industrial labour, particularly in a situation in which employers paid food rations in kind. In the absence of any notable technological progress in Katangan industry during the 1920s, such a situation was conducive to a lasting crisis which could only be resolved by two possible solutions. The first was through improvements in production techniques coupled with the creation of a skilled labour force, with the consequent abandonment of the migrant labour policy—an experiment attempted by some of the larger employers of labour from 1927. The social and political consequences of such a step would be the eventual emergence of an African urban proletariat. The second solution was to subjugate extensive rural areas to the interests of private industry by compelling them by administrative and political measures to engage in poorly rewarded agricultural production. Because African agriculture could sustain itself outside the capitalist sector, a lowering of the purchase price could reduce it to below labour costs, especially since the reproduction of the farmer was realized outside the capitalist sector. In the same way the cost price of industrial labour could be stabilized and even considerably reduced while maintaining wages at a low level. Thanks to the policy of compulsory cultivation in conjunction with fixed prices, as well as the trading monopoly which was greatly intensified during the Depression, and thanks also to the fact that the railway network was finally completed on the eve of the Depression, the second solution became practicable during the 1930s.

At the end of the 1920s however, the Belgian colonial administration, in the company of the great European powers, had opted for the first solution. At that time a political decision was taken in Katanga in favour of incorporating the entire colonial society within the capitalist system—a move conducive to economic development, but at the same time fraught with political dangers. The coming of the Depression presented the central administration with the opportunity to subjugate the economic life of the colony to the interests of the metropolitan economy and a few local vested interests. In order to reduce costs in the capitalist sector to a minimum and, despite the poverty of its technical resources, to make the Congolese capitalist economy competitive on world markets, large sectors of non-capitalist agriculture were handed over to it. The choice of unequal development, to the detriment of African agriculture, became entrenched during the Depression and was in fact maintained throughout the rest of the colonial period. This model, which ensured cheap labour and food supplies for the economy and particularly for capitalist industry, rapidly imposed severe constraints on the internal market. Despite numerous attempts, starting from 1948–50, to modify this situation, the commercialization of African agriculture was not possible within a framework which involved placing the African farmer out of reach of the market. The underdevelopment of internal consumption, a direct consequence of agricultural stagnation, was subjected to a twofold pressure: from the 'traditional' authorities maintained by the administration in accordance with its 'indirect rule' policies, and from the colonial and metropolitan capitalist sector demanding cheap manpower and raw materials, which by the end of the 1950s had taken a stranglehold over the Congolese economy.

Though the administration succeeded in raising urban wages, rural

## FIGURE 1—Food and Labour Supply Statistics, 1920–33[89]

**I: Food imports into HKI (in tonnes)**

(a) From Belgian territory

|  | 1920 | 1921 | 1922 | 1923 | 1924 | 1925 | 1926 | 1927 | 1928 | 1929 | 1930 | 1931 | 1932 | 1933 |
|---|---|---|---|---|---|---|---|---|---|---|---|---|---|---|
| Maize and millet | 1,411 | 1,114 | 822 | 3,462 | 3,866 | 5,875 | 5,535 | 6,090 | 3,734 | 3,723 | 4,436 | 2,301 | 4,207 | 2,648 |
| Cassava meal | 1,493 | 6,479 | 4,091 | 4,886 | 4,488 | 4,577 | 3,240 | 5,974 | 6,586 | 10,207 | 7,718 | 7,565 | 4,935 | 7,050 |
| Rice | 186 | 1,439 | 1,034 | 1,095 | 690 | 1,114 | 2,083 | 595 | 1,341 | 1,215 | 1,610 | 711 | 466 | 417 |
| Beans | 562 | 2,008 | 821 | 886 | 160 | 451 | 178 | 2,223 | 598 | 244 | 911 | 315 | 256 | 400 |
| Groundnuts | 540 | 338 | 631 | 592 | 900 | 892 | 1,259 | 1,829 | 1,310 | 876 | 1,220 | 974 | 619 | 651 |
| Palm oil | 169 | 210 | 447 | 391 | 402 | 429 | 790 | 1,289 | 3,452 | 2,275 | 2,441 | 1,682 | 608 | 688 |
| Total | 4,361 | 11,588 | 7,846 | 11,312 | 10,506 | 13,338 | 13,085 | 18,000 | 17,021 | 18,540 | 18,336 | 13,548 | 11,091 | 11,854 |

(b) From outside Belgian territory

|  | 1920 | 1921 | 1922 | 1923 | 1924 | 1925 | 1926 | 1927 | 1928 | 1929 | 1930 | 1931 | 1932 | 1933 |
|---|---|---|---|---|---|---|---|---|---|---|---|---|---|---|
| The Rhodesias and South Africa | 5,097 | 3,214 | 5,979 | 3,950 | 5,215 | 5,927 | 11,488 | 8,815 | 8,704 | 10,839 | 9,130 | 5,029 | 278 | 38 |
| Angola | — | — | — | — | — | — | — | — | — | — | 1,241 | 1,053 | 176 | — |
| GRAND TOTAL | 9,458 | 14,802 | 13,825 | 15,262 | 15,721 | 19,265 | 24,573 | 26,815 | 25,725 | 29,379 | 28,707 | 19,630 | 11,545 | 11,892 |

**II: African commercial production in the Upper Luapula district**

|  | 1920 | 1921 | 1922 | 1923 | 1924 | 1925 | 1926 | 1927 | 1928 | 1929 | 1930 | 1931 | 1932 | 1933 |
|---|---|---|---|---|---|---|---|---|---|---|---|---|---|---|
|  | 1,800 | — | — | 1,298 | 1,812 | — | 1,082 | 1,820 | — | 2,457 | 2,394 | 2,743 | 843 | 1,055 |

**III: The African labour force in Katanga**

(a) The total labour force

|  | 1920 | 1921 | 1922 | 1923 | 1924 | 1925 | 1926 | 1927 | 1928 | 1929 | 1930 | 1931 | 1932 | 1933 |
|---|---|---|---|---|---|---|---|---|---|---|---|---|---|---|
|  | 35,825 | 38,098 | 35,573 | 39,000 | ? | 64,133 | ? | 55,165 | 54,010 | 71,486 | 72,947 | 40,010 | 28,530 | 21,879 |

(b) Labourers from Northern Rhodesia

|  | 1920 | 1921 | 1922 | 1923 | 1924 | 1925 | 1926 | 1927 | 1928 | 1929 | 1930 | 1931 | 1932 | 1933 |
|---|---|---|---|---|---|---|---|---|---|---|---|---|---|---|
|  | 9,000 | 8,759 | 4,587 | 4,387 | 8,781 | 6,111 | 4,425 | 6,021 | 6,089 | 5,606 | 1,800 | — | — | — |

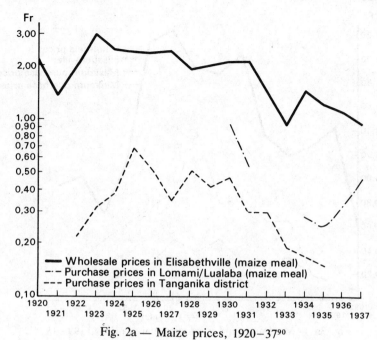

Fig. 2a — Maize prices, 1920–37[90]

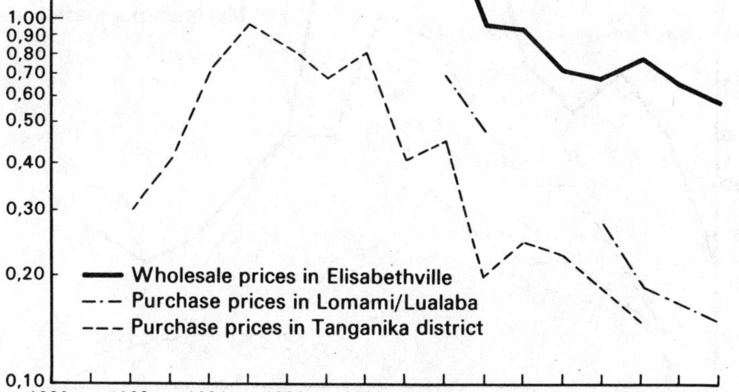

Fig. 2b — Cassava meal prices, 1920–37[90]

Fig. 3a — Maximum and minimum maize prices, 199–35.[90]

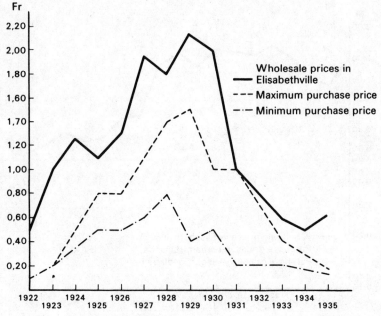

Fig. 3b — Maximum and minimum cassava meal prices, 1922–35.[90]

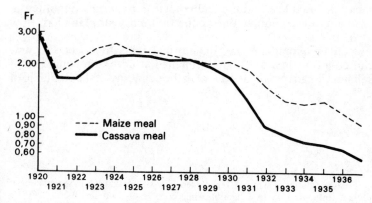

Fig. 4 — Triennial mean pattern of wholesale prices in Elisabethville, based on 1931 standard francs.[91]

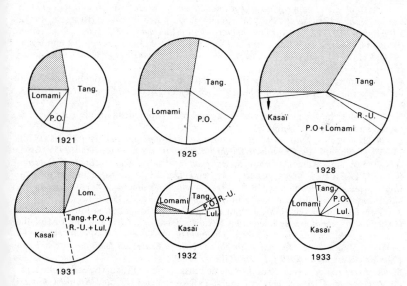

Fig. 5 — Imports of 'native' foodstuffs into KHI by region of origin.[92] (Tang. = Tanganika district; P.O. = Province Orientale; R.-U. = Ruanda-Urundi; Lom. = Lomami; Lul. = Lulua; the shaded areas = imports from the south — from the Rhodesias and South Africa, and after 1929 from Angola.)

incomes remained low and the technological modernization attempted throughout the country during the first ten-year plan (1949–59) ended in failure.

Unequal development was the normal inheritance of the new African governments, and the entrenched structural inequalities of the Belgian Congo remain dominant in the economy of the Republic of Zaïre.[93]

## NOTES

1.    The taxes and duties paid by UMHK played a very important role in the revenue of the colonial state. B. Fetter, 'L'Union Minière du Haut-Katanga, 1920–1940: La naissance d'une sous-culture totalitaire', *Les Cahiers du CEDAF, 6,* 1973, 10.

2.    I have analysed the politics of the Depression in a paper (in Polish) presented to a conference on the The Great Depression 1929–1935, held in Warsaw in October 1974: 'La grande crise économique 1929–1935 dans une économie coloniale—Congo belge'.

3.    'Peneplain' is a term introduced by the American geomorphologist W.M. Davis to denote a surface of very limited relief ('almost a plain'), produced in a landscape after a very long period of erosion, usually by the action of running water and associated processes. Thought to have been formed near to sea level, many peneplains are now found in apparently uplifted positions. This geographical section is based upon: M. Robert, *Géologie et géographie du Katanga, y compris l'étude des ressources et de la mise en valeur* (Brussels, 1956); M. Robert, *Le Katanga physique* (Brussels, 1927); J.D'Hoore, *Note sur l'utilisation et la conservation du sol dans la Province du Katanga* (Brussels, 1952); J. de Wilde, *Introduction à la géographie du Katanga* (Lubumbashi, 1971); J.H. Vandersmissen, *Aperçu sur l'économie agricole de la Province du Katanga* (Brussels, 1956).

4.    The importance of the problem is underlined in E. Leplae, 'L'agriculture du Congo belge: Rapport sur les années 1911 et 1912', *Bulletin Agricole du Congo Belge, 4,* 1913, 434.

5.    The valley in the middle stretches of the Lufira is practically useless for agriculture. Vandersmissen, *Aperçu,* 39.

6.    A. Huybrechts, *Transports et structures de développment au Congo* (Paris, 1970), 14–37; *Compagnie du Chemin de fer du Bas-Congo au Katanga, 1906–1956* (Brussels, 1956); S.E. Katzenellenbogen, *Railways and the Copper Mines of Katanga* (Oxford, 1973); E. Esteves, 'Chemin de Fer Tenke-Dilolo: Construction et implications sociales et économiques (1928–1950)', mémoire de licence en Histoire, Université Nationale du Zaïre, Lubumbashi [henceforth UNAZA], 1972–3.

7.    For Katanga, see R.M. Kibambasi, 'Occupation économique du Shaba (1920–1940)', mémoire de licence en Histoire, UNAZA, 1974. For the rest of the country, see M. van de Putte, *Le Congo belge et la politique de conjoncture* (Brussels, 1945); G. Vandewalle, *De conjoncturele Evolutie in Kongo en Ruanda–Urundi van 1920 tot 1939, en van 1949 tot 1958* (Ghent, 1966).

8.    *Archives régionales du Shaba,* Note de l'inspecteur de l'industrie et du commerce du Katanga au CDD du Haut-Luapula, 29 November 1917, and *Rapport Annuel Economique du Katanga,* 1919.

9.    *Archives régionales du Shaba,* Note..., 29 November 1917, and *Rapport...,* 1919.

10.    *Bulletin des Renseignements de l'Office Colonial,* 1920, 105.

11.    In 1923 Sakania sold 540 tonnes of meal to traders, and Kambove 405 tonnes. *Bulletin des Renseignements de l'Office Colonial,* 1924, 141.

12.   In 1929 they produced 7,500 tonnes of 'native' foodstuffs, and devoted over half of their acreage under cultivation to such crops. *Comité Régional du Katanga*, 1930, 23.

13.   The basis of estimation and the sources change too often. Sometimes they concern local traffic on the CFK, at other times estimates of the Service des Affaires Economiques. It is clear that the 1922 production was greater than 300 tonnes, which represented only millet, produced principally in the Sakania district: Sakania sold 270 tonnes to traders in 1922. *Comité Régional du Katanga*, 1925, 64; *Bulletin des Renseigements de l'Office Colonial*, 1924, 141.

14.   The data are difficult to compare. The figures for the end of the 1910s give both African and European production and are taken from the *Rapports Annuels Economiques*. The figures for the end of the 1920s are based upon my own estimates.

15.   For the period in question, see *Archives des Titres Fonciers du Shaba*, Dossier Colonisation; Comité Spécial du Katanga, *Rapports et bilans*.

16.   *Archives des Titres Fonciers du Shaba*, Observations au sujet de la note de M. Sprendre remise à M. le Gouverneur Général, (Sprendre, 'Suggestions intéressant la colonisation agricole').

17.   'Theoretically,' wrote Colonel Wangermee, 'it will always be possible to bring the necessary foodstuffs from afar, but in practice this is very expensive. We cannot count on native production. In the Cataractes district, for example, the blacks will doubtless soon be attracted by the good wages in the mines and will abandon their agricultural labours.... One could of course expand native cultivation quite a bit, but it is easy to see that this in itself will not be enough. We must therefore have recourse to other means, and it seems to me that the only choice we have is to establish European farmers in Katanga.' Leplae, 'L'agriculture', 329–30.

18.   For an analysis of the situation as seen from the other side of the border, see M.C. Musambachime, 'Labour Migration from Mweru–Luapula 1900–24: A Study of African Response to Wage Labour', in R.H. Palmer (ed.), *Zambian Land and Labour Studies*, Vol. 2, National Archives of Zambia Occasional Paper 3 (Lusaka, 1974), 39–65.

19.   *Comité Régional du Katanga*, 1930, 108–10.

20.   *Archives régionales du Shaba, Rapport sur un voyage d'études effectué dans l'Angola du 13 septembre au 2 novembre 1930 par M. Strythagen, Directeur de l'Office Central du Travail du Katanga*.

21.   *Archives des Titres Fonciers du Shaba*, Dossier Questions économiques, Agriculture au Katanga, Culture du maïs; *Comité Régional du Katanga*, 1931, 107–8; *Compte-rendu de la Sous-Commission pour l'étude du problème de la fourniture des vivres pour indigènes*.

22.   For figures on the growth of copper production, see F.L. Coleman, *The Northern Rhodesia Copperbelt 1899–1962* (Manchester, 1971), 21, 75, 145.

23.   The following table records the growth of food exports from Katanga to Northern Rhodesia (in tonnes). It is based on *Conseil de Province du Katanga*, 1936, 16; *Rapport Annuel Economique du Katanga*, 1937, 6.

|  | 1933 | 1934 | 1935 | 1936 | 1937 |
|---|---|---|---|---|---|
| Maize and maize meal |  | 359 |  |  |  |
| Cassava meal |  | 17 | 108 | 53 | 362 |
| Rice | 19 | 3 | 17 | 28 | 59 |
| Palm oil | 1,282 | 2,316 | 3,962 | 4,791 | 6,210 |
| Groundnuts | 178 | 278 | 320 | 738 | 337 |
| Beans | 296 | 500 | 306 | 398 | 297 |

24.   K. Khang-Zulbal, 'Histoire économique du district du Tanganika (1935–1940)', mémoire de licence en Histoire, UNAZA, 1973–4; M.K. Mwendanga, 'Occupation économique du district du Tanganika–Moëro (1920–1947) d'après les rapports annuels du Tanganika-Moëro (Archives régionales du Shaba)', mémoire de licence en

Histoire, UNAZA, 1972–3.
25. The later figures have not been included in the tables because of the changes in the administrative boundaries.
26. Leplae, 'L'agriculture', 319–30; R.H. Palmer, 'Land in Zambia', in Palmer (ed.), *Zambian Land and Labour Studies, Vol. 1*, National Archives of Zambia Occasional Paper 2 (Lusaka, 1973), 56–66.
27. La Compagnie Foncière, Agricole et Pastorale du Congo was created in 1909 on the initiative of King Léopold II with the aim of establishing Belgian agricultural settlement in Katanga. Its first mission arrived in Katanga in 1910. Its capital of one million francs was quickly wiped out and the state took over the running of its establishments in 1912. In the meantime the Mission agricole du Katanga was given the task of establishing in the shortest possible time Belgian settlement and cultivation in the mining area. For the comparable situation in Rhodesia, see Chapter 9, R.H. Palmer, 'The Agricultural History of Rhodesia'.
28. 'From the viewpoint of agriculture settlement, this overestimation of the amount of land occupied by the natives presents great inconveniences. One of the most important problems which we have to resolve will be *to find the means to increase native agricultural production, while cutting down the amount of good land actually occupied by the natives.*' Leplae, 'L'agriculture', 434. Emphasis added.
29. Musambachime, 'Labour Migration', 52–4.
30. E. Leplae, 'Histoire et développement de cultures obligatoires de coton et de riz au Congo belge de 1917 à 1933', *Congo, 14*, 1, 1933, 645–753; E. Leplae, 'Résultats obtenus au Congo belge par les cultures obligatoires, alimentaires et industrielles', *Zaïre, 1*, 1947, 115–40.
31. Comité Spécial du Katanga, *Rapport et bilan de l'exercise 1923* (Brussels, 1924).
32. *Archives du Parquet d'Elisabethville*, Lubumbashi, Governor, Katanga, to Governor-General, 7 October 1926.
33. *Archives du parquet d'Elisabethville*, Lubumbashi, Governor-General to Minister of Colonies, 28 September 1926.
34. One might note here the response of Chief Kaponda on being forced to leave one reserve for another following the expansion of UMHK activities: 'Formerly we were made to leave our villages to come and live in the reserves. The Government told us: "now these are your lands and no other white men can come and live here." Now we are being chased away once again. In a few months they will come and ask for something else and eventually we will have to move again.' *Archives du Parquet d'Elisabethville*, Lubumbashi, Note by Governor Bureau, 30 November 1926.
35. The Conseil Colonial was a legislative council which gave advice to the Minister of Colonies in Brussels. *Compte-rendu de la Sous-Commission pour la protection des indigènes*, 1923–4; *Comité Régional du Katanga*, 1925; *Conseil Colonial*, 26 June 1926, 3 and 10 July 1926.
36. The Congrès Colonial was an occasional unofficial gathering of people representing all interest groups in the Congo, which held open discussions and published reports. O. Louwers, 'Le IIe Congrès Colonial Belge', *Revue Générale, 115*, 1926, 333–49; P. Coppens, 'Le IIe Congrès Colonial de Bruxelles', *Le Flambeau, 8*, 1926; G. Moulaert, *Les problèmes coloniaux d'hier et d'aujourd'hui* (Brussels, 1946).
37. *Archives du Parquet d'Elisabethville*, Lubumbashi, Note relative à l'exécution de la convention conclue le 20–4–1922 avec Kaponda . . . , October 1926.
38. *Archives de la Direction Régionale des Affaires Sociales du Shaba*, G. Heenen, Projet de décret constituant les 'Communes indigènes'; F. Grevisse, *Le Centre extra-coutumier d'Elisabethville* (Brussels, 1951), 9–10.
39. Heenen had for some years been an advocate of planning in this matter. In 1921 he suggested a division of Lomami into two distinct zones, food-producing and cotton- and palm-producing. *Archives de la Direction Régionale des Affaires Politique du Shaba*, Heenen, District Commissioner Lomami, to Assistant District Commissioner, 10 March 1921.
40. In 1924 it was stated that vegetables sold at the market were 30 per cent cheaper

than those sold in the town shops. *Bulletin des Renseignements de l'Office Colonial*, 1924, 398.
41.  *Comité Régional du Katanga*, 1930, 113.
42.  The idea of settling Ruandan immigrants in Katanga dates back to the Governor of Ruanda–Urundi during the Marzorati era. Heenen said of the proposal, 'This experiment, which needs to be carried out with great prudence and on a small scale, should be most interesting. Perhaps on the basis of its results we will be able to achieve a type of emigration quite different from the normal type of recruitment, *Rapport sur la Commission Provinciale de la main-d'oeuvre du Katanga tenue à Elisabethville du 30 juillet au 6 août 1928* (Elisabethville, 1928), 10.

At the same time the Franciscan mission at Kanzenze proposed a settlement plan whereby Christian families would produce cassava with the help of the mission, which would then sell it. The mission wanted to organize the scheme on its own lands, hence on 'non-native' lands. *Archives de la Direction Régionale des Affaires Sociales du Shaba*, Appendix to Agricultural Report, Kanzenze Mission, 1927–8, and Memo presented to the Vice-Governor-General of Katanga on native agriculture in collaboration with Europeans, 1929.

At the end of the 1920s a number of collaborative projects between Africans and Europeans with respect to agriculture were put forward: *Congo*, 8, 1, 1927, 428; *Bulletin Agricole du Congo Belge*, 21, 1930, 220–51.
43.  *Archives de la Direction Régionale des Affaires Politiques du Shaba*, Rapport Semestriel Politique du Lomami, II semestre 1919, I and II semestre 1920.
44.  *Archives des Titres Fonciers du Shaba*, Note au sujet d'un projet de colonisation aux mines de l'Ouest: installation des colons indigènes du R–U, 13 May 1929.
45.  *Archives de la Direction Régionale des Affaires Politiques du Shaba*, Note pour la Commission Provinciale de la main-d'oeuvre.
46.  *Archives des Titres Fonciers du Shaba*, UMHK to Prime Minister, 23 September 1927.
47.  Comité Spécial du Katanga 1900–1950, 256–60.
48.  Province of Katanga, *Commission Provinciale de la main-d'oeuvre, Compte rendu analytique de la réunion du 13 mars 1933* (Elisabethville, 1933), 25–8.
49.  *Comité Régionale du Katanga*, 1930, 112.
50.  See the statement by Valkenbergh, Director of the *Comuele* Company, who was invited to the session by the Governor: *Comité Régionale du Katanga*, 1930, 107.
51.  Note to the Economics Office, 30 March 1934, *Conseil de Province du Katanga*, 1934, 113.
52.  The Office Economique was created in 1933 to help with economic planning, and particularly with agricultural policy. It was an advisory committee, comprising representatives of the provincial government and of commercial, industrial, and transport firms. It was convened once a year and outlined a proposed agricultural policy for the following year. Sub-committees were created in the districts.
53.  *Conseil de Province du Katanga*, 1934, 80.
54.  One should remember that in the administrative reorganizations of 1933, the northern part of Lomami had been taken away from Katanga.
55.  Programme of food production for the Province, *Conseil de Province du Katanga*, 1934, annexe 10, 2.
56.  *Conseil de Province du Katanga*, 1934, 96–7. In 1932 the Managing Director of the Lubilash Company wrote to the Katanga Director of Agriculture, 'I have the honour to send you the enclosed note concerning the cost price of native maize production in order to enlighten you about the exploitation by European buyers to which the natives are now victims. The Europeans are actually in a position to impose an arbitrary purchase price which will effectively destroy agricultural endeavour in Katanga.' In the note he defended the interests of the settler farmers who grew food crops before the Depression, and found themselves subsequently facing competition from African-grown food which had been bought by big business at ridiculously low prices. *Archives des Titres Fonciers du Shaba*, Managing Director, Lubilash Company, to Katanga

Director of Agriculture, 20 February 1932.
57.   *Conseil de Province du Katanga*, 1934, 98.
58.   *Conseil de Province du Katanga*, 1934, 98–9, 103–4.
59.   *Conseil de Province du Katanga*, 1934, 101–2.
60.   One might almost speak of a psychosis relating to subversive action. In Katanga the newly created Comité Secret and the Service de la Sûreté were vigorously active.
61.   *Comité Régional du Katanga*, 1933, 170. Similar feelings were voiced by business circles in Léopoldville.
62.   A decree of 1917 had laid down compulsory measures for cotton and rice cultivation, and the use of compulsion as an economic instrument grew progressively. Paradoxically, after the Duke of Brabant's speech announcing that African agriculture was to be modernized and intensified, which conflicted to some extent with a system of compulsory cultivation, the 1933 decree in fact reintroduced the old restrictions and even reinforced them.
63.   *Archives de la Direction Régionale des Affaires Politiques du Shaba*, Note du Chef du Service Provincial des AIMO du Katanga, 12 March 1932.
64.   *Conseil de Province du Katanga*, 1936, 65. In fact compulsion increased considerably during the Depression, even though the terminology remained discreet. For example, one spoke of Africans who cultivated 'par la nécessité de se procurer l'argent nécessaire au payement de l'impôt ou encore par obligation vu les décisions du Commissaire de District.' *Archives des Titres Fonciers du Shaba*, Managing Director, Lubilash Company, to Katanga Director of Agriculture, 20 February 1932.
65.   *Archives régionales du Shaba*, Dossier Commerce, Cultures cottonnières au Tanganika, 1931, 1932, 1935. Cited in Mwendanga, 'Occupation économique', 128.
66.   The legality of this decree was raised by the Elisabethville Tribunal du Parquet on the grounds that the compulsion was of an individual nature, while the decree of 5 December 1933 imposed collective compulsion, which was subsequently to be apportioned by the chiefs. *Conseil de Province du Katanga*, 1937, 52.
67.   *Conseil de Province du Katanga*, 1936, 54. The proposal did not in fact become law, and it was not until the Second World War that the limit was raised to 120 days per year to help the war effort. An earlier increase, in 1938, was unofficial.
68.   *Archives de la Direction Régionale des Affaires Politiques du Shaba*, Documents pour établissement du Rapport AIMO du Katanga, 1939, Section B, chapitre XX, 'Travaux imposés aux circonscriptions: Programme des cultures obligatoires'.
69.   *Conseil de Province du Katanga*, 1936, 14.
70.   The only exception was during the First World War, when the administration organized the feeding of the troops. *Archives de la Sous-Région du Tanganika*, Dossier Guerre 1914–1918.
71.   *Archives Zone de Pweto*, Registre des borderaux: Transport marchandises expédiées par l'administration aux frais de la Colonie, 1924–6.
72.   Y.T. Kasimba, 'Mission de Recrutement des Travailleurs de l'UMHK au Kivu-Maniama (1926–28)', mémoire de licence en Histoire, UNAZA, 1972–3; B. Cirhagarhula, 'Les migrations de travailleurs dans le contexte de l'histoire sociale et économique de l'ancien district de la Lulua (1920–1940)', mémpire de licence en Histoire, UNAZA, 1973–4.
73.   Regulations governing 'native' markets were laid down in the governor-general's decrees of 20 April 1894 and 15 February 1905. In 1912 competitions were introduced to attract sellers, and the administration tried to 'protect' the markets from unrecognized traders. The governor-general's ordinance of 26 March 1918 gave district commissioners powers to fix maximum prices in markets in the main centres. A. Lycops and G. Touchard, *Recueil usuel de la législation de l'Etat Indépendant du Congo, Vol. 3* (Brussels, 1904), 103; O. Louwers and G. Touchard, *Recueil usuel de la législation de l'Etat Indépendant du Congo, Vol. 5* (Brussels, 1909), 389; *Journal Administratif du Katanga*, 2, 1912, 154, 160; 5, 1915, 82; *Bulletin Administratif et Commercial du Congo Belge*, 7, 1918, 222.
74.   One could put forward the hypothesis that the departure of large numbers of men

to the urban centres diminished home consumption needs and hence exercised only a slight influence on productivity, given the fact that it was the women who normally worked the fields. This supposition would seem false for two reasons. First, men were particularly important in clearing land for cultivation, and secondly at this period, when there were still many wild animals about, they played an important role in protecting the fields against animal attacks. On this second role, see Leplae, 'L'agriculture', 538.

75.  *Archives régionales du Shaba, Rapport Annuel Economique du Katanga*, 1924.

76.  Similar, and even higher, increases were reported from other centres in HKI. *Bulletin des Renseignements de l'Office Colonial*, 1924, 404.

77.  M.M. Malungu, 'La politique de l'administration envers le commerce africain au Katanga d'après l'inventaire d'une collection provenant des Archives régionales du Shaba', mémoire de licence en Histoire, UNAZA, 1972–3, 84–93.

78.  At the beginning of 1923, traders entered the Sakania region and agreed to fix the price of a (90 kg) bag of cassava brought to Sakania at 30 francs. However competition quickly pushed the village purchase price up to between 33 and 35 francs per bag, which in turn raised the price in Sakania to between 42 and 48 francs, or 50 per cent more than the original agreement. For details of this incident, and the issue of competition among traders, see *Bulletin des Renseignements de l'Office Colonial*, 1923, 146; *Archives Zone Sakania*, Shaba, Registre des Renseignements politiques du Territoire de Sakania, 1920–8.

79.  Kibambasi, 'Occupation économique', 223.

80.  The ordinance of 7 December 1932 which allowed the fixing of minimum prices was never renewed. *Archives régionales du Shaba*, Provincial Commissioner Katanga to District Commissioner Lualaba, 17 October 1933.

81.  *Archives des Titres Fonciers du Shaba*, Dossier Questions économiques, Agriculture au Katanga, Culture du maïs. There were however occasional clashes of interest, as for example in 1937, when UMHK tried to free itself from what it by then considered the burdensome monopoly of Interfina and Amato, by giving a special price to European-produced maize in an attempt to create its own independent source of supply. *Archives des Titres Fonciers du Shaba*, Representative of CSK to the President, 16 April 1937.

82.  *Congo, 3*, 1922, 108; *Archives régionales du Shaba*, Rapport Semestriel Economique du Tanganika–Moëro, II semestre 1924, 27, II semestre 1925, 51.

83.  *Archives Zone de Pweto*, Postmaster Pweto to Administrator Kasanga, 10 September 1932.

84.  M.S. Kamalundua, 'Les interventions administratives dans la fixation du niveau de vie des travailleurs du Haut-Shaba (1920–1945)', mémoire de licence en Histoire, UNAZA, 1972–3, 50.

85.  *Comité Régionale du Katanga*, 1930, 100–06.

86.  *Archives du Parquet d'Elisabethville*, Lubumbashi, *Sous-Commission du Katanga de la Commission pour la Protection des Indigènes, Comptes-rendus des réunions*, 1936.

87.  Mwendanga, 'Occupation économique', 129.

88.  *Rapport aux Chambres législatives sur l'administration de la Colonie du Congo Belge* (Brussels, 1932), 236; *Archives régionales du Shaba, Rapport Annuel Economique du Katanga*, 1937, 36.

89.  The sources from which Figure 1 had been compiled are: *Rapports aux Chambres législatives sur l'administration de la Colonie du Congo Belge*, 1920–33; *Rapports Annuels Economiques du Katanga*, 1924–5, 1929–30, 1933; Comité Spécial du Katanga, *Rapports annuels*, 1920–33; *Bulletin des Renseignements de l'Office Colonial*, 1920–33; *Comité Régional du Katanga*, 1920–33; *Archives régionales du Shaba, Rapport Economique Annuel du Haut-Luapula*, 1926, 1929.

With reference to the figure of 4,361 tonnes of food from the Belgian possessions in 1920, another source, *Comité Régional du Katanga*, 1921, gives 7,860 tonnes, which would seem more likely and would raise the overall total from 9,458 to 12,957 tonnes.

90.  In Figures 2A and 2B, 3A and 3B, wholesale prices in Elisabethville, in standard

francs, are based on the annual average prices fixed by government adjudication. See *Rapports Annuels Economiques du Katanga*, 1919–24, 1929; *Bulletin des Renseignements de l'Office Colonial*, 1920–1939. Purchase prices, in standard francs, are based on the purchase price to the producer in the Tanganika district. Given that in a number of cases the exact date when prices were recorded is not known, the gap between minimum and maximum prices (Figures 3A and 3B) reflects both geographical location and annual contingencies. Prices which are accidentally either too high or too low have theoretically been eliminated by virtue of the fact that the administrators provided either average prices or those which occurred most frequently. The calculations given are based on : *Archives régionales du Shaba, Rapports Semestriels Economiques du District du Tanganika*, 1924–1931; *Cours des transactions locales des territoires du Tanganika*, 1933; *Conseil de Province du Katanga*, 1936; Mwendanga, 'Occupation économique'; Malungu, 'La politique'. Figures 2A and 2B are based on the same sources as 3A and 3B, but are completed for Lomami on the basis of: *Archives régionales du Shaba, Rapports sur la situation des vivres indigènes*, 1931; *Cours des transactions locales*, 1934; *Conseil de Province du Katanga*, 1937. The semi-logarithmic scale makes it easier to see the evolution of the two curves in relation to each other, given that the gap between them is exactly proportional to their inter-relationship.

91.    In Figure 4 the standard franc of 1931 is calculated on the basis of the sources cited in note 91 and on the import price index worked out by Huybrechts, *Transports et structures*, 309–19. Given that a consumer price index exists only for European consumers, the calculation of a wider index is only possible on the basis of import prices.

The estimated wholesale prices in Elisabethville are arithmetic means for the year. Such an approach, though highly imperfect, was the only one possible. For some years I have two or three different price adjudications without unfortunately knowing the quantities bought, and it has therefore been impossible to balance my means. Seasonal variations in agricultural prices are much less important in Africa than in Europe, but cannot be altogether excluded. HKI has traditionally known a period of hunger at the beginning of the year. However, considerable purchases of food from the north of the province, where the climate is not the same as in the south, have played a moderating role. This triennial mean pattern allows us to remedy the haphazard character of certain unbalanced data.

92.    The sources from which Figure 5 has been compiled are: *Rapports aux Chambres législatives sur l'administration de la Colonie du Congo Belge*, 1921, 1925; *Rapports Annuels Economiques du Katanga*, 1928, 1932; Comité Spécial du Katanga, *Rapport Annual*, 1924; *Comité Régional du Katanga*, 1928–32; *Archives régionales du Haut-Zaïre, Rapport Annuel AIMO de la Province Orientale*, 1926.

93.    J.Ph. Peemans, 'The Social and Economic Development of Zaïre since Independence: An Historical Outline', *African Affairs*, 74, 295, 1975, 148–90.

# CHAPTER 14

## Thwarted Development: A Case Study of Economic Change in the Kabwe Rural District of Zambia, 1902–70

## MAUD MUNTEMBA

### Introduction

The part of Kabwe Rural district (to be referred to as Bulenje)[1] with which this chapter is concerned lies between the two important towns of Kabwe (formerly Broken Hill) and Lusaka, Zambia's capital since 1935. Kabwe has experienced a steady growth since 1906. In that year the railway, which in 1909 was to link South Africa and Southern Rhodesia to the copper mines of the Belgian Congo (now Zaïre), reached Broken Hill. This marked the beginning of the town's growth as the country's leading mining centre (lead and zinc), a position it held until the late 1920s when the Copperbelt mines came into full production. A depot for the railways was also established in the town, and in 1908 the *boma* (administrative post) for the Broken Hill sub-district was transferred there from Mwomboshi, some 20 kilometres to the south. Lusaka, on the other hand, did not expand as a town until it became the country's capital, though previously it had been the centre of a settler farming district and also contained a small limeworks industry which had attracted a few workers.

To the local people of Bulenje the towns and settler farmers provided a market for their agricultural produce and their fish. Despite the availability of such markets, however, Bulenje experienced setbacks which proved an impediment to rapid economic development. In isolating the reasons for these setbacks, the problem of marketing facilities aggravated by poor communications stands out as one of the most important. In 1950 T.S.L. Fox-Pitt, Provincial Commissioner for the Central Province of Northern Rhodesia, wrote:

> At present the will of the cultivator to turn his production to cash crops is often influenced by his confidence, or lack of it, in his ability to market his produce. Existing communications are poor, present marketing facilities are improvised and elementary. Consequently the primary producer of many areas has to take the risk of selling his surplus crops or of leaving them to rot uneaten. It is believed that there are many who, in present circumstances, are unwilling to take the risk.[2]

Generally speaking, this situation has continued into the 1970s. Lombard and Tweedie, writing in 1974, noted that although Zambia was rich in agricultural resources, it had thus far failed to exploit them. Some of the reasons for this failure lay in marketing difficulties arising from transport problems: 'There is the difficulty of actually moving the inputs to farmers on time, aggravated by the high cost of transport. . . . Many commodities can be grown only near their final markets because of their nature, and perishable crops in particular must be produced near markets.'[3]

Pricing policies and price fluctuations have also influenced the degree to which people participated in commercial agriculture as well as the types of crops they grew for the market. Thus, for example, at one time people turned from sorghum to maize because of the higher prices offered for maize.[4] But maize production slumped disastrously in 1969–70 and Zambia was faced with the problem of how to feed its population. Following a number of good crops and the creation of a substantial surplus, the government had tried to diversify farmers away from maize by reducing the price and restricting credit. The result was the slump of 1969–70.

Other constraints on Bulenje's economic development were a result of twentieth-century socio-political developments. The fact of colonialism meant that African participation in agriculture in terms of prices and what crops to grow was determined by the needs of the metropolitan economy. Furthermore, the country's internal market (provided by the mines) was officially monopolized by settler farmers, who insisted, often successfully, on the elimination of competition from African cultivators. African participation in the urban market was further handicapped by the creation in 1929 of 'native reserves', modelled on the Southern Rhodesian pattern, which effectively moved people farther away from the towns and main lines of communication. Land alienation and the consequent dislocation also deprived people of access to some of the best arable land in the country, and led to overcrowding and land shortage in some areas as population grew.

In Broken Hill the colonial government and the local mine management introduced the '5 acre plot' scheme, under which people could buy or rent plots on the outskirts of town, on which they grew vegetables and raised poultry. This was of great advantage to the urban workers, but it had the effect of undercutting the selling power of the rural people.

Finally, the period 1902–70 witnessed technological and technical innovation. This led to changes in the means of production and the distribution of labour, the result of which was an increased agricultural output but also the deprivation and consequent migration to urban centres of many women, despite the fact that women are generally the most productive unit in a non-highly-mechanized agricultural system.[5]

In order to understand the nature of twentieth century change, however, it is necessary to look briefly at the pre-colonial economic situation in Bulenje.

## The pre-colonial economic situation

A reconstruction of economic developments in Bulenje in the period before the twentieth century is greatly handicapped by the lack of sources. Furthermore, what sources are available are biased in favour of trade. Hardly any material exists as yet on the agricultural economy.[6]

It appears that the Lenje people were involved in long-distance trade with the Portuguese at Zumbo from the second half of the eighteenth and throughout most of the nineteenth century.[7] Sources suggest that in the early stages the Lenje used to journey to Zumbo, but that later the Portuguese agents, the *mussambazes,* travelled to Bulenje. It is possible that the Bisa, reputed as middlemen, acted in this capacity between the Portuguese and the Lenje.[8] In the nineteenth century the Arabs and the Ovimbundu (Mambari) traded with the Lenje, the latter coming in from Angola through Bulozi and Ilaland. The main items which the Lenje got from the traders were firearms, gunpowder, knives, cloth, and beads in return for ivory and slaves. It is not clear whether any currency was used. Some shells were found at Chief Chitanda's court, but except for one, they do not correspond with the shells commonly used for currency.[9]

Intensive inter-regional trade also existed. The Lenje traded with the Soli, from whom they obtained iron ore; with the Ila and Sala, from whom they got salt, cattle, copper, and ivory in return for iron ore; and they sold both iron ore and slaves to the Tonga in exchange for ivory, cattle, and salt.[10] In addition to this circular trade, the Lenje traded among themselves in commodities which were abundant in one area but scarce in another. Thus the people near the Lukanga Swamps traded fish for grain with 'mainland' cultivators.[11]

Despite the extent of such trade, it is clear from oral sources that industrial specialization was absent at this period, as was the case with the Shona, described in Chapter 1. Thus, for example, blacksmiths were involved in the same agricultural tasks as the rest of the population, while neither long-distance nor inter-regional trade generated the type of large-scale professional entrepreneurs who appeared in West Africa.[12]

Furthermore, the chiefs do not appear to have obtained a firm monopoly over long-distance trade, though clearly they had many advantages over individual entrepreneurs. Ivory and slaves were the main items of trade, for both of which chiefs were potentially a good source of supply. They were entitled to one tusk of each elephant killed by an individual under their jurisdiction, while tusks were also given to chiefs as tribute or as presents. Chiefs also tended to own substantial numbers of slaves, some of whom had been bought, others captured in raids, and others enslaved for debt. Because of such factors, traders tended to approach chiefs directly.[13] On the whole, any surpluses accumulated by the chiefs were used to build up their political power and hence redistributed to headmen and others of influence.

An interesting example of the impact of trade upon chieftainships is the frequent reference to Chipepo (Mamba or Momba) in the written sources.[14] Chipepo was not only nearer to Zumbo than the other Lenje chiefs, but after the break up of the unitary political system in the late eighteenth century, he retained the most important title of the *Mukuni,* the founder of the Lenje chieftainships.[15] Access to Zumbo meant that he was able to acquire more ivory and slaves and hence a larger following than his main rival, Chitanda, the most senior Lenje chief.[16] Between them, these two chiefs were the main participants in trade. Their areas, together with that of Chief Mukubwe, border on the Lukanga Swamps, where a fishing industry was established, and were also rich in iron and other minerals which the people worked.[17] The Lenje farther south, around what later became Lusaka, also worked iron, though the Soli were reputed to have been more prolific.[18]

## Pre-colonial agriculture

A comprehensive study of the dynamics of Bulenje's agriculture awaits further research. The discussion which follows is based on limited material and naturally tends to reflect the situation as it was in the latter part of the nineteenth century.[19]

Although maize may have been grown in Bulenje from the eighteenth century,[20] sorghum was the main crop produced and was the staple food. The scale and quantity of production have yet to be established, but by the second half of the nineteenth century the people were producing sufficient to escape the famines which hit neighbouring peoples and indeed to supply the Lamba when Lamba country was hit by famine in 1891–2.[21] Under precisely what terms this was done we do not know, but what is important is that surpluses existed. Long-distance trade may well have stimulated agricultural production, since those engaged in such trade had to be fed. A number of questions arise. Did the people, towards the end of the nineteenth century, consciously increase production with a view to selling the surplus, or did they merely sell surpluses when they happened to have them? The answer might well lie in the varying environmental factors. The ecological survey of the 1930s established that the areas farther away from the Lukanga Swamps were more suited to maize-growing than those closer to the swamps. It is likely, therefore, that those near to the swamps rarely produced a surplus, while those farther afield, situated on more productive soils, were able to aim at producing surpluses for sale. Maize, which was grown on a smaller scale than sorghum and was secondary to the people's own consumption, was almost certainly grown with a view to sale. This was certainly the pattern for most of the twentieth century.[22]

Land tenure in Bulenje can be described by the loose term

'communal ownership', if by this term we mean the right of every adult to have access to some land for purposes of cultivation. Land was vested in the chiefs and the headmen under him, who allocated it to the people for use. Provided there were no other claimants, a person could expand his boundaries as far afield as he could cultivate,[23] in accordance with the extensive system of agriculture practised. In the event of death, the rightful successor (except for slaves) could inherit the land if he so wished. Thus as long as an individual and his family used the land, he was considered to be its owner and the chief could not reclaim or reallocate it. Women also were allowed to own land[24] and hence every adult had access to some land.

The Lenje have practised a hoe cultivation for a long time. In the area around Lusaka, iron-making dates back to the eleventh or twelfth century,[25] while an early date has also been proposed for the workings in the eastern part of Bulenje.[26] In the nineteenth century the Lenje traded iron and hoes with the Soli. It can therefore safely be assumed that although the people practised a form of *citemene*,[27] the hoe was used to turn the soil. The axe too played an important role in agriculture, in cutting the trees in preparation for the *citemene*. Cattle were kept but did not play any significant part in agriculture. They could not be employed as draught animals before the introduction of the plough, and there is no evidence that manure was ever used for agricultural purposes.[28] Cattle seem to have been used for trading, for consumption, and for conspicuous wealth.[29]

The main Lenje labour unit was the family, comprising the man, his wife or wives, and unmarried wards. The man was responsible for clearing the fields, cutting the trees and digging up the soil in readiness for planting. However, in cases where the soil was not too hard, women could also dig. Women did the planting, weeding, scaring off of birds, harvesting, and storing. Sometimes villages organized work parties, and when this was done the same division of labour was observed.

It is clear therefore that while the man's productivity rate may have been higher than that of the woman in spheres such as hunting and warfare, in agriculture it was the woman who was dominant. The practice of rotating cultivation, the use of the hoe, the nature of the soil and the crops grown all necessitated high female participation. As a result, women had the right to dispose of the produce from their own fields as they wished.[30] Also, because some of the produce from men's fields went as tribute obligation, women were in a particularly advantageous position to trade their surplus.

## Twentieth-century change

In 1890 Alfred Sharpe declared the area west of the Luangwa and north of the Zambezi 'to be under British Protection'. By virtue of this declaration, Bulenje subsequently came under the colonial rule of

Cecil Rhodes's British South Africa Company.[31] This heralded an intensification of economic change by the strengthening of ties with the capitalist Southern African economic region.[32]

As the BSA Company was primarily interested in minerals, Bulenje and areas to the north, known to be mineral-bearing, were subjected to a great deal of prospecting, and some old mines were indeed found.[33] In order to tap these resources effectively, the Southern Rhodesian railway was extended northwards, crossing the Zambezi at the Victoria Falls in 1905. Lead, zinc, and vanadium were found at Broken Hill in 1902, and from 1906, when the railway arrived, the mine was in regular production. After the First World War production expanded, and by 1940 the African workforce totalled some 3,500.[34] The town grew in other spheres as well. In 1932 Rhodesia Railways moved their Northern Rhodesian headquarters from Livingstone to Broken Hill.[35] Government and missions also expanded their activities, and a number of independent workers were attracted to the town. By 1940 the total male workforce numbered 6,460, with a further 1,040 described as 'visitors and temporarily unemployed'.[36] To the north, the Copperbelt opened production in the late 1920s. In 1927 the mines were employing some 8,000 Africans, a figure which rose to 32,000 in 1930. Then came the Depression and the numbers showed a sharp decline, but rose again to over 30,000 by 1941. By 1946 the total African population of the Copperbelt towns was estimated at 200,000.[37] Lusaka also witnessed urban growth after being made the capital in 1935. In 1946 its African population was thought to be 15,000, rising to 50,000 by 1951.[38] Today Zambia is the most urbanized country on the continent after South Africa, with between 40 and 60 per cent of its population domiciled in the urban areas, some temporarily but most of them permanently.[39] Thus a large internal market was created by this growth of an urban population dependent upon others for supplies of food.

Another crucial aspect of economic change was the encouragement of settler farming by the colonial administration. The first trickle of settler farmers came in after the South African War in 1902, but despite the fact that land was extremely cheap—between 3d and 8d per acre for a while[40]—the number remained very small. By the end of 1904 there were only an estimated 850 Europeans in the entire country, many of whom were administrative officers, missionaries and mining prospectors. In 1911 there were some 159 white farmholdings, mainly concentrated along the line of rail, with a few at Abercorn (now Mbala) in the Northern Province and around Fort Jameson (Chipata) in the Eastern Province. By 1919 the number of settler farms along the line of rail had risen to 250, and remained at about this level until after 1940.[41] In spite of such discouraging figures, the BSA Company administration and the Northern Rhodesia government, which succeeded it in 1924, retained a firm belief in a future influx of white settlers. To make way for such an influx, land was alienated and 'native reserves' designated in 1928–9 along the line of rail and around Fort Jameson and Abercorn.[42] Soon after Africans were moved into these reserves, land shortages became apparent in the Eastern, Copperbelt, and part of the Central Province. Many of the areas from which Africans were evicted were given the label 'silent lands' because they remained unoccupied and in some parts attracted only the tsetse fly. Along the line of rail, where a settler influx might logically have been expected, many 'silent lands' were not taken up until after the Second World War, when there was an expansion in settler farming as the tobacco boom provided Northern Rhodesia with its first reliable export crop. Much of the land was abandoned once again in the 1960s, as many settlers left when Northern Rhodesia became Zambia. It was in the light of such circumstances that Governor Hubert Young and the Pim Commission of 1938 recommended a major overhaul of land policy, advocating the introduction of a 'native trust land' system, which would 'return' land to African use. This was finally adopted in an Order in Council of 1947.[43]

## African economic responses

Labour migration is one of the main factors which indicate the economic links which territories to the north of South Africa had with that country; it demonstrates the unequal nature of the relationship since most of the labour was channelled to the southern mines; and through it we discern some of the mechanisms employed to make the capitalist economy operate.

One of the earliest mechanisms used was that of tax. Ostensibly tax was introduced in order to pay for the costs of administering the territory, but it was also used effectively to push people out into wage-employment. Taxation was first imposed in North-Eastern Rhodesia (under whose jurisdiction Bulenje initially fell) in 1902, but the people of Bulenje did not respond enthusiastically to the call to become wage-labourers. One reason for this was the weakness of the administration and the consequent fact that tax was initially collected only in areas close to the *bomas*. In addition, early tax figures suggest that most people paid their tax in kind, in the form of agricultural produce or of 'free' labour.[44]

Indeed it was of crucial importance that the people were able to raise cash through agricultural sales. As the town of Broken Hill grew after 1906, so the market for such produce grew, and by 1915 a 'substantial number' of people were reported to be engaged in this means of raising cash. As a result, in that year only sixty-one people from the district were reported to be out at work in Southern Rhodesia, while none at all were said to have gone to South Africa. Two hundred and ten were working in the mines locally and at the Chilanga limeworks south of Lusaka. Some sub-districts reported that no people at all were leaving their homes in search of wage-labour. Year after year the colonial reports stressed the difficulties of recruiting labour from Bulenje. Moreover, those few who did go out to work did not earn the reputation of good employees; they tended to work for only six months at a time, and at the period when this did not clash with their own agricultural needs—a fact greatly resented by the settler farmers, who habitually complained of a shortage of labour.[45] In addition, Bulenje workers frequently 'deserted' and hence earned the name of 'here today, gone tomorrow'.[46] Thus in 1925 the District Commissioner for Broken Hill concluded sadly that 'the local native is not a keen labourer because of the many ways in which he could obtain money'.[47] The numbers of migrants did rise in the Depression years of the 1930s, but in 1938 the rate of absentees (10 per cent) was the lowest in the whole country with the exception of Livingstone (5 per cent), and in marked contrast to most parts of the Northern, Western, and Eastern Provinces which had absentee rates of over 40 per cent.[48]

It would appear therefore that people from Bulenje were among the earliest documented peasants in Northern Rhodesia. From the early 1910s and perhaps before, Bulenje cultivators could be termed peasants, if defined as 'those whose ultimate security and subsistence lies in their having certain rights in land and in the labour of family members on the land, but who are involved, through rights and obligations, in a wider economic system which includes the participation of non-peasants',[49] or as 'rural cultivators whose surpluses are transferred to a dominant group of rulers that uses the surpluses both to underwrite its own standard of living and to distribute the remainder to groups in society that do not farm but must be fed for their specific goods and services in turn'.[50] From 1915 there are constant reports of people taking advantage of the market and selling milk, eggs, poultry, vegetables, and grain to the growing towns.

That the people of Bulenje seized the opportunity to produce for the growing urban market leads on to the question of agricultural change in terms of crops, land tenure, and means of production. We noted earlier that in the nineteenth century sorghum was the most widely cultivated grain. In the twentieth century, however, there was a shift to maize production. This was due to the fact that maize demanded less labour and, as a non-perishable, was transportable and hence marketable over longer distances. Following the 1936 Maize Control Act, when the government fixed prices for the first time, Bulenje producers found it more profitable to grow maize than sorghum.[51]

After the Second World War the Northern Rhodesia government began for the first time to take a serious interest in African agriculture. Prior to this, its main concern had been to 'protect' settler farmers from African competition, as in the case of the quota system established by the Maize Control Board in 1936, which guaranteed three-quarters of the internal market to settler farmers. Though the Director of Agriculture complained about the lack of help for African agriculture in 1938,[52] he was ignored. The awakening of interest after 1945 was in fact directly related to the unhealthy state of the metropolitan economy and the perceived need to strengthen it by encouraging the colonies to produce 'economic', i.e. exportable, crops, such as cotton, groundnuts, tobacco, etc. Thus in East Africa, for example, the notorious 'groundnut scheme' was started in Tanganyika in 1946. It was also thought necessary to maximize industrial production and hence increase the urban working force. Agricultural production was required to expand to feed the new proletariat.

In Northern Rhodesia, in conformity with the new policies, the Kafue Basin, which included Bulenje, was earmarked for intensive agricultural development. The 'improved' and 'peasant' farming schemes were introduced in 1946 and 1948. They aimed at increasing production by teaching cultivators belonging to the schemes improved methods of farming, and by according them easier access to loans and fertilizers. A bonus scheme was also introduced which rewarded large producers. Prices for agricultural produce rose steeply after the war.

After some initial hesitation and suspicion, people responded favourably and in fact began to take the initiative, establishing farmers' co-operatives. A consumer co-operative, set up to supply inputs to local farmers, was established in 1948. This was abandoned in 1953 in favour of a producer co-operative which had two branches in Bulenje, each commanding two to three depots, and which acted as a buying agent on behalf of the producers. Bulenje's favourable response is reflected in the steady increase in production (with the exception of the poor season of 1949), as illustrated in the following table on maize production:

| Year | Central Province | Broken Hill district |
|------|------------------|----------------------|
| 1948 |                  | 19,000 bags[a]       |
| 1949 |                  | 3,350 bags           |
| 1950 | 38,000 bags[b]   |                      |
| 1951 | 75,000 bags[c]   |                      |
| 1953 | 132,433 bags     |                      |

[a]  Some maize was left unsold due to a shortage of bags.
[b]  Mainly from Mumbwa and Broken Hill districts.
[c]  Mainly from Broken Hill district.

The 1960s however witnessed great fluctuations in maize production as a result of unstable prices. When, in the face of a substantial maize surplus, government lowered the price and restricted credit, the producers in large number stopped producing in 1969–70, and Zambia 'literally scoured the world for maize'.[53]

There was also an upward trend in crops such as cotton and legumes. Cotton was introduced as a cash crop to the Central Province after 1961. 'In 1964, Africans sold 33 per cent of the crop; by 1971 almost all the marketed cotton came from Africans', the largest proportion from that part of the Central Province to the west of Lusaka, an area which includes Bulenje. By this time both the quantity and the quality of the crop had risen tremendously.[54]

This increase in output is sometimes attributed to the arrival in the Kabwe Rural district of Shona and Ndebele farmers from Southern Rhodesia. There is certainly some truth in this, but since the majority of these farmers entered the country after 1953, by which time the increase in production was already becoming marked, we need to look to changes in the means of production for a more adequate explanation.

We have already seen that the people of Bulenje practised a hoe cultivation which enabled some of them to produce a surplus. But these surpluses must have remained limited in quantity since the area cultivated by a family at any one time was never more than a few acres.[55] The introduction of the ox-drawn plough, however, beginning on a small scale in the 1920s, enabled the people to cultivate larger acreages which in turn gave them larger yields. Though only a total of 1,777 ploughs were recorded for the district in 1953, this does not mean that only that number of families utilized ploughs, since they generally served more than one family, while some plough-owners found the hiring out of ploughs a lucrative business. Indeed it has been recorded from one district of the Central Province that some plough-owners actually preferred to do this rather than produce marketable crops themselves.[56] The use of the plough, as well as other agricultural implements such as weeders and scotch carts, led to the incorporation of cattle, as draught animals, into agriculture. Thus a new dimension in people's attitude to cattle was generated, as cattle became an investment and a saleable commodity with enhanced economic value.

By the late 1950s only a few people were able to afford tractors, and it was not until after political independence in 1964, when loans were made available, that the tractor began to make an impressive appearance in Bulenje. We do not know the numbers of tractors bought and used in the district, but at the time of independence, some 94 per cent of the 257 African-owned tractors in the country were concentrated in the Southern and Central Provinces.[57] However, a substantial number of people who bought them found that they were costly and difficult to maintain. The government thus found it extremely difficult to recover the loans granted, and by the end of the 1960s the reliance on tractors as a means to rapid economic development was abandoned, and there was a general return to the use of the ox-drawn plough.

Alongside change in agricultural technology went advance in agricultural techniques. That the people had always been aware of the need to fertilize the soil can be seen in the practice of the *citemene,* but the intensive labour required for this limited the acreage which could be cultivated and hence the resulting yields. *Citemene* was still in use in Bulenje in the 1930s,[58] and possibly also in the early 1940s.

After the war, and especially after 1964, people were encouraged by government to use artificial fertilizers and also to practise crop rotation. Slowly they responded to this, and by 1970 the use of fertilizers was commonplace. Other technical information such as the use of anti-pest sprays and the necessity and methods of avoiding soil erosion were being slowly disseminated and appreciated. It cannot be denied that such developments affected the productivity rate and production output advantageously.[59] It is in the light of this technological and technical change that we must understand the Shona and Ndebele contribution. Most Shona and Ndebele who came to the district in the 1950s came equipped with the technological knowledge they had acquired in Southern Rhodesia. Indeed it has been shown that a large proportion of those who moved to Northern Rhodesia had left their homeland precisely because they were unable effectively to utilize their knowledge, and had suffered economic frustration as 'progressive' farmers.[60]

The question of technological change leads us to consider the nature of production units during this period. We have noted that despite the advent of the tractor, the ox-drawn plough remained the main agricultural tool. Moreover, in spite of the use of other implements, a fully mechanized agriculture has not yet emerged, and most of the work continues to depend upon human power. The ox-drawn plough is itself a labour-intensive implement requiring at least four people—to lead the oxen, handle the plough, hold the rear, and to plant. By 1970 a few people were able to afford occasional hired labour,[61] but in the main the family continued to be the major production unit and work parties still operated.

But there was a shift in the distribution of labour roles. Because the plough and the growing of cash crops are so labour-intensive, people could not afford to stick to their traditional roles if they were to succeed. The movement away from the *citemene,* technological change, and the nature of the dissemination of new knowledge (which was officially confined to men since to the colonial mind only men could be farmers), all contributed to a new distribution of labour roles, with a much less clearly defined division of labour than hitherto. Compared to former days, the productivity rate of men began to increase. In such circumstances, Boserup argues, the productivity rate of women tends to drop or remain static.[62] This does not seem to be the case, however, where women are as involved in cash-crop growing as men. Rather, the female productivity rate also increases, so that their rate of productivity remains higher than that of men.

Another industry that took on new dimensions in the twentieth century was that of fishing. We have noted that in the earlier period the Lukanga fisherman traded in fish with 'mainland' cultivators. In the twentieth century the growth of urban markets stimulated large-scale fishing. In 1926 fish was mentioned as one of the items, together with agricultural produce, which was sold at the Broken Hill mine market; by 1928 Lukanga fishermen were supplying the town with all its requirements; and from the 1930s fish from Lukanga were sold in Kitwe, and later in Luanshya and Lusaka.[63] Reports indicate however that in the late 1920s and early 1930s the industry was not as prosperous as it might have been, given the expanding market, and the colonial government at one point contemplated offering assistance.[64] There is no evidence that this was ever done. From the 1940s onwards the industry became more prosperous as a result of the people's own initiative. In 1948 the 'Lenje Native Treasury' realized £100 from the sale of fishing licences, and a number of fish pedlars were reported in 1952. A fish marketing survey estimated that there were some 600–700 people earning their living by fishing in the year 1964–5. The number would certainly have been higher had the definition of fishermen been stretched to include those who fished part-time.[65]

The fishermen did not travel to town themselves but used middlemen. Who these were has yet to be firmly established, but it is likely that in the initial stages it was mostly the local people themselves, with people from other parts of the country moving in later. Certainly by 1935 this had become the case, for in that year the 'Lenje Native Authority' took steps to restrict the actual fishing to local people, while offering no objection to middlemen coming in to buy.[66] This decision was probably taken because more and more local people were engaging themselves in agriculture. This can be seen in the 'Lenje-ization' of the Twa, the traditional fishermen. The 'mainland' Lenje have always had a certain aversion to fishing, and had left it in the hands of the Twa. By 1970 those Twa who claimed to be Lenje had also adopted this attitude and had become agriculturalists. By this time most of the fishing villages and camps consisted of Luvale peoples from the Northwest Province, Malawians, and some people from the Luapula and Northern Provinces. Nevertheless, the arrival of such people enlarged the fishing industry, and the establishment of a fishing camp and installation of a refrigeration plant on the eastern side of the swamps after independence has boosted the industry further.

There were few trading stores or hawkers in Bulenje. As late as 1950 the local district commissioner bewailed the fact that 'apart from the retail of normal consumer goods, African trade is largely limited to the sale and purchase of agricultural produce and fish'.[67] The following year he commented 'There is little evidence that Africans are much interested in commerce and that those in the towns who have a commercial bent are anxious to venture out in the countryside.'[68] The few shops that were established in the area were in the hands of Asians, but these were on the outskirts of the 'Lenje Reserve' since the 'Native Authority' refused to issue licences to Asians, for fear that they might undercut potential local businessmen. Within the 'reserve' itself a few shops were established in the 1960s, mainly by people from outside the area. There was little local involvement in handicrafts either; what was produced came mostly from the Luano valley, the most infertile area in Bulenje and the one most hampered by lack of transport. Such negative responses do not reflect a lack of business aptitude, but rather a realization that commercial ventures involved both heavier capital investment and a slower rate of profit than either agriculture or fishing. The people of Bulenje deliberately chose activities which were more immediately rewarding.

## Constraints on economic development

The above account of twentieth-century developments shows how Bulenje became more agriculturally oriented whereas earlier there had been greater participation in other areas of trade, and how the people responded positively to the opportunities of the new urban market. But at this point we need to examine the nature of the various constraints on development.

This paper began with quotations from Fox-Pitt in 1950 and from Lombard and Tweedie in 1974, to the effect that the greatest handicap to Zambia's agricultural development was the existence of numerous marketing difficulties connected with the transport problem. Thus we find that although markets existed in Broken Hill, Lusaka, and the Copperbelt towns, the problem of communications in some parts of Bulenje remained acute.

Until 1936, when the Maize Control Board was established, the Northern Rhodesia government had not concerned itself with African agriculture. It followed that no facilities were made available. Thus although commodities such as vegetables, eggs, milk, grain, and fish were sold, the lack of marketing facilities meant that not many people were able to participate in the sale of these perishable commodities. Consequently, only those who lived in close proximity to the towns benefited from such trade. This state of affairs had not changed by 1970, when the people living away from the towns and the main lines of communication remained excluded from trade in perishables.

The core of the communications network was the railway. It was adjacent to the line of rail that the towns grew up, that white settlement occurred, and that the main road was built. Communications were thus concentrated in this narrow area, with a few feeder roads leading off to administrative stations. With this in mind it is possible to appreciate the economic discrepancies which emerged in Bulenje. To take the two areas discussed in the pre-colonial period, Chipepo's and Chitanda's, which had both participated in long-distance trade: Chipepo's area included the site on which the town of Broken Hill grew, and hence many of his people were able to sell perishable foodstuffs to the town; Chitanda's area, however, lay at some distance to the south-west, and consequently while some of his people did trade with the town, the trade was confined to non-perishable grains, such as maize, and to dried fish. But even here the means of transportation, initially walking, which took some days, and later bicycles, when they became available, precluded extensive participation in trade. When after 1945 the government began to buy more directly from the people, distances from the villages to the main feeder roads, on which the depots were located, determined to what extent people were able to sell. Furthermore, distances affected the amount of money people finally received for their produce. Those from Chipepo's got more, and therefore had greater incentive than the people from Chitanda's. With regards the fishing industry, the feeder road running through Chitanda's did not reach the Lukanga Swamps. Another road, improved since independence, runs from Kabwe to the eastern side of the swamps (in Chipepo's area), where the fishing camp and refrigeration plant are situated. Thus in both agriculture and the fishing industry Chitanda's area was participating less than it might have done, and economic activities tended to shift from the area largely because of the marketing difficulties.

Another major constraint was closely linked with the question of colonialism and capitalism. When the BSA Company extracted its fraudulent concessions from African chiefs and established itself as an administration, it undercut African participation in small-scale mining industries. The quality and quantity of African mining is immaterial; what is important is the fact that the BSA Company determined what areas and roles of economic participation Africans would henceforth be assigned to. Trade in minerals and in ivory was denied to them, and the development of a diversified economy, such as had existed before, was precluded. Their role in such industries was one of supplying labour, while the profits accrued now went into foreign hands.

Because they had become tied to the world capitalist economy, the people could no longer determine the prices of their produce, with inevitable effects on their rate of production, as witnessed during the Depression. What crops they could grow and the amount of aid they could get from government were also determined by the needs of the metropolitan economy. Thus African agriculture was neglected for many years, and when official interest was at last expressed, it was to the effect that the people should grow 'economic' crops and those which 'could not be converted into beer'[69]—a neat way of saying that they should grow crops for export. The fact that choices were determined by the needs of the metropolitan countries clearly limited the people's participation in agriculture, since those who could not grow 'economic' crops, either because they lacked the expertise or because their ecology and geographical location did not permit it, were excluded.

Further limitations were imposed by the alienation of much excellent land to settler farmers. The Land Commission of 1946, discussing the Broken Hill district, observed 'In the central and the southern portion immediately south of Broken Hill and at Chisamba, there occur stretches of the Upper Valley types of soils . . . which

constitute the best yet found for general agricultural purposes and
also the best grazing land. Nearly all the available Crown Land of this
category has already been taken up by Europeans.'[70] The 'Lenje
Native Reserve', into which Africans were moved after 1929, totalled
some 17,300 sq. km, of which 5,200 sq. km comprised the Lukanga
Swamps. Of the remaining 12,100 sq. km, less than 40 per cent was
cultivable.[71] Some of the 40 per cent comprised the 'Older Ironstone
Soils', about which the 1937 Ecological Survey had commented,
'Under this head are designated partially denuded soils of the older
land surfaces. . . . These "fossil" soils are exemplified on the Lusaka
limestones, but are best preserved along the Congo border and
towards the Lukanga Swamp. . . . Except that they are employed by
natives for finger millet cultivation, they are agriculturally useless.'[72]
Yet finger millet, easily convertible into beer but not as easy to grow
as maize, was not a marketable crop.

It is in the context of land alienation that we must appreciate the
nature of congestion and land shortage in the 'Lenje Native Reserve'.
The 1946 Land Commission noted that there was congestion in the
eastern part of the 'reserve' due to soil infertility and a lack of water,
which led to a concentration along the Mufukushi river.[73] The census
of 1969 showed a population increase of 19.8 per cent over that of 1963
for Kabwe Rural district as a whole, and revealed a man to land ratio
of ten persons per square mile (about four per sq. km). This figure
may not appear disastrous when compared to much higher densities
in the Southern and Eastern Provinces, but the nature of the soils in
the 'reserve' meant that there were high concentrations in the more
suitable agricultural areas. Thus areas whose ecology was suited to
cash-crop growing became densely populated and land shortages
ensued; in Chief Mungule's area the 'peasant farmer' scheme could
not be introduced because there was insufficient land available. The
shortage of land was further reflected in the enhanced value which
land had acquired by 1970, by which time there was a shift from
territorial to local (i.e. individual) land disputes.[74] It is possible too
that land has become a commodity to be rented or sold under the
pretext of 'improvement' sales. While this development might well
lead to increases in output, it also means that some people who have
always had access to land will find themselves landless or assigned to
less productive land. The result will be, and indeed has already been,
a movement towards the urban centres on the part of the less
privileged.

It is within this context that we must understand female migration.
Most women in the district, belonging to a matrilineal (Lenje) society,
had been entitled to own and inherit land. With the new developments
discussed in this chapter, however, more inheritance rights were
being challenged and some widowed women no longer had as much
access to the best lands as hitherto. Added to this was the fact that the
colonial mind had never associated agriculture with women, hence all
the advice, loans, etc. were restricted to men, a practice unfortu-

nately continued after independence;[75] that women were forced
therefore to deal through men; that by the removal of the market from
the home base, they were no longer in a position to handle their own
sales—all this produced frustrations in women, who had previously
been quite economically independent of their menfolk. The 1969
census revealed a total of 52,496 men and only 50,611 women in
Kabwe Rural—an unusual male preponderance in a country where
typically males have migrated to the urban areas in large numbers.
Since the female productivity rate in agriculture was higher than the
male, this emigration by women must have had adverse effects on
production.

Land alienation and the creation of the 'Lenje Native Reserve' also
had the effect of moving the people farther away from the markets,
and, given the nature of the transport available, this must have
affected the quantities of their sales. The movement also set limits on
participation in the sale of perishable commodities. The local people
around Kabwe, for example, had always supplied milk to the town.
People from slightly farther afield had often brought their cows into
villages near the town, milked them, and sold the milk in town. The
demarcation of the 'native reserve' in 1929 moved the people over 30
km from the town and also deprived them of their grazing lands.
Consequently, milk vendors experienced great hardships as they
were forced to rent land for pasture near the town, while those from
farther off had to abandon their sales altogether.[76]

We have also to consider the influence of the settlers on the
government. Despite official protestations concerning the
'paramountcy of native interests', there was in practice a strong bias
towards settler and South African interests. Thus until 1936 the
supply of grain and cattle to the mines and townships was theoretically a preserve of the settler farmers.[77] Only if they failed to meet the
requirements could these be bought from Africans, who tended to
conduct their sales mainly on a door to door basis in the compounds
and at the compound markets. This attempted monopoly obviously
meant that Africans were unable to sell as much as they might wish.
When the sale of maize from Africans could no longer be effectively
controlled, settler farmers pressed successfully for the Maize Control
Act of 1936, which guaranteed them the lion's share of the internal
market.

Lastly, the Broken Hill mine management introduced the '5-acre
plot' scheme in the late 1920s. The object was to retain its labour force
which might otherwise have been tempted by the higher wages being
offered at the newly opened mines on the Copperbelt. It was also
hoped to procure a cheaper supply of vegetables for its workers, but
this was abandoned in the face of government opposition. The
government supported the scheme in the hopes of luring older miners
and independent workers away from the mining townships. By 1940
some 6,670 men, women, and children out of a total population of
15,000 were living on c.920 plots.[78] Here they grew grain and

vegetables in large quantities, and raised poultry. While this directly benefited the plot-holders themselves, it had the effect of depriving rural sellers of about half of the Broken Hill market. As a result they were obliged to turn to the more distant markets of Lusaka and the Copperbelt towns.

## Conclusion

In this paper we have identified typical problems confronting a rural economy within a colonial capitalist framework. We have shown why, despite the presence of expanding urban markets, twentieth-century economic changes did not lead to progressive development for Kabwe Rural district as a whole, or for Bulenje in particular. The market was there, the will of the people to take full advantage of this was there also, but the operational framework with vested interests elsewhere imposed serious constraints. Peasant agriculture has become the basis of the economy of Bulenje, but peasant agriculture was and is part of a market system regulated by the demands of the mining sector, and therefore ultimately by the Western capitalist metropoles. Peasant agriculture was essentially subordinate to capitalist estate agriculture, run by white settlers, which took the best land and the best market terms and communications. This subordination has remained part of the given structure of the post-colonial state, since Zambia is an appendage of international capitalism. Consequently the people's aspirations continue to be only partially fulfilled and a move towards progressive 'rural development' thwarted.

## NOTES

1.  Bulenje derives its name from the majority of its residents, the Lenje. The area falls under the jurisdiction of six Lenje chiefs, although there are a number of non-Lenje: Tonga, Kaonde, Ila, Mbwera, plus Shona and Ndebele from Southern Rhodesia, and some people from Tanzania. From 1899 to 1905 Bulenje formed part of North-Eastern Rhodesia, after which it was transferred to North-Western Rhodesia (and from 1911 Northern Rhodesia) and fell under the jurisdiction of four administrative units: Mumbwa sub-district, Ndola district, Chilanga sub-district, and Broken Hill sub-district. When 'native reserves' were created in 1929, all four components were brought together to form the 'Lenje Native Reserve' in the Broken Hill district. The boundaries of Bulenje have remained unaltered since then and today Bulenje comprises the largest part of the Kabwe Rural district.
2.  National Archives of Zambia, SEC/NAT/66B, Report of the P/C Central Province for the year 1950.
3.  C.S. Lombard and A.H.C. Tweedie, *Agriculture in Zambia since Independence* (Lusaka, 1974), 1, 19.
4.  Interview with G. Shipekwa and S. Shibeleka, 1 March 1975.
5.  Ester Boserup came to this conclusion after studying agricultural change in many Third World countries: E. Boserup, *Women's Role in Economic Development*

(London, 1970), 31–5, 53–7.

6.  The current research of the author will focus on this question and it is hoped that this will throw some light on the pre-colonial agricultural economy.

7.  N. Sutherland-Harris, 'Zambian Trade with Zumbo in the Eighteenth Century', in R. Gray and D. Birmingham (eds), *Pre-Colonial African Trade* (London, 1970), 231–42.

8.  A.D. Roberts, 'Pre-Colonial Trade in Zambia', *African Social Research, 10*, 1970, 728–9.

9.  National Archives of Zambia, KDA 2/1, Broken Hill District Notebook; also inspected by the author, 1969.

10.  M.P. Miracle, 'Plateau Tonga Entrepreneurs in Historical Inter-Regional Trade', *Rhodes-Livingstone Journal, 26*, 1959, 34–50; interviews collected in the field, 1969, 1971.

11.  The Twa people of the swamps are said to have built their shelters on the swamp marshes. They were moved to the 'mainland' in the 1920s in order to facilitate taxation. F.B. Macrae, 'The Batwa in the Broken Hill District', *NADA, 7*, 1929, 63–75; H.P. Haile, 'Chilwa Island in the Lukanga Swamp', *Northern Rhodesia Journal, 3*, 1958, 381–6.

12.  A.G. Hopkins, *An Economic History of West Africa* (London, 1973), 8–123.

13.  Part of the rivalry between the chiefs Chitanda and Chipepo dates back to this period. M. Muntemba, 'The Evolution of Political Systems in South-Central Zambia, 1894–1953', MA thesis, University of Zambia, 1973, 34–5.

14.  Sutherland-Harris, 'Zambian Trade', 236–7; National Archives of Zambia, KDA 2/1, Broken Hill District Notebook.

15.  Muntemba, 'Political Systems', 28–31.

16.  Muntemba, 'Political Systems', 34–8.

17.  In 1902, a representative of the BSA Company noted, with reference to Chitanda's area, that 'people own cattle but secrete them away. They are great workers in iron, country full of iron ore, oxide.' Public Record Office, London, CO 468/2, British South Africa Company, Information as to Mining in Rhodesia, 1902.

18.  D.W. Phillipson, 'Excavations at Twickenham Road, Lusaka', *Azania, 5*, 1970, 112–18.

19.  One topic which particularly requires further examination is the relationship between trade and the agricultural economy. Did trade stimulate agricultural production; did an assurance of food supplies strengthen trade, releasing men to engage in trading activities; might this not push back further in time the date when the region became tied to the world economy?

20.  Maize came into Central Africa with the Portuguese. The introduction of the crop into Bulenje may have come from direct trading contacts with the Portuguese or as a result of movements of people into Zambia from Angola. Further research should elucidate this.

21.  W. Allan, *The African Husbandman* (Edinburgh and London, 1965), 46–7; C.P. Luchembe, 'Rural Stagnation: A Case Study of the Lamba-Lima of Ndola Rural District', in R.H. Palmer (ed.), *Zambian Land and Labour Studies, Vol. 2*, National Archives of Zambia Occasional Paper 3 (Lusaka, 1974), 24.

22.  This was the opinion expressed by G. Shipekwa, S. Shibeleka, and E. Shipekwa, interviewed 1 March 1975.

23.  Nevertheless due to the implements used, the acreage under cultivation was not vast. By the 1930s most people still cultivated about four to five acres. C.G. Trapnell and J.N. Clothier, *The Soils, Vegetation and Agricultural Systems of North Western Rhodesia* (Lusaka, 1937), 34–5.

24.  The Lenje, who form the majority of Bulenje's residents, are a matrilineal society where women are entitled, by right, to ownership and inheritance of property, and to have access to land.

25.  Phillipson, 'Excavations', 77–118.

26.  Personal communication from David Phillipson.

27. The local word is in fact *cibibi*, but *citemene* is used technically as the word most commonly found in the literature.

28. In the twentieth century, some cultivators attempted to use manure. But because a cattle *kraal* was used by more than one person, this presented problems and was abandoned. Interview with G. Shipekwa *et al.*, 1 March 1975.

29. R.J. Fielder, 'The Role of Cattle in the Ila Economy: A Conflict of Views on the Uses of Cattle by the Ila of Namwala', *African Social Research, 15,* 1973, 327−61. Here Fielder looks at cattle as a social and economic investment, and there are some similarities between Ila and Lenje socio-cultural modes.

30. See also Boserup, *Women's Role,* Chapters 1−3. Current research by the author will further elucidate this *vis-à-vis* Bulenje.

31. L.H. Gann, *A History of Northern Rhodesia: Early Days to 1953* (London, 1964), 62. J.H. Clarke, in charge of the Broken Hill beerhall, claimed in 1926 that separate treaties had been extracted from the Lenje chiefs which were never acknowledged by the BSA Company. But until such time as these are located, we shall continue to treat this statement with caution.

32. Early traders and travellers such as Westbeech and Selous first established links with the Southern African region, but it was only when full-blooded capitalism in the form of the BSA Company arrived that such links were noticeable and felt.

33. Public Record Office, CO 468/2, British South Africa Company, Information as to Mining in Rhodesia, 1902; J.A. Bancroft, *Mining in Northern Rhodesia* (Salisbury, 1961).

34. G. Wilson, *An Essay on the Economics of Detribalization in Northern Rhodesia, Part 1* (Livingstone, 1941), 19.

35. A.H. Croxton, *Railways of Rhodesia* (Newton Abbot, 1973), 173.

36. Wilson, *Detribalization,* 19.

37. L.H. Gann, 'The Northern Rhodesian Copper Industry and the World of Copper: 1923−52', *Rhodes-Livingstone Journal, 18,* 1955, 6, 7, 10.

38. National Archives of Zambia, SEC/NAT/66B, Report of the P/C Central Province for the years 1946 and 1951.

39. Lombard and Tweedie, *Agriculture in Zambia,* 1.

40. R.H. Palmer, 'Land in Zambia', in Palmer (ed.), *Zambian Land and Labour Studies, Vol. 1,* National Archives of Zambia Occasional Paper 2 (Lusaka, 1973), 57. See also M.Y. Jones, 'The Politics of White Agrarian Settlement in Northern Rhodesia, 1898−1928', MA thesis, University of Sussex, 1974, 33−4.

41. F. Carpenter, 'The Introduction of Commercial Farming into Zambia and its Effects, to 1940', in Palmer (ed.), *Zambian Land and Labour Studies, Vol. 1,* 4.

42. Palmer, 'Land in Zambia', 58−60.

43. Palmer, 'Land in Zambia', 63−4.

44. British South Africa Company, *Reports on the Administration of Rhodesia, 1900−02* (London, 1903), 408.

45. Taken from various annual reports.

46. National Archives of Zambia, KDA 2/1, Broken Hill District Notebook.

47. National Archives of Zambia, KDA 8/2/1, Report of the D/C Broken Hill for the year ending March 1925.

48. J.A. Hellen, *Rural Economic Development in Zambia, 1890−1964* (Munich, London, and New York, 1968), 96.

49. J.S. Saul and R. Woods, 'African Peasantries', in T. Shanin (ed.), *Peasants and Peasant Societies* (Harmondsworth, 1971), 105.

50. E.R. Wolf, *Peasants* (Englewood Cliffs, NJ, 1966), 3−4.

51. Interview with G. Shipekwa *et al.*, 1 March 1975. On the impact of the Maize Control Act in the Southern Province, see K. Vickery, 'Aspects of Plateau Tonga Economic History', in R.H. Palmer (ed.), *Zambian Land and Labour Studies, Vol. 3,* National Archives of Zambia Occasional Paper 4 (Lusaka, 1977), 70.

52. *The Minutes of Proceedings at the First and Second Meetings of the Native Development Board* (Lusaka, 1938), 12−17.

53.   Lombard and Tweedie, *Agriculture in Zambia*, 22. See also S.C. Nolutshungu, *South Africa in Africa* (Manchester, 1975), 200.

54.   Lombard and Tweedie, *Agriculture in Zambia*, 34.

55.   Trapnell and Clothier, *The Soils*, 34—5.

56.   N. Long, *Social Change and the Individual* (Manchester, 1968), 24.

57.   Lombard and Tweedie, *Agriculture in Zambia*, 81.

58.   Trapnell and Clothier, *The Soils*, 33—5.

59.   Mutsau cites figures of Shona and Ndebele farmers producing between 460 and 1,002 bags in 1972. R.J. Mutsau, 'The Shona and Ndebele Settlements in Kabwe Rural Area, 1953—63', in Palmer (ed.), *Zambian Land and Labour Studies, Vol. 1*, 46.

60.   Mutsau, 'The Shona and Ndebele', 43—6, R. H. Palmer, *Land and Racial Domination in Rhodesia* (London, 1977), 244.

61.   Until September 1971, the minimum daily agricultural wage was 55 ngwee. It was then raised to 70 ngwee, a figure which most peasant farmers are unable to pay.

62.   Boserup, *Women's Role*, 53.

63.   Taken from various annual reports.

64.   *Report on the Native Fishing Industry by J. Moffat Thomson* (Livingstone, 1930), 5—6.

65.   *Results of a Fish Market Survey in Zambia, 1964—1965* (Lusaka, 1969).

66.   *Native Affairs Annual Report for the year 1935* (Lusaka, 1936), 17.

67.   National Archives of Zambia, SEC/NAT/66B, Report of the D/C Broken Hill for the year 1950.

68.   National Archives of Zambia, SEC/NAT/66B, Report of the D/C Broken Hill for the year 1951.

69.   Public Record Office, CO 795/3, Governor Stanley to Colonial Secretary, October 1924.

70.   *Report of the Land Commission* (Lusaka, 1946), 35—6.

71.   *Report of the Land Commission*, 38.

72.   Trapnell and Clothier, *The Soils*, 5.

73.   *Report of the Land Commission*, 38.

74.   The anthropologist Richard Canter, who has worked in Bulenje since 1970, has noted that many cases which ostensibly centre on other issues are in fact basically land problems. Personal communication from Richard Canter.

75.   The Keembe Farm Institute did arrange courses for women prior to independence, but these were mostly confined to poultry. In 1975 the Chipembi Farm College had only one woman enrolled in a course.

76.   Wilson, *Detribalization*, 25; Interview with G. Shipekwa *et al.*, 1 March 1975.

77.   Public Record Office, CO 795/85, Memorandum on Policy in Northern Rhodesia, 1936.

78.   Wilson, *Detribalization*, 20, 22, 24.

# CHAPTER 15

## Railway Development and Colonial Underdevelopment: The Nyasaland Case[1]

### LEROY VAIL

*It is a gigantic task that we have undertaken when we have determined to wield the sceptre of empire. Great is the task, great is the responsibility, great is the honour.* Joseph Chamberlain, 1897

*I loathe everything to do with Nyasaland Railways.*
Sir John Campbell, financial adviser to the Colonial Office, 1938

## Introduction

Nyasaland was known as the 'Cinderella' of the British Empire as early as the 1920s.[2] As a Cinderella she has long been recognized in Southern Africa as an important supplier of human labour for the area's mines. In this chapter I shall argue that her role as an exporter of labour was forced upon her by the working out of two policy decisions made early in her colonial history. First, the imperial government's decision to rely upon a small and undercapitalized white settler community on the Shire Highlands resulted in the treating of the African peasant community as little more than a source of labour for these settlers, accompanied by neglect of the possibility of establishing an African peasant cash-crop economy. Secondly, decisions to construct the railway that serviced Nyasaland were taken in such a way as to prevent a shift from reliance on the chronically unprosperous European settlers to reliance upon African peasant agriculture when the error of the first decision was fully realized in the 1920s. The railway development, which was not initially conceived of as benefiting Nyasaland, in the 1920s and 1930s functioned as an impoverishing factor that prevented the Protectorate's government from establishing a viable internal economy and ultimately caused her to pursue a policy of encouraging labour migration to the mines. Although it has been assumed that Nyasaland's railways were of benefit to her development, I shall demonstrate that they did her and her people great harm in the colonial era and that they were the principal reason for the Nyasaland Protectorate's emerging from the colonial situation to independence with a distorted and dislocated economy.[3]

365

## Settlers, labour supplies, and the Shire Highlands Railway, 1892–1908

For both the imperial government in London and the colonial administration in Zomba, the British Central African Protectorate was, in the early years of this century, little more than the Shire Highlands and the Shire river valley. Enjoying fertile soil, abundant rainfall, and a hospitable climate, the Highlands were considered the only area of the country that was potentially suitable for large-scale European agriculture. Colonies and protectorates were expected to pay their own way, and from the beginning of the Protectorate's administration the government saw the European settlers as potentially important sources of tax revenue. Although missionaries such as Alexander Hetherwick argued that 'the one hope of British Central Africa is in the cultivation of its own soil by the hands of its own children', the colonial administration did not see the situation in this way.[4] It viewed the settlers as economically paramount and endeavoured to satisfy their wishes and needs as best it could. Coffee, cotton, tea, and tobacco were all envisaged as crops that would turn the Highlands into a Central African El Dorado and thus provide the economic base that would pay for the costs of the local administration. None did, but the hope was always present.

From the beginning of European settlement one of the settlers' main concerns was the problem of securing adequate labour supplies. Their inefficient plantations were labour-intensive, and labour was chronically in short supply.[5] That the plantations were not the sole important employers of labour in the Protectorate greatly aggravated this problem. The planters had to compete with the various transport companies that served British Central Africa and, via Lake Malawi, the areas around Lakes Mweru and Tanganyika. These transport companies needed abundant labour for the porterage of head-carried loads from depots on the Lower Shire river up the steep escarpment to the Shire Highlands, and thence from the Highlands to the Upper Shire river for transport on water to the Lake and northwards. The demand for such porterage was immense as this route was the principal route into Central Africa from the east, and there were generally inadequate numbers of men, women, and children to handle the task. In late 1899, for example, 100,000 loads were lying in store on the Lower Shire river awaiting transport up the escarpment.[6] The planters well realized that the casual labour demanded by the transport companies was a constant drain upon the Protectorate's labour reserves and a constant threat to their own survival.

To this challenge and to the challenge presented by the recruitment of labour within the Protectorate for work outside it, the planting community responded vocally. They successfully lobbied the local administration in 1899 to forbid the recruiting of labour inside the Protectorate for work outside it, hoping thereby to preserve their pool of cheap local labour.[7] And to divert labour from the transport companies to the plantations, the settlers pressed for many years for the construction of a railway that would permit goods to be imported and exported without the use of large numbers of African porters. It was argued that such a railway would free tens of thousands of African labourers for work on the coffee plantations, thereby ensuring their successful operation.[8] To this planter lobby were added humanitarian pressures from the local Scottish missionaries who argued that the use of human porterage—especially women and children—was unsuitable for the conveyance of heavy goods and that 'the inhumanity of the system is becoming more apparent as the traffic increases'.[9]

In the Protectorate's early days two railway routes were mooted. As early as 1892 John Buchanan, a former Vice-Consul and an important planter in the Shire Highlands, noted the need for such a railway and circularized the public for support of such a venture.[10] In 1895 Harry Johnston, the commissioner, asserted that if a railway were built, the Protectorate would be 'as valuable as Ceylon' and began negotiating with the authorities in Portuguese East Africa regarding the possible construction of a short railway from Blantyre down to Quelimane, on the Indian Ocean coast.[11] Although some preliminary surveys were done, a second route was soon suggested as an alternative. One of the Highlands' leading businessmen and planters, Eugene Sharrer, originated a scheme to construct a railway from the Lower Shire river up the escarpment to Blantyre. The rationale for such a route lay in the fact that Portuguese customs duties that could be levied on goods shipped via Quelimane would be avoided if the goods were shipped by water up the Zambezi and Shire rivers and then by rail to Blantyre. This was the case because the Treaty of Berlin of 1885 stipulated that the Zambezi and its affluents were open to trade without the payment of customs duties. Sharrer's projected route also ran through his own plantations for much of its length. To forward this scheme Sharrer founded a company in London in which such influential figures as Lord Balfour and Sir Charles Euan Smith took part.[12]

Both early plans came to nothing, however, because of inadequate financial backing, because of the British Foreign Office's refusal to guarantee the interest charges on the capital necessary to construct a railway, and because of inconclusive bickering between Sharrer's company and the African Lakes Company as to who should construct and run the proposed new line.[13] It was generally agreed in London that a railway was needed, but the will to build one was lacking. Although Johnston and the Crown Agents both urged the Foreign Office to finance the railway itself, it was unwilling to do so.[14] Nothing was done, and then the demands of the South African War of 1899–1902 ensured that no further action could be taken until the war's end. After it was over, however, vigorous settler and humanitarian pressure at last prevailed, and the imperial government agreed in principle to the construction of a line from Blantyre to the

Lower Shire. Once again the settlers in British Central Africa and the Crown Agents in London urged that the imperial government should itself build the railway.[15] The Foreign Office remained committed to private enterprise, however, partly because of Treasury unwillingness to risk imperial money upon a risky venture and partly because of the Foreign Office's own reluctance to become involved in colonial affairs, something beyond its usual experience.[16] In early 1903 it let a contract for the building of the railway to Sharrer's company, the Shire Highlands Railway Company, which was now under the control of Sir Alexander Henderson, MP. It was the Foreign Office's reluctance to assume the responsibilities of railway building that resulted in Nyasaland alone, out of all the tropical colonies Britain had in Africa, having a privately run railway system. Nyasaland was indeed unfortunate in being placed under the authority of the Foreign Office, which was largely ignorant of African affairs. The new private railway was to extend from Chiromo, a port on the Lower Shire, to Blantyre. Any possibility of linking British Central Africa with the coast by a railway to Quelimane was thus precluded, at least for the time being.

Once this decision had been taken, a new problem appeared almost immediately. Lake Malawi and the Shire river have no fixed depths, and wide fluctuations occur from year to year. In the late nineteenth and early twentieth centuries both the Lake and the river were receding, and it soon became evident that the Lower Shire was no longer deep enough to allow boats of any substantial draw to sail as far as Chiromo at all times of the year. If the obnoxious human porterage was to be eliminated wholly, then, the railway would have to be extended from Chiromo southwards to Port Herald, a village on the border that was still open to Zambezi craft at all times of the year. After many delays the railway between Port Herald and Blantyre was opened in 1908, thereby linking the Shire Highlands with the outside world without the use of human porterage.

While the settlers on the Highlands were having their rail links pushed outwards from the Protectorate, others were contemplating the building of railways inland from the coast to meet the new Shire Highlands Railway, hoping to tap the supposedly rich resources of the Zambezi Basin as a fillip. One such line was to extend from Quelimane to the border between Portuguese East Africa and British Central Africa. Another suggested line was to go from Beira to the Zambezi, traversing territory administered by the Mozambique Company under Portuguese royal charter. The decision as to which of these two routes would ultimately serve Nyasaland was an important one for the future of the Protectorate, but its story lies largely outside the scope of this chapter.[17] Here it will be enough to say that for reasons of international imperial politics the route ultimately chosen was the Beira route. In 1913 a line linking the Shire Highlands Railway with the Zambezi river was completed. This was the Central African Railway. At the same time, Libert Oury, a leading capitalist in

Portuguese East Africa who controlled the Mozambique Company and the Port of Beira, pressed for British support for the proposed Beira–Zambezi route. After several years of inconclusive negotiations, the Beira plan stalled. In late 1916 Bonar Law, the Chancellor of the Exchequer, refused Oury's request for an imperial guarantee for the Beira line and the project seemed dead.[18] In the meanwhile Portuguese colonial interests had pressed ahead with their plans for a line from Quelimane to the Nyasaland border, but the war brought this project also to a standstill.

## The Trans-Zambesia Railway, 1919–22

In 1919 the British Colonial Office, which had assumed responsibility for Nyasaland in 1903, faced a new situation in South-East Africa. Germany, the constant threat to British interests in the area in the years before the war, had been defeated. Fresh from her victory on the battlefield, Britain determined to consolidate her position in Portuguese East Africa so as to prevent Germany from pursuing any economic activity there and thus driving a wedge between the Tanganyika Mandate and South Africa. The part of Portuguese territory immediately south of Tanganyika was administered by the moribund Nyassa Company. This company had almost fallen into German hands during the war, and imperial politicians were determined not to allow this to happen after the war. Thus the imperial government energetically supported a British takeover of the company through the acquisition by British interests of shares formerly held by the Germans. In this way Portuguese susceptibilities would be protected. As General Smuts of South Africa noted, this method would ensure that the imperial government would secure the Company 'very cheaply indeed, and the danger of German intrigue with an insolvent Portuguese Company or Government will be averted'.[19] Imperial politicians, led by Smuts, Amery, and Milner, argued that such a takeover was imperative 'for reasons of high policy'.[20] They chose the Union Castle Steamship line as the instrument of British policy, and Smuts warmly welcomed the choice as 'of great advantage to the Union of South Africa'.[21] Thus it was arranged that the Union Castle Company should buy up German-held shares in the Nyassa Company from the Custodian of Enemy Property. The precedent established in this decision was to shape imperial policies elsewhere in Portuguese East Africa and affect profoundly the economic health of the Nyasaland Protectorate in the process.

Once again the construction of a railway from Nyasaland to the coast was to be considered. The Quelimane route could have been adopted, especially as the promoters of the Beira route had failed utterly to obtain financial backing for the route and as the Portuguese authorities had expressed a willingness to grant substantial tax concessions to goods being transported to and from Nyasaland over the Quelimane line.[22] Moreover, the Quelimane line was far shorter than the Beira route, and no broad Zambei needed to be crossed. But the Colonial Office's thinking was not dominated by such considerations as the cost of building the railway, its length, or its potential profitability. Nor were the interests of Nyasaland to be consulted.

Although unable to raise the capital, the promoters of the Beira line still desired it greatly, as it would enhance the Port of Beira, their principal concern.[23] Therefore Thomas Gilmour, Oury's London agent, suggested to the Colonial Office that to ensure that the needed capital could be raised, the imperial government should guarantee the interest of the debentures that would be issued. The Colonial Office's permanent officials, while not unfriendly to Gilmour and Oury, were puzzled as to why the imperial government should make such a guarantee at a time when the Portuguese were pressing ahead with their own more rational railway from Quelimane and were willing to grant tax concessions.[24] Their hesitancy was heightened by the gloomy financial prospects for the proposed Beira line. As Oury himself noted, 'Owing to the disturbance created by the war it is not possible to obtain any reliable statistics as to the traffic which could absolutely be relied upon by the new railway.'[25] But if the permanent Colonial Office officials were doubtful, and if the railway promoters were uncertain, expansive imperial politicians were both more positive and more sanguine.

Lord Milner, the Colonial Secretary, was not influenced by the gloomy economic outlook for the line, nor was he swayed by any reflections as to what policy would be best for Nyasaland. What weighed foremost in his mind was the position of British interests in Portuguese East Africa. The forward move to take control of the Nyassa Company had strengthened Britain's position in the north of the colony. It was in Britain's interests, Milner calculated, to bolster Britain's economic position in the south as well, especially as he thought that there was an imminent American commercial invasion of the area in the offing.[26] The price of informal empire was eternal vigilance.

Oury was well aware of such apprehensions in Milner, and in a secret memorandum addressed to Milner, he wrote headily of his proposed railway as a link in a projected Cape to Cairo route that would everywhere pass through British territory or, as in Portuguese East Africa, through British-dominated territory.[27] Milner was convinced. Realizing that his government could do nothing officially, Milner thought that the best procedure for consolidating British interests in the area was to use the railway scheme as an instrument in the game of commercial imperialism in much the same way as the Union Castle Steamship Company was being used in northern Portuguese East Africa. Milner put his case to Austen Chamberlain, the Chancellor of the Exchequer, and Chamberlain agreed that, in the interests of Britain's dominant position in the area, financial guarantees should be given to Oury's Beira project to thwart the threatening American commercial penetration of southern Portuguese East Africa. A Colonial Office official thus explained the situation:

> On grounds of high policy it is very necessary that this country should lose no opportunity of strengthening its position in Portuguese East Africa, and the construction and operation of this line, under what, in practice, will amount to British control is an important step in that direction. It is known that American capital is beginning to interest itself in this region.[28]

Because it was in Britain's interests to allay Portuguese fears of possible British designs towards her colony, the imperial authorities decided that it would be wisest not to guarantee the debentures of the new Trans-Zambesia Railway with an imperial guarantee. They instead cast their eyes about for a puppet to handle this aspect of the arrangement, and the nearest candidate for this unwholesome role was the government of the Nyasaland Protectorate. Thus it was arranged. Only after the decision was made did Milner telegraph to the Protectorate's Governor to inform him. Rather cynically in the circumstances, Milner asserted that 'it is clearly in the interests of Nyasaland that the line should be built'.[29]

Therefore, in spite of the fact that Nyasaland had not been consulted, in spite of the fact that the railway was to lie wholly outside Nyasaland, and in spite of the fact that the line gave no promise at all that it would ever pay its own way, the imperial authorities, without consulting the British Parliament, compelled the Nyasaland government to guarantee the interest at 6 per cent of £1,200,000 worth of debentures for twenty-five years. The Colonial Office candidly explained the arrangement:

> In view of the suspicions and susceptibilities of the Portuguese Government, it was recognised that any proposal for a direct guarantee by the Imperial Government would wreck the whole project, and it was in these circumstances that it was decided, without preliminary consultation with the Government of Nyasaland, to arrange for a guarantee in the name of that Government as being likely to be less distasteful to the Government of Portugal.[30]

The situation in London was a curious one. There was a great deal of misunderstanding between the Treasury on the one hand and the Colonial Office on the other over the exact implications of Nyasaland's guarantee. When the Chancellor of the Exchequer had agreed to the guarantee of the Trans-Zambesia Railway debentures, he apparently thought that the Treasury would willingly supply funds out of the imperial Exchequer to cover the guarantee. This was also Milner's assumption at the Colonial Office. But is was not the assumption of the permanent Treasury officials. The result was a wrangle as to who should actually bear the costs of the guarantee. In

October 1920 the Treasury wrote to Milner, noting that 'it will be for the Protectorate to provide as far as possible for any payments falling due under the guarantees. . . . Any assistance from the Exchequer can only be given in the last resort and will be in any case by way of loan only.'[31]

Replying to the Treasury's policy statement, the Colonial Office protested with considerable perception that 'such a condition would render development and even decent administration impossible and would probably make the Protectorate a charge on Imperial funds for an indefinite period'.[32] A Treasury official, surprised and uneasy, observed, 'The whole story shows that the Colonial Office are not an equal match for the railway promoters.'[33] The dispute lay dormant for a time, for the Nyasaland government was not yet due to pay any interest on the debentures as the railway was not as yet completed.

In mid-1921 the Colonial Office again raised the matter with the Treasury. Churchill, the Colonial Secretary, argued that 'too little attention has been paid to the Imperial side of the question,' and proposed certain compromises to lessen the burden on Nyasaland, but the Treasury was deaf to his entreaties.[34] The result was that Nyasaland was required to devote half of all her revenue over a 'standard revenue' figure of £275,000 per annum to the liquidation of the Trans-Zambesia guarantee.[35] Desiring to avoid friction in Whitehall, Churchill acquiesced to the Treasury, and Nyasaland was left holding the Trans-Zambesia bag.[36] The most the Treasury could do was to suggest that Nyasaland should practise economies and increase her taxes so she would be able to meet the guarantee charges that she soon would be facing.

The response in Nyasaland to the unforeseen responsibilities that she had had thrust upon her was one of anger and despair. The *Nyasaland Times,* the settlers' voice, complained immediately after the contract with the Trans-Zambesia Railway was made public that the Protectorate was being exploited and that its development would be impeded:

> In return for this expenditure, what are we to get? Nothing but the privilege of sending our goods over the new line and paying such rates as may be fixed. . . . The agreement seems to us to be entirely one-sided and we thus see the extraordinary position that we are to be taxed to construct a railway in a foreign country and for the benefit of a foreign chartered company. The worst feature, however, is that this burden of taxation for these railways in foreign territory will hamper us in developing our own country.[37]

Rankine, the Protectorate's Chief Secretary and Acting Governor, echoed this tone of protest when he wrote to Churchill:

> I do not consider however, that it can reasonably be held that the Trans-Zambesia Railway, in respect of the guarantees on which the

Protectorate was not consulted was built directly and only in the interests of Nyasaland.... Native taxation is high enough in the present circumstances of the Native population. Any increase in it would simply lead to the demand, which could not be resisted, for higher pay for agricultural labourers which would fall on the European planters....

Reduced by the charges for guarantees and annuities on account of the Trans-Zambesia Railway, as is insisted upon by His Majesty's Treasury, the possibility of improving or providing means of communications is remote. Development cannot take place and the object of the Imperial authorities to obtain raw products from their colonial possessions is defeated and future prospects jeopardised.[38]

Finally, in 1922, Sir George Smith, the Governor, wrote an anguished letter to Churchill, linking the Trans-Zambesia guarantee obligations with African attitudes in the Protectorate and forecasting gloomy economic prospects if the conditions of Nyasaland's responsibility remained unaltered:

It is when we come to consider the more material and direct advantages the native has derived from our rule, and these are matters which mainly govern his appreciation of that rule, that one cannot but feel how much remains to done if we are to secure his contentment . . . . [T]here is unquestionably a growing and more articulate feeling among the more advanced natives that they contribute to the revenue out of fair proportion to the benefits they derive from our administration. There is a pressing need for extending more directly in their behalf the expenditure on Medical Services and Education.

I have wrought hard in the eight years I have been here ... to build up our finances with as little recourse as possible to Imperial funds; but I foresee that all further effort will be in vain unless the Treasury can be moved to assume a different attitude towards the Trans-Zambesi Railway guarantee and treat it as an Imperial obligation. With that load off our shoulders.... I am sanguine in the hope that we shall be able to balance our revenue and expenditure.[39]

In the post-war slump, however, the Treasury was not to be moved by such pleas from Nyasaland and the Colonial Office, and the Protectorate entered upon what a later Governor called the 'Times of Starvation'. Nyasaland was prevented from devoting her revenues to such things as African education, medical services, road-building, agricultural development, and the establishment of veterinary services. Instead, so as to pay off the debt charges without recourse to imperial aid, the Treasury urged Nyasaland to pare £1,000 from its already too-meagre medical services and to practise a range of other economies.[40] Thus a decision taken to counter the rumoured machinations of American capitalists south of the Zambezi was to affect adversely hundreds of thousands of Africans living in the Nyasaland Protectorate, as the financial obligation proved of vital significance to the potential development of that country. Nyasaland increasingly became a colony of the railway interests, and her government was increasingly constrained in the formulation of developmental policies by the fiscal realities of the Protectorate *vis-à-vis* the railways.

## Agriculture and freight rates

From the earliest days of the Protectorate, both the local administration and the imperial government considered the white settlers as of primary economic importance to the country. They believed that prosperity among the European settlers would ensure prosperity to the Protectorate's economy as a whole, and as late as 1921 Churchill linked hopes of future economic successes in Nyasaland with the possibility of an influx of settlers to the country from South Africa.[41] In fact, however, in the first years of the century hopes for a European coffee bonanza had faded, and tobaccco and cotton had also proved disappointing. The result was that, as the Protectorate failed to pay its own way, it remained under Treasury control. The small settler population could not provide a sound base for the country's economy. It was too weak, the international markets were too unstable, the plantations depended upon undernourished and inefficient labour that was paid too little and was, as a result, disinclined to sell its labour within Nyasaland, and transport difficulties hindered the export of cheap bulk crops.

In such a situation, one answer would have been to develop a peasant-based agricultural economy to replace that of the chronically insolvent European settlers. If such had been achieved, overhead costs would have been reduced, and the agricultural potential of this relatively fertile country could have been at least partially realized. Yet the development of a peasant-based agricultural economy required such initial investments as good seeds, agricultural and veterinary experts, teachers, improved medical facilities, and, above all, the local government's willingness to allow Africans to cultivate their own lands instead of working for the European settlers. In the early days none of these prerequisites existed. Because of the incessant clamour for cheap labour by the planters of the Shire Highlands, the government adopted tax policies that were calculated to encourage Africans either to seek employment with local planters or to seek their fortunes in the mines of Katanga, the Rhodesias, and South Africa. For not only were taxed to be paid, but also a 'labour certificate' had to be obtained for each year, showing that the bearer had actually worked for a specified time within Nyasaland.

Additionally, as the Protectorate's budget was usually not in balance, it was impossible for the government to find the funds necessary to educate Africans in agricultural techniques, to provide seeds and equipment, to build roads and marketing facilities, to eradicate disease, and to do all those other things necessary for the

improvement of the people's welfare. The local administration was
caught in a situation in which it did all it could for the European
settlers in the country, in the hope that they would one day strike it
rich and provide the country with a sound economic base, and in
which it neglected the Africans, except to force them to work for the
settlers. The settler success never materialized, however, and in the
years immediately prior to the First World War serious thought began
to be directed towards the possibility of using the·African population
for production of cash crops at the village level—as the missionary
Hetherwick had urged in 1903.

The first move towards such an approach were made at the end of
the first decade of the century. In 1909 a newly established
Department of Agriculture decided to concentrate its attention on
fostering African production of cotton.[42] African agriculturalists
responded to the opportunity, and by 1912, 964 tons of cotton were
produced.[43] The British Cotton Growing Association welcomed this
development and began to re-evaluate its earlier policy of helping the
European settlers. In a letter to Lewis Harcourt, the Colonial
Secretary, the Association's secretary in 1912 wrote that there 'is not
the least doubt that the introduction of white planters into tropical
countries such as Nyasaland. . . . brings difficulties and complications
which do not arise when the industry is solely in the hands of the
natives'.[44]

The Association and the Protectorate's government co-operated to
encourage further African cotton production and found the African
peasantry most willing. The district commissioner in the far north of
the country, for example, noted with satisfaction that 'the cotton
industry has occupied the chief energies of the district. If there is a
failure it will certainly not be from any fault or lack of willingness on
the part of the natives. . . . '[45] Although the Association complained
that the settlers' constant demands for labour were hurting the
prospects of a peasant-based industry, the cotton crop rose to 1,198
tons in 1914.[46]

These initial attempts by the British Cotton Growing Association
and the Nyasaland administration to foster peasant production of
cotton were frustrated by the war's disruptions and the tremendous
demands made upon the male population for service in the Carrier
Corps in the East African campaign.[47] After the war, the government
tried to revive production by supporting, in the face of stiff settler
opposition, an Association's buying monopoly in order to stabilize
prices and encourage peasant growers.[48] Although these efforts met
with initial success,[49] the new financial obligations to the debenture-
holders of the Trans-Zambesia Railway and higher rail rates thwarted
all the good intentions aimed at developing a solid, peasant-based
agriculture in the country. The intention was not lacking, but British
Treasury decisions did not permit the implementation.[50] Nyasaland
functioned under the so-called half-and-half principle. When she had
a budgetary deficit, the Treasury granted her loans at 7 per cent.

When she had a surplus of revenue over the base figure of £275,000, half of the excess had to be applied to the liquidation of past Treasury loans. Nyasaland's Governors had always ardently desired to escape this position, and in the years after 1911 a precarious revenue surplus was in fact achieved, and the Governor made plans to break away from Treasury control. But war loan debts and the Trans-Zambesia Railway guarantee condemned Nyasaland to continued Treasury control and to a continuation of the same policies that had been followed in the early years of the century, with the same lamentable results. Attention to the European settlers, neglect of the African population and decisions in favour of still more railway building marked the twenties, as the imperial government, enmeshed in the Trans-Zambesia guarantee, frantically sought ways of making the railway pay, thus releasing it from the guarantee's obligations. In 1921 the government found itself with one arm in the railway tar-baby. By the end of the 1920s it was almost wholly engulfed. And the more deeply involved with the railways that the administration became, the less able it was to operate freely in the realm of policy-making.

The privately-owned railways affected Nyasaland's economy adversely in two ways during the 1920s and 1930s: in railway rating and in railway financing. As soon as the imperial authorities arranged the Trans-Zambesia guarantee, the private enterprise Shire Highlands Railway and the Central African Railway increased their rates dramatically. Some of the Shire Highlands' rates went up by as much as 50 per cent, while the Central African Railway increased some of its rates by 103 per cent. To beat the still formidable river competition, the railways proposed to charge less for goods shipped all the way to the railways' end than for goods shipped only to the Lower Shire, where they could be trans-shipped for water carriage on the Zambezi to the ocean. Because of the Protectorate's interest in the health of the railways, Governor Smith was forced to support the railways, much to the fury of the white planting community.[51] Whenever similar situations arose, the government tended to support increased railway rates against the public welfare because of its financial commitments to the railways.

When the railways raised their rates in the early 1920s, a price war broke out between them and the river transport companies. Finally, unable to beat their competitors, the railways decided that they would have to buy them out so as to ensure their monopoly position. But because they had no liquid assets of their own, the railway interests approached the imperial government, requesting an increase in the Nyasaland guarantee to allow the railways to purchase the river transport companies' equipment. Reluctantly the Treasury agreed to a further £40,000 loan to the railways from the Protectorate and a closing of the British concession at Chinde, at the mouth of the Zambezi,[52] so as to close down much of the competing Zambezi traffic. As soon as the river competition was exterminated, the railways felt free to raise their rates again and tighten their monopoly.

In 1924 the Empire Cotton Growing Association complained that the high freight rates were frustrating African production of cotton because they did not allow for a suitable rotation crop to be grown for export. Thus, cotton yields were falling and the soil was becoming exhausted.[53] In the same year a Colonial Office committee reviewing the poor financial position of Nyasaland reported that 'in our opinion the first remedy for the present unsatisfactory position is a reduction of freight rates'. Only through such a reduction could low-priced African-grown crops be exported.[54] In 1927, in a confidential report to the Treasury, the railway expert, General F.D. Hammond, saw the necessity of reducing rail rates if any substantial agricultural development were to take place in the Protectorate.[55] In spite of these calls for lower rates, however, nothing could be done to curb them. This was so partly because the railways enjoyed a monopoly, partly because they were privately owned and hence beyond the control of government, and partly because the government was, in any case, in a special relationship with the railways which usually resulted in governmental policy being oriented in such a way as to favour the railways at all times. Those who suffered from the situation were the European planters and the African peasant producers.

## The Zambezi bridge, 1921–9

But although railway rates continued to be a damper on the Nyasaland economy throughout the inter-war years, it was in the realm of railway financing that the most dramatic developments occurred. In 1923 the Trans-Zambesia Railway requested a further extension of its guarantee by £200,000 for the purchase of additional rolling stock. This rolling stock was to allow the railway to carry the sugar produced by the Sena Sugar Estates Ltd, a British-owned company that operated on the south bank of the Zambezi in Mozambique Company territory.[56] Furthermore, the railway decided to charge the Sena Sugar Estates only 2d per ton mile to Beira, whereas it charged 4$^{1}/_{2}$d per ton mile for sugar produced in Nyasaland and sent over the same track.[57] Thus, although they were being requested to increase Nyasaland's guarantee obligation to underwrite the export of sugar from estates outside the Protectorate at costs that would make sugar produced inside the Protectorate uncompetitive at Beira, the imperial authorities could see no alternative to giving the railways the money they requested.[58]

While Nyasaland was being further stuck in the quagmire of railway financing, the controller of the Trans-Zambesia Railway, Libert Oury, was pursuing two other schemes that were to affect Nyasaland adversely. One was to build a bridge over the Zambezi to link the Central African Railway directly with his own Trans-Zambesia Railway. The other was a multi-faceted programme of development in those parts of Portuguese East Africa in which he was interested. The two plans were interlocked, and both involved the imperial government and the Nyasaland administration.

With the completion of the Trans-Zambesia Railway, the rail route to the coast was complete except for the Zambezi itself, where a ferry operated. Oury was anxious to have the river bridged, partly to speed transport, but primarily to enable him and his fellow financiers to develop certain coal deposits at Moatize, on the north bank of the Zambezi, opposite Tete. If there were a bridge across the Zambezi, it was argued, coal could be sent to Beira economically; without the bridge, there was no possibility of exploiting the coal.

As early as 1919 Oury had urged upon the Colonial Office the desirability of building such a bridge.[59] By 1921 the desirable had, for him, become the essential. For the first time there appeared the standard argument that the railways used in subsequent years: that if Nyasaland and the imperial government were to be freed from the burden of the Trans-Zambesia guarantee, then they would have to be willing to spend more money on railway developments.[60] Oury wanted as much development as possible, for such would benefit his railway and port, but he was unable to find development capital himself. He therefore sought aid from the British, and they were very reluctant, fearing still deeper involvement in the financial morass.

Oury was at this time extending his interests in Portuguese East Africa. With ever-increasing traffic to and from Rhodesia and Katanga, the Port of Beira was becoming inadequate to handle it efficiently. In 1922 Oury formed the Port of Beira Development Company, and in 1923 he decided to construct deep-water wharves to handle the increasing traffic and allow for further expansion.[61] Inland, he was investigating the mineral potential of the Zambezi Basin, and in 1924 he formed the Zambezi Mining Development Company to exploit the rich coal measures near Tete and prospect for other minerals. To bring the coal to Beira for bunkering required a bridge over the Zambezi.

By 1924 Oury was energetically pressing the imperial authorities to build this bridge, arguing that if it were built, the coal passing over it would pay for both the bridge itself and the Trans-Zambesia Railway. The Treasury, increasingly apprehensive about the long-term costs of the railway guarantee, was initially inclined to see Oury's plan as a possible release from a position that was becoming ever more embarrassing. Sir George Barstow, a high Treasury official, wrote to the Colonial Office in support of the plan:

> I feel myself that the Bridge will have so marked an effect upon the earnings of the TZR that it would be worth Nyasaland's while to guarantee a part of the cost of the Bridge, because I doubt whether the guarantee in respect of the Bridge with the TZR will come to more than the cost of the TZR without the Bridge.[62]

One cannot help but feel that the wish engendered the belief. Support for the bridge came from other sources as well. A committee studying railway development in Nyasaland recommended that the bridge be built to facilitate the shipment of coal from Moatize to Beira, thus reducing 'the heavy burden on the finances of the Protectorate incurred by the Trans-Zambesia guarantee'.[63] Governor Bowring himself was exceedingly sceptical of this report and its recommendations, yet he too succumbed to the desire of freeing Nyasaland from the debenture obligations as quickly as possible and embraced the bridge as a possible means to fiscal salvation, in spite of deep misgivings. Rather wistfully, he summed up his position: 'It may, I think, be safely assumed that once the bridge is built the annual contributions by the Government in respect of the Trans-Zambesia guarantee will decrease.'[64] Lastly, the influential Ormsby-Gore Report of 1924 also endorsed the scheme enthusiastically, asserting that the coal would pay for it.[65]

There was opposition to these favourable opinions. European planters in Nyasaland submitted a petition against Nyasaland's backing the bridge, asserting that the volume of traffic could not justify its construction. If it were built with Nyasaland's guarantee, it would cause 'financial chaos in those territories it serves'.[66] As there were but slightly over 300 planters in Nyasaland and as African agriculture was receiving scant encouragement, one cannot but feel that their prediction was well-founded.

By this time, too, the Colonial Office was becoming chary of the perpetual optimism of Gilmour and Oury, disillusioned as it was by the gigantic failure of the Trans-Zambesia Railway.[67] In its first year of operations it had netted only £35,669, while in its third year its profits sank to £23,000. In every year, then, Nyasaland had to make up the difference between the actual revenue and the 'break-even' figure of £72,000. The *coup de grâce* to the bridge scheme was dealt by the East African Guaranteed Loan Report when it expressed profound doubts as to whether Beira could be developed as a bunkering port and when it stated that only if Beira could be so developed could the bridge be justified.[68] By late 1925 the Treasury had accepted the Report's implications and had reconciled itself to postponing the bridge to a later date. A Treasury memorandum reflects this growing awareness of the dangers of dealing with the railway promoters:

> Unless some guarantee can be obtained for the construction of the coal railway and the development of the mines, there is clearly the danger when we have built the bridge . . . that we should be pressed to guarantee funds for the construction of the line and the development of the coalfields. Our experience with the Trans-Zambesia Railway is a warning.[69]

The bridge scheme was shelved, although throughout 1925 and 1926 the promoters agitated both privately and in the press for the imperial authorities to reconsider their decision and denounced the findings of the East African Commission.[70] At length the Colonial

Office yielded to the blandishments of the bridge promoters and their own fears that they would never be free of the Trans-Zambesia guarantee obligations. It appointed a commission under General Hammond, already well known for investigations in Nigeria, East Africa, and Rhodesia, to go to Nyasaland to study the feasibility of the bridge and to see whether it could be paid for under the terms of the East African and Palestine Loan Act of 1926.

Quite astonishingly though, Leopold Amery, the Colonial Secretary, instructed the Hammond Commission not to investigate the workings of the Port of Beira or the actual prospects of the coal near Tete 'because he understands from Mr. Oury and Mr. Gilmour, who visited him on Saturday, that the suggestion that this should be done has caused a great deal of annoyance both in Belgium and in Portugal'.[71] Not for the last time would an official commission of inquiry be handcuffed from the start at the behest of the powerful railway interests, interests who were fearful lest the Colonial Office learn the truth about their operations. Amery was deceived by the wiles of Oury and Gilmour, who assured him that the 'risk which the Nyasaland Government would incur of having to make good any shortfall in revenue from the existing lines is, in fact, negligible'.[72]

But while Amery in London was succumbing to Gilmour and Oury, the Nyasaland government was extremely apprehensive over the fresh interest shown in the bridge in London. Rankine, the Acting Governor, urging caution, wrote that 'for the main development we must look to native agriculture', and suggested that the bridge would not be a 'vital necessity'. A better way to spend any money available under the East African Loan Act, he suggested, would be on an extension of the railway system within Nyasaland and on the development of feeder roads through the countryside. In this way, peasant-grown produce could be marketed and the flow of Nyasalanders to foreign territories staunched.[73] In January 1927 the *Nyasaland Times* editorialized that an improvement of the ferry services at the river would be far preferable to the construction of a costly bridge.

In any event, General Hammond and his colleagues came to Nyasaland, took evidence, and produced their findings in 1927. Their report was a most influential document, for Hammond had, as part of his terms of reference, the duty to review Nyasaland's economy and recommend whatever changes he thought necessary to make the railways pay. In short, he was asked to design a plan that would free Nyasaland from the debenture responsibilities. Hammond's brief was wide, but not really wide enough, for he had been prevented from investigating both the Tete coalfields and the Port of Beira, with which Nyasaland's economy was inextricably linked.

One important conclusion that the investigators reached was that if Nyasaland were to become prosperous, African agriculture would have to be developed, and that if this were to occur, medical treatment would have to be widely extended to Africans to make them more efficient workers. The Commission noted that 80 per cent of the people suffered from hookworm, and that this endemic condition impeded efficiency.[74] The Commission also recommended the extension of the railway system northwards to open up the Central and Northern Provinces, and it stated that a bridge over the Zambezi would be essential for solving the problem of conveying low-priced exports across the river cheaply enough to make African agriculture pay.[75] At the same time, the commissioners said that the success of the railway and bridge depended ultimately on the construction of more roads in the country, an overhaul of district administration, more attention to improving African agricultural techniques, and the extension of educational and medical facilities to a far wider spectrum of the population.[76] Such would produce a peasant-based agricultural infrastructure adequate to produce large quantities of export goods needed for the transport system. At last, the error of the administration's earlier reliance solely upon European agriculture was being realized in London. The existence of a transport system without an infrastructure for peasant agriculture was recognized as pointless. In order to allow money to be spent, the Commission argued that the 'standard revenue' figure be increased from £275,000 to £400,000 in order to preserve Nyasaland from the necessity of using her monies to pay off the Trans-Zambesia guarantee liabilities.

The one critical point left untouched, because it was excluded from the Commission's terms of reference, was the Tete coalfields, the very thing that had generally been recognized as the only factor that could make the bridge a financially feasible proposition. Although nothing was published about the Tete coalfields, General Hammond wrote a secret memorandum to Amery to make the point that the Tete coal was highly speculative, that Natal coal would almost surely undercut Tete coal, and that the British South Africa Company, with its large influence in the Port of Beira, would surely use that influence to block improvements that would be at the expense of the Wankie coal industry.[77]

This then was the situation. The bridge was not really wanted, except by a handful of promoters, but the financial position of Nyasaland seemed to call for some move, for the *status quo* was merely resulting in the Protectorate's sinking further into insolvency with each passing year. Bowring, the Governor, grasped at the straw and was willing to have the bridge built even though he thought it would result in higher freight rates, higher hut taxes, higher import duties, and the establishment of a poll tax.[78] More imaginative and more realistic, Schuster, of the East African Loan Commission, wrote to Amery to criticize the Trans-Zambesia guarantee liability as 'a dead weight around the neck of the country', saying that if local development was to be achieved in Nyasaland, all the public debt should be wiped out and African production of export crops stimulated.[79] The Colonial Office had come to agree with Schuster, and an official minuted:

I can only express the hope that this [Treasury] attitude may be overcome so that a condition of affairs which is discreditable to the Empire and in danger of causing grave scandal may be removed.... In any case, the problem at present before us is to give the native (already the best educated and, under decent conditions, the most efficient worker in East Africa) a chance to develop his own country and thus improve his sunken condition.[80]

It was recognized that Nyasaland was the Empire's slum.

The Treasury still hesitated to assume new capital commitments on the basis of the very equivocal recommendations of the Hammond Report, and it refused to raise radically the standard revenue figure of £275,000 and to shift from a reliance upon European settler production to a reliance upon African peasant production, the shift that Hammond had recommended.[81] The fundamental disagreement between the Colonial Office and the Treasury surfaced in mid-1928, when Amery wrote to Churchill, now the Chancellor of the Exchequer, to urge a moratorium and limit on the Nyasaland government's repayments to the Treasury in respect to past debts. He painted a desperately gloomy picture of the situation in Nyasaland, hoping thereby to dissolve the Treasury's obduracy:

[Nyasaland's] social services, particularly sanitation, education and technical services are at a scandalously low ebb. The death rate is disgraceful. The inhabitants are emigrating. Owing simply to present poverty everything in Nyasaland is below the standard of other African colonies.... In a total revenue of less than £400,000 you charge over £50,000 interest and sinking fund for past loans besides taking a considerable bite towards the Trans-Zambesia Railway contribution....
In present circumstances this African Cinderella cannot pay for necessities let alone raise money for bridges and railways.[82]

Although Amery's bluntness shocked the Treasury, it remained firm. Nothing was done except for the raising of the standard revenue figure to £325,000. Between the Treasury and the Colonial Office, it was the former who had the upper hand. In the late 1920s then, an impasse had been reached, but this deadlock was not to last.

With the Treasury's apparent rejection of the Zambezi Bridge, opinion began to swing in favour of a total reorientation of Nyasaland's transport system towards Quelimane, the idea that Harry Johnston had pursued in 1895. In London, the Crown Agents agreed that a bridge over the Zambezi was unfeasible and suggested that a rail link with Quelimane be constructed.[83] The *Nyasaland Times* editorialized in a similar vein, while an imperial official visiting Nyasaland wrote:

The more I see of the Zambezi Bridge site, the less I like it, and I still think that although the Zambezi and Shire were a blessing to Nyasaland in the old days, the lure of them and of Beira has been a curse. Neither the Trans-Zambesia Railway nor the Central African Railway should ever have been built.[84]

But it was not to be Quelimane! Nyasaland once again had her destiny thrust upon her. Again it had a 'Made in England' label upon it. Outside forces intervened, and the decision was made for her by her masters. In 1919 the external force had been the apparent threat of American commercial expansion into Mozambique. A decade later a far different factor made its impact upon Nyasaland's fate. This time it was British political concern with the state of the metropolitan economy. In October 1928 a memorandum was circulated in Whitehall, spotlighting the high level of unemployment that existed in Britain and noting that:

> Widespread industrial irritation is apt to find expression through the Ballot Box to the detriment of the Government in power; and this is of special importance in view of the election in the early summer of 1929. If substantial orders for three or four millions' worth of railway and constructive materials could be placed now, it would produce a favourable effect in many of the depressed industrial areas during the coming winter; and it would do something to counterbalance the cry for an immediate measure of safeguarding in the steel industry.[85]

Amery, the Conservative Colonial Secretary, responded quickly and pushed forward the Zambezi Bridge scheme as a way of countering unemployment in Britain, stipulating carefully, however, that Nyasaland should not be saddled with any further debt charges.[86] Amery's idea of using imperial funds for colonial development in this manner was anathema to the Treasury officials, even with the need of reducing unemployment at home pressing upon them.[87] Instead, they hit upon the alternative of building the bridge under the terms of the Colonial Development Act of 1929. This Act, formulated to reduce unemployment in Britain, involved the giving of loans to cover the debentures necessary for capital developments in the colonies.[88] Nyasaland would be liable to repay the loan and the interest on the debentures, beginning five years after the bridge's completion. The decision to build the bridge was, in this form, as much a cure for the Protectorate's economic problems as a month in a swamp would be a cure for malaria. But, then, it was not meant to cure Nyasaland's problems, but rather as a benefit to Britain.

## Development plans and the Depression, 1929−35

While the Treasury had been far from generous in its bridge decision, the coming to power of the new Labour government in 1929 signalled a decisive change in imperial attitudes towards Nyasaland. To complement the decision to proceed with the bridge, the Colonial

Office, now under Lord Passfield, the former Sidney Webb, decided to remove Governor Bowring from office and replace him with a younger, more dynamic man. It chose Sir Shenton Thomas, a senior official in the Gold Coast.[89] Thomas had a lofty vision of Britain's role in Africa and was appalled by the decrepitude of his new charge. Soon after his arrival, he wrote a long and impassioned letter to Passfield lamenting the errors of the past and setting out his ideas as to what should be done for Nyasaland in the future. He blamed the Trans-Zambesia guarantee for causing the Protectorate's starvation of funds during the 1920s and noted that the entire country was sunk in lethargy. The Africans were leaving the country to work elsewhere because of the high local taxes and the lack of any local economic developments that would induce them to remain in their homeland. The civil service also was deeply disillusioned. Little money was available to it, the number of officers was far below establishment, and because of this there was an 'inevitable feeling of despondency and despair' permeating the service. He concluded:

> The question at issue is simply whether we intend to carry out our duties as trustees of the native population and, though I realize fully that considerations of finance cannot be completely ignored, I do suggest that the matter is one which should be judged from the higher ground of equity and justice. These people look to us for guidance, and it is our bounded duty to help and protect them. . . . If I am given the help for which I ask, though I cannot guarantee prosperity, I will at least guarantee that the reproach which now lies upon us will be removed.[90]

Thomas's appeal found a response in Lord Passfield, who, with great candour, wrote to the Treasury to request a more lenient attitude towards the impoverished Protectorate:

> It is recognised that any power which takes responsibility of governing uncivilised races should, in the words of the Covenant of the League of Nations, 'apply the principle that the well-being and development of such peoples forms a sacred trust of civilisation.' In this duty the British control has failed . . . [I do] not intend to suggest that the administration of Nyasaland can be brought up to the standard of the Belgian Congo or French Madagascar, but the Protectorate should be at least maintained in a condition to avoid grave public discredit which would attach to HMG both in this country and abroad should the present scandalous state of Nyasaland attract attention.[91]

With three-quarters of a million Nyasalanders with no medical facilities available to them at all, with the mortality rate among infants as high as 60 per cent in some districts, and with almost no money being spent on education, Nyasaland was a monstrous slum. The Colonial Office was at last recognizing that this situation was unacceptable.

As a result of this fresh appeal to the Treasury, the old 'starvation principle' was abandoned, and the standard revenue figure was raised to £450,000, thereby transferring all the immediate obligations of the Trans-Zambesia guarantee to the imperial government.[92] Nyasaland's public debt continued to increase, though, because the Treasury insisted that the guarantee obligations be fulfilled through the lending of interest-bearing loans to the Nyasaland government. Additionally, a development plan was drawn up for the period 1931–4 to prepare the Protectorate for the opening of the bridge. Large expenditures were scheduled for public works, agriculture, medicine, and education, to be financed out of the Colonial Development Fund, with the basic goal being the largest possible expansion of African agriculture.[93]

The coming to power of Labour and the arrival of Governor Thomas seemed to herald a bright new era for Nyasaland, but the initial gleam was soon tarnished by the Great Depression's impact on the British Empire's economy. In Nyasaland the decline in the territory's economy was coupled with the increasing of railway rates to pay for new railway construction. And once again, the Nyasaland administration found itself caught in the middle of a dilemma between the desire to have the railways function for the benefit of Nyasaland and the need to have the railways run profitably. When the railways raised their rates, the local European community urged that the government take them over and run them as a public utility. Thomas refused, arguing that they were not profitable and would therefore probably involve the Nyasaland administration in even deeper debt if they were acquired.[94] On the other hand, he was irritated by the railways' attitude towards the establishment of a local groundnut industry. In 1929, as a step towards encouraging African peasant production, the government sought to persuade Africans to grow groundnuts. In the same year, a factory for the local manufacture of soap was opened, and this served as a market for the groundnut oil. To protect this new industry, the government instituted a protective tariff over the strenuous objections of Lever Brothers,[95] who valued the Nyasaland market for their imported soap products. But the government had reckoned without the railways. Seeing that the replacement of imported soaps by locally produced soaps would result in declining freight revenues, the railways took steps to force the local manufacturer out of business. They decreased the rail rates on imported soap in an effort to allow it to compete effectively against the local product. This attitude angered Thomas, and he asked to be placed on the railways' boards of directors, so that the administration would have a direct influence upon rating policy and make the railways work more to the benefit of the Protectorate.[96] The Colonial Office, ever-fearful that the railways would take offence, refused the request as being wholly out of the question.[97]

With the failure of the local administration to get some control over railway rating policies, the tea planters of the Shire Highlands

decided to stop using the railways entirely and to send their produce
by road to Mocuba, in Portuguese East Africa, and thence by rail to
Quelimane. By so doing, the planters could save 14s 6d per ton.[98] In
1931, encouraged by this change, the Portuguese promised to reduce
the freight rates on the Quelimane line to such an extent that the
savings to be gained would be 42s 11d per ton.[99]

The railways were horrified at this competition and responded
quickly. But their response did not take the form of lowering their
rates. Instead, they requested the imperial authorities in London to
compel the Nyasaland administration to suppress this competition by
closing the border so that the tea would be forced back on to the
railways. Because of the ever-growing Trans-Zambesia guarantee
debts, the imperial authorities were easily persuaded and took
preliminary steps to close the Quelimane route to tea and suppress all
competing road transport throughout Nyasaland.[100] Governor
Thomas was reluctant to do the railways' bidding, especially as he
had grave doubts about their efficiency and management. At last,
however, after much harassment by the railway interests, the
Colonial Office approved special legislation designed to force all
traffic on to the railways by closing down the road competition.[101]

A furore greeted this legislation in Nyasaland. The planters sent a
petition of protest to Whitehall. The *Nyasaland Times* fulminated
against 'this Transport Tyranny'.[102] The so-called 'Beira Monopoly
Bill' passed the Legislative Council by a vote of 4−3, with the three
settler representatives voting against it. The Portuguese viewed the
measure as an anti-Portuguese action, and Oury, with his Mozambique interests in mind, was appalled by the Nyasaland government's
lack of subtlety. In a private letter, one of Oury's associates wrote
that the railway interests could not 'understand how it was that the
local Government, even if they desired to aim the legislation
exclusively at the Portuguese, did not embody in their bill a whole list
·of other roads . . . in order to mask in some measure their design'.[103]

In any event, the imperial government was compelled to take
measures that were neither popular nor calculated to benefit
Nyasaland in any way. Enmeshed in the railway tar-baby, it felt
constrained to do the railways' bidding in the hope that such action
would somehow lessen the financial burden weighing down the
Protectorate. That none of the decisions worked as was hoped did not
deter the authorities from taking fresh similar decisions when the
railways requested them.

The early promise of the Thomas administration was not to be
fulfilled. Passfield was replaced as Colonial Secretary in the new
National government of 1931 by the protectionist Philip Cunliffe-
Lister. In 1932 the Treasury, reacting to Britain's economic crisis and
the continuing langour of the Nyasaland economy, decided to
terminate the Protectorate's development programme. It directed,
over Thomas's strenuous objections, that any surplus of revenue over
expenditures should henceforth be directed towards the accumula-

tion of a large reserve balance, rather than being expended on local development projects.[104] The seal was placed upon this change in policy by the transfer of the capable and energetic Thomas back to the Gold Coast and the appointment of Sir Hubert Young as his replacement.

From 1932 onwards the picture in Nyasaland became gloomier and gloomier. The railways, in a wild attempt to maintain their position, increased their rates again and again over the constant protests of the Governor. The economy stagnated and the railways remained a liability. The Tete coalfields, which were envisaged in the 1920s as the one possible justification for the building of the Zambezi Bridge, were kept from operating by the imperial government's decision to block any development of African coalfields that would compete with the sale of Welsh coal to South Africa.[105] When suggestions were made that maize production should be encouraged in Nyasaland to provide a cheap bulk crop for export, Cunliffe-Lister brusquely vetoed them. Imperial considerations ruled out such a possibility, he argued, for Nyasaland maize might compete with maize from Kenya and Southern Rhodesia.[106] And while maize production was being forbidden, the one crop that Nyasaland did produce in abundance, tobacco, was being throttled by high freight rates. In 1936 Nyasaland tobacco cost 0.97d per pound to be transported from Limbe to Beira, while Rhodesian tobacco was transported the same distance from Rhodesia to Beira at only 0.17d per pound.[107]

The Zambezi Bridge was opened in 1935. But the event, which ought to have signalled an improvement in Nyasaland's economic condition, was marked only by deep despair. In 1934 Sir John Campbell, the able economic and financial adviser to the Colonial Office, reviewed the history of the Trans-Zambesia Railway and concluded that it might be in the interests of the government if the debenture-holders of the railway were allowed to foreclose when the Nyasaland guarantee expired.[108] In Nyasaland, the Director of Public Works regretted the whole transport system with which Nyasaland had been lumbered, saying that he felt that

> had the interests of Nyasaland been the sole consideration and had independent expert authority planned its communications before ever the Central African Railway and the Trans-Zambesia Railway existed, we would have had an easily graded railway less than 300 miles long. . . . Transportation by that route could have been as cheap as elsewhere under similar conditions. It is inconceivable to me that the route from Luchenza down to and across the Zambesi (involving the construction of one of the world's longest bridges) would have been adopted had not the interests of Nyasaland been merged with those of the Mozambique Company, the Port of Beira, Sena Sugar, Tete coal, etc.[109]

The one mistake in his assessment is that he says that Nyasaland's interests had been 'merged' with the others'; in actuality, Nyasaland's interests had been annihilated by the others.

In 1935 a Colonial Office official noted that the railway's receipts were tumbling and that only transporting railway building materials for the bridge had kept the railway going at all.[110] A Treasury official, summing up the situation at the same time, was also unbelieving and rueful:

> From the financial point of view it certainly is a strange story. Government investigators seem to have started off from the premise that Nyasaland was at a dead-end without an outlet to the sea via a bridged Zambezi. This is a negative argument. Railways make opportunities for traffic, they do not create it and the experts' views in the matter of development in the area were intensely hypothetical.[111]

Imperial authorities were at last realizing that the establishment of a highly sophisticated railway infrastructure was no substitute for the development of an African-based agricultural infrastructure. But this basic error of policy was perceived too late. The imperial government was by now unwilling to devote any further expenditure on the encouragement of African agriculture, especially if the goods produced were going to compete with goods from other colonies.

Instead, rather, a change in general developmental policies occurred, and with it came a change in the official attitude towards labour migration. In 1935 Cunliffe-Lester vetoed various developmental projects proposed by Governor Kittermaster and urged that 'the most rigid economies' be practised.[112] He made this decision in spite of the fact that while the taxes paid by Africans amounted to £230,796 in 1935, only £122,130 was being spent on providing services to the African population, with such services including headings like 'Police', 'Prisons', and 'Provincial Administration'. Only 3 per cent of the entire budget was allocated to 'Agriculture'. At the same time, the total indebtedness of the Protectorate had risen to over £5 million and was increasing daily.

## The export of labour, 1934–6

Cunliffe-Lister's retrenchment edict demanded some hard decisions in Zomba. New policies towards the African population were called for, especially in the area of labour migration and recruitment. The basic policy of the government prior to the mid-1930s was that Nyasalanders could not be recruited for work outside the Protectorate. It had been accepted that it was desirable for Africans to remain at home to develop Nyasaland's potential, if only to provide freight for the railways.[113] Earlier, in 1929, Governor Thomas had determined that, with the good prospects of developing agriculture, everything should be done to discourage emigration to the mines and farms of the Rhodesias.[114] In 1931, when Thomas was pressured to allow recruitment in Nyasaland of workers for the mines of Northern

Rhodesia, he rejected the proposition, asserting that:

> At the very time this Government is embarking on an extensive
> programme of development, when the construction of the railway
> extension to the lake is about to commence, when we are at last in a
> position to promote the cause of native agriculture on which the future
> prosperity of this country is believed to depend, Your Lordship has been
> asked to agree to a suggestion which will deprive the country of thousands
> of its strongest men.[115]

Although the imperial government acquiesced to Thomas,[116] with the
failure of development plans and the higher rates of the railways, this
labour retention policy gradually became untenable.

In early 1934, the Chief Secretary of the Protectorate made a
speech which illustrated the dilemma in which the administration was
finding itself. He said that there were two possibilities open to
Nyasaland. Either the government would have enough money to
stimulate, encourage, and teach the Africans to produce crops for
export, or, if this were impossible, the Africans would have to be sent
off to work in the mines of the south. In lieu of agricultural produce,
Nyasaland would export human beings.[117] In late 1934 the Protectorate's government took a step towards the future that it knew lay
ahead of it when it permitted a Rhodesian firm to recruit 100 Africans
in Kasungu and Mzimba districts.[118] The die had been cast.

At this very time a new situation was developing in the gold mines
of the Rand. South Africa's abandonment of the gold-standard had
raised the price of gold to such an extent that it became profitable to
work mines that had hitherto been unprofitable. A great expansion in
deep mining activity on the Rand resulted in a growing demand for
new workers, especially so-called 'Tropicals', who were thought to
be particularly well-suited for the hot mine depths. At the same time
there appeared in Nyasaland the Lacey Report, which drew attention
to the depressed state of the rural areas, embarrassed the Colonial
Office thereby, and called on the government of the Protectorate to
allow the controlled recruitment of labour.[119] Responding to these
pressures, the administration decided that henceforth it would be
willing to have Nyasalanders go to the mines of South Africa and
Northern Rhodesia and to the farms and mines of Southern
Rhodesia.[120] Agreements were signed to this effect in Johannesburg
and Salisbury in 1936. Henceforth, Nyasaland would be a conscious
exporter of people, and the government would no longer hope for the
development of African agriculture. Through errors of judgement, the
railway experiment, which had originally been embarked upon for the
wrong reasons, dragged the Protectorate's economy and government
into a situation from which there was no apparent escape other than
the mass migration of her citizens—the Protected—to the mines to
work. In reviewing the failures of the attempts to develop Nyasaland
through the construction of an expensive railway system charged to

the Nyasaland government, Sir John Campbell summed up the whole situation in 1936 when he grimly noted, 'We *are* in a mess; the thing has been done and cannot be undone.'[121]

As the years passed, the railways continued outside the local government's control, no peasant agriculture was developed and the economy stagnated, with the country sinking further and further into debt. In the years after 1936 the Nyasaland government continued to fight for freedom from the incubus of the railway, but always in vain.[122] In 1945, indeed, to placate the Portuguese, the imperial authorities agreed to a renewal of the Trans-Zambesia guarantee.

## Conclusion

So then, between 1914 and the end of the Second World War Nyasaland suffered a chronic lack of economic development, not because developmental plans were lacking, but because Nyasaland was a chattel of the railways, a Protectorate in which the railways were the Protected, a colony which had been used as a pawn in imperial designs without regard to the effects that decisions taken in London would have upon the welfare of the people of Nyasaland. From the evidence of history, by the end of the Second World War it could be said that the Nyasaland *Protectorate* had been misnamed. Onerous railway and bridge charges, the impact that these had upon the imagination and efficiency of the local administration, and the frustration by financial strictures of many development projects led to the creation and perpetuation of Protectorate-wide slum conditions, conditions which necessitated labour migration. The experience of colonialism, with decisions taken outside the colony and for reasons that had no relevance to the colony, left Nyasaland with a distorted and dislocated economy at the end of the colonial period, a condition not yet wholly remedied.

## NOTES

1.   This chapter is based upon research carried out between 1970 and 1973 in the Archives of the Malawi Railways, Limbe, Malawi; in the National Archives of Malawi, Zomba, Malawi; the British Museum; the Library of the Royal Commonwealth Society; and in the Public Record Office, London, where Foreign Office (FO), Colonial Office (CO) and Treasury (T) files were consulted.
2.   A.J. Wills, *An Introduction to the History of Central Africa* (London, 1964), 276.
3.   For a totally opposing view, see B. Pachai, *Malawi: The History of the Nation* (London, 1973), 152, where the author asserts that 'the railway development and concurrent loans represent a most positive contribution by the British Government'.
4.   A. Hetherwick, 'Letter to the Editor', *The Scotsman,* 17 February 1903.
5.   FO 2/690, Sharpe to Salisbury, 27 December 1899.
6.   S.H.F. Capenny, 'Railway Schemes in Relation to British Central Africa', *Scottish Geographical Magazine, 17,* 1901, 369. See also, in the same volume, A. Sharpe, 'Trade and Colonisation in British Central Africa', 134.

7. *Central African Planter,* 11 November 1899.
8. *Central African Times,* 6 January 1900. The Nyasaland case, in which white planters preceded the building of a railway, was unusual; in Southern Rhodesia, Northern Rhodesia, and Kenya they only arrived to take up land after a railway had been built.
9. FO 2/691, Minute of the Church of Scotland Foreign Mission Committee, 20 November 1900.
10. J. Buchanan, 'Industrial Development in Nyasaland', *Geographical Journal, 3,* 1893, 253.
11. FO 2/689, Sharpe to Salisbury, 27 January 1897, Memo by Johnston, 20 November 1896; H. Johnston, 'England's Work', *Proceedings of the Royal Colonial Institute, 27,* 1896−7, 55. Some years earlier, Johnston had spoken of Nyasaland as 'another Brazil'. FO 84/2052, Memo by Johnston, 29 December 1890. Cited in R.H. Palmer, 'Johnston and Jameson: A Comparative Study in the Imposition of Colonial Rule', in B. Pachai (ed.), *The Early History of Malawi* (London, 1972), 295.
12. FO 2/689, Memo by Stanmore, 18 November 1898.
13. See FO 2/689, Moir, African Lakes Company, to Salisbury, 1 December 1896, Memo by Johnston, 20 November 1896. Johnston was extremely critical of the African Lakes Company's intervention, noting that 'in the present state of the country the Lakes Company reap very large profits from the very imperfection of the transport system that others deplore'. He saw the Company as trying to obscure the issue and thus postponing the building of a railway that would compete with the Company's transport business.
14. FO 2/689, Memo by Johnston, 20 November 1896, Ommaney, Crown Agents, to Stanmore, 15 December 1896, Stanmore to Johnston, 30 January 1897. The Crown Agents for the Colonies was an official agency in London which handled business and financial transactions on behalf of the governments of British colonies. It was often consulted by the Foreign Office, *c.* 1891−1903, about the proper procedures which the FO should adopt in transacting business on behalf of the British Central Africa (Nyasaland) Protectorate.
15. *Central African Times,* 10 November 1900 and 23 February 1901; FO 2/691, Ommaney to Hill, 30 August 1899; FO 2/693, Blake, Crown Agents, to Lansdowne, 27 June 1902.
16. FO 2/691, Minute by Eyre-Crowe, 30 January 1901.
17. For a full discussion of the background to the ultimate decision, see L. Vail, 'The Making of an Imperial Slum: Nyasaland and her Railways, 1895−1935', *Journal of African History, 16,* 1975, 89−112.
18. National Archives of Malawi [henceforth NAM], GOA 2/4/29, Oury to Smith, 18 January 1917.
19. CO 525/70, Memo by Smuts, 15 January 1918.
20. CO 525/88, Bottomley, Colonial Office, to Buckley, Treasury, 19 April 1919.
21. CO 525/81, Philipps to Read, 11 September 1918.
22. CO 525/64, Officer Administering the District of Quelimane to the British Consul, Quelimane, 9 July 1914.
23. Malawi Railways Archives, Oury to the Mozambique Company, undated.
24. CO 537/844, Fiddes to Gilmour, 2 May 1919.
25. CO 537/844, Memo by Oury, 19 April 1919.
26. CO 525/85, Read, Colonial Office, to Barstow, Treasury, 18 August 1919.
27. CO 537/844, Memo by Oury, 19 April 1919. The Mozambique Company had long been in the hands of British shareholders and had functioned as Britain's instrument of informal imperialism in the area of Portuguese East Africa south of the Zambezi. L. Vail, 'Mozambique's Chartered Companies: The Rule of the Feeble', *Journal of African History, 17,* 1976, 389−416.
28. CO 525/85, Read to Barstow, 18 August 1919.
29. NAM, S2/44/19, Milner to Smith, 17 July 1919.
30. CO 525/85, Read to Barstow, 18 August 1919.

31.  T 161/64/S.4625/1, Barstow to Milner, 30 October 1920.
32.  T 161/64/S.4625/1, Read to Barstow, 12 November 1920.
33.  T 161/64/S.4625/1, Upcott to Barstow, 24 November 1920. The guarantee prescribed that Nyasaland should make up any difference between the actual profit of the railway and £72,000 per annum.
34.  T 161/64/S.4625/1, Read to Treasury, 13 August 1921.
35.  T 161/64/S.4625/1, Barstow to Read, 9 September 1921.
36.  T 161/64/S.4625/1, Read to Barstow, 8 October 1921.
37.  *Nyasaland Times,* 29 April 1920.
38.  CO 525/98, Rankine to Churchill, 24 November 1921.
39.  NAM, S1/38/21, Smith to Churchill, 12 June 1922.
40.  NAM, S1/1644/23, Treasury to Colonial Office, 5 March 1923. This explains the persistent, and unsuccessful, demands for more educational and medical facilities by the 'native associations' in the 1920s.
41.  T 161/120/S.9781/1, Read to Barstow, 17 August 1921.
42.  M.L. Chanock, 'The Political Economy of Independent Agriculture in Colonial Malawi: The Great War to the Great Depression', *Journal of Social Science, 1,* 1972, 114. See also B.S. Krishnamurthy, 'Economic Policy, Land and Labour in Nyasaland, 1890–1914', in Pachai, *Early History,* 384–404.
43.  NAM, S1/557/20, 'Cotton Statistics'.
44.  CO 525/46, Hutton to Harcourt, 20 March 1912.
45.  NAM, NNK 2/4/2, Report of the D/C North Nyasa for the month May 1912.
46.  CO 525/46, Hutton to Harcourt, 30 March 1913; NAM, S1/557/20, 'Cotton Statistics'.
47.  NAM, S1/557/20, Smith to Milner, 16 August 1920.
48.  NAM, S1/1702/21, Smith to Churchill, 15 May 1922.
49.  For example, African production of cotton rose from 315 tons in 1920 to 747 tons in 1923, while the cash value for cotton grown in the Lower Shire had reached £15,000 by 1924. NAM, S1/481/24, 'Report on the Native Cotton Industry'; Chanock, 'Political Economy', 119.
50.  For example, when the Nyasaland administration received some money under the terms of the British Cotton Growing Association's buying monopoly, it wished to use this money for the development of African agriculture. The Treasury insisted that this money should instead be used for the recurrent costs of the administration. NAM, S1/1702/21, Rankine to Devonshire, 25 April 1923.
51.  CO 525/93, Smith to Milner, 20 October 1920. See also NAM, S1/55/20, Acting Chief Secretary to Nyasaland Chamber of Agriculture and Commerce, 2 October 1920.
52.  CO 525/103, Meiklejohn, Treasury, to Churchill, 7 September 1922.
53.  NAM, S1/1851/24, Empire Cotton Growing Corporation to Under-Secretary of State for the Colonies, 6 October 1924.
54.  NAM, GOB G/6, 'Report of the Departmental Committee on Nyasaland Railways, 1924'.
55.  T 161/698/S.28440, Memo by Hammond, 1927.
56.  NAM, S2/25/22, Trans-Zambesia Railway to Nyasaland Government, 16 February 1922.
57.  NAM. GOA 2/4/29, Smith to Gilmour, 1 January 1922. It is worth noting that Oury was a director of the Sena Sugar Estates Ltd.
58.  CO 525/106, Barstow to Devonshire, 19 July 1923.
59.  CO 537/844, Memo by Oury, 19 April 1919.
60.  CO 525/100, Oury to Churchill, 27 April 1921.
61.  E. d'Erlanger, *The Construction and Financing of the Rhodesian Transport System* (n.p., n.d. [London, 1938].), 46–8.
62.  CO 525/110, Barstow to Read, 27 May 1924.
63.  NAM, S1/874/23, 'Report of the Stevenson Committee, 1924'. See also T 161/225/S.22987/01.
64.  NAM, S1/874/24, Bowring to Amery, 21 January 1925.

65. *Cmd. 2387, Report of the East African Commission* (London, 1924), 13–14.
66. CO 525/110, Petition of Nyasaland Planters, May 1924. See also *East Africa,* 19 March 1925.
67. CO 525/113, Minute by Green, 29 May 1925.
68. *Cmd. 2701, Report of the East African Guaranteed Loan Committee* (London, 1926), 107.
69. T 161/741/S.28440/1, Memo by Treasury, 15 November 1925.
70. CO 525/115, Gilmour to Colonial Office, 26 July 1926.
71. CO 525/115, Minute by ?, 27 July 1926.
72. CO 525/115, Gilmour to Amery, 26 March 1926.
73. CO 525/115, Rankine to Amery, 4 October 1926.
74. *Report on the Nyasaland Railways and the Proposed Zambesi Bridge,* Colonial No. 27 (London, 1927), 10. [Henceforth *Hammond Report.*]
75. *Hammond Report,* 13. This assumed that the imperial authorities would allow cheap things, such as maize, to be produced for export. When the opportunity arose, however, Whitehall refused to countenance such schemes.
76. *Hammond Report,* 46–56.
77. CO 525/117, Hammond to Amery, 17 June 1927. By this time the British South Africa Company-dominated Rhodesia Railways controlled the Beira Works Company, which held the concessions for port developments at Beira.
78. CO 525/122, Bowring to Amery, 11 April 1928.
79. CO 525/122, Schuster to Amery, 21 June 1928.
80. CO 525/122, Minute by ?, 26 June 1928.
81. T 161/741/S.28440/3, Minute by Hardman, 2 December 1927.
82. T 161/742/S.28440/4, Amery to Churchill, 18 July 1928.
83. *Nyasaland Times,* 19 February 1929; CO 525/129, Lambert, Crown Agents, to Bottomley, 10 April 1929.
84. CO 525/129, Jeffares to Anthony, cited in Anthony to Carmichael, 6 April 1929.
85. T 161/291/S.33978, Memo by Treasury, October 1928.
86. T 161/291/S.33978, Amery to Churchill, 26 November 1928.
87. T 161/291/S.33978, Hopkins to Churchill, 21 January 1929, Churchill to Amery, 23 January 1929. One Treasury minute characterized Amery's proposal as 'so preposterous that it is hardly necessary to argue it seriously. . . . The scheme is sheer financial immorality.' It is small wonder that the Treasury and the Colonial Office failed to see Nyasaland's problems in the same light.
88. See the speech by J.H. Thomas in 229 HC DEB. 5s., 12 July 1929, col. 1255.
89. CO 525/131, Memo by Wilson, 19 March 1929.
90. CO 525/137, Thomas to Passfield, 30 January 1930.
91. CO 525/137, Bottomley to Treasury, 11 April 1930.
92. NAM, S1/1248.A1/29, Hopkins to Colonial Office, 30 June 1930, in which the Treasury official admits that there is 'no room for doubt that the burden of the existing scale of contributions towards the service of the Trans-Zambesia Railway guarantee is preventing the proper and necessary development of the Protectorate'.
93. NAM, S1/1248.C/29, Minute by Thomas, 24 November 1929. The development programme, as outlined by Thomas, was ambitious, with an initial expenditure of £195,525, in the first year, with similar amounts projected for both capital and recurrent expenditures down to 1934–5. See NAM, S1/702/30 for the details.
94. CO 525/135, Thomas to Passfield, 4 October 1930.
95. NAM, S1/852/29, 'Groundnut Oil Industry'; NAM, S1/1382/29, 'Increased Duties on Imported Soap'. The Lever Brothers representative wrote in an attempt to have the tariffs reduced, threatening that his company might henceforth refuse to send any soap at all to Nyasaland. He continued. 'I need hardly point out the inconvenience and uncleanliness that would follow if the country were left short of Soap. The reduction from 7/- to 5/- per cwt. would further help British Manufacturers to sell better quality soaps, such as CARBOLICS, so necessary to NATIVE cleanliness and Hygiene.' NAM, S1/1382/29, Casson to Nyasaland Treasurer, 25 September 1929.

96.  CO 525/145, Thomas to Cunliffe-Lister, 19 March 1932. Especially repugnant to
Thomas was the railways' tendency to place most of the costs of transport on the
non-guaranteed Shire Highlands Railway and to allow the guaranteed Central African
Railway and Trans-Zambesia Railway to charge relatively low prices. Thus, for
example, tea cost £7 19s per ton from Luchenza to Beira, with fully £6 10s being
charged on the very short Shire Highlands Railway and the remainder on the other two
lines. This policy, which was general, resulted in the guaranteed railways always
needing government support and in the Shire Highlands Railway always paying a
dividend to its shareholders. See CO 525/135, Thomas to Passfield, 4 October 1930.
97.  CO 525/135, Minute by Downie, 12 December 1930.
98.  CO 525/135, Thomas to Passfield, 7 November 1930.
99.  CO 525/139, Thomas to Passfield, 24 January 1931.
100.  CO 525/139, Passfield to Thomas, 6 July 1931. See also NAM, S1/734 I–II/31,
'Road and Railway Transport Competition'.
101.  CO 525/144, Hamilton to Hall, Officer Administering the Government, 28 July
1932.  The Chief Secretary, Hall, was exceedingly unhappy with the Colonial Office's
decision even at this stage, noting 'Protection of the railway should mean increased
freightage, and not an opportunity to put on any rates the railway cares to adopt. . . . I
suggest that a lowering of freight rates can be demanded in return for protection against
road competition.' NAM, S1/734 I–II/31, 'Notes for a Leg. Co. Meeting, September
1932'. Needless to say, freight rates were *not* dropped in return for such protection.
102.  *Nyasaland Times,* 7 October 1932.
103.  CO 525/143, Secretary, Trans-Zambesia Railway, to General Manager, Nyasaland Railways, 16 December 1932.
104.  CO 525/144, Hamilton to Hall, 10 August 1932. The Governor of Northern
Rhodesia was obliged to pursue the same policy, with the result that 'Experience of the
depression generated a philosophy of penny-pinching and near despair among the
officials of the Secretariat'. E.L. Berger, *Labour, Race, and Colonial Rule: The
Copperbelt from 1924 to Independence* (London, 1974), 22–3.
105.  Speech by Sir O. Mosley in 230 HC DEB. 5s., 18 July 1929, col. 694.
106.  CO 525/147, Minute by Cunliffe-Lister, 2 March 1933.
107.  CO 525/162, Kittermaster to Ormsby-Gore, 8 October 1936. High freight rates
also prevented the development of an export-oriented groundnut industry.
108.  CO 525/151, Minute by Campbell, 23 July 1934.
109.  NAM, S1/734[111]/31, Director of Public Works to Duncan, 11 January 1933.
110.  CO 525/152, Calder to Grieve, 1 October 1935.
111.  T 161/S.28440/08, Memo by Grieve, 1935.
112.  CO 525/155, Calder to Treasury, 10 April 1935.
113.  CO 525/154, Minute by Greenhill, 25 July 1934.
114.  NAM, S2/4[1]/31, Thomas to Maxwell, 3 January 1930. A Southern Rhodesian
labour report of 1928 noted with alarm that 'In Nyasaland too there are, we understand,
already some 57,000 natives growing tobacco on their own account . . . and if this is so
to-day we cannot expect but that there will be many thousands more native tobacco
growers there in the near future and our labour supply for this reason alone enormously
decreased.' National Archives of Rhodesia, S 235/426, 'Report of the Native Labour
Enquiry Committee, 1928', 15. This interpretation of Thomas's desires and plans is at
variance with that of Chanock, 'Political Economy', 127–8, where Chanock attributes
Thomas's impotence to his conservative economic beliefs, not to his inability to break
from the bonds of Treasury control and the obligations of the railway guarantee. While
Chanock is correct in saying that Thomas did not like the idea of artificially maintaining
prices, he did seek, vainly, to maintain cotton prices by persuading the railways to
reduce their high freight charges for cotton. Eventually Thomas did agree, with
Whitehall's approval, to support cotton prices at the rate of $^1/_4$d per lb. Even with this
support, though, cotton suffered a severe setback. See NAM, S1/941/31, Treasurer to
Thomas, 1932.
115.  NAM, S2/4[1]/31, Thomas to Passfield, 7 May 1931.

116. NAM, S2/4¹/31, Thomas to Thomas, 16 September 1931.
117. Speech by Hall, reported in *East Africa,* 25 January 1934.
118. NAM, S2/4¹¹/31, Minute by Hall, 20 August 1934.
119. *Report of the Committee Appointed by His Excellency the Governor to Enquire into Emigrant Labour, 1935* (Zomba, 1936).
120. CO 525/158, Kittermaster to Cunliffe-Lister, 1 February 1935.
121. CO 525/163, Minute by Campbell, 20 October 1936.
122. When, for example, in 1944 Governor Richards suggested that the railways be nationalized, the suggestion was rejected by London, and the Nyasaland government's Director on the Railways' Board, General Hammond, aghast and amazed, remonstrated that 'what the Government of Nyasaland apparently wanted was to use the railway for improving the condition of the people in Nyasaland'. CO 525/197, Minutes of a Meeting held in London, 3 April 1944.

# CHAPTER 16

## Agricultural Change and Continuity in Malawi

## MARTIN CHANOCK

### Introduction

That Malawi is, and was during the colonial period, a predominantly agricultural country, is a statement which can be made by the most cautious of scholars without recourse to a footnote. It seems reasonable to postulate, therefore, that it has an agricultural history and indeed in recent years historians throughout much of Central, Southern, and East Africa have at last recognized the need to provide adequate explanations of rural change.[1] Once a move had been made away from an over-riding concern with policy-making in the metropolis to a search for the political realities within Africa itself, it became clear that such histories would have to be based not so much upon the often ephemeral political activities of élites, but rather upon an understanding of the material world in which they took place. In one sense this was yet another move away from a concern with Europe rather than with Africa—away from the centre towards a localized and small-scale view of change. But an adequate account of the agricultural and economic life of each locality must equally be linked back to the centre, for the major change which has taken place in the twentieth century has been the linking of the African economy to the capitalist economy, which was, and is, dominated from outside the continent. The agricultural historian is thus engaged upon two tasks; he must both illuminate rural activities at the local level and show how these activities were influenced by the impact of outside forces.

In Malawi, agricultural patterns have been varied. Different geographical conditions, social organization, and economic opportunities have produced characteristically different rural economies in the Lower Shire, the Shire Highlands, the Central Plateau, the Lakeshore and the north, each of which have in turn been affected in varying degree by the demand for labour, the alienation of land, and the introduction of exportable crops. In addition, there are several 'peripheries' linked to different 'cores'—the peasant economies of the Lower Shire and the Central Region primarily to British, but also to South African, markets; those living on the Shire Highlands to the local settler and plantation economy; and those in the north to the mining economies of Central and Southern Africa.

## Economic historiography

Despite the growing sophistication of the literature on the economies of Central Africa, a bedrock of old interpretation remains. This rests upon the supposed contrast between subsistence and surplus-producing farmers, and sees the colonial era essentially as a period which brought about a change from a 'subsistence economy' to one of an entirely different order. The historian will rightly be uneasy with the characterization of pre-colonial African economies as simply 'subsistence'. It is not difficult for him to point to African economic activities which for a long time have rested upon and been shaped by exchanges with the outside world. The products of different areas have long been exchanged, and the growth of the caravan trade with East Africa in the nineteenth century produced important changes in patterns of supply and demand.

Nevertheless, there comes a time when changes in scale are such that they become changes in essence, and it might still be more useful to see the pre-imperial and subsequent periods in terms of contrast rather than continuity. The newer literature, though it contains a customary genuflection towards the importance of understanding the dynamics of pre-colonial economies, still sees the capitalist economy as transfiguring the market relations of the bulk of the population with the outside world—the peasantry proper being created by colonialism.[2] While it does not, as the subsistence/cash school did, write off the complexity of the pre-colonial economy, it does, because of a lack of information combined with an eagerness to provide an alternative conceptual framework, effectively share the same departure baseline, which is the beginning of the European colonial period. Yet in the case of Malawi, virtually the entire area was linked to the outside world in a particularly exploitative trading relationship during much of the nineteenth century, and the slave/ivory trade must have been malformatory long before the introduction of a cash economy oriented towards Britain and South Africa. The notional baseline, either for the change from a 'subsistence' to a 'cash' economy, or for the take-off into underdevelopment, must therefore be pushed further back in time.[3]

There remain other concepts which, however useful they may be as analytical tools, have the effect of impeding a coherent understanding of the world created by colonialism. The concept of the 'dual economy' and the obfuscations of the 'backward sloping labour supply curve', and the attendant controversies regarding African responses to wage and price incentives were prominent in economic analyses of the colonial era.[4] Non-economists too have tended to separate the lives of men into confusing and unnecessary categories. Kettlewell, for example, who as Director of Agriculture during the Federal period (1935–63) had a hand in the formulation of policy, writes that Malawians were 'engaged in subsistence cropping, supplemented by the cultivation of cash crops [and] casual employment in towns or on European farms'.[5] This separation of the world in which people lived into 'subsistence' and 'cash' sectors is built upon a model of a self-contained African economy to which an external exchange system was added, and does not allow either for the dynamics of the pre-colonial economy, or for the way in which the 'subsistence' rural world was shaped by being a part of, rather than separate from, the colonial one. The fact is that families lived within a single system with inter-dependent parts, in which wage income was depressed because of the existence of the 'subsistence' sector, while the wealth derived from the latter remained low because of supplementation by wages.

Perhaps the most important contribution that a historical study of agricultural change can make is to reintegrate the divorced categories of politics and economics, and to present a coherent picture of economic change which fully takes into account the political context in which it takes place. A study of pre-colonial agricultural history cannot take place outside the context of the group relationships which determined land use, labour relations, patterns of production, and terms of exchange. This is even more obvious for the colonial and post-colonial periods, throughout which state power and intervention grew. The colonial polity gave land to some and denied its use to others; for some people it created new opportunities and incentives, and, above all, it controlled them and ruled (or, when it could not, appeared to rule) the terms of exchange between the rural areas and the outside world. It is therefore important to understand how the peasantry adapted to its new political position, though in Malawi, which achieved political independence as a result of successful peasant revolt, remarkably little interest has so far been shown in the roots of rural anti-colonialism.[6]

## Rural poverty

In the earlier literature there was an assumption that underdevelopment and rural poverty were a natural part of the 'subsistence' world which pre-dated colonialism, and that colonialism itself, however slowly and for whatever reasons, created additional wealth by increasing the flow of cash (earned both by peasants and migrants) into the rural areas. Later analyses of Central Africa have stressed the ways in which colonialism created rural poverty—destroying the self-sufficient peasantry and forcing them on to the labour market. Concern has been with declining peasant production and with migrancy, which drained labour away from peasant agriculture and into mining, capitalist agriculture, and secondary industry.[7] In one specific challenge to Hancock's conclusion that Nyasaland was poor because of the poverty of her resources, Krishnamurthy criticizes the administration for not actively promoting African cash crop production, and sees migrancy flowing from this, and from the dominant South African capitalist pressures which prevented the country 'taking control of its labour'. Consequently, he writes,'Nyasaland, in effect, became part of the economic system of the South'.[8]

Yet Malawian agriculture does not quite fit into the gloomy southern picture, and migrancy does not appear to warrant the importance it has so often been given. Diagnoses of the effects of migrancy have varied greatly. Some have stressed the disintegrative impact on rural life; others the local cohesion which migrancy maintained in addition to providing increased economic opportunity; and others again the malformatory effects, seeing migrancy not as distributing wealth from the rich areas to the poor, but being a vital part of the development of those areas to which it goes, and creating an ever-widening imbalance between them and the areas it leaves.[9] One feature which is clear is that in Malawi the main areas affected by labour migration were not, and never have been, the major areas of agricultural production. The Lacey Report of 1935 estimated that in only a handful of districts in the north, or formerly Ngoni-dominated, or both, were more than 10 per cent of the adult male population absent migrants.[10] During the second half of the nineteenth century, the rulers of these districts had profited from slave-trading and crop-raiding, but when the economy was smashed by colonial conquest, not only migrancy, but often an increase in agricultural production in surrounding areas, resulted. No doubt the continual drain of male labour combined with an unbridgeable distance from colonial markets contributed to the continuing depression of the north, but migrancy could hardly be said to have damaged an ongoing peasant economy. In the 1930s, after the Depression, it is clear that the rate of migration from the cash-crop producing areas did increase, but the absentees were still a small minority and were only away for short periods.[11] And if one considers the territory as a whole, the inter-war influx of permanent Lomwe settlers from Mozambique more than compensated for the loss of labour from temporary absentees.[12]

Migrants also remitted and brought home money, and there *was* more in the 'Dead North'. Money could be used to buy education, and the convenient mission presence meant that the élite which later became the mouthpiece of rural discontent was far from being a new class created by new relations of production in the major agricultural areas. (Looked at from this angle, the change in the class composition of the Malawi leadership since 1964 is not so much a 'counter-revolution'[13] as the correction of a process of malformation.) Yet if Malawi does not quite fit into the southern model of proletarianization and rural impoverishment, it is clear that colonialism left Malawi poor, and other areas of explanation need to be looked at. But it is at least worth posing the question of whether it could have 'developed' at all. Territorial compartmentalization tends to produce even greater absurdities in the field of economic history than in any other. Though Malawi as a unit was obviously affected by the particular policies of its own administration, it makes far more sense to treat its problems in either a narrower or a wider context. Indeed, the very act of writing a national agricultural history would be dangerous if it encouraged the habit of thought that present problems are soluble within and by the present national structures.

## Pre-colonial agriculture

Accounts of the agricultural life of Malawi in the pre-colonial period are scattered and sketchy, and we are forced to rely in the main upon the *ad hoc* observations of travellers and missionaries, many of whom wished to give a particular impression (Livingstone with his exaggeration of the extent of cotton cultivation being the prime example), or who generalized widely from superficial impressions. Lists of crops grown and animals kept in themselves tell us little about the 'hows' of change. The two major changes of the recent pre-colonial past were the (probably nineteenth-century) spread of maize as the major food crop in the wake of increasing population, and the diffusion of cattle-keeping after the Ngoni invasions from the south.[14] But we know very little of the processes of these major innovations. For the period for which we have detailed observations it can be seen that the main food crops and their method of cultivation have not significantly altered.

From the early nineteenth century at least, it seems that the 'Marave' peoples were the producers of an agricultural surplus which supplied not only Portuguese settlements, but other African groups as well. In mid-century the coming of the Ngoni imposed not only new political and cultural forms but also new economic relationships, and Ngoni rule rested upon both the exploitation of the labour of conquered peoples and the continuing appropriation of the product of peoples outside the immediate Ngoni sphere of influence. In parts of the Central Region of the country, agriculture prospered. John Nicholl, who crossed the Kirk Range in 1894, commented 'Nowhere in the length and breadth of Central Africa have I seen cultivation which so readily excited my imagination. I am however persuaded that this is due indirectly to the Angoni, who give some measure of protection to their Amarawi bondsmen, to whom directly is due the credit for such work.'[15] Margaret Read likewise persuaded herself, with the help of Ngoni informants, that the Ngoni were responsible for the prosperity of agriculture in the area.[16] Yet it seems more realistic to see the Ngoni as Nicholl described them, in spite of his odd choice of the word 'protection', as overlords of a tribute economy and the exploiters of an agriculture which was often damaged, rather than created, by their presence. There is little difficulty in finding accounts of the inhabitants of the Central Region abandoning their cultivation in the face of Ngoni activity, and although this picture depends upon missionary and administrative accounts which wished to present the colonial conquest as a process of liberation, it is a version which finds definite support in Chewa accounts as well. Colonial conquest disrupted the Ngoni system of rural exploitation, and led to considerable changes. Cultivation and settlement increased in areas which had formerly been subjected to Ngoni raids, and the first twenty years of the century provided the basis of an expanding agriculture upon which the growth in cash cropping was to be built. In Ngoni areas themselves, cultivation declined and men migrated. A similar pattern of change can be found in southern Malawi, where the Yao, who had formerly appropriated a surplus produced by others, became servants of the colonial economy once the political basis of their economy was smashed. And while in the early colonial period the Yao areas were continually judged to be economically backward, the Mang'anja were able to use the new situation to create a new surplus, which they disposed of to new rulers.

## Colonial policies and misconceptions

European views on the technological capacity of African agriculture were generally highly unfavourable. Harry Johnston's view was typical: African farming was 'conducted on a heedless system, ruinous to the future interests of the country'.[17] Johnston, and the white planters, agricultural officers, and administrators who followed him, all opposed what they regarded as wasteful land use by Africans. After the establishment of the colonial administration, and the subsequent increase in population and in the amount of land under cultivation, the virgin forest lands and plentiful wild game of the Protectorate began to disappear. There was a strong white reaction to the waning of the happy hunting-grounds and the tropical wilds, and there began the long story of European conservation attempts, which constitute one of the major themes of the agricultural history of colonial Malawi. A stereotyped view of African agriculture as 'slash and burn', which would lead quickly to deforestation, erosion, and rural disaster, prevailed throughout white Central and Southern Africa. As a result, the Department of Agriculture adopted conservation policies, culminating in the adoption of compulsory methods, which brought it into conflict with African cultivators, to whom the aims and motives cf their rulers were unclear. The emotional tinge behind the conservation drive was only a part of the fundamental disapproval of African methods. The wastefulness of 'slash and burn' was seen as a symptom of a social system which encouraged thriftlessness. It was thought to be fundamental to the inculcation of good farming habits to change entirely African ideas of land use. Harry Johnston wrote, 'One of the greatest lessons we have to teach the Central African negro is fixity of tenure, the need of settling permanently on one piece of land and by careful manuring, the constant raising of crops from within a definite certain area.'[18] Even when the Jackson Land Commission estimated in 1921 that, taking into account all food needs for the next thirty years, there would still be a surplus of over $2\frac{1}{2}$ million acres of land (of which it suggested 700,000 acres could be set aside for European use), it looked to 'improvement in the methods of native agriculture and for greater economy of the soil', and suggested that charges should be made for land which Africans used to cultivate cash crops.[19] Two types of rationality clashed.

To a community living in a situation in which there was no land shortage, neither conservation nor intensive methods of cultivation appeared necessary. The colonial rulers, on the other hand, were accustomed to intensity of land use and were convinced that 'slash and burn' and population growth would rapidly exhaust the supply of available land. The land surplus clearly did begin to be reduced during the twentieth century, but the sense of impending doom which coloured the policies of the Department of Agriculture was, in its time, unrealistic. Such attitudes increased political tension, especially during the Federal period, when the tendency to emphasize the difference between European technological skills and African backwardness was especially marked. It was not generally appreciated that this technological 'gap' had been artificially created by the vast investment of money and research devoted by administrations in Central and Southern Africa specifically to the problems facing settler farmers. Such advice offered to Africans which did aim at increasing crop production tended to be confined to cash, rather than food, crops. But the high risks involved in applying the results of new research were more easily borne by the settler sector, where the risk was reduced profit, or at worst bankruptcy, rather than starvation. In any case, where no land shortage was perceived, output was increased by planting a greater area instead of employing labour-intensive innovations. Kettlewell reflects the tone of the 1945—60 period, which he perceives as a time of rural crisis during which population pressure was leading to mono-cropping in maize, which in turn caused soil exhaustion and land shortage. Erosion was being accelerated by the cultivation of steep terrain and the overgrazing of land. All this, he wrote, was happening too quickly for traditional patterns to cope with.[20] Thus in 1946 the administration decided on the necessity of compulsion to hasten the change from mound to contour cultivation, and the first object of the 1947 Nyasaland 'Development Programme' was the 'conservation of soil, soil fertility, and natural resources'.[21] The subsequent decisions to apply compulsion to methods of conservation, and, following the poor rains of 1948—9, to early planting, were the culmination of fifty years of government unease and frustration with African land use methods.

While the Europeans were quick to forecast potential land shortage and exhaustion of resources, Africans perceived a different and more immediate kind of shortage. For while the colonial conquest of central Malawi had brought liberation to Chewa agriculturists, the conquest of the south was followed by the large-scale appropriation of land for settler estate farming. In the Southern Region it appeared obvious to African cultivators that the main reason for pressure on land was the existence of large settler estates, and there were continuous and bitter complaints about the unjustified appropriation of land by settlers and companies.[22] The air of desperation in this most densely populated part of the Protectorate was captured by Principal Headman Mtenje, when he said in 1937, 'As I look on the Crown Land, I see no land remaining where so many of my people could go. I look in the air, I see I cannot fly there, then I come to the point that I say, what is the use of living.'[23]

These protests grew in intensity during the 1950s, when Federation was seen as heralding a possible expansion of white landholdings. During the post-Depression period, the administration had looked less favourably on peasant agriculture and had sought to increase the Protectorate's revenue by encouraging white settlers and the growth of tea estates. Later the white takeover bid which would have made Nyasaland a colony of Southern Rhodesia *was* a serious one. Nationalist politicians consistently called into question the legitimacy of the arrangements which had given land in freehold to foreigners, contrary, it was said, to what had been the intention of the chiefs at the time.[24] To the Europeans, however, estate land was being put to the most rational economic use of which they could conceive and was in no way connected with a land shortage clearly attributable to wasteful African methods of agriculture. Plantation agriculture, with its 'natural' markets in Southern Africa, was of vital importance to the export-oriented economy of Malawi, and the nationalist challenge to it was in fact a brief one. The care and favour with which the plantation sector had been treated during the colonial period continued after independence in 1964, and the settlers and companies which had looked to Federation as their shield were to find a new and adequate protector in the Malawi government, which has courted, and attracted, considerable political unpopularity on the Shire Highlands as a result of its determination to assist the plantation sector and its southward exports. As the Minister of Finance promised in 1965, the Malawi government would 'give every facility and encouragement to the production of agricultural commodities by large estates with commercial capital'.[25] The Shire Highlands were thus spared the fate which overtook the Kikuyu 'White Highlands' of Kenya.

## Land tenure and differentiation

Closely associated with the clash of concepts over conservation, land utilization, and scarcity was the vital question of land tenure. Two things about Malawian land-tenure systems struck the colonial rulers as being most obviously undesirable. The first was the absence of negotiable individual title in land. In Malawi, as elsewhere on the continent, the most common prescription for agricultural progress was the introduction of individual tenure, which would, it was felt, produce a rational economic man, eager to improve and enrich himself. As Kettlewell wrote of the post-war period, official policy was one 'of concentrating on the most progressive individuals. This policy was rooted in the belief that the foundation of a prosperous agricultural industry would eventually depend upon the individual yeoman farmer with a secure, heritable title over sufficient land to enable him to be efficient and to enjoy an improved level of living.'[26]

Yet this was not all. Over much of Malawi there appeared to be another obstacle in the way of the creation of a landowning, individualist, profit-motivated yeomanry. The matrilineal system, it was felt, was a part and parcel of backwardness, as a man apparently had no incentive to improve his land, 'over which he had tenuous and transitory tenure and no prospect of handing it on to his son'.[27] The fact that during the colonial period it was the matrilineal areas which, outside the estates, rapidly became the main producers of the agricultural surplus, and the patrilineal ones where agriculture appeared to decay, apparently passed unnoticed. The administration continued to aim, by and large, at individual title in male hands as the key to economic advance. The large part played by women in agriculture was seen as an impediment to the adoption of new methods, which, it was thought, they met 'with derision'. From the beginning agricultural instruction had been aimed at men, despite the fact that missionaries and district officials consistently complained that food production was in female hands and that men were unproductively lazy. In short, the colonial government was unable to take proper cognizance of the agricultural role of women because there was no way of fitting it into its stereotyped model.

The Nyasaland government thus made sporadic attempts to bring about a social and economic revolution for which no conditions existed, and which they had neither the resources nor the political will to carry out. Yet there was, nevertheless, an important legacy which outlived the colonial period; the legacy of the 'advanced' farmer. The colonial period witnessed the creation of new forms of privilege. To the 'advanced' farmer went permission to grow certain crops, tenure, and title; to the less 'advanced', the refusal of licence, marketing facilities, and advice were the means adopted to force them from the cash-cropping system. As a way of maximizing production, it may have had its advantages, but there were social implications which were never considered important by the economists. The importation of alien social values, linked in part with the adoption of new techniques in a parcel labelled 'modernization', continues today, reflecting the interests of an élite of agricultural entrepreneurs and its neo-colonial advisers.

Though rural economic progress seemed to the colonial rulers to depend upon increasing socio-economic differentiation, this was slow in coming about. Before colonialism attacked the tribute economies and domestic slavery, a section of society had been able to live off the agricultural labour of others. But the abolition of slavery must have reduced economic differentiation, arrested any trend towards the accumulation of wealth, and levelled the countryside back to production based upon the small family unit. This was reinforced by official policy on the size of gardens. A maximum of three acres for cash-crop growers was recommended in 1921,[28] and this appears to have been enforced by district officials, especially after the Depression. Throughout the cash-crop revolution, it was this unit which remained the basis of production. There was no overall shortage of land and therefore no landless mass to provide the basis of a rural labouring class. In the tobacco-producing regions, plots were of family size and were worked by members of the family. No employer–employee relationship based upon ownership of land developed, though there is some evidence of chiefs and headmen making use of traditional labour obligations, but not to the extent that this developed elsewhere in Africa. Where surplus labour was required it was supplied from outside the Protectorate; Lomwe immigrants provided the basis of the landless labour force which served the settler plantations, so that even these created little disturbance by their demand for labour, while in the cotton producing areas of the Lower Shire, Lomwe workers came across from Mozambique on a seasonal basis. Since landholdings could not be increased and income was too small for the accumulation of capital, class formation had to wait on the more energetic application of policies designed to accelerate it.

## Cash crops and the marketing problem

One of the greatest problems which faced the colonial rulers was that the economic system which to them appeared to be a rational and coherent one failed to deliver the goods to the African farmer. The Depression of the late 1920s and early 1930s clearly demonstrated that the capitalist world was not an orderly and predictable one. Even the traumatic experience of the Depression did not free planners from their delusions. In 1934, shortly after the collapse of markets, officials were steadfastly urging Africans to produce more: 'Prices at the time were known to be low, but this circumstance seemed to render it more necessary that the native cultivator should increase his output', in order to 'increase prosperity and to feed the railway'.[29] (For the importance of the railway, see the previous chapter by Leroy Vail.) But it was not easy for a cash-cropper to make much money. A report of 1939 estimated that three months' hard work was put into the average half-acre tobacco plot, from which the average income earned was under £2. (Following the Depression, the administration deliberately depressed tobacco prices each year to provide funds for price support should there ever be a second disaster.) An unskilled labourer on the South African mines would have earned, after deductions, approximately £25 for a year's work, while average wages were closer to £40. The rise in the price of goods imported into and bought in the rural areas was continuous, and was in no way related to fluctuations in the prices of rural products. Though wages in the south did rise fairly consistently from the mid-1930s onwards, there is considerable evidence of the great distress caused by the falling value of money in the rural areas.[30] Yet in the administrators' eyes, the existence of rural poverty was attributable to failures in African social institutions and agricultural practices, rather than to the restrictions which the colonial structure placed upon rural enrichment, and many seemed to share the feeling that peasants were getting rich too quickly, and that 'material development is outpacing moral development'.[31]

The uncertainty, resentment, and political tension produced by price fluctuations are an important factor in the political history of the colonial period. The settlers, too, suffered during the Depression, and the government-controlled marketing system which was subsequently introduced deprived them of the opportunity to profit from the marketing of peasant crops. By 1938 there were only sixteen purchasers of the country's tobacco crop, with the two largest, Imperial Tobacco and Conforzi, buying 65 per cent.[32] Thus the system limited the number of its beneficiaries. The prices received for crops rested, of course, upon 'supply and demand'; European markets determined price levels. But hugely different values were put upon different kinds of work, and the value placed upon the hours worked by the farmer in the production of his leaf was very much less than that placed upon the work of handlers, graders, shippers, and so on. A peasant farmer in the colonial period could do nothing about this, and certainly his rulers had no intention of doing anything about it: they perceived the differences as being the result of immutable economic laws which had nothing to do with, and could not be changed by, political intervention. The Nyasaland government, in fact, was unenthusiastic about any interference with the operation of a free market. All the arrangements that were made were seen as temporary and undesirable expedients. As Leubscher observed, summing up the attitude of the time, price stabilization arrangements were only permissible as tending to help towards 'the ultimate object, as implied by the principle of trusteeship [which] may be briefly defined as the strengthening of the forces which encourage voluntary effort and the facilitating of the evolution towards an increasingly differentiated and more individualist economic system of African society'.[33]

## Rural development

The agricultural experts, the administrators and the missions all aimed at the creation of a prosperous countryside, and in spite of the poor economic opportunities which agriculture offered in comparison with migrancy, all those in authority bemoaned the southward flow of labour, blamed the backward position of the rural areas on it, and looked forward to a time when it would be arrested. Missions such as the Dutch Reformed Church and the South African General Mission were in the forefront of those which pressed for policies, educational and other, which would keep villagers in the village, and their vision was in tune with the accepted wisdom of the day. What better example of the colonial way of thought could be found than Bell's discussion of the possibilities of cloth production in Malawi, entirely within the context of village crafts and the relative competitiveness of hand-loom weaving, and without any hint of the British government's recent rejection of the Protectorate's desire to allow the creation of a locally run cotton mill?[34]

Yet the idea that Malawi's wealth would be based upon a prosperous, individualized peasantry was a curious one. The societies from which the administrators came had, after all, grown rich as a result of migration, voluntary or otherwise, from the countryside to the towns. In the colonial, political and economic structure, a comparable development would have meant the expropriation of the African peasantry by settler or company estates, and the creation of a landless rural class forced by circumstance into colonial towns or mining belts as labourers. With the examples of South Africa and Southern Rhodesia before them, all of 'trusteeship' and anti-colonial opinion was combined vociferously against such a development. Rural development, rural preservation, rural-based education seemed to be the alternative. The wilder industrial visions of some of the early Scots missionaries seem very quaint retrospectively in the face of later predominant opinion, yet it is at least worth remarking that the rural enthusiasts were suggesting a developmental path for which there was no historical precedent. Their assumptions have carried over into the post-colonial period, where, in spite of the fact that the structure of extreme exploitation associated with urban development under colonialism has become more controllable, the faith of developers is still placed in a line of rural development by which no society has yet succeeded in significantly enriching itself.

## Conclusion

It is tempting, when considering the agricultural history of Malawi, to take it as a field in which to demonstrate essential continuities between pre-colonial and colonial history. Crops, land tenure, and methods of production have all carried over the past hundred years. Furthermore, it is equally tempting to emphasize the disjuncture in agricultural history between the colonial and post-colonial periods. The 1950s were a period of high political tension during which both nationalist politicians and chiefs focused attention on problems of land shortage and on the hated Department of Agriculture, and its enforcement of conservation and planting rules. The cry was 'no more agriculture because agriculture means nothing but European domination'.[35] Yet it would seem more realistic to emphasize the essential continuity between the colonial and post-colonial periods. The 1960s did see the abandonment of coercion—the uprooting of crops, fines, and imprisonment—but no change in the fundamental direction of policy. In contrast to Tanzania, efforts were not made to base rural activity on a traditional ethic. The emphasis on individualism, the need to expand the scope for entrepreneurial ability, and the willingness to promote the central position of the estate enclave in an export oriented economy did not cease to be operative at the end of the colonial period. Capitalist development, along the lines and within the framework handed on from the colonial period, was intensified and accelerated, rather than interrupted.

## NOTES

1. This chapter is based upon my earlier paper, 'Notes for an Agricultural History of Malawi', *Rural Africana, 20,* 1973, 27–35.
2. For example, J.S. Saul, 'African Peasants and Revolution', *Review of African Political Economy, 1,* 1974, 41–68; K. Post, ' "Peasantization" and Rural Political Movements in Western Africa', *Archives Européennes de Sociologie, 13,* 1972, 223–54.
3. E.A. Alpers, *Ivory and Slaves in East Central Africa* (London, 1975).
4. For the Rhodesian case, see C. van Onselen, 'Black Workers in Central African Industry: A Critical Essay on the Historiography and Sociology of Rhodesia', *Journal of Southern African Studies, 1,* 1975, 228–46.
5. R.W. Kettlewell, 'Agricultural Change in Nyasaland: 1945–1960', *Food Research Institute Studies, 5,* 1965, 235.
6. An exception is I. Linden, *Catholics, Peasants and Chewa Resistance in Nyasaland, 1889–1939* (London, 1974).
7. For examples of both, see W.K. Hancock, *Survey of British Commonwealth Affairs, Vol. 2, Part 2* (London, 1942); G. Arrighi, 'Labour Supplies in Historical Perspective: A Study of the Proletarianization of the African Peasantry in Rhodesia', *Journal of Development Studies, 6,* 1970, 197–234.
8. B.S. Krishnamurthy, 'Economic Policy, Land and Labour in Nyasaland, 1890–1914', in B. Pachai (ed.), *The Early History of Malawi* (London, 1972), 399.
9. M. Read, 'Migrant Labour in Africa and its Effects on Tribal Life', *International Labour Review, 45,* 1942, 605–31; F.E. Sanderson, 'The Development of Labour Migration from Nyasaland, 1891–1914', *Journal of African History, 2,* 1961, 259–71; J. van Velsen, 'Labour Migration as a Positive Factor in the Continuity of Tonga Tribal Society', *Economic Development and Cultural Change, 8,* 1960, 265–78; R.B. Boeder, 'The Effects of Labor Emigration on Rural Life in Malawi', *Rural Africana, 20,* 1973, 37–46.
10. *Report of the Committee Appointed by His Excellency the Governor to Enquire into Emigrant Labour, 1935* (Zomba, 1936), 36.
11. E. Dean, *The Supply Response of African Farmers* (Amsterdam, 1966), 26–7.
12. Census figures are given in *Report of the Commission Appointed to Enquire into the Financial Position and Further Development of Nyasaland,* Colonial No. 152, (London, 1938), 12. [Henceforth *Bell Report.*]
13. A. Ross, 'White Africa's Black Ally', *New Left Review, 45,* 1967, 93.
14. M. Miracle, 'The Introduction and Spread of Maize in Africa', *Journal of African History, 6,* 1965, 39–55; S. Agnew, 'Environment and History: The Malawian Setting', in Pachai, *Early History,* 43–6.
15. P.T. Terry, 'African Agriculture in Nyasaland, 1858–1894', *Nyasaland Journal, 14,* 1961, 34.
16. M. Read, 'The Ngoni and Western Education', in L.H. Gann and P. Duignan

(eds), *Colonialism in Africa, 1870–1960, Vol. 3;* V. Turner (ed.), *Profiles of Change: African Society and Colonial Rule* (Cambridge, 1971), 367–9.

17.   H.H. Johnston, *British Central Africa* (London, 1897), 424.

18.   Johnston, *British Central Africa,* 424–5.

19.   *Report of a Commission to Enquire into and Report upon Certain Matters Connected with the Occupation of Land in the Nyasaland Protectorate* (Zomba, 1921), 7, 9, 33. [Henceforth *Jackson Report.*]

20.   Kettlewell, 'Agricultural Change', 238.

21.   *The Nyasaland Development Programme* (Zomba, 1947), 5.

22.   The large landowning companies were in many ways the real beneficiaries of the colonial system: 'These companies acquired extensive landholdings (over 700,000 acres in the Shire Highlands) in the early days of the Protectorate, and some indication of their dominance was revealed in the 1926 census, which showed that 63 per cent of all African tenants lived on the land owned by just five large companies.' R.H. Palmer, 'European Resistance to African Majority Rule: The Settlers' and Residents' Association of Nyasaland, 1960–63', *African Affairs, 72, 288,* 1973, 261.

23.   Public Record Office, London, CO 525/165, Minutes of the Chiradzulu District Native Association, 23 May 1937.

24.   B. Pachai, 'Land Policies in Malawi: An Examination of the Colonial Legacy', *Journal of African History, 14,* 1973, 682–3.

25.   Cited in C. McMaster, *Malawi: Foreign Policy and Development* (London, 1974), 73.

26.   Kettlewell, 'Agricultural Change', 243.

27.   Kettlewell, 'Agricultural Change', 238.

28.   *Jackson Report,* 8.

29.   *Bell Report,* 46.

30.   *Report of a Commission Appointed to Enquire into the Tobacco Industry of Nyasaland* (Zomba, 1939) [henceforth *Tobacco Report*]; G.N. Burden, *Nyasaland Natives in the Union of South Africa* (Zomba, 1940); Dean, *Supply Response,* 58–60; M.L. Chanock, 'The Political Economy of Independent Agriculture in Colonial Malawi: The Great War to the Great Depression', *Journal of Social Science, 1,* 1972, 121–5.

31.   Governor Thomas to Colonial Secretary Passfield, 6 December 1930. Cited in Chanock, 'Political Economy', 127.

32.   *Tobacco Report.*

33.   C. Leubscher, 'Marketing Schemes for Native Grown Produce in African Territories', *Africa, 12,* 1939, 187.

34.   *Bell Report,* 92–4; L. Nthenda, 'From Trade to Manufacture: Britain's Delemma in the Face of Colonial Industrialization, 1913–1938', *Journal of Social Science, 1,* 1972, 103–5.

35.   Nyasaland Protectorate, *Proceedings of the . . . Legislative Council,* 5 July 1960, 55.

# POSTSCRIPT

## The Economics of Eliminating Rural Poverty

## ANN SEIDMAN

### The problem: development of underdevelopment

Almost every one of the more than forty African states that have attained political independence in the last two decades has pledged major efforts to stimulate 'rural development'. Unfortunately, the consequences of these efforts have tended in most cases to augment the growing gap between the so-called 'modern' and 'productive' growth of the export economy and the poverty of the masses in the rural areas. Schemes to extend marketing facilities, to provide rural credit, to mechanize agriculture, to build co-operatives, have barely altered the fact that the vast majority of Africans still struggle to survive on the threshold of hunger. Increasing numbers of peasants drift annually into the cities, crowding into urban squatter compounds, swelling the ranks of the tens of thousands of unemployed. This is as true among the more recently independent countries of Central and Southern Africa as it is of those farther north.

Extensive debate has emerged among development theorists as to the nature of the inter-relationship between the rapid growth of the export enclaves and the persistent rural poverty of the masses. The significance of this debate rests in the fact that the effectiveness of the solutions to the problems of underdevelopment depends on the validity of the explanations given for them. If the explanation of the growing gap between the 'haves' and 'have nots' in Central and Southern Africa is inadequate, the proposed solutions will inevitably fail to improve life for the masses.

Traditional Western economic theory has argued that export growth should serve as an engine of development, stimulating the spread of modern productive activities to the countryside through a 'multiplier' effect. The cause of the obvious failure of this approach in independent Africa, these theorists maintain, is to be found in the characteristics of the rural population: their attitudes and traditional institutions hinder the emergence of the necessary entrepreneurial behaviour required to take advantage of the new opportunities created by the expansion of the export sector.[1]

South Africa is held by some conventional economists, despite its oppressive racist rule, to be the paradigm of success. Building on the export of gold to world capitalist markets, a determined white minority government has, in the post-Second World War years,

successfully fostered manufacturing growth at one of the highest rates
in the Western world. Multinational firms have enthusiastically
contributed capital and technology. South African investment in the
1960s was the largest single source of British profits from overseas.
American investment there has more than doubled in the last seven
years. Over 80 per cent of all American manufacturing investment in
Africa is located in South Africa.[2] South Africa's outreach to the
north is conceived as a form of 'multiplier' to stimulate economic
growth there. Over time, some still insist, this growth will ultimately
trickle down to the masses of impoverished Africans.

Other Western theorists, repelled by South Africa's racist doc-
trines, argue that the failure of export-oriented growth to spread
development to African populations in the independent states reflects
the failure to create the appropriate institutions to provide them with
the necessary market incentives. Once these are created, African
peasants may be expected to behave like 'economic men' and
augment output rapidly, setting the 'multiplier' effect into motion.[3]

Growing numbers of political economists have rejected both
variants of this traditional Western explanation. The fundamental
causes of the widespread rural underdevelopment still characteristic
in Africa, they hold, are to be found not in traditional attitudes and
institutions, not even in the lack of market incentives, but in the sets
of institutions and class relationships shaped in the process of carving
out the externally dependent export enclaves during the colonial era.
Colonialism systematically undermined pre-existing agricultural and
trading systems in order to coerce Africans into providing the
low-cost labour needed to produce cheap raw materials for export to
the factories of Europe.[4]

Most political economists espousing this explanation of underdevelopment have focused their analyses on the institutions and class
relations which emerged in the export enclave itself, rather than
starting such analyses from conditions in the rural areas. They have
shown how the export enclave was geared to the production of one or
a few raw materials for export. Simultaneously, the import of
manufactured goods for the associated high-income group provided a
market outlet for the surplus output of metropole factories in Europe
and North America. The basic industries, foreign and internal
wholesale trade, and banks are dominated directly or indirectly by
foreign firms, which mesh the export enclaves firmly into the external
dependency network of the world capitalist system. The profits,
interest, and high salaries drained from the continent by these foreign
firms constitutes a major loss of investible surpluses for national
development. Moreover, since independence a newly emergent
group of highly paid civil servants and politicians has become
increasingly linked to the foreign firms in a variety of new ways.
Together, these increasingly intertwined groups have tended to
perpetuate and aggravate the lopsided, externally dependent growth
initiated during the colonial period.

This is not to argue that theory must begin its analysis in the rural periphery rather than the export enclave, but that such theory needs more sophistication in relating itself to the specifics of rural poverty. It is essential to probe more deeply into the historical roots and continuing inter-relationships between the expansion of the export enclave and mounting rural and urban poverty in Africa today. This is the key to understanding the way the new institutions and class relationships, which dominate the export enclave, continue to distort and undermine development in widespread rural areas in Africa. The evidence needed to warrant this explanation cannot be uncovered by any one scholarly discipline alone. Neither the problems involved nor the explanations come in boxes neatly labelled 'economics', 'history', 'sociology', or 'political science'. What is required is systematic inter-disciplinary analysis employing a time scale.

Herein lies the value of the chapters presented in this book. They shed considerable light on the way the historical process of underdevelopment has taken place in Central and Southern Africa. They lay the basis for the articulation of a theoretical model exposing the causal nexus between the growth of the export enclaves and the deeply rooted poverty of the rural areas of the region.

## The explanation: colonial origins

Despite the obvious differences in the historical development and colonial-imposed ties of the various Central and Southern African countries into the world commercial system, the evidence in this book exposes the basic similarities in the process of the development of underdevelopment in the rural areas of the region. This postscript therefore seeks to set forth an explanatory model[5] of the origins of the problem, flexible enough to identify key variables while still accommodating the variety of the case studies presented in *The Roots of Rural Poverty*.

The imposition of export enclave production varied in detail from area to area, but the underlying pattern in all cases was that of carving out export production sectors as intermediate centres between the European metropole and the vast labour reserve of the Central and Southern African economies in the context of the world capitalist system.

The growth of the export enclaves contributed to the impoverishment of the rural areas in two ways. Directly, through the extraction of surpluses produced by the low-paid wage-labour generated out of the vast rural reservoir. Indirectly, in the form of surpluses accumulated from the sale of high-priced manufactured goods sold by the big trading firms and their agents in both rural and urban areas. A major share of these surpluses was shipped out of the country by the giant firms dominating the mines, trade, and finance.

The export enclaves of Central and Southern Africa therefore were developed at the expense of the rural African populations. In all the countries, laws and administrative controls had the cumulative effect of turning control and ownership of vast mines and estates over to foreign firms and settlers.

Initially in some areas—as illustrated in Chapters 8–14—the expanding labour force on the mines and plantations provided growing markets for food and crops produced by neighbouring peasants. Not a few Africans successfully expanded their food crop output, despite the almost universal failure of the colonial governments to provide funds or technical assistance. In some cases, disease and drought destroyed their crops or animal wealth. In almost all cases, the settler-dominated governments ultimately took steps to end this African peasant competition, especially when the Great Depression of the 1930s sharply reduced overall demand for agricultural produce. In effect, natural calamities combined with restrictive governmental policies deprived Africans of the opportunity of participating in the use of the new means of production introduced in the export enclaves, except as members of a low-wage labour force.

Sir Harry Johnston, an architect of British colonial policy, explained that the colonial goals of acquiring cheap raw materials and markets for European factories could be achieved 'if the European capitalist can be induced by proper security to invest his money in Africa and if native labour can be obtained by the requisite guarantees of fairplay towards native rights'. He made quite clear what he meant by 'proper security' for European investment: 'The White capitalist ... must have something conceded to him. The native must be prepared to guarantee a fairly handsome return for money hazardously invested.'[6] He had earlier spelt out what he considered 'fairplay' to the African: 'A gentle insistence that the native should contribute his fair share to the revenue of the country by paying his hut-tax, is all that is necessary on our part to secure his taking that share of life's labour which no human being should evade.'[7]

The imposition of hut and poll taxes, requiring Africans to earn cash, was not the only means of 'gentle insistence' applied in Central and Southern Africa. Africans were typically forced off the best lands, particularly those located near roads and railway lines leading to cash markets. These lands were turned over to European settlers who received extensive technical and financial assistance from government agencies to expand their output. Complex marketing and quota arrangements excluded Africans from producing cash crops in competition with them. In those areas like Shaba/Katanga (see Chapters 12 and 13) where Africans were permitted to continue to grow cash crops due to the settlers' failure to produce sufficient amounts, administrative coercion, reinforced by the violent impact of economic fluctuations emanating from the world market, destroyed peasant initiative. Foreign-owned import houses and their associated agents were encouraged to sell manufactured goods mass-produced in European factories throughout the colonies. Government licensing and other restrictions on local productive activities and trade completed the process of undermining and destroying traditional African handicraft industries. The money and banking system, created to finance the imposed system of production and trade, intertwined the export enclaves still more closely into the international commercial system. Africans were explicitly denied credit on the grounds that they were poor risks. In some cases, legislation was passed making it illegal for banks to lend them funds.

As a result of systematic policy decisions, then, Africans in many areas were given little opportunity to earn cash except by joining the vast migratory wage-labour force required to expand the production of the foreign-owned mines and plantations (see Chapters 4–8). As Sherilynn Young points out in Chapter 2, the previous status of women as independent cultivators in some areas was undermined and destroyed. Tens of thousands of young African men were forced out of the villages to search for wage employment. Forty to sixty per cent of the men aged twenty to forty years old might be out of a village at any given time. The women, children, and older men who stayed at home had difficulty in maintaining the levels of agricultural productivity previously attained. As traditional irrigation and cultivation practices fell into disuse and the soils became increasingly eroded, the vast majority of the young men growing up in rural areas were even more narrowly restricted to seeking jobs on the large mines or plantations.

The wages paid to men who worked on the mines and plantations were actually subsidized by the rural areas. Women were expected to remain there, and to continue to provide housing and foodstuffs for the children. Cash wages were only expected to pay for the men's subsistence, with a little left over for taxes and perhaps a few 'extras', like a bicycle or a new suit of clothes. In other words, the colonialists did not even expect wages to cover the minimum defined by Marx as essential under capitalism: i.e. the socially necessary labour time required to maintain and reproduce the labour force. This system has been institutionalized by *apartheid* in South Africa and increasingly in Rhodesia, but it remains a dominant characteristic of the economies of the black-ruled states of Central and Southern Africa even today.

As the rural areas became meshed into the monetary sector through the sale of labour and the purchase of trade goods, the class relationships there became increasingly dependent on the dominant institutions of the export enclave. Chiefs were enticed or coerced into participating in extensive labour recruitment networks. A few entrepreneurial types, co-operating with the big trading firms, established small village stores or a bar. They gradually accumulated wealth. Those who benefited from the limited educational facilities available obtained posts as teachers or as clerks and petty officials in district offices north of the Zambezi, or in mines and private businesses south of the Zambezi. In a few areas, where cash-cropping was permitted, so-called 'emergent' or 'progressive' farmers expanded their output. They extended their land areas and hired their neighbours at a few pence per month, adding the resulting surpluses to their income. New class relationships gradually emerged in this way, with a clique of relatively well-to-do traders, farmers, and low-level civil servants benefiting from the extension of the commercial system from the enclaves into the provinces.

## The problem today: post-colonial perpetuation

The attainment of political independence in Central and Southern Africa has done little to alter the fundamental institutions and class relationships which emerged during colonial rule. The new governments there, as elsewhere on the continent, began to expand their social and economic infrastructure. Zambia, with the highest per capita income and tax revenues in independent Africa,[8] was perhaps the most successful in building up a national network of schools, roads, and electric power facilities. In part, this was a response to the popular demand for 'development'. In part, it reflected orthodox economic theory that the establishment of infrastructure contributes to the creation of an 'hospitable investment climate', which will attract foreign firms to build manufacturing industries, thereby providing employment and stimulating development throughout the economy. It was assumed that, eventually, given the appropriate opportunities and market incentives, African entrepreneurs would begin to benefit from and contribute to the resulting 'multiplier' effects, spreading development into the rural areas.

But even where newly independent governments could afford to finance the rapid expansion of social and economic infrastructure—as in Zambia—this did not change the basic institutions which tied the allocation of resources to the export sector, dominated by European and South African interests. On the contrary, its impact tended to aggravate the inherited, externally dependent dualism.

Zambia's experience is typical. On the one hand, the civil service multiplied rapidly to provide personnel to man the new projects created. This required funding, which necessitated increased current tax revenues merely to cover operating costs. The immediate source of new revenues was perceived to be the expansion of copper exports, an added argument for further investment in mining. When the price of copper fell on the world market, the government was forced to borrow internally and externally. The former added to domestic inflationary pressures, the latter to future burdens on the balance of payments and ties to multinational banking interests. This still further aggravated external dependence.

On the one hand, the new foreign investment attracted into Zambia's (import substitution) manufacturing sector tended to produce more and more luxury items for the limited high-income élite associated with the export enclave, along with a few profitable mass-produced goods, like beer and cigarettes. This remained true even where government had purchased a majority of shares in the businesses, for government personnel adopted the same import substitution criteria as their foreign partners.[9] Beer and cigarette output, for example, expanded rapidly. By 1972, it had reached 40 per cent of the manufacturing value added in Zambia. Pharmaceuticals, radios, television sets, air conditioners, even private cars, are now being 'produced' locally in last-stage assembly and processing factories using imported parts and materials. The import of finished luxury items for high-income groups, in other words, is gradually being replaced by the import of some machinery and equipment and the continuing import of parts and materials, instead of developing local resources. The resulting finished products are often sold at higher than world prices in the tariff-protected markets. The fact is that the complex industries required to produce such luxury items cannot be established in the truncated markets of Zambia or any other African state for a long time to come. Typically, moreover, the machinery and equipment imported for these kinds of industries are relatively capital-intensive, so that the number of new jobs created is limited. The new factories are generally built in the already developed export enclave to take advantage of existing external economies and the urban high income market. Few new job opportunities are spread into the rural areas. Peasants seeking to escape rural poverty still have little choice but to crowd into urban slums.

Although Zambia's greater per capita wealth may have facilitated the more rapid expansion of its social, economic, and political infrastructure, as well as its manufacturing sector, the situation is different in degree rather than in kind in Zaïre, Malawi, Botswana, Lesotho, and Swaziland.

In all of the ex-British and ex-Belgian states of Central and Southern Africa, a new class of Africans, termed by some the 'bureaucratic bourgeoisie', has emerged rapidly with the growth of the civil service and the upper echelons of the ruling political parties. Although at the outset its members did not control the major means of production—still owned outright by foreign firms and settlers—their positions in the government gave them a base from which they could attain a status of dependent participants in that control. They tended, from the beginning, to be linked with the more advantaged, well-to-do groups in the villages. Some used their high salaries and newly acquired facilities to obtain bank credit to invest in large estates, as well as in trade and speculative real estate in burgeoning urban communities. Government 'Africanization' policies combined with licensing powers rapidly endowed the 'bureaucratic bourgeoisie' with *oligopolistic* status as intermediaries between the firms dominating the export enclave and the impoverished populations. While they generally lacked the expertise and capital to acquire a significant share of the rapidly expanding (import substitution) manufacturing and mining sectors, selected individuals began to participate in the managements and as members of the boards of directors of newly formed parastatals in which governments had invested directly. Thus they became directly associated with the foreign firms and banking businesses which continue to handle the management, the marketing networks, and, in most cases, own a major share of the capital invested in the export enclave.

Widespread appeals for peasants to exert greater efforts to expand rural production have, as might be expected, been ineffective in such a context. Mere appeals cannot create new sets of institutions or contribute to expansion of new sectors of the economy in any way which might restructure the narrow choices of impoverished rural dwellers. New factories are not built to provide markets for local agricultural raw materials or to increase the productivity and living standards of the rural poor.

Marketing institutions designed to collect agricultural produce tend to purchase crops produced by the estate sector, in which the new dominant class now has a stake, and to pay premium prices for the produce. Government spokesmen argue that it is cheaper to purchase maize or tobacco by the ton than to buy a few bags from one small farmer here, a few more from another several miles away. But the fact remains that, as leading political figures and civil servants have become owners of large estates, their attention has become primarily focused on ensuring the profitability of their own operations.

The foreign private banks, still operating primarily in accord with traditional lending criteria, continue to finance larger farmers who can prove secure title to their land. Government civil servants and politicians may now have some access to bank credit, but the small peasant in remote rural areas is still excluded.

The smaller African peasant, unable to expand his sales in competition with the larger estate farmers, inevitably finds himself squeezed out. His only remaining channel for escape from rural poverty is to flee the countryside, vainly hoping to share in the conspicuous consumption which political independence has bestowed on a lucky few of his compatriots.

## The implicit solution: new institutions and class relations

In short, the explanation for the perpetuation of rural poverty in Central and Southern Africa lies rooted in the historically developed institutions and class relationships exposed above. Self-evidently, the white minority rulers of South Africa and Rhodesia will seek to perpetuate these institutions and class relationships for all time, relying on racist policies to admit only a tiny but significant minority of African collaborators to luxury consumption patterns, and to restrict the majority of the population to underpaid labour. But it is becoming increasingly obvious that replacement of the white rulers by an emergent class of wealthy Africans in the context of the inherited sets of institutions has not fundamentally altered the situation in the black-ruled countries of Central and Southern Africa. It is true that more social and economic infrastructure has been built than ever before—but the *nouveau riche* has greater access to its benefits than the masses of rural poor. In fact, there appears to be some evidence that their own newly acquired comfortable status, combined with the pressures of the economic crisis currently engulfing the capitalist world, is rendering this emergent class increasingly hospitable to South Africa's outward-looking policies.

If the above model is valid, as the evidence accumulated in this book suggests, it indicates that the only way to uproot rural poverty in Central and Southern Africa is to implement fundamental changes in the inherited class relationships and institutions. This implies, in the first place, the necessity of carrying through the national liberation struggle until all the nations of the region are politically independent under governments which represent all the people. The recent victories of the liberation movements of Mozambique and Angola have accelerated the timetable. South Africa remains the bastion of colonial minority domination, backed by extensive foreign investment. It seeks to consolidate and indeed to expand its position, though its domination of the region is increasingly threatened by guerrilla successes in Zimbabwe, by the struggle in Namibia, and by growing numbers of strikes by workers in South Africa itself.

The post-independence experience of Central and Southern African states, however, especially when viewed in the context of the explanations exposed above, suggests that African accession to political power is not in itself enough. Fundamental restructuring of the regional political economy is essential to end the continuing development of underdevelopment. Proposals along these lines, stemming logically from the explanations embodied above, are tentatively outlined here as possible guides for further investigation and evaluation in terms of their potential contribution to more effective attainment of 'rural development'.[10]

## 1. Rural focus

Every effort should be made to create new opportunities for the rural population to expand their productive activities and improve their living conditions. This requires creation of new rural institutions to encourage all peasants, not just the few wealthy ones, to participate in discovering new ways of increasing productivity and benefiting from new industrial and agricultural activities. Appropriate backwards and forwards linkages must be forged between these rural institutions and those controlling the 'commanding heights' to ensure that they supplement, rather than contradict, each others' efforts. Our model has shown how the development of underdevelopment in rural areas is the obverse side of the growth of the externally dependent export enclave dominated by foreign firms and settlers. Hence attainment of rural development requires that the institutions and class relations created in the rural areas be accompanied by fundamental measures to attain a balanced, nationally integrated, independent political economy capable of providing productive employment and higher living standards in every region.

## 2.  The political arena

New political institutions need to be shaped to ensure the effective participation in government at all levels of those classes which would benefit from rural development, particularly the masses of low-income rural peasants, the wage-earners on plantations, in mines and factories, and the growing numbers of urban unemployed. Appropriate channels of communication and feedback should be shaped to enable these groups to take part in critical decisions relating to reallocation of resources and creation of new productive activities designed to stimulate rural development.

## 3.  Government machinery

The inherited colonial sets of government ministries were designed primarily to facilitate the expansion of social and economic infrastructure to simulate private investment in productive sectors. The entire structure of governmental administrative machinery and parastatals needs to be redesigned so that it is capable of coordinating measures to ensure the spread of *productive* industrial and agricultural activities into remote rural areas.

## 4.  A long-term physical plan

Such a plan, covering, say, twenty years, should be formulated to create balanced industrial and agricultural sectors to increase productive employment opportunities and raise living standards in the countryside, while reducing external dependence. This does not imply that the economy should no longer produce exports. Rather, the export sector should be increasingly characterized by production of more finished products in place of low-cost raw materials. A greater share of the inputs and outputs of the export sector should come from and contribute to the expansion of employment and production in other sectors. New manufacturing industries created should be explicitly designed to increase productivity and improve the consumption patterns of the rural population. Poles of growth should be established to stimulate the spread of agricultural and industrial activity in each geographical region. Local resources should be developed and processed to contribute to the greatest possible local spread effect in the rural areas. Appropriate technologies, based on available labour and skills, should be introduced to advance overall productivity as skills and domestic investible surpluses are augmented in each stage of the plan.

## 5.  A long-term financial plan

Such a plan should be formulated to ensure that all available investible surpluses are directed to fulfilment of the planned physical perspectives. This would require a national incomes policy—which co-ordinated taxes, profits, prices, wages and salary payments, as well as bank credit—to direct surpluses, previously accruing to the 'haves', to productive activities providing jobs and incomes for the 'have nots'.

## 6. The 'commanding heights'

The government, involving the masses of the population at every step, would need to exert control of the 'commanding heights'—that is, basic industries, banks, and foreign and internal wholesale trade—to enable it to implement long-term physical and financial plans. Basic industries could then be directed to providing parts and materials for essential manufacturing and agricultural development, at appropriate levels of technology, in planned locations in all areas, as well as adding to national foreign exchange earnings and investible surpluses. The banks could facilitate check-ups on financial implementation of physical plans, as well as provision of credit to planned industries and agricultural development in the rural areas. Foreign and internal wholesale trade could be reshaped to support planned expansion of domestic productive sectors. No goods would be imported in competition with planned local projects. New trade channels would be opened to bring domestic inputs to new factories and to spread their products at reasonable costs into the most remote local markets. Efforts could be made to expand foreign sales of new manufactured products.

## 7. Regional co-operation between states

Potential economic development in both industry and agriculture is severely limited at present by the inherited colonial borders which fragment Central and Southern Africa into coastal and landlocked states. Only South Africa has the wide array of natural resources and integrated infrastructure which has enabled it to practise economies of scale and benefit from modern technology to diversify production and expand its market. So long as the rest of Central and Southern Africa does not realize its great potentials through regional co-operation, especially to create basic industries that individual states could not attain alone, South Africa will retain its economic advantages over its northern neighbours.[11]

## Conclusion

Pledges by independent governments in Central and Southern Africa to foster 'rural development' appear to have failed to achieve the promised goals. Analysis of the historical evidence presented throughout this book permits the formulation of a model which may help to explain why. The causes lie embedded in the institutions and class relationships which perpetuate and aggravate the inherited externally dependent dualism characteristic of Central and Southern

African economies. If this explanation is valid, it suggests specific areas for new policy measures to change those institutions and class relationships. These have been outlined here for further critical evaluation in the light of evidence as to the historical validity of the explanations which lie behind them, as well as possible consequences of their adoption. This, then, presents a new challenge to interdisciplinary teams of researchers seeking to contribute to the formulation of more effective policies for rural development. Not only is further information required as to the historical development of the causes of underdevelopment. Systematic study is also needed, in the light of that essential historical background, of the consequences of policies adopted in efforts to restructure the political economy today.

## NOTES

1. See, for example, D.C. McClelland, *The Achieving Society* (Princeton, 1961), especially 36–106; E.E. Hagen, *On the Theory of Social Change: How Economic Growth Began* (London, 1964); B.F. Hoselitz (ed.), *Economies and the Idea of Mankind* (New York, 1965).
2. R. First, J. Steele, and C. Gurney, *The South African Connection* (Harmondsworth, 1973); United States Chamber of Commerce, *Survey of Current Business* (Washington), October 1969, October 1971, August 1974.
3. See W.O. Jones, 'Economic Man in Africa', *Food Research Institute Studies, 1,* 1960, 107–34; M.P. Miracle, 'Capitalism, Capital Markets, and Competition in West African Trade', in C. Meillassoux (ed.), *The Development of Indigenous Trade and Markets in West Africa* (London, 1971), 399–410; P. Hill, *The Migrant Cocoa-Farmers of Southern Ghana: A Study in Rural Capitalism* (Cambridge, 1963).
4. Perhaps the best known is Samir Amin, head of the Institute for Development and Economic Planning, Economic Commission for Africa. See his 'Underdevelopment and Dependence in Black Africa—Origins and Contemporary Forms', *Journal of Modern African Studies, 10,* 1972, 503–24.
5. There is a growing literature on model-building for the social sciences. The following have been found useful in formulating the model presented here: G.C. Homans, 'Contemporary Theory in Sociology', in R.E. Faris (ed.), *Handbook of Modern Sociology* (Chicago, 1964), 951–77; M. Black, *Models and Metaphors: Studies in Language and Philosophy* (Ithaca, 1962); I.D.F. Bross, *Design for Decision* (New York, 1965); M.W. Riley, *Sociological Research, Vol. 1, A Case Approach* (New York, 1963).
6. H.H. Johnston, 'The Importance of Africa', *Journal of the African Society, 17,* 1918, 186–7, 192.
7. Public Record Office, London, FO 2/106, Johnston to Salisbury, 29 April 1896, 'Report on the British Central Africa Protectorate from April 1st, 1895, to March 31st 1896'. Quoted in R. Oliver, *Sir Harry Johnston and the Scramble for Africa* (London, 1957), 270.
8. For data on Zambia's investible surplus, see A. Seidman, 'What To Do with the Copper Surplus', *African Development, 8,* October 1974, Z.59–Z.61.
9. See, for example, A. Seidman, 'The Distorted Growth of Import-Substitution Industry: The Zambian Case', *Journal of Modern African Studies, 12,* 1974, 601–31.
10. For more elaboration, see A. Seidman, *Planning for Development in Sub-Saharan Africa* (New York and Dar es Salaam, 1974).
11. R.H. Green and A. Seidman, *Unity or Poverty? The Economics of Pan-Africanism* (Harmondsworth, 1968).

# Select Bibliography

This very brief bibliography contains works which many of our contributors have found to be particularly valuable, and which readers may find helpful in providing a general introduction to the various themes discussed in *Roots*.

Allan, W., *The African Husbandman* (Edinburgh and London, 1965).

Alpers, E.A., *Ivory and Slaves in East Central Africa* (London, 1975).

Amin, S., 'Underdevelopment and Dependence in Black Africa—Origins and Contemporary Forms', *Journal of Modern African Studies, 10,* 1972, 503–24.

Arrighi, G., 'Labour Supplies in Historical Perspective: A Study of the Proletarianization of the African Peasantry in Rhodesia', *Journal of Development Studies, 6,* 1970, 197–234.

Arrighi, G. and Saul, J.S., *Essays on the Political Economy of Africa* (New York and London, 1973).

Boserup, E., *Women's Role in Economic Development* (London, 1970).

Bundy, C., 'The Emergence and Decline of a South African Peasantry', *African Affairs, 71,* 285, 1972, 369–88.

Chanock, M.L., 'The Political Economy of Independent Agriculture in Colonial Malawi: The Great War to the Great Depression', *Journal of Social Science, 1,* 1972, 113–29.

Denoon, D., *Southern Africa since 1800* (London, 1972).

Fielder, R.J., 'The Role of Cattle in the Ila Economy: A Conflict of Views on the Uses of Cattle by the Ila of Namwala', *African Social Research, 15,* 1973, 327–61.

Ford, J., *The Role of the Trypanosomiases in African Ecology* (Oxford, 1971).

Gluckman, M., *Economy of the Central Barotse Plain* (Manchester, 1968).

Gray, R. and Birmingham, D. (eds), *Pre-Colonial African Trade* (London, 1970).

Hellen, J.A., *Rural Economic Development in Zambia, 1890–1964* (Munich, London, and New York, 1968).

Iliffe, J., *Agricultural Change in Modern Tanganyika,* Historical Association of Tanzania Paper No. 10 (Nairobi, 1971).

Johnstone, F.A., *Class, Race and Gold* (London, 1976).

Meillassoux, C., 'From Reproduction to Production: A Marxist Approach to Economic Anthropology', *Economy and Society, 1,* 1972, 93–105.

Meillassoux, C., 'The Social Organisation of the Peasantry: The Economic Base of Kinship', *Journal of Peasant Studies, 1,* 1973, 81–90.

Palmer, R.H., *Land and Racial Domination in Rhodesia* (London, 1977).

Palmer, R.H. (ed.), *Zambian Land and Labour Studies, Vols 1, 2, and 3,* National Archives of Zambia Occasional Papers 2, 3, and 4 (Lusaka, 1973/4/7).

Phimister, I.R., 'Rhodes, Rhodesia and the Rand', *Journal of Southern African Studies, 1,* 1974, 74–90.

Ranger, T.O., *The Agricultural History of Zambia*, Historical Association of Zambia Pamphlet No. 1 (Lusaka, 1971).

Rodney, W., *How Europe Underdeveloped Africa* (London and Dar es Salaam, 1972).

Saul, J.S. and Woods, R., 'African Peasantries', in Shanin, T. (ed.), *Peasants and Peasant Societies* (Harmondsworth, 1971), 103–13.

Terray, E., *Marxism and 'Primitive' Societies* (New York, 1972).

van Onselen, C., 'Black Workers in Central African Industry: A Critical Essay on the Historiography and Sociology of Rhodesia', *Journal of Southern African Studies, 1*, 1975, 228–46.

van Onselen, C., *Chibaro: African Mine Labour in Southern Rhodesia 1900–1933* (London, 1976).

van Onselen, C., 'Reactions to Rinderpest in Southern Africa, 1896–97', *Journal of African History, 13*, 1972, 473–88.

van Zwanenberg, R., *The Agricultural History of Kenya to 1939*, Historical Association of Kenya Paper No. 1 (Nairobi, 1972).

Wilson, F., 'Farming, 1866–1966', in Wilson, M. and Thompson, L. (eds), *The Oxford History of South Africa, Vol. 2, South Africa 1870–1966* (Oxford, 1971), 104–71.

Wilson, F., *Labour in the South African Gold Mines, 1911–1969* (Cambridge, 1972).

Wilson, F., *Migrant Labour in South Africa* (Johannesburg, 1972).

Wilson, G., *An Essay on the Economics of Detribalization in Northern Rhodesia, Part 1* (Livingstone, 1941).

Wilson, M. and Thompson, L. (eds), *The Oxford History of South Africa, Vols. 1 and 2, South Africa to 1870 and 1870–1966* (Oxford, 1969 and 1971).

Wolpe, H., 'Capitalism and Cheap Labour-Power in South Africa: From Segregation to Apartheid', *Economy and Society, 1*, 1972, 425–56.

# INDEX